The Crusade for Justice

The Crusade for Justice

CHICANO MILITANCY AND
THE GOVERNMENT'S
WAR ON DISSENT

Ernesto B. Vigil

THE UNIVERSITY OF WISCONSIN PRESS

The University of Wisconsin Press
2537 Daniels Street
Madison, Wisconsin 53718

3 Henrietta Street
London WC2E 8LU, England

Library of Congress Cataloging-in-Publication Data

Vigil, Ernesto B., 1948–
The crusade for justice : Chicano militancy and the government's war on dissent /
Ernesto B. Vigil.
487 pp.   cm.
Includes bibliographical references and index.
ISBN 0-299-16224-9 (pbk. : alk. paper)
ISBN 0-299-16220-6 (cloth : alk. paper)
1. Mexican Americans—Civil rights—Southwest, New—History—20th century.
2. Civil rights movements—Southwest, New—History—20th century.   3. Mexican
Americans—Southwest, New—Politics and government.   4. Southwest, New—Ethnic
relations.   5. United States—Ethnic relations.   6. United States—Politics and
government—1945–1989.   I. Title.
F790.M5V54   1999
323.1'16872079—dc21   98-51514

This book is dedicated to those who fight for social justice and to those who have been deprived of it.

Contents

Preface

Many books begin with an obligatory and boring scholarly introduction, and this preface may join their number. I hope not, because that would be a disservice to the countless people who contributed to this work through their involvement in the political movement that it seeks to recount. This movement became known as the Chicano movement, and unique contributions to it came from a powerful and effective grassroots organization in Colorado, founded by Rodolfo "Corky" Gonzales and named, in its articles of incorporation, the Crusade for Justice, Inc.

When I decided in 1980 someday to write the history of the Crusade for Justice, it was already evident that its decline was inevitable. Yet its accomplishments, history, and long struggle against injustice were too important to neglect. The racism currently evident in English Only legislation, attacks on bilingual education, and the promotion of immigration hysteria only confirms this conviction.

The Crusade for Justice was a catalyst for uncompromising political activism on behalf of people of Mexican descent at a time when our population was growing and becoming urbanized. Spanish-surnamed people are about to become the nation's largest minority, and Mexicanos and "Chicanos"—people of Mexican descent born in the United States—account for over 60 percent of this population. The irony of seeing Mexicans portrayed as "foreigners" in the "American Southwest" is a tempting target for comment, but the brevity called for in a preface does not allow this. This narrative, hopefully, will give readers an idea of who we are, why longstanding grievances provoked an outpouring of angry but creative political activism in the 1960s, and how this movement was blunted in the 1970s.

Though I spent years gathering material, my intention was given a great boost in 1989 when a member of Rodolfo Gonzales' family offered me the funding that would free me to begin writing. I was also given access to some files from the large archives the family then maintained.

Some of their funds, proceeds from the sale of the property where Crusade headquarters was once maintained, were donated to the Center for the Studies of Ethnicity and Race in America (CSERA) at the University of Colorado at Boulder. Dr. Estevan Flores and Dr. Evelyn Hu-de Hart of CSERA facilitated my becoming a research associate, and I produced a very rough draft, nearly 700 pages, that was reviewed by Dr. Flores and Prof. Manning Marable. Unique circumstances, however, impeded the granting of the final third of the fellowship funds, and this, compounded by my subsequent bouts with employment, unemployment, and underemployment, resulted in several more years of delay. One benefit, however, was that the final product became a much better book.

The manuscript was reviewed several times, most recently by Prof. Rodolfo Acuna, Prof. Jeff Garcilazo, and Dr. Jerry Mandel, whose comments were invaluable. Rosalie Robertson, senior editor at the University of Wisconsin Press, patiently assisted me throughout the last two difficult years and displayed a forbearance from which I would do well to learn. The eagle-eye editing of Ms. Jane Barry, the copy editor, greatly impressed me. She understood what I was trying to do and helped it be done better.

Numerous people shared their time, opinions, and reminiscences about the Crusade for Justice and the Chicano movement, and it bothers me not to mention everyone by name. Others have to be named because they shared their files, constructive criticisms, photographs, labor, and contacts, or gave moral and financial support, putting food on my table or a roof over my head, or loaning their shoulders to cry upon when such was needed. This book could not have been written without them. Without specifying who assisted in which manner, I think the following people, note that it is not possible to rank them by the importance of the assistance rendered, and delete their titles, credentials, and degrees because they are buena gente, good people, and their egos don't require it.

They are: Esther Acosta and Jay Alire, Ralph Arriola, Herman Baca, Vera Benavidez, Pablo, Shirley, Dennis, Dino, and Danny Castro, Vincent and Rosario ("Chayo") C' de Baca, Everett Chavez, Levi Crespin, Johnny Davis, Eugene Deikman, Rolland Dewing, Frank Dillon, Jerry Duran, Seferino Garcia, Cecilia ("Tuni") Garrison and Dusti Garrison, Walter Gerash, Estanislado Gonzales, Sue Green, José Angel Gutiérrez, Richard Gutman, David Hermosillo, Sr., Howard ("Uncle Howie") Hollman, Duane E. Howell, LeRoy Lemos, Jr., Michelle (Sanchez) Lopez, Mike Lopez, Ricardo Lopez, Esequiel ("Kelly") Lovato, Jr., Apaxu Maiz, Alberto Mares, Cleo Martinez, Manuel (Emanuel) Martinez, Carlos Montes, Ed Montour, Mike Montoya, Willie Ray Montoya, John Nichols, Julian Nieto, Tom Noel, Lorena Oropeza, Ken Padilla, Alex Pappas, Danny Pedraza, Ken Portuese, Richard R. Rodriguez, Roseanne (Olguin) Rodriguez, Suzi

Rodriguez, Ross Romero, Ryan Ross, Raul Ruiz, Joan ("Tinko") Salas, Josie Salinas, Al Sanchez, Jr., Antonio Sanchez, Fred Sandoval, Jr., Sandra Santa Cruz, the late Rudy Schware, Christine Serrano, Sam Sierra, Michael Evans-Smith, Alicia Torres and Luis Torres, Patrick Gutierrez-Trane, Fernando Edmund Valencia, Ernesto, Jr., Jessie, and Maria Rosana Vigil, Tracey Salvador-Vigil, James Patrick Walsh, Luther Wilson, and Reba (Garcia) Yepes.

I have depended on written sources over interviews even though written words can be as flawed as spoken ones. Some comments on these sources are now warranted.

This work makes frequent use of citations from Federal Bureau of Investigation (FBI) documents that have been released under the Freedom of Information and Privacy Acts (FOI/PA). Alberto Mares, whose reason for interest in these files will become evident in Chapter 16, obtained many of these documents in 1992 and shared them with me. Other documents surfaced elsewhere. It took the FBI more than four years to respond to my 1994 FOI/PA request for my personal file, the Denver FBI field office file on the Crusade for Justice, and numerous related internal security files. My personal file was released too late for use herein, and the FBI informed me that releasing documents from all the files I requested would require an additional five-year wait and cost thousands of dollars. About 6,000 pages of the Denver FBI field office file on the Crusade for Justice are scheduled for release in 1999.

Documents currently available show that the FBI routinely sought to link the subjects of their investigation to the Red Menace bogey-man and thereby justify the Bureau's surveillance and disruption of government critics and other wrong-thinkers. I surmise, however, that anyone who waits for the FBI to prove that the Chicano movement was guided by Cuba or the Kremlin will first die of old age. It is ironic, moreover, that KGB files are more likely to be released in a timely fashion than those of the FBI. Even though the Red Menace no longer exists, the FBI, for example, still finds it desirable to withhold documents on Chicano activism in the Nixon and Vietnam war era "in the interest of national defense or foreign policy."

The FBI also frequently withholds documents on the grounds that their release might "constitute an unwarranted invasion of personal privacy," ironic words from an organization that compiled files on untold hundreds of thousands—if not millions—of people over several decades even though its charter did not authorize it and the attorney general forbade it. The FBI, however, was not the only witch-hunter at work. The FBI refuses to release documents that would cast some light on the Bureau's working relationships with local law enforcement bodies. Some comments on this are now appropriate.

Police intelligence files are hard to obtain, in part, because most people do not realize that their police departments conduct political surveillance. Most state and local laws do not authorize political spying, but neither do they forbid it, so the work goes forward and the unwitting public has no access to these files because no mechanism is in place to allow review. After all, no remedy can be prescribed without a diagnosis that something is wrong. In any case, the right to review police intelligence files is a weak defense against powers they should never have to begin with, powers that make them the Praetorian Guard of the status quo, intervening in politics and suppressing civil liberties under the guise of anticommunism and "counterterrorism."

In spite of the difficulties entailed, police documents and information about police intelligence practices do surface. The Denver Police Department Intelligence Bureau, for example, maintained information on me as early as May 19, 1968; nor did these practices cease with the closing of the Watergate era. One Denver officer admitted in a phone conversation in 1990 that the intelligence Bureau had conducted an inquiry on a small group of people who participated in a local commemorative protest that year. The inquiry was made at the request of Los Angeles Police Department intelligence officers, though neither department believed that any law had been broken. Denver, by the way, is not within the LAPD's jurisdiction. A Denver intelligence command officer subsequently denied that the LAPD had made the request and that his officers had conducted the inquiry. He was anxious to know the identity of the officer who made the admission. Neither officer realized that I was taping our phone conversation.

Special thanks are due to three active and retired Denver officers for their valuable assistance, including the naming of names, the provision of copies of documents, and the confirmation of long-held suspicions. Two others read drafts of Chapters 10, 11, and 12, and I was gratified when they offered no protest against my interpretation of the facts. Both officers, moreover, asked the same question and offered the same advice: "You don't keep all your documents in the same place, do you? You need to make extra copies and keep them in different places."

Special thanks are also owed a clerical staffperson in an FBI field office whose location cannot be revealed. Three of the aforementioned parties, whose acquaintance I made in the last 10 years, graciously consented to taped interviews; the decision to forgo their use was mine alone.

It is my hope that something can be learned from this work that will someday enable us to remedy the social inequities which the Crusade protested and whose resolution was resisted and postponed in the era documented herein.

The Crusade for Justice

One

Rodolfo Gonzales' Crusade for Justice

Power is respected in this society. . . . Are we endangering the economic system, the political system, by saying that? I think that the system should be endangered. It is a system built upon racism and imperialism. That is why the low-income people and the minority people across the nation are rebelling. Unless the system changes, there will be more rebellions. Those who advocate change will save the country, not destroy it. Those who are resisting change are destroying the country. If there is no change by peaceful assembly, by demonstration, by sitting down to discuss changes, then there will be frustration. Out of the frustration will come real violence, not riots. Unless everyone gets an equal share in this country, there won't be any country.

Rodolfo Gonzales, June 25, 1968, speech at
California State College at Los Angeles

"Unless everyone gets a share in this country, there won't be any country." The FBI latched on to that single sentence as an indication of the radical and potentially violent politics of Rodolfo "Corky" Gonzales and the Crusade for Justice, Inc., the organization he found in 1966. Rodolfo Gonzales was the sole founder of the Crusade and its undisputed leader, but to make their names synonymous is to oversimplify both. The Crusade was more than a dependent of its charismatic founder. At the same time, it would never have risen to the prominence it achieved without the vision, dedication, and inspiration Gonzales provided. No one has adequately chronicled the political activism of Gonzales and the Crusade. This book is not meant to be his biography, but no account of the Crusade would be complete without a description of its founder and home town.

3

DENVER IN THE 1920S

In 1920 about 15 percent of Denver's population was Catholic. Its 6,000 African Americans lived in a segregated neighborhood in Northeast Denver; the Jews were concentrated on West Colfax Avenue; Italian Americans lived in North Denver; and Mexicans lived around Larimer Street, in the Auraria neighborhood west of downtown Denver, and in the "Bottoms" of North Denver or elsewhere near the Plate River.

In the mid-1920s, Colorado's Governor Clarence Morley was a loyal member of the Ku Klux Klan. The Klan tapped the various prejudices of the community: anti-Semitism, anti-Catholicism, and anti-immigrant and antiminority biases. Its political clout did not subside until the early 1930s. Denver's Mayor Ben Stapleton denounced the Klan's anti-Semitic and anti-Catholic rhetoric but held KKK membership card no. 1,128. (The mayor's friend, Dr. Galen Locke, led the state KKK). Stapleton was not the only politician to join the Klan from conviction or for convenience. In seeking Klan support, he is reported to have said, "I will work with the Klan and for the Klan in the coming election, heart and soul. And if I am re-elected, I shall give the Klan the kind of administration it wants."[1]

The "manager of safety" is the title of the Denver police chief's immediate superior. Mayor Stapleton appointed the Klansmen Rice Means and, later, Ruben Hershey to be managers of safety. Other KKK members became justices of the peace and district court judges. Eventually, Stapleton appointed the Klansman William Candlish to head the police department. The new chief urged Protestant policemen to join the Klan. Those who did not were sent to work with Catholic and Jewish cops, doing night shifts or patrolling undesirable beats. Chief Candlish issued an edict prohibiting the employment of white women in businesses owned by blacks, Greeks, Japanese, Chinese, or Mexicans. On August 13, 1924, the *Denver Post* declared that the previous day's election "proves beyond any doubt that the Ku Klux Klan is the largest, most cohesive, and most efficiently organized political force in the State of Colorado today." Though the KKK fell into disarray a few short years after it blossomed, it gave ample evidence of the strength that could be mustered by rallying Colorado's resident reactionaries. Stapleton lost his third mayoral campaign in 1931, but recaptured the office in 1935 and held it until the campaign of 1947.

RODOLFO GONZALES

Early Years

Rodolfo Gonzales was born in a Denver hospital on June 18, 1928. Two years before the Great Depression began, his parents were working the beet fields north of Denver. He was one of eight children, and as he later recounted, "I would have been born in Keenesburg, but they didn't allow Chicanos in the hospital."[2] Denver would remain Gonzales' home town.

Gonzales' father was from the state of Chihuahua, Mexico; he had served in Pancho Villa's army during the 1910 Mexican Revolution. His mother, who died while he was a toddler, was from southern Colorado. His father never remarried. At the age of 10, Rodolfo began working alongside his father as a stoop laborer in Colorado's agricultural fields each spring and summer. His fall school semester started late and his spring semester ended early because of the need to follow the crops.

Following the crops also meant that his family moved frequently. Gonzales at one time or another lived in every barrio in the city. He graduated from high school in 1946 at the age of 16, two years ahead of schedule, after attending four grade schools, three junior high schools, and two high schools. He attended the University of Denver for one semester. Little is known about his brief period as an undergraduate. Highly motivated and ambitious, Gonzales went on to a string of sports, business, and political accomplishments.

Boxing Career

Gonzales' prominence in political circles was preceded by his success in the ritualized mayhem of the boxing ring. He became interested in boxing when he was 15 years old, but he entered no tournaments until he was 17 because tournaments were suspended during World War II. Boxing took him from the barrio and exposed him to new horizons.

Gonzales was no Depression-era "plug ugly." He read poetry before his fights to calm his nerves and pump up his adrenaline: "The Charge of the Light Brigade," or poems by Federico García Lorca, the assassinated Spanish poet. He read Tolstoy, Steinbeck, Hemingway, and books with social themes. He noted that there was little literature written about Mexicans, about Chicanos.

With only three recreation center fights to his credit, he decided to fight as a 112-pound flyweight in amateur boxing's elite "open class" division in the 1946 Golden Gloves tournament. Speed and counterpunching were his trademarks. His first fight was in Denver against a Texan, former

Golden Gloves champion Armando Delgado. After winning the division championship in Denver, Gonzales went to Chicago to compete in the national tournament. There he lost a split decision to Keith Nuttal, who went on to win the national championship. Though Gonzales lost, he made an impressive showing and was chosen as an alternate in the 112-pound division of the Golden Gloves "Inter-city Matches," where mid-western and western champions fought eastern seaboard champions.

In 1947 Gonzales again won the Colorado open class division and went to the National Golden Gloves Tournament, where he lost a split decision to Bobby Bell. He then fought in the National Amateur Athletic Union tournament, where his five victories won him the National AAU championship in the 118-pound bantam-weight division. Gonzales entered the professional ranks with an amateur record of 50 fights, 47 wins, and three losses.

His first professional fight took place in Sioux City, Iowa, in June 1947, the first of 24 straight wins. Of the 24 fights, only two were fought in Denver. The balance were out of state, a fact that Gonzales attributed to the racism of the boxing commission run by Eddie Bohn. Gonzales' professional fights in Denver took place in the Stockyards Arena and at Mammoth Gardens.

In his first Denver professional fight, Gonzales faced Eddie Marotta, a former National Golden Gloves champion who had already fought many of the division's top fighters. Gonzales, who never lost twice to the same opponent, was beaten by Marotta and then was victorious in two rematches. Gonzales had no coach and managed all the business aspects of his fight career.

His go-it-alone methods may well have limited his success in the professional ranks, where financial backing and connections in fight promotion have much to do with one's advancement. He believed that animosity between himself and Boxing Commissioner Bohn undercut his opportunity to fight for the bantam-weight championship held by Manuel Ortiz. In any case, Bohn refused to sanction the fight.

Gonzales' professional fight career included three matches with Charlie Riley, then ranked as the number-three contender for the title held by Sandy Sadler. Gonzales earned the number-three position by twice beating Riley. Among the world-class fighters Gonzales faced in the 1940s and 1950s were Harry LaSane, Eddie Burgin, Jackie Graves, Gene Smith, and the legendary Willie Pep. When he was 25 years old, he retired from the professional ranks with a record of 65 wins, 9 losses, and 1 draw.

An article in the May–June 1978 issue of *El Chicano Boxing Magazine* chronicled Gonzales' amateur and professional career, reporting that he fought 125 times in eight years, with only 12 losses and 1 draw. He quit fighting in 1953 but made a comeback in 1957. His last fight was a benefit for the Latin American Education Fund. Gonzales was inducted into the Colorado Sports Hall of Fame on February 15, 1988, the first Chicano to be so honored since the Hall of Fame was established in 1966.

Gonzales' life and political views evoke many analogies from the fight game. Fighters' rankings are constructed like a pyramid. Those who successfully climb the pyramid do so individually in a merciless struggle that pits one against all. Competition is the rule, but not all rules are written.

The fight world is split into divisions and classes. Strength, speed, intelligence, courage, determination, discipline, preparation, endurance, and discretion are required for success. No one factor guarantees success; it results from a combination of factors. The fight game, like politics and life, is not inherently fair. One can win the fight and still lose the decision when favoritism is involved, when the rules are bent.

Though cruel, the fight game has its science, logic, and beauty. Gonzales was a crowd favorite because of his speed, courage, and mastery of his science. He coached numerous fighters from his own amateur days until the early 1980s. He coached them so that they maximized their chances of winning—though winning was not guaranteed.

One fighter's strength could be countered by another's speed or skill. A short fighter could beat a taller one by fighting on the inside, where the taller fighter's reach advantage became a hindrance. A taller fighter would do well to fight at a distance, damaging his opponent while himself avoiding injury. An injured fighter should not run, but tie up the opponent while conserving strength and clearing his head. A good fighter might excel at offense or defense, a great fighter mastered both. Courage was needed to fight, but brains were needed to win. The ideal was to hit without being hit.

Many good fighters made bad coaches. Gonzales was a good coach in a brutal sport. He and his boyhood chum Raul Luna would later train boxers at the Crusade for Justice headquarters. Their style was learned through years of blood and sweat. both men fought well and taught others who followed. Their fighters were allowed to adapt individual styles (left-handed, counterpuncher, etc.) and were well-conditioned and scientific. No one put on the gloves until he was confident, was ready for the ordeal, and knew the basics.

A smart fighter often does not look like a fighter at all. Pictures of Gonzales as a boxer show a handsome young man with a boyish grin. After 125 fights his face was remarkably untouched. Gonzales laughed at the braggarts who said they could "take a punch." He believed that the broken nose and cauliflower ear were, more often than not, signs of an unskilled fighter with no "class." These fighters often spent their later days with slurred speech and scrambled brains, mumbling about bygone days of splendor when they could "take a punch."

Gonzales' ring humor exemplified his wit. As a young, devoutly Catholic fighter, he knelt in his corner and made the sign of the cross before the match. In later years, someone asked if making the sign of the cross really helped. "Sure," came his answer, "if you know how to fight."

An eager novice once asked if there was a secret to winning fights. Gonzales, without smiling, answered, "There's three rules: Keep your hands up, your chin down, and your ass off the canvas." When neither contender in a fight showed "heart," Gonzales would quip, "One of 'em is scared, an' the other's grateful."

Business Career and Early Organizing Efforts

From 1952 to 1958 Gonzales owned a popular lounge called "Corky's Corner." He later started a bail bond company, in part because of his ownership of the bar. As he recounted in a September 1977 interview in *La Cucaracha,* a community newspaper:

> [Corky's Corner] was a neighborhood bar, and I knew everyone. Someone would go to jail for disturbance, and I'd lend them money. I became sort of an advisor. In the bonding business, I went back to the same thing I saw in the streets; people being brutalized; kids with their scalps open. . . . I decided to get out of the bonding business because it wasn't the kind of a business I wanted to make a living off of.

Gonzales was self-employed from the age of 18, except for appointments to the directorship of Denver's War on Poverty (later called the Office of Economic Opportunity, OEO) and the Neighborhood Youth Corps, an employment program serving low-income youth. This history of self-employment may well have been a factor in his strong sense of self-reliance and fierce independence. His business endeavors were matched by his involvement in efforts to elevate the conditions of the Chicano community.

In the 1950s, Gonzales was a founding board member of the Latin American Educational Fund, the Colorado GI Forum, and the Latin American Research and Service Agency. He also served on the national board of Jobs for Progress and on the board of directors for the Job Opportunity Center. He was president of the National Citizens Committee for Community Relations and member of the steering committee of the Anti-Poverty Program for the Southwest.

Even earlier, in the late 1940s, Gonzales campaigned in the Chicano community for Quigg Newton, who challenged and unseated incumbent mayor Ben Stapleton. In 1955 Gonzales and three others ran against State

Representative Elvin Caldwell seeking election to the Denver City Council. He lost in a runoff election when Caldwell tallied 2,000 more votes. His strong showing, however, soon led to his becoming Denver's first Chicano Democratic district captain in the heavily Chicano Westside. He put his organizing talents to work to turn out the vote for John Carroll, who successfully ran for the U.S. Senate one year after Gonzales' City Council race.

Gonzales subsequently led the Democratic Party's "Viva Kennedy!" campaign, and his district turned out the highest Democratic vote in Denver for the 1960 election. He remained an organizer in Chicano districts and worked to register voters. Though his star was rising within the party, his career was marked by his outspoken manner.

Gonzales was in the headlines in the summer of 1964 when he ran for the House of Representatives seat for District 7, where he was the Democratic district captain, even though he resided in District 16. On July 31, 1964, the *Rocky Mountain News* reported that Colorado Attorney General "Duke" Dunbar had ruled him ineligible to run for the seat because he did not reside in the district. "Duke Dunbar isn't infallible," Gonzales retorted. "He's just another lawyer."

Gonzales was a surprise candidate in this race. Helen Lucero, a member of the Denver Democratic Assembly, which selected the party's candidates, was also seeking the post, but she withdrew and threw her support to Gonzales, giving him the top-line designation in the primary. Gonzales was taking advantage of a recent Colorado Supreme Court ruling that subdistricting was unconstitutional, bringing district residency as a qualification to run into question. The court ruling, however, was held in abeyance until the Colorado General Assembly reconvened in January 1965. Gonzales' move was a bold one. When the Attorney General refused to certify him for the race, Gonzales took the matter to the district court, where Judge Saul Pinchick ruled in his favor on August 8, 1964. Pinchick ordered Attorney General Dunbar to certify Gonzales. This decision was later overturned on August 27, and Dunbar's was upheld.

Militant Vision

Gonzales' political battles lasted longer than his ring career. A January 6, 1988, article in Denver's *La Voz* newspaper reported, "His name was mentioned in the same breath as Stokeley Carmichael and Angela Davis. But his heroes were Martin Luther King and Cesar Chavez."

This article is laudatory and generally accurate. The last sentence, however, is open to question. King and Chavez were Gonzales' contemporaries; he knew both and respected them as organizers. Yet unlike them,

ᵣes was not guided by a spiritual pacifism. He entertained no no-
of redeeming the souls of those he viewed as oppressors. Gonzales
ᴀired Chavez and praised his dedication to the cause of farmworkers,
ᴀt he—like Chavez himself—saw the latter mainly as a labor leader. He
viewed King as a martyr, but his own nationalist politics and sentiments
were closer to those of the assassinated Malcolm X.

Gonzales saw politics and life as a struggle in which there were winners
and losers. He had made a living for himself and his family with his fists
and literally fought the toughest men in the world in his weight division.
He beat most of them.

If Gonzales had a personal hero, it was Emiliano Zapata, the indomi-
table peasant revolutionary. Gonzales admired his independence, integrity, strategy of popular autonomy, and spirit of unceasing struggle. He
may have learned lessons from King and Chavez, and, indeed, he studied
the struggle of African Americans: "I learned from the Black movement.
Look at Watts [the 1965 African American uprising in Los Angeles]. The
day after the riots the government was dumping millions of dollars to
help the people. They felt threatened, so they give a little. They never give
a lot, just a little. I've been taught that five loose fingers by themselves are
nothing. Bring them together and you have a fist."[3]

The last years of Gonzales' fight career coincided with his entry into
mainstream politics as a liberal Democratic Party activist. He brought his
fighter's caginess with him. This was demonstrated when Gonzales, then
a Democratic district captain, was arrested on July 26, 1958, on misdemeanor charges of assault and battery on Denver Patrolman Frank Michaelson. An article on the incident says that the officer suffered facial
cuts and a broken ankle while attempting to break up a brawl at Club
Ciros on East Colfax Avenue.[4] Charges against Gonzales were dismissed
after a January 1959 trial that resulted in a hung jury, but the officer sued
him for $75,000 in damages. Gonzales' attorneys, Ben Klein and Bert
Gallegos, countersued for $1 million, the legal equivalent of a counter-
punch.[5] Neither suit resulted in a monetary award.

Gonzales' version of the altercation was more detailed than the media
accounts. He had been at the nightclub when Michaelson arrested a
young Chicano. The officer, according to Gonzales, used unnecessary
force and viciously beat the young man with his nightstick, even though
the youth offered no resistance. The sight brought back memories of
events Gonzales had witnessed in the barrios in his youth.

Gonzales said he intervened only to stop the beating, and the officer
then turned on him and hit him repeatedly with the club. After deflecting
several blows, Gonzales hit the larger officer, who fell, twisting and break-

ing his ankle in the process. Gonzales was not noted for remaining passive when he felt that principle called for action.

POLITICS AND POLICE MISCONDUCT

Headlines about police brutality, corruption, and scandal have regularly appeared in Denver newspapers since the last century. Furthermore, Chicanos were becoming urbanized and were already Denver's largest minority when Gonzales began his political career. They bore the brunt of police abuse.

George Kelly's *The Old Gray Mayors of Denver* credits Mayor Quigg Newton with modernizing reforms in municipal government, including the "establishment of a Community Relations Commission years in advance of the clamor for recognition by minorities." Yet he notes elsewhere that in 1946 a grand jury indicted 17 officers on "charges [that] ranged from burglary to brutality. After 16 policemen had been exonerated in separate trials, the 17th case was dismissed by the D.A."[6]

Brutality was not the only charge leveled against Denver police. A series of 1955 articles by *Rocky Mountain News* reporter Tom Gavin focused on the controversial practices revealed by Omar E. Garwood, a Denver attorney and former municipal judge. Garwood asserted that police routinely arrested and held people without charge in violation of their constitutional rights.

At issue was the "checkout" practice that allowed the Denver police to arrest people whom they did not immediately charge, or did not charge at all. Suspects were held for indefinite periods while the police "checked them out." During the checkout period suspects could be interrogated repeatedly by officers, who sometimes were able to obtain incriminating information without advising suspects of their Fifth Amendment rights.

Suspects were held incommunicado until the police decided to release them or file charges. Garwood complained that this practice violated a person's right to bail, since no bond could be set until charges were filed. Meanwhile, the checkout system allowed police to gather evidence and file charges, or not file charges, while the person remained in custody. The system was ripe for abuse. Officers could continually arrest suspects without justification.

The Colorado Supreme Court recognized the legal principle that police could arrest and hold a suspect for a period of investigation, and held that the police must be given reasonable latitude in such circumstances. No one, however, had defined "reasonable." Suspects who knew their rights, and had access to attorneys, could begin habeas corpus proceedings. The police would then have 48 hours to show the court why the person should continue in confinement. Without sufficient reason, the person would have to be released.

Many did not know their rights, and those held incommunicado could not contact attorneys. According to one of Gavin's articles, Chief Walter "Bud" Johnson said, "We don't volunteer to call a lawyer for every drunk. We don't tell a man as soon as we put him in jail to keep his mouth shut. We don't work against our own interests."[7] The police would allow suspects to call attorneys only if the suspect could name a specific attorney. Accompanying Gavin's August 30, 1955, article was a photograph of the city jail sheet, which logged arrests. Of 18 people listed, 16 had been arrested under the checkout system.

All was not well in the Denver Police Department when Ed Geer was appointed manager of safety in 1955. Police Captain Tom Branch saw poor morale, poor administration, and loose discipline on the force. Kelly's *Old Gray Mayors of Denver* recounts that Branch met with Mayor Bill Nicholson and expressed his concerns freely. Branch subsequently wrote a report on the matter and sent it to Mayor Nicholson, who then sent it to the manager of safety, who forwarded it to Chief Johnson. Johnson promptly suspended Captain Branch.

Branch fought the suspension and hung on to his job. He did not have an easy time: "My phone was tapped and I had to use a public phone four blocks away or a neighbor's phone, even to call Joe [his attorney]," he told Kelly. "At one time we were fearful that Joe's phone was also tapped. Officers who called me or stopped by the house were plainly told not to do it again—or else." Department charges against Branch were dropped in July 1956, but instead of returning to duty at headquarters, Branch was assigned at night beat in Denver's Eastside Five Points neighborhood.

"The idea was that exertion or perhaps a physical attack would kill me. I walked the beat nights for two months, or so, when they finally gave up that plot and reassigned me to headquarters captain." Kelly writes, "Every competent observer who sought causes for the departmental disgrace that surfaced in 1960 reached the same conclusions [as Branch]. The scandal, the experts said, resulted from loose and careless administration, lax discipline and poor leadership, the very liabilities the tough-talking captain tried unsuccessfully to expose."[8]

Mayor Nicholson declined to run again in 1958, so he was out of office in 1960 when the police burglary scandal broke. Republican Richard Batterton won the May 19, 1959, election.

Mayor Batterton appointed John M. Schooley to be the manager of safety, but 1960 would not be a good year for Batterton or Schooley.

Rumors about police corruption had circulated throughout the 1940s and 1950s. In April 1959 an iceberg surfaced that was hard to ignore.

Early one morning in April 1960, two on-duty Denver policemen attempted to stop a vehicle carrying two men in downtown Denver. The car sped off. As the officers followed, a large, dark object spilled out of the trunk of the fugitives' car and was nearly struck by the pursuing patrol car. The fleeing vehicle was pulled over, but the driver asked the officers to let him leave the area, explaining that he, too, was a Denver police officer. The passenger in his car was a sheriff from a nearby county. The two men were allowed to drive off after the driver showed his police identification. The two on-duty officers returned to the object that had fallen into the street and loaded it into the cruiser. The heavy object was a safe that had just been stolen from a nearby coffee shop.

The two on-duty officers, John Bates and Robert Green, did not immediately report the incident, but when Bates revealed it several days later, a police burglary scandal that drew national attention to the city began to unravel. In time, 53 members of the Denver police department were suspended from duty, with 30 confessing to their crimes or being found guilty in criminal court. Some officers were tried and acquitted. About a dozen more "resigned" from the force.

Others were allowed to enter no-contest pleas or were disciplined via internal administrative hearings conducted by the department. These officers did not face criminal charges because the crimes they had committed fell outside the statute of limitations. Of the 30 who confessed or were convicted, all were patrolmen, except for one sergeant. Investigators at one time thought the number of implicated officers would rise above 100. A question that was asked then, and never fully answered, was how such a large ring could grow in the ranks and not be noticed by the command structure.

People joked that Denver kids played "cops and cops," and one local jokester related that a woman had called the police to report a burglar in her basement. According to the joke, the woman was advised to get the burglar's badge number and told, "We'll pick him up at roll call."

MOVEMENTS STIR

The police scandal, and attendant jokes, had faded by 1964, when Rodolfo Gonzales campaigned for the last time as a Democratic politician. His campaign was unsuccessful. In the four years from the onset of the police burglary scandal to Gonzales' 1964 campaign, America's first Catholic president had been elected and assassinated, the CIA had launched an invasion of Cuba, and the United States had steadily increased its military involvement in faraway Vietnam. Changes were brewing.

Throughout the 1950s and 1960s, the nation was forced to focus on its own system of apartheid: racial segregation in the South. African Americans had won Supreme Court victories against segregation and forced the system to live up to the rhetoric of freedom and democracy with which it cloaked its actions abroad. Could America fight for freedom abroad while it denied freedom at home?

The nation had launched a "war on poverty" to eliminate the social inequalities that were highlighted by the civil rights struggle. The expectations of poor people and communities of color were rising. Some reform efforts, however, were struggles to give people rights they supposedly already had, like the right to vote. For exercising these rights, African Americans were murdered while southern law enforcement and court systems either ignored or collaborated in the abuses. The civil rights struggle looked to Washington for endorsement and protection and found them lacking.

The civil rights movement, moreover, caught the Democratic Party in a contradiction: the party had to please both the African American voting block and its own segregationist wing, controlled by powerful southern Democratic congressmen. The increasing segregationist violence brought on resistance by African Americans. Younger militants began to change the rhetoric of the debate from civil rights to human rights and Black Power.

The tinder that would feed the flames of the Chicano movement was also being gathered. In May 1964 the newspaper *Viva!* cited demographic information in an article captioned, "The Spanish American in Denver." It noted the U.S. Census Bureau's estimate that 11.8 percent of the 1960 population of the five southwestern states was Spanish-surnamed, approximately 3.5 million people.

"There are over 60,000 Spanish Americans in the Denver metropolitan area: over 43,000 of them live in the city," the article noted. In 1960, 9 percent of Colorado's population was Chicano, a total of 157,173. Seventy-nine percent lived in urban areas; 76 percent of the males in the labor force were manual laborers, and 31 percent of the urban families had yearly incomes of $3,000 or less.

Earlier, in 1950, the Denver Area Welfare Council had conducted an "Exploratory Survey on the Spanish American of Denver." Researchers stated that "Spanish Americans are Denver's largest 'minority' group and the one with the lowest level of employment, housing, and income."

At the time of Rodolfo Gonzales' birth in 1928, only 20 percent of the southwestern Chicano population was urban. Eighty percent lived in rural areas. Richard Gardner's *Grito!* interpreted the significance of these figures:

> For the majority of those forced to leave their villages and farms, moving to the city meant living in shanty towns sprawled along the railroad tracks or in tumbledown tenements close to the urban core: The Barrios. . . . The movement from the country to the cities had, of course, been taking place in the United States for half a century, but the latest wave of migrations had a particular significance. The cities had originally been built and populated by predominantly white populations, who had in general enjoyed increased affluence beginning with the Second World War and who had set in motion a reversal of the in-migration movement, moving out of the rapidly congesting and increasingly uninhabitable centers into . . . the suburbs.[9]

Other changes accompanied urbanization.

In 1962 the Filipino Agricultural Workers Organizing Committee, led by Larry Itliong, and Cesar Chavez' National Farm Workers Association campaigned to unionize California field workers. In 1966 the groups would merge into the United Farm Workers Organizing Committee. In New Mexico's northern counties impoverished people bitterly resented the violation of a treaty of which most Americans had never heard: the Treaty of Guadalupe Hidalgo. Meanwhile, in Texas, community activists aspired to take control of local government in counties where people of Mexican origin were the majority.

The United States has never been fully cognizant of its second-largest ethnic minority, people of Mexican descent. Some view them as foreigners—even though Mexicans and their Spanish and Indian forebears lived in today's "American Southwest" before the 13 colonies were established on the Atlantic coast. Two articles written in the 1960s dealt with a question that underlay the polemics, tactics, and philosophy of the coming Chicano movement, a question of identity and history. It manifested itself in arguments about who Chicanos were, and what they should be called.

Less than a week after Mayor Thomas Guida Currigan appointed Gonzales as director of the War on Poverty in Denver, an article appeared in the September 5, 1965, *Denver Post*. "Spanish-origin Citizens: People Without a Name" put forth the views of a Denver academician, Dr. Daniel Valdez:

> Most of the Spanish-name people in the Southwest are not Mexican. . . . "Spanish Americans," whose ancestry goes back 300 years in the United States and whose forefathers were of Spanish background, resent being called Mexican or even Mexican American. They justify their position

by pointing out that they are not Mexican citizens, that they are not mestizos (mixed Spanish and Indian ancestry), and that they were citizens of Spain for more than 200 years, but of Mexico only less than 25 years before being conquered by eastern U.S. Anglos. . . . [Their] culture is Spanish, not Mexican. . . . The primary fact is that the first explorers in the Southwest United States were Spanish, and that nearly all the Spanish-name people in Southern Colorado and New Mexico are descendants of these settlers. . . . The term "Hispano" is a term which can most properly be used to label all the people with Spanish names in the Southwest. . . . Among educated, or well-informed, people of all backgrounds, the terms "Hispano" or "Hispanos" are the ones winning the most respect and popular acceptance.

In contrast to Valdez' views is a February 24, 1963, *Los Angeles Times* article by Ruben Salazar. In "Spanish-speaking Angelenos: Culture in Search of a Name," Salazar recounted arguments he had overheard in East Los Angeles, where Chicanos were debating among themselves over what they should be called.

However ludicrous such arguments may seem, they demonstrate how difficult it is to pinpoint just what more than 700,000 Los Angeles area residents really are. The complexity of definition is further aggravated by those who speak of Los Angeles' "Spanish heritage." Romanticists like to think that El Pueblo de Nuestra Reina de Los Angeles de Porciuncula was settled by Spanish grandees and caballeros, sophisticated descendants of the "conquistadores."

Salazar interviewed Father Zephyrin Engelhardt, whose research on Los Angeles' first Spanish-speaking inhabitants showed that these *pobladores,* or settlers, were:

Jose de Lara, 50, a Spaniard, with an Indian wife and 3 children; Jose Antonio Navarro, 42, a Mestizo, with a mulatress wife and 3 children; Basilio Rosas, 68, an Indian with a mulatress wife and 6 children; Antonio Mesa, 38, a Negro, with a mulatress wife and 5 children . . . ; Antonio F. Felix Villavicencio, 30, a Spaniard, with an Indian wife and one child; Jose Vanegas, 28, an Indian (Los Angeles' first "alcalde," or mayor), with an Indian wife and one child.

The original "Spanish" settlers of Los Angeles, in fact, were "two Spaniards, one Mestizo, two Negroes, eight mulattoes, and nine Indians. Their children were four Spanish-Indian, five Spanish-Negro, eight Negro-Indian, three Spanish-Negro-Indian, and two Indian." Salazar continued:

The reason the "Spanish heritage" is propagandized out of proportion at the expense of the Mexican-Indian heritage is the Anglo American's attitude toward the so-called non-white races, several educators charged at a recent Mexican American seminar in Phoenix. "The Mexican American is a victim of confusion, frustration, and insecurity because he has been taught through social pressure to be ashamed of, and even disown, his ethnic ancestry," says Marcos de Leon, teacher of Spanish at Van Nuys High School. "A very practical teaching of mental hygiene is that one cannot run away from himself, or what he is. To do so is to invite disaster. Somewhere along the way the Mexican American must make a stand and recognize the fact that if there is to be progress against those barriers which prevent and obstruct a more functional citizenship, he must above all retrieve his dignity and work as a person with a specific ethnic antecedent, having a positive contribution to make to civilization. No man can find a true expression for living who is ashamed of himself or his people."

Two

Politics, Police Controversies, Surveillance

The Advent of the Crusade for Justice

In the 1960s Chicano communities in the American Southwest—Mexico's northern provinces in the previous century—blossomed in a period of political activism known as the Chicano movement. Colorado had a role in this movement far out of proportion to the size of its Mexican-origin population. The spearhead of the movement in Colorado was the Crusade for Justice under the leadership of Rodolfo Gonzales. Gonzales hoped the Crusade would be a national model for organizing urban Chicanos to resolve chronic problems and achieve self-determination.

A small, male-dominated organization in the mid-1960s, the Crusade would become a multifaceted, multi-issue organization with hundreds of members before its fortunes wavered, then declined, in the mid-1970s. Its achievements have been poorly chronicled, and the Crusade is often recalled for the controversies in which it was embroiled, rather than for its accomplishments in the face of adversity.

"WE ARE BRINGING THIS MATTER
TO YOUR ATTENTION . . ."

On July 7, 1962, Edward Larry Romero, aged 19, was shot and killed in Northeast Denver by Officer Gordon L. Thomas, who was working a second job at the Cowboy Drive Inn, a 3.2 beer establishment, on 33rd and Downing Street. Romero reportedly became involved in an altercation with Officers Thomas and Charles Cullen near closing time. As they were taking him from the establishment, he broke away and ran. Thomas chased him. Just as Romero turned a corner, Thomas claimed, someone yelled, "Look out, he's got a gun." A police representative later reported that Thomas said he "thought he heard a shot."[1]

Romero fled to an alley behind the 300 block of Curtis Street and ran between two houses. Thomas said he fired a warning shot before firing the shot that killed Romero. On July 7, 1962, the *Denver Post* reported that Romero was shot in the chest, and Chief of Detectives James Schumate said, "To the best of my knowledge, the officer took every precaution possible before he fired at the boy."[2] No gun was found on Romero, and the next day's *Post* revealed that Romero had been shot in the back, though Thomas said he'd shot "toward the legs."[3]

Two cousins, Tony Trujillo and David Cordova, aged 17 and 16 respectively, were in one of the two houses between which Romero fled before he was shot. According to the *Post*, Trujillo was in the kitchen when he heard three shots; he later recounted, "As soon as we heard that guy (Romero) fall, we turned out the lights and went into the parlor." The *Post* reported that the cousins looked out the window and saw Romero and Thomas. They heard Romero say, "What did you shoot me for? I didn't do nothin'." Thomas responded, "If you didn't do nothing, what did you run for?" Trujillo said Romero then "tried to talk to the policeman, but he just couldn't."[4] Romero died in the ambulance, and Officer Thomas returned to duty on July 12.

In response to protests over Eddie Romero's death, mayoral candidate Thomas Currigan promised to create an independent review board to investigate such killings if he was elected. This promise motivated Denver's Mexican leadership, including Gonzales, to campaign for Currigan in the 1963 mayoral election. After the election, Chicano activists were angered when Currigan announced that he would not establish a review board because a closer look at the one he wanted to copy, the Philadelphia Police Advisory Board, showed that it did not work well.

One year and eight months later, on Saturday, March 7, 1964, Officers Michael Dowd and Warren Beard were working at a 3.2 beer establishment called the Westway in Denver's Westwood neighborhood. A disturbance erupted, the officers reported. Officer Beard struck Alfred Salazar with his nightstick and arrested the 19-year-old for disturbance and resisting arrest, although Salazar's friends claimed that he was not involved in the altercation. Salazar was booked at City Jail around 1 a.m. on March 8. He complained that his head hurt, but no injury was found. His parents went to Gonzales' bail bond office, made arrangements for their son's release, and, accompanied by Gonzales, went to the jail. There they found Salazar incoherent and unable to sign his name. He was taken to Denver General Hospital, where doctors found that his skull was frac-

tured. He died. The March 10 *Denver Post* reported an inmate's claim
that jailers had struck Salazar and that sheriffs physically threw him into
a cell. The autopsy showed that Salazar had an exceptionally thin skull,
half the average thickness. His death was ruled accidental. Ultimately,
Officer Beard was cleared.

Salazar's death aroused the Denver chapters of the American GI Forum
and the Congress of Racial Equality (CORE), the Denver Luncheon Club,
the Committee Against Police Brutality, the United Mothers, and Los Voluntarios—the precursor to the Crusade for Justice. Los Voluntarios was
a mainstream, not a "radical," organization, founded in the spring of
1963 to advocate for "the Spanish-speaking people of Colorado."[5]

Los Voluntarios, under Gonzales' leadership, took the forefront in the
Salazar controversy as recounted in its own newspaper, *Viva! The Battle
Cry of Truth.* On Sunday, May 5, a community meeting was held at the
AFL/CIO headquarters. Gonzales led the meeting, which was attended
by city and state government officials. *Viva!* reported that the 500 people
in attendance "proclaimed in a single voice that the investigation of purported police brutality remains an issue for the people to see and hear
until just action had been taken." Gonzales said, "We are regarded as a
voting block and if in four days we can raise 500 people to show up here,
we can raise 5,000 when we march on City Hall."[6]

Viva! reported that the grand jury investigating Salazar's death recommended the abolition of the police Internal Affairs Bureau and urged an
election to amend the city charter to permit a citizens' board to hear
charges of police misconduct.[7] The mayor, however, believed that misconduct could be investigated by the Internal Affairs Bureau and the Commission on Community Relations, each acting as a check on the other.
Gonzales, dissatisfied, wrote to Currigan:[8]

> Since it is our experience that your Mayor's Citizens and City and
> County Employee Commission has no legal powers to investigate, sub-
> poena, or enforce any action against policemen who use unnecessary
> force, we are bringing this matter to your attention for immediate action
> on these incidents.

Gonzales cited incidents of alleged brutality that occurred in June 1964.

> We suggest immediate suspension or removal of those officers in-
> volved. A complete investigation by an independent investigator and at-
> torney to be selected by civil rights organizations such as SNCC [Student
> Nonviolent Coordinating Committee], CORE and Los Voluntarios. We
> must have an objective and thorough investigation. Only then can we
> expect positive results.

Gonzales reminded Currigan that in May 1964 a grand jury had recommended abolishing the police Internal Affairs Bureau and establishing a citizens' review board.

> Our first approach is to seek redress in a diplomatic fashion, the weight of positive decisions lies in your hands. Once before I advised you that relief for those who are abused and mistreated cannot be expected unless you as Mayor . . . use the position of your office to insure maximum safety for the citizens of this city and . . . to reprimand and penalize those officers guilty of misconduct. The community can no longer wait patiently while their complaints are aired by anemic boards appointed by the mayor to absorb and confuse issues. It is time for positive and responsible action.

Viva! reprinted part of an April 22 *Denver Post* article by Tom Gavin detailing the mayor's 1963 campaign promise to establish an independent police review board to review accusations of brutality. Currigan had said:

> In fairness to both the officer and the citizen involved in such a complaint, it would seem that a body completely separated from the police department could receive and hear grievances with greater detachment than a unit of the police force. I would strongly urge the creation of such a board in Denver and feel that it would not only protect the policeman from unfair charges, but give the public an opportunity to present grievances against improper police action.[9]

Gavin wrote that Currigan's "promises to the spokesmen of the groups in question have not been kept and these people are justifiably angry."

DENVER'S WAR ON POVERTY

Though he was a political maverick, Gonzales was a popular community leader and a force within the Democratic Party. Los Voluntarios' successful voter registration drives, and the voter turnout among Denver's Spanish-surnamed voters in the 1960 presidential election may never have not been equaled since. So it was not altogether a surprise when, on September 1, 1965, Currigan appointed Gonzales, then 37 years old, to head the Denver War on Poverty, the keystone program of the social reform agenda initiated by President Kennedy.

The article reporting the appointment was accompanied by a photograph of Gonzales with Lady Byrd and Lynda Byrd Johnson, Lyndon Johnson's wife and daughter. Though Gonzales worked in the political mainstream, he was not a rubber-stamp for anyone's policies. As usual, Gonzales had something quotable to say. "I'm an agitator and a troublemaker. That's my reputation and that's what I'm going to be. They didn't buy me when they put me in this job."[10]

He criticized unidentified people whom he described as "coyotes" and "generals of the banquet table." Moreover, he considered organizing a Denver contingent to picket on behalf of people angered because an Anglo had been appointed to head the War on Poverty in Pueblo, Colorado—a city that was nearly half Chicano. Poverty programs, he said,

> only scratch the surface, sure. But there's kind of a mass hypnosis. Somebody makes it, and those around them see them make it and want to make it themselves. They begin to see how you do it. Just like in politics, where you throw a job to your brother or your uncle—these people get a job through the poverty program and learn how to go about wrangling a job for a brother or a man from the community.

Gonzales did not believe the programs were perfect. He continued:

> We have to keep an eye on the agencies and make sure they hire people from the community. All over the country, the poverty jobs and the administration have gone to the professionals, and nothing has trickled down to the people. That's not the way. You have to get people involved, and the way to do that is to live among the people, to hear what they are saying, and to agitate them.

He took to heart the antipoverty guidelines of the Washington, D.C., office of Sargent Shriver, the national head of the Office of Economic Opportunity. The guidelines promoted the "maximum feasible participation of the residents of the area or neighborhood" and allowing "residents (of poverty areas) to influence the ways in which policy decisions are made and carried out." Gonzales' responsibilities as head of the Denver War on Poverty included raising local matching funds. "We'll be getting $7 million a year from Washington. . . . The city has to appropriate (10% matching) money, and private industry has to involve itself. Maybe that's where a mass rally of the poor would come in—in waking people up."

The "war on poverty" stirred controversy throughout the nation. Community involvement in decision-making meant shifting local balances of power in which ruling elites had a stake. Gonzales' vision of community empowerment made some people uncomfortable, including A. Edgar Benton, a Denver War on Poverty board member, who voted against Gonzales' becoming chairperson. "Aura is not irrelevant," Benton said. "There is the basic issue of one's reputation in the community, which I find here to be a disqualifying factor. . . . The legislation calls for the local contribution to step up from 10% now to 50% next August. I question whether Gonzales can relate to the community at large in such a way as to win a local commitment of such funds."[11] Benton apparently recognized the contradiction between leading marches against local government and businesses and raising funds from them.

Though Gonzales ended 1965 with a prestigious political appointment, within months he was being criticized for his administration of the local War on Poverty and the Neighborhood Youth Corp (NYC), a youth employment program.

CONFLICTS OVER RACIAL TERMINOLOGY

Controversy over police record terminology strained relations between Denver Chicanos and the city administration in early 1966. Police records listed suspects by race. For Chicanos, the terms were "Spanish," "Mexican American," or "Latin American," suggesting that police saw people of Mexican origin as Spanish, Mexican, or Latin before they were "American." The February 17 *Denver Post* reported:

> Safety Manager Al Capra announced . . . that . . . persons of Spanish descent will be classified "White" or "Caucasian" on police arrest records. . . . Police had listed such persons as "Spanish American" or "Latin American." Capra said police will use only three designations of race on police booking slips: Mongolian, Caucasian, and Negro. "We will now use the term race in its scientific connotation," he said, "and as far as I'm concerned, Spanish Americans are now a member of the white race."[12]

Mayor Currigan "applauded" this new policy. "'It's been a long time coming,' the mayor said. He said the words Spanish-American and Latin American had 'no bearing on law enforcement. It's been a tradition with no purpose.'"[13] One newspaper reported some criticism of the reforms:

> Capra informed the Denver Luncheon Club, a Latin American group, of the new policy. . . . Bert Gallegos, club member and former State Representative, blasted the new policy as "an idle gesture." [Gallegos said Currigan] "has been talking out of both sides of his mouth" on this question and cited recent conflicting orders over whether County Jail escapees will be identified by race or ethnic group. Gallegos said the new policy "is merely a token thing for publicity purposes. It doesn't begin to touch the problem." Gallegos said Currigan probably made the announcement because he—Currigan—plans to run for re-election next year.[14]

Criticism and publicity might have subsided but for further remarks by Capra. On February 23, Capra met with Public Defender Edward

Sherman, who asked him to post Spanish-language notices of constitutional rights in the City Jail. The safety manager refused, saying, "Just a week ago I liberated these people. . . . I made them white people, and they like it."[15]

Once Capra's remarks were published and had prompted an outcry, he modified his statement: "As to making them white men, no one of course can make anybody a white man. They are white men. I merely insisted they be designated as members of the white race on public records." In the end, the Spanish-language advisement was not posted at the City Jail because, Capra reasoned, this "would be like throwing salt into an open wound."[16] Interestingly, this failure to post the advisement generated no community protest.

Police Chief Dill likewise was sensitive about charges of racism against his department: "We have no riots, no problems, and a respect for the law. There are a lot of good (Spanish-Americans) who have been tremendous help to us. We have some on the police department, and you can't get finer men."[17] Yet Dill had not in fact hired many of them. In 1967, one year after his defensive remarks, there were only 13 Spanish-surnamed police out of more than 800 officers in a city that was 10 percent Spanish-surnamed. Only three had command positions: one lieutenant and two sergeants.[18]

A local John Birch Society leader, the Reverend James Miller of the Montclair Community Church, expressed his resentment of police criticism in a letter to a Denver newspaper:

> I can speak with authority for I make it a practice to spend an evening now and then as an observer in a Denver patrol car. . . . The likelihood of a race riot in Denver is remote. . . . All this [criticism of police] sounds too much like what the Communists have achieved in China and Vietnam and plan to instigate between Negro and White in our country—American fighting American with only the Communists standing a chance to gain.[19]

BREAKING WITH THE DEMOCRATS

Gonzales' incessant activism brought him into conflict with the Democratic Party. He sought to empower his community by building a voting bloc that would make the party and local government responsive to community needs, and consciously employed pressure tactics to do so. His "work-through-the-system" strategy was about to change.

Publicity about Gonzales' criticism of the status quo was embarrassing to Mayor Currigan and the party. Gonzales was a rising star in the party, but his criticism of the establishment did not subside as he rose politically, and the party's failure to address concerns he raised caused him to re-examine his strategy.

On April 23, 1966, Gonzales spoke at Denver AFL/CIO headquarters to a liberal coalition that sought his participation. Gonzales said he "canvassed the community, both the leadership and the grassroots. As a person who has been given the opportunity to make this statement, I must speak from my own personal feelings and observations what the feelings and attitudes are of a majority of our people."[20] He said he felt "torn between the intense desire to involve myself in a new and dramatic move to unite the strength of groups who would work towards the goal of better government, and my dedication to my own ethnic group . . . [but] I must say to Herrick Roth and the fine members of the committee that we agree wholeheartedly with the philosophy of the coalition."

Gonzales was guided by a new vision in which ethnic solidarity and urban organizing took priority over coalition-building and electoral strategies involving politicians and processes he deemed untrustworthy or unworkable:

> We are bound to no one . . . we cannot dilute our strength . . . we will be a bargaining power committed to the economic, social, and academic betterment of the Spanish named people in the state of Colorado. We can no longer be exploited or taken for granted by any political party, city, state, or Federal agency. . . . We must struggle to unite the factions within our own group and we must guarantee to ourselves and the people in the entire community that we are one group, united and strong. It is at this time, in good conscience, that I cannot bring myself to ask my group to commit themselves to this new exciting idea. . . . I also want to make it clear that our reluctance at this time not be construed as a negative decision, but that we will support the objectives and goals of organized labor, we will support the programs and legislation to aid the aged. We are still committed to fight for equality for the Negro, all races, ethnic, or religious groups.

Gonzales had decided to build an autonomous, grassroots movement to fight for social change, and his break with the establishment was fast approaching. The setting for this break involved his administration of the Neighborhood Youth Corps.

Gonzales was angered by a *Rocky Mountain News* article that insinuated that his administration placed Chicano youths ahead of others on an NYC waiting list. In effect, he was being charged with discrimination. His administrative assistant, Peter Papageorgiou, charged that the NYC suffered from disorganization and mismanagement. Gonzales countered that Papageorgiou was not up to his own job's challenges, and "lack[ed] administrative ability." He contested the charge of by-passing names on the NYC waiting list, saying: "If a kid comes along from a family of 10 children where the income is $2,000, he gets a job quicker than a kid from a family of 4 with a $4,000 income. If that's favoritism, then let it be that way."[21] Because of this alleged bias, according to the *Rocky Mountain News,* officials were "keeping a wary eye" on Gonzales. Gonzales called for a newspaper boycott and picketed the newspaper, conduct Mayor Currigan said was improper for a public official.[22]

On Monday, April 24, the day after Gonzales addressed the liberal coalition, Mayor Currigan fired him as director of the NYC, citing the boycott as the reason for the dismissal. Gonzales called Currigan's action "a gutless, weak-minded decision. But you have to remember—he's easily influenced and led. He can't stand up to pressure because he's got very little courage."[23]

Gonzales said Currigan had written to Sargent Shriver after publication of the article alleging bias in his administration: "Currigan told Shriver how successful our program here is, then on Sunday he terminates me. I think the real reason I was fired was because of my calling the boycott on the *News.* . . . I told Mayor Currigan when I took the Youth Corps job that he was not buying me. I said I would always express my views as a private citizen. I guess I'm the cannon fodder who has to pay the price because I didn't agree with the power structure."[24]

"THE SPARK OF A CRUSADE FOR JUSTICE"

Gonzales and his associates organized a rally at Denver's Civic Center to protest against his dismissal, and 1,200 people attended. "This meeting is only the spark of a crusade for justice which we are going to carry into every city in Colorado," he announced.[25] His rejection of mainstream politics now opened the way for a strategy of militant grassroots organizing and independent political action in which Chicanos would decide their destiny independent of institutions controlled by others.

A year after being fired, Gonzales wrote a scathing letter to Democratic Party County Chairman Dale Tooley:

> I watched for some time to see if there would be any changes in the party under your leadership. I looked hopefully for the restoration of dignity and respect for the individual and maybe, much too idealistically, a change on the status quo and conventional attitudes which the Democratic Party has been guilty of in the past. It is clearly apparent that the party has not progressed on any of the pre-mentioned planes, but instead, has regressed so far back that the Party is certainly in jeopardy of antagonizing those people who have accepted the party with open arms. . . . From my point of view, party politics have traveled backward

instead of forward. The individual who makes his way through the political muck of today's world—and more so the minority representatives—suffers from such a loss of soul and dignity that the end results are as rewarding as a heart attack, castration, or cancer![26]

Gonzales criticized Tooley for "arrogant intimidation of career service city employees to vote for the mayor on the thread of not being promoted, placed, or employed," and charged that Tooley pressured Democratic municipal employees to "pay part of their earnings to the campaign of the Mayor." Tooley, as a party official,

> chose to appoint to party leadership in the districts, except for one grassroots person, Barbara Santistevan, a blue ribbon crew of Uncle Toms and political hacks to represent people who they do not communicate with, let alone identify with. . . . You and your cohorts have been accomplices to the destruction of moral man in this society. I can only visualize that your goal is the complete emasculation of manhood, sterilization of human dignity, and that you not only conscientiously [*sic*] but purposely are creating a world of lackeys, political bootlickers, and prostitutes.

This letter signaled the end of Gonzales' ties to the Democrats. Tooley would later cross swords with the Crusade many times in his role as Denver's district attorney.

THE FBI AND "A WANTON, RUTHLESS WAR"

Gonzales' evolving politics included international issues and an economic critique of society, as seen in his speeches against the Vietnam war. In August 1966 he charged that American society was run for, and by, "the ruthless financial lords of Wall Street" and by "great and powerful corporations." Gonzales' departure from mainstream political coincided with his entry into the files of the FBI. The Denver FBI field office reported:

> On August 6, 1966, the Denver Stop the War Committee sponsored an anti-Vietnam march and rally in Denver and the march culminated in a rally at the State Capitol building in downtown Denver. At the rally were members of the Denver C[ommunist] P[arty] and DBSWP [Denver branch, Socialist Workers Party]. [Gonzales] was one of the speakers at the rally.[27]

The antiwar movement had yet to reach its peak, and Gonzales' pioneering speech would put him in the vanguard of Chicano opposition to the war:

> My expressions from this platform do not represent any particular group, organization, or political party. My feelings and emotions are

aroused by the complete disregard of our present society for the rights, dignity, and lives of not only people of other nations but our own unfortunate young men who died for an abstract cause [*sic*] war that cannot be honestly justified by any of our present leaders. . . . The American people are daily faced with news that attempts to brainwash them into approving of a war that can only bring shame and disgrace to the most powerful nation in the world along with misery and destruction to weak and helpless people. Would it not be more noble to portray our great country as a humanitarian nation with the honest intentions of aiding and advising the weak rather than to be recognized as a military power and hostile enforcer of our political aims? What the American people should recognize and evaluate is that political doctrine is not the issue in Vietnam. It is not the real issue here at home. The real issue is economics. At present the economic stabilization of our country is dependent upon the war in Vietnam. The ruthless financial lords of Wall Street are the only real recipients of the tremendous profits to be made by the conduct of a wanton, ruthless war. The great and powerful corporations who control our industries, who control the purse strings of the nation, calmly play a chess game trading the lives of innocent American boys, confused and bewildered Vietnamese men, women, and children for green dollars that do not show the red stain of blood, the anguish and torment of grieving parents, the guilt for rape of a weaker nation. . . . Who reaps the profits? If in essence we are sharing in this prosperity by our own personal good life, then we are prospering at the expense of the blood and bones of fellow human beings. If our own economic gain must be earned by such a grisly trade, then we are truly a very sick society. . . . Prolongment of the war means isolation of the most powerful military country in the world, frowned on and hated by millions of people on all the continents of this planet.[28]

Gonzales' broad social critique raised questions that needed to be asked—and resolved—about the organization, tactics, and strategy necessary to bring about social change in this crusade for justice. What was the nature of the struggle, the basis of oppression? What were the role of a leader and the tasks of the oppressed to win freedom and recoup their human dignity? Though Gonzales and the Crusade never fully resolved these questions, his words now described an inherently oppressive society divided by class, race, and nationality.

The FBI's wariness about political dissent, clearly shown in its files on the Crusade, was shared by local reactionaries, including a group called the Soldiers of the Cross who harassed early Denver antiwar marches. The Crusade's politics did not include pacifism; its members would fight back. Crusade members' participation in antiwar marches may have ended the abuse peace marchers had suffered—this, at least, was a claim made by Gonzales and Crusade activists who engaged in antiwar activity during this period. Esequiel "Kelly" Lovato, Jr., son of Esequiel and Eloisa Lovato and a founding member of the Crusade, wrote in *El Gallo* about a 1967 protest at the State Capitol.

> There is nothing that fans the fires of the cross-burners like police pro-tection. . . . The right-wing fascists were represented in uniform and out of uniform. Out of uniform they call themselves "Soldiers of the Cross," the cheap and easy way to put God on the side of John Birchers, Min-utemen, and other false patriots. . . . At one point in the rally we wanted to have a direct "talk" with the "dukes of Dixieland," and we were stopped by the gun-toting goons of the Denver Police Department. . . . [Denver police] weren't interested in stopping violence. Later in the rally, Chief R. D. Potter, Chicano-hating policeman, led the Soldiers of the Cross up the steps in an attempt to break up the rally. As people at the rally went to the defense of their leaders, we expected the bullets, clubs, and fists to be flying. . . . Those of you Chicanos who might also be interested in hearing the truth and have, up to now, thought that peace marchers are sissies and cowards, come to the next rally and face "the Man's" goons. War has many forms; even in Vietnam two-thirds of the soldiers are not actually fighting, but just supporting. By not supporting a rally you show your support for "the Man," the same guy who beats you, jails you, and sends you up or shoots your brother in the back. . . . Wake up minorities; unite![29]

Opposition to the war in Vietnam put the Crusade to the left of the American political spectrum, and the organization's position on other matters steered the organization into exciting, and perilous, political waters.

BLACK POWER AND BROWN POWER

The FBI carefully noted Gonzales' and the Crusade's links to the Black Power movement. On January 6, 1966, the police arrested a group of protestors at the FBI office in Denver's Federal Building. The protestors, identified as the Denver Friends of the Student Nonviolent Coordinating Committee, were protesting against the slaying in Tuskegee, Alabama, of Samuel Younge, Jr., who had attempted to use a segregated facility. The protestors were found guilty of disturbance in County Court on May 4 and later appeared for sentencing. When the defendants left the court-room, the FBI reported, "they were joined by several persons who had been spectators in the courtroom, as well as Rudolph (Corky) Gonzales and some of his followers. They all joined hands and sang. 'We Shall Overcome.'"[30]

While monitoring a 1966 meeting of the Denver Friends of SNCC at Mount Girard Church, at which "the Reverend Clifton Whitley of the

Democratic Freedom Party [*sic*] in Mississippi" was the guest speaker, the FBI noted that the discussion included a new term: "Black Power." The FBI reported that Reverend Whitley "stated that Negroes in Denver should work with [Gonzales] to form a united front with the Spanish-American people."[31]

The FBI also reported on Gonzales' efforts to form the new organization, the Crusade for Justice, including the protest rally that launched it:

> [Gonzales] was quoted as saying that he had been accelerating his efforts to organize the Spanish-speaking community and stated he hoped that the May 21, 1966, rally "will be the biggest rally in the history of the state." GONZALES was quoted as saying that the May 21, 1996, rally would be held under a "Crusade for Justice" organizational blanket which would include a number of participating organizations. He stated he hoped to have as a speaker, CAESAR [*sic*] CHAVEZ, leader of the National Farm Workers Association Strike Against the Grape Growers in California's Delano County.[32]

THE NEW MEXICO LAND GRANT STRUGGLE

For the FBI, Gonzales' antiwar politics and ties to Black Power activists, leftists, and progressives were overshadowed by his association with Reies López Tijerina and the dramatic New Mexico land grant struggle. Tijerina and his organization, the Alianza Federal de Mercedes, sought to reclaim millions of acres taken by force and fraud from native New Mexicans after the 1846–1848 Mexican–American War. The Alianza, founded in 1963, sought return of these lands based on provisions of the Treaty of Guadalupe Hidalgo, which formally ended the war.

Gonzales attended the Alianza's 1966 convention, and ties evolved, based on a spirit of common struggle. The Alianza's escalating efforts to recover land grants met with increasing hostility from local officials. At stake were millions of acres in 277 Spanish and Mexican land grants.

In October 1966 the Alianza dramatized its demands by gathering at the Echo Amphitheater in New Mexico, part of U.S. Forest Service holdings and—more importantly for the Alianza—part of the San Joaquin del Rio de Chama Land Grant. Forest Rangers arriving at the scene were "arrested," "tried," and "convicted" for trespassing on the grant and then released. The Alianzistas, in turn, were arrested on assault charges. On March 25, 1967, Reies López Tijerina sent a letter to Gonzales. Translated from Spanish, it reads:

> Corky . . . this summer the people will take over San Joaquin del Rio de Chama once and for all. The people, or, as I call them, "The Sons of San Joaquin," are aroused and full of ardor and longing not ever seen in the

history of New Mexico. The people of New Mexico have moved to-gether in a miraculous manner which causes joy in the soul of the natives but great fear and terror in the strangers who arrived in New Mexico but yesterday. The taking of San Joaquin del Rio de Chama will be about the third day of June. And those valiant ones from Denver who wish to be present are invited and can personally see the valor of the "Sons of San Joaquin." We would like it if there could be one witness from among you so that this person could give first-hand details to you all.[33]

By May, incidents of vandalism and arson were reported in northern New Mexico. New Mexico authorities tried to forestall the Alianza by a preventive arrest of the members who gathered in Coyote, New Mexico, on June 3. Angry Alianzistas boldly responded on June 5, whey they ar-rived at the Tierra Amarilla courthouse, in northern Rio Arriba County, to make a citizens' arrest of District Attorney Alfonso Sanchez for order-ing the June 3 arrests. In the ensuing confrontation, two officials were wounded by gunfire. The Alianzistas fled into the countryside and were later captured. The courthouse raid drew national attention as National Guard troops, with armored personnel carriers, flooded the area.

Though the Crusade sent no observers in response to Tijerina's March 25 invitation, it monitored these developments. Gonzales and a small Colorado delegation visited New Mexico on June 8 for a firsthand view. Returning to Denver on June 9, Gonzales "drafted a telegram to President Johnson, Attorney General Ramsey Clark, Civil Rights Commission Di-rector William Taylor, New Mexico Governor Cargo, and Rio Arriba County District Attorney Alfonso Sanchez."[34] Tijerina had just been ar-rested. The telegram stated:

> It is with great concern that we ask your immediate consideration and attention to afford far and impartial administration of justice to those individuals arrested and now in custody. . . . Areas of concern are fair and reasonable bond, legal aid, and a thorough investigation of the le-gality of all arrests, warrants, interrogation, search and seizure proce-dures, etc. . . . It is of imperative importance that the incidents, long-standing problems, and complete disregard of the law [i.e., the Treaty of Guadalupe Hidalgo] be thoroughly studied, evaluated, and acted upon in order to prevent future problems and misunderstandings.[35]

The next day, at a rally at Denver's Sunken Gardens park, Gonzales called for "dedicated and concerned members of our community . . . not only in Denver but in the entire Southwest . . . to support a just and hon-orable cause."[36] A Denver FBI report chronicled developments in Denver and New Mexico, referring to the Alianzistas as "armed desperadoes" and to Tijerina, in particular, as a "terrorist leader."

On June 8, 1967, an article appeared in the *Rocky Mountain News,* indicating that RUDOLPH (CORKY) GONZALES, militant leader of Denver's Crusade for Justice, called for a public rally to support the claims of TIJERINA to thousands of acres of New Mexico land. According to the newspaper article . . . he stated that the rally would be held . . . on Saturday, June 10, 1967, at Sunken Gardens Park. . . . GONZALES reportedly stated that after the rally he and some of his followers will leave for Tierra Amarilla, New Mexico. . . . GONZALES said, "We must find out for ourselves what the situation is and in what manner we can offer assistance." GONZALES called TIJERINA'S claims "a just and honorable cause" that should be supported by Spanish-Americans in Denver and throughout the Southwest. GONZA-LES stated that the Treaty of Guadalupe Hidalgo, under which TIJER-INA makes his claims, has been disregarded by the courts, "the establishment," and the United States government.[37]

The FBI monitored the rally and noted the numbers attending. Two days later Gonzales and the Crusade organized a caravan to New Mexico to support the Alianza and assist it in the absence of its leadership.

Crusade members were present when arrested Alianzistas appeared in court in Santa Fe, as chronicled in the June 23 premier edition of *El Gallo,* the Crusade's newspaper. It recounted how cries of "Viva Tijerina!" went up as Reies, in handcuffs, was led through the hallway into the courtroom. Charges against Anselmo Tijerina, Reies' brother, were dropped. When asked how it felt to be free, Anselmo answered, "It is no different being out here than in the penitentiary. Our people are still not free."[38] *El Gallo* reported:

Crusade members were warmly received by Tijerina supporters and offers of dinner, homes and accommodations and hospitality were graciously and sincerely exchanged. . . . A new spirit of confidence prevailed over the past few days of gloom and people were now talking freely and refused to be intimidated as they had been by the arrests, questioning, and harassment instigated by the DA of Santa Fe.[39]

The New Mexico state police had in fact stopped the Crusade delegation outside Santa Fe, but this did not deter them.

On June 28, Gonzales reported on the New Mexico trips at a Crusade-sponsored meeting at Denver's Santa Fe Theatre, telling the gathering that Tijerina had given him a letter authorizing him to take over the New Mexico movement. The letter asked the Alianza's branches to cooperate with Gonzales, who promised: "I will offer as much advice as I can on such things as organizing and moving forward with the movement there. . . . The United States government itself is part of a criminal conspiracy in taking these people's lands, making out fraudulent titles, and selling the land to others."[40] Gonzales stayed in New Mexico from July 12 to July 22, operating from Alianza headquarters.[41] Tijerina was released on bond on July 23 and announced that the Alianza would hold a national conference for land grant heirs in August 1967 in Albuquerque.

The historic and family ties between Colorado and New Mexico Chicanos were seen in a letter from a jailed Alianzista, Jose Madril of Velarde, New Mexico, to Juanita Dominguez of the Crusade for Justice:

> I can't find the words to express the great feeling that came to our hearts when we heard inside the prison that the Crusade for Justice was supporting us. . . . I also want you to know that I was born in La Jara, Colorado [in southern Colorado]. I lived in La Jara most of my life. This morning on this date, 6/26/67, I met Mr. Corky Gonzales for the first time and I wished we could have more people like him and the ones that are helping us. . . . I will close my letter with this, give me liberty or give me death. Y que viva la justicia! May God bless each and all of you.[42]

Not all Nuevomexicanos appreciated the Crusade's expression of solidarity. Garcedan Madrid of Chaperito, New Mexico, wrote:

> We from New Mexico have never attempted to solve your people's problems . . . Why, then, should people from your great state try to stick their noses into affairs which are strictly New Mexico's . . . We have competent people in New Mexico capable of handling any and all situations. We strongly resent intrusions and assure you that yours is neither desired, needed, nor appreciated.[43]

Waldo Benavidez, of the Crusade, responded with his own letter:

> Most of the [Colorado] people who went to Santa Fe are originally from New Mexico, knowing of the problems, and not outsiders, and even if they were, they still believe in a common cause and the human rights of all people. . . . I might add that the "competent people" Madrid mentions are probably the same ones that have created this situation in the first place. They have sold out their pride and honor to the highest bidder for money, positions, etc. Now they are desperately trying to regain a semblance of leadership, but the people are no longer buying this.[44]

PROTESTS OVER POLICE KILLINGS

Killings by Denver police roused protest during Gonzales' absence from Colorado. Louis Piñedo, aged 18, was killed on July 12, 1967, and the death on July 3 of a young African American, Eugene Cook, angered the African American community. Crusade and Black Panther representatives sought march permits; the manager of safety granted Black Panthers a permit while refusing one to the Crusade, which wanted to bring a contingent from the nearby Westside housing projects. His explanation was that the march would interfere with the free flow of traffic.

African Americans and Chicanos converged in a two-pronged march on police headquarters on July 23. The *Denver Post* reported 125 protestors at the noisy demonstration; *El Gallo* reported over 300. There was a tense moment at the police building's entrance when demonstrators insisted on talking with Chief Harold Dill. Dill, with Division Chief Clifford Stanley and eight helmeted officers, pushed the crowd from the door. Emilio Dominguez, Crusade vice chairperson, said, "This will be the last time we come here in peace; we want to do right, but we're not left alone. Our people are shot in the back."[45]

Dominguez' remarks about people "shot in the back" revealed the cause of the protestors' anger. Both major newspaper accounts of Piñedo's death said he was shot in the chest by Officer John E. Cain. *El Gallo,* however, contradicted them: "A copy of the coroner's report proves that Piñedo was shot in the back."[46]

Press accounts reported that Cain found Piñedo stealing car parts from a car dealership. Piñedo allegedly stabbed Cain with a sharp metal object, a knife or screwdriver, and Cain then shot him. The Crusade's unofficial Police Review Board was led by Desiderio "Desi" de Herrera, a former town sheriff from southern Colorado, who demanded a copy of the death certificate from the coroner's office. After much resistance, he got the document. Three words told the cause of death: "gunshot wound, back."[47]

Though the Crusade demanded action, an *El Gallo* editorial revealed the organization's skepticism:

> In 1964 demonstrations were held against the Denver Police Department for the killing of Eddie Romero and Alfred Salazar. A Grand Jury investigation was held in connection with the Salazar death. The officers were vindicated [and] although the Grand Jury recommendations [for an independent review board] were objective and meaningful, they have since gathered dust in the vault of Denver's district court. Now comes the killing of Louis Piñedo and Eugene Cook. . . . What now? Another grand jury investigation to handle the hot potato long enough to cool the situation down? Or complete disregard by the Police Department, District Attorney, and city administration?. . . . The time has come for action. . . . Our people who are hiding behind closed doors hypnotized by TV sets, trying to identify with Anglo success figures, had better come awake and start fighting their brother's battle. The power structure, meaning this society, only recognizes reaction or power, and action produces both. Where are you?[48]

Shooting controversies did not subside, On August 20, Officer Harold McMillan critically wounded 23-year-old Andrew Garcia at a local tavern. *El Gallo* reported:

Andrew Garcia, 23, . . . was shot and critically wounded outside of Joe's Buffet . . . by Harold E. McMillan, off-duty Denver policeman, who claims Garcia stabbed him. As usual the two daily Denver newspapers reported only the police reports. Witnesses interviewed by Crusade for Justice Police Review Board Chairman, D.C. de Herrera, claimed Garcia was shot as he ran from the officer and then after falling, Officer McMillan clubbed him with his pistol until it went off a second time. A number of calls came into the editorial office of *El Gallo,* telling of past incidents in which Officer Harold McMillan has been involved. . . . Denver has had no riots to date, but the toll of injured and killed in the Mexican American community continues to climb. The people contacted in the neighborhood scoff at what they term "phony meetings with the Mayor." The Police Community Relations Division is considered a public relations division and that the Man is encouraged to, rather [than] discouraged from, assaulting Mexicans.[49]

In a harshly worded *El Gallo* editorial, Gonzales included community apathy among his targets:

The Mayor holds meetings with responsible leaders of the Mexican American and the Negro community. The *Denver Post* gives the Mayor, Police Department, and spokesmen full coverage on statements and intent. So what now, or rather, just "So what?" Andrew Garcia gets shot and pistol-whipped by a policeman acting as a paid bouncer while he wears a police uniform, badge, and the authority vested in him by the City and County of Denver. The minorities look at each other and say, "What now?" Do we picket? Do we demonstrate? Do we force a Grand Jury investigation so that the recommendations gather dust in the District Court? Shall we have police command–community leaders conference's; shall we hold hands and play ring-a-round-the-rosy? Shall we just keep watching our TV sets, drinking our beer, and say, "It's his problem, not mine?" Shall we pretend it didn't happen and turn our other cheek just in case it really did? After seeing what is happening across the nation, the Denver Mexican Americans should start analyzing the situation. Police are not afraid of us. They can mistreat one Chicano, and a hundred looking on won't make a move. We fight each other at the drop of a hat. The young tough cats shoot each other down, cut each other up, and don't blink an eye. The policemen are not afraid of Mexican Americans and, until they are, they will never respect us.[50]

New Mexico's controversies now surfaced in Denver. On September 12, Danny Tijerina, Reies López Tijerina's son, was arrested at Denver's West High School and detained at Juvenile Hall. Danny was staying with his mother in Denver when he was arrested on a warrant issued by the district attorney of Santa Fe and charged with assault with intent to commit murder and kidnapping at the Tierra Amarilla raid. *El Gallo* reported:

When interviewed by *El Gallo* representatives, Danny said he was never given an explanation of rights or advised about securing an attorney. Maria Escobar, Danny's mother, contacted the Crusade for Justice office, who called on Eugene Deikman, one of Denver's finest attorneys, to represent the Tijerina boy. . . . Deikman said, "The public should know what the District Attorney of New Mexico is trying to do." Certified papers and amended warrant had not yet been received although [Danny Tijerina] had been arrested and held in custody and brought before the court. . . . Danny said that he was not at the Tierra Amarilla when the shooting started June 5th. He remained in camp at Canjilon, 11 miles from Tierra Amarilla, with 40 others. It was at Canjilon where the state National Guard kept them hostage in a sheep pen.[51]

Danny's extradition proceedings were scheduled for October 2, but the Denver District Attorney's office requested a continuance to seek more information from Santa Fe. The Crusade considered the grounds for extradition flimsy. *El Gallo* reported:

Deikman termed the request [for extradition] "ridiculous" and "Alice-in-Wonderland law." He objected to any delay and stated that the juvenile court had no jurisdiction over Danny Tijerina. Judge Ted Rubin, conducting his court in the fair and impartial manner that has won him the acclaim as being one of the finest judges in the country, agreed with Deikman that his court had no jurisdiction over Danny who was being charged with numerous counts of kidnapping and attempted murder in Tierra Amarilla. The confused Santa Fe D. A. also sent letters to Danny and his mother ordering their return to New Mexico. It makes one wonder if the D. A. at Santa Fe got his law degree by saving up cereal box tops or Gold Bond stamps.[52]

The effort to extradite Tijerina was dropped.

The Crusade's focus shifted again when young Robert Gene Castro was killed by Detective Paul Montoya, one of Denver's few Spanish-surnamed police officers. Controversy now erupted in another public forum, as a Denver FBI report informed FBI headquarters:

On October 3, 1967, a public meeting was held at Baker Junior High School in Denver, sponsored by some unknown group concerned with police community relations. The program was carefully planned and functioned smoothly without interruption until [Gonzales] and other members of his Crusade for Justice organization entered and disrupted the meeting by shouting "police-brutality" type insults at the police officers who were on the panel. . . . Several of Gonzales' group started to shout, "Shoot them all!" Gonzales himself started to shout about revolution and stated that his group would arm themselves, if necessary. At this point almost everyone in the meeting began shouting insults back and forth at each other which approached an actual disturbance.[53]

Three days later, Gonzales wrote to the mayor and police chief: "Because we no longer intend to use the meaningless methods of attempting to gain redress for the injuries sustained by our people, we demand the immediate dismissal of the . . . officers (please do not confuse dismissal with suspension). We expect immediate action. Patience and time is running out. Awaiting an immediate reply." [54]

The Crusade's takeover of the October 3 conference may or may not have "approached an actual disturbance," but it was prompted by the group's anger, desire for direct action, and sense that community grievances were neither heard nor heeded. Anger was also directed at unnamed persons, former associates of Gonzales in Los Voluntarios, who were derided as "worn-out race horses that are still listening to the bugle of the past and still dancing to the tune of the power structure for their daily bread"—jobs, political appointments, and other benefits that they were unwilling to jeopardize in protests. Gonzales wrote:

> They went through the same pretension that they had in the past and will in the future. They shadowboxed, growled ferociously, pledged undying brotherhood, fawned over each other, and strutted like gladiators. Only there is one thing wrong. They never finish in the winners circle. In fact, they'll never finish the race. Weren't those the same faces that tried to form a council of Latin American groups some years back? It flopped! How many of those people were members of Los Voluntarios, an organization that was comprised of a cross section of the community? Los Voluntarios, a political organization [that was] the fore-runner of the Crusade for Justice [and] was the initiating or employment bridge for almost every self-acclaimed leader in Denver's "Spanish-surnamed" community. That's why sounds of demonstration, riot, and militancy coming from people who ran like thieves when Los Voluntarios took up the cause against police brutality sounds not only ridiculous, but impossible.

He described them as "old left-wingers who now fear the mention of red, the old bulls who were castrated years ago, . . . young, ambitious status seekers, the bootlickers and the malinches of our times." He predicted that they "will be scorned and cast out by a social revolution led by the young who will not buy hypocrisy or be bought by money. . . . It is no wonder that the young shy away from politics and phony meetings. They just aren't buying it." [55]

For the Crusade, the October 18 acquittal of Officer Cain for first-degree murder in the death of Louis Piñedo was evidence that the courts would not provide remedies. Attorney Eugene Deikman described the trial in *El Gallo:*

> The trial was set up by the District Attorney's office to clear Cain so that criminal charges could not be filed against him in the future. . . . One

juror admitted that he was a neighbor of a police officer and had a relative on the Little Rock, Arkansas, Police Force. Ordinarily [Prosecutor] Ettenburg would have challenged him off the jury. He did not do so this time. Neither side challenged jurors. . . . The family of Louis Piñedo and Mexicans, in general, were excluded from the courtroom as the jury was picked and during the opening statement of the District Attorney. Meanwhile, Anglo witnesses sat in the courtroom. . . . Ettenburg neglected to mention at all the fact that the victim was shot in the back but made excuses in advance by pointing out that the defendant could not have seen well as he had no flashlight.[56]

Deikman's article discounted the testimony of Officer Vandervelde, Cain's partner, who had not seen the actual shooting:

Vandervelde peered through the fence of the lot from the east side while Cain rushed to the west side and quickly climbed over the barbed wire topped fence. Vandervelde saw someone's feet between the cars and yelled to Cain. Cain went between the cars, and Vandervelde heard him "groan" and, immediately after, heard a shot. . . . Vandervelde was worried and called out. After a prolonged silence Cain said, "I've been stabbed. You'd better call an ambulance." Meanwhile, the boy was writhing on the ground bleeding to death from a bullet in the back, but Cain wanted an ambulance to come take care of his one-half inch wound. . . . After calling for an ambulance Vandervelde climbed over the fence. . . . Vandervelde went over to his partner, and they stood over the writhing body of the victim discussing Cain's one-half inch wound. Vandervelde had to be reminded even by Ettenburg that there was a mortally wounded boy present, and Vandervelde said, "Oh, yeah, the kid was on the ground. I thought he was shot through the chest." Later, when the court dismissed the murder charge against Cain, the victim's brother, Henry, furious and humiliated by this travesty, spat full in Cain's face as Cain slunk past him near the courtroom. Vandervelde jumped Henry Piñedo and brutally handcuffed him. "He's my brother," Henry gasped. Vandervelde sneered, "He was your brother." "You're proud of what you've done aren't you?" Henry screamed. Vandervelde smiled and spat in Henry's face.[57]

The indignation shown in Deikman's article was indicative of tensions mounting in the summer of 1967, a summer that saw over a hundred riots in African American communities throughout the United States and led the FBI to launch its infamous "Black Nationalist Hate Group Counterintelligence Program," an effort to derail—and defame—African American activism. A key target was Dr. Martin Luther King, Jr.

THE CRUSADE AND "INTERNAL SECURITY"

Police controversies were not the only focus for Gonzales' energy. On August 31, 1967, Gonzales—accompanied by Crusade vice chairperson Emilio Dominguez—was invited to Chicago to attend the National Conference for New Politics. The conference organizers' goal was "to enable those who work for peace, civil rights, and an end to poverty to register the greatest impact by concentrating money and manpower on direct political action."[58] The gathering was heavily infiltrated by government informers, including some from the Chicago Police Intelligence Unit who stole the conference organizers' files. Years later, as a result of a successful suit against the Chicago police, the files were turned over to the Chicago Historical Society.[59]

Gonzales intended to develop ties with other Latino groups at the conference, though Latinos were scarce, numbering two dozen or so. The Mexican population was concentrated in the Southwest, but national political, financial, and media centers were located in eastern seaboard cities and the industrial Midwest, factors that Gonzales felt impeded Latinos' impact at the Chicago conference. He noted the clout wielded by African Americans, but he felt that whites had little sense of who Chicanos and Latinos were. In *The Sixties,* Todd Gitlin recounted that "at the chaotic National Conference for New Politics convention in a Chicago hotel over Labor Day weekend, some three hundred blacks in a conference of two or three thousand demanded—and in an orgy of white guilt were granted—half the votes on all resolutions."[60] Gitlin's book, incidentally, makes almost no mention of Latino issues, activists, or organizations.

Whether or not black impact was tied to white guilt, which did not concern him, Gonzales felt that Latino impact was tied to unity on a regional and national level, so he proposed that Latinos operate as a caucus at the convention. He also called for a national Latino gathering in the spring of 1968. This proposal met with enthusiasm from the Latino activists, and the Crusade volunteered to host the gathering.[61] Informers reported the proposal to the FBI. Though Gonzales did not involve himself with the National Conference for New Politics after that initial gathering, Crusade member Eloy Espinoza attended a followup meeting in Chicago on February 11, 1968. The FBI apparently mistook Espinoza for Gonzales because both men were short, dark Mexicans with mustaches.[62]

The proposed gathering was a major topic of correspondence between the Chicago office of the FBI and FBI headquarters. An April 24, 1968, report, called an "Airtel" in FBI jargon, was obtained under the FOIA. Though heavily edited, it made it clear that many Latinos who had attended the Chicago Conference were subject to surveillance afterward.[63]

How the Chicago FBI office learned the identities and hometowns of the activists need not be left to conjecture: the list of participants was among the documents stolen by informers and delivered to police intelligence officers who worked with the FBI. FBI reports show that the bureau classified the proposed Latino gathering as an "internal security" matter.

In the spring of 1968, the Crusade for Justice embarked on the Poor People's Campaign, and the national gathering was postponed. Still, communications between headquarters and various FBI field offices showed confusion about the proposed conference, Gonzales' whereabouts, and the possibility that the Crusade owned a ranch in New Mexico that might be linked both to the conference and to Gonzales' activities.[64]

Gonzales was closely monitored by the FBI after the spring of 1967, especially his association with Reies Tijerina and the Alianza. On January 22, 1968, the Denver FBI office sent headquarters a "Nonprosecutive Summary Report" on Gonzales. Headquarters responded on February 7:

> Bureau feels instant investigation should not be closed at this time. The active leaders of the Alianza Federal de Mercedes, aka (AFDM) are currently undergoing trial on state charges in New Mexico. If they are found guilty and sentenced, it is not impossible they will be removed from positions of leadership in the AFDM thereby placing [Gonzales] as a likely candidate for the leadership of this militant Mexican American organization. Subject's activities with the Crusade for Justice indicate that the organization may be similar in nature to the AFDM.[65]

On February 28, headquarters informed the Denver FBI field office that Gonzales "has been approved for inclusion on the Rabble Rouser Index (RRI). . . . There seems to be no question that his activities pose a threat to the internal security of the United States. . . . Subject is leader of organization called Crusade for Justice. . . . His activities also warrant his inclusion on the Security Index."[66]

Having judged Gonzales' activism to be an internal security threat, headquarters took the next logical step the very next day, and targeted the entire Crusade organization. FBI headquarters instructed its Denver office as follows: "Since [the Crusade for Justice] has been active for a number of years . . . it is felt that investigation should be conducted to determine the true nature of the organization . . . and investigation of the organization is, therefore, being ordered."[67] The Special Agent in Charge (SAC) of the Denver FBI field office soon noted:

> On November 19, 1967, an article appeared in the *Denver Post* captioned, "TIJERINA Vows Appeal to U.N." The article dealt with the appearance of REIES LOPEZ TIJERINA . . . before the first anniversary celebration of Denver's Crusade for Justice. . . . Approximately 500 indi-

viduals were present at this meeting, including [Gonzales]. The article quoted TIJERINA as saying that the Spanish land grant dispute that goes back at least 100 years in northern New Mexico would be taken to the United Nations by some nation, even Castro's Cuba, if necessary.[68]

Though the reference to Cuba interested the FBI and local media, *El Gallo*'s account of Tijerina's visit merely recorded his itinerary in the Denver area. For example, Tijerina spoke at the University of Colorado and the University of Denver, was interviewed on radio programs and television, and was the honored guest at a reception at La Fiesta nightclub, hosted by owners Tim and Luisa Garcia and by the Crusade for Justice. At the Crusade's anniversary dinner, two 13-year-old boys recited "I Am Joaquin," an epic poem written by Gonzales, and a five-member dance troupe, including three of Gonzales' daughters, performed Mexican dances. Three New Mexico artists—Cleofes Vigil and John and Rini de Puy—and Manuel Martinez of the Crusade for Justice auctioned their work. Proceeds went to the Crusade. Cleofes Vigil, a farmer and multitalented folk historian from San Cristobal, was prevailed upon to sing an *alabado* (a traditional penitente song) to 81-year-old Teresina Romero, Gonzales' mother-in-law. *El Gallo*'s article on Tijerina's visit concluded with the names of the Crusaders who had offered him hospitality: Luis Ramirez, Eloisa Lovato, and John Haro.[69]

October and November 1967 were busy months for Gonzales. As he traveled to fulfill speaking engagements, the FBI's eyes and ears followed:

> On October 12, 1967, a meeting sponsored by the United Mexican-American Students at California State College at Los Angeles was held and approximately 200 individuals were present. . . . [Gonzales] was one of the featured speakers along with REIES LOPEZ TIJERINA. . . . In his speech before the crowd GONZALES stated that the present American middle-class society is sick. GONZALES called for all Mexican Americans to rebel from the present standard way of life. GONZALES stated that the widespread frustration of the Mexican Americans of the Southwest United States will eventually lead to violence. He stated that large-scale violence would be resorted to unless the Federal government changes its ways. He stated there would be large-scale rebellion unless the government provides basic needs of the Mexican-American people.[70]

Three days later:

> On October 15, 1967, an anti-Vietnam war protest and rally, sponsored by the Peace Action Council, was held at East Los Angeles College Stadium. . . . [Gonzales] was one of the speakers at this rally and he was

introduced as a former boxer and a Southwest leader of the Mexican Americans. Subject spoke of his work in Colorado to help the oppressed Mexican Americans to find jobs, learn English, and in some instances he stated that he fed and housed these Mexican Americans.[71]

On October 20 Gonzales attended an Albuquerque conference sponsored by the Alianza. Tijerina was trying to broaden the Alianza's support among peoples of color and draw activists from throughout the nation to conservative Albuquerque. Also attending were José Angel Gutiérrez of the Mexican American Youth Organization (MAYO); Ralph Featherstone and Ethel Minor of SNCC; Eliezer Risco of *La Raza* newspaper; Maulana Ron Karenga of US; Thomas Banyacya, a Hopi traditionalist; Bert Corona of the Mexican American Political Association; James Dennis of CORE; Anthony Babu of the Black Panther Party and the Black Student Union; and Walter Bremond of the Los Angeles Black Congress. The conference closed with participants signing a Treaty of Peace, Harmony and Mutual Assistance, which was printed and distributed by the Third World Committee of Karenga's organization. The treaty was symbolic and led to no formal alliance. Gonzales did not sign the treaty but was soon involved in another conference.

"BRAVE WORDS . . . AND NO ACTIONS"

Gonzales' presence at a gathering of Chicano activists in El Paso, also drew FBI scrutiny:

> On October 27, 1967, a public meeting was held at the Sacred Heart Gymnasium, EL Paso, Texas, in connection with the travel to El Paso by President Gustavo Diaz Ordaz of Mexico. [Gonzales] was one of the speakers at this meeting, and he told the group that the Mexican Americans in the Southwest would demand their rights and obtain justice for all. Also a speaker on that date was Reies Lopez Tijerina.[72]

The October 27 gathering was a protest against the Cabinet Committee Hearings on Mexican American Affairs, sponsored by the federal Inter-Agency Committee on Mexican American Affairs. The hearings were highlighted by a visit from President Gustavo Diaz Ordaz and by the return to Mexico of a parcel of land known as the Chamizal. The return of this land, due to a change in the course of the Rio Grande, was supposed to symbolize the United States' good intentions toward its southern neighbor. The hearings on Mexican American affairs, however, were called in response to a walkout by activists at the March 1966 meeting of the Equal Employment Opportunity Commission in Albuquerque. Gonzales had participated in the walkout, which protested against government neglect of civil rights concerns in Mexican communities. President Johnson promised to hold a White House conference for Chicano leaders following the Albuquerque protest, but the conference never materialized because Johnson feared another walkout. Instead, the El Paso hearings were held to demonstrate government concern, but activists like Gonzales, Tijerina and Cesar Chavez were not invited.

The Johnson administration's concern about the growth of militancy was evident in its efforts to defuse it. The El Paso conference was planned in Washington D.C., and in secret. The *Rocky Mountain News* reported:

> Although reporters were barred from the [planning] meeting, reports of dissension among the delegates from Colorado, New Mexico, and Texas leaked out. . . . The White House reportedly decided to split up the meetings to keep harmony between more militant Spanish-American groups and more moderate members of the Southwest's Spanish-speaking communities. A source said there was fear one large pre-conference session might produce a repeat of last year's meeting of the Equal Employment Opportunity Council in Albuquerque. Militant Spanish-Americans including Rudolph "Corky" Gonzales marched out of that conference. The planned White House conference grew out of a promise by President Johnson to take up Spanish-American problems and complaints this fall . . . [and was] in response to criticism for not including Spanish-Americans in a national White House civil rights conference last summer. Spanish-Americans long have complained about treatment they have received from government officials who, they charge, court them only around election time. . . . But the White House in recent months has become increasingly alarmed by what seems to be a growing move among Spanish-Americans in the Southwest, where they are the largest minority, to abandon their traditional support for the Democratic Party.[73]

The protestor's declaration, the "Plan de La Raza Unida," was more moderate than subsequent Chicano rhetoric and blends patriotism with anger over American racism. Its more militant signers included the Crusade, the Alianza, the UCLA chapter of United Mexican American Students (UMAS), Chicago's Latin American Defense Organization (LADO), and northern California's Mexican American Student Confederation (MASC). The American GI Forum and others represented more moderate activists. The diversity of views is reflected in the proclamation:

> On this historic day, October 28, 1967, La Raza Unida organized in El Paso, Texas, proclaims the time of subjugation, exploitation, and abuse of human rights of La Raza in the United States is hereby ended forever. . . . We have demonstrated and proven and again affirm our loyalty to the Constitutional democracy of the United States of America and to

the religious and cultural tradition we all share. We accept the framework of constitutional democracy and freedom within which to establish our own independent organizations among our people in pursuit of justice and equality and redress of grievances. La Raza Unida pledges to join with all our courageous people organizing in the fields and barrios. We commit ourselves to La Raza, at whatever cost.[74]

The proclamation demanded housing, education, and labor rights, and an end to police abuse; demand number six, (of eight) reads: "We demand the strong enforcement of all sections of the treaty of Guadalupe Hidalgo, particularly the sections dealing with land grants and bilingual guarantees."

Maclovio Barraza of the United Steel Workers of America signed the proclamation, participated in the picket, and attended the government conference, where he called for the empowerment of the poor:

> It takes the poor to understand the problems of the poor and to be involved in the plans and decisions aimed at the solution. It is equally true that one has to be a Mexican American living in the Southwest to know and understand the problems of this people, who today are among the most disadvantaged segments of our society and for whom the door of opportunity is, in most instances, more tightly shut than even the American Negro. . . . While I personally welcome the invitation to present my views, I cannot refrain from informing you that several important organizations equally concerned with the problems of the Mexican Americans view this conference with suspicion. They hold little or no expectation that it will result in anything meaningful. . . . These groups consider this meeting as being politically motivated at a time when the Federal election season approaches. They charge that the conference is structured so as to have only the "safe" Mexicans participating.[75]

This gathering proved to be another landmark in the growth of the Chicano movement. *El Gallo* recorded the Crusade's sentiments and role:

> Twelve Crusaders traveled to El Paso to take part in La Raza conference, which took place at the same time as the President's Conference on Mexican American Affairs. Yes, we picketed, we demonstrated, we marched, and we're still mad. A crowd of 300 out-of-state delegates led by Reies Tijerina and Rodolfo (Corky) Gonzales marched through the streets of downtown El Paso to a meeting of 1,000 people at the Sacred Heart Gym. Unity was the pledge.[76]

The Crusade contingent, moreover, encountered peculiar difficulties prior to the march.

> We arrived in El Paso at 2 a.m. and immediately went to a church where the Alianza members were supposed to be staying for $.75 a cot. It was

closed. No one answered the door. No one answered the phone. We called the Paso del Norte Hotel and asked for Reies Tijerina. The woman answered, "That man who is raising all kinds of Cain ain't here." (The next day we found out he was there.) We then went to Juarez, where our bus and cars were stopped and searched. We went to a cheap hotel managed by an old friend of Manuel Martinez. He was scared to death, he explained, about the government men from Mexico City, and he refused us rooms. There were no rooms available for Mexicanos Norte Americanos in all of Juarez. We were there 45 minutes and we were searched going back across the bridge to El Paso where we finally found room at the YMCA.[77]

After resting for the night and getting their bearings, Gonzales and the Crusade delegation led a march to Texas Western University, where Vice President Hubert Humphrey spoke. Texas Rangers barred the protestors from entering. According to *El Gallo:*

When we arrived at the gate, the farm workers of Laredo, Texas, were picketing the conference. Crusaders immediately joined the line. The Laredo people had been told by the police and Texas Rangers that they couldn't go on the grounds to demonstrate in front of the auditorium. The Crusade confronted the Texas Ranger and led the demonstration past the gate. The Ranger insisted that we have official business to be on the grounds and that a new policy or law was in effect to keep strangers off the campus. Our answer was that it was a tax-supported college and that it was having a conference on Mexican American Affairs and we were Mexican Americans. We marched in to the campus directly to the auditorium and demonstrated. All of the OEO, Labor, and government agency employees went out the side doors and got in buses rather than walk through the front to see their brothers who were demanding justice.[78]

Gonzales felt that the President's Conference lacked "any positive direction or militant action and rehabilitation. What resulted was a lot of brave words, promises, motions—and no action."[79]

A little-noted resolution by a young Crusade member, Manuel Martinez, criticized conference participants as "opportunists, tio tomases, coyotes" and describe the educational shortcomings affecting Mexican Americans. His resolution stated:

We . . . support those leaders who truly represent the feelings of the poor and who have taken a public stand denouncing the war in Vietnam. Furthermore, we support them in their efforts to secure justice with dignity for our people. Two of these leaders being . . . Reies Tijerina of New Mexico and Rodolfo "Corky" Gonzales of Colorado.[80]

Gonzales' travels continued into November 1967, and his speeches denounced the Vietnam war. Though he had publicly criticized the war one year earlier, as an individual, his criticism now reflected the official Crusade position. The FBI reported:

> On November 5, 1967, the *People's World* (West Coast communist newspaper) held its annual fund-raising banquet at the Miramar Hotel, Santa Monica, California. [Gonzales] was one of the featured speakers at this banquet. In his speech GONZALES dwelled on the oppression of the Mexican Americans in the United States by the "anglos". He traced the history of the Mexican Americans. . . . He stated that the young people should be told the truth about the racist policies of the U.S. government. He stated that the battle in Vietnam is really an extension of the imperialistic racist policies of the United States. GONZALES further stated that the "battle" should be in Los Angeles, in Denver, in Albuquerque, and throughout the Southwest. He stated that the "battle" should be in the Southwest and not in Vietnam.[81]

THE UNITED FARM WORKERS UNION

The FBI monitored Gonzales' involvement with cultural events as well as his speeches before communist audiences. The Crusade sponsored Teatro Campesino, a theater troupe that worked with Cesar Chavez' farmworkers union, at its first performance in Denver, which took place at the Santa Fe Theatre on August 8, 1967. On the same occasion Crusade troupers performed "The Revolutionist," a play by Gonzales. The FBI's theater review noted:

> Among those present were members of the Denver C[ommunist] P[arty]. "The Revolutionist" is a play about a typical Mexican American coming into a large city with a great deal of ambition and finding that willingness to work is not enough to get along in the city. The individual then becomes a "revolutionist" when he finds himself an outcast.[82]

Gonzales invited Chavez to Denver in December 1967, and the Crusade sponsored his visit. Though this was Chavez' first visit, his union was already represented in Denver by Louis Melendrez, who had received housing at the Crusade for Justice headquarters at 1265 Cherokee Street. This small, two-story apartment building owned by Gonzales was used as office space for the Crusade, and one unit served as a combination coffee house/crash pad for young artists and activists. Chavez stayed with Melendrez during his visit. He arrived on December 20 and was busy with interviews the following day. At a dinner in his honor at the Annunciation Church in Northeast Denver, Chavez briefly addressed the issue

of police brutality, saying, "For those who have never suffered police brutality, it was impossible to discuss the problem and, for those who had,
nothing was more degrading and barbarous than police brutality."[83]

Chavez' visit and those of Tijerina and the Teatro Campesino demonstrate the contacts, talents, and political contributions of Rodolfo Gonzales in the Crusade's early years. Gonzales was not merely a participant in
political activity; he was often its initiator. He was a leader who could
speak to the powerful and voice the outrage of the powerless. Those he
criticized sought to minimize his words, beliefs, and sentiments as unrep-
resentative of the community.

DILL'S RESIGNATION: "CHANGE OR EXCHANGE?"

At 4 p.m. on November 17, 1967, Police Chief Dill met with Mayor Currigan and Manager of Safety Hugh McClearn, Dill's immediate superior.
Currigan told Dill, "McClearn is going to resign and is going back into
private practice. Getting down to the meat of it, Harold, I want you to
resign, too."[84]

Dill later recounted that the mayor wanted him to decide the date of
his departure within a week. On November 21, Dill announced his resignation, effective December 31, 1967, thus ending a career that began on
May 1, 1935. A newspaper wrote:

> From that brief City Hall meeting [on November 17] to this day [Janu-
> ary 1, 1968], there has been no further meeting between the Chief and
> the Mayor as to why the resignation was demanded. . . . [or] the Chief's
> status on pension, accrued leave time, or other matters generally dis-
> cussed between two men in such administrative positions. . . . They are
> not only long-time past friends, but both are indebted to each other.
> When Currigan became Mayor, he removed Dill from "Siberian banish-
> ment" as jail captain. . . . Chief Dill . . . played no small role in Curri-
> gan's weight at the polls when he was up for re-election last year. While
> the two are reluctant to discuss their differences, it's generally believed
> the split between the former friends stems from one boiling issue. The
> issue isn't one of Denver concern alone. . . . It touches every city which
> has persons classified as the minority—those who are hungry, jobless,
> poverty-stricken. When these minority groups rebel over their years of
> frustration, their first target is the police—symbols of authority with
> whom they are in the most frequent contact. The dispute between the
> Chief and his boss stemmed over how this explosive problem should
> be handled.[85]

Reporter Al Nakkula—who was apparently given documents on the
rift between Currigan and Dill—revealed that the mayor wanted police–

minority relations handled "with kid gloves," while Dill "insisted on maintaining full police powers as the symbol of authority." The mayor himself described the situation as one in which the two were poles apart.[86]

A three-page, single-spaced letter to Safety Manager McClearn depicted Currigan's emotional stresses as he dealt with a situation he feared could lead to riots. Another document provided to Nakkula revealed the mayor's concern about three confrontations involving the police and minorities, two of which occurred in the African American Park Hill neighborhood. Dill was present at one, and police car windows were broken. Unnamed community leaders felt that the police presence incited the crowd's anger and urged Dill to withdraw his men, a suggestion Dill rejected. The third incident cited was the 1967 Crusade for Justice—Black Panther Party protest at police headquarters over the deaths of Louis Piñedo and Eugene Cook.[87]

The Crusade took an unsympathetic view of Currigan's stress and Dill's resignation. A front-page cartoon in *El Gallo* shows the mayor accepting Dill's resignation, as the latter with a big retirement check protruding from his pocket, crosses his index and middle fingers to indicate that he is lying. Ignored by the mayor and the chief, two policemen are beating an elderly, cane-carrying Mexicano in the background.[88] The Crusade's views were also conveyed in an editorial titled "Change or Exchange?"

> Police Chief Dill has resigned or, as those supporters of the Mayor would say, "Currigan fired him." Now what? Is he replaced by another career cop who has been with the DPD for 20, 25, or 30 years, like Dill? If so, the same attitudes toward minorities and humanity will prevail that prevailed 20, 25, and 30 years ago in our fair city of conservative moths who scream from their cocoons that police brutality, harassment, and inhumanity is only a figment of the poor people's imagination. . . . There is a new cry arising from the Mexican American areas of Denver, and it has changed from a cry of pain to a cry of anger. "An eye for an eye and a tooth for a tooth, bullet for bullet; instead of cracked skulls, bullets in the back, justice in the alley." As [Dill and Currigan] go their separate ways, tight-lipped about each other's problems, Dill will receive vacation pay, back pay, and retirement pay. [Currigan] will remain on as mayor, praised by the Uncle Tom Negroes and the Tio Taco–Vanishing Spanish Americans who retain their jobs and are in the good social graces with the patron.[89]

On November 9, a week before Currigan summoned Dill to his office, a public forum became an ugly confrontation. This incident may have influenced Currigan's decision. The meeting was to be moderated by Colorado Labor Council President Herrick Roth. Manager of Safety McClearn was present, and Ted Yoder, another participant, was to provide the discussion format. The police department was represented by Division Chief Ralph Potter and Police Technician Al Nieto.

The meeting was disrupted when Desiderio de Herrera of the Crusade went to the stage, took the microphone from Mr. Yoder, and denounced the police department. Another, unnamed Crusade member said angrily:

> "If you shoot our kids in the back, we're going to shoot policemen in the back." Herrick Roth then invited Rodolfo "Corky" Gonzales to speak. Gonzales supported the militant spokesman 100% and then let the Police Department know that the Mexican American would no longer take insult, abuse, harassment, beating, or killing from the police. "If it takes retaliation and violence to gain justice and equality, that's what is going to be."[90]

These words drew FBI scrutiny and were cited in subsequent FBI reports. The Crusade's speakers, however, may have felt that they were merely stating the facts: Chicanos saw neither their rights nor their lives respected in society, and if the only option to gain rights and respect was to take arms in self-defense, or in retaliation, they gave notice that they stood ready. Were these words, deeds, and beliefs justified? And were there other questions that needed to be asked and answered?

Did police routinely abuse people and sometimes murder them? Did politicians lie and cover up because of expediency, incompetence, or racism? Who—or what—was at fault? Though the answers to these questions may not be clear, it is clear that the issue of police brutality had become highly polarized.

Dills firing, or "retirement," led to his replacement by George L. Seaton. Chief Seaton had risen through the ranks like his predecessor. He was appointed on December 29 and sworn in on January 2, 1968. Harold Dill was conspicuous by his absence at Seaton's swearing-in ceremony. The media trumpeted its high opinion of Seaton, and editorials proclaimed; "Chief Seaton Off to a Good Start" and "Seaton Impresses Minority Leaders" (the "leaders" went unnamed).[91] Francis Salazar, an attorney, wrote to the *Denver Post* editor urging minority support for Seaton:

> I have read the comments of Denver's new Police Chief, George L. Seaton, and he sounds almost too good to be true. He sounds sincere, educated, and enlightened. . . . As sick as it may sound, there are people who hope that [Seaton] fails in his very difficult undertaking. . . . There are others who hope to profit by strife and riot, would-be-leaders who do not care about the consequences of their reckless statements. . . . Currigan's actions in changing Police Chiefs were courageous and right: he suffered with dignity and restraint a great deal of unjust and unwarranted criticism.[92]

Seaton realigned the department's policy and command structure, saying: "We are aiming at human relations, with everyone we serve, and legalities and trying to dispel any suspicion and hostility that may exist among them. Policemen are going to have to get smart. . . . Many times, by what he says, a police officer gets himself in trouble. . . . I hope to release men from less critical areas for community relations and delinquency control."[93] Similarly, the *Rocky Mountain News* reported that "key [administrative] appointments appear in line with Seaton's previously stated intent to emphasize improvement of community relations . . . and a heavily accelerated war on juvenile crime."[94]

The Crusade, however, continued its protests.

A "SICK AND CORRUPT" SOCIETY

On January 28, 1968, a Denver chapter of the American GI Forum hosted a panel discussion titled "Will the Mexican American Riot?" Among the panelists were Armando Rodriguez, of the U.S. Office of Education's Mexican American Affairs Unit; Dr. Phil Montez, identified as a California dentist; and Dr. Ralph Guzman of Los Angeles, California. The discussion did not go as planned.

As the panel began, a large Crusade contingent arrived. Members were in no mood to hear out-of-town speakers. They were tired of panels, discussions, and experts. According to the *Denver Post*, "Gonzales and his group of vocal supporters made their presence known quickly. . . . Shouts demanding that Gonzales be allowed to speak had interrupted panelists, and when it was agreed that Gonzales should come to the speaker's rostrum, cries of 'Viva! Viva!' went up."[95] Though Gonzales did not predict riots, he said, "I don't think that there won't be people who will be putting names on lists" and predicted "guerilla warfare in the Southwest."

Gonzales linked the government's Vietnam policy to domestic racism, saying that Chicano casualties made possible "the millions and millions of dollars being made on Vietnam by the industrialists and politicians." He said American society was racist, and "if we say we want to be a part of this society, then we are sick because this society is sick and corrupt." A *Rocky Mountain News* article on the event quoted three of the 11 panelists, but did not report that the Crusade commandeered the meeting. Gonzales and the Crusade, in fact, were not mentioned at all.[96]

Gonzales traveled to California three weeks later. The FBI reported: "On February 18, 1968, [Gonzales] attended a mass rally held at the Los Angeles Sports Arena. . . . Approximately 5,000 people were in attendance. STOKELY CARMICHAEL and H. RAP BROWN, militant black nationalist leaders, were the main speakers. [Gonzales] was introduced and spoke in favor of REIES TIJERINA."[97]

Gonzales, in company with Tijerina, subsequently spoke at a press conference at the New Left School in Los Angeles on February 22. The FBI reported that Gonzales said he was "training young people there [in Denver] on the idea of who their enemy is and how they can be taught this principle instead of being brainwashed and used to go to Vietnam, to fight the battle 'here' instead of Vietnam. They must learn to operate in the 'open' instead of underground methods."[98]

That year President Johnson asked Congress to provide $6.3 billion to American cities for antipoverty efforts, including rent supplements, mass transit planning, and a proposal to build six million housing units for the poor in ten years. While conservatives decried these liberal policies and the growth of the "welfare state," Gonzales criticized liberals and conservatives alike.

Gonzales, the former head of the Denver War on Poverty, held a jaundiced opinion of these programs and of society's potential to reform itself voluntarily. He believed that conservative opposition to social programs was motivated by racism. Conservative farmers who received subsidies to *not* grow food while the poor went hungry, he reasoned, were also welfare recipients. Both major parties routinely supported farm subsidies.

Gonzales saw war in Vietnam, which both parties also supported, as a mechanism to provide profits to corporations producing airplanes, ships, and weaponry, while poor and minority soldiers paid the price in blood and the Vietnamese landscape and people were laid waste. This, he felt, was a welfare state for war contractors and wealthy corporations.

His criticism of liberal politicians was equally scathing. He believed that politicians used money allocated for poverty programs as patronage; more money went for salaries and overhead than trickled down to the poor. Dependency and control resulted, not reform.

Distributing food commodities helped conservative farmers; the poor received mere crumbs, and were then despised and stigmatized as though they deserved their misfortunes. Rent subsidies passed through the hands of the poor and returned to municipal public housing bureaucracies. Food stamps were passed to the poor and then redeemed by the chain stores where they shopped. Who was really on welfare: the poor, the rich, or the bureaucrats?

Gonzales felt that these programs were minor concessions to the poor, not true remedies for social inequality, mechanisms to pacify communities without empowering them. The political patronage dispensed by the system served to buy minority "leaders" with jobs and social prestige.

"Yesterday's militant is today's government employee," Gonzales frequently said. He called people who returned to the community as government-funded leaders "boomerang Chicanos" while administrators who went from one government job to another like monkeys swinging from tree to tree, were "limb-swingers."

Society's responses to social problems were not limited to government programs and subsidized "leaders." The Ford Foundation, for example, made a $221,164 grant to the System Development Corporation to expand a pilot study project of Spanish-surnamed students in Los Angeles. Dr. Julian Zamora, of the University of Notre Dame, used Ford Foundation money to study U.S.–Mexico border issues. The Ford Foundation also made available $150,000 to increase the number of Spanish-surnamed attorneys in the Rocky Mountain region, where 9 percent of area's-population was Spanish-surnamed, "but of over 2,000 lawyers in the (Denver) metropolitan area, less than 10 are of Spanish-American descent."[99] Ford's generosity in one instance helped create an "alternative leadership structure."

According to one well-placed Ford man: "Ford's first direct contact in New Mexico was in the spring of 1967. The key (Ford) man here was Bill Watts, who was active head of the Office of Government and Law. Ford was very anxious even at that point to build some reasonable alternative to Tijerina and the Alianza. Within a month after the raid at Tierra Amarilla, a team was dispatched to New Mexico. Their purpose was to create as quickly as possible a leadership structure alternative to Tijerina. Actually, the team had two objectives: The first was to divert attention from Tijerina and the land question by creating an alternative leader, someone to whom they could point as a spokesman for the Mexican Americans in New Mexico. The HELP [Home Education Livelihood Program] was existent, under the direction of Alex Mercure, so Ford decided to make Mercure that leader. A few months after the team was sent to New Mexico, Ford approved a $453,450 [research and development] grant to HELP as part of the program to knock Tijerina and create this alternative leadership structure." After Ford's initial $453,450 grant. . . . Mercure became known as "The Empire Builder" among his poverty program colleagues and was named to national commissions, advisory boards and panels as a "Mexican American leader." When Congress called hearings after the Tierra Amarilla incident . . . it called Mercure to testify, not Tijerina or Alianzistas. . . . .Watts is no longer with Ford; at last report he was working as a staff secretary of the National Security Council in the Nixon Administration under Henry Kissinger, an old personal friend of Ford Foundation President McGeorge Bundy. . . . In the fall of 1967, Ford moved, under a $21,839 grant, to bring together a select group of Mexican Americans at a meeting in Los

Angeles. Out of that gathering eventually came the Southwest Council of la Raza, designed as an umbrella organization covering the Southwest, funded by Ford to the tune of $630,000 in February 1968. The Council's first executive director was Herman Gallegos, who resigned his job as a Ford Foundation consultant to accept the new position. Alex Mercure was immediately appointed to the Council's Board of Directors.[100]

All this concern for Spanish-surnamed communities resulted, in Gonzales' and the Crusade's view, from independent leadership, autonomous organization, and forceful action on the issues. The activism of Gonzales and Tijerina drew the attention of the nation's antiwar and civil rights movements as well. In Chicago for the 1967 National Conference for New Politics, both men met Martin Luther King. King invited them and others to participate in an upcoming national protest. The stage was being set for a "poor people's campaign" in the nation's capital in the spring of 1968.

Three

The Poor People's Campaign

In the last years of his life, Martin Luther King broadened his political agenda beyond integration to include eloquent criticism of American militarism, the Vietnam war, and the unequal distribution of wealth and power inherent in America's social order. His call for a "poor people's campaign" to unite the disenfranchised was symbolic of his transformation.

Though Gonzales' rhetoric and nationalism separated him from King's pacifism, he viewed the Poor People's Campaign with enthusiasm as another forum for the budding Chicano movement. Though Gonzales expected the Campaign to fall short of its goals, he eagerly awaited the opportunities it presented.

"GONZALES AND TIJERINA HAD MET WITH DR. KING . . ."

In a March 12, 1968, interview on KBTR, a Denver radio station, Gonzales announced that he was going to Atlanta, Georgia, to meet with King and discuss the march on Washington being planned by the Southern Christian Leadership Conference (SCLC). The Denver FBI reported to Director J. Edgar Hoover, "Gonzales hopes to have poor Spanish-Americans join King's march, along with poor Negroes."[1] The March 15 *Denver Post* reported, "Corky Gonzales . . . was in Atlanta . . . to confer with the Rev. Dr. Martin Luther King, Jr., on the role the Southwest will play in a national demonstration of the poor in Washington, D.C., April 22."

An 18-page Denver branch report, captioned "Rudolph Gonzales, Internal Security . . . Field Office File #100–9290," and dated April 26, was sent to FBI headquarters, which forwarded it to the State Department, the Secret Service, the 113th Military Intelligence Group, and the CIA. The FBI reported:

> On March 14, 1968, Reversed Martin Luther King, Jr., President of the Southern Christian Leadership Conference (SCLC) attended a meeting of representatives of minority groups held . . . [in] Atlanta, Georgia. The purpose of Reverend King's address was to solicit support of minority groups for the SCLC's Washington Spring Project. . . . [T]he SCLC . . . press release . . . showed that at the meeting a "National Poor People's Steering Committee" was selected. The name "RODOLFO CORKY GONZALES, Crusade for Justice, Denver, Colorado," was shown as a member of this committee.

Page 8 of the same FBI report then cited the April 9 *Denver Post:*

> Rodolpho (Corky) Gonzales, chairman of the Crusade for Justice . . . flew to Atlanta, Ga., Tuesday for the funeral of the Rev. Dr. Martin Luther King, Jr. Gonzales said he would confer in Atlanta with Reies Lopez Tijerina. . . . Gonzales and Tijerina had met with Dr. King to plan Mexican American involvement in Dr. King's "poor people's march" on Washington.

FBI surveillance of Dr. King was intense enough to tell the bureau what transpired in his bedroom, but not adequate to prevent his assassination.

The Campaign's strategy was to make demands on the federal government on poor people's behalf and to bring Washington to a standstill by militant civil disobedience if the government did not respond. Dr. King's assassination deprived the SCLC of its ablest, most inspiring leader, and the anticipated civil disobedience campaign never occurred on the scale some feared and others hoped for.

The SCLC continued organizing for the Poor People's Campaign after King's assassination, and Gonzales' and Tijerina's support boosted Mexican and Native American participation.

The southwestern "poor people's" contingent they organized was exotic mix. There were Native Americans from Colorado, New Mexico, Arizona, Nevada, and Oklahoma; young California Black Berets and Brown Berets; elderly New Mexico land grant heirs and Asians from California's Bay Area; Black Panthers, hippies, and white radicals; pacifists and advocates of revolution.

Gonzales' brother-in-law, Richard Romero, had gone ahead to Washington to develop contacts and resources for the rest of the group. The whole contingent arrived in Washington and settled at the private Hawthorne School. The main body of protestors was housed in an encampment called Resurrection City.

Before leaving Colorado, Gonzales advised Crusade members that making demands in Washington would not in itself bring about change. The main things to be gained by participation in the Campaign, he stressed, were opportunities to develop ties with other activists and gain national visibility for Chicanos. The real work, building bases of power, would remain when the activists returned.

Upon arriving in Washington, Gonzales decided that the Chicanos in his group would not move into Resurrection City but would remain at the Hawthorne School. Since the Poor People's Campaign was to symbolize the solidarity of poor people, this decision troubled the SCLC leadership.

INTERNAL CONFLICTS

Diversity was a factor in some conflicts among participants in the Poor People's Campaign, but more frequently critics targeted the SCLC leadership, protest strategy, and allocation of resources. Sometimes personality conflicts were involved.

Tijerina loudly criticized the SCLC for, among other things, overlooking the land grant question: "The poor have been completely mocked. Never have I seen the poor so betrayed. . . . I say now that only the public can put a stop to this shameful, hypocritical campaign that was supposed to have been established in the name of God and the poor."[2] It was not the Crusade's understanding that the Campaign had been established for reasons related to the Almighty, although it too disagreed with SCLC strategy (and sometimes with Tijerina, as well). Crusade members' children, for example, took to calling Reies Tijerina—whom they saw as zealous for publicity—"Reies TV-rina." Similarly, Reverend Ralph Abernathy, with his Southern Baptist rhetorical style, became known as Reverend Blabbernathy.

SCLC leaders visited the Hawthorne School to urge Gonzales to ask Chicanos to move to Resurrection City. They warned that the media might insinuate that Chicanos chose to remain separate because of racial antipathy. Various SCLC reverends, each with a different oratorical style, attempted to influence Gonzales. The Reverend Hosea Williams, a scowling, blustery, and burly man, probably had the least appropriate manner. Gonzales remained adamant. When individual meetings failed, a meeting was called at the Hawthorne School for all SCLC reverends, Gonzales, Tijerina, and others.

Gonzales criticized the poor management of Resurrection City and said that it was his responsibility to provide the best he could for those who had come to Washington with him. He would not subject his group to the conditions prevailing at the encampment, especially when the leading figures of the SCLC were housed in hotels and motels, a pointed criticism to which the SCLC leaders were at a loss to respond. The meeting lasted for hours, but the Hawthorne School contingent remained where it was.

Another, unspoken consideration motivated Gonzales. Mexicans were a regional minority with little impact on national consciousness and would remain a minority-within-a-minority under the SCLC umbrella at Resurrection City. A distinct Chicano presence at the Poor People's Campaign was necessary to guarantee the visibility for which the Hawthorne School provided the base. Though the Hawthorne contingent was under Chicano leadership, people of all backgrounds stayed there because it was well administered.

INDIGENOUS RIGHTS AND THE POOR PEOPLE'S CAMPAIGN

As Chicanos asserted their autonomy by refusing to move to Resurrection City, Native Americans asserted their autonomy by leaving the Hawthorne School. Not long after arriving in Washington, Native Americans at the school packed their belongings and moved to a nearby church, where they joined Native Americans from other areas. There were no hard feelings, but they never discussed their decision: they just left. Gonzales laughed and spoke admiringly of their independence. Who could require native people to consult with anyone, much less ask permission to leave?

Issues of Indian sovereignty and primacy of rights had arisen on the caravan to Washington, when publicity-minded "militants" bickered over who would lead the march across the bridge between St. Louis, Missouri, and East St. Louis, Illinois. Gonzales stated that Native Americans were the first people of the Americas, had suffered genocide, and lived in unsurpassed poverty while their comrades sniveled over who should lead marches on their land. Rather than argue, Gonzales declared that native people would lead the march across the bridge. The march was led by native people. All others followed.

Indigenous rights were also the issue in the most dramatic protest of the Poor People's Campaign. Native Americans met with the Hawthorne School contingent to seek support for a protest at the Supreme Court that the SCLC hesitated to endorse. Gonzales agreed to support it. His decision to remain at the school was politically calculated, but his decision to back the protest was principled. It was the right thing to do. The SCLC was told that the Hawthorne School contingent would support the Supreme Court protest, the inference being that SCLC permission was not needed, but that the organization was being informed as a courtesy.

There were far fewer Native Americans in the Poor People's Campaign than Chicanos, whose support would add the strength of numbers to the protest. African American and white protestors at Resurrection City were also impatient for action, and they responded favorably upon hearing of the protest. The reluctant SCLC leadership had no choice but to participate, since it would take place with or without them.

Native peoples from Washington State targeted the Supreme Court to protest against violation of the 1854 Medicine Creek Treaty.[3] In return for the "right" to fish in their ancestral waters (in common with "all citizens of the territory"), native people lost 2,240,000 acres to the United States. By the late 1950s, they were accused of overfishing the salmon, though they took less than 1 percent of the state harvest.

On May 29, Puyallup-Nisqually people led several hundred protestors to the Supreme Court. The building's great metal doors were shut, and the protestors denied entrance. *El Gallo* reported:

> Hours were spent in negotiating with low-rank officials before reaching an agreement as to the size of the delegation that would be allowed to enter. The agreement was finally reached and a delegation including Hank Adams and Al Bridges, fishermen, Corky Gonzales and Reies Tijerina along with Rev. Abernathy, was finally allowed to enter. When they came back out, a press conference was held on the steps of the Supreme Court that was guarded by 85 young Chicanos who comprised the tight-knit security guard headed by Sal Candelaria, a Black Beret from San Jose, California.[4]

The dramatic, well-orchestrated demonstration incurred the hostility of the police. About 300 officers had gathered around the Supreme Court by the day's end.

> As the marchers left the Court to return to Hawthorne School and Resurrection City, the police marched along the opposite curb. Finally, at the corner of 1st and Independence, the police got what they long wanted—a chance to crack heads. The security guards, with arms linked, had stopped in the intersection waiting until the last of the marchers had passed. At this time the police drove two motorcycles through the security line and into the mass of men, women and children in an attempt to break up the march.[5]

The resulting scuffle led to the arrest of six of the security guards: Danny Tijerina and his friend, Miguel Trujillo, both 17 years old; Billy Joe Cheek, a white youth who claimed to be of Cherokee and Mexican Indian descent, from Oakland, California; and Mark Jaramillo, Al Sanchez, Jr., and the author, all members of the Crusade for Justice.

FBI AND MEDIA REPORTS

The FBI was monitoring Gonzales' activity during the Poor People's Campaign. One FBI document reported, "[Gonzales] is currently on the Security Index and the Agitators Index. He is a known Mexican-American rabble rouser and current summary report has been furnished to the intelligence community."[6] The FBI noted the rifts among the protestors, including Native Americans' criticism of Abernathy, Gonzales' criticism of Tijerina, Tijerina's criticism of the SCLC, and Hosea Williams' disagreements with Gonzales.

On June 3, demonstrators assembled at a press conference at the Department of Justice. Speakers at the demonstration included Father James Groppi of Milwaukee, SCLC Reverends Jesse Jackson, James Bevel, and Hosea Williams, Gonzales, and Tijerina.[7] SCLC leaders criticized the lack of progress in the investigation of King's assassination, and Chicanos protested against the arrest of over a dozen California activists on conspiracy charges following massive East Los Angeles school walkouts in March 1968. (This case is described in Chapter 7.) Brown Beret Carlos Montes, who was present at the Justice Department protest, learned of his indictment by Los Angeles authorities when Gonzales told him about it.

The demonstration began at 1:15 p.m. Activists demanded that Attorney General Ramsey Clark meet with a 100-person delegation, but Clark only wanted to meet with 20. After negotiations involving Gonzales, Williams, and Hank Adams, an Assiniboin-Lakota living in Washington State, Clark agreed to meet with the 100 representatives at 10 a.m. on June 4.[8] Protestors from Resurrection City returned to the encampment about 8 p.m., but 150 Chicanos stayed on at the Justice Department to pressure for the release of the Los Angeles defendants. Gonzales disbanded the rally at 10:40 p.m. after learning that the defendants had been freed. At the June 4 meeting, Gonzales read Clark a statement calling his attention to the Los Angeles indictments.

By June 10, less than half of the original 400 members of the southwestern contingent remained in Washington. An FBI "source" reported minor differences between Gonzales and Abernathy over what strategy should be employed after the Poor People's Campaign ended. Gonzales pressed for representation reflecting the movement's diversity and used every opportunity to press Chicano issues. The Washington FBI field office reported to Hoover's office:

> Gonzales indicated that he wanted a coalition of all ethnic groups to follow through after the [Campaign ended]. . . . He [also] said that his

group will demonstrate here to coincide with an undisclosed demonstration scheduled at San Jose State College and will join with Reies Tijerina, Albuquerque, New Mexico leader of the Mexican-Americans in a
demonstration at the U.S. Department of State (USDS) June thirteenth
next. . . . The San Francisco Office is requested to advise any info which
it may have concerning planned demonstration at San Jose State
College.[9]

On June 10, as the Campaign neared its end, Abernathy listed its
accomplishments at a press conference, as recorded by an FBI source:

1. US Department of Agriculture Secretary Orville Freeman agreed to
   release food to the neediest counties in the country,
2. $270 million released by the Department of Agriculture for the poor,
3. $25 million dollars had been released by the Office of Economic Op-
   portunity for the poor,
4. A housing bill had been passed by the Senate.[10]

The press conference, like the Campaign itself, did not proceed
smoothly. The FBI noted:

During the conference an Indian American, Kahn Tineta Horn, from
Quebec, Canada, presented a letter of complaint to Abernathy about
POCAM [Poor People's Campaign]. She stated that the Indians' aims
are different and refused any spokesman for Indians except an Indian
. . . while at the same time she requested a cessation of exploitation of
Indian Americans for purposes not related to their goals.[11]

Gonzales flew to Denver on June 10 and held a press conference to
announce the formation of a steering committee to coordinate poor
people's demands after the Campaign ended in Washington:

One prime interest of the [steering] committee, Gonzales said, isn't
only to change the present national structure to allow greater opportunity for poor people and minority groups, but also to make the changes
while preserving cultural ties and values. . . . Specific demands by ethnic
groups within the general group will also be worked out.[12]

Gonzales focused on issues like land grants, economics ("industries
which come into the Southwest should use human resources available
there, rather than place our people in the bondage of welfare by bringing in outside labor"), and cultural rights ("the continued ignoring of
our cultural rights has resulted in psychological destruction of our
youngsters").[13]

When questioned about conflicts among protestors, Gonzales sought
to minimize the squabbling and blamed the media for misrepresenting
disagreements between himself and Tijerina. Media reports implied that

the differences resulted from a power struggle; in fact, they were primarily over strategy. Gonzales, and the Crusade in general, felt that Tijerina's style was marked (or marred) by personal flamboyance at the expense of sound organizing. The differences were not about jealousy or personal power, and Gonzales believed that exposing the differences to the media was not in the movement's interest: "Any fights within our family, we keep within the family." He accused the media of "looking for cracks in a negative [journalistic] approach."[14]

Gonzales wanted to purchase the Calvary Baptist Church at 1567 Downing Street to anchor the Crusades operations. The old office on Cherokee Street, a few blocks from downtown Denver, was in a precarious position.

In 1966 Gonzales was fired as director of the Neighborhood Youth Corps, resigned his War on Poverty directorship, and dropped his lucrative bail bond business. He lost the Cherokee Street office when he could no longer make payments. Gonzales envisioned the three-story church building as a cultural and community center.[15] Buying it would be a bold move, since the Crusade had few resources and a small membership. Gonzales returned to Washington after exploring the feasibility of the purchase.

Subsequent demonstrations in Washington included a June 13 protest at the State Department, the June 15 Puerto Rican Day demonstration, and a June 21 Indian and Chicano protest at the Justice Department, where Mad Bear Anderson, Hank Adams, Tijerina, and Gonzales spoke. The Poor People's Campaign culminated with a June 19 Solidarity Day rally. The FBI monitored the protests, sometimes using inaccurate sources, as exemplified by a report on a June 18 youth protest.

A July 15 FBI memo reported that a group of about a hundred young marchers "led by Rudolph Gonzales" departed from Resurrection City to demonstrate in front of the White House, but

> was met by the police and when the group insisted upon demonstrating, a confrontation ensued with the police using night sticks resulting in superficial and minor injuries to several demonstrators and policemen. A number of the demonstrators were arrested. . . . They were charged with disorderly conduct and one was charged with assaulting a police officer.[16]

Contrary to the FBI's "source," the protest was not led by Gonzales, totaled far fewer than 100 protestors, and did not depart from Resurrection City. The White House protest was planned as a youth demonstration, and demonstrated the ill-conceived and impatient qualities of youth, not the well-calculated tactics of Rodolfo Gonzales.

On the evening of June 17, a small group of youngsters had complained that the adults who organized activities at the Hawthorne School and in the Poor People's Campaign were not providing enough action. They felt that youths should have their own voice and, by implication, their own demonstration. The idea for the youth protest was initiated by Los Angeles Brown Berets, including Ralph Ramirez and Carlos Montes, and endorsed by other young people. Consultation with adults was minimal.

On the morning of June 18, young activists decided to march to the White House to demand a meeting with President Johnson. If denied entrance by White House guards, the protestors vowed to scale the White House fence, charge across the lawn, and enter the president's dwelling. With their strategy decided, two or three dozen youngsters set out from the Hawthorne School, among them members of the Brown Berets, the Black Berets, the Crusade, the Alianza Federal de Mercedes, and others. After a few blocks, the group was followed by plainclothes agents in unmarked cars who photographed them. They marched from the Hawthorne School to Resurrection City, then to the White House.

The protestors' strategy, like the FBI memo, was deficient in its details. President Johnson was not in Washington, much less at the White House, that day. Few adults participated in the protest, but among the few who did were Eloy Espinoza of the Crusade and Ruben Maldonado, a Spanish-speaking Indian from Arizona. The marchers drew increasing police scrutiny as they approached the White House.

As they turned a corner and approached the guard post at the White House entrance, buses arrived. Dozens of helmeted, club-carrying police took up positions in a three-line formation. As the protestors advanced, they were ordered to disperse by police. When they refused, the first line of police moved forward to prod and hit them with riot batons. Marchers who pushed through the first line were clubbed to the ground by a second line of officers. The third line picked up the protestors, handcuffed them, and took them to jail.[17] So ended the youth march on the White House.

THE END OF THE CAMPAIGN

Resurrection City closed on June 24, 1968, and Gonzales returned to Denver. A rally was held at the Annunciation Church two days later. In September 1968 a press conference in Denver announced that a "Poor People's Embassy" was to be established to provide leadership training and lodging for groups visiting the nation's capital, and serve as "a communications center for numerous . . . groups which have allied themselves with the Poor People's Campaign."[18] Gonzales was the temporary chairman of the embassy's board.

Represented in the effort were the National Welfare Rights Organization, the United Farm Workers Organizing Committee, SCLC, and others. The embassy's co-directors were Anibal Solivan, a Puerto Rican from New York, and Ivanhoe Donaldson of the Institute for Policy Studies. The embassy was supposed to receive $24,000 from two small foundations to establish itself temporarily in New York City while its leaders sought $1.5 million from larger foundations. Temporary office space had not even been rented at the time of the announcement.[19] The plans for the embassy went nowhere, and the Crusade held no serious internal discussions on the matter.

Gonzales did not believe social change would come from Washington, but felt that building autonomous power bases at the grassroots level was the key to social change. When asked by a reporter if he would leave Denver to join the staff of the proposed embassy, Gonzales simply answered, "I'm going to stay with my group."[20]

Though the Poor People's Campaign did not "turn the nation around," as its rhetoric promised, the Crusade noted with satisfaction that media coverage of minorities increasingly referred to "Mexican Americans," "Chicanos," or Spanish-speaking communities. Crusade activists and other Chicanos increased their contacts with other ethnic groups and organizations, including the tribal nations from the Southwest, the Plains states, the Pacific Northwest, and elsewhere. They met African American activists from the Midwest, Northeast, and Deep South, as well as Puerto Ricans from the Midwest and Northeast. They met poor whites from Appalachia, who reminded them of New Mexico mountain villagers, and their veteran organizers like Miles Horton of Kentucky. Moreover, Chicanos began to know each other better. Spanish-speaking Tejanos met English-speaking Chicanos from Denver; urban activists met heirs to ancient New Mexico land grants; and a generation of middle-aging activists, like Gonzales and Tijerina, exposed a younger generation to political activism.

Four

Youth Activism and the Crusade's New Headquarters

In February 1968, a college dropout and 20-year-old draft resister, I joined the Crusade for Justice, struck by its fervor and dedicated activism. The Crusade was then headquartered at 1265 Cherokee Street in a small office that was open five days a week, but whose principal function was the holding of Wednesday night meetings. On those nights working-class, middle-aged men gathered to hold political discussions that served as community forums on the issues of the day. These "Fishermen's Meetings," a Biblical reference to the disciples of Christ who served as "fishers of men," were not attended by women—a practice I never questioned at the time. It would change thanks to criticism from Gonzales' wife, Geraldine, after the Crusade contingent returned from the Poor People's Campaign.

Most Crusade members were nearly a generation older than myself; younger members included the artist Manuel (Emanuel) Martinez, long-haired Esequiel "Kelly" Lovato, Jr., and a few others. The median age of the nation's Mexican-origin people is significantly younger than the national norm. By joining the Crusade, I had the privilege of viewing the stirrings of political activism in my generation.

The years 1966 to 1968 were significant ones for the Chicano movement, and the vigor and strength of youth were central to its mushrooming growth, influenced and guided by the preceding generation. As the historian Juan Gomez-Quinones later noted,

> Of immediate organizational and ideological influence and relevance to the student movement were the National Farm-Worker Association of California led by Cesar Chavez, the Crusade for Justice of Denver, Colorado led by Corky Gonzales, and the Alianza of New Mexico led by Reies Tijerina. This influence was reflected in issues, political style and rhetoric. . . . Both in the community and on some campuses each leader,

especially the former, greatly impressed and influenced the fledgling student movement.[1]

The most significant Denver youth protest would be a series of school walkouts among barrio youths during March 1969, but college students were mobilizing, as well.

THE UNITED MEXICAN AMERICAN STUDENTS

The assassination of Martin Luther King prompted the University of Colorado to develop programs to bring more minority students to campus through the Summer Tutorial Program (STP). Simultaneously, in the summer of 1968, a chapter of United Mexican American Students (UMAS) started at the University of Colorado at Boulder. California students founded UMAS in 1967, and UMAS members were among the leaders of the historic 1968 Los Angeles school walkouts. The Boulder UMAS founders were older and more politically moderate than the radicalized youths who arrived on campus in the next few years or their California counterparts. Yet they too promoted ethnic solidarity and greater educational opportunities for Chicanos. Among the Boulder UMAS goals were:

To foster unity among the Spanish surnamed.
To encourage dignity and respect for the Spanish-surnamed people.
To further justice and equality for the Spanish-surnamed people in Colorado and at C.U.
To encourage a greater admission of the Spanish-surnamed to C.U. . . .
To further education on Mexican-American cultural and historical contributions to the U.S. among the Spanish-surnamed and the Anglo population.
To foster self-respect and identity among the Spanish-surnamed and those with Mexican-American culture and heritage.
To encourage those graduating to return to their communities and do all that is possible to better the lot of the Mexican-American.[2]

The Crusade, always believing that concessions were the fruits of struggle, not society's gifts, was skeptical about STP.

The Summer Tutorial Program was a piece of window-dressing adopted by the University of Colorado to show good faith and concern for minority students after the assassination of Dr. Martin Luther King. The STP cost was $66,000 for a summer orientation program and about the same amount in financial assistance. This program accounts for 47 Negro and Mexican Americans who plan to attend CU this fall. . . . With lots of luck there might be thirty Chicano students at Boulder this fall. We, at the Crusade, congratulate the University of Colorado for being

so liberal as to have thirty of the Chicano students among its total enrollment of 16,000.[3]

Other statistics hinted at the educational challenge affecting the Mexican
community: only 74 of 4,247 teachers in Denver's public school system
(less than 2 percent) were Spanish-surnamed.

THE CHICAGO CONSPIRACY CASE

The FBI's interest in Gonzales and the Crusade mounted as political activism grew. The Chicago FBI field office, in an Airtel dated September 30,
1968, ordered the Denver field office to interview Gonzales about a possible federal antiriot law violation. The FBI believed that Gonzales played
a role in the August 1968 riots during the Democratic National Convention in Chicago because he had, the year before, attended the National
Conference for New Politics, where the demonstrations were proposed.
(As noted above, Crusade representative Eloy Espinoza attended a subsequent Chicago gathering in February 1968, and the FBI apparently mistook him for Gonzales.) Neither Gonzales nor the Crusade was involved
in the Chicago protests.

The government was preparing to indict protest leaders on felony
charges. The sensational trial that resulted is remembered as the Chicago
Seven trial; the eighth defendant, Black Panther Bobby Seale, was tried
separately. The FBI's principal suspects in the fall of 1968 were Dave Del-
linger, Rennie Davis, Tom Hayden, Don Haverquist, and Rodolfo Gonzales. The FBI's intention to indict Gonzales was not publicly known, and
the details of its investigation have never been published. The federal antiriot law (ARL in FBI jargon) went into effect on April 4, 1968. The Chicago FBI office sought an indictment against Gonzales based on the February 11 meeting that Gonzales had not attended.

Ordered to interview Gonzales in preparation for prosecuting him, or
to obtain evidence from him to use in prosecuting others, the Denver field
office concluded that both courses of action presented problems. They
notified headquarters on October 4 that:

> Gonzales is [Security Index] subject and also on Rabble Rouser In-
> dex. . . . It is noted [by the Denver field office that] the meeting on 2/
> 11/68, at Chicago for plans by subjects against [Democratic National
> Convention] took place before effective date of ARL Statutes (4/11/68).
> In view of the foregoing and the SI status of GONZALES, interview of
> GONZALES [in] this matter will not be conducted.[4]

Further, an October 7 headquarters Airtel to the Denver field office
shows that the Chicago field office notified headquarters on October 3

that Gonzales had not been present in Chicago at the Democratic Convention, thus eliminating him from participation in the riot. Headquarters was unhappy that the Denver field office had decided not to interview Gonzales, however. The Denver office was instructed by headquarters that, although "ARL prosecution [of Gonzales] has been lessened":

> the fact that the [February 11] meeting occurred prior to enactment of the ARL statutes is no bar to the use of evidence developed should information be obtained pertinent to these investigations. Likewise, the fact that Gonzales is on the Security Index is no bar to his interview concerning the criminal violations alleged in these cases. Denver should complete investigation requested by Chicago including interview of [Gonzales] and [submit response] as soon as possible. NOTE: It appears that while subject may not be successfully prosecuted for ARL, he might prove to be a valuable witness concerning some of the principals under investigation.[5]

In other words, Gonzales was targeted for prosecution even though the FBI had no facts placing him at the crime scene or in the conspiracy.

Ironically, Gonzales had not agreed with the Chicago organizers' strategy, believing some of their resources should be used to build grassroots organizations rather than holding media-centered protests that left no organization in the aftermath. Gonzales advocated this course, when he attended the August 1967 gathering in Chicago, but he put no further energy into their efforts when his proposal was not adopted.

Acting on headquarter's orders, the Denver FBI contacted Gonzales, who consented to be interviewed on October 8, 1968. The interview, recorded in stilted FBI prose in an October 17 report, revealed Gonzales' opinions on the following subjects.

On the FBI and the Chicago Democratic Convention protests: "GONZALES expressed criticism of investigation of groups involved in the disturbances . . . and stated the investigation should be directed against the police who suppressed the demonstrators and were thus engaged in suppressing dissenters and in violating civil rights."

On Chicanos: "The Mexican American is a victim of discrimination by virtue of the simple fact that he has a Mexican name and is a victim of police oppression by virtue of his residence in a Mexican ghetto."

On minorities and Vietnam: "Mexican Americans and Negroes are drafted or volunteer for service because they are denied the advantages of the Anglo American in United States society. Gonzales charged that the United States is in the Vietnam war through the influence and for the profit of Anglo-controlled corporations such as Morrison-Knudsen construction company and Boeing and Douglas Aircraft corporations to name a few."

On radicals and mainstream political parties: "He said it was much easier for him to identify with radical groups than with either major political party in the United States. . . . He was a ward leader in a Mexican American area of Denver, but disassociated himself because the party, which he alleged to be controlled by the affluent Anglo-American, merely uses minority groups while furthering its own interests."

On the term "wetback": "He stated that in his opinion the term 'wetback' could be compared to the use of the word 'Kike' to identify a Jew or 'WOP' to identify an Italian."

On Gonzales' conflict with the Denver politicians: "He has brought suit against the Mayor of Denver, Colorado, Thomas Currigan, charging that he had illegally gained the office of mayor. He stated that he found considerable pleasure in obtaining subpoenas at a cost of $1.50 each to compel the affluent supporters of Currigan to testify in court."

On Fidel Castro and Cuba: "He explained that the United States broke off relations with Castro after he had nationalized American holdings in Cuba, whereas Castro was justified, because for many years the United States had been draining the wealth from Cuba. . . . He said he is not sympathetic to Cuban refugees who have arrived in Denver, as he considers them to be of the middle-class strata who have had 'some of the fat cut off their side' which they did not share with the poor people in Cuba in the past years."

On Mexico and the Philippines: "Mr. Gonzales stated he also considers the recent problems in Mexico involving armed conflict between the police and students in Mexico City to be the result of a resurgence of United States financial investments in Mexico. . . . That these American investments lead to discontent in Mexico because wealth is taken out of the country at the expense of underpaid workers. Mr. Gonzales continued his comments on what he described as American capitalists growing more affluent at the expense of underdeveloped countries. He questioned that the United States had truly liberated the Philippines during the Spanish-American War because the Philippines, in the opinion of Gonzales, became a dependent of the United States in the sense that financial control was assumed by the United States."[6]

Meanwhile, Gonzales went about his business not knowing until a decade later that his indictment had been considered.

DOWNING STREET HEADQUARTERS

By purchasing the Calvary Baptist Church building at 1567 Downing Street in the summer of 1968, the Crusade obtained a huge physical plant for its operations at a time when its full-time membership was still very small.

"Battles of the Bands"

Gonzales' older daughters, Nita and Charlotte, found one use for the building: raising funds and holding social activities for barrio youth. Thus began regular Friday-night youth dances.

Some dances featured contests ("battles of the bands") in which neighborhood bands competed for prizes and recognition. Bands had ready-made followings, and the Crusade provided the venue. Leaflets were distributed announcing the dances. With time the dances became a social institution in the barrios and provided young Crusade activists with opportunities to interact with barrio youth. The dances were held in the downstairs cafeteria. Crusade youths organized the dances, collected admission, provided security, cleaned the facility, and drove young people home after the dance. Problems were encountered.

After youngsters realized that a basement window was level with the alley, they opened the window to gain free entrance; the window was subsequently nailed shut. When liquor bottles were found after the dances, and weapons were brandished on the dance floor, Crusade youths implemented tighter security. It was out of the question, on principle alone, for Crusade members to call the police to handle problems. The new security measures required coats and purses to be opened before anyone could enter. The security crew confiscated liquor and weapons, but patiently explained that this was done so people could enjoy themselves without problems. Rather than eject people with weapons or alcohol, the security allowed them to enter but took the contraband. On one occasion, for example, a young man hid a machete under his trenchcoat. It was returned at the end of the night. In time the firm but nonpunitive discipline gained the respect and confidence of the poorest, roughest of barrio youths.

The bands were neighborhood bands, and a battle of the bands could easily end as a battle of the neighborhoods. The Crusade organized a youthful security crew that would intervene if fights occurred. The security crew separated combatants while telling them that "the system" benefited from disunity, a message not automatically understood or heeded. Some youths assumed that talk of unity and peace indicated weakness or cowardice. Though many security crew members were scrawny teenagers, some took boxing lessons from Ralph Luna, a boyhood companion of Gonzales and former prize-fighter who had trained many prominent amateur fighters, in a large room in the Crusade building that had been converted to a gymnasium. When persuasion did not keep the peace, the security crew was prepared to fight to get across the point that Chicanos should not fight among themselves, logic that can seem contradictory to those who were not street-wise.

At this time the Crusade drew much of its membership from families, and the middle-aged men whose children organized the dances would arrive at the Crusade building an hour or so before the midnight closing time and drink beer in the upstairs lounge. If needed, these adults were the final authority in maintaining order. Crusade members tolerated little abuse; Gonzales set the example, and on one occasion he was an enforcer of the peace.

Other Battles

One youth clique (or "gang") that attended the dances—the 23rd Street Boys—came from the Eastside, a mixed Mexican and African American neighborhood. The "gang" was composed entirely of Chicano youths, yet their leader was an African American youth nicknamed "Doc." The 23rd Street Boys were not disruptive, but Doc, being the oldest in the gang, a Golden Gloves boxer, and a bully, caused many problems. He was the leader by virtue of his size and fighting ability, since none of his followers could whip him. Doc had often started disturbances but had not been barred from the dances. At one dance, he picked fights with smaller youngsters while trying to take their dance partners from them. Near closing time, Doc hit one of the security crew from behind after being cautioned for harassing a smaller youth. Doc was restrained, but not hit, by security members.

Rodolfo Gonzales entered the dance area at this moment, saw the disturbance, and ordered Doc to leave. Doc responded with a stream of obscenities and threats and reached into his pocket to draw a knife but was disarmed by another adult. Another man grabbed a metal drum stand and prepared to bash the foolhardy young man in the head, but Gonzales stopped him. Doc, possibly enjoying being the center of attention, vowed to return to the Crusade with a gun. Gonzales told those restraining Doc to release him and told the young man he did not have to wait if he wanted revenge. Gonzales removed his wristwatch as Doc danced about cursing and threatening him.

Gonzales squared off with Doc and let the bigger youth throw his first, and last, punch, which missed, before Gonzales flattened him. Humiliated, Doc sprang to his feet swearing to return to kill Gonzales. He walked to the door while making threats, but Gonzales stood between him and the exit. While the 23rd Street Boys watched, Gonzales told Doc to "put up or shut up." Realizing that Gonzales would block his way as long as he continued to make threats, the young man fell silent. He left, never returned, and lost his status as the leader of the gang.

Young Activists and Barrio Unity

The Friday night dances became orderly events where young people could enjoy themselves without fighting. The dances continued from 1968 until 1970. Though they were not particularly successful in attracting youth membership, they served to establish ties between barrio youth and the Crusade. The political sentiments of Crusade youth were heartfelt. Though they were young, they were highly motivated and expressed themselves in terms understood by other young people, as exemplified by Andres Valdez. After returning to Denver from the Poor People's Campaign, Valdez and others donned black berets and formed the first Colorado Black Beret chapter, though it did not last long. Valdez' sentiments on the need for unity are expressed in an *El Gallo* article titled, "Attention Chicanos":

> Hey you! Chicano, Mexican American, Spanish American, Hispano, whatever you call yourself. Think you're bad because you carry a blade or gun and you fight your people? . . . The Westside fights the Northside, the Eastside or Westwood or Goat Hill. Chicanos are always fighting each other. . . . One of us will turn in sudden anger for little reasons that can be settled with a little understanding. If we Chicanos are so bad why do the cops shoot our people, beat our people, why do "tough guys" run when the cops come? . . . who should you be fighting? Do you live in the projects that Uncle Sam put up to keep us happy while they took our lands? Or do you live in slums that have toilets that don't flush right, torn-down doors and walls? Or maybe your mom lives on Welfare and she is unable to get a job to buy a little more food. Maybe you go to school and they tell you that Washington is your forefather. Does he look like any of us? . . . Stop and look around you! Stop fighting each other. We need unity and our people. The power structure is our real enemy![7]

THE CHICANO PRESS: CHRONICLING THE MOVEMENT

Though the arrival of cold weather in the fall of 1968 slowed the pace of activity, a review of *El Gallo* from September to December of 1968 reveals the growth of Crusade activism and community organization. In January 1968, *El Gallo* listed nine newspapers belonging to the Chicano Press Association (CPA), a total that grew to 13 by September 1968. All were based in the Southwest with two exceptions: *Latin American Defense Organization* of Chicago (named after its parent organization), and *La Voz Mexicana* of Wautoma, Wisconsin.[8]

El Gallo articles reported that the Boulder UMAS group marched with the Crusade for Justice and the Students for Democratic Society (SDS) to support Cesar Chavez in California.[9] A new student organization, Mexican Americans Committed for Equality (MACE), was formed in Fort Collins, and Los Latinos was organized at Colorado State College in Greeley.[10] In late 1968 *El Gallo* reported that Yvonne Sanchez and Al Sanchez, Jr., children of Crusade members, had circulated a petition at Denver's Lincoln High School to support the California grape boycott and gathered over two hundred signatures.[11] The Crusade walked on union picket lines at the Brown Palace Hotel and the Kitayama greenhouse in Brighton, Colorado, where greenhouse workers attempted to unionize.[12] Suzette Bridges and Roxanne Allen, fishing rights activists, spoke at the Crusade auditorium about Native American struggles in Washington State.[13]

Art Melville, a former Maryknoll priest, spoke to an audience of 300 about the guerrilla struggle in Guatemala, from which he had been expelled by the government.[14] The October *El Gallo* contained a small picture of the Latin American revolutionary Ernesto "Che" Guevara and his famous quotation: "Wherever death may surprise us, let it be welcome if our battle cry has reached even one receptive ear and another hand reaches out to take up our arms." This edition also reported the massacre of protestors in Mexico City by the Mexican army under President Gustavo Diaz Ordaz. A second article, apparently reprinted from a California publication, commented favorably on Fidel Castro and critically on the Mexican government.[15]

The January 1969 *El Gallo* reported on events in San Antonio and Edcouch-Elsa, Texas, in Los Angeles and Oakland, California, and on the acquittal of Reies Tijerina in Albuquerque on charges stemming from the Tierra Amarilla courthouse raid. The paper published two pages of poetry. The front page featured a photograph of students Daniel Reyes and Juan Garcia, from San Jose, California, members of the Mexican American student Confederation (MASC), who visited Denver in December 1968.

The Crusade now prepared to host the national gathering that Gonzales first proposed in Chicago in 1967 but postponed because of the Poor People's Campaign. Once its new headquarters formally opened on September 16, 1968, the organization was ready to proceed. The conference was announced in the January 1969 *El Gallo* with the banner headline, "Chicano Youth Conference to Be Held in Denver." No article described the conference; readers were merely instructed to "see page 8," where a full-page announcement was laid out in bold print. The conference was scheduled for March 27–31 and was called the Chicano Youth Liberation Conference. This page included a blank to be cut out and mailed to the

Crusade for advance registration. There were to be both "Cultural workshops" and "Social Revolution workshops [on] issues, problems, organizational techniques, political philosophy, communications, self defense, civil disobedience and demonstration." The conference purpose was described as the "New Chicano Revolution." Housing was to be provided by the Crusade.

With this simple, even sketchy, advertisement, the Crusade announced one of the landmark gatherings of the Chicano movement. By February 1969 confirmations of attendance were received from Los Angeles, Oakland, San Jose, Kansas City, and Albuquerque. Gonzales' March speaking engagements in Dallas, Houston, and San Antonio also served to promote the conference. Before the conference took place, however, another youth-related issue arose. The Crusade would now rally to the defense of one of its young members who had refused induction into the armed forces to protest against the Vietnam war.

RESISTING THE DRAFT: "COURTS OF LAW, NOT OF JUSTICE"

In November 1967 the author dropped out of Vermont's Goddard College and moved to Philadelphia for a short time. One consequence of leaving college was losing the deferment from military service that college students then enjoyed. I read of the indictment of Dr. Benjamin Spock, a renowned pediatrician, for urging youths to resist the draft, and in January 1968 I mailed my draft card to the Denver office of the Selective Service System. The draft card was accompanied by a poem composed for me by a hippie friend, and a letter I myself wrote on my twentieth birthday. It stated:

> I hereby submit my draft card as a gesture of my dissatisfaction and disaffection for the social, governmental, and political system of this nation. This is the gesture of a free person with a free will and should be understood as such for it is also a token of my determination to remain so. My country is not my god; I will—and must—first serve the dictates of my mind, heart, and conscience. There are laws and values that are higher than those of this nation's government, and sometimes these come from the conscience of one lone individual: they cannot be legislated by politicians, nor enforced by policemen and soldiers. In this belief I now state that I will not fight the war of a power and system that I feel is unjust, hypocritical, deceitful, inadequate, and detrimental to the happiness and best interests of its own people and the people of the other nations of the world.[16]

I returned to Denver in February 1968 and sought out Rodolfo Gonzales and the Crusade for Justice. The Crusade was notable for its opposition to the war at a time when opposition in the Chicano community was equated with cowardice or Communism. Thus began my 13-year affiliation with the organization.

The law obligated young men to carry draft cards. Returning them to the draft board promptly brought protestors to the attention of the Selective Service System, then headed by General Westmoreland. Such protestors were classified as delinquent and called for induction. I was fully aware of the consequences. The Crusade referred me to the local American Friends Service Committee draft counseling office to apply for status as a conscientious objector. The application would be rejected, since my grounds for opposing the war were political and ethical, not based on religious convictions (I had none). The Selective Service System ordered my appearance for induction at the Armed Forces Examining and Entrance Station at the New Customs House in Denver on May 7, 1968.

Induction involved a physical examination, and my unsuccessful attempt to fail the vision and hearing tests. An interview elicited creative responses: I said I used many drugs and once overdosed on barbiturates in an attempted suicide due to depression (a lie). Nevertheless, a May 7 "Request for and Results of Personnel Security Action" document signed by "D. C. Anderson, 1Lt., USAF," found that "Registrant is mentally, morally, and physically qualified for military service" (another obvious lie). I then refused to step forward to take the oath required for the induction ceremony, or to sign any forms. The above-cited document states, "Ernest Benjamin Vigil, a registrant under the Universal Military Training and Service Act, was this date given an opportunity to execute DD Form 98 and in my presence he refused to do so." Federal felony charges were filed, but I remained free on bond posted by the Crusade.

After I returned home from the Poor People's Campaign in June 1968, a hearing was held at the Federal Courthouse. Defendants were required to wear a tie to enter the magistrate judge's chambers. Draft resisters faced prison sentences, and the tie requirement seemed to be another arbitrary, petty humiliation. I could not understand why people wore strips of cloth around their necks in the first place, felt they were useless, did not own one, and refused to wear the silly one brought me by the bailiff. The attorneys entered the chamber by themselves but quickly returned. The charges were dropped because the Selective Service System had failed to process my application for conscientious objector status and was in violation of its own procedures, a fatal flaw for its case.

The application was subsequently processed and, after I underwent a brief interview with the local draft board, denied. A new induction notice ordered another appearance, this time at 7 a.m. on February 27, 1969.

Though I had resolved to resist induction, options to avoid induction—any options—now seemed more attractive. Gonzales suggested exile to Canada, but Canada was too cold, and there were not enough Mexicans there. Someone sought the assistance of a middle-aged Crusade member who owned a small jewelry store. Plan A—to the extent that there was a plan—was as follows: I would break the store windows on the night before induction and wait to be arrested at the scene for attempted burglary. The charges could later be withdrawn by the store owner. Someone in jail could not be inducted or charged with refusing induction. Or so the reasoning went.

A group of us stayed at the Crusade building after the Fishermen's Meeting on the evening of February 26; I drank to calm my nerves (maybe to bolster my courage). We were notified shortly before midnight that Plan A had fallen through because the store owner backed out. Upset and frustrated, we continued to drink until the early morning hours. We woke up with hangovers in one young man's Volkswagen, and then improvised Plan B. This plan was based on the assumption that the Selective Service System would not want to induct a dope-smoking subversive.

On February 27, Plan B went into effect. Gilbert Quintana and I appeared at the induction center nearly five hours late. We carried antiwar pamphlets and literature, subsequently described in the 113th Military Intelligence Group's Agent Report (dossier no. 522626434) as including "pamphlets, one entitled 'American Atrocities in Vietnam,' . . . 'The Movement,' a Black Power newspaper, . . . and a one-sheet pamphlet of antiwar nature expounding subscription to *The Daily Worker*."

We walked to an office to announce our arrival. I requested instructions while smoking a joint. The uniformed recruiting officer apparently was not familiar with marijuana, for he merely lectured us sternly for being late. We were told to proceed to another office down the hall.

We quickly drew the attention of one Milton T. Johnson as we distributed the antiwar literature to the young inductees. According to dossier no. 522626434, Johnson "advised [us] of action that could be taken against [us] for interfering with the orderly processing of inductees." When he was ignored, "Johnson warned both individuals could be ejected from the building if they did not cease. Johnson called CAPT Thomas M. Cooper, Chief, General Service Administration Guard Force . . . and reported the disturbance."

Cooper appeared, ordered a halt to the distribution of "unauthorized" literature, demanded that the material be surrendered to him, and said that distributing it was against the law. We refused to surrender the material and responded that our actions were protected by the Constitution; if we were breaking the law, Cooper should show us the statutes. A growing number of recruiting personnel, filing clerks, and other uniformed men gathered in the hallway.

Cooper then called the U.S. Marshall's office across the street and reported a disturbance. A U.S. marshall responded to the scene and walked past us seeking someone who could identify the persons causing the disturbance. When we were pointed out, the marshall approached us and after a brief discussion told Quintana he was under arrest. I told the marshal that if Quintana was arrested, the marshal should take me too, since we were involved in the same activity. We would accompany him peacefully, but would not surrender our material and did not want anyone to lay hands on us. He agreed. Plan B appeared to be working, though not exactly as planned. The goal was to be rejected by the military, not arrested by a marshal.

As we were leaving, a uniformed man approached and told the marshal that only Quintana should be arrested as I was scheduled for induction. The procession came to a halt, but Cooper grabbed Quintana by the neck to pull him away from the scene. Quintana resisted, and several men threw him down. One pinned him on the floor and grabbed his throat, choking him. I grabbed the marshal, who was also on top of Quintana, and attempted to pull him off. The scuffle that ensued pitted us against more than eight others. We were handcuffed and taken to a holding cell at the marshal's office until the Crusade posted bail. Plan B resulted in unforeseen problems. We were not charged with misdemeanor disturbance but with felony charges of assaulting a US marshal.

The case went to trial in October 1969, and Eugene Deikman and Harry Nier of the National Lawyers Guild were the defense attorneys. The defense and prosecution accounts of events were similar, with minor, but legally significant, differences. A key detail in the marshal's testimony was that only Quintana had been arrested. Both sides agreed that distributing literature was legal. Further, the disturbance to which the marshal responded was in question, since he had passed us in the hall and had to ask who was creating the disturbance. If a disturbance took place, it had—at the least—subsided by the time of the marshal's arrival. The Marshal, by law, could arrest persons only for misdemeanors that occurred in his presence, and the marshal was in his office across the street when the disturbance was reported.

Federal Judge Alfred A. Arraj instructed the jury that the arrest of Gilbert Quintana was unlawful. Quintana, therefore, had the right to resist arrest and was not found guilty. The marshal, however, testified that I had not been arrested. My grabbing the marshal in the scuffle was ruled to be an illegal act constituting assault, the "unlawful laying upon of hands," since the marshal was acting erroneously but not capriciously. The jury found me guilty. On the date of sentencing, Judge Arraj asked if I wanted to speak before sentence was pronounced. In my response I noted that the Vietnam war had been denounced by scholars and others as illegal, since Congress had sole authority to declare war and had never done so.

Further, if federal jurists ever confirmed the war's illegality (unlikely as that was) Presidents Johnson and Nixon and other government officials would not find themselves in court to face sentence for violating the Constitution, for murder, and for war crimes. Having been found guilty of assault, I noted that the judge refused to rule on the war's legality but stood ready to pronounce sentence on me. "I have been found guilty in a court of law, not a court of justice," I announced.

The judge, flushed and seemingly angry, ordered a three-month "presentence observation" period at the Federal Correctional Institute in Englewood, Colorado. After the observation period a sentencing recommendation would be made to guide the judge's final sentence. We felt that Arraj ordered the observation because he would have appeared unduly harsh had he immediately imprisoned a defendant who had no record of prior convictions. My attorneys said that the probation office, which wrote a routine presentence report for the judge, considered me hostile and resentful of authority. An unfavorable report from the prison would justify a prison sentence. The conviction was appealed but upheld two years later.

My presentence observation period began in March 1971. Opposition to the war, however, had increased greatly in the two years since my trial. The Crusade campaigned for my release, and slogans were painted on barrio walls throughout Denver. The graffiti were noticed by the authorities, and the prison administrators held meetings in anticipation of riots and demonstrations. The prison guards were trained in riot control at nearby Camp George West, and automatic weapons were issued to the watchtower, a practice previously abolished after a warning shot fired at a prisoner attempting to escape over a fence ricocheted and killed him.

These measures had unforseen results. The counselor assigned me during my incarceration was a young college graduate who was opposed to the Vietnam war and had participated in Denver antiwar demonstrations. He felt that the prison was overreacting and imposing unduly harsh scrutiny in my case. He warned me that many staff members were military veterans and did not look kindly on war resisters.

This counselor wrote the sentencing report, sent it to Judge Arraj, and told me the recommendation would be favorable. He also revealed the date on which Arraj would pronounce the final sentence. Arraj could still ignore the counselor's recommendation and order the maximum penalty. The Crusade was notified of the date—information usually kept from inmates. Judge Arraj was surprised and angered to find the courtroom packed on the day of sentencing. He canceled the proceedings, ordered me returned to the prison, and rescheduled the sentencing for an unspecified date. At the second hearing, in an empty courtroom, Judge Arraj pronounced a sentence of three years federal probation. If successfully completed, this sentence would result in expunging of the felony conviction from my record under the provisions of the Federal Youth Corrections Act.

The granting of probation was a victory for the Crusade, the antiwar movement, and the organizing and legal defense strategy. Activists had packed the federal courtroom every day of the trial. Whatever happened in the court was witnessed by working-class Chicanos and antiwar activists who sat quietly and grimly for the trial's duration. The lawyers' strategy was to bring the war in Vietnam into question and into focus and to have the courtroom serve as a classroom.

The case, in this sense, did not involve a crime of violence, but was a protest against the violence in Vietnam and racism at home. Motions were entered based on the Treaty of Guadalupe Hidalgo, the treaty that finalized the invasion of Mexico by the United States, a Vietnam-style conflict of the preceding century. Though the judge could reject the motions, everybody had to listen as they were made. Though a conviction resulted, the war in Vietnam, and the guilty verdict itself, were still subject to the ongoing tribunal of public opinion. Slogans condemning the war in Vietnam appeared on the walls of every barrio in the city. The authorities were powerless to overrule the community's verdict.

The probation granted was a victory for a whole people and a movement whose strength resulted not from the letter of the law, but from a determined spirit and unrelenting struggle for justice in spite of the law. This trial signaled the growth of Chicanos' militancy and of the Crusade's organizational strength. It was also a tribute to Rodolfo Gonzales, who bravely articulated, and helped popularize, Chicano opposition to the war in Colorado and the Southwest.

A REMINISCENCE

In February 1968, Rodolfo Gonzales was puzzled by the longish-haired college dropout who appeared unannounced at the Crusade office on Cherokee Street. The young man liked to use big words and even attempted to speak with the accent of the upper-middle-class students he had known in college. Gonzales listened attentively to the opinions and sentiments that led his visitor to mail his draft card back to the Selective Service System, its rightful owner. Military induction would be resisted regardless of the consequences. My opposition to the war in Vietnam was tinged by a vague pacifism, soon abandoned, and Gonzales clearly saw me as a test case of opposition to the war. He never revealed his first impressions or his deeper thoughts on that occasion.

It was apparent, however, that Gonzales did not know how to pigeonhole me, and could not fully mask his puzzlement . . . or suspicion? He did not ask me to join the Crusade, and clearly left the decision to me. He praised my stance on the war and, a week or two later, said that if I joined the Crusade, he felt I could become a "leader." I vaguely felt that he was appealing to my ego, and this puzzled me. I had no interest in being a leader—or a follower—but said I wanted to join the Crusade because it was dedicated to defending the interests of our people. The response may have puzzled him. Though he was cordial, he did not demonstrate complete confidence. This situation prevailed until the demonstration at the Supreme Court, mentioned in Chapter 3, when I attempted to punch a cop who drove his motorcycle into the crowd of protestors. The punch missed, and I was thrown to the ground and beaten by several officers. Gonzales' cordiality thereafter was warm, not formal.

Gonzales quickly declared, in the May 1968 *El Gallo,* that I was the first Chicano to refuse induction. I wrote an article about returning my draft card, but Gonzales wrote the headline: "First Chicano in Southwest Refuses to Kill in Vietnam." It is probable that no one then knew who was the *first* such resister; finding out would require a search of federal court records in the Southwest.

Rodolfo Gonzales and the Crusade were in the forefront of Chicano antiwar sentiment in Colorado, and Crusade members believed (and boasted) that the Crusade was the first Chicano organization in Colorado to officially oppose the Vietnam war. It was not. Gonzales publicly opposed the war in August 1966 but stated that his views were his own. No documentation shows that the Crusade, as an organization, opposed the war until 1967.

The first group in Colorado that officially opposed the war declared its stand in 1966 and called itself the "New Hispano Movement." This group advocated independent political action during elections and sought to establish an independent political party or organization. Its leaders were attorney Levi Martinez of Pueblo, Joe Lucero of Littleton, and Tom Pino of Denver. In November 1966, Lucero advocated U.S withdrawal from Vietnam and the admission of mainland China to the United Nations, very radical positions at the time. These men were middle-class "Hispano" professionals, not working-class militants. The New Hispano Movement quickly folded. Gonzales criticized their efforts, saying that they would benefit Republican candidates at election time by drawing away Mexican votes that traditionally went to Democratic candidates.

At this time the Crusade and Gonzales had not completely abandoned mainstream politics. Ironically, in view of his criticism of the New Hispano Movement, Gonzales and the Crusade endorsed Republicans in the 1966 elections.[17]

Five

School Protests and
Youth Liberation

On March 20, 1969, student protest at West High School resulted in solidarity walkouts in every secondary school in Denver's barrios. The following day, walkouts became city wide, leading to the bloodiest school protests in Denver's history. Within a week, the Crusade for Justice held the first National Chicano Youth Liberation Conference. The conference became one of the landmark gatherings of the Chicano movement, and the walkouts radicalized a generation of Denver's Chicano youth, who soon swelled the Crusade's membership.

THE SCHOOL WALKOUTS

Racism at West High School

In March 1969 *El Gallo* reported that a student had called the Crusade to complain about a teacher: "Mr. Schafer, my social problems teacher, said the people from the Crusade were ignorant and uneducated." [1] The Crusade had known about Schafer for some time, alerted by two friends who became the catalyst for subsequent events: Jeanine Perez and Priscilla Martinez. Perez' father, José Muñiz, had been a southern Colorado coalminer; he learned leftist politics as a trade unionist, and was an early Crusade member.

When the Crusade for Justice returned to Denver after the Poor People's Campaign, it organized a small summer youth program called the "freedom school," where—to instill ethnic pride—youths were taught rudimentary "Chicano" history, culture, and politics. One result was that Perez began to correct public school teachers who mispronounced her surname.

During roll call in Harry Schafer's class, she corrected him and asked that he pronounce her name correctly. Instead, Schafer ridiculed Perez and deliberately began to pronounce her surname as "Paris." When she contradicted him about history, citing what she had learned during the freedom school, Schafer challenged her to bring Crusade members to speak in his class.

Gilbert Quintana and the author went to West High School, where Schafer demonstrated his disdain by refusing to stay for our presentation. His absence allowed students to speak freely about their experiences with him, and allowed us to share our views with students (we urged them to organize). The students' stories demonstrated the teacher's callous attitude, and when class was over, we waited in the hallway to discuss the incidents the students had reported. When he returned, Schafer turned his back on us when we addressed him; he then entered the classroom, pointedly shutting the door.

Because we believed Schafer would deny his remarks and conduct, we asked students to document their experiences and, later to provide their parents names and phone numbers so that Crusade adults could visit them. We needed to cultivate parental support because, as Gonzales noted, parents would tend to disbelieve their children and order them "to respect the teacher."

Gonzales called West High to arrange a meeting with the principal. Those present at the meeting, which took place on February 27, included Gonzalez, Howard Johnson of the central school administration, Edgar Benton, a liberal school board member, and a Catholic priest, Father James Groppi from Milwaukee, who was speaking in Denver at the Crusade's invitation.[2]

Father Groppi had spoken to an audience of 500 at Crusade headquarters the previous evening. "We live in a society that says it is wrong for you to stand up for your God-given rights," he said. "We've reached our breaking point. 'The Man' will not listen." Groppi recounted how the Milwaukee media questioned his support for the African American community during protests and civil disorders because of violence that occurred. He bluntly stated, "Nothing else has worked. One gets tired of walking picket lines, attending school board meetings, and being carried in paddy wagons to face racist white juries. Our people who participated in that violence did not feel any guilt whatsoever. We don't talk about the morality of tactics, we talk about the effectiveness of tactics. Christ was a revolutionist and was put to death because he dared to confront the system."[3]

In preparation for the meeting, students circulated a petition demanding Schafer's dismissal. More than 20 students, parents, and Crusade members filled the office and described Schafer's conduct for the principal, who said he was unaware of what had been going on.

Among the remarks that Schafer allegedly made were: "All Mexicans are stupid because their parents were stupid, and their parent's parents (before) them were stupid," and, "If you eat Mexican food you'll look like a Mexican." Schafer defended his remarks as intended solely to elicit responses in his social studies class. The adults endorsed the students' demand for his transfer or dismissal. The meeting closed with the principal's indication that Schafer would be removed from the school. Gonzales responded, "Either you take care of it your way, or we'll take care of it our way." [4]

If Gonzales' words reflected the group's spirit, the front page of the April 1969 *El Gallo* graphically illustrated students' sentiments. Accompanied by a headline in block letters that read "West High Blowout" was a photograph of a teenager standing on the hood of a Denver police car and bashing a cinderblock on its roof. School authorities had refused to act on the students' demands: several days after they, their parents, and community leaders met with the West High principal, "the administration handed down its decision. Schafer would not be fired. Schafer would not be transferred. That was how the school ignited the spark, and the students took the initiative." [5]

When the students learned of the authorities' inaction, they began leafletting at West High to inform and rally fellow students. Teachers, in reaction, passed around their own petition in support of Schafer.

On Wednesday night, March 19, several West High students, including Jeannie Perez, Priscilla Martinez, Auggie Botello, and Donald "Archie" LaForette, attended the Crusade's Fishermen's Meeting. They informed the Crusade that students intended to walk out of school, and although the decision had been made impulsively by the students, it as apparent that the walkout would proceed. They were excited but nervous and full of questions. Should they gather on the school grounds or in the park across the street? Should they picket? Or just go home? When asked how many students would participate, they estimated 50 to 75.

A plan was improvised when the meeting ended. Students would arrive at West High the next day, March 20, and distribute leaflets calling for students to walk out at 9 a.m. Crusade members would be present as a support group and to monitor the authorities. Students began leaving their classes in two and threes at the appointed time. Then, slowly, small groups of four and five began to walk out, and increasing numbers followed. The crowd, including adult supporters and others, grew to around 300. Crude picket signs, made the previous night at the Crusade building, were carried. The crowd marched three blocks to Baker Junior High School, where the doors and windows had been locked. Some Baker students broke windows and climbed out to join the protestors. The crowd returned to West High.

Police in riot gear now stood in formation at the entrance to the school. The marchers gathered on the school's front steps, and speakers began to address the crowd with a small bullhorn. As Gonzales began to speak, police ordered the crowd to move across the street. Without giving them time to respond—those in the rear of the crowd had not even heard the order—the police waded into the crowd, pushing and prodding with riot batons. Students fell down the stairs, some pushed and kicked by the police. Pandemonium resulted as students fought back and police began to use Mace and club people with full force. Young women were dragged in the street by their hair and loaded into patrol wagons. Gonzalez was wrestled to the ground, Maced, and arrested when the disturbance began. Among others arrested were Manuel Martinez, Nita Gonzalez, Manuel Lopez, Gil Quintana, Ernie Espinoza, Larry Aragon, and Carlos Santistevan; all but Aragon, a Westside resident, were Crusade members.

A lone policeman chased a student into Sunken Gardens park across from the school and was mobbed by other students, who left him unconscious and ran off with his riot helmet. As the patrol wagons hauled away the arrested, one group of protestors returned to Baker Junior High, another started walking north to the City Jail, and a third group went to the nearby City and County Building.

The groups returned to West High as Crusade members and other adults arrived. Desiderio de Herrera gathered the crowd for another march, providing a semblance of order. While leading the march past St. Joseph's High School, de Herrera later said, a police officer told him that a nun at the school wanted to speak with him. When he arrived at the school office, the angry nun denied that she had summoned him and called him a communist. De Herrera was then arrested for trespassing as he attempted to leave. Led by the other adults and student leaders, the march passed Baker Junior High. The school grounds emptied as students on lunch break joined the march, which proceeded to the Crusade building, nearly two miles away.

The fourth floor of the old City Jail was crowded with those arrested, the smell of Mace hung in the air, and jailers were angry with protestors, who noisily shouted "Viva La Raza!" and other slogans. The cells continued to fill as new arrests were made. About 4 p.m. the chanting quieted as people pondered their situation. When would they be released? Who would post bonds? What next?

Car horns and remote shouts from outside were heard. Climbing to the top bunks in the cells, some protestors could look down into the street. They began to shout, "Look out the windows! Look out the windows!" One block east of the jail, rounding the corner at 14th Avenue and Champa Street, came a crowd of hundreds led by Crusade members.

The street was filled from curb to curb. They came to demand the release of those arrested. Cries of "Viva La Raza!" and "We want Corky!" filled the air.

The jail rocked with the shouts of protestors outside and the replies of protestors inside. Tension mounted as the police closed the building's entrance, becoming captives themselves. Picket lines formed, and slogans were chanted. The sheriffs initially told those arrested that they would be held "under investigation" for 72 hours before charges were brought. People detained under investigation are not entitled to release on bond, thus subjecting them to a three-day jail sentence without first being found guilty in court. The crowd on the steps appeared to have changed the authorities' mind. Gonzales was told he would be bonded out and was urged to inform the crowd that all others would soon be released. Gonzalez refused bond, saying he would not sign his bond papers until all protestors were freed. Shortly after darkness fell, the last protestor, Gonzales, was released.

The morning's events were captured by reporters and television camera crews, including an African American cameraman, Vernon Rowlette, who was also arrested.[6] Graphic scenes were broadcast in the early evening; home from work and having dinner, Denver residents watched televised arrests and violent beatings. Middle-class Denver was stunned, city government angered, and the barrios outraged.[7]

That night hundreds gathered at the Crusade auditorium for a mass meeting attended by the media. African American and Chicano students from East High School and Manual High School pledged to walk out the next day, March 21, in solidarity with the students at West and Baker.[8] Many more schools would participate: a walkout of all barrio schools was underway.

Barrio Schools Unite

A crowd estimated at 1,200 to 1,500 gathered at West High the next morning. Students came from West, North, Manual, Lincoln, and East High Schools; from Cole, Kunzmiller, Lake, Horace Mann, Skinner, Morey, Baker, Smiley, and Kepner Junior High Schools; and from Adams City Junior and Senior High Schools and Kearney Junior High in neighboring Adams County.

The overwhelming majority of students were Chicano, but many African American and white students were present. The UMAS chapters from the University of Colorado campuses at Boulder and Denver were present, as were Students for a Democratic Society (SDS) and the Denver Black Panthers. Inside the school, student leaders and their parents negotiated with school officials, who were now attentive to student demands. The April 1969 *El Gallo* reported. "Now the officials were very eager to listen and to talk. They also made promises. 'We're looking for more Chicano teachers; we're looking for a culture and history curriculum; we're making new committees, etc., etc., etc.'"[9]

Protestors marched to Lincoln Park, where a rally was held. Some young men rashly called for the crowd to march into downtown Denver, about a half-mile to the east. The protest needed focus and discipline, not further complications. Moreover, the young men were not from the Westside, were not Mexican, and had lent no hand to the organizing work done by activists. West High students spoke among themselves; then one addressed the crowd: "We are going back to West. West is a Chicano school, and we're doing a Chicano thing. If you want to support us, fine. Decide what you want."[10]

With this simple statement, the crowd assembled in the streets and marched back to West High School. Police cars lined the streets, many with broken windows from sporadic rock- and bottle-throwing. As the ranks of outside supporters dwindled, around 3 p.m., violence between police and the crowds escalated. Shots rang out, and a middle-aged man was wrestled to the ground and arrested for firing a pistol at police. Police depleted their Mace, sent for new supplies, and brandished drawn weapons with increasing frequency. Teargas drifted throughout the neighborhood, and a police helicopter passed overhead, dropping some chemical irritant.

Police formed lines and marched in the streets, but the crowd would vanish into yards, alleys, and side streets and reemerge as police passed. Rock- and bottle-throwing continued. The crowd refused to disperse. Especially violent confrontations occurred at the intersection of 9th Avenue and Galapago Street, one block west of the high school. A squad car stalled at the intersection and was pelted with bricks and stones. The panicked driver was unable to restart the car. The windows were shattered but did not collapse until a youth stepped off the curb and hurled a cinderblock at the driver's window. The glass gave way, the officer catching the full force of the blow on the side of his face. He was hospitalized but not seriously injured. Later, at the same intersection, an intoxicated 26-year-old man stepped into the street and yelled belligerently at a group of police about thirty yards away. Officer James A. Hartford, Jr., took several steps toward the intersection and fired his shotgun, and the man fell wounded with birdshot.

The police were ordered to withdraw from the area, and the violence ceased dramatically, though the city remained tense. Around 5 p.m. a small crowd gathered at the steps of the Denver Inner-city Parish on the northeast corner of the intersection. Gonzales addressed the crowd, urging people to return to their homes. The crowd dispersed, and the disturbance ended. Twenty-five police vehicles were damaged, and 17 policemen were treated for injuries at a nearby hospital.

Protests were reported on Monday at Baker and Kepner Junior High and at St. Joseph's High School, three blocks from West High. Other walkouts were reported at Adams City High School and in a suburban Englewood school few Chicanos then attended. School officials, under pressure, granted amnesty to students who had walked out. Telegrams of support arrived from California, Texas, New Mexico, and elsewhere. If anyone believed that the discontent and criticism voiced by Gonzales and the Crusade were the rantings of a few misfits and malcontents, the events at West High School indicated that the number of malcontents and misfits was much larger than some people realized. Mexicans were no longer an "invisible minority."

THE IRON TRIANGLE: POLICE, FBI, AND MILITARY INTELLIGENCE

The emergence of Mexican community activism was not a threat to democracy, but the rising of a stifled voice to participate in it. This was a dissenting voice, however, one that challenged the way things were and demanded change. Though the nation was conscious of, and frequently uncomfortable with, the growing antiwar, civil rights, and Black Power movements, the nation's second-largest minority did not have the same national impact, since Chicanos were concentrated in the southwestern states. In these states, people of Mexican descent tallied numbers far greater than any other community of color. Powerful forces with vested interests in maintaining the established order felt threatened and reacted accordingly. The reaction to the "threat" posed by the Chicano and other movements can be seen in the transformation of police departments, the guardians of the status quo. Denver's police department would mirror changes taking place nationally.

The Denver Police Department, though reorganized by Chief George Seaton when he took office in 1968, seemed little different from that of Harold Dill. Both men shared hardline law-and-order views, and the transformation of their department did not involve a shift in attitudes. Seaton's remarks early in his tenure gave insight into his approach to police work.

Chief George Seaton

In a wide-ranging interview in the *Denver Post* on July 22, 1969, Seaton expressed his views on a various topics, such as hippies and strong-arm tactics:

> Naturally you see a lot of strange characters walking around today and, of course, an officer runs into the worst part of society. . . . A lot of the weirdos or hippies, you might call them, are involved in many of the crimes involving moral turpitude—narcotics, prostitution, things of this sort.
> . . . I went into police work in '46, and I've never seen third-degree methods used. I think this cry of police brutality is an overused thing. This is a tool that revolutionaries use, Communists use. All kinds of revolutionaries use this. It's designed to disrupt and influence other people. It just isn't so as far as I'm concerned.[11]

Though Seaton expressed concern about people "trying to tear down the structure in this city or nation," he claimed to respect their right to hold their views: "It doesn't make any difference to me what they think. They're free to think anything they want to. If they're revolutionaries, I suppose they have that right. . . . I'm not trying to change their minds."[12] Though Seaton's critics might assume he disliked communists, hippies, weirdos, and strange characters who were naturally seen walking around, he distinguished "militants" from "revolutionaries." Yet here too he indicated the limits of his tolerance:

> Now I'm not talking about militants, I'm talking about revolutionaries. Some people will say it's all right to be militant—well, that's all right, too, I agree with them. But when it comes to the point where they preach revolution and tearing down and burning and looting, well, this is disruption. And we've got plenty of it, not only here but in every city across the nation. In fact, there's a group in town now with that aim—disrupt, tear down. That's the American Liberation Front. . . . We watch 'em day and night. . . . I'm not going to elaborate on this: That's intelligence work, and I don't want to discuss it.[13]

Perhaps Seaton's constant vigilance discouraged the American Liberation Front, a group of which no one had heard, because the front never disrupted (much less tore down) the Mile High City, Denver.

This group was not Seaton's only target. In 1968 he lashed out at the local Black Panther Party at a meeting with business owners in Northeast Denver, saying, "They don't want any white honkies telling them what to do."[14] Though he announced that Denver police would not tolerate discrimination in the department and that "police brutality was a thing of the past," he went on to say that the police "were through being re-strained," an apparent reference to the Black Panthers. He claimed that "black and white revolutionaries"[15] controlled the community relations board of Denver's Model Cities program, an antipoverty agency. In an-nouncing that police would deploy their recently acquired helicopter, the *Denver Post* reported, Seaton said that it would be used for burglary pa-trols, "especially those committed by black revolutionaries seeking arms."[16] In September 1968 the *Rocky Mountain News* reported Seaton's assertion: "They (who he didn't specify) are trying to stockpile weap-ons. . . . One of these days they are going to try to take over, and that's probably going to be before the election. But if anything happens, the people breaking the law are going to jail, and they're going to be prose-cuted."[17] In spite of his prediction, no armed militants—Black Panthers or otherwise—attempted to hijack Denver's 1968 elections.

Criticizing unnamed liberals in Mayor Currigan's administration, Seaton complained, "We've been told by some of the 'enlightened' people . . . that if a bunch of youngsters are breaking windows with rocks, and if we go in and arrest them, we're over-reacting. . . . Now don't get me wrong. Mayor Currigan is a good Mayor, but he's got people up there in his programs who don't know the time of day. They're feeding us a bunch of hogwash."[18]

When the *Denver Post* asked Currigan about Seaton's remarks, the mayor said they were "well timed and expressed [Seaton's] opinion as well as mine." As for the armed takeover of city government by militants, Currigan said he was unaware of the plot but added, "I would assume that the police department intelligence division has such information."[19]

Seaton's concerns about insurrection were shared by Police Captain Le-onard Johnson, a division chief who met with the Northeast Park Hill Civic Association in February 1969, the month before the West High walkouts. He spoke about race relations in Denver and said, "As of now, I do not envision a full-blown riot in Denver this summer. I do anticipate incidents or guerilla-type activities. These will probably take the form of attacks on buildings and property rather than on individuals."[20]

Police Reorganization and Riot Preparations

Seaton and Johnson's overheated views were widely shared in the era of Richard Nixon, who was elected in 1968, in great part, because of a law-and-order campaign. These views, furthermore, had consequences. The rhetoric signaled a transformation of America's police forces because these views were shared, and maybe originated, at the highest levels of the FBI bureaucracy. These views also had funding and organization, factors that mark qualitative differences between the pre-1968 administration of Harold Dill and the post-1968 administration of George Seaton.

On January 27, 1968, soon after his appointment, Seaton returned to Denver from Warrenton, Virginia, where he and 30 other police chiefs attended a meeting that focused on "riot prevention." On January 29, he and five of Denver's finest went to the San Francisco Bay Area to study race relations and student violence.[21] What he learned on these trips may have guided his reorganization of the department, though it began before them.

By January 14, 1968, Seaton had established a program under which the FBI trained "police riot control 'platoons.'" The training began on January 25, and at least 60 officers (five 12-officer "platoons") were trained in riot and crowd control methods. The police K-9 corps was to be used, and the program included an intensive 16-hour class taught "by FBI specialists from Denver and Washington D.C. and by Denver command officers."[22] The first platoons came from the downtown area and District 2 in Northeast Denver. The Crusade for Justice was headquartered in the downtown district, only a few blocks from the boundary with District 2.

On March 6, Seaton announced the formation of a 31-member, highly mobile police task force called the Special Services Unit (SSU), the name by which today's Special Weapons and Tactics (SWAT) team was then known. Officers in the SSU "were among the first to receive the new riot control training now being given every man on the 841-officer department." The new unit was to be operational by April 1968. Training began on March 11 and included "legal methods of search and seizure, field interrogation of suspects, community relations, and other constantly changing areas of police work."[23]

Seaton said the SSU was "created for crime control purposes and any other purposes for which we have to use it," citing an increase in bus robberies and purse snatching. SSU officers were to work in "teams" composed of two four-member "squads" in unmarked cars directed by sergeants and available for use by any district commander. The SSU, "not tied to radio calls for routine assignments . . . would be able to concentrate solely on the assignment, as district patrols cannot."[24] It was, coincidentally, the SSU that confronted students on the front steps of West High School on March 20, 1969.

Seaton, a former detective captain, brought other changes to the department. A January 3, 1968, *Denver Post* article by Harry Gessing reported the creation of a new Administrative Division to handle personnel, training, education, and "planning" functions. The Intelligence Bureau, then under the Investigations Division, was shifted to the Administrative Division.

On January 4, the *Denver Post* added details about the Intelligence Bureau in an article on staff transfers. Sergeant Jerry Kennedy was transferred from Intelligence to the new Juvenile Division, which Seaton upgraded from its bureau status. Youth, apparently, was becoming a priority target for police. Though the three highest-ranking officers were transferred from the Intelligence Bureau, Seaton named no replacement to head the bureau at that time. His subsequent appointment to the post of Lieutenant (later Captain) Glenn Reichart went unpublicized. Seaton clarified that the shift of the Intelligence Bureau to the Administrative Division from the Investigations Division was a shift in name only. "They will, in effect, be right under me and work out of my office," he said.[25]

Captain Doral Smith would take command in a newly redrawn District 2. The boundary shift between the downtown district and District 2, effective October 1, 1968, was prompted by "several confrontations . . . between area residents and police" in Five Points, an African American neighborhood where the Black Panthers were active. This shift put the Crusade building in Captain Smith's District 2, which now had 33 additional officers. Also, eight K-9 Corps officers were transferred to the SSU commanded by Lieutenant Stan Stortz, bringing the total to 40 officers.[26]

From 1968 to the early 1970s, Denver police intelligence officers met at least monthly with army intelligence and research officers from Fort Carson in Colorado Springs, where 25 army officers were involved in intelligence operations with police and FBI. Half of these officers performed undercover assignments requested by Denver police and approved by army division headquarters in Colorado Springs. The Crusade for Justice was among its targets. Members' names and pictures were taken and shared with the FBI and military installations.[27]

The FBI's Crusade File

The FBI Internal Security file on the Crusade, Bureau file (Bufile) 105-178283, lists the 113th Military Intelligence Group (MIG) among recipients of FBI reports on the Crusade. The 113th MIG—one of seven MIGs operating nationally in regional, field, and resident offices—was headquartered in Evanston, Illinois. It received its first FBI report on the Crusade in May 1968 (document 105-178283-2), which covered the investigative period "3/1–5/6/68." An FBI report on Gonzales (document 105-176910-1) was sent even earlier, January 1968.[28]

All MIGs confronted a minor legal problem: their activities were banned by the U.S. Constitution and by Congress. According to Frank J. Donner, an attorney:

> The Constitution and specific statues, and the republican principle they implement, subject the Army to civilian direction and control, and confine military intervention in domestic affairs. Article I, Section 8, of the Constitution entrusts to the Congress the power to authorize domestic use of the military but solely to repel invasion, suppress insurrection, and execute the laws. The President is authorized to use troops only if it is necessary to protect the state against invasion and against domestic violence, and in the latter case only on prior application of state authorities. Congressional enactments further precondition the use of troops by the President to repel an invasion on the issuance of a proclamation ordering the dispersal of the invading forces and, in the absence of such a proclamation, ban the use of any part of the Army or the Air Force, as a Posse Comitatus or otherwise, to execute the laws.[29]

Hoover's FBI, however, was not about to let the Constitution or Congress impede its holy war against radicals, communists, and wrong-thinkers. The collaboration among the police, the FBI, and military authorities continued with business as usual.

The FBI and "Mexican American Militancy"

The first National Chicano Youth Liberation Conference proved to be of special interest to J. Edgar Hoover's FBI, which had monitored the conference's progress since Gonzales first proposed a national Latino gathering in Chicago in 1967.

The Chicago FBI field office, in a document of April 24, 1968, notified headquarters "that the national convention in Denver is to be hosted by an organization headed by a militant Latin named 'Corky' Gonzales."[30] FBI documents dating from that time also refer to a mysterious FBI file captioned "Mexican American Militancy," whose contents and purpose have yet to be revealed. Copies of the Chicago FBI memo were sent to FBI field offices in Albuquerque, Denver, El Paso, Los Angeles, Milwaukee, Phoenix, Sacramento, San Antonio, San Diego, and San Francisco.[31] The Chicago FBI knew the home states of Latino activists who attended the 1967 Chicago gathering and notified FBI field offices in those states afterward.

Significantly, on August 25, 1967—before Gonzales proposed and subsequently postponed the 1968 Denver Chicano conference—the FBI ordered an illegal counterintelligence program (COINTELPRO) that targeted African American groups ranging from the Nation of Islam to the pacifist SCLC. The order referred to "black nationalist, hate-type organizations" and became known as the "Black Nationalist Hate Group COINTELPRO." FBI headquarters informed the Albany, Georgia, field office that "the purpose of this new counterintelligence endeavor is to expose, disrupt, discredit, or otherwise neutralize the activities of black nationalist, hate-type organizations and groupings, their leadership, spokesmen, memberships, and supporters."[32]

This COINTELPRO sought to prevent the black militants' movement from gaining respectability (among both blacks and whites), influence among youth, and coalitions with other African American groups; it also aimed to block the rise of a leader who could unify the movement.[33] It is not yet known if the FBI launched an all-encompassing COINTELPRO against the Chicano movement.

On March 13, 1969, one year and nine days after launching the nationwide Black Nationalist Hate Group COINTELPRO, headquarters notified the Denver SAC that:

> Information has been received from another Government intelligence agency that [the Crusade for Justice] is sponsoring a National Youth Convention to be held in Denver, Colorado, March 27–31, 1969 . . . and is attracting support from throughout the West and Southwest. Rudolph "Corky" Gonzales, Chairman of the Crusade for Justice (CFJ), announced that in addition to young Spanish-speaking militants from New York and Chicago who are planning to attend the conference, delegations are being organized from San Antonio and Kingsville, Texas, and from Seattle, Washington, and unknown places in Oregon. . . . Consequently, offices receiving this communication are to contact appropriate sources to determine the identities of individuals and the extent of participation in the above conference and advise Denver [FBI field office] and the Bureau [headquarters].[34]

Headquarters sent copies of his order to Chicago, Houston, New York, Portland, San Antonio, and Seattle.

The Denver FBI field office responded to headquarters "Airtel" in a teletype dated March 26, 1969, but the copy deletes data that show what the Denver FBI did. Copies of the Denver teletype were sent to FBI offices in Albuquerque, Dallas, El Paso, Los Angeles, San Francisco, Phoenix, Sacramento, and San Antonio.[35] FBI field offices in Houston, El Paso, San Francisco, Phoenix, and New York responded to Hoover's order to "determine the identities of individuals and the extent of participation."

The FBI's interest in the 1969 conference resulted in a separate, ongoing FBI Internal Security file on that and subsequent Denver youth conferences.[36] The Crusade had little knowledge at that time of the extent of FBI interest in its activities. It is safe to say that many former and current members still have little detailed knowledge of it. FBI files were released to Rodolfo Gonzales in the late 1970s, but for reasons known only to himself, he never shared them with the Crusade's leadership or its members.[37]

"LIKE IT OR NOT, AMERICA LISTENS TO VIOLENCE"

The Denver school walkouts had a significant impact. Until then the Crusade for Justice had been an organization of working-class, middle-aged activists; its younger membership comprised a few persons in their twenties and some teenage children of members. The walkouts radicalized a generation of youths once absorbed by neighborhood rivalries but now showing remarkable solidarity in barrio-wide protests stemming from West High. They faced the same opponents, marched, and were beaten, gassed, and arrested together.

Further, the Crusade's persistent activism granted others a forum, though this was not necessarily its intent. This phenomenon, to which the Crusade did not comfortably adapt, was described by State Senator Roger Cisneros: "Corky is aspiring for the same goals all of us aspire for, and I think we owe him a vote of thanks for bringing this to a head. He is influential. He represents people who could not be reached by the established leaders. He is capable of carefully articulating the basic differences within the society and calling for cures. Corky gives the more conservative leaders an opportunity to move in later."[38] Gonzales' assessment was different. He drew an analogy of militants shaking an apple tree and everyone else walking off with the fallen apples.

The media's interest in Chicanos intensified. A *Rocky Mountain News* article by George Lane and Clemens Work cited statistics on problems confronting the community, including an average educational attainment level three years behind African Americans and four years behind whites: "The recent disturbances at West High School, where 38% of the students are of Hispano origin, took many persons by surprise, at least those who had not been following the issues closely, but it was expected by many members of Denver's West Side and by persons in the educational system." Lane and Work perceived the significance of the students' demands:

> The students who presented the demands asked for amnesty from reprisal for the demonstration. Other demands asked that students in ROTC and graduating seniors not be negatively affected by the action. These demands seem to indicate the students acted because they saw no other way, even thought it might hurt their chances for the future—chances that are vitally important to them.[39]

Amnesty was granted. Other demands were granted "in principle," including a more adequate treatment of Mexican history and culture, bilingual education, and "Chicano" literature; young men would no longer be counseled to enter the military. As the Crusade had long argued, concessions were won through pressure, through Chicano power, not through the institutional generosity of a purportedly democratic society.

The article quoted no one from the Crusade, but the words of community members reflected long-simmering anger. Helen Lucero of the Mile Hi American G. I. Forum said:

> Whether we like it or not, America listens to violence and if violence is what motivates this community, even a "stupid Mexican" can see the course he has to follow. If you want attention, an audience, or results, you allow a few persons to get knocked around by antagonized policemen. You allow the police department to have a few cars damaged. You even allow some personal injuries. And then all Denver wants to know your needs. But you didn't want this, and we surely didn't want it. But, for over 200 years of "Si, señor" and "Excuse me," we have reached the point where it has begun to choke us.

Antonio Ortiz, of the Southwest Action Center, said, "It's time to get rid of bigoted teachers and get together around a negotiating table and come up with results. . . . It is everybody's fight at West." Mark Saiz, a school employee, said, "We don't have to be Anglicized to be Americans. We are entitled to the benefits accorded Americans, but if it means becoming Anglicized, forget it."

Gonzales' leadership was noted; "Responses from the community, from students, legislators, community developers and other leaders indicate, to a perhaps surprisingly unanimous degree, that . . . Corky has done more good than harm for their cause. Some are a good deal more enthusiastic about him, but very few Hispanos have no use for him." A West High School student said, "You have to admire him, because he has aroused the community and he has helped matters at West. Chicano student leaders tried for months to start a Chicano club at West, but in the end they were forced to go out and recruit Corky." Said another, "Maybe our parents are against demonstrations. But the younger generation is getting involved. Before, our people moved out when they made it. Now some of them are coming back. We're staying here. We're going to give our people a hand. We're going to stay and fight."

THE 1969 CHICANO YOUTH LIBERATION CONFERENCE

After the Crusade announced the Chicano Youth Liberation Conference in January 1969, preparations proceeded quietly. Crusade women secured cots and blankets for youths who were to be housed at the Crusade building; young women and families were housed by local activists. Registration cards were printed and issued to participants, and no one was allowed to enter without a card. Security personnel, coordinated by Anselmo "Sal" Candelaria of the San Jose Black Berets, were posted at the door. The Crusade had announced that "only Mexican Americans will participate,"[40] but many youth groups arriving from Chicago and other areas reflected the composition of local gangs with Latino, black, and white members. The "Mexicans Only" rule was unenforceable; literal enforcement would have eliminated Puerto Ricans and Central Americans, as well, which was never the intent.

The Crusade originally expected several hundred participants. As registration proceeded, it became apparent that initial projections were far too modest. Not all details of the conference were fully chronicled (as was the case with the resolutions of the women's workshop), and the most detailed *El Gallo* account was an article by Maria Varela, a journalist and photographer, in the April 1968 issue.

Varela noted that a hundred Puerto Rican youths from New York and Chicago attended, making this first major gathering of Latino youths. More than a hundred organizations were represented, and over 1,500 people attended. People came from Texas, Oregon, California, Washington, Utah, Arizona, New Mexico, and Colorado.[41] Chicanos also came from midwestern cities like Detroit, Saginaw, Kalamazoo, Milwaukee, St. Paul, St. Louis, Kansas City, and Chicago.

Central Americans came from San Francisco and elsewhere. One young Nicaraguan distributed posters of Augusto Sandino and explained that he represented for Nicaraguans what Zapata represented for Mexicans. He wore bell-bottomed pants, flowered shirts, and a brown beret on an enormous Afro-style hairdo. In sessions in the Crusade's cafeteria, he read fiery poetry with Guadalupe Saavedra, Rodolfo Gonzales, and other poets. He was a member of the San Francisco Brown Berets and, in addition to being a poet, was a Golden Gloves welterweight boxer. His name was Roberto "Beto" Vargas; in the 1980s he represented the Sandinista government in the Nicaraguan embassy in Washington, D.C.

Varela's article described a rally at the State Capitol where the Mexican flag was raised on a flagpole after the American flag was lowered. A young man in the crowd drew a knife and slashed the U.S. flag after the protestors lowered it, an incident recorded in the FBI's Crusade file.

El Gallo published only two resolutions of the many passed at the conference; most of its pages were devoted to the school walkouts or photographs of the conference. The artists and culture workshop resolution, written by Crusade member and artist Manuel Martinez, proclaimed,

"Arte de Aztlan is a social, revolutionary art, reflecting the greatness and sacrifices of our past and clarifying and intensifying our present desires. . . . When liberation comes, then artists can do art for art's sake, but until then we must do art for the sake of liberating humanity."[42] The other resolution proposed to establish a Chicano institute where students and youths would collaborate with workers in educational and organizational projects.[43]

The social highlight of the conference was the marriage of Gonzales' oldest daughter, Nita. *El Gallo* reported, "The bride wore a simple, richly-embroidered, white full skirt and blouse. . . . The princess was made even more regal by the covering over the head and body by a rebozo de bolita, a shawl of dainty clusters laced together by a fernlike pattern."[44]

El Gallo published photographs of conference participants Valentina Tijerina, representing an agricultural cooperative in Tierra Amarilla; Sal Candelaria of the San Jose Black Berets; Francisco Martinez, who was indicted in the 1968 East L. A. school walkouts; Manuel Gomez, a student activist, poet, and future draft resister; Alberto "Alurista" Urista, a San Diego poet; Luis Valdez of Teatro Campesino; Obed Lopez of LADO (Chicago); and Ignacio "Nacho" Perez of MAYO, forerunner of the Texas La Raza Party.

Uncaptioned photographs of male activists dominated *El Gallo,* and Patricia Borjon and other California women in fact criticized sexism at the youth conference.[45] Though women had always been a crucial part of the Crusade's labor force and, since the Poor People's Campaign, had been involved in organizational planning, administration, and decision making, the organization's conservative cultural orientation cast women in "traditional" familial and gender roles: wives, sisters, daughters, sweethearts. Crusade men were puzzled by the feminist criticism and attributed it to a few women "intellectuals." Even some Crusade women were offended by the feminist criticism but lacked a framework with which to challenge it.

EL PLAN ESPIRITUAL DE AZTLAN

The first Denver youth conference is best known for a proclamation called *El Plan Espiritual de Aztlan,* published in English and Spanish and consisting of a preamble and a less well known three-point "Program of Action." The three-paragraph preamble read:

> In the spirit of a new people that is conscious not only of its proud historical heritage, but also of the brutal "Gringo" invasion of our territories, We, the Chicano inhabitants and civilizers of the northern land

of Aztlan, from whence came our forefathers, reclaiming the land of their birth and consecrating the determination of our people of the sun, Declare that the call of our blood is our responsibility, and our inevitable destiny.

We are free and sovereign to determine those tasks which are justly called for by our house, our land, the sweat of our brows, and by our hearts. Aztlan belongs to those that plant the seeds, water the fields, and gather the crops, and not the foreign Europeans. We do not recognize capricious frontiers on the Bronze Continent.

Brotherhood unites us, and love for our brothers makes us a people whose time has come and who struggles against the foreigner "Gabacho" who exploits our riches and destroys our culture. With our heart in our hands and our hands in the soil, We Declare the Independence of our Mestizo Nation. We are a Bronze People with a Bronze Culture. Before the world, before all of North America, before all our brothers in the Bronze Continent, We are a Nation, We are a Union of free Pueblos, We are Aztlan—Por La Raza Todo, Fuera de La Raza Nada. March 1969[46]

"Aztlan" referred to the land of origin of the Nahuatl-speaking Mexica of Mexico, who are commonly, but incorrectly, known as Aztecs. They came from somewhere in northern Mexico or the present-day American Southwest. The Mexica, who are not specifically named in the *Plan,* arrived nearly one thousand years ago in the Valley of Anahuac, after a long odyssey, and rose to power and splendor until their subjugation by the Spaniards. The location of Aztlan, their homeland, is difficult to ascertain: Somewhere between Nayarit, Mexico—400 miles northwest of Mexico City—and the present-day U.S. Southwest. Who could locate, with precision, Aztlan, the ancestral Mexica homeland? Incidentally, no account of Aztlan locates it near Denver, which is 120 miles north of the Arkansas River, Mexico's northern border at the time of the American takeover.

"AZTLAN" RECONSIDERED

The wording of the *Plan* demonstrates ethnic pride in its consciousness of a "proud historical heritage," but its poetic wording creates great interpretive difficulties. It declared unity in gender-based terminology ("brotherhood unites us, and love for our brothers makes us a people whose time has come"). It spoke of "tasks which are justly called for by our house, our land, the sweat of our brows, and by our hearts." But what were these tasks for which our hearts called, and what, exactly, was it time to do?

And what did indigenous nations have to say about this grand plan declared in their absence? They clearly have their own myths, legends, and histories of origin that surpass, equal, predate, or displace Aztlan. What did the *Plan* mean to the tribal nations of the present-day American Southwest, if this is where Aztlan was once located, tribal nations who had engaged Spaniards and Mexicans ("mestizos") in bloody warfare for encroachment on lands they occupied. Or was their input needed, since Chicanos were really "Indian," or at least mestizo, anyway?

While declaring the "Independence of our Mestizo Nation," the plan says nothing about these peoples and nations, nor about African Americans or the role—if any—that the foreign "gabacho" would play in the nation it proclaimed. Its wording implies the solidarity of the Americas, since it does "not recognize capricious frontiers on the Bronze Continent." But how were Chicanos to commune with their "brothers" across these borders? And what was meant by a "Bronze People with a Bronze Culture"?

The *Plan* declares, "We are free and sovereign. . . . We are a Nation." Was this to be a new Chicano nation called Aztlan? And how would Aztlan relate to Mexico? Or would it? Was the *Plan* a literal declaration of independence from the United States? If so, where were the limits of these lands, since Mexico's borders were drawn by Spanish imperialists anyway, and, at the time of the American takeover, vast regions were populated not by Mexican mestizos, but by sedentary or nomadic tribal nations? In what sense did "Chicanos" have "their hearts in their hands and their hands in the soil"? What did this interesting imagery mean?

The verbal and theoretical imprecision of this declaration leaves room for many interpretations. Whatever "Aztlan" meant, the word spread rapidly after the conference. Students, for example, soon adopted the name Movimiento Estudiantil Chicano de Aztlan (MEChA)—the Chicano Student Movement of Aztlan.

The *Plan* was, as noted above, a two-part document; Gonzales wrote the program, while the poet Alberto Urista wrote most of the preamble. The program sees nationalism as an ideology around which Chicanos would rally:

> The Chicano (La Raza de Bronze) must use their nationalism as the key or common denominator for mass mobilization and organization. Once we are committed to the idea and philosophy of *El Plan de Aztlan,* we can only conclude that social, economic, cultural, and political independence is the only road to total liberation from oppression, exploitation, and racism. Our struggle then must be the control of our barrios, campos, pueblos, lands, our economy, our culture, and our political life. El *Plan* commits all levels of Chicano society: the barrio, the campo, the ranchero, the writer, the teacher, the worker, the professional, to la causa.[47]

Nationalism was so important that a restatement of it served as *punto primero* (point one): "Nationalism as the key to organization transcends all religions, political, class and economic factions or boundaries. Nationalism is the common denominator that all members of La Raza can agree on." Gonzales believed nationalism should, and would, transcend those factors that divided Chicanos. Leftists and many intellectuals at the youth conference, however, argued that "La Raza" itself was divided into classes with divergent interests, and that, at its worst, primitive nationalism could be racist. For them, nationalism alone would not transcend class privilege and bias. The *Plan* did not address these issues.

The resolutions of the Crusade's youth conferences of 1969, 1970, and 1971 reflect the prevailing nationalist sentiments of conference participants. Nationalism may not have been a comprehensive political theory, but it prevailed in the conferences' rhetoric, emotion, spirit of unity, and youthful enthusiasm. Philosophical conflicts arose between nationalists and those advocating theories based on class, and though the *Plan* did not cause these conflicts, being merely an expression of pre-existing nationalist sentiment, neither was it an adequate framework to comprehend or resolve them.

For all its conceptual murkiness and rhetorical quirkiness, the *Plan*'s preamble and program denounced exploitation and advocated liberation and self-determination, calling for driving out exploiters and "occupying forces." It was provocative in its advocacy of "revolutionary acts" by youth and was traditionalist, or conservative, in its defense of culture, morals, and values like "respect" and "family and home." It was idealistic in advocating "love," "humanism," and "dignity." It criticized and rejected American society and government and served as a radical voice that spoke to many ideas, emotions, visions, and issues within the community.

The Denver walkouts and the national youth conference demonstrated the involvement and growing militancy of Chicano youth, but were not its only manifestations. The issue of *El Gallo* covering the 1969 conference records student walkouts in Tucson, Arizona, and Kingsville, Texas. Three thousand protestors marched in Del Rio, Texas, after 32 youths were arrested in a demonstration. On March 4, 1969, Chicano students in Fort Collins, Colorado, led by student Manuel Ramos and leaders of MACE, demanded that the Colorado State University increase Chicano enrollment.[48]

TWO ALIASES: "JUAN GOMEZ" AND
"ANTONIO EL GUERRILLERO"

In the summer of 1969, *El Gallo* reported an incident in San Francisco's Mission District that resulted in the arrest of a group of young Latinos who became known as Los Siete de La Raza, though only six were apprehended. The seventh suspect, Gio Lopez, escaped capture. The arrested suspects—Mario Martinez, Rodolfo Martinez, Jose Rios, Nelson Rodriguez, Jose Melendez, and Gary Lescallet—were charged with the death of San Francisco patrolman Joseph Brodnik in a confrontation between the young men and Officers Brodnik and Paul McGoran. A Denver FBI report, dated June 30, 1969, citing an unnamed informer attending the May 28, 1969, Fishermen's Meeting, reported that

> another speaker at [the] meeting was an individual from San Francisco, California, believed to be named [name deleted] who spoke concerning the arrest of seven Mexican Americans at San Francisco on May 1, 1969, on charges of murder. He alleged that the charges were false and that these seven Mexican Americans are being persecuted by the police. During the meeting this individual requested funds be donated for the defense of those arrested at San Francisco and a sum of approximately $100 to $200 was collected from the group attending the meeting.[49]

Contrary to the FBI report, Los Siete were Central Americans, not Mexican Americans, and the speaker, Oscar Rios, later said he raised only $28 on his Denver visit.[50] (Whatever the amount was, the Crusade provided other assistance to the cause of Los Siete.) The June 30 FBI report also shows that an informer attended at least three Fishermen's Meetings and

> advised that the regular weekly meeting of the CFJ. . . . June 11, 1969, . . . was addressed by a guest speaker from San Antonio, Texas, who was one of the founders of the Mexican American Youth Organization (MAYO). [Name deleted] stated there were about 100 persons in attendance at the meeting. The guest speaker spoke on the topic of poverty among Mexican Americans and how Mexican Americans would have to end conflict among themselves and direct their efforts to obtaining concessions from the general population of the country.[51]

The unnamed speaker was José Angel Gutiérrez.

The FBI report did not mention what happened after the meeting. Prior to Gutiérrez' Denver visit, another young man arrived in town and was taken in by the Crusade. Quiet and reserved, he said he had been active with MAYO in Texas and wanted to be active in Denver. He was about 5 feet, 7 inches tall, with a dark complexion and curly hair. After Gutiérrez' presentation at the Fishermen's Meeting, activists who had accompanied him gave some Crusade members additional information about this visitor. The young man had indeed been active in Texas until he aroused the suspicion of the MAYO activists with whom he lived. He left the house every day saying he was going to work, but it was discovered that the rode buses all day and had no job. He left Texas and appeared in Denver.

At this point Crusade members asked the young Texan to accompany them on a security check of the premises. He was surrounded in the gymnasium and accused of being an informer. He hung his head in silent response. He was punched and nearly struck with a heavy metal object before his would-be assailant was restrained. He was told to leave the building or face consequences. He left and was not seen again.

The would-be assailant called himself Antonio Medina and sometimes used the name Antonio El Guerrillero ("Antonio the Guerrilla"). El Guerrillero angrily searched the Crusade vicinity for the young Texan. A copy of an FBI file on the Crusade refers to El Guerrillero as Antonio Gustavo Medina.[52] Medina was an interesting character and claimed at various times to be Puerto Rican, Chicano, Mexicano, Venezuelan, and/or descended from the indigenous people of an island off Venezuela's coast.

In fact, Antonio Medina was a Latin mulatto who took pains to deny his African heritage. He spoke a fluent, rapid Spanish without a Mexican accent and was familiar with "calo," a border slang. He came to Denver just before the 1969 conference and said he was a member of the Los Angeles Brown Berets, and, indeed, he wore a brown beret. He stayed on at the Crusade after the conference. Medina was loud, provocative, seemingly quick-tempered, and emotional. He claimed this was due to his father's (or his brother's) having been tortured for revolutionary activity in Venezuela. He claimed his father (and/or brother) fought with the famed revolutionary Ernesto "Che" Guevara, and that his father (or brother, or both father and brother) was (or were) killed. He claimed that he, too, had been subjected to fierce torture by the Venezuelan government. His autobiography was skeptically received by Crusade members. He spent his time boasting, drinking, and womanizing.

Medina once accompanied Crusade member Gilbert Quintana to a meeting of the School District 14 Board of Education in nearby Adams County, where community members were presenting grievances related to a student walkout subsequent to the Denver walkouts. Medina told board members, "If you don't meet our demands, we will deal with you mentally and physically."[53]

That same summer, another young man appeared at the Crusade building and was introduced as Juan Gomez. He was young, about 5 feet, 9 inches tall, with shoulder-length black hair, a sparse beard, and medium build. His barrio-accented English was softly spoken. Looking like a barrio-bred Che Guevara, he seemed cocky yet withdrawn. He was popular with young women in the growing social circle of youth activists. He worked as a resident janitor at the Crusade building and seldom left the premises.

Gomez disliked El Guerrillero. Like many youths, Gomez smoked marijuana and, on more than one occasion, offered pot to Medina, who politely declined. When, rarely, he smoked with Gomez, Medina became nervous and agitated and soon departed. Medina was uncomfortable around Gomez. Though Gomez spoke little, he apparently also thought little of Medina, whom he beheld with an amused but coolly menacing contempt.

Gomez became close friends with many younger Crusade members and with some adults. In the fall of 1969, he left Denver as quietly as he came. He was, in reality, Gio Lopez, the fugitive seventh member of Los Siete de La Raza.[54] On November 7, 1970, Los Siete de La Raza were acquitted of murder in the death of Officer Brodnik. Antonio El Guerrillero, as will be related, left Denver several weeks later.

"SPLASH-INS" IN BARRIO PARKS

The pace of Chicano youth activism quickened over the summer of 1969. Two events were especially significant: the "nationalization" of a Westside park and the September 16, 1969, school walkouts. The first event provided a base for Denver organizing well into the 1970s, and the latter greatly assisted in the revival of Mexican (or "Chicano") cultural consciousness.

In 1969, two young couples moved into the Lincoln Park housing projects in the Westside: Gilbert and Carol Quintana, and Manuel Martinez and his wife, Sally. Also moving to the Westside were Kelly and Sue Lovato. All were Crusade members. Other young Crusade members began socializing in the Westside, which was then Denver's largest barrio and a turf-conscious neighborhood.

Crusade members worked with Westside residents like Germaine Aragon and her son Larry, who had been arrested during the school walkouts. Their intention was to begin organizing neighborhood youths who congregated around the swimming pool in the local park, then named Lincoln Park, which provided both the locale and the target population for organizing. The housing projects were constructed in two parts, the red projects and the yellow projects, named after the color of bricks used in their construction. Lincoln Park was situated between the two projects.

Earlier in the summer, the media had reported that the city was considering closing the swimming pools in the Westside and Eastside because, the city said, it did not have the money to maintain the facilities. Closing the swimming pools would have deprived these neighborhoods of needed services. Rodolfo Gonzales used a creative protest called a "splash-in" to pressure the city to allocate resources for the pools. The Crusade organized Eastside and Westside youths and took them to Mamie Eisenhower Park in middle-class Southeast Denver to draw attention to the neglect of facilities in low-income communities.

Scores of youngsters, led by the Crusade, invaded the swimming pool in street clothes and without paying the fee. The staff was unable to prevent their entry, and some were pushed into the water. Local youths quickly abandoned the pool, and neighborhood residents gathered on their lawns and sidewalks, initially intimidated by the rambunctious crowd. In time they approached to ask why "their" pool had been taken over and were told that the protestors did not want to be in Southeast Denver but had no choice, since the city was about to close facilities in the barrio. Gonzales, who understood that middle-class Denver had political clout, told them they should call city officials to urge allocation of resources to the low-income parks.

These residents were soon chatting amiably with the protestors, and their children returned to the pool to swim and splash with their inner-city counterparts. It may have been their presence that prevented the use of force by the police, who reported to the area in riot gear. As usual, this protest did not escape the attention of the FBI:

> The June 29, 1969, issue of the "Denver Post" . . . reported that Rodolfo "Corky" Gonzales termed inadequate and outdated swimming pools in low income areas. The article reported that the followers of Gonzales voiced chants of "Chicano Power" and went into the pool wearing their street clothes. Also present at the "splash-in" was Lauren Watson, head of the [Black Panther Party], Denver, and some of his supporters who also entered the pool.[55]

Four months later, the *Rocky Mountain News* reported the results of the demonstration:

> Gonzales got support from several groups and many individuals last June, when he organized a "splash-in" of 100 Hispano youngsters at Eisenhower Park pool in affluent Southeast Denver. . . . [The splash-in] also served to contrast Eisenhower's well-maintained facility—heated water, an adequate filtration system, and a wading pool for tots—with run-down and neglected pools in Lincoln Park and Curtis Park, two minority areas. All three pools are public, city-owned facilities. . . . The splash-in brought results: the city has taken steps to remedy conditions at both Curtis and Lincoln.[56]

Westside youth activists now addressed another concern relating to recreation facilities: barrio swimming pools usually employed middle-class white youths who often showed little interest in their work and less interest in the day-to-day life of the community. The young Westside organizers raised pointed questions. Why were outsiders employed in the barrio when neighborhood youth were unemployed? Couldn't neighborhood youths run their own facilities? Didn't they need and deserve jobs as much as others?

Pool managers and lifeguards, key staff, had to receive certification as "water safety instructors." Westside youths, many of whom were adept swimmers, could easily obtain such certification, but those employed there were not going to vacate their jobs voluntarily. The resentment and high spirits of barrio youth did not make it easy for the middle-class staff to exercise authority. It was one thing to eject troublesome but compliant youngsters from the pool or ban them from using the facility, but what could be done when youths refused to leave and were willing to fight to stay? As if to emphasize community grievances, someone once drove a vehicle into the swimming pool after the staff left for the day.

The Department of Parks and Recreation declared its willingness to employ qualified neighborhood youths. Young activists quietly trained for certification as lifeguards, anticipating that the regular employees would not be able to deal with the new stresses of the job. When employees began to quit, surprised Parks and Recreation bureaucrats found neighborhood youths ready to replace them. This would soon lead to the first "park nationalization" in Denver. A small piece of Aztlan was about to be liberated.

"CHICANO LIBERATION DAY"

Meanwhile, in North Denver, Manuel "Rocky" Hernandez, son of Crusade members Luis and Cordelia Ramirez, was quietly organizing young men and women to form a Denver Black Beret chapter. Hernandez was a musician who performed at Crusade youth dances. At the 1969 youth conference, he met Sal (or "Chemo") Candelaria of the San Jose Black Berets. Though some Denver youths returned from the Poor People's Campaign wearing black berets, Hernandez' group became the first functional chapter of Black Berets in Denver. In September the Black Berets organized a walkout at North High School, and participated in Denver's second citywide school walkout.

In the summer of 1969, the Crusade planned a massive demonstration to establish Mexican Independence Day as an ongoing event in the city of Denver. The FBI opened an Internal Security file on the event: Bufile 105–197022 captioned "Chicano Liberation Day, September 16, 1969, Internal Security–Spanish American."[57] The first reference to the Mexican Independence Day protest in the FBI's Crusade file is found in a report dated July 30, 1969. The report's "Synopsis" states, "CFJ plans a nationwide boycott of schools by Mexican American students on 9/16/69, the anniversary of independence of Mexico, to protest alleged inequities to Mexican American students."[58]

The September 16 protest was called for in *punto tercero* of the *Plan*

Espiritual de Aztlan action program: "September 16th, on the birthdate of Mexican Independence, a national walkout by all Chicanos of all colleges and schools to be sustained until the complete revision of the educational system, its policy-makers, administration, its curriculum and its personnel to meet the needs of our community."[59] This was a grandiose undertaking, since the Chicano movement lacked the organization, communications network, and unified leadership to force the "complete revision of the educational system," but, then, no one had envisioned the overwhelming response to the convening of the conference. Who was to say it could not be done?

An FBI report on the walkout, citing an informer whose name is deleted, indicates close scrutiny:

> [Name deleted] stated that the idea for the "Chicano Liberation Day" celebration, to be held on September 16, 1969, began with a youth conference sponsored by the CFJ in Denver during March 27–31, 1969. [Deleted] stated that it was at that same conference that "El Plan Espiritual de Aztlan" was given impetus and that this plan called for the unification of Mexican Americans within the influence of their heritage derived from the land of "Aztlan," which is the name given to northern Mexico and the Southwestern part of the United States, and which land was to be regarded as still belonging to its earlier settlers of Spanish and Mexican-Indian descent.[60]

The event was envisioned as a protest, not a celebration, and the Crusade hosted a gathering on August 29–31, 1969, to organize the upcoming walkout. Crusade members and youths drawn to the Crusade since the walkouts attended. Workshops were held in rooms at the Crusade building, and various social service agencies and professional groups were present.

In the education workshop, educators listed the demands they wanted made at the rally: the hiring of more Spanish-surnamed teachers and advancement for teachers who were presently employed. The militancy of youth was evident, and politically astute Crusade members noted that the educators, consciously or not, asked only for reforms benefiting themselves while leaving youth unmentioned. Were schools to serve students or teachers? As happened repeatedly, the pressures generated by the grassroots seemed about to be harnessed by a small middle class that equated its advancement with social change for the masses.

When a young man suggested that the schools provide books teaching the history of Chicanos, one middle-aged, middle-class educator impatiently asked him to name specific books. The young man suggested *North from Mexico* by Carey McWilliams; the educator retorted that the book was out of print. In fact, the book had been published in paperback the previous year. This educator had been hailed, in 1964, for her "key role in community leadership" after Mayor Tom Currigan appointed her to one of his commissions. Her flattered response to this honor: "I hardly thought about being part of the Spanish-American community until I got caught up in the Mayor's Commission."[61]

By September 16 the demands were finalized and reflected the spectrum of community concerns on education. Denver's Commission on Community Relations helped the Crusade obtain a parade permit. The September 13 *Rocky Mountain News* wrote that "hundreds of Mexican Americans in the Denver area are expected to participate in the observance of Mexican Independence Day."[62]

The demonstration started at the Civic Center and traversed the length of downtown Denver's two main thoroughfares, 15th and 16th Streets. The march ended in a rally at the State Capitol, after which the Crusade hosted festivities at its headquarters. Students were to be excused from parochial and public schools and were "requested" by school authorities to present written excuses from their parents before the walkout. Police Chief Seaton also demonstrated his concern by asking priests and ministers to join the protestors, saying, "We hope that you will wear your clerical garb, so as to be clearly recognizable, and will thus exert a quieting and constructive effect upon those individuals who might otherwise be inclined to be disruptive."[63]

Though press accounts referred to protestors as "children" and called the protest a "celebration," they recognized an unprecedented showing of community support. According to the *Rocky Mountain News:*

> Public school officials . . . reported absenteeism high at all schools with a large number of Hispano and Negro children missing from class. They estimated that 1,500 elementary pupils and nearly 1,800 secondary students walked out. Officials said others stayed away from school. At Baker Junior high 168 students walked out of class, leaving 172 in school. School officials estimated nearly 500 students failed to report. The Denver march ended in front of the Capitol, where Crusade for Justice leader Rodolfo "Corky" Gonzales told the nearly 2,000 persons, "We didn't come here to tear anything down—we came here to build a new movement for the Chicanos."[64]

The *Denver Post* estimated the crowd at 2,500 to 4,000 and reported:

> The turnout for the Mexican Independence Day celebration, led by the Crusade for Justice, was far greater than the city had expected. One official close to the city's preparations for the event told the Denver Post last week that the city was expecting the parade and rally would draw

300 to 500 persons. The day began when more than 3,300 students walked out of more than a score of metropolitan area schools to join the downtown parade.[65]

The *Denver Post* dedicated nine lines to the demands of the Congress of Hispano Educators and one line to Gonzales' keynote speech, but noted that "the real meaning of the event was captured by Rodolfo (Corky) Gonzales, leader of the Crusade, when he told the huge crowd gathered on the west lawn of the Statehouse, 'Everybody thought it couldn't be done.'"[66] The massive protest impressed the *Post*'s reporter, who observed:

> It was unprecedented. On Sixteenth Street there was a virtual army of people, linked arm and arm, jamming the street from curb to curb chanting "Chicano power" at the top of their lungs. The parade stretched more than six blocks long and even the leaders expressed amazement as they began walking back on Fifteenth Street toward the statehouse and looked over toward 16th Street at the intersections and saw people still marching. . . . Civil rights and racial groups have conducted protest marches through downtown Denver before, but their number has never exceeded 500.[67]

An article printed in *The Militant* listed Donald ("Archie") LaForette, Manuel ("Rocky") Hernandez, Al Sanchez, Jr., and Linda Bustos as the respective walkout leaders at West, North, Lincoln, and Adams City high schools.[68] Walkouts occurred in 31 schools, many teachers joined the protestors, and a solidarity speech was given by Salvador Herrera Gomez, a Mexican student attending the University of Colorado at Boulder.

El Gallo dedicated five pages to the protest, which drew participants from Englewood, Boulder, Adams City, Commerce City, Brighton, Fort Lupton, Greeley, and Lafayette. The front-page article mentioned walkouts in Monte Vista, Alamosa, Antonito, and Colorado Springs.[69] A map on page two indicated walkouts in Fort Collins, Greeley, Longmont, Trinidad, Del Norte, and Grand Junction as well.

An *El Gallo* article criticized "the same old people asking the same old questions" about the protest and provided a response:

> "Aren't you going about this the wrong way? . . . Why are you people starting trouble, we have no problems?" These questions came from people who did not know, and who did not care to know, that immediately after the blow-out the school administration promoted 9 Chicano teachers into administrative positions. This fall the Denver Public Schools recruited 20 new Chicano teachers. These were the teachers who one year ago had a hard time getting an interview. And still people ask, "What do you hope to accomplish?" . . . Now, after the [September

walkouts], over $100,000 in government funds has been allocated for the Westside schools.[70]

Twenty-one years before the Denver walkouts, Beatrice Griffith, a social worker and author, wrote in *American Me:*

> It is in the schools that children of Mexican ancestry learn of America: American life, American history, her great men, her cities and government. Here they make their dreams—and often lose them. The school records of these youngsters are affected by the same factors that influence any other underprivileged children—poverty, bad housing, under-nourishment, and ill health. Added to these are the bilingualism and segregation which make even worse the hard lot of underprivileged childhood.[71]

Another generation of neglect followed the publication of Griffith's book, and resulted in school protests in Colorado and throughout the Southwest at the end of the 1960s. Though some criticized the walkouts, the pressure they created led to reforms. Yet the Mexican community did not gain control over the education of their children. The crisis faced by children of Mexican descent in public schools remains to this day. The dismal pushout rate has not changed.

On the other hand, the solidarity, pride, and vigor of this protest movement forced the powers-that-be to take into account the existence of the largest and fastest-growing community of color. This movement woke the Sleeping Giant, and changed the Mile High City forever.

Six

Militancy and Counterreaction

BLACK BERETS AND BROWN BERETS

September 16, 1969, marked the advent of Denver's first well-organized "beret" youth group, the Northside Black Berets.[1] Its founder was Manuel "Rocky" Hernandez; the membership included Dan Pedraza, Freida Rangel, Sheryl Ritchie, Danny Martinez, Juan Trujillo, Ron Freyta, Walter Cordova, and Luis "Junior" Martinez (Junior Martinez would be killed by the Denver police on March 17, 1973).

Organized over the summer of 1969, the Black Berets provided security for the renaming of Lincoln Park in Denver's Westside. Activists wanted to change the name to Aztlan Park; it is now officially named Alma Park. Young Crusade members and Westside youths organized a renaming dance at a small amphitheater in the park on September 26, 1969. Hundreds of young people attended.

Police in the area attempted to stop a car carrying several young people, but the driver sped away. The car was stolen. It stopped near the southwestern edge of the park, and the occupants ran, but police captured one young man, whom they handcuffed and beat. Dozens of youths gathered at the scene and grew increasingly angry as they watched the beating. They yelled for the police to stop and began to throw rocks and bottles when the beating continued. "Some Black Berets started to push the crowd back but by this time several carloads of [police] had arrived. They singled out the Black Berets and four [police] gave Black Beret Ronnie Freyta a severe beating."[2]

The incident escalated and led to an hour of fighting between police and youths. Police fired birdshot and used Mace and teargas canisters, which they threw into the nearby housing projects. The crowd fought back with fists, rocks, and bottles. Freyta was arrested, and 14 policemen were reportedly treated for minor injuries at Denver General Hospital.

Crusade members and Black Berets held a protest the next day at police headquarters, and Freyta was released on bond.

The Northside Black Berets had their counterpart in the Eastside Brown Berets, a group organized in the autumn of 1969. The Eastside Berets had over two hundred members by March 1970, including junior high and high school students as well as youths who no longer attended school.[3] This Brown Beret group was formed by Roddy Miera (an amateur boxer and leader of a gang known as the Curtis Park Boys), Margarito "Muggsy" Berzoza (another boxer), and Ray Zaragosa. When Miera spoke about peace and brotherhood to his former rivals in other gangs, the young men listened; he was widely known for his courage, temper, and fighting ability. Most members of his gang joined the Berets, and the gang ceased to exist. These young organizers contacted youths from several Eastside neighborhoods, and all these areas were represented in the Eastside Brown Berets. Many went by nicknames with a distinct barrio flavor: Peso, Masa, Buzzard, Fat Tony, Caveman, Muggsy, Crusher.

Another Brown Beret group was formed later and led by such activists as Carlos Zapata, Aaron Duran, Bobby Ward, and David Madrid. It drew most of its members from the Northside but, like all Denver Brown Beret or Black Beret groups, had members from other barrios as well. The Brighton Brown Berets were based in a small agricultural town 30 miles or so northeast of Denver. Later, another Black Beret organization was led by Van Lucero and Marcos Martinez, brother of Junior Martinez.

The longest-lived of these organizations was the Brown Berets of Pueblo, a southern Colorado city of about one hundred thousand where Chicanos were almost a majority. The town's economy was then dominated by the steel mills of Colorado Fuel and Iron (CF&I). The Pueblo Brown Berets, in conjunction with the Pueblo La Raza Unida Party, paralleled the Crusade for Justice in strength and organization and were its closest political allies. Among the many Pueblo activists of note were Maria Serna (Subia), Eddie Montour, Clifford Martinez, Alfredo "Freddie" Archer, Albert Gurule, Martin Serna, and Edmund Roybal. Many of these activists, in turn, had been influenced by older women like Mrs. Bea Roybal and a women's group known as the Mothers of Casa Verde (Casa Verde being the small community center where activists gathered).

Many of the Northside Black Berets who provided security at the renaming of Lincoln Park were students at North High School. Tensions arose when Principal Pete Shannon forbade them to wear their berets in school. Ironically, Shannon had been promoted to principal because of the walkout demands for more Chicanos in administrative positions within the schools. (His mother was Latina). The conflicts at North High

School led to walkouts at North, West, and Manual High Schools in early 1970, coordinated by the Northside Black Berets, the Eastside Brown Berets, and the Crusade for Justice. The youths were influenced by a nationalism that looked to the culture and revolutionary traditions of Mexico for its inspiration, but others had contrary views.

BARRIO NATIONALISM AND "REAL AMERICANISM"

The stirring of barrio activism also produced a reaction among the small but growing middle class. These people served as a conservative political current in opposition to that of militant nationalism, while the status quo accommodated pressures generated by nationalists by increasing opportunities for Spanish-surnamed people, especially the middle class. The number of Spanish-surnamed politicians grew, especially among the Democrats, and local and federal governments allocated more funds for the War on Poverty in the barrios. Universities recruited more Chicano students and staff and developed Chicano Studies programs and departments. These affirmative action programs generated leadership within mainstream channels, with increased opportunities for employment and social prestige. The possibility of employment, material advancement, and prestige was attractive to many people, who sought inclusion in the system rather than rejecting it. After all, wasn't getting ahead what it was all about?

Nationalism did not have the same attraction for all Spanish-surnamed people, and the word "Chicano" was disdained by some, who preferred "Hispanic" and "Hispano" as designations for Denver's Mexican-origin community. These generic terms, while leaving Mexico unmentioned, evoke visions of Spain, a European nation Chicano activists spurned as the imperialist oppressor of Mexico and Latin America.

The concern about proper terminology was nothing new, and a booklet published at the time reflects how the debate was repackaged. *The Heritage and Contributions of the Hispanic American* was the brainchild of the Congress of Hispanic Educators. An article on the booklet's publication quoted Uvaldo "Sam" Chavez, a Denver teacher:

> Sixty percent of the Spanish-surnamed people of the Denver Metro area are descendants of the Spanish colonials of New Mexico, dating way back to and following 1598–1821, during part of which time the area was called the Kingdom of New Spain, in the name of the Catholic King of Spain. . . . To trace one's ancestry to these people is to boast of one's real Americanism. . . . The heritage of the Southwest really has nothing to do with the Mexican revolution.

It was evident that Chavez was at odds with the spirit behind the recent protests:

> ["Chicano" is] no word, it's an utterance. Personally, I detest it. . . . The point I would make here is that the Spanish-speaking peoples of the Southwest are not Mexican, nor are they Spaniards. Mexican, Spaniard, these are political terms—but these people are Americans, uniquely so, the only term acceptable seems to be "Hispano." That describes their ethnicity and stops there. The only legitimate political term I would use might be "colonial Americans of the Southwest."[4]

Though ethnic pride popularized the word "Chicano," nationalist sentiments did not completely rule the day. Nor were the movement's goals for education reform fully attained. The students' demands for a curriculum that included the contributions, history, and culture of their people were never fully implemented. While activists affirmed Mexican heritage (and militant politics), there were countering trends of denial.

"MILITANCY . . . HAS BEGUN TO GROW"

The beating of a young Chicano named Pat Apodaca by a teacher sparked walkouts at Lake Junior High School on October 7 and 8, 1969.[5] The walkout was supported by students from North High School, West High School, and Crusade members. North High Black Berets who supported the students at Lake had their own problems, as the October 8 *Rocky Mountain News* reported: "Ten students were suspended from North for refusing to take off berets before attending classes. The North principal, Pete Shannon, Jr., said it was not the headgear itself, which has become the symbol of militancy, but the attitude of the students that caused the problem."[6]

The "attitude" problem was not further explained, but youth activism everywhere revealed their attitudes. Young people were refusing to be sent to wars they did not start by governments for which they did not vote. They were willing to fight police rather than be beaten by them, and they challenged schools that failed them (and then blamed them for the failure). Young people quit gangs and started activist organizations, and since more than 50 percent of Denver's Mexican-origin population was under 19 years old, their attitudes were a problem for some people. The *Rocky Mountain News* reported:

> Militancy, activism, or whatever word you choose, has begun to grow in stature among Chicano youth as a tool for advancement of their people. Its turbulence and occasional violence is condemned by many older and middle-class Hispanos, who admit in the next breath that they, at one

time or another, have fallen victims to Denver's . . . ethnic discrimination in employment, housing or other opportunities for the good life. . . . Many young involved Chicanos also deplore the violence that sometimes springs from militant confrontations, but feel equally strong that without a strident challenge to business and government establishments, the circle of poverty and urban neglect will continue to trap many of their people. . . . While Gonzales' circle of active followers is limited largely to those of high school age, and while his tactics sometimes spark controversy, his ability to highlight inequities and his emphasis on Chicano pride have prompted many young Chicanos who disown him as a leader to become more aware of themselves, and of the potential destiny of their people. . . . The seeds have already been sown. As one Chicano youth put it: "Making it to me is when ALL our people make it."[7]

Rodolfo Gonzalez, the Crusade for Justice, and the Chicano movement played a key role in changing young people's attitudes in Denver and elsewhere. Activists were heartened by youthful attitudes that others found distressing.

ANTIWAR ACTIVISM

The San Francisco Vietnam Moratorium: Autumn 1969

The Crusade's concern with education issues was matched by its concern about the Vietnam war. The "Synopsis" of a November 28, 1969, Denver FBI report to Washington headquarters reported on the Crusade's participation in the Vietnam War Moratorium activities in San Francisco on November 15. It was one of many reports on Chicano antiwar activity.[8]

The Crusade, although it did not consider itself a "peace group," went to San Francisco to protest against the war as a Chicano organization. A two-day Chicano Symposium was held prior to the moratorium at California State College in Hayward. One session was to address the theme "Why a Chicano Party?" Among the speakers were Gonzales; Roger Alvarado, a 1968 San Francisco State College student strike leader; Aaron Manganiello, who had been associated with the College of San Mateo; Antonio Mondragon, who worked at Cal State Hayward; Froben Lozada, a Merritt College (Oakland) faculty member and Socialist Workers Party (SWP) activist; and Antonio Camejo, also a SWP member and Merritt College instructor. This all male line-up did not escape critical notice. One young Latina asked why no women were on the panel and commented: "When I look at the panel and see all these men with mustaches and beards, it reminds me of a picture of the Last Supper." The men's replies were awkward.

An additional speaker was provided time to address the symposium on

November 14. Rosalio Muñoz, whose draft induction refusal was reported in September–October *El Gallo,* proposed to the gathering that Chicanos hold their own moratorium to mobilize opposition to the war in Chicano communities. Muñoz said that the antiwar movement had succeeded in generating opposition to the war mostly among middle-class white youths who were being replaced by Chicanos and other minorities. Muñoz took advantage of the gathering of antiwar forces in San Francisco to propose an autonomous "Chicano moratorium."

"Great Pressure to Prove Loyalty"

Statistics confirmed the disproportionate casualty rate for Chicanos in Southeast Asia. Though people with Spanish surnames accounted for less than 12 percent of the population in five southwestern states, the Chicano casualty rate from this area stood at 19 percent. In a study entitled "Mexican American Casualties in Vietnam," Dr. Ralph Guzman wrote, "Chicanos tended to serve in those branches of the military that entailed high-risk duty, the Army and the U.S. Marines. . . . Mexican Americans have been seen as a suspect, 'foreign' minority. Like the Japanese Americans during World War II they have been under great pressure to prove loyalty to the United States." Several factors contributed to this casualty rate, Guzman suggested. Chicanos entered military service as a way out of poverty, few received student deferments, since few attended college, and Mexican American veterans' organizations "have long proclaimed the sizable military contributions of the Mexican American soldier," thus popularizing military service among Chicano youth. These factors led to higher draft and enlistment rates and to heavy casualties. Guzman's research showed that the Chicano combat casualty rate was 25.9 percent of Colorado's total casualties between January 1961 and February 1967.[9]

Later studies showed that minority veterans suffered higher rates of psychological disorders following military service in Vietnam. One study showed that 27.9 percent of all Latino veterans suffered psychological disorders, and 48.4 percent of Latinos who served in higher-stress war zones were affected. Figures for white veterans were 13.7 percent overall and 34 percent for those who served in the higher-stress areas.[10]

These statistics fueled opposition to the Vietnam war, and Muñoz' proposal met with enthusiasm. After the San Francisco protest, the Crusade hosted an antiwar gathering in Denver on December 6–7, which was attended by Muñoz, Ramses Noriega, Roberto Elias, and other California activists. From Chicago came Fred Aviles, a recently paroled draft resister and Puerto Rican independence activist. Colorado resisters included myself and Arturo Cordova, a college student and Crusade member. The

California activists announced the first of many Chicano moratoria, a protest scheduled for December 20 in East Los Angeles.[11] About 70 persons attended the Denver gathering.

THE DEPARTURE OF EL GUERRILLERO

An incident that occurred at this time resulted in the departure from Denver of the previously mentioned Antonio "El Guerrillero" Medina. On December 5, the night before the first full day of the Crusade's antiwar conference, several young men who had arrived for the conference went to a Westside nightclub with young Crusade members. Some entered the club, but one person—the author—had failed to bring identification and was denied entrance. The remainder of the group stood at the entrance while one person entered to tell those inside that all of the group should leave. El Guerrillero, who was with the group at the entrance, begun arguing loudly with two off-duty policemen who were checking IDs. He shoved one officer, knocked the flashlight from the other's hand, and was chased out the door by the officers.

The rest of the group then left the establishment and were confronted by the returning officers. After a brief argument on the sidewalk, the group began to walk to the Crusade building. After walking about two blocks, we heard sirens, and several police cars converged on the scene. The group scattered in various directions, but Roberto Elias and myself were caught and beaten. Elias, a Californian, was briefly hospitalized.[12] El Guerrillero was nowhere to be seen. Misdemeanor charges of disturbance, resistance, interference, and public intoxication were filed against Elias and the author. We were subsequently acquitted.

In a meeting the next day at the Crusade building, El Guerrillero said that after being chased from the nightclub he engaged pursuing officers in a furious fistfight, when police reinforcements set their dogs on him, he fought both dogs and reinforcements. After a long foot-chase through the Westside, he escaped by hiding under a parked vehicle. His story of valiant battle was not consistent with anyone's recollection, or with testimony in subsequent trials.

During the meeting El Guerrillero informed Gonzales and those gathered in the office that he was being called to Texas to attend to Brown Beret business. Perhaps the stony silence of the assembled group indicated that his departure was a wise move. On December 20, the first Chicano moratorium was held in California. In a picture taken of the protest in Los Angeles, El Guerrillero is shown marching in the front line. Though he never returned to Denver, to anyone's knowledge, Crusade members saw him again over three years later when Gonzales was invited to California to attend a fundraising dance for Ricardo Chavez-Ortiz, who had been convicted of air piracy.[13] El Guerrillero approached Gonzales and his companions and spoke cordially and briefly.[14]

THE SCHOOL BUS BOMBING AND THE ARREST OF BALTAZAR MARTINEZ

On February 3, 1970, a massive bombing destroyed or heavily damaged 38 school buses parked in the terminal lot on 6th Avenue and Federal Boulevard in Denver's Westside. Black and white middle-class integration activists had been pressing the city to integrate its public schools. Denver responded by busing students to schools outside their neighborhoods to achieve racial "balance."

School busing to achieve integration was of little interest to Denver's Chicano activists, who had other priorities: bilingual education, community empowerment, and curriculum reform. For them, integration was misguided "liberalism," a mere cosmetic reform premised on the assumption that minorities could be well educated only when whites were physically present. Moreover, indifference to busing was not confined to the Crusade. In the 56 demands listed by Chicano students in metropolitan Denver in three massive protests between March 1969 and February 1970, the words "busing" and "integration" were never mentioned.[15] (This was also true of the 38 demands of the 1968 East Los Angeles walkouts).

Though minority communities might share concerns about the failings of the public school system, their strategies were not identical. Yet power may have been a common issue: if middle- and upper-middle-class communities enjoyed better public education systems for their children, for example, it was because these communities had economic and political power. Chicano activists felt that controlling schools—having power over policy, staffing, administration, and methodology—was central to educational reform. How well Mexicans did in school was related to the attainment (or deficiency) of power and resources, not the absence of white or black students among them. Though the Mexican community was poor, it was populous. Effectively organized, the community could exercise the power of its numbers to reform the schools.

So when some culprit—or culprits—scaled a barbed-wire fence on a cold February night and detonated enough explosives to blow a fleet of school buses to smithereens, the Crusade felt no special interest; members merely assumed that responsibility lay with white racists. It was impressive, however, that someone had the skill, motivation, and resources to carry out this commando-like mission and go undetected and unpunished (to the present).

The Crusade, therefore, was very surprised when Denver police announced four days after the bombing that their key suspect was Baltazar Martinez, 25, of Tierra Amarilla, New Mexico. Martinez was a member of the Alianza and a key participant in the Tierra Amarilla courthouse raid of 1967.

The police claimed that a man walked into an ambulance company on 10th and Federal Boulevard, four blocks away from the bus lots, shortly after the blast. The man allegedly sought first aid for deep cuts on his right hand, purportedly explaining that he "had cut them climbing a barbed wire fence."[16] Shown pictures by the police, an ambulance company employee identified Martinez as the man with injured hands. Why police would have Martinez' picture for display was not explained.

The *Rocky Mountain News* headline read, "Bus Bombing Suspect Linked to Militant Tijerina Band." The *Denver Post* headline read, "Bus Bombing Suspect Named," and the article described Martinez as "an Albuquerque demolitions expert." The newspaper articles recounted details of the Tierra Amarilla courthouse raid, writing that Martinez had entered the courthouse "with a stick of dynamite attached to his body" and "threatened to blow up the courthouse"; they noted that he was found not guilty "by reason of insanity."[17] "Though the press dragged in the [Tierra Amarilla] incident, the Alianza, and Tijerina to cloud up and distort the issue," *El Gallo* reported, "they do not mention such things as the fact that the Alianza itself has been the victim of four dynamite bombings in the past two years."[18]

Baltazar Martinez was also surprised by his new notoriety in Denver. He was living in a mobile home park in Englewood, a Denver suburb, when a friend told him about the news accounts. Martinez later recounted that he made his friend swear that he was telling the truth before he would believe him. He called the Crusade for Justice and asked it to guide him through this crisis, and the organization took him in for the night. Crusade members were unaware that he was in Colorado until he called.

The next day, Sunday, February 8, the Crusade summoned Harry Nier, a National Lawyers Guild attorney, and called a doctor and a photographer as well. The doctor examined Martinez' hands, and the photographer took pictures of them. Both hands were free of any injury. A brief afternoon meeting at the Crusade building assembled "Chicanos from all walks of life: OEO (Office of Economic Opportunity) officials, lawyers, college students from United Mexican American Students (UMAS), Eastsiders, Northsiders, Westsiders, old and young, Black Berets and Brown Berets, husbands and housewives, and the Crusade for Justice leadership. As they left the meeting that afternoon they spread the word on our Chicano grapevine."[19]

That evening a community meeting was held in the Crusade auditorium, and all seats were taken. Before the meeting Martinez sat in the building's lounge, where an *El Gallo* photographer took pictures that show Martinez sitting at a table with his hands showing no cuts or injuries. Martinez addressed the crowd in Spanish, saying, "No hice nada. Aqui esta la prueba" (I didn't do anything. Here is the proof), and presenting his hands to the crowd. The Crusade notified newspapers and television stations that Martinez was at the Crusade building, and invited them to cover his surrender to police. The television stations quickly sent camera crews. The *Rocky Mountain News* and *Denver Post* reporters arrived last.

As the cameras began filming, a young Chicano entered the rear of the auditorium with his clothes bloodied and in disarray. He said he worked at a parking lot near police headquarters and had argued with an officer who parked a car in the lot and did not want to pay the parking fee. He said the policeman became angry, beat him, and then took him into the police building, where he was beaten further. His head was held in a toilet by the first cop as another flushed it. He came to the Crusade to report the beating. Though he stood there bloody, disheveled, and angry, the cameras and reporters completely ignored him.[20]

The police were informed by phone that Martinez was at Crusade headquarters and ready to surrender. They took 45 minutes to get there. When they arrived, two command officers were led into the Crusade auditorium, where they walked down a long aisle between two lines of Black Berets and Brown Berets as the crowd chanted "Chicano Power!" and "Off the pigs!" Martinez surrendered to the police, and the assembled crowd followed him and the officers out of the auditorium. Many went to police headquarters to await his release.

The next day one newspaper reported that a suspect "who claimed he was Baltazar Martinez" had surrendered to the police and was released shortly thereafter. This account reported that Martinez refused to say if he was from New Mexico or an Alianza member. Though Baltazar Martinez spoke heavily accented English, and always preferred to speak rapid-fire Spanish whenever possible, there was no way the newspapers should have mistaken his fervent claim to his identity, his relationship to the Alianza, and his deep anger as a land grant heir who felt he had been defrauded.[21]

Martinez was, as the newspaper stated, released shortly after arriving at police headquarters. He posted no bond, no charges were ever filed, and the police tersely announced that there had been a case of mistaken identity. Martinez wrote a brief letter to the Crusade after the incident: "This is my feeling, my hot boiling blood for Justice, and what I have to say. There is not a way I can thank enough the Crusade for Justice and my Raza that helped me. I am a freedom fighter myself. That pig, Robert Gilliland from the New Mexico State Police and the FBI were the main cause of the trouble I had, not mentioning the pigs here in Denver. . . . The pigs, John Birchers, and Minutemen's plan failed." The letter closed, "Para Justicia, una Revolucion." (For Justice, a Revolution.)[22]

The bus bombing remains unsolved. It was, however, recalled seven years later in the *Straight Creek Journal,* a small Denver newspaper, where an article detailed the career of FBI informer Timothy Redfearn. Redfearn had spied on dozens of political organizations and scores of activists in Denver for several years until his arrest on burglary charges in 1976, one of many run-ins with the law.

The *Straight Creek Journal* reported that Redfearn was recruited by the FBI—according to Redfearn—before graduating from high school in 1969. He claimed that his recruiter was FBI Special Agent James O'Connor. O'Connor later testified to a grand jury that he was not sure of the time and circumstances of their first meeting: "I tried to check that bus bombing case to see if I could determine how I first happened upon this fellow (Redfearn) and I couldn't really find it. . . . But it evidently was in connection to [the bus bombings] because I found a reference to the fact that he advised [us] concerning an individual who was believed to be in possession of dynamite."[23] Redfearn's account of his dealings with O'Connor was more detailed.

> The first time I ever heard anything about the school buses was from a friend of mine. He told me he had a good idea who did it. That's when I first dropped a line to O'Connor and that's when I first decided to work for them. As I recall I told him I wanted to talk to him about the school bus bombings. He came out to talk and I gave him a guy's name and address—a guy who lived in Boulder who supposedly went to work for some mining company to get access to explosives. The FBI is supposed to be interested in that sort of thing—supposed to be really hot on that kind of thing. But it was as if they had gone out and done it. O'Connor took a few notes but he was more interested in when I was gonna start work for them.[24]

Apparently Redfearn's leads were unproductive. A few months later, in September 1970, his home was raided by four Denver narcotics officers who had tried to bust him the previous year. This time they found him in possession of a considerable amount of drugs, and according to the *Straight Creek Journal,* Redfearn offered to spy for the Denver police. The officers left his home but told him to report to the police station the next day. Redfearn said, "I went down there voluntarily. I was scared shitless. I met with Keith Mullihan [Mollohan] . . . of the Intelligence unit. It turned out they wanted me to look into the SDS and I joined [SDS] the next day."[25] Redfearn now worked for both the FBI and the Denver Police Intelligence unit. That was all the *Journal* had to say about the Martinez fiasco. This was not, however, the last appearance of the Denver Police Department, informers, explosives, the FBI, and the Crusade for Justice in the headlines during the 1970s.

THE FEBRUARY 1970 SCHOOL WALKOUT

As the nonarrest of Baltazar Martinez faded from the headlines, Denver witnessed further school protests stemming from the suspension of Black Beret members at North High School the previous October.

Initially, there was no conflict between the Black Berets and the newly appointed principal, Pete Shannon. The students openly prepared for the September 16 walkout, wearing their uniforms, or "colors." On October 7, 1969, Shannon informed the Berets that they would no longer be allowed to wear their berets in school. Manuel "Rocky" Hernandez, founder of the Northside Black Berets, and nine Black Beret members were suspended after they were called to the principal's office that day. When Hernandez asked the specific reason for his suspension, school officials refused to respond. Hernandez simply returned to class and took his seat. "Later on that day," *El Gallo* reported, "the principal of North High (a Hispano) sent three pigs into Rocky's classroom where they dragged him out of the classroom, out of the building, and into jail. He is now out on a $1,000 bond charged with disturbance and unlawful acts in or about school. All because he asked a simple question: 'Why am I suspended from school?'"[26]

When told that wearing berets was against the rules, the Berets asked why ROTC members and cheerleaders could wear uniforms, but the Berets could not. In addition to their annoying questions, the Berets irritated school authorities in other ways. They would not stand for the Pledge of Allegiance and challenged their teachers when they believed the teachers were wrong. They were argumentative if they found teachers' remarks or behavior to be demeaning. They acted as though they believed the schools were made to serve them, and teachers and administrators should be accountable to students and the community. They even believed they had the same constitutional rights as adults, and that these rights did not end at the school door. The rising tensions at North High School led to the third major Chicano student walkout in less than a year. As explained by a protestor:

> After the West High walkouts of last March, the shrewd anglo administration placed various Hispanos (and that's what they are because they

sure in the hell ain't Chicanos) in prominent positions, like principals of schools or on community relations boards, just to mention a few. These Hispanos [who] don't live in the community, became the Establishment "firemen" for only Uncle Toms can prevent ghetto fires. It's these Uncle Toms or Tio Tacos that became the mouthpiece of the Establishment, that initiated and sparked this walkout. . . . We've been told to organize all our life. . . . Well we organized for West High. What happened? . . . [One] of the reasons for the Wednesday walkout is the Black Berets por la Justicia organized so well that they were told to stop. The reason? Not because they wore berets, but because they exposed the real issue: a Racist education. They have one way or another been expelled, have dropped out because of teacher harassment by so-called teachers and the few that remained walk the thin line. The Berets have to go to court because one of these Hispanos put the finger on them. There is a conspiracy against the brothers. Can you see a judge in the court and who would he side with? Some so-called troublemakers or a nice principal with a suit and tie who never tells a lie, just sucks a lot of ass?[27]

Angered by Hernandez' suspension and frustrated by the ongoing conflict with North High School administrators, the Black Berets decided to organize a school walkout. In preparation, the Northside Black Berets met with the Eastside Brown Berets, West High School students, and young Crusade for Justice members. The Black Berets organized Northside schools, and the Brown Berets organized Cole Junior High and Manual High School for the February 11 walkout. Students from West High School and Southwest Denver schools also participated.

The different barrio contingents converged in downtown Denver and marched to the school administration building, which was then located at 404 14th Street (14th and Tremont). There was a tense moment when protestors were denied entrance. Some youths tried to enter the building, and Special Services Unit officers stationed there rushed down the narrow hallway leading to the entrance. The police were bottlenecked at the doorway, but those who pushed their way out used riot batons. A number of young men pulled billy-clubs from their coats and swung back at the police. A brief scuffle followed, resembling a sword fight with billy-clubs. Older Crusade members intervened and kept the disturbance from escalating.

The police regrouped in loose formation outside the building while reinforcements arrived. Some officers milled around in the street as though unsure who was in command. While the officers seemed to wait for directions from the police hierarchy, older Crusade men convened a march to the Crusade headquarters to defuse the tension. No one was hurt or arrested.

The Eastside Brown Berets held dances at the Curtis Park Community

Center and Annunciation School, using the proceeds to support their activities. They had taken the proceeds from one dance and purchased the entire stock of billy-clubs at a surplus store. These were their weapons in "sword fight" at the administration building.

Student demands were read and explained by an ad hoc group called the Chicano Student Movement Council at a press conference on February 13 at the Crusade building. Its members were Margarito Berzoza, Laura Valdez, Sheryl Ritchie, Mark Martinez, Carl Patron, Solomon Romero, Manuel Hernandez, and Gina Gonzales.[28] In the wake of the walkout, many Black Berets remained suspended or quit school. Within a year, the Crusade would establish its own school.

THE 1970 CHICANO YOUTH LIBERATION CONFERENCE

The second Chicano antiwar moratorium preceded Denver's second national youth conference. It took place in East Los Angeles on February 28, 1970, and was attended by about 2,000 protestors, who marched more than an hour in pouring rain. Among the California marchers were groups from Delano, Oakland, San Francisco, San Jose, and San Diego. Out-of-state groups included MAYO from Texas, the Alianza of New Mexico, the Puerto Rican Young Lords from New York, and the Crusade for Justice.[29] Among the speakers were Gonzales, Rosalio Muñoz of the Chicano Moratorium Committee, Alicia Escalante of the Welfare Rights Organization, attorney Oscar Zeta Acosta, Santiago Anaya of the Alianza, Woodrow Diaz of the Young Lords, Sal Castro, the Los Angeles schoolteacher indicted for his participation in the 1968 East Los Angeles school walkouts, and David Sanchez of the National Brown Berets. The growing momentum for the establishment of an independent political party was evident at the second moratorium. Woodrow Diaz stated:

> This social system is killing our brothers in Vietnam. We have one enemy, the capitalist system and their agents in the Democratic and Republican Parties. We must organize independent political parties along with Puerto Ricans including poor working whites in a political coalition. The Third World must lead the way because it is the most oppressed. We must control every aspect of our lives. Something beautiful will be happening in Denver March 25 when we begin to organize our own political party. I say this is right on![30]

The second National Chicano Youth Conference was held in Denver in March 1970 and drew more participants than the 1969 conference. It was the subject of numerous FBI reports and Airtels between FBI offices in Denver, San Antonio, New York, Sacramento, San Francisco, Los Angeles, Chicago, Albuquerque, and Washington. The CIA and the White House were recipients of copies of these FBI reports, which circulated among the FBI's top officials. The earliest is dated March 16, 1970, and the last is dated September 2, 1970.

The second conference called for the establishment of an independent third party, La Raza Unida Party, and for the creation of a national congress, the "Congreso de Aztlan," to govern the political party.[31] Not everyone agreed with the proposal to make La Raza Unida a national party, however. MAYO activists were based in south Texas counties where Chicanos were the majority population and, if effectively organized, could control county and municipal governments. Indeed, the name of the proposed party had originated in Texas before the youth conference. MAYO, founded by José Angel Gutiérrez and other Texas activists, conducted voter registration campaigns and employed bold tactics to build an extensive base under adverse conditions. To see the Texas party subsumed by a national party was a departure from their original plans. Still, it would have been awkward for the Texas activists to oppose the push to make La Raza Unida a national party.

The new party was not the sole focus of the conference. Workshops focused on community control, women's rights, Vietnam, economics, political prisoners, art, youth, and education.[32] The women's workshop resolution called for women to struggle for the liberation of La Raza and for "self determination of the women." It criticized traditional conservative concepts regarding women:

> We must change the concepts of the alienated family where the woman assumes full responsibility for the care of the home and the raising of the children to the concept of La Raza as the united family . . . [and the liberation of women] must be included in the ideology of the La Raza Independent Political Party so that everyone, men and women, will work consciously towards the goal of the total liberation of our people.[33]

The community control workshop passed no resolution but issued a call for control of various institutions in the barrio, including police, the education system, and social service agencies. La Raza would be empowered at the grassroots level through community control.

Resolutions were adopted seeking freedom for political prisoners held throughout Latin America, including prisoners in Mexico, Peru, Brazil, Puerto Rico, Bolivia, and the Dominican Republic. The resolution expressed solidarity with struggles of oppressed people and stated that Chicanos "are tied by blood to the people of Latin America." It continued: "We know that the government in Washington, D.C., supports and aids all efforts to keep the people of Latin America subservient to the United Fruit (Company), Standard Oil, Anaconda, etc." The workshop called for "the US government [to] withdraw all military missions, troops, and aid to the dictators of Latin America." The resolution also addressed trials involving activists in Colorado, Illinois, Texas, and California. Among defendants to be supported were Los Catolicos por La Raza and the Biltmore Ten in Los Angeles, Los Siete de La Raza in San Francisco, and "Cha-Cha" Jimenez, a former gang member and founder of the Puerto Rican Young Lords Organization in Chicago. New Mexico activists drafted a resolution urging freedom for Reies Tijerina, who was then incarcerated in a federal prison.[34]

Youthful idealism and enthusiasm mark many resolutions. One rather naive statement reads, "Resolved: to nationalize our college students to the point that they will be willing to put their life on the line for their demands"—as though this could be accomplished by passing resolutions.[35] Other resolutions, however, show the movement's persistent concern with education; one calls for the "inclusion in all schools of this nation the history and culture of our people and our contributions to this country."[36]

Three brief paragraphs addressed the war in Vietnam. One proposed that the youth conference "endorse and support a National Chicano Moratorium, Saturday August 29, 1970, in Los Angeles."[37] The others urged conference participants to hold local moratoria, to build delegations to the August 29 moratorium, and to circulate antiwar petitions. Though these paragraphs appeared on the last page of *El Gallo,* the conference was undoubtedly an important factor in the massive turnout of 20,000 to 30,000 antiwar protestors in East Los Angeles in the summer of 1970.

LA RAZA UNIDA PARTY

The conference was the springboard for establishing La Raza Unida Party (LRUP) as a *national* party, something Gonzales had anxiously awaited since his break with the Democrats in 1966.[38] A state convention was held in Pueblo in mid-May 1970 to launch the Colorado branch of the party, and a lengthy speech by Gonzales served as its ideological basis:

> The truth is that both parties, the Elite Republicans and the party of promises, the Democrats, operate for their own selfish interests. They are both ruled and controlled by money and racism. . . . THE TWO PARTY SYSTEM IS ONE ANIMAL WITH TWO HEADS EATING OUT OF THE SAME TROUGH. HOW DO WE PROVE THIS? Very simple. Start checking out who sits on the same board of directors at your local bank, who are the

people who have shares in the same companies. . . . Find out the political affiliation of the lawyers who are running for office and the [affiliation of their law partners]. Check out the country clubs and you'll find out that the two-party boys drink together, hold hands together, and vomit together in the same toilets. Meanwhile, Chicanos go around saying "*my* President" . . . "*my* party" and they have to deliver their people's votes and get castrated at the same time for a pat on the head or a small favor while Gringo businessmen can buy any politician in this state or this nation. Some people will question my statements and ask, "How do you know?" I know because I was an organizer for the Democratic Party. I was the first Chicano District Captain in the history of Denver. . . . Yes, I learned the hard way that I was a stooge for the party delivering my people's vote. And, when I asked for social change, when I demanded jobs for people, they winked and I could have gotten a liquor license under the table, a zone change for a paying businessman, or a political job that was equipped with a gag to keep your mouth shut. Our people are energy that creates power, but in the past we gave that power away. La Raza is a generator of power, those people like myself in the past, who take that power to the "The Man," are like a copper conduit or wire that takes our energy and power and gives it away. When we cut that wire, the power that is generated stays with the people. . . . I can just hear them running around saying you have to vote for the lesser of two evils. If four grains of arsenic will kill you and eight grains of arsenic will kill, which is the less of two evils? You're dead either way. Another statement you often hear is that "We must work within the System, we'll make the changes by using them." Let me tell you that you can't walk into a house full of disease with a bottle of mercurochrome and cure the disease. You end up sick yourself. Look around at our politicos today and ask them . . . if they have done away with unemployment, racism, discrimination, irrelevant education, police brutality, political corruption, organized crime, do-nothing service agencies, bad housing, high interest rates, and WAR.[39]

Albert Gurule of Pueblo and George Garcia of Denver were Colorado LRUP's first candidates for the posts of governor and lieutenant governor. The party platform addressed law enforcement, economic opportunity, agricultural reform, and redistribution of wealth. It called for radical change in American society: lands taken by force from Chicanos would be returned with compensation; all education was to be free of fees, dues, or tuition, and would reflect Chicano history and culture; unions would be established for workers, tenants, and social service recipients.[40]

COMMUNITY ACTIVISM AND POLICE BRUTALITY

The Beating and Arrest of Richard Castro

As the Colorado LRUP launched its first statewide effort, still another police controversy stirred Chicano activists. On April 14, 1970, police officers in Denver's Eastside attempted to arrest four Brown Berets—Tony "Fat Tony" Ornelas, Miguel "Masa" Renteria, Carlos Chavez, and Leonard Trevino. Officers said they saw the young men driving a vehicle over the lawn at Curtis Park (now Mestizo-Curtis Park). The officers involved were Michael Davin, Buckley Stewart, Hendrik Duyker, and Harold McMillan.[41] The young men reportedly resisted arrest. A 23-year-old passerby, Richard Castro, approached the officers to inquire about the commotion. He was clubbed, arrested, and driven from the scene in a patrol car. Castro later said one of the arresting officers "turned around in his seat and sprayed Mace directly in my eyes while I sat handcuffed in the back seat." Another officer at the police station, "without any provocation, gave Tony Ornelas a karate kick in the chest. Tony was still handcuffed. [The officer] then picked Tony up by the handcuffs and dropped him on his face on the floor two or three times."[42]

The beatings were followed by a series of meetings and community protests. People were angered when Police Chief George Seaton charged that the protests against the beatings were the work of "left-wing radicals" and further angered when Safety Manager William Koch, on April 21, said he found no "substantiating evidence" supporting the brutality allegations. Protestors pointed out that none of those arrested had even been interviewed by authorities, and one city councilman "wondered aloud whether [the Internal Affairs Bureau] made any significant effort to contact and interview the five persons arrested in the case."[43]

Mayor Bill McNichols favored a grand jury investigation of the matter. Safety Manager Koch agreed to the grand jury probe and conducted an investigation of his own as well. A citizens' group including State Senator Roger Cisneros met to draft a proposal for a citizens' police review board to submit to City Council. Community critics called for an independent investigation and issued a statement criticizing the investigation of police by police. Among those who endorsed the statement were the Religious Council on Human Relations, Trabajadores de La Raza, the Asian American Alliance, the West Side Action Ministry, the American Friends Service Committee, the Human Relations Commission of the Catholic Archdiocese, the NAACP, Black United Denver, and GI Forum. Some activists also demanded the firing of Chief Seaton and the suspension of the officers involved.[44]

On April 20, protestors went to the City Council meeting and found the controversy listed as the last agenda item. "After a few hours of listening to their bullshit several young Chicanos took over the meeting, suspended the business at hand, and started to call up community people to the microphone to talk about the brutality issue. At this time the City Council members showed their deep concern by adjourning the meeting and walking out after a small confrontation with several young Chicanos."[45] Later that month a community meeting was held at the Curtis Park Community Center. City Councilmen Elvin Caldwell and Ernest Marranzino attended. Those present were angry, and the council members were repeatedly shouted down. People later demonstrated at the home of Officer McMillan.

Protestors returned to City Council on April 27. "Twenty-one speakers, 19 of them supporting the Hispano cause, exhorted the council for two hours," the *Denver Post* reported. "The two who didn't were loudly booed." The two were identified as Ron Karron of the Metro Denver Support Your Local Police Committee and Reverend James Miller, "a leader in the John Birch Society." Miller tried to preface his remarks by saying, "The history of the human race is the history of man's inhumanity to man. All men are by nature sinful men," but the crowd was in no mood for socioreligious pronouncements.[46]

On the more recent controversy, the *Denver Post* reported, "The Hispano crowd and its Anglo supporters wouldn't buy Miller's and Karron's viewpoints. The meeting was theirs. The councilmen just listened without question. Steve Levine (a 17-year-old whose column appears in the *Denver Post*) remarked: 'You could set up some sort of a civilian review board—but you won't.' There was little chance of that, he said, because of the political power of the police which, he added, 'seems at times to be the only government we have.'" Another speaker said, "There are no longer any silent Mexicans in Denver. There must be sweeping reforms of the Denver Police Department."[47]

Richard Castro agreed to take a polygraph test given by an independent expert if the city government would pay the bill. His attorney, Don Nicholls, reported that he "received written confirmation from a polygraph . . . operator that Castro was telling the truth when he [the polygraph expert] asked questions primarily related to Castro's written statement alleging brutality."[48] Castro had already submitted a detailed written statement to the manager of safety. Koch did not attend the polygraph testing, claiming that he understood that the test was not going to be administered. He did not explain his assumption.

The *Rocky Mountain News,* apparently out of touch with developments in the case, published an article indicating that the polygraph test had not been given. It further reported that the grand jury had not decided whether to conduct an investigation into the matter, and that not all Castro's supporters were in favor of the grand jury involvement, although "they concede that it is a step in the right direction."[49]

Though the Crusade and its affiliates attended initial meetings, their participation was limited. Gonzales, who had long experience in these matters, felt that continuous meetings with government officials and bureaucrats would entangle the community and dissipate energy with no positive results. Indeed, further confusion and delays resulted when the grand jury refused to conduct an investigation until Koch's investigation was complete. Meanwhile, the safety manager said his investigation would be hampered by a desire to protect the identities of witnesses he would call.

On May 6, Koch and Minoru Yasui, director of Denver's Commission on Community Relations, released a report that stated, "There was no reason to believe the alleged brutality occurred or to take any disciplinary action against the patrolmen." The great majority of witnesses interviewed for this report were policemen, sheriffs, or firemen employed at a station near the scene of the incident. Bal Chaves, another attorney for Castro, said, "We who have been involved on the part of the community, in attempting to present the truth of Mr. Castro's observations, expected the city to dodge the reality of police brutality existing in Denver."[50]

Koch and Yasui were invited to a May 10 community meeting at the Centro Cultural in the Westside to discuss their findings. Koch did not indicate if he would attend and never arrived. Yasui did, and his remarks were revealing: "The finding was not that there was no police brutality; the finding was that no brutality could be proven. . . . We can't prove brutality, although there is a doubt in the back of my mind."[51]

The new Colorado LRUP had a voice in the controversy through its candidate for lieutenant governor, George Garcia, a consultant on Chicano affairs for the Commission on Community Relations. At its founding convention, the party had adopted a position on law enforcement: "We resolve an immediate suspension of officers suspected of police brutality until a full hearing is held in the neighborhood of the event."[52] On May 18, Garcia was dismissed from the commission. He attributed his dismissal to anti-Chicano bias on the part of its director, Minoru Yasui. In a *Denver Post* article, Yasui blamed Garcia's "continued violations of directives set forth by the mayor's office and Career Service Authority rules and regulations,"[53] directives he said Garcia violated by his involvement in the Castro controversy.

Garcia retorted that criticism of his professional actions was really a criticism of his community advocacy: "This is because I took a stand when I joined the commission that my commitment was to the Chicano community and has always been since." The article continued, "Garcia said the reference to his professional actions probably resulted from his failure to go out into the community, and try to convince Chicanos that the recently completed investigation into police brutality wasn't a whitewash. . . . Garcia said that instead of supporting the investigation report, which discounted the allegation, he wrote a memo to Yasui calling the entire investigation 'garbage.' "

Others involved with the Commission on Community Relations were drawn into the growing conflict. State Senator Cisneros and Armando Atencio resigned from the commission. Cisneros' letter to Mayor Bill McNichols stated, in part: "I don't begrudge the commission members voting their convictions, much as I might disagree with them. However, I feel that in this day and age of turmoil and disturbances, that it is important for all agencies to review their role and not be reluctant to change to meet the new demands of the 1970s." The commission, in his opinion, "has outlived its usefulness to the Chicano community."[54]

Some of Castro's supporters now considered complaining to the Federal Commission on Civil Rights or to the U.S. Department of Justice that a violation of civil rights had occurred. On June 6, the grand jury under District Attorney James "Mike" McKevitt found no evidence to support brutality charges against the policemen.[55] "This latest whitewash only confirms our belief that we cannot expect justice if we seek it with our hat in our hand," *El Gallo* wrote. "The Denver Pig Department had also better realize that if they think they've had trouble with the Chicano community up until now, THEY'VE ONLY SEEN THE TIP OF THE ICEBERG."[56]

Castro's supporters distributed a flyer criticizing the handling of the incident and called for Mayor McNichols to fire Yasui if he did not resign. Endorsers of the flyer included the executive board of the West Side Coalition, the Metro State College UMAS, the Skyline and Mile High chapters of the GI Forum, and the Crusade for Justice. McNichols had responded to earlier demands to oust Yasui by saying, "I intend to commend him for the good job he has done."[57] He did not change his mind. This became one incident in a long series of community demands for a civilian review board countered by mayoral opposition—a series that extended into the administrations of Federico Peña and Wellington Webb, Denver's first minority mayors.

Richard Castro, incidentally, was a protege of Waldo and Betty Benavidez, Democratic Party activists who had once been Crusade members.[58] Based in nonprofit agencies promoting social services and economic development, they and others like them filled the void created when Gonzales left the Democratic Party and the War on Poverty four years before.

Tensions and hostility would later arise between the Crusade and Chicanos in the Democratic Party–service agency–business ranks.

More Protests

Police controversies continued throughout the spring and summer of 1970. A case involving officers Dale Lawless, Joseph Catalina, and William Martin was submitted to the Denver grand jury on May 12, 1970. The three officers, searching for a Colorado State Penitentiary escapee, Toby Gallegos, broke into a hotel room, where Lawless shot a suspect in the right hand and left shoulder. The suspect was the wrong man, and Gilbert E. Franco, through attorneys Ken Padilla and Walter Gerash, later won damages in civil suit.[59]

Police–community conflicts, moreover, were not limited to urban settings. Fort Collins, 70 miles north of Denver, was the scene of another controversy involving the police, the City Council, and the Chicano community. At issue in April 1970 was the conduct of Officer Terry Rains in the arrest of Joe Serna, one other Chicano, and three Anglos. The Chicano community was upset, in part, because the three Anglos were released on lower bonds than Serna and the other Chicano, a disparity that indicated a double standard. These sentiments were reinforced when Serna's 18-year-old sister went to the station to post bond. She claimed that Officer Rains threatened to arrest her for loitering and would not let her post Serna's bond. "I gave him no reason for his conduct towards me. He said if he had broken Joe's neck, that it would have been okay."[60]

Chicanos alleged that Rains was the subject of six previous verbal complaints—made to no avail—and that he had been suspended from duty in August 1968 when a superior officer found it necessary "to pull a gun on Terry Rains in order to disarm him. Rains was suspended for insubordination but in a matter of months was back in good standing with the police force." While Rains's supporters attended City Council meetings holding "Support Your Local Police" signs, the mayor of Fort Collins reportedly told members of the Chicano community: "I know that you've felt an injustice was done you and I don't know that I can say you're wrong."[61]

On August 10, nearly four hundred marchers protested against police harassment in Fort Lupton, a small town 30 miles northeast of Denver. Participating organizations included the GI Forum, the United Farm Workers, Migrants in Action, the Boulder chapter of UMAS, and the Crusade. UMAS students had surveyed Fort Lupton arrest records, and their findings showed that 67 percent of 486 arrests in a 14-month period (ending in April 1970) were of Chicanos and Mexicanos, though they were only 23 percent of the local population. Some marchers chanted, "Down with the pigs!"[62]

Onlookers were often hostile. One bystander said, "Sure I resent them. Most of them are from out of town anyway. I'd say about 30 percent of the marchers live here. Not all the Mexicans here feel that way. If they want what I have they can go out and work for it." Another bystander, who would not identify himself, said, "You know what I'd do if I had a shotgun? I'd kill every one of them. They're trying to get something for nothing. If they went out and worked like us white people and took care of themselves the police would leave them alone."[63] This would not be Colorado activists' last experience of anti-Mexican bigotry that month, though they could not imagine what awaited them on August 29, 1970.

Seven

East Los Angeles, August 29, 1970

On September 16, 1969, in Los Angeles, California, Rosalio Muñoz prepared to refuse induction into the armed forces as a protest against the war in Vietnam and racism at home. Muñoz, who had been student body president at UCLA in his senior year, issued a statement:

> I accuse the government of the United States of America of genocide against the Mexican people. Specifically I accuse the draft, the entire social, political and economic system of creating the funnel which shoots the Mexican youth into Vietnam to be killed and [to] kill innocent men, women and children. I accuse the United States Congress and Selective Service System which it has created of reinforcing these weaknesses imposed upon the Chicano community and of drafting their laws so that more Chicanos are sent to Vietnam in proportion to the total population than White youth. I accuse the entire American social and economic system of taking advantage of the machismo of the Chicano male, widowing and orphaning the mothers, wives and children of the Chicano community, by sending their men into the front lines where our machismo has given us more Congressional Medals, Purple Hearts and deaths in proportion to the population than any other race or ethnic group in the nation. This is genocide.[1]

Events set in motion that day led to a surge of activism that culminated 12 months later in the largest Chicano protest the nation had yet seen, an event that drew in the national leadership of the Chicano movement and in which Crusade was to be uniquely and intimately involved.

RUBEN SALAZAR

If any name is linked in the public mind with the August 29, 1970, Chicano Antiwar Moratorium in East Los Angeles, it is that of Ruben Sala-

133

zar, a reporter for the *Los Angeles Times*. In 1967 Salazar's name was entered in an FBI report that described him as "most cooperative when interviewed" by FBI agents seeking information about Stokely Carmichael, the African American activist credited with coining the phrase "Black Power."[2] Carmichael, who later changed his name to Kwame Ture, spoke at the Latin American Solidarity Organization conference in Havana, Cuba, which concluded in August 1967.

Though Salazar had no way to know it when the FBI interviewed him, his work in the subsequent 36 months would bring him into contact with American reds, white conservatives, black radicals, brown militants, and men in blue. At the time the FBI interviewed him about Carmichael, the bureau maintained data on Salazar that predated by a decade and a half the files it kept on the Chicano movement. These data would, at some unknown date, be made part of FBI Internal Security file 105-23153, of which Salazar himself was the subject.

Salazar's career started in El Paso, Texas, in 1955, and he began working for the *Los Angeles Times* in 1961. He served as its foreign correspondent from 1965 to 1968. Returning to Los Angeles in 1969, he reported on the growing Chicano movement. Later he would become news director for KMEX, a Spanish-language television station that served Los Angeles' huge Mexicano community. No one who knew him personally or professionally described him as a militant or leftist, except for the Los Angeles Police and Sheriffs Departments and their informers.

LAPD Chief Edward M. Davis wanted to tear "the hide right off [Salazar's] back" for an article he wrote on March 13, 1970, describing the chief's meeting with Latino reporters, who, Salazar emphasized, were "not Chicano underground press types."[3] Student walkouts had started up again, spreading from Roosevelt High School on March 5, to Lincoln High School, to Huntington Park High School, to Excelsior High School in Norwalk. Fifty people were arrested. According to an article reprinted in *El Gallo*, the protestors at Roosevelt High were targeted by a "police squad composed of Mexican Americans, known as Special Operations Conspiracy (SOC), [that] pointed out those to be arrested."[4]

Salazar's article on the dinner with the Latino press corp may have embarrassed Davis by illustrating the bigotry implicit in his foot-in-mouth remarks, which the chief may have perceived as more damaging than references to police improprieties at school protests. At the dinner Davis boasted that he had written a chastising letter to President Nixon, thus demonstrating the strength of American democracy, wherein common citizens could criticize even the highest public officials without suffering consequences. He went on to contrast this privilege with Mexico's

"Napoleonic" system of "tyranny and dictatorship." These remarks were very coolly received by the journalists, especially those who worked for Mexican newspapers. Some of these journalists, moreover, had that very week seen police beating students at Roosevelt High School. A police captain physically prevented one cameraman from filming by putting his hand over the camera lens. An editor with 25 years experience was denied entrance to the school because he carried a Sheriff's, but not an LAPD, press card. Some members of the group sitting down to dinner with Davis had been berated by the police at Roosevelt for covering the event. The irony of Davis' lecture about tyranny and dictatorship was a tempting target, but, as Salazar himself wrote in another context: "The implications . . . are staggering and too complicated to go into here." [5]

In retaliation for Salazar's article, Davis ordered the LAPD to open an intelligence file on him. A "reliable confidential informer" for the LAPD who worked at the *Los Angeles Times* judged Salazar to be "a slanted, left-wing oriented reporter," [6] a judgement that must have pleased Davis. Davis' anticommunist views justified the placement of police informers in minority organizations or their cultivation in the largest newspaper west of the Mississippi River, from which the chief once sought to have Salazar fired. [7]

TARGETING THE BROWN BERETS

The professional demands of their jobs gave Salazar and Davis some mutual acquaintances, among whom were Los Angeles Sheriff Peter Pitchess and District Attorney Evelle Younger. Pitchess and Younger were law-and-order Republicans, former FBI agents; Pitchess still had close connections with the bureau. During his five-year FBI career, Younger once embarrassed the bureau by being caught burglarizing the room of labor leader Harry Bridges. [8] Davis, Pitchess, and Younger, in turn, were familiar with others known by Salazar: Rodolfo Gonzales, Oscar Zeta Acosta, Sam Kushner, the Brown Berets, the Crusade for Justice, the National Chicano Moratorium Committee, La Raza Unida Party, and, yes, the Communist Party USA (CPUSA). Tying all these together is a web of political controversies, police acronyms, convoluted motives, and FBI files.

The FBI was in the midst of a surging investigation of "rabble rousers" when, on December 13, 1967, the FBI agents in Mexico City asked Ruben Salazar if he could obtain a tape recording of Stokely Carmichael's speech. The FBI, as usual, was monitoring for signs of a conspiratorial network of revolutionaries that might imperil the nation, the government, democracy, and capitalism—all, purportedly, one and the same.

The net cast to catch these rabble-rousers was stitched together by FBI Internal Security investigations. It is well documented, though possibly poorly appreciated, that the FBI launched illegal attacks against a broad spectrum of targets, ranging from Dr. Martin Luther King, Jr., to the Communist Party USA. It is far less well known and publicized that the FBI waged a similar campaign against the Chicano movement.

On February 29, 1968, FBI Supervisor S. S. Mignosa, on J. Edgar Hoover's authority, ordered an Internal Security investigation of the Crusade for Justice organization (Bufile 105-178283). Mignosa's name is found on numerous FBI documents relating to the Crusade and other organizations. He was, for example, the recipient of a courtesy copy of an FBI headquarters document to the Los Angeles field office. The sender of the document was "J. H. Trimbach," who wrote under Hoover's authority on March 5, 1968, to chastise the L. A. field office for its laxity in monitoring the Young Chicanos for Community Action, the original name of the National Brown Beret Organization, headed by David Sanchez.[9] Trimbach (noting that "'the Brown Berets' is apparently a new organization") was alarmed when the L. A. field office reported that two Brown Berets were arrested on February 25, with a weapon reportedly stolen from the Marine base at Camp Pendleton in Oceanside, California. The FBI variously reported that the weapon was a fully automatic M-16 or a semi-automatic AR-15.

In response, the Los Angeles Special Agent in Charge (SAC) quickly wrote to headquarters asking for authorization to launch an internal security investigation of the Brown Berets (Bufile 105-178715). The National Brown Beret Organization, as its "Prime Minister" David Sanchez referred to those chapters who accepted his leadership, saw three of its leaders (Sanchez, Ralph Ramirez, and Carlos Montes) indicted with other activists in June 1968 on felony conspiracy charges stemming from the March 1968 East L. A. school walkouts. The indictments followed an undercover investigation ordered in early March by D. A. Younger and conducted by detectives from the LAPD and the Sheriffs Department (LASD), as well as investigators from the District Attorney's office. Younger announced the indictments on June 1 after several of the 13 defendants had been arrested. Disturbing a school and disturbing the peace were misdemeanors. Conspiracy to commit these misdemeanors, however, was a felony.

Ramirez and Montes were in Washington for the Poor People's Campaign at the time of Younger's announcement. When the Chicano contingent there learned of the indictments, it held a protest at the Justice Department to demand that the activists be released (see Chapter 3). The FBI, though aware of Ramirez' and Montes' presence in Washington, did not want to risk an arrest that could result in violence, or, worse, negative publicity.

The Los Angeles 13, as the walkout defendants became known, were later victorious in court, where they were provided an inspired, effective, and unorthodox legal defense by attorney Oscar Zeta Acosta. In May, the Sheriffs Department planted an undercover deputy sheriff, Robert Acosta, in the National Brown Beret Organization, after recruiting him from the Sheriff's Academy.[10] In November Fernando Sumaya infiltrated Sanchez' Brown Berets; a graduate of the LAPD Academy, Sumaya was recruited for undercover duty by Sergeant Ceballos of the LAPD Intelligence Division.[11] Additionally, LAPD Sgt. Abel Armas of the Special Operations Conspiracy (SOC) Squad operated in uniform to monitor the Brown Berets after participating in a SOC Squad–Criminal Conspiracy Section orientation. Armas later said his supervisors were a Lieutenant Deemer and, later, Lieutenant Robert A. Keel.[12]

Montes, arguably the most observant and articulate member of the Brown Beret leadership in Sanchez' constituency, claimed that LAPD Officer Robert Avila also infiltrated the Brown Berets around March 1968 and, according to Montes, urged members to shoot police officers.[13]

Ruben Salazar reported on all these personalities and events. He also wrote about Rodolfo Gonzales and the 1969 and 1970 Crusade for Justice youth conferences. In time he developed friendships with activists, including Oscar Zeta Acosta, who ran for sheriff of Los Angeles in 1970. Acosta proposed to reconstitute the Sheriff's Department as the "People's Protection Department." Governed by civilian review boards, it would serve "as a shield, not a sword," because "justice for all members of the community must always precede claims for 'Law and Order.'"[14]

On June 2, 1970, Salazar reported on Acosta's campaign in an article headlined, "To the Chicanos, It Is How Narrowly a Candidate Lost":

> A Chicano who had an impressive loss was Oscar Z. Acosta, a militant attorney who received more than 100,000 votes for sheriff. During the campaign, he defended the establishment-shaking Catolicos por La Raza, spent a couple of days in jail for contempt of court, and vowed if elected to do away with the Sheriff's Department as it is now constituted. Acosta, easily recognized in court by his loud ties and flowered attache case with a Chicano Power sticker, didn't come close to Sheriff Pitchess' 1,300,000 votes but did beat Everett Holladay, Monterrey Park Chief of Police.

Within three months of writing the article, Salazar would die at the hands of a Los Angeles sheriff's deputy, shot through the head with a 10-inch-long metal teargas projectile when a riot erupted during the Chicano

Moratorium. And Oscar Acosta, who won 100,000 votes while campaigning to dismantle the Sheriff's Department, would be the defense attorney for Rodolfo Gonzales, arrested on a weapons charge during the riot.

THE CHICANO MORATORIUM

On August 29, 1970, an estimated 20,000 to 30,000 Chicano protestors marched in East Los Angeles to protest against the Vietnam war. The march was the largest minority protest against the war, the largest protest gathering of Chicanos until that time, and probably the largest antiwar protest composed of working-class people.

Nearly a hundred Colorado activists attended the Moratorium, including a busload of Crusade members and affiliates. Other than the misadventures that inevitably occur when driving a decrepit school bus a thousand miles, everything went smoothly until the bus was stopped by law enforcement officers in San Bernardino, California, who demanded to know its destination and told the driver that state law allowed only school buses to be painted yellow. The officers were told that the group was going to the beach.

The Moratorium march started peacefully on the morning of August 29 at Belvedere Park and proceeded to Laguna Park (now Salazar Park) on Whittier Boulevard. Some people scattered in the crowd threw bottles and rocks at police cars stationed on the march route, but these minor incidents did not escalate. When the crowd arrived at the rally site, people found places to sit on the lawn and listened to music by the Teatro Campesino and a Puerto Rican band. The rally site was peaceful. Among the scheduled speakers were Gonzales, Mario Compean of MAYO, and Cesar Chavez, who did not arrive.

Police Riot

Since the march was long and the day hot, Junior Martinez, 18 years old, and I left the park shortly after arriving to buy something to drink. Approaching a nearby liquor store, we saw that the place was filled beyond capacity and that some customers in the store were taking advantage of circumstances and leaving without paying. Patrol cars arrived. Several officers left their cars and beat people standing on the sidewalk, clubbing guilty and innocent alike. People on the northern fringe of the park shouted at the police and threw a brief flurry of rocks and other missiles at them.

The officers stopped clubbing people, and the rock throwing stopped.

The incident appeared to be over. Some long-haired whites—alleged members of a small Maoist group—tried to stir the crowd on the sidewalk to more violence, but since they were not Mexican, they were ignored. Martinez and I returned to the park and found places to sit by the speakers' platform, where most Crusade members were gathered.

While the crowd waited for the music and performances to end, a commotion began at the rear of the crowd. Crusade member Antonio Salinas recalled seeing what he thought was a soda can land on the stage near where he was standing. From the object came a white cloud of teargas.[15] People near the stage stood and turned to see what was causing the commotion. They saw scores of uniformed police and sheriffs file into the park in full riot gear and riot formation. No orders to disperse were heard. Having decided to use the incident at the liquor store to break up the gathering, the officers went on the offensive. Speakers on the stage attempted to calm the crowd, telling them to remain seated, but teargas canisters were landing everywhere.

Some people briefly formed a line between the police and the crowd and tried to keep the two groups separated, but the police kept advancing and firing teargas. Thousands streamed from the park to escape the gas, while hundreds, incensed at the police assault, fought back with sticks, rocks, fists, and bottles. The angry crowd rushed the police and sheriffs and twice drove them from the park, catching and beating many officers. The officers returned in greater numbers and finally occupied the park, beating and arresting hundreds.

Most of the Crusade delegation remained together near the front of the stage. Others attempted to leave the area in school buses parked nearby. Police tossed teargas into the buses, and many people were dragged from them and beaten. At least two helicopters flew above. A large group of Crusade members and their associates piled onto a flatbed truck and drove from the area but returned when children were found to be missing. Leaving again, the truck's occupants noticed that they were being followed by one of the helicopters. About a mile and a half from Laguna Park, the truck stopped at a red light at the far end of an underpass. The helicopter hovered above. When the light turned green and the truck proceeded into the intersection a large contingent of police officers with drawn weapons stopped the truck and ordered everyone to lie on the ground. "As the [police] were making people get off the truck, they were telling each other 'Look for Corky! He's the one with a mustache.'"[16] Confusion resulted when police found many men with mustaches.

Everyone in the truck was arrested, and many were beaten. Frank Luevano, 16, was handcuffed and beaten in police custody. His ribs were fractured. Antonio Salinas was struck on the head with a shotgun. Eddie

Padilla, 16, escaped arrest but returned to Denver with an injured back. The most severe injury was suffered by Daniel Lopez, who became separated from the Colorado delegation in the confusion at the park. He stooped to pick up a child in danger of being trampled. As he lifted the child, an advancing officer lunged, sticking his riot baton into Lopez' face. Lopez lost his right eye.

Those arrested on the truck were held on "suspicion of robbery" because Gonzales had $370 in his possession. Hunter S. Thompson, a friend of Oscar Acosta and a contributor to *Rolling Stone* magazine, quoted Gonzales as saying: "Only a lunatic or a fool could believe that 29 people would rob a place and then jump on a flatbed truck to make their getaway."[17]

On the truck were some of the most visible leaders of Colorado's major movement organizations: Colorado La Raza Unida Party, the Crusade for Justice, and the Black Beret and Brown Beret organizations. Five members of La Raza Unida's first slate of candidates were arrested: Al Gurule, George Garcia, Carlos Santistevan, Martin Serna, and José Gonzales, who were running for governor, lieutenant governor, state senator, congressman, and state representative respectively. The protest gathering ended in the largest urban uprising in California by people of color since the Watts uprising of 1965.

The Moratorium police riot led to disturbances as far west as Wilmington and as far east as Barrio Casa Blanca in Riverside. About 500 officers were deployed to put down the disturbance in East Los Angeles, and 178 businesses were hit by rioters, at least seven of which were extensively damaged by fire. Approximately 400 arrests were made on August 29 and 30, nearly half after the initial disturbance on Whittier Boulevard and vicinity.

An eight-block stretch of Avalon Boulevard in Wilmington was the scene of a disturbance shortly after 9 p.m. on Sunday night, August 30. Hundreds participated until "massive reinforcements were brought in to clear the area," centered on Avalon Boulevard and Anaheim Street. Among the reinforcements were five squads of the Metropolitan Division from downtown headquarters. Approximately 24 young adults were arrested.[18]

Meanwhile, Riverside's Barrio Casa Blanca experienced a

> night of disorders . . . during which four policemen were wounded by one shotgun blast. . . . The officers were seeking sniper suspects in the backyard of a home on Diamond St. when hit by the single blast from an unknown assailant. . . . The trouble started in the Villegas Park area where a few small fires were ignited and a fire bomb was thrown at a police car. . . . About 120 police officers and California Highway Pa-

trolmen were in the community during the evening hours. Police said carloads of youth tried to box in patrol cars. Ten arrests were made by officers.[19]

Riots would continue into 1971. Activists faced a dilemma well summarized by Jerry Mandel and Jay Alire: "Unwilling to turn to violence and unable to find another way of raising their concerns peacefully, many of the Mexican American activist groups, including the Moratorium Committee, gradually faded from sight, leaving a vacuum which was filled only gradually over the following decade."[20]

"A Well-planned Conspiracy"

The arrest of Gonzales and the Coloradans, was the LAPD's largest group arrest during the riot and the largest single arrest of non-Californians.[21] An early article stated that they "were arrested as they rode down Olympic Blvd. in a truck reportedly carrying ammunition and three rifles, all said to have been recently fired."[22]

The initial police version was that Gonzales and the others were stopped for a traffic violation at Olympic Boulevard and Lorena Street because passengers were hanging over the guard rails on the truck bed. Police said that they found three revolvers and claimed that one was found when they noticed Gonzales hiding what appeared to be a revolver in the floorboard of the truck cab, where he was a passenger. The story had changed by the following day:

> Police gave conflicting reports Sunday regarding the arrest of Chicano militant Rodolfo (Corky) Gonzales of Denver and 25 of his staff members and followers. . . . Upon approaching the vehicle, officers said, they observed Gonzales, a passenger in the cab, hide what appeared to be a revolver on the floorboards. . . . The original police report Saturday said officers found one .38-caliber revolver and two .22-caliber revolvers . . . and reported that "a large amount of ammunition"—some of it spent— was also discovered. In addition, two shells from the .38-caliber revolver had been fired". . . . A supplementary report filed with the Police Department's Criminal Conspiracy Section said all three weapons were fully loaded and that no additional ammunition was found. Inspector John Kinsling refused to comment on the discrepancies.[23]

Kinsling said those arrested were held on suspicion of robbery because "any time we stop a traffic case and find that there is a weapon in the car and that is occupants have a sizable amount of cash . . . we always book them for suspicion of robbery." Gonzales, as noted above, was carrying $370.[24]

Similarly, the press reported that three "militant Brown Berets" from

San Jose and Oakland were jailed by the LAPD on Sunday, August 30. The three Californians, like the Coloradans, were initially stopped "for a traffic violation" on East Whittier Boulevard and then held on suspicion of robbery. The LAPD found "revolutionary literature and a cache of weapons" during the arrests at 3617 E. Whittier. The "revolutionary literature" was a paperback copy of *The Diary of Che Guevara*, a copy of the *People's World* newspaper, and two Stanford University publications.[25] The weapons were reported to be two M-1 carbines, a shotgun, two revolvers, a rifle with scope, two walkie-talkies, ammunition, and three daggers. A picture accompanying the article shows LAPD Lt. Robert A. Keel holding one of the carbines in his left hand. The suspects were identified as Jesse Dominguez, 24, of San Jose, Louis Charles Camacho, 18, and Juan Antonio Espinoza, 17, both of Oakland.

The next day the LAPD issued an "all-points bulletin" for two cars from the San Diego area, bringing "Brown Beret militants" to Los Angeles "specifically to commit acts of destruction." Within minutes of the bulletin, a sheriff's patrol car stopped one of the two cars at Ferris Street and Whittier Boulevard, where police arrested five men and a woman who refused to give their addresses. They were held for investigation after being found with a starter's pistol that shot blanks and a bottle of volatile liquid that was not further described.[26]

The rioting sparked fears of commies, outsiders, malcontents, and wrong-thinkers in the minds of city officials. On September 2, County Supervisor Warren Dorn said, "It was a very bad revolutionary situation . . . a well-planned conspiracy. It was going to be the biggest possible emotional disruption and, after that, further attempts ([would be made]) to divide the community." Another city official said the events "proved that the Mexican American community was ripe for exploitation by confrontation-seeking agitators [and outside] troublemakers."[27]

"Hundreds of provocative acts were committed by known dissidents who came to the location to incite and foment trouble," L. A. Sheriff Peter Pitchess declared.[28] Newspapers reported that Pitchess told the Board of Supervisors that "leaders of the Chicano power movement came from Denver, Oakland, San Jose, and San Diego to participate in the antiwar march and said he is asking the FBI to investigate such movements."[29] The former FBI agent did not need to ask the bureau to look into the matter.

FBI offices in Denver, Los Angeles, San Antonio, Washington, Chicago, Albuquerque, and elsewhere had been aware of the upcoming August 29 protest as early as May 22, when a Denver FBI report on the Crusade briefly noted: "During 3/25–29/70, CFJ held Second Annual Chicano Youth Conference at Denver attended by estimated 3,000 person from throughout the country. This conference planned a political party known as 'La Raza Unida'; it also voted to hold an anti–Vietnam war rally at Los Angeles, Calif., on 8/29/70."

Pages 21 and 22 of the report were captioned "Anti-draft and Anti-war Activities of the CFJ" and "Relations of the CFJ With Other Groups." Page 21, obtained under the FOIPA, was entirely blacked out; page 22 was withheld from release. A Chicago FBI Airtel sent to FBI Director Hoover on June 2 suggested: "Los Angeles [field office], if not already in possession of *La Causa* [the National Brown Beret Organization's newspaper], should consider obtaining copies of this paper for intelligence purposes. [The] Los Angeles [FBI office] should note National Chicano Moratorium scheduled for 8/29/70." [30]

The Crusade Bufile documents mention antiwar activity, but the exact nature of the FBI's interest and involvement in the Moratorium is hard to ascertain. The FBI refused to release the entire contents of 34 pages from six FBI documents on the youth conference, documents dated from March 16 to May 22, 1970. Further, the Crusade Bufile jumps from the May 22 report to a September 2 report on the Moratorium riot. One document has Hoover's initial and the comment, "OK." These documents, however, show that they were channeled to the highest officials in FBI headquarters: W. Raymond Wannall, Clyde Tolson, Cartha De Loach, William Sullivan, Charles D. Brennan, John Mohr, Alex Rosen, and George C. Moore (head of the FBI's "Racial Intelligence Section").

The details that the FBI had at its disposal about the Moratorium are still unknown, while other matters have not been fully recounted. Press accounts never mentioned the helicopter that followed the truck in which Gonzales and the others were riding. No official mentioned it. The police and sheriffs did not mention it, preferring instead to focus on "troublemakers," "communists," "confrontation-seeking agitators," and "known dissidents."

Communists were, in fact, involved in the Moratorium riot controversy, if only to the extent that their newspaper covered the events. Sam Kushner of the CPUSA *People's World* wrote about the ill-treatment accorded Oscar Acosta when he tried to visit Gonzales in jail. Acosta said, "When [Gonzales] was arrested, I went to the East Los Angeles Sheriff's substation to interview him. I was prevented from entering the station at the point of three rifles by armed uniformed deputies at that station." Upon his release from jail, Gonzales said, "The disturbance, we feel, was planned to disrupt the greatest, the biggest, the most historic march against the war by Chicanos in the history of this nation. This racist society was going to prove to us that we could not demonstrate, we could not go out in a fiesta-like event to say we are concerned about the war, we are concerned about the death of our young people."[31] The *People's World* also reported the death of Ruben Salazar.

The Death of Ruben Salazar

Salazar was killed in the Silver Dollar Cafe on Whittier Boulevard, some distance from the scene of the rioting. The initial press accounts of his death, like reports on Gonzales' arrest, were based on information from the authorities and were plagued by inaccuracies. The *Los Angeles Times* initially reported:

> The dead man was identified as Ruben Salazar, 41, award-winning *Times* columnist and news director for television station KMEX. . . . ([Sheriff's]) Deputies found him sprawled on the floor inside the Silver Dollar Bar, 4945 Whittier Boulevard, with a bullet wound in the head. The deputies had surrounded the bar and ordered it evacuated after receiving a report of a man carrying a gun inside. Tear gas—but no bullets—was fired inside, deputies said. When no one came out, they entered and found Salazar. . . . Although deputies said they had fired no shots before entering the bar, they speculated that Salazar might have been killed by errant gunfire during clashes between police and rioters near the bar earlier in the evening.[32]

In fact, Salazar was killed by a deputy sheriff who fired a high-powered teargas canister through the curtain of an open doorway from a distance of about ten feet. The 10-inch metal projectile struck Salazar in the temple, passing completely through his head. This "Flite-Rite" projectile was designed to be used against barricaded criminals and was capable of penetrating a one-inch pine board from 100 yards. According to reports, the projectile that killed Salazar was not intended for use in riot situations but was to be fired only when there was no other way to rout a dangerous criminal and then only upon command of a supervisory officer in the field.[33] Some believe Salazar died because he was in the wrong place at the wrong time. Some felt, or speculated, that he was murdered. No criminal charges were ever filed over his death.

Ruben Salazar was neither a cynic nor a militant. He wrote an optimistic article ("A Beautiful Sight: The System Working the Way It Should") when charges were brought against seven law enforcement officers for killing two unarmed Mexicanos, cousins Guillermo and Beltran Sanchez.

The Sanchez cousins were living in Los Angeles without the benefit of immigration papers. Officers went to their apartment looking for a murder suspect—who no longer lived at the location—and the cousins, fearing deportation, attempted to flee. Police killed both men. The suspect the police sought was himself later shown to be innocent. The only crime the Sanchez cousins committed was entering the country "illegally." Or maybe, as some muttered, it was that they were Mexicans.

One of Salazar's articles reported that a member of Congress had called for a federal grand jury to investigate the Sanchez killings. A white reporter challenged the congressman, noting the killing of two Border Patrol officers by Mexicanos and asking why he had not called for a federal grand jury investigation of those killings. Salazar wrote:

> When the Border Patrolmen were killed it was crystal clear what had to be done. The murderers had to be found and punished. When a policeman kills a civilian things aren't that clear. When there is a question about the officer's comportment in such a death, the case is sometimes turned over to the county grand jury where it is handled in secrecy. . . . Anyone who has worked a police beat as a reporter, as I have, knows that policemen tend to have different attitudes toward enforcing the law depending on the social, financial, and racial makeup of the people they deal with. This is not a special police attribute, but it becomes very important when an armed policeman has some sort of confrontation with an unarmed civilian. . . . Some time ago I asked a high police official to confirm or deny information which I had which showed that a policeman who had just shot a Mexican American boy had been suspended twice before, once for threatening another boy with a cocked pistol. "Before I answer that," the police official said, "let me remind you that the release of such information will hurt your community more than it will hurt mine." The implications of that statement are staggering and too complicated to go into here. But one of the implications was that certain communities, in this instance, Mexican Americans, cannot handle certain kinds of information.[34]

Salazar decided to play on KMEX interviews with two witnesses to the incident in which the Sanchez cousins were killed. Two policemen visited him and "warned me about the 'impact' the interviews would have on the police department's image. Besides, they said, this kind of information could be dangerous in the minds of the barrio people."[35] Incidentally, charges filed against the officers involved in the Sanchez killings were later dropped. Such circumstances led many Chicano activists to doubt that Salazar's death was accidental and to surmise that a conspiracy led to his death.

The dominant conspiracy theories, however, were those of L. A. city officials. Sheriff Pitchess, Police Chief Davis, and other law enforcement officials believed outside agitators, troublemakers, hard-core subversives, known dissidents, and others had deliberately gone to Los Angeles to start a riot. Davis believed there was a conspiracy involving the California

Communist Party. Speaking to the American Legion's annual convention in Portland, Oregon, he blamed the Moratorium violence on a "small hard-core group of subversives" that had infiltrated the rally: "Ten months ago, the Communist Party in California said it was giving up on the Blacks to concentrate on the Mexican Americans. One per cent can infiltrate and turn any group into a mob."[36]

Though Davis believed the reds had given up on the blacks in order to concentrate on the browns, Chicanos had other theories. When Gonzales and the Coloradans were jailed, a *Los Angeles Times* correspondent phoned Denver to speak to Crusade representatives. He was told that the news of the arrest "came as no surprise," that it resulted from "a national conspiracy" against Gonzales by law enforcement agencies.[37]

THE GONZALES–GURULE TRIAL

Gonzales' arrest and trial kept the Crusade focused on developments in California. He and co-defendant Al Gurule, defended by Oscar Acosta, were tried in November and December of 1970. Acosta demonstrated a style Gonzales liked, based on the assumption that the best defense is a good offense. Acosta was no wallflower and more than once was jailed for contempt of court for his contentious approach to judges. He was jailed for 24 hours on November 13 for interrupting Municipal Judge Joseph R. Grillo, who admonished him for his questioning of prospective jurors about their potential racial bias.[38]

Acosta was intimately involved with Chicano antiwar protests in Los Angeles and had spoken at an earlier rally. His rhetoric on the speaker's platform equaled his flamboyance in court. At the February 1970 Moratorium in Los Angeles, he proclaimed:

> Ya es tiempo! The time is now! There is only one issue. Not police abuse. We are going to be clubbed over the head for as long as we live because we're Chicanos! The real issue is *nuestra tierra*, our land. Some people call us rebels and revolutionaries. Don't believe it. Emiliano Zapata was a revolutionary because he fought other Mexicans. But we're not fighting our own people but gringos! We are not trying to overturn our own government. We don't have a government. Do you think there would be police helicopters patrolling our communities day and night if anybody considered us real citizens with rights?[39]

During the Gonzales–Gurule trial, police testified not that they saw the defendants with weapons, but that weapons were found after the two made furtive motions. Acosta did not deny the presence of the two guns, but argued that his clients had the constitutional right to carry them.

Though the right to carry a loaded weapon is greatly restricted by California law, one exception allowed business owners to carry weapons in defense of their property. Acosta argued that the right of people to protect their lives needed equal protection. In a defense bulletin Acosta wrote. "It is about time somebody spoke out in court about the right of a poor person to protect the only thing he has—his life. We will rest our defense on the 'Businessmen's Exception' and the self-defense exception contained in Section 12031 of the California Penal Code."[40]

Gonzales admitted that weapons were present on the truck: "I don't carry a gun, but the men with me are armed and they will continue to be armed. It is their legal right, and for us, it is a matter of survival. This decision for armed defense was made to protect lives by our members." Acosta spoke of the violence at the Moratorium, in the barrios, and in police practices. Justifying the carrying of weapons by besieged civilians like Gonzales, Acosta said, "If you are going to be in a war zone, you had better be equipped."[41] Defense witnesses testified that they themselves had carried the weapons found by police. One witness, Antonio Salinas of Colorado, even requested from the stand that his weapon be returned to him.[42]

The prosecution challenged the credibility of some defense witnesses by alleging that they were not present at the arrest scene or by pointing out minor discrepancies in their testimony. In response, Acosta asked a marshal to hand him one of the weapons taken in the arrest. Acosta turned and pointed it at the surprised jurors, all the while speaking heatedly and brandishing the gun in their faces. Lowering the unloaded weapon, Acosta then asked the jurors if they had any idea what the judge and Gonzales were doing while he flashed the gun in their faces. He asked the jury to attribute any discrepancies in witnesses' testimony to the loaded pistols and shotguns pointed at them by angry and excited policemen during the arrests.

Cesar Chavez was a character witness for Gonzales. He testified about Gonzales' reputation for "truth, honesty, and integrity," and said that these traits were recognized by others as well. He named the Reverends Ralph Abernathy and Jesse Jackson as two others who shared his opinion of Gonzales. Chavez was asked if his opinion would change if police had negative opinions of Gonzales. "Considering the information I have about the police," Chavez responded, "their opinion would have no effect."[43]

The testimony concluded on December 4. The jury, eight women and four men, acquitted Gurule but split the Gonzales verdict: eight for acquittal, two for conviction, and two undecided. The prosecution usually decides to drop charges in cases involving hung juries. Judge Grillo, how-

ever, decided to refile the charges because the jurors who voted for acquittal did so immediately after testimony ended and refused to consider any
other verdicts. This upset Grillo, and the charges were refiled.[44] Gonzales
was retried in 1971 and convicted. On January 27, 1972, he flew from
Denver to Los Angeles to serve a 40-day jail sentence.

MALE EGOS AND SIMMERING CONFLICTS

Unlike those who saw communists lurking in the shadows of the Moratorium violence, activists believed local and federal agencies provoked the
riots to halt the growth of Chicano activism. This does not mean that the
Chicano movement was impeded only from without, or that it was free
of egotism, divisiveness, incompetence, stupidity, or other human frail-
ties. The movement, at times, was less than harmonious.

An example of these failings can be found in *La Causa,* the newspaper
of the National Brown Beret Organization. Feeling that they had been
slighted by the National Moratorium Committee, members of the organization wrote articles that could be called threatening, thuggish, and stupid. Or laughable and poorly written.

> Rosalio Muñoz, Ramses Noriega, and Bob Elias allowed members of
> the Chicano Moratorium Committee to use the Moratoruim [sic] Com-
> mittee as a vehical [sic] for sabatoge [sic] of the Brown Beret Natl. Or-
> ganization. For months the Chicano Moratorium Committee said we
> could not have a speaker at the Natl [sic] Chicano Moratorium . . . it
> was not until we recently applied pressure, they then said maybe. . . .
> Also, money from the Natl. Chicano Moratoruim [sic] Committee was
> used for travel expenses of a rumor and scandel [sic] team of which we
> have received reports from Fresno, Frisco, Oakland, and Denver, in their
> purpose to sabatage [sic] and cut off Brown Beret National resources.
> We have not yet caused great harm to any of this team because we are
> a deplomatic [sic] organization that moves with fairness and without
> implication. We disassociate our selves [sic] from the Natl. Chicano
> Moratorium Committe [sic], because too many ego-trippers and oppor-
> tunist [sic], who in the name of the movement, became the pig establish-
> ment. We demand a written and read statement of apology to the Brown
> Beret Natl. Organization and to Mr. David Sanchez, Prime Minister.[45]

Frictions arose between Prime Minister Sanchez' National Brown Beret
Organization and the Crusade long prior to the Moratorium protest.
Gonzales met the organization's leadership at their Piranya coffeehouse
late in 1967 when the group formed. He was initially enthusiastic about
their potential, but relations with some individual Brown Berets soured
at the 1968 Poor People's Campaign. One National Brown Beret member—a huge young man who became aggressive and bullying when intox-

icated—assaulted Reies Tijerina's bodyguard and subsequently challenged Crusade member Luis Ramirez to a fight. Though outweighed, Ramirez, who sometimes served as Gonzales' bodyguard, severely beat the Brown Beret.

The Crusade remained cordial with certain Brown Beret leaders, such as Montes, but the relationship with others cooled after 1968. The Crusade was favorably impressed with Montes, who was articulate and analytical. The National Brown Berets, however, were deprived of his skills nine months before the Moratorium, in January 1970, when Montes fled Los Angeles, alleging that Sgt. Abel Armas, of the LAPD SOC Squad, had threatened his life in July 1969. Several months later, Sgt. Ceballos of the LAPD Intelligence Division allegedly told Montes, "I'm either going to kill you or see that you spend the rest of your life behind bars."[46]

In the August 29, 1970, issue, *La Causa* printed a veiled message, one that was clumsily written and poorly considered: "The Brown Beret Organization in Denver is being Harassed [sic] by certain people who are affraid [sic] of Denver going all Brown Beret. These people are causing disunity by usage of smear tactics and scandalizing. If the 'cork' doesn't stop the spoiled beer, then we will break the bottle. PEACE."[47]

Crusade members who read the article did not like it. Their Colorado associates who accompanied them on the bus ride from Denver—Colorado Black Berets and Brown Berets—also failed to appreciate it. Moreover, the group's reception in Los Angeles had been less than hospitable. When they arrived in the city the night before the protest, the Colorado activists reported to a storefront office staffed by Moratorium organizers to arrange accommodations. A group of young men insisted on taking charge of their accommodations and security arrangements and told the Coloradans to accompany them.

Colorado Black Berets and Brown Berets, Crusade members, and others filed from the bus and assembled before their would-be hosts, whose offer lacked a cordial tone. A Colorado spokesperson, possibly Ricardo Romero, said that the Colorado group was in charge of its own arrangements. One of the Californians attempted to interrupt but was cut off and told the decision was final. The sullen young men fell silent and left. A cramped bus ride, a crude reception, and too little sleep did not predispose Colorado activists to appreciate anonymous, incoherent grumbling about corks, "spoiled beer," and the peaceful breaking of bottles when they read *La Causa* the next day.

ALPHABET SOUP: SOC, CCS, PDID, ATF, LEIU

Though some believe the Moratorium riot was the result of a police or federal conspiracy, and it is well known that police and federal agents infiltrated and disrupted organizations, no one has convincingly explained how the disruption and violence were planned and carried out. The first of the Chicano moratoria was organized by National Brown Beret chapters in December 1969. As noted previously, Los Angeles police and sheriffs had infiltrated the National Brown Beret Organization. Further, the FBI file caption for the organization is "Young Citizens for Community Action," the Brown Beret's original name, indicating that the Berets had been monitored since their inception.

One important Brown Beret leader, Carlos Montes, was indicted with several others for conspiracy to commit arson at the Biltmore Hotel during an educational conference held on April 24, 1969. Activists attending the conference protested against the presence of Gov. Ronald Reagan, and small fires were started in the hotel. The key prosecution witness was undercover officer Fernando Sumaya, who had infiltrated the National Brown Berets and was present at the Biltmore protest, where, Sumaya claimed, the activists conspired to disrupt the conference and start fires. The defendants, however, held Sumaya himself responsible for advocating violence and setting the fires. Oscar Acosta was the attorney for the Biltmore defendants, who were subsequently acquitted.

One exception was Montes, who fled California before the trial and went underground in January 1970. (He was arrested on May 30, 1977, stood trial, and was also acquitted). Montes, the Brown Berets' Minister of Information, said he was the subject of surveillance, intimidation, and death threats by law enforcement agencies from December 1967 till January 1970. The officers he named belonged to special entities of the LAPD and the LASD, including the LAPD's Criminal Conspiracy Section (CCS), Special Operations Conspiracy Squad, which the LAPD proudly pronounced "Sock Squad," and the Public Disorder Intelligence Division (PDID). Sumaya, Robert Avila, and Robert Acosta were three of four LAPD and LASD undercover agents identified by Montes. According to him, these police operatives not only infiltrated the Berets but advocated illegal activity, including shooting cops.[48]

Officer Sumaya, code name S-257, gave a written declaration during court proceedings against the Biltmore defendants. It states that Sgt. Ceballos of the LAPD Intelligence Division described the Brown Berets as "militants involved in disruptive activities, however, [Ceballos] never described any current criminal cases against the Brown Berets. . . . I would only occasionally meet Sgt. Ceballos in a face-to-face contact. I never made any field notes or written reports of any kind."[49] Sumaya also reported to Sgt. Armas of the SOC Squad. He insisted he knew of no other law enforcement bodies involved in the Beret infiltration.

In a similar declaration, Armas described the Brown Berets as "potential law-breakers" and detailed the political intelligence work he and the SOC Squad did.

> The function of the Special Operations Conspiracy Squad was to monitor and determine what were the common denominators that had caused disruption throughout the City of Los Angeles. School disruptions had taken place at the high school, junior college, and college level. I was assigned to the East Los Angeles area since I had been in the Hollenbeck Division, and I was of Mexican American ancestry and spoke the language. I understood the Brown Berets to be a militant organization who were agitators, dissenters, and potential law violators. At the time I originally began investigating the Brown Berets, there was no current criminal investigations pending. However, I had determined that they were likely to create or commit crimes in the future because of their disruptive acts in the school system. I had attended an orientation meeting where officers that were then assigned to a new section called the Criminal Conspiracy Section were given an overview of the school disruptions and how to handle this.[50]

Armas also maintained that he had no "communication or contact with other agencies" in the investigation and infiltration of the Brown Berets.[51] His supervisor was Lt. Keel, and he acknowledged occasional contact with Sgt. Ceballos of the LAPD Intelligence Division. Armas also emphasized that no notes, ledgers, reports, or notebooks were used in his activities, or that any that existed had been discarded and were no longer available.

The SOC Squad investigated the Biltmore fires. Officer A. I. Priest, for example, wrote a report on April 30, 1969: "It was learned through Intelligence Division, Officer Ceballos, that certain members of the Brown Berets and La Vida Nueva had formulated a plan to disrupt the Conference."[52] Priest's report, incidentally, was submitted to the O.I.C. (Officer-in-Charge) of the SOC Squad: Keel.

Other agencies were involved in the infiltration of Sanchez' National Brown Berets. When Robert Acosta was recruited from the Los Angeles County Sheriff's Academy to spy on the Berets in May 1968, he was supervised by a Sgt. Morales. In his seemingly contradictory declaration, Acosta stated that Morales had told him that "the Brown Berets were a subversive organization who may be involved in bombings, starting fires, and killing of police officers. At the time I infiltrated the Brown Berets, I had no information that they had been involved in any criminal conduct nor that any criminal activities should be investigated."[53] Acosta also knew nothing of other agencies' involvement in the infiltration of the Brown Berets and, like Sumaya and Armas, neither kept notes nor wrote reports on the matter.

Eustacio Martinez, the Orbiting Satellite

Another informer and provocateur was Eustacio "Frank" Martinez, a Texan recruited in July 1969 by the Treasury Department's Bureau of Alcohol, Tobacco, and Firearms (ATF). His targets in Texas were MAYO and the Texas Brown Berets. Martinez arrived in L. A. from Texas in October 1970, was given the code name "Twenty-Seven Adams," and joined the National Moratorium Committee, where he represented the National Brown Beret Organization.

The traditional September 16 Mexican Independence Day parade in Los Angeles came two weeks after the Moratorium police riot. It too ended in a riot. Fearing more violence, Moratorium leader Rosalio Muñoz wanted to cancel future demonstrations, but he was accused of being "too soft" by Martinez and removed from his position. Martinez, after instigating factional strife on the Moratorium Committee, became its new chairperson, a position he held during the riots of January 9 and 31, 1971. During this time Martinez reported to ATF agents Fernando Ramos, Jim Riggs, and Tito Garcia.[54]

On November 13, 1970, Los Angeles police raided the Moratorium Committee office with drawn weapons and swinging clubs because someone had paraded with a shotgun on the sidewalk in front of the office. The person with the shotgun was Eustacio Martinez. Three people were hospitalized in the aftermath of the raid. Martinez recounted his role in this incident:

> They told me, you know, that ... the main reason they wanted me [in Los Angeles] was because they wanted me to get the information and everything—in other words—the purpose was to eliminate the—all the organizations. So in order to cause confusion within the organizations, to provoke incidents. ... I had pressure [from the ATF]. ... I was being pressured, and how come I wasn't givin' them information, and how come there were no busts, you know? ... So I was under pressure, so in order to get them off my back ... by walkin' out with the rifle so the pigs could see it, so that was the purpose, to get raided.[55]

When Ed Davis blamed the Moratorium violence on infiltration by a "small, hard-core group of subversives," he was not referring to his officers and Eustacio Martinez. In an interview with a news reporter, Davis referred to Martinez as an "orbiting satellite," laughingly recounting how the LAPD broke up the Chicano Moratorium Committee.

> We had a satellite that ... went around ... we had this orbiting satellite. That's the way I'll put it (laughter), and when they'd walk out with brass knuckles, we made all those arrests, for an illegal gun or something. ...

We were knocking them off right and left. That's what this whole thing is about. . . . They went to court . . . and they never did figure, you know, how it was happening. But what they didn't know is that in the Mexican community the great bulk of people are very law abiding and very anti-Marxist and very supportive of the police and very respectful of the uniform.[56]

Martinez' snitch career in Texas and California was marked by disruption and violence. During the Los Angeles riots of January 9 and 31, one person was shot to death by police, and 13 to 24 others were wounded by gunfire. Martinez said he helped provoke the riot on January 31 by "shouting and throwing things at the East Los Angeles Sheriff Station and talking about doing in police and throwing a reporter in the river."[57] He claimed his LAPD and ATF handlers wanted him to infiltrate groups they thought were linked with the Chicano Liberation Front, a group that claimed responsibility for a series of bombings. He said his handlers urged him to engage in bombings, for which they would have provided the explosives.

Louis Tackwood and the Glass House Tapes

In a 1973 book, *The Glass House Tapes,* Louis E. Tackwood recounted his career with the LAPD, for whom he had worked as an informer and agent provocateur since 1964. In 1965 his LAPD controllers were assigned to a special downtown squad, the Special Identification and Investigation Squad, and Tackwood went with them. Tackwood claims the LAPD Intelligence Division was caught flat-footed by the August 1965 Watts riot and set about reorganizing itself. One result, according to Tackwood, was the creation of the Criminal Conspiracy Section (CCS), which operated on the street level to infiltrate militant organizations: "They [CCS] are in charge of all the militants. They've got a room on the eighth floor of the Glass House [the Parker Center Police Administration Building] with files and pictures of all radicals—Brothers, Brown militants, and White boys, too. It's a top secret place where they keep information on everyone . . . they got files on people [from] all over the country. CCS is a super police agency. They can go anywhere."[58]

Tackwood knew Lieutenant Robert A. Keel, whose name has been mentioned previously in connection with recruiting spies. Keel was the Officer-in-Charge of the SOC Squad in the unsuccessful Biltmore conspiracy case and posed for the press holding an M-1 carbine allegedly confiscated from "militant Brown Berets" after the Moratorium police riot. It was Keel's CCS that gave the press misinformation about the arrest of Rodolfo Gonzales and Colorado activists.

Tackwood recalled his first meeting with Keel:

> My first meeting was held at the Glass House on the third floor where I
> met the head man in charge of a new department called Criminal Con-
> spiracy Section. His name is Lieutenant Keel. His partner was a Sgt.
> Sherrett. Before they started talking, they gave me a hundred dollars. Lt.
> Keel said, "Listen, man, you're just the man we want. You have all the
> experience we need. . . ." I said, "Well, yeah, the money looks good.
> Who are you?" Keel said, "Criminal Conspiracy Section." I found out
> later that's just what they're doing too. They spend all their time cooking
> up criminal conspiracies against militants, particularly against groups
> like the Panthers, Angela Davis, and people like that. . . . I will tell you
> something about the staff of CCS. Lt. Robert Keel, a prejudiced-type
> redneck, runs his ship like a well-trained Army thug.[59]

To untangle and interpret the names, acronyms, and intertwining chro-
nologies of past controversies is a challenge. What may be more important than each obscure detail is the awareness that the clandestine work
of entities like the SOC Squad and PDID signaled the transference of
Vietnam-era military intelligence theory to domestic intelligence practice.
The Citizens Research and Investigation Committee traced this process:

> California took a leading role in the coordination and up-lifting of the
> role of intelligence. The California police had used this method for years
> and in 1955 they led the nation in the creation of a formal nationwide
> organization of Municipal Intelligence Departments: now known as the
> Law Enforcement Intelligence Unit. The LEIU was created by a special
> conference of a select group of police officers from seven states. The
> need for some means of organization in law enforcement to exchange
> confidential information on certain individuals and organizations as
> well as a central clearing house for this information was outlined to the
> group by the conveners of the conference, San Francisco's Chief of Police
> Frank Ahern and Captain Hamilton of the Intelligence Division of the
> Los Angeles Police Department. . . . "The purpose of this organization
> shall be the gathering, recording, investigation, and exchanging of infor-
> mation concerning any local or known individual or organizations
> whose background, activities, or associates identify them with [orga-
> nized crime]." . . . What was organized ostensibly for syndicated crimi-
> nal activities became an intelligence center for the surveillance of politi-
> cal activity.[60]

In July 1978, an LAPD document revealed that nearly two hundred
political organizations were under PDID surveillance, including more
than twenty Chicano organizations. Among them were the Brown Berets,
the Crusade for Justice, the United Farm Workers of America, La Raza

Unida Party, and MEChA. When a reporter asked LAPD Chief Daryl Gates about charges of "police spying" in the surveillance list controversy, Gates responded, "I don't know what police spying is."[61] Gates headed the LAPD Intelligence Division from June 1963 to 1968, when he became deputy chief. Gates's 1992 book, *Chief: My Life in the LAPD,* makes interesting reading, especially when compared with former LAPD intelligence officer Mike Rothmiller's *L.A. Secret Police: Inside the LAPD Elite Spy Network.*

Though Gates claims no knowledge of police spying, Rothmiller's book details Gates's direct involvement with it and the various LAPD entities named in this chapter (and others that are not mentioned). Rothmiller discloses that the LAPD maintained files dating back to the 1930s and operated on an international scale. He cites one incident in which the LAPD spied on Sheriff Sherman Block, and another in which Chief Gates ordered a deputy chief investigated in the belief that the subordinate was spying on Gates. Rothmiller left the LAPD in 1983 after a mysterious attempt on his life.

Ruben Salazar: Bufile 105-23153

There are many ironies in the life and death of Ruben Salazar. Salazar, described as "most cooperative" when the FBI interviewed him about Stokely Carmichael, was himself the subject of an FBI internal security file. The FBI files on Salazar, Bufile 105-23153 and Los Angeles FBI file 100-57253, included data on his 1950–52 military service. Salazar was born in Mexico, was raised in the United States, and entered the U.S. military as a resident alien. He hoped that military service would help him become a U.S. citizen.

Salazar appears to have drawn the FBI's attention during the Korean War era, when he corresponded with a person who may have held pacifist views. This Anglo woman lent Salazar a sympathetic ear when he wrote to her in frustration after learning that the army had lost his application for U.S. citizenship. The fact that this woman had somehow attracted the FBI's attention was sufficient reason for the FBI to maintain data on her correspondent.

The FBI interviewed Salazar on December 13, 1967, in their effort to build a case against Carmichael, who had embarrassed the U.S. government with his fiery speeches denouncing American racism and the Vietnam war at the July 28–August 5 Latin American Solidarity Organization conference in Havana, Cuba. Carmichael was born in the Caribbean, and the FBI apparently hoped to build a case for revoking his citizenship. The

FBI reported that Salazar believed such a case would be weak, and "felt it would be a shame" to prosecute "Carmichael on a weak charge, and [make] a 'martyr' of him."[62]

If Carmichael's words at the Havana conference were to be used against him, however, the FBI needed a witness to testify about his speech or procure a taperecording of it, since, at Carmichael's request, the U.S. media had been barred from the presentation. The FBI reported:

> Salazar was informed that the interview was being conducted at the request of Mr. J. Walter Yeagley, Assistant Attorney General, Internal Security Division, U.S. Department of Justice. Pertinent statements attributed to Carmichael which were included in Mr. Yeagley's letter to the Director, FBI, dated August 30, 1967, were shown to Salazar. Salazar commented that the statements were what he had been told Carmichael said.[63]

Salazar, however, told the FBI that he could not be a witness about the speech because he was not present when Carmichael spoke. The FBI asked if Salazar could obtain a tape of the speech from Mexican journalists who had been present. Salazar agreed to do so, but his response implied that he would let his Mexican colleagues know that the FBI would be getting the tape. This seemed to present a dilemma. Mexican journalists might have been indifferent to the FBI's subversion of the Bill of Rights—the Constitution and its purported guarantees of a free press and free speech were, after all, meant for *norteamericanos,* not Mexicans, so this was not the dilemma. Instead, the FBI seemed to fear that Mexican journalists would expose FBI intelligence gathering on Mexican soil and thereby create an embarrassing incident. Salazar's offer was one the FBI could not accept, and they apparently did not pursue the matter.

The Communist Connection

The Crusade for Justice met many leftists and communists in the course of its career and was willing to collaborate with those who demonstrated competence and a sincere concern for the Mexican community (as opposed to those who merely wanted to line up Chicanos behind their ideological banners). The fact remains, however, that the Crusade was unwilling to accept ideological domination by any outside group. Police, spy agencies, and ultrapatriots sought to taint the reputation of dissident groups by linking them to communists, as though commies were bogeymen hiding in the shadows of domestic unrest. Ironically, there was a communist link—of sorts—between Ruben Salazar and the Crusade for Justice. The link was Sam Kushner, a writer for the *People's World* newspaper of southern California.

When Salazar flew to Denver in March 1969 to cover the National Chicano Youth Liberation Conference for the *Los Angeles Times,* his story was nearly aborted when the Crusade refused to allow him to enter. Salazar's *Los Angeles Times* credentials did not help him and, in fact, were the reason he was refused entrance. The Crusade was skeptical that mainstream journalists would do anything other than disparage the Chicano movement, and so it barred all mainstream reporters, Spanish-surnamed reporters included, from the conference. Salazar knew Sam Kushner, and Kushner pleaded his case to Gonzales, who exempted Salazar from the media ban on Kushner's assurance that he could be trusted to be fair. Salazar's articles about the conference were published in the *Los Angeles Times* on March 30 and April 1, and the Crusade paid them little notice.

During his stay at the conference, Salazar was nervously quiet and stayed in the background. Though his initial reception may have unsettled him, it seemed more likely that he was stunned by the militant fervor of the gathering. He had, after all, been posted outside the United States for three years and returned to Los Angeles when the Chicano movement was in its first flush of vigor. His March 30 article concluded by quoting a statement from the conference's "revolutionary caucus": "Revolution is the only means available to us. We owe no allegiance, no respect, to any of the laws of this racist country. Our liberation struggle is a war of survival." Salazar's April 1 column concluded, "Many of the youths who returned home Monday will be preaching Chicano nationalism, liberation, and 'Corky' Gonzales to their fellow students."[64]

The LAPD and LASD tended to equate social unrest with communist control or influence. Ed Davis, for example attributed the violence at the Moratorium protest and subsequent riots to "swimming pool Communists" and Brown Berets "sophisticated in Bolshevik tactics." According to Davis, "[communists] saw the black people were not going to hold still and be exploited by the Communist Party, so they concentrated on the Mexican American community."[65] As proof of his allegations, Davis provided reporters with photographs taken by the LAPD at a January 1971 protest by Chicanos in front of the Parker Center, (i.e., the Glass House). One photo shows Sam Kushner, who covered the demonstration for the *People's World,* walking among the demonstrators. Though Kushner had no swimming pool, he was clearly a communist.

To equate Ruben Salazar's journalism with advocacy of the views he reported was a failure to recognize the obvious. Salazar reported what he saw, (inaccurately at times); he was not a closet militant. Though he became critical of the Vietnam war, which the articles he wrote while in Vietnam had failed to criticize, he was not a closet communist, either.

The Anticommunist Connection

The LAPD also had files on Salazar. As noted above, the LAPD intelligence file was ordered by Chief Davis after Salazar wrote about Davis' references to Mexican "tyranny and dictatorship." The article was published on March 13, 1970, and the LAPD intelligence file followed within days. The Intelligence Division was responsible for keeping this file, and Salazar may have inspired additional police hostility with an April 3 article about LAPD Sgt. Robert Thoms, who had worked as a "community relations" officer with barrio and ghetto groups from March 1967 to February 1968 before being transferred to intelligence work.

In January 1970 Chief Davis sought to cut funding for community groups in Los Angeles by sending Thoms to testify before the Senate Internal Security Subcommittee. According to Frank Donner, "Thoms charged that the subversive groups [in Los Angeles] had been subsidized to the tune of $5 million by the government, over $1 million by the Ford Foundation, and over $200,000 by the Episcopal, Methodist, and Unitarian churches."[66] Among Thoms' targets for defunding were the California State College (now University) Educational Opportunities Program and the Brown Berets. Thoms said he could document that 43 of 124 EOP beneficiaries at Cal State Los Angeles belonged to "militant organizations."

Salazar's article noted that Thoms was questioned about his sources. Thoms said the information was from a reliable source who had made the information public in Chicago in May of the previous year. When questioned further, Thoms admitted that he himself was the reliable source. Salazar's article concluded, "Thoms' report should be read by all Americans concerned with the problem of the credibility gap."[67]

"If I Survive . . ."

Salazar's articles recount that Los Angeles law enforcement officials were unhappy with his reporting and let him know it. After his death Sam Kushner wrote, "Salazar had been a staunch advocate of the rights of his people. His broadcasts and his columns have often . . . brought the police to his office. They urged him to tone down his criticism and reporting."[68] His family saw his behavior change in the weeks before the Moratorium. When the station manager of KMEX told Salazar that he would see him Monday after the Moratorium protest, Salazar responded, "Yeah, if I survive, you'll see me."[69]

Salazar was gathering material for a series on Los Angeles police, entitled, "What Progress in 30 Years of Police–Community Relations?" He confided to the KMEX station manager that he thought police were following him. He believed that someone had gone through his desk at KMEX, so he began to keep research materials in his car trunk. Activist Bert Corona recalls that Salazar was concerned about the FBI. The night before the protest, he told Corona that he had reason to believe that the Moratorium Committee and Prime Minister Sanchez' Brown Berets had been infiltrated by provocateurs. He was afraid that the police would take action against the protest. Corona says that the police were deliberately shooting teargas at Salazar's film crew to impede their filming when the riot erupted; he notes that the riot film and research material kept in Salazar's car trunk have never been seen since.[70]

The role played by the law enforcement agencies in disrupting the August 29 Moratorium will remain a tangled mystery until the files of the LAPD, LASD, LEIU, FBI, ATF, and other collaborating agencies are opened to the taxpayers who fund their endeavors. That day may never come.

Eight

Colorado in the Early 1970s
Education, Elections, Parks, and Prison Activism

Though the violence at the L. A. Moratorium was a serious setback for the Chicano movement, the loss of momentum was felt most strongly in California. When Colorado activists returned to Denver after the Moratorium, they found that the pace of events actually quickened. The Crusade and its allies organized the second annual September 16 protest and launched their first statewide campaign under the banner of La Raza Unida Party (LRUP). The Crusade also started its own school, Escuela Tlatelolco.

EDUCATION

Escuela Tlatelolco

The expulsions that accompanied school activism in 1969 and 1970 motivated the Crusade to start a school. As early as 1967 the Crusade, had voiced its intent to "direct and administer a school of Culture and Arts which will offer our students and membership the History and contributions of our people to this country."[1] Escuela Tlatelolco became the focus of the Crusade's material and human resources throughout the 1970s. Tlatelolco, which did not need government accreditation because state law did not require accreditation of private schools, enrolled more than 200 students from first to twelfth grades in its first year and operated a Bachelor of Arts program under the auspices of Vermont's progressive Goddard College. The school's name commemorated the hundreds of Mexicans gunned down by army troops in the Plaza de Tlatelolco in Mexico City in the fall of 1968.[2]

The connection to Goddard College, indeed the opening of the school, came about when a carload of Crusade youths drove to New Mexico in May 1970 to visit former Crusade member Kelly Lovato, who was living in a small village near Taos. They found him in the company of some long-haired Goddard students who were studying in the area through an arrangement known as a "vest-pocket college." Lovato and the Crusade youths thought that the vest-pocket concept of a school that went with the students to the locales best suited to their studies could be implemented in Denver and Taos. If it was well-directed by activists, the concept would allow for student empowerment and relevancy of studies. The Goddard students in New Mexico were enthusiastic about the idea of autonomous Chicano projects.

Gonzales, though interested in working with Goddard, opposed any arrangement if Lovato was involved in a similar project in New Mexico. He argued that two projects would stretch the resources needed to make one project successful—and Gonzales was determined that the one project would be in Denver.[3] Rather than involve himself in a dispute over the issue, Lovato sought his own resources and began his own educational project in Taos.[4]

Tlatelolco was not a mirror image of the public school system, but a reflection of Mexican culture and the movement's politics. Many, if not most, of its adolescent students were youth activists who had attended the schools where the 1969 and 1970 walkouts occurred. Tlatelolco included a preschool, and Crusade members and Tlatelolco staff were given priority in enrolling their children there. Because it lacked the financial base of other schools, the Crusade could not build libraries, science labs, or other facilities, and so it offered few elective courses. The school emphasized the basics—reading, writing, 'rithmetic—and, given the Crusade's ideological orientation—the social sciences.

Tlatelolco students quickly accumulated credit hours that enabled them to graduate before their public school counterparts. Those students who returned to public schools, even mediocre students, often did well, an outcome the Crusade attributed to the confidence instilled at Tlatelolco. A 1973 brochure recounts Escuela Tlatelolco's early days:

> *Tlatelolco's beginning:* Following the National Chicano Youth Liberation Conference in 1969, the Crusade for Justice . . . began a summer Freedom School . . . to provide Chicano children and youth in the Denver area an opportunity to study their history and to reinforce pride in their language, culture and to identify as Chicanos. One hundred and fifty students ranging in ages from four to eighteen . . . learn Spanish, history, music, folkloric dancing, geography, printing, sculpturing, and contemporary world and national affairs. . . . In the summer of 1970,

Freedom School enrollment doubled. Three professors were recruited from Monterey, Nuevo Leon, Mexico, to teach advanced Spanish, Mexican history, economics, political science and mathematics. . . . Students who attended the summer Freedom School expressed dissatisfaction with public and parochial systems . . . [for not] relating curricula and teaching methods to their needs. They also experienced frustration with instructors' inability, unpreparedness, and unwillingness to correlate their educational methods and material with the increased social, historical, and cultural awareness of the students. . . . It also surfaced resentment which caused them to doubt the veracity of their past and possible future education. . . .

Tlatelolco's Educational Philosophy: Tlatelolco's philosophical objective goes beyond effecting academic competency. We perceive education not only as the intellectual development of the individual for his benefit but as a social orientation and development process for social change which will benefit a collective group.[5]

Escuela Tlatelolco opened its doors at the Crusade headquarters on 1567 Downing Street after the 1970 Mexican Independence Day ("Chicano Liberation Day") protest organized by the Crusade for Justice and its allies. The September protest was peaceful and massive. Participating organizations included the Black Berets and Brown Berets, the Denver and Boulder UMAS chapters, the Colorado Migrant Council, the Westside Youth Center, the Hispano Youth Congress, the Westside Health Board, the Colorado Civil Rights Commission, and others.

More School Protests

Through the mid-September walkout and demonstration were peaceful, violence closed two schools later in September and in October. Confrontations involving African American students at George Washington High School occurred on September 24 and 25 and on October 20. Police were called to the school and, students said, used unnecessary force when they arrived. Other problems arose at West High School on October 22.

Violence erupted among Chicano and black students at West and resulted in the arrest of seven students. The media reported that Chicanos were angered because black students controlled the music played in the school social room. About 20 students participated in the initial fighting, which teachers halted. A gun was reportedly flourished by a student. Violent clashes recurred between classes. Police arrived at the school in response to a fire alarm around 1:30 p.m. and reported that a gang fight seemed imminent, Molotov cocktails had been thrown at school buildings, and a car with young Chicanos brandishing firearms had been seen. Hundreds of Chicano students gathered north and west of the school when police vehicles arrived. A car was stopped at 11th Avenue and Fox Street, where a shotgun was confiscated and two juveniles were arrested. Arresting officers were showered with rocks, bricks, and bottles, and at least one policeman was seen throwing rocks and bricks back at the students. A tense peace was restored an hour or so after the false alarm.[6]

That night African American students from George Washington and Chicanos from West High appeared at a regularly scheduled school board meeting to complain about the schools and the police. Minority parents, community activists, and concerned whites criticized the use of police to solve social problems. The George Washington students wanted police removed from the school, saying that much of the violence was a reaction to their deployment. Chicano students voiced similar views regarding occurrences at West.

The meeting began at 7.30 p.m., with the young people's concerns at the end of the night's agenda. As the board's budget reports were presented, Chicano students yelled, "The idea of West needs to be discussed." The conservative board president replied, "You'll have to wait until the scheduled speakers are heard." A student replied, "Either you listen to us, or we're not going back to school." Another shouted, "We haven't got time to wait. If you haven't got a school, you haven't got a budget. People are more important than money."[7]

Clarence Briscoe, an African American job counselor, asked the board, "Why are you putting up a front when you merely have to vote on the question of police in George Washington? You're asking the Black and Chicano communities to trust you when you don't trust them. You're bigots."[8]

Board members Steven Knight and Frank Southworth, conservatives who favored keeping police in the school, did not want to vote on the issue. Though students, faculty, and neighborhood residents attended the meeting, most of the crowd was black or brown. When Southworth remarked, "The school [George Washington] isn't represented in its entirety here tonight," the crowd felt that he was saying that not enough whites were present, as though their desires were the hinge on which all matters hung. Knight said, "I feel we'd be derelict in our duty to allow ourselves to be intimidated. I believe the police are necessary at George Washington and that a large number of people agree with me."[9]

The board vote was 3–3, and the impasse meant that police would remain at the school. Shouts and angry comments greeted the vote, and students were further angered when the board president tried to temporarily adjourn the meeting at 11:00 p.m. Students packed the speaker's podium and momentarily blocked the passage of board members.

Board members conferred among themselves for about an hour and then returned to the meeting to report that the board would meet with the faculty at George Washington to seek their permission to remove the police. Students and others announced a sit-in at the board chambers until action was taken to remove police. Denver attorney and former school board member A. Edgar Benton voiced the sentiments of concerned whites:

> As a personal gesture to the importance of the removal of the police from this school, I intend to stay in this room until some action is taken. I feel you must call upon parents, students, teachers, and community leaders to help you solve these problems which are so deeply imbedded in our society. . . . Application of force, police power, isn't going to solve the problems. And, as a first step toward de-escalating the problems in this community and creating a calm atmosphere, where anguish now exists, we need to remove the police.[10]

One week later Chicano, African American, and white students were back at the school board, seeking the removal of the South High School principal. "His ears are never open to student grievances," according to students Madeline Dudley and Becky Peters. African American students complained because the Confederate flag was hung in the school hallway and the school's football team was called the Rebels. Lena Garcia complained of the school's insensitivity, saying minority teachers were needed and that parental involvement was important. She said parents were consulted only when "they are called to the school to take us home."[11]

THE 1970 LA RAZA UNIDA CAMPAIGN

A Nationwide Movement

The Crusade for Justice was a major influence in the Chicano movement. It was, however, a Denver-based organization and remained so by choice. Though there was tentative discussion about establishing other chapters as late as 1968, this strategy for extending the Crusade's influence was never attempted. Gonzales hoped that the Crusade would serve as a model for those wanting to build autonomous, urban organizations, but he realized that it could not guarantee the accountability or political integrity of dispersed chapters. He also felt that the millions of people of Mexican descent in the United States would not become powerful enough to defend their interests unless they were organized on a national level under their own initiative, agenda, and leadership. But how could a national organization be built?

Gonzales felt that it was one thing to galvanize a political movement and another to build a solid organization. Both tasks were needed, but the Crusade for Justice was the organization Gonzales would build, and with it he could influence the course of events and the political direction of the larger movement. Gonzales closely guarded the Crusade's autonomy but yearned to see the emergence of a national organization compatible with its ideals. He viewed Chicanos as a conquered, colonized people, and when he spoke of self-determination, he meant it literally. Chicanos, he felt, had the right and the duty to free themselves from their colonizers. Gonzales read about the Zionist organizations of the Jewish Diaspora that brought Israel into existence from bases outside their Biblical homeland. What would be the potential for people of Mexican descent who still lived in the lands on which they had evolved?

A national organization, or network of working alliances, needed to be built. Gonzales hoped that an independent political party, La Raza Unida, would become a vehicle to coordinate political activism on a national level. LRUP was adopted as a national political party at the 1970 National Chicano Youth Liberation Conference, and Gonzales, the Crusade, and other Colorado groups began to organize the Colorado LRUP. The Crusade hosted a "political caucus" in Denver to initiate the party on April 27, 1970. Eight "regional conferences" were held from May 16 to August 22 to launch the party's statewide campaign. LRUP candidates announced their campaigns in June 1970, and additional candidates stepped forward over the summer.

Denver and Pueblo were the party's areas of urban activism, Gonzales was the state chairperson, and Crusade members who campaigned for office included Carlos Santistevan, Lionel Sanchez, José Gonzales, Pete Lopez, and Eloy Espinoza. Seven Denverites ran for office, as did six Puebloans (including Pueblo Brown Beret Bruno Medina, a Vietnam veteran, who ran for sheriff).

LRUP attacked law-and-order campaigns by Republicans and Democrats as hypocritical or superficial. Education was a key theme; LRUP candidate Salvadore Carpio said, "We must begin to focus more attention on education. We must make the political decision-makers realize that when this nation's economic pie is being sliced, education must receive the first slice, not the last." [12]

Women, College Students, and Labor in LRUP

College activists and women played a role in the party's early stages. Eight LRUP candidates were college activists from Boulder, Denver, and Pueblo; at least four were Boulder UMAS members. Among Colorado LRUP's founders were Liz Montoya and Priscilla Salazar, who left the Democratic Party to help form the new party. [13] Four women were listed as candidates on the first Colorado LRUP slate: Flor (Lovato) Saiz campaigned for a seat on the Board of Education; 21-year-old Ann Garcia ran for county assessor in southern Colorado; Marcella Trujillo campaigned for the University of Colorado Board of Regents; and Mrs. Patricia Gomez, a candidate for the state legislature, was described in *El Gallo* as "a housewife who intends to CLEAN HOUSE."

Marcella Trujillo's campaign received significant publicity and support. She opposed links between the University of Colorado and the military (ROTC and war-oriented research), supported minority students against an administration that was "pulling them to the confrontation line because of reneging on promises and funds," and said she would fight discrimination against women and people of color.[14]

Colorado LRUP, as a third party, needed only to obtain signatures on petitions in order to be on the ballot (300 signatures were needed to run for governor). LRUP's petitions were challenged by a Spanish-surnamed Democrat who was campaigning to be Colorado secretary of state. Al Gurule and George Garcia's petitions were challenged because they were under 30, the minimum age to hold the offices sought. At hearings held in September 1970, attorney Eugene Deikman of the National Lawyers Guild represented LRUP candidates, who charged that the legal challenge against them was set up to benefit Lt. Gov. Mark Hogan, then running for governor; the argument was that Hogan feared that LRUP would drain votes from the Democrats. Secretary of State Byron Anderson, a Republican, ruled that pending their election, the issue of candidates' age was premature. Anderson's ruling did not hurt his party, since it attracted few Spanish-surnamed voters.[15]

Organized labor opposed Magdaleno "Len" Avila's LRUP campaign for secretary of state. Avila organized farm workers in the southern Colorado town of Center on behalf of the United Farm Workers Union. Cesar Chavez supported the Democratic Party, the party supported his union, and both opposed Avila's candidacy. In October, Avila announced that he was ending his campaign because of pressure from the Democrats and organized labor.[16] Organized labor's position was articulated by Herrick Roth, president of the Colorado Labor Council and a former colleague of Gonzales during his Democratic career: "I think [Avila] should have remained as the candidate, but he should not pose as a trade union leader of the farm workers. Avila has to make up his mind whether he wants to be a trade union leader for the good of the farm worker or a political leader in a separatist movement." Avila charged that Roth threatened to withhold support for a lettuce strike with which Avila was involved "unless we joined the (Democratic) Party."[17]

Building LRUP in Colorado

LRUP also found support. Columnist Tom Gavin interviewed Salvadore Carpio, LRUP congressional candidate, and traced the roots of Carpio's political thought. Gavin quoted him as saying: "To be a Mexican American is a thing to be proud of. We've learned from history that no one's going to do it for us. We have to start doing it ourselves. . . . It has to be on a basis of equality." Gavin asked his readers: "Do you know what that is? That's the rhetoric of Corky Gonzales, of the Crusade for Justice, of La Raza Unida. That's what the Chicano militants are saying."[18]

Carpio told Gavin: "I decided to run because of the lack of responsiveness in either of the two parties toward the Chicano community. . . . For too long, power has been something that works from the top down. To me, it should be the other way around: from the bottom, from the people up. . . . Everything that concerns the lives of people, there's a political decision behind it." In 1975 Carpio was elected to the Denver City Council as a Democrat.

Colorado allowed a party obtaining 10 percent of the votes cast in an election to become an established party that no longer needed to get on the ballot via petitions. About 70,000 votes were needed in 1970 to establish LRUP as a permanent party, since it was projected that 700,000 votes would be cast. Gonzales realized that immediate victories were improbable, though elections might be won in certain counties in southern Colorado, in Denver barrio districts where Chicanos were a majority, or in places like the steel-mill city of Pueblo, where Chicanos were nearly a majority. The Colorado LRUP sought to use election campaigns as educational, agitational, and organizational forums. Gonzales took the community's psychology into consideration, knowing that people did not like to lose or be considered losers. He portrayed the electoral effort as an act of dignity, not as a campaign for a losing cause. The lack of community participation in elections, which LRUP sought to change, was seen not as a sign of apathy among Spanish-surnamed voters, but as a sign that the community did not trust the electoral system to protect rights or interests.

If the Chicano electorate stayed home during elections, this, in effect, was a protest vote: the community voted with its feet by walking away from the voting booth, rather than to it. The role of the party was to rally this community to challenge the system and make changes. The gains would not necessarily be election victories, but changes in the way the community viewed itself and society. If the community was motivated by pride and sought power, Chicano power, this mattered as much as winning elections. The party wanted to win elections, but if the community challenged the system and lost elections, was not it better, at least, that the community had stood up? Some Colorado LRUP candidates received 5,000 to 9,000 votes in the November 1970 elections. In contrast, the Texas LRUP won elections in Crystal City, Carrizo Springs, and Cotulla. Whatever vision Gonzales and the Colorado LRUP had of the party, other visions existed as well. The different visions, circumstances, and strategies of the Colorado and Texas parties would later result in conflict over the role of the party in the Chicano movement.

Political Concerns of Denver Police and Teachers

The 1970 elections marked the halfway point of the Nixon-Agnew administration's first term. Denver's election reflected national social conflicts and the rightward drift of national politics as well as local issues like discontent among teachers and police, student protest and nonconformity.

As the elections drew near, Juvenile Judge Ted Rubin found himself the focus of attention by those who blamed delinquency on "liberal" policies and "lenient" judges. In September, the Denver Police Department's Delinquency Control Division prepared a study of crime statistics to deliver to the Chamber of Commerce. Why the police believed the Chamber was interested in these figures was not made clear. The *Denver Post* article about the report bore the headline "Juvenile Policy Lenient," and law enforcement officials concluded that "the survey substantiates our previous opinions that laws, some court policies and some police procedures are not effective. . . . The survey shows that the policy toward juveniles is lenient, tolerant, permissive, and, in some cases overprotective to the point that there is great detriment to the community." [19]

In preparing the report, a "spot check" was done on 226 juveniles who accumulated 2,335 arrests, according to case history cards the police kept on juveniles they arrested five or more times. The police then made an "estimate" that for every one arrest, the juveniles committed eight offenses that went undetected. The police provided no scientific data to support this ratio but used it to conclude that the 226 juveniles had "committed 18,680 offenses." Having found a veritable crime wave of juvenile offenses that had apparently eluded public attention until that point, the police report concluded that "lenient" enforcement of the juvenile code "is a major contributor to the rising crime rate in Denver." [20]

Judicial leniency was also attacked by some teachers. On October 20, the Representative Council of the Denver Classroom Teachers Association (DCTA) passed a resolution urging voters "to vote 'NO' on the issue of whether Judge Rubin should be retained in office when such issue is placed before them in the general election on November 3."[21] DCTA President Max Bartram said the decision followed a detailed discussion of the George Washington High School disturbances. Another outcome of the meeting was a decision to poll the DCTA's 3,300 members about Rubin's retention over the following three days. DCTA Director Clarke Ballinger told the *Rocky Mountain News:* "Teachers around the city are pretty unhappy with the Children's Code and the way it has been administered. Students have been dismissed from school for serious offenses and the judges sent them back immediately. . . . We are now actively soliciting teachers to document their frustrations with the Juvenile Court."[22] The DCTA Council apparently was confident that it could survey 3,300 members by October 23, analyze the data, and report its findings before Election Day.

A week before the election, the *Denver Post* reported that the DCTA poll, by a three-to-one margin, recommended against Rubin's retention. "The problem of assaults on classroom teachers continues to rise," Ballinger complained in the *Rocky Mountain News.* "Yet students who commit these assaults are permitted to return to school before the teacher can receive first aid." On October 30, four days before the election, 29 assistant principals wrote in a letter to the *Rocky Mountain News* that their efforts "have often been frustrated as a result of little or no action taken against those juveniles who are repeatedly guilty of breaking city and state laws."[23]

The DCTA did not reveal how many of its members were surveyed, nor was the hasty poll conducted in standardized language. The *Rocky Mountain News* on October 31 noted that teachers at East High School and Smiley Junior High blasted the poll, saying it was neither "a total response" nor "an honest cross section." Craig Spellman, an East High history teacher, said that in many schools the poll was conducted only among teachers who favored ousting Rubin. The teachers at East and Smiley charged that the DCTA was "looking for a scapegoat." The DCTA anti-Rubin factions "seem to feel that Judge Rubin and the Juvenile Court are somehow responsible for the breakdown in discipline within our schools," they wrote. "As educators, we feel the responsibility lies squarely within the schools and the community at large." Teachers at East and a majority of teachers at Smiley, including the principal, circulated their own letter in support of Judge Rubin, whose conduct on the bench they found to be "superior."[24]

On November 3, 63,935 voters opposed Rubin's retention, against 60,950 favoring it. Rubin noted, "I am not a permissive judge, I am a careful judge, a thorough judge, a rehabilitation-oriented judge as I must be and should be." He attributed his defeat to the DCTA attack, to poor media coverage of the complexities of his work, to the high profile given Police Chief George Seaton's criticism of the "social work ideology" of people who dealt with juveniles, and to the "national Nixon-Agnew hysteria about law and order."[25]

LIBERATED TERRITORY: ALMA, MESTIZO, AND LA RAZA PARKS

Though law-and-order politics had the edge in the polls, activists continued to gain ground in the barrios. During the summer of 1970, young political activists and community residents took over the public swimming pool in the Northside's Columbus Park, a tactic patterned after the 1969 takeover at Lincoln Park. The pool at Curtis Park was taken over in 1971, and the three parks were renamed La Raza Park, Alma Park, and Mestizo Park. In West Denver, the Alma Park staff included Gil Quintana, Danny Martinez, Jerry Garcia, Manuel "Rocky" Hernandez, and the artist Manuel Martinez, who painted a series of murals on the park walls and in the community.[26] Though it lost influence over Alma Park in the early 1970s, the Crusade for Justice continued as the key influence at the Eastside and North Denver parks, which became centers of community organizing, leading to conflicts with local authorities.

Conflicts at Mestizo Park

Youth activists in the Eastside pressured employees at Curtis Park to quit their jobs in 1971, and replaced them with staff from the community. Among the new employees were Artie, Victor, and Tomas Ornelas, Danny Castro, Ray Zaragosa, Philip Miera, and others. The Mestizo Park takeover led to unforeseen complications. Chicano youths were well organized and highly politicized through their participation in school walkouts and involvement in the Berets and the Crusade for Justice. Though the African American community in the Eastside is larger than the Chicano community, Chicanos predominated in the immediate area of the park. African American youths were also employed at the park, but conflict arose when some resentful black youths felt that "the Mexicans had taken over."

Community activists recall that some of the African American youths had recently moved to Denver from the Deep South or were staying with Denver relatives during the summer months. Unfamiliar with Mexicans, some of these youths viewed Chicanos as dark white people. In the summer of 1972, conflict escalated when Chicano youths reported that they had been assaulted or bullied by this particular group of youngsters. The park staff sought them out and told them that both groups suffered discrimination and should get along peacefully. The staff reported that this attempt to forge unity was misinterpreted as weakness and fear. After another run-in with these youths, the Chicanos challenged them to meet them in the park at night to settle matters.

The 20 or so black youths who arrived that night found themselves outnumbered. Shots were exchanged, and one Chicano suffered a minor wound, reportedly from a rifle shot. The Chicano youths had small-caliber pistols and missed their targets in the exchange of gunfire. Representatives of the black youths went to the park the next day saying they wanted to establish a "peace treaty." The Chicanos responded that this was what they had wanted before the violence escalated, but the previous night's incident had changed the situation. A Chicano was shot, while their rivals suffered no injury. The Chicano youths made a counteroffer. Both groups were to show up that night. At the appointed hour of 9 p.m., the black youngsters were told, they must, as a sign of good faith, shoot at the first police car to pass through the area. Chicanos would then join the battle. Sporadic gunfire was heard during the day as Chicano youths shot out street lights. By nightfall two city blocks around the park were in complete darkness. Over a hundred Chicano youths from different barrios gathered in the darkened park.

Police cruised the area, but the 9 p.m. deadline passed without incident. A messenger was sent to inform the African Americans that the Chicanos would wait until 10 p.m. for action to be taken. People with police scanners monitored police communications, so youths in the park were aware that riot-equipped police were congregating four blocks away and that the nearby fire station was in radio communication with the police to report developments. The 10 p.m. deadline also passed. A patrol wagon ventured into the area and was met with gunfire from Chicanos in the park. It quickly retreated. Many volleys of gunfire were then directed at the housing units in the nearby projects where the black youths lived. After 11 p.m. the police marched into the area, but found the park abandoned, thanks to police scanners. No arrests were made. The next day organizers from the Crusade for Justice and the Black Panthers were called in to negotiate an end to the violence, and conflict between the two youth groups ended.

Conflicts at La Raza Park

The takeover of La Raza Park, one year earlier, ignited a political transformation in Denver's Northside. Columbus Park was renamed when Chicanos became the majority population in an area formerly known as Little Italy. Italian Americans were prominent in the Democratic Party apparatus and owned most of the area's small businesses. Among the young activists organizing La Raza Park were Arturo Rodriguez, Antonio Archuleta, and Donny Marquez; many had participated in the school walkouts or gone to the University of Colorado after being recruited by UMAS activists. Returning to the Northside in the summer, these youths began to organize.

Previously, in June 1970 dozens of Northside youths congregated in the park and decided to take down the fence. Police responded. Some determined youngsters jumped into the pool and challenged police to enter the water to make arrests. Rocks and bottles were thrown at police vehicles and the windows of Italian American businesses.

At that time the park's staff would close the pool on the slightest pretext and paid little attention to park upkeep. The restrooms were dirty, and broken glass littered the park and pool. Many youths returned to the park at night to climb the fence and go swimming. Often they cut their hands badly on the dilapidated chainlink fence.

La Raza Park soon became a gathering place for hundreds of youths from all of Denver's barrios. It also became the focus of intense police patrols.[27] Denver police deployed large detachments to the park to arrest youngsters for violating the 11 p.m. park curfew, a curfew seldom enforced previously. Conflicts with police continued into 1971 and were aggravated by the election on June 15 of North Denver tavern-owner Eugene DiManna to the City Council. The Spanish-surnamed vote in District 9, where La Raza Park was located, was split between Hispanic Democratic and Republican candidates in this nominally non-partisan race, allowing DiManna to win over Pete Garcia, a former priest, by 4,339 votes to 4,104. As *El Gallo* later characterized DiManna's victory: "[Hispanic] Republicans and [Hispanic] Democrats . . . were drowning in their slobber and tripping over each other in their mad scramble to get the council seat, [and] become the new token Mexican so they could proudly say they are 'working within the system.' They split the Chicano vote and DiManna walked away with the position."[28]

As tensions mounted with DiManna's election, police began to demonstrate sophisticated tactics that were matched by the increasing militancy of youth and community residents. The Northside substation initially deployed patrolmen from the Northside district to La Raza Park, but youths would draw police units away from the park area by driving through neighborhoods setting off fire alarms. They knew that it was police practice to dispatch a patrol car to accompany firetrucks responding to alarms. With time, however, police from other districts were deployed to the park while Northside police continued their routine patrols. Police formations entered the park at 11 p.m., curfew time, from two or three directions in order to channel the crowd in the direction where other units were stationed to make arrests. Plainclothes officers stood on adjacent blocks while patrol cars slowly cruised the streets during confrontations. The police cars would draw people's attention and give plainclothes officers time to identify ringleaders and coordinate arrests.[29]

Neighborhood activists monitored police scanners, decoded these ploys, and developed countermeasures. Since most police parked their vehicles before entering the park, youths learned to monitor the nearby places that would accommodate a large number of cars. These staging areas included a vacant lot opposite the southwest corner of the park and a restaurant parking lot on 37th Avenue and Navajo Street. The most frequently used staging area was a school parking lot two blocks northeast of the park. Young boys and girls on bicycles cruised these areas and reported police deployments to their older brothers and sisters in the park. Young people would drive long nails through boards, spray them with black paint, and leave them in the alleys the police used to approach the park.

The takeover of La Raza Park was complete by 1971. It was renamed at a "grand opening" organized by the park staff. The celebrations continued every year during the 1970s. The Italian American community, however, viewed the removal of the Columbus Park sign as an insult to Christopher Columbus. While community resentments simmered in North Denver over the summer of 1971, they erupted in gunfire at the close of the season in West Denver.

Gun Battle at the Platte Valley Action Center

The area around the Westridge Housing Projects in West Denver was the scene of a violent clash on August 8, 1971. The Platte Valley Action Center, a social service agency, organized an outdoor fiesta to raise money to build a swimming pool so neighborhood youths would no longer have to walk to Alma Park. Security was provided by Brown Berets from the Northside and East Denver, along with Northside Black Berets. On the last night of the three-day fiesta, near closing time, a white male became involved in a dispute with his Chicana girlfriend. Several young men beat and then stabbed him before the security force intervened. He was taken inside the center and cared for while an ambulance was called.

Police arrived at an intersection that was crowded with people and vehicles. Two plainclothes officers pulled a young man from the crowd to arrest him, claiming he was wanted on an arrest warrant. When the young man resisted, the officers clubbed him into submission while uniformed officers pulled pistols and retrieved shotguns from their cars.

The crowd began to throw rocks and bottles at the police. One officer pulled a small carbine from the trunk of his vehicle and began firing. After the police had fired many rounds, people in the crowd and from the surrounding community engaged police, including some from the Special Services Unit, in a gun battle lasting until 3 a.m., when police were ordered to withdraw from the area. Patrolman Dennis Rice suffered a gunshot wound to the shoulder during the confrontation.

Tomas Rios, 21, and Mike Sanchez, 15, were wounded by police gunfire. Rios said he watched as a policeman took aim and shot him with no provocation. He fell to the ground and lay there until residents were able to remove him to the nearby housing projects. People who came to his aid were shot at by the police. He waited in the projects until an ambulance was finally allowed into the area. Two arteries in his leg were severed; the delay in receiving medical attention almost cost him his leg.[30] Six years later, in 1977, Rios and Sanchez were awarded $70,000 in damages in a civil suit filed initially by attorneys from the Mexican American Legal Defense and Education Fund and concluded by National Lawyers Guild attorneys.

Police Chief George Seaton claimed that the Brown Berets had lured the police into an ambush. Nearly a hundred people who sought refuge in the Action Center building were arrested though most were released without charges. Many reported that the police never returned wrist watches and money taken during their arrests. Over 40 firebombings were reported in seven days, 36 of them in the first four days after the clash. Police responding to firebombings in the Lincoln Housing Projects were met with sniper fire.[31]

"I Want Them Mexicans Out of the Park"

The La Raza Park controversy flared up in March 1972 when park activists demanded the removal of Joe Ciancio, manager of the Denver Parks and Recreation Department. Ciancio had refused to rehire Arturo "Bones" Rodriguez as manager at La Raza Park because of poor attendance. Rodriguez said the decision was "political" and had been engineered by Ciancio and Councilman DiManna.[32] The summer of 1972 saw further disturbances at the park as youngsters were beaten and arrested by police officers who came almost every night to enforce the park curfew. DiManna, who had a police radio in his car and his own code name, Ocean 9, began to order police sweeps in the park. He was present when arrests were made.

On June 27, several people were arrested on curfew violations, and many were beaten. DiManna was reportedly overheard directing the police actions: "I want them Mexicans out of the park and if you have to break heads to do it, then do it." [33] One *El Gallo* article addressed itself to Denver police:

> Attention police department! DiManna has provoked our people into violence and it is you who nightly have to face guns and [fire]bombs because DiManna ordered you to protect his interests. While the Mafia makes money on theft, gambling, and drugs you get shot at. While DiManna has you arresting kids for an 11 p.m. curfew, his friends in organized crime are making their coin in nearby Northside bars in bookkeeping operations and you know which bars these are. We realize you are racist, but the next time you are putting yourself on the line, remember who you are doing it for and who really gains from it. Certainly you don't. We are aiming to control our own community and to clean it up. . . . Think twice, Denver pigs! How does it feel to be the new Mafia hit-men? [34]

El Gallo repeated information from mainstream Denver newspapers about DiManna's links to organized crime figures, employing Mafia stereotypes. DiManna did in fact write letters of recommendation for Robert Woolverton and Mike Pauldino, who had been convicted of burglary. Woolverton, DiManna wrote, was "of good, substantial character." As for Pauldino, DiManna wrote that he had known him "for 30 years. During this period Mr. Pauldino has enjoyed a good reputation and, to my knowledge, is of honest and good character." *El Gallo* pointed out that both men were "recognized by the D. A.'s Organized Crime Unit as associates or belonging to Denver's gambling syndicate." [35]

The June 27 beatings stirred activists to call a press conference to protest against police violence. The conference was attended by Captain Paul Montoya, who headed the Northside police district, and two officers from a nearby police storefront office. One of them, Daril F. (Frank) Cinquanta, would become well known in Denver barrios and activist circles. Montoya told over 200 angry residents that if the park was not cleared by 11 p.m. that night, "then I have my job to do." [36]

Over 500 defiant youths from all the barrios congregated at La Raza Park on June 28 to defy the curfew. When the police formations marched into the park, the youngsters quickly dispersed but then congregated on 38th Avenue on the park's south end and in surrounding side streets. They barraged police cruisers with rocks, bottles, and gunfire in a disturbance lasting an hour and a half. Thirty-one people were arrested, and eight false alarms and five firebombings were reported, including one at the police storefront office on 38th Avenue. The storefront never reopened. One officer was slightly wounded by gunfire.[37]

On July 3, DiManna addressed the City Council. The city administration "put the handcuffs on police and will not let them go in and do their job,—" he complained. He asked the council to give them back "the power to use their badges to enforce law and order, the power to use their clubs to maintain it, and the power to use their guns to protect themselves. . . . It's high time the Council put the pressure on the judicial system and tell the judges we want the laws enforced."

As the conflict grew, La Raza Park activists held community meetings at Our Lady of Guadalupe Church, five blocks from the park. On July 7, José Lara, a long-haired Spanish priest from the church, was invited to a meeting at St. Patrick's Church to discuss the controversy. Present at the meeting were DiManna, Councilman Larry Perry, Lou Sinopoli of the Northside Community Center, and Lt. Les Gebhardt of the police department. When Lara left the meeting, DiManna waylaid him and beat him up. Lara minimized the incident, fearing the anger it would arouse.

The next day 200 protestors marched through the community, pointedly passing DiManna's tavern. DiManna himself appeared at a park meeting, "There will be no changes in the curfew," he said. "There are ordinances, and they will be enforced." DiManna had to be escorted to his car by the Brown Berets. Later that day he reportedly went to the Northside Legal Services office, where young attorneys had been assisting youths arrested in park disturbances, and told the staff, "If anything happens to my business or family, I hold you responsible, and I'll come and get you." He allegedly made it a point to let the staff see a sidearm he was bearing.

On July 10, over 200 people packed the City Council chambers. Angry about rumors of the priest's beating, they demanded a vote of no confidence in DiManna. The council refused. *El Gallo* analyzed this decision:

> [Instead,] the Council appoints another phony, time-wasting study committee to meet with Northside Chicanos. The obvious purpose of the committee is to tie up Chicanos in a merry-go-round of useless meetings from which the committee would write a whitewashed report of the incident or make recommendations that would never be acted on anyway. . . . The committee is to be headed by Larry Perry, a Northside Italian [actually, half-Italian] who was present when DiManna attacked Father Lara. Perry is part of the same Northside business-politician-Mafia group as is DiManna and Joe Ciancio, director of Denver Parks and Recreation. . . . Maybe it's just one of those coincidences. Also on the committee is Councilman Burke who already has stated he backed "DiManna to the hilt." Is this another coincidence?

On July 12, José Lara broke his silence and issued a public statement recounting his assault by DiManna. Activists refused to meet with the City Council committee and, during a July 13 press conference at La Raza Park, declared that they would not recognize the council's authority or intentions. The activists announced a petition drive to recall DiManna and said that "Chicano control over the Chicano community was the only solution."

Though Colorado law provided for the recall of elected officials, no successful recall effort had taken place in the state's history. The La Raza Park Steering Committee, an ad hoc group, spearheaded the effort. Its representatives included Mrs. Ursula Garcia, Santiago Valdez, and Florencio Granado. Recall supporters included the Crusade for Justice, the Brown Berets, UMAS and MEChA chapters, and attorneys Ken Padilla and Ralph Torres of the Mexican American Legal Defense and Education Fund (MALDEF), sometimes assisted by attorney Francisco Martinez.

Resolving Drug "Problems"

Confrontations at La Raza and Mestizo Parks were not always with police. Young activists sometimes clashed with drug dealers over the sale of drugs in the park. Many dealers voluntarily moved their operations. The park staffs opposed the use or sale of hard drugs, especially heroin, having seen its effects on people they knew and the related problems of arrests and imprisonment. The law's harsh penalties and stigmatization made some addicts particularly vulnerable to becoming police informers, and this was an important motive for the antiheroin stance.

Some dealers viewed the parks as their turf, as well. Yet the parks drew hundreds of children, families, adolescents, and adults on a daily basis. Two to three hundred young people could easily be found there on a warm, pleasant evening, strolling, talking, flirting, or lounging on the lawn. Some listened to music, others drank beer, and still others played on the basketball courts or climbed the fence to take a plunge in the pool. It was the community's public ground, defended against police, politicians, and the city bureaucracy. The staff would not let the park become a hard-drug market.

Drugs and weapons were sometimes physically taken from dealers and users. Those who became belligerent and resisted left the park bloodied. On one early occasion several young men were approached when it became known that they were dealing. They apparently had been drinking, too, and when confronted they rallied close to one who acted as their spokesman. He drew a gun from his waistband, and some of his group made motions as though to pull guns on the group that approached them.

They changed their minds when they heard ominous metallic sounds, saw with peripheral vision that a number of hands holding objects were already extended in their direction, and then realized that numerous people who had been casually sitting, strolling, or standing nearby had apparently moved into position around them. The park staffs never called police, preferring to handle their own affairs.

The antidrug attitude was less harsh toward marijuana, about which few people were concerned. Staff members were not to buy, sell, or smoke pot during working hours. What people smoked on their own time was their business; their own time might also include lunch hour or their 15-minute break.

Though both parks were centers of controversy, the fact remained that they were well managed by the activists. Park employees directed youth summer employment programs and cultural events, as well as swimming, softball, volleyball, basketball, and horseshoe tournaments, work that was not called for in their job descriptions. Funds and equipment were begrudgingly made available by the municipal government. Gang activity was not permitted by the staff at either park. In fact, most gangs ceased to exist by the early 1970s, and new ones were not formed. The barrio gang mentality largely disappeared after the 1969 and 1970 school walkouts, as youth activism displaced gangs. Fights in the parks were quickly broken up by the staff and—in many instances—by bystanders, usually other community youths.

People who wanted to fight were told to take their problems elsewhere, and this was usually enough to restore calm. When it was not, it was made clear that continuing a fight would lead to intervention by the activists, who came from the same streets as everyone else. They were not missionaries or do-gooders, and the message was clear: peace would prevail one way or another.

The first two directors at La Raza Park were Antonio Archuleta and Arturo Rodriguez, followed by Tony Marquez, who ran the park for over seven summers. Marquez came from a large family, and his younger brother, Donny, was involved in the original takeover. Marquez was known as "Big T" because he was over six feet tall. Big T was as popular with the Northside residents as he was physically imposing, qualities that served him well in his job. Residents respected him for his deep commitment to the community and its youth. During his tenure at La Raza, the park was a popular place. Most residents of the community were not bothered by these nightly gatherings of young people, who were usually respectful of the area's residents. The conflicts with police enforced community solidarity as the youths and residents rallied to each other's defense. The 1972 effort to recall DiManna further cemented the strong community spirit that marked the history of La Raza Park.

Launching a Recall Election

La Raza Park activists circulated recall petitions against Councilman Di-Manna (the sponsoring signers being Santiago Valdez, Arturo Rodriguez, and David Madrid) and obtained thousands of signatures. Because no previous recall had been successful, the courts had little precedent to guide them. Election Commission President Jim Bayer invalidated the signatures of signers who did not live in District 9, though the recall law did not specify that residency in the district was required. Bayer argued that it was "logical" to invalidate such signatures. "Are we dealing with logic or with the law?" MALDEF attorney Ralph Torres retorted.[38]

DiManna's was largely a North Denver District, but it also included parts of West Denver around the Lincoln housing projects, where various Hispanic Democrats were based, often employed in social service agencies. On June 8, 1973, after La Raza Park activists received an unfavorable court ruling that threatened to derail the recall effort, Richard Castro of the Westside Coalition held a press conference to announce that his organization was considering a recall campaign against DiManna for his abstention on a vote that killed an urban renewal project in the Westside. Some activists suspected that the Westside group was trying to sow seeds where the Northside had plowed the ground, wanting the original recall to fail so that they could launch their own campaign while resentment against DiManna was still high. Any LRUP candidate who entered the race could, ironically, be accused of vote-splitting and dividing the community. The park activists communicated with some of these Democrats in the early stages of the recall, but decided against working with them because they "were ready to run for office, but none of them were ready to do the work"—that is, work for the recall.[39]

The La Raza Park Steering Committee held a press conference on June 12, and Florencio Granado announced, "The La Raza Park Committee will not have another recall. As far as we are concerned, the petitions we have in court are valid and there is no need for another recall."[40] Activists pointedly noted that the press conference was held in the park "because here's where DiManna has no political pull . . . he has no say-so here . . . the people run this park." It was the park activists who were keeping things going on a daily basis at the park and in the Northside. They were also there on a nightly basis when the squad cars and police formations entered the park to enforce curfew. Hispanic Democrats, however, were a rare sight at those times. The remark about "having no say-so" at La Raza Park was not directly solely at DiManna.

The Westside Coalition's recall initiative fizzled, but political rivalry resurfaced when the La Raza Park recall was validated. On April 1, 1974, the Colorado Supreme Court ruled that the Denver Election Commission did not have grounds for rejecting 1,490 recall signatures.[41] The park activists announced no candidacy because the April 1 ruling did not resolve all the legal questions raised, and it was also doubtful that a recall election would be scheduled soon. It was not, and DiManna retained power for nearly three years of his four-year term.

The persistent efforts of the activists, however, resulted in Colorado's first successful recall of an elected official when, in 1975, the courts ruled that all recall requirements had been met. This was a unique accomplishment of the Chicano movement. DiManna lost his seat on the City Council, but now the park activists found themselves confronting a former LRUP member who moved back into North Denver from Montebello, a Denver subdivision, and changed his affiliation to the Democratic Party.

On July 17, 1974, the *Denver Post* reported that Salvadore Carpio, a 1970 LRUP congressional candidate and now a registered Democrat, had announced his candidacy against Eugene DiManna for the council seat for District Nine. His press conference was held at Our Lady of Guadalupe Church, where he was a parishioner. As a Democrat, Carpio would have financing and favorable media coverage that LRUP never had. Further, the community wanted DiManna replaced by a Chicano, but showed no preference for LRUP over a Spanish-surnamed Democrat. Activists felt that the rewards of their victory would now be reaped by those who did not participate in, much less lead, the recall effort.

The conflict with Hispanic Democrats over District Nine was not new but was actually an episode in the long-term rivalry for political leadership between those seeking to bring change through the electoral process and those who believed the system did not work, or did not work for the poor, and who sought social change through pressure politics based in autonomous community organization. The Hispanic Democrats viewed the activists as crude and violent, and the activists viewed the Democrats as naive, weak, or self-interested.

A Headstone for the Grave of La Raza Park

Challenging Carpio put LRUP in an awkward position. It was feared that the media, after the community's long campaign to get rid of DiManna, would portray the contest as a petty power struggle. Not challenging Carpio, however, meant surrendering the victory for which so many had fought. In the spring of 1975, the Denver chapter of LRUP decided to run a candidate against Carpio. After a meeting at the Crusade headquarters, the author became that candidate, in a race that LRUP was not confident of winning but was determined to carry forward. The campaign drew enough votes (15 percent of the total) to deny the top vote-getter, Carpio, a majority and force the mainstream candidates into a run-off election. Carpio won the run-off, but resentment for the role he played led to years of bitterness between the activists and the district's elected representative.

Activists continued to run La Raza Park—to have the "say-so"—until 1982. Though Councilman Carpio represented the district into the mid-1980s, he was never invited to speak in the park, nor was his campaign literature allowed to be posted there. Paul Roybal, a community activist and employee of Servicios de La Raza, a North Denver social service agency, gathered documentation about funds spent in District Nine in 1981. His research on Community Development Act programs located one document showing $5,940,500 allocated for the Northside ("Sunnyside, Jefferson Park, and Highlands" neighborhoods) and the nearby Globeville neighborhood. Not one cent was spent in the Sunnyside neighborhood where La Raza Park was located. The sole paragraph in this financial document underlines the point: "*Sunnyside:* No projects have been funded although a proposal was submitted for Land Acquisition and Park Expansion at La Raza Park—$30,000 but evidently dropped from consideration."[42]

The park's facilities deteriorated to the point that the city could justify closing the swimming pool rather than make costly repairs. The pool was closed permanently after the summer of 1982, when Carpio still represented the district, and was demolished in 1984, when Denver had its first Hispanic mayor, Federico Peña. Promises were made to replace the pool with a better facility at the Aztlan Recreation Center, five blocks from La Raza Park. The new swimming pool was much smaller than the old one, and it was not, as promised, a heated, year-round facility. Though a kiosk constructed in the style of a Mexican pyramid stands on the site of the old pool, critics say it is merely a headstone on the grave of La Raza Park. With no swimming pool and no staff, the park is no longer a popular gathering place, much less a site of political activism.

LADS: POLITICAL ACTIVISM IN THE STATE PRISON

The Latin American Development Society (LADS), a prisoners' self-help group, was formed in the summer of 1969 at the Colorado State Penitentiary in Canon City.[43] This was a unique political development. LADS represented Mexicans, the largest ethnic group in the prison, and exerted considerable influence there. Among LADS leaders were Toby Gallegos, Alfredo "Freddy" Archer, José "Big Joe" Gaitan, Gene Cisneros, Ricardo Librado Mora, Trino Cisneros, Philip "Piccolo" Gonzales, and, in 1974, Lawrence Carbone Pusateri, alias Luis "Tingo" Archuleta. LADS persuaded prison authorities to allow community organizations to enter the prison and establish contacts that would assist parolees in obtaining jobs, counseling, and educational opportunities upon their release.

Rodolfo Gonzales spoke at the first LADS meetings in the prison in June 1969. LADS became a remarkable and highly motivated organization with ties to activist organizations throughout Colorado. Community groups attended LADS meetings in the auditorium at the maximum security facility called "Old Max." LADS developed programs that brought convicts to speak to youth groups and civic organizations throughout the state. It established contacts to sell art work and prison-made crafts and got cultural groups to perform at its meetings. It circulated petitions seeking parole for terminally ill members, sought transfers for young prisoners to the lower-security reformatory at Buena Vista, and mediated racial conflict among convicts, a crucial effort in a prison where Mexicans ("Chicanos" and "Mexicanos") and African Americans made up over 50 percent of the population, and the balance were mostly poor, working-class whites, including some rough characters. It was, after all, a prison.

LADS protected young prisoners from the institution's predatory environment by establishing a committee to greet new inmates upon their release into the prison population. Young prisoners were counseled by the older cons in LADS. Among the LADS subcommittees were the Committee to Assist Young People (CAYP) and the Committee to Assist Youth Understand Drug Abuse (AYUDA). Some LADS members established a security committee known as the "Zapatistas," a group that made notable progress in the daunting task of discouraging the prison commerce in heroin.

Among LADS leaders and members were people convicted for narcotics offenses, armed robbery, homicide, and jewel thefts—yet race riots, drug trafficking, and homicides declined in prison through the effort of LADS and its counterpart, the Black Cultural Development Society (BCDS). At the height of LADS' influence, the group organized a statewide conference behind the walls of Old Max to establish links with outside organizations through a "Concilio de Unidad" on which LADS would have representation. The conference occurred on September 24–25, 1971. Gonzales was the keynote speaker on September 24, and Mrs. Lupe Briseño, who organized women floral workers in Brighton, Colorado, in 1968–69, was the keynote speaker on the 25th. Authorities allowed women prisoners to attend the conference on the second day.

The LADS youth workshop resolution exemplified the conference spirit. "The youth of today are the future of our people and we are committed to them as to ourselves. We are deeply concerned at the extent to which their lives are leading to drugs, crime, and institutionalization and we are committed to changing the conditions that surround and misdirect them."[44]

LADS became influential enough to draw the resentment of the prison guards, who felt, with some justification, that prisoners were running the prison. LADS supporters countered, also with justification, that the prison was run better at the time of LADS dominance than previously (or, it should be noted, subsequently). The influence of LADS and the BCDS declined after November 1971, when prison authorities disbanded the groups and abolished their programs. On November 2, 1971, inmates staged a prison strike, refusing to report for dinner. By the next day, "the strike had spread to 1,023 men which included 686 inmates at the main penitentiary, plus 283 prisoners at the medium security Pre-parole Release Center, six miles west of the prison and 54 prisoners at the . . . Honor Farm."[45] The guards pointed to the strike as proof that the prisoners had too much power. The groups were first restricted, then, over time, disbanded, and the prison returned to the conditions that prevailed before the era of convict activism.

In 1973, José Gaitan, a key LADS leader, orchestrated the release of documents from the prison administration's files. The documents, obtained by convict file-clerks, disclosed that food and supplies meant for prisoners were being diverted to the personal use of the wardens and guards, and that this had gone on under three wardens' administrations. A warden and a captain of guards were convicted of felony offenses stemming from these revelations and given deferred sentences.[46] Could politicians and bureaucrats learn from the LADS experiment with prisoner empowerment? Considering that the incarceration industry grew almost threefold from 1980 to the mid-1990s, it seems doubtful.

Nine

La Raza Unida Party
Fights about Ideology and Structure

The 1972 presidential campaign continued the right-wing shift of national politics. Though the word "Watergate" had no meaning for the public in the early months of 1972, the polarization of society that followed Nixon's 1968 election continued apace. A gathering in California, meanwhile, helped set the stage for a divisive battle over the direction of La Raza Unida Party.

SAN JOSE: THE FIRST NATIONAL CHICANO
POLITICAL CAUCUS

LRUP had grown quickly since 1970, with chapters throughout the Southwest and Midwest. In April 1972, the party showed its potential clout at the First National Chicano Political Caucus, organized by the Mexican American Political Association in San Jose, California. The conference was attended by 800 delegates, including notable grassroots and mainstream political figures like Reies Tijerina, recently paroled from federal prison, and New Mexico's Lieutenant Governor Roberto Mondragon, who called for an end to the Vietnam war and criticized Republicans because they "feather the nest of a few Chicanos and let the rest go to hell."[1] He added that Democrats were not much better.

Spanish-surnamed Republicans and Democrats attended this gathering, but the contest was not between them. LRUP members outnumbered Democrats and Republicans combined two to one. The gathering became polarized when LRUP activists challenged mainstream politics and took over the proceedings. In a stormy opening session, proponents of the independent party pushed for its endorsement. Herman Baca of National City, California, declared, "The only way this caucus will have any rele-

184

vance is by ignoring Democrats and Republicans, and to endorse the concept of La Raza Unida."

Black Berets twice had to restore order on the speakers' platform. The bulk of the delegates later walked out and reconvened in San Jose's Eastside barrio in order to be more accessible to the community. There they endorsed La Raza Unida Party. Professor Carlos Penichet gives an account of the caucus in "Reflections on the Chicano Political Caucus Held in San Jose." Penichet criticized caucus sponsors for their emphasis on inviting politically connected professionals and "bureaucrats in state and Federal government [,causing] a great deal of disgruntlement in many sectors of the Chicano movement and community since the vast majority of the Mexican American population are workers." He acknowledged the lack of structure in the national LRUP, and noted that whatever "form the party will eventually take is not known and must be resolved in the coming months. And the form and tactics it develops will determine its success in the future."[2]

Penichet believed the San Jose gathering was an indication that activist groups were moving to the forefront of community politics because they functioned "on a day-to-day basis at the grassroots level, providing services to the community and organizing effective political lobbies, [unlike] rhetorical, convention calling, self-anointed 'spokesmen' [who spent] most of their time calling meetings and conventions [while] neglecting to actively sustain organizational efforts in the communities." He criticized the "self-annointed 'spokesmen'" for being legitimized "through the media and government agencies, and not by an organization base through the people. This curious paradox is now coming to an end."[3]

THE NATIONAL LA RAZA UNIDA PARTY CONVENTION

"Pragmatism" Versus Idealism

After the April 1972 San Jose Caucus ended, the Crusade and the Colorado LRUP heard of a proposal by José Angel Gutiérrez, founder of MAYO and the Texas LRUP. Gutiérrez had suggested to the San Jose gathering a strategy of negotiating for concessions from the two major parties. He believed that LRUP could, and should, tip the scales in favor of whatever mainstream party offered it the most. This "pragmatist's" strategy clashed with the idealistic vision of the Colorado LRUP. Gutiérrez articulated his position in a letter to the National Chicano Political Caucus:

> We need to keep white America divided evenly between Democrats and Republicans. And, we need to shift our [LRUP] block of votes from elec-

tion to election as needed for the maximum feasible benefit. In 1972, because we do not have a presidential candidate, the Chicano Raza Unida Party will be the balance of power. To Nixon we say, "Show us how badly you want our vote. How about two Chicano Federal Bank Charters for every state that has at least 10,000 Chicanos? How about 100 million dollars in government contracts for Chicano economic enterprises every year? How about fully funded Chicano Universities in every Southwestern state plus Michigan, Illinois, Wisconsin and Ohio? How about 10 million acres of Federal Land in occupied Aztlan?" To the Democratic challenger we intend to demand the same and more. In the event we are ignored by either or both parties, we will vote a straight LRU ticket.[4]

If LRUP was a bargaining chip, the incumbent party, the party in power, had the most to offer. This was the Republican administration of Richard Nixon. The Crusade and the Colorado LRUP criticized that administration for its campaign against political dissidents, for prolonging the Vietnam war while claiming to "Vietnamize" it, and for its appeal to domestic racism and reaction under slogans of "law and order" in the name of a "Silent Majority." The Colorado LRUP saw no way any "deal" could ever be struck with Nixon. A deal with either party, it reasoned, was merely a sellout of the party's independence. The Colorado LRUP felt that the party was for making change, not making deals.

Though LRUP was projected as a national party, the leadership of its state chapters had never met in a nationally sanctioned gathering. There was, in fact, no sanctioning mechanism. LRUP held power in South Texas towns, and chapters were active in the Southwest and Midwest. Because 1972 was a presidential election year, pressure mounted to hold a national gathering, and a party convention was convened by the Texas LRUP that summer. Other state parties anxiously awaited the gathering, to be held in El Paso, because the Texas LRUP strategy proposed in San Jose fueled speculation about the party's future course.

Gutiérrez also sought to implement an alliance between California and Texas chapters in advance of the national convention. These states were home to the largest Mexican populations in the country. "California and Texas undoubtedly are the focus for our national strategy," Gutiérrez wrote. "We must work together for our people. I tried to open a dialogue between all of us in the Raza Unida, primarily between Tejas and Califas. I succeeded only with Southern California and some from the North [of California]."[5] Gutiérrez' limited success could plausibly be credited to many activists' doubts about, or opposition to, the strategy of negotiating with the major parties.

Preparing to counter this strategy at the approaching national convention, the Colorado LRUP met in the Spanish Colony, a barrio of Greeley, Colorado, on August 5. The Colorado LRUP drafted a resolution, which was published in *El Gallo:* "We reaffirm and restate our position as an independent political party, making independent decisions and actions, and not as an endorsing organization." *El Gallo* added the editorial comment that the resolution "was significant because there had been some pre-convention talk that some Raza Unida people were still under the illusion that there were gains to be made 'through the system.'"[6]

The Colorado activists believed that the Texas LRUP had used its contacts to create bogus state chapters in the Midwest and elsewhere in order to stack the convention. They also suspected the Texas of planning to put other states at a disadvantage in the allocation of delegate votes. Two carloads of Colorado activists drove to El Paso for a preconvention meeting to devise the voting formula for state delegates. *El Gallo* explained the issues:

> If delegates were chosen on the basis of [a] state's population alone, bigger states would be in a position to put smaller states at a disadvantage. If delegates were chosen solely on the basis of past La Raza Unida activity then states who hadn't been working on La Raza Unida would be at a disadvantage. Finally, the formula decided upon for choosing delegates was a combination of standards taking into account the state population of Chicanos, the percentage of Chicanos in individual states and consideration for the number of years of known La Raza Unida organizing.[7]

Colorado LRUP members believed that the electoral strategy they favored was at stake, and it was important that they be represented at the preconvention meeting that would set the framework under which the convention would operate.

The Death of Ricardo Falcon

The death of one of Colorado's most promising young leaders stunned the Colorado LRUP delegation. Ricardo Falcon was killed on August 30, while en route to the El Paso preconvention meeting. Falcon was a popular activist who had been involved with the Boulder chapter of UMAS since its 1968 inception. He was especially active in rural northeastern Colorado, but traveled throughout the state, bridging the gap between campus and community activism. He was an adept organizer, whether working with youth or adults, rural or urban activists, intellectuals or working people, and was a fiery speaker with an equally fiery temper.

The car with Falcon stopped repeatedly in the New Mexico desert as its radiator leaked and overheated. Its riders urged those in the other vehicle to proceed to El Paso so the Colorado LRUP would be represented at the meeting. They would arrive later.

The two-car caravan separated near Alamogordo, New Mexico, the lead car passing quickly through Orogrande, New Mexico, to El Paso. The other vehicle stopped in Orogrande to fill the radiator at a filling station owned by Perry Brunson. Brunson was a member of the American Independent Party, founded by the segregationist presidential candidate George Wallace. Brunson told the group not to spray water over the radiator to cool it—he reportedly wanted to charge for the water. Falcon argued with Brunson and followed him into the office, where their argument turned violent.

Four shots were heard, and Falcon's close friend, Florencio Granado, entered the office, where he found the two struggling on the floor. Granado told Falcon to go to the car. Falcon stood up, took a few steps, and fell. He had been shot twice in the chest and died at the scene. His death deprived Colorado of one of its most effective young organizers. His killer was tried for manslaughter and acquitted. The Colorado Chicano movement had its first martyr. He would not be the last.[8]

A National Platform

The convention began in El Paso on September 1. Twenty-five states and Washington, D.C., were represented. The biggest delegations, from Texas, California, and Colorado, had over 300 members each. Gutiérrez was elected chairperson of the tension-filled convention, and delegates held lengthy discussions over planks in the party's platform, lobbied state delegations for votes, and engaged in procedural wrangling. A key procedural disagreement concerned whether state parties would cast their votes as a bloc or would allow minority blocs to cast individual votes. The latter position prevailed 214–201 with the support of the Texas delegates, and state parties were split. The Colorado LRUP continued to cast unanimous votes.

LRUP launched no presidential candidacy under its banner, and the Texas LRUP did not repeat its proposal that the party endorse a Democratic or Republican candidate in a trade for concessions.

The Colorado LRUP had no contingency plan to respond to these circumstances and was thus prevented from implementing its strategy to rally convention delegates around its banner. The national platform that was adopted was a hodge-podge of various state party positions. The underlying ideological conflicts remained unaddressed and unresolved. Tensions continued.

On Sunday, September 3, Gutiérrez and Gonzales were nominated to direct the Congreso de Aztlan, which would convene after the convention ended. The Texas faction again won the vote (256–175) and the bitter rivalry continued, fed by the misconception that the party split was merely a power struggle between two men and their supporters, rather than between related but differing ideologies and strategies.

One account suggests that Gonzales called the national convention in the first place, and some accounts of the El Paso convention state that he hoped to be nominated as LRUP presidential candidate, as though he were some ego-ridden buffoon with laughable personal ambitions. None of these writers, however, cites any primary source, other than interviews, for these assertions. No written documentation is cited because none exists. The initiative to call the conference came from Texas, and Gonzales never wanted to run for president of the United States. The Colorado LRUP never raised this possibility or planned for it.

Just as the lack of political clarity kept any faction of the party from unifying it, similar confusion aborted the establishment of the Congreso de Aztlan. The Congreso de Aztlan was a conceptual congress of the "Chicano nation," of "Aztlan." It would be similar to a government-in-exile in as much as it claimed legitimacy in opposition to the colonizing power that claimed Mexicans as subjects. In this case, however, the Congreso was not in exile but operating in occupied territory. The Congreso de Aztlan was born out of the vision of Rodolfo Gonzales, who proposed it at the 1970 national youth conference in Denver. Initial publicity about the El Paso convention indicated that Gonzales' brainchild would be on the El Paso agenda, but the Colorado activists did not know what the Texas LRUP had in mind regarding it.

On Saturday, September 2, the day before Gutiérrez was elected to direct the Congreso, Gonzales spoke to the national convention. He said, in part:

> The one thing we want to establish is that the Chicano movement— its concept and philosophy of self-determination, of even sovereignty— cannot be prostituted by politics, although [electoral] politics can be incorporated into the Chicano movement. . . . You cannot base any logical argument about the fact that it takes money to free us—it takes people. It takes people in action. . . . [The Congreso de Aztlan], in handling the issues that are necessary for us, would take such positions as making the decision of ridding ourselves of the [military] draft, for taking us out of wars that we didn't make, for becoming allies with Indian nations. . . . To make alliances with emerging peoples, to free colonies like Puerto Rico, to set up cultural, educational relationships with Mexico, Cuba, all of South America.[9]

Neither the Texas LRUP, the Colorado LRUP, nor any other faction completely dominated the politics at the national LRUP convention. It ended on September 4, after four acrimonious days.

In the November 1972 elections, Texas LRUP candidates Ramsey Muñiz and Alma Gonzales received 210,000 and 128,755 votes in their races for governor and lieutenant governor. In Colorado, Mike Montoya won 6,428 votes in his race for the State Board of Regents, Florencio Granado won 22,580 votes for the University of Colorado Board of Regents, and José Gonzales won 18 percent of the vote in a Denver-based race. The national party, however, was disintegrating. LRUP in fact, was less a national party than an umbrella stretched over incompatible groups and ideas.

Unable to resolve the conflicts that had emerged, the El Paso convention delegated responsibility to the Congreso de Aztlan to resolve the party's differences and plot the party's and the Congreso's future. Expecting the Congreso to constitute itself while retroactively putting the LRUP house in order was wishful thinking. The Congreso de Aztlan was misunderstood, or misinterpreted, by those who sought to form it. This was not too surprising, since the Congreso itself did not exist, except, like "Aztlan," as a concept.

The Roots of Divergence

At the 1970 Denver youth conference, enthusiasm for a Chicano party favored the adoption of La Raza Unida as a national party. This decision, however, did not fit the strategy developed for South Texas by MAYO/Texas LRUP activists, as explained in Chapter 6.[10] The Congreso de Aztlan called for at the 1970 conference, as perceived and conceived by Gonzales, was a Chicano people's national congress. It was the Crusade's position that LRUP was merely the electoral vehicle for the Chicano congress; the Congreso itself would decide the party's direction, platform, and so on. This concept subordinated the party to a "congress" that did not yet exist—the Congreso, unlike the party, did not take form after the 1970 conference that called for it. In fact, it never came into being. LRUP, however, did exist, even though its chapters were divergent. Yet the Crusade had great expectations for the Congreso. This vision was as clear for the Crusade for Justice as the Texan view of the party was clear for the Texas LRUP. The visions were also mutually exclusive.

Although the Congreso did not exist, the concept appealed to many activists. It was to be their "congress," as LRUP was to be their "party." Unfortunately, LRUP activists in Colorado, Texas, California, and elsewhere saw how to use the party locally more clearly than how to agree about its national role. The visions of the Congreso were even more divergent. In retrospect, it is easy to argue that appeal was no substitute for clarity. Many of these grand undertakings of the Chicano movement may have been destined to fail at that time. There was no precedent to which activists could look for guidance. Mistakes were inevitable.

The party was a national party in name only and never had a clear, central ideology other than the antiestablishment nationalism prevalent in the movement. It had no central command structure, common revenues, or strategy. In practice, state parties did their own thing in the absence of a unifying structure, strategy, or ideology. Some hoped that the 1972 El Paso convention would resolve these problems and build the necessary party structure, but by then the party's divergences and shortcomings were insurmountable.

Most of the antagonists had probably never fully considered the position(s) of their rivals. The Colorado's LRUP view of the Texas LRUP and Gutiérrez himself was less than charitable. Was there another perspective, maybe valid in its own terms, that needed to be more fully appreciated?

La Raza Unida Party, after all, started in Texas, which was the only place where its candidates were elected. It was the creation of young and committed activists with bases in South Texas, where Mexicans historically were the majority, and was also active in cities like San Antonio and Houston. Many Texas LRUP activists were militants of the Mexican American Youth Organization, whose principal spokesperson and theorist was Gutiérrez. Since MAYO's inception, Gutiérrez' stature as a national leader had grown within the Chicano movement, and his name ranked with those of Tijerina and Gonzales, though he was nearly a generation younger. Gutiérrez was a brilliant tactician and orator, confident and capable of defending his positions. His stature and capabilities made him a formidable opponent.

MAYO and the Texas LRUP, moreover, operated in cowboy conservative Texas, a part of the South and home of the Alamo. MAYO conducted massive school walkouts in South Texas. Its leaders boycotted the Mexican American Affairs Conference in 1967 and participated in the Alianza's 1967 national convention, the 1967 National Conference on New Politics in Chicago, the 1968 Poor People's Campaign, and the 1970 Chicano Moratorium. The Texas activists had a clear vision of what LRUP could do in South Texas: it could win political power in elections. In 1970 they won school board elections in Crystal City and city council elections in three cities.

Their work was impressive, ambitious, and daring. They were also highly pragmatic. By winning office, the Texas LRUP could control taxes, budgets, and public policy. And if this was not social change, what was? Based in the party's birthplace, the only place the party held power, the Texas LRUP could justifiably argue that they had the largest stake in the party's future. The Denver conference that adopted La Raza Unida as a national party in 1970 was a national youth conference, not a national La Raza Unida conference.

Once the youth conference adopted LRUP as a national party, activists returned to their home areas and set about building the party according to local conditions, their own concepts, and their own capabilities, with no national newspaper, no national offices or officers, no national command structure, platform, or strategy. And none ever came to exist. Perhaps it was inevitable that the 1972 national convention would be the rock upon which the party's skeletal structure was shattered. And the growing divisions in the Chicano movement did not end here.

THE CONGRESO ON LAND AND CULTURAL REFORM

Reies Lopez Tijerina appeared at the El Paso convention as a speaker and José Angel Gutiérrez' guest on the platform from which the convention was conducted. Though he belonged to no LRUP chapter, he was a living symbol of the land grant struggle. At the national LRUP convention, Tijerina announced his own "congress"—the Congreso on Land and Cultural Reform—and invited LRUP activists to attend. The event might have gone better for him had some of these activists not attended.

There had been little communication between Gonzales and Tijerina, or the Alianza and the Crusade, since the 1968 Poor People's Campaign. At the National Chicano Political Caucus in San Jose, Tijerina's remarks seemed to indicate approval of presidential candidate George McGovern, whom he described as not "beating around the bush" in his political statements. He also said, "I don't dig the political philosophy of the Third World. We are here. We have what it takes. I don't go for outside ideologies."[11] The first comment suggested that Tijerina became receptive to mainstream politics after his release from prison, and the second bordered on red-baiting.

El Gallo contained nearly four pages of criticism, in English and Spanish, of Tijerina's Congreso on Land and Cultural Reform, held in Albuquerque on October 20–22, 1972. This conference, like the San Jose gathering, was attended by both mainstream politicians and movement militants.

Tijerina's letter of invitation to his "Congress" stated that the gathering would "be the greatest atempt to develop Awareness of Unity and Brother-hood among all the Spanish-speaking organizations and people. So, PLEASE HELP US." Addressed to "Dear Brothers," the invitation read:

> On June 1972, we, (by we I mean all the Spanish-speaking Organizations) got together and for a day, we discussed and agreed to have a

National Congress for Land and Cultural Reform, with "Unity before ideas leaders or Organizations" and with the spirit of Brother-hood Awareness among Chicanos, Mexican Americans, Latin Americans etc. We are all indebted to the Commission of Unity and Brotherhood—to accomplish this, we must rid ourselfs of all envy, jealousy and hate. Our bright age of Science and technological accomplishments is on our side, so it won't be difficult.[12]

Colorado activists did not see how a political movement could exist without ideas, leadership, or organizations to confront the issues of the day. Though the word "unity" appealed to activists, the slogan "Unity before ideas . . ." had no meaning or content. Some statements ("Our bright age of Science and technological accomplishments is on our side, so it won't be difficult") sought to convey optimism but fell short of coherence.

Problems in Albuquerque ranged from a dispute over a mural done by Denver artist Manuel Martinez to ideological conflicts. In his book, *Mi Lucha por la Tierra,* Tijerina recalled:

In the Congress that took place in Albuquerque I realized that our youth, although not all of them, still have a mentality that is conditioned by the education of the Anglosaxon. And in their resentment against the Anglo they have embraced foreign ideologies. Without repudiating the Anglosaxon mentality they have tried to believe in imported ideologies. This has involved them in such confusion that, without knowing it, they serve the Anglo.[13]

Rodolfo Gonzales' pointed critique of the gathering found targets other than the "imported ideologies" of the youth. Gonzales rescinded his earlier promise to attend, citing "commitments here at home and my own uncompromising philosophy." *El Gallo* published Gonzales' letter to Tijerina, which read, in part, "In the past I have disassociated from those people who confuse and mislead, the gullible Government representatives. I want no type of alignment with political prostitutes; I have no intention of creating reaction for the profitable benefit of the professional program managers."[14]

Here Gonzales emphasized his ideology. Ideological differences had to be articulated, considered, and, hopefully, resolved. Though concerns over ideology could result in division, as well as debate, in the ranks of the movement, vague generalities like Tijerina's "Brotherhood Awareness" no longer sufficed to unify activists.

Gonzales also wrote a statement ("Message to El Congreso on Land and Cultural Reform") that was read at Tijerina's gathering by Colorado LRUP representatives. It attacked Tijerina's unity-before-ideas formula by proposing unity "based on ideals and principles." Gonzales typically criticized those who deviated from his ideals by listing their presumed character defects. In his statement Gonzales stressed abstract ideals ("dignity," "equality," "liberation, and freedom," etc.) which he mixed with political criticism aimed in personal terms at unspecified parties to whom he referred as "opportunists, capitalists, promoters, charlatans, demagogues, carpetbaggers, and parasites." In Zapatista-like rhetoric, Gonzales asked (and answered) his own question about the land issue:

> [Who] are the heirs to the land irregardless of patent and title or family claim? We are all heirs, we are all children of the earth, and the land will belong to those who work it and those who fight for it. . . . The struggle for land cannot be for the opportunists and financial gain of a few. The struggle for land must be a people's struggle.[15]

Gonzales felt that Tijerina overemphasized the Treaty of Guadalupe Hidalgo and that his concern over particular land grants detracted from the collective concerns of a conquered people. Near the conclusion of Gonzales' statement, he issued his trademark appeal to idealism by quoting the Mexican radical Ricardo Florez Magon, who said, in Gonzales' paraphrasing, "When I die my enemies will say, 'Here lies a madman.' My friends will say, 'Here lies a dreamer and a fool,' but no one can say that I was a coward or traitor to my ideals and principles."

Gonzales' proclamation to the Albuquerque gathering and his speech at the El Paso convention were full of purist rhetoric and idealism. This, like Tijerina's "Brother-hood Awareness," was not enough to unify the movement. Further, the movement's growing internal contradictions were now compounded by external calamities like the Moratorium violence and the death of figures like Ruben Salazar and Ricardo Falcon.

Gonzales' message at Tijerina's gathering, aside from the personal antipathy it conveyed, was ideologically based. Gonzales' speeches denounced any political strategy that called for collaboration with a political system he viewed as corrupt. He argued for self-determination and the building of mass, autonomous bases from which to wage a struggle for power. Electoral politics, seen from this perspective, was just one arena of struggle, and to believe electoral politics was the sole arena was to dangerously misread the nature of the struggle. The heated rhetoric in the struggle between Texas and Colorado LRUP activists, and Gonzales' scathing criticism of the Tijerina gathering, precluded collaboration between them. It is also likely that by 1972 the momentum behind the divergent visions and strategies had already sealed the party's fate.

THE CONGRESO DE AZTLAN

The Albuquerque Congreso on Land and Cultural Reform was now followed by the Congreso de Aztlan, meeting on Thanksgiving weekend in Albuquerque. The conflicts deferred at the national LRUP convention continued. Colorado delegates were reluctant to accept an agenda prepared by José Angel Gutiérrez. The agenda for the first full day of business was prepared by the Texas LRUP with no input from other states and, among other items, included proposals dealing with the structure of the national party, the establishment of regional offices, and party financing. Discussion of these items was scheduled for 9 a.m. to 5 p.m., and Gutiérrez scheduled a 7 p.m. session to deal with proposals from other state chapters.

Colorado LRUP delegates resented and distrusted Gutiérrez. They felt that accepting the agenda meant yielding the initiative to him and would put the Colorado LRUP at a disadvantage in the political maneuvering at the meeting. Colorado delegates were under no illusion that things would go smoothly. Texas, Colorado, California, Nebraska, Illinois, and other midwestern chapters were present, but many state chapters that participated in the El Paso convention failed to send delegates to the Albuquerque Congreso de Aztlan meeting, depriving the Texas LRUP of the votes they had mustered in El Paso. For their part, the Texans who prepared the Albuquerque agenda and outlined a structure for the Congreso may have resented the fact that work was held up by the resistance of Colorado in conjunction with other state parties.

A bloc formed composed of Colorado, New Mexico, Illinois, Nebraska and some California delegates (the Californians were split between pro- and anti-Texas factions). This bloc, using the voting formula established at the El Paso convention, outvoted Gutiérrez at the Albuquerque meeting. The anti-Texas bloc convened a caucus and worked late into the evening to draw up a unified proposal that was presented the next day. This counterproposal called, among other things, for establishing the party's national headquarters in New Mexico. Gutiérrez charged that this proposal would hamstring his ability to operate as the head of the national party, since he lived in Texas.

Colorado later took the position that Gutiérrez had been "elected Congreso Chairman and National La Raza Unida Convention Chairman (1972) not National La Raza Unida Party Chairman."[16] This was an important distinction for Colorado because it undercut Gutiérrez', authority. The Coloradans may well have been incorrect in this interpretation, and no primary source documentation available to me clarifies this point.

Though Colorado activists had no reservations about making proposals to impede Gutiérrez' ability to function, they were more concerned about the role of the Congreso than about the party. The party could play a role in electoral politics, but the Crusade saw this as playing in an arena controlled by rules and power relationships governed by the status quo.[17] The Crusade's concept of a people's congress would symbolize the sovereignty of the Chicano people and supersede the party. The Crusade and the Colorado LRUP based this position on political workshop resolutions from 1970 Denver youth conference:

1. Begin a nation of Aztlan.
2. Establish an independent La Raza Unida political party with *El Plan Espiritual de Aztlan* as the initial platform with the understanding that the Congress will expand and put forth a more detailed platform. This Party will not be concerned merely with elections, but will work everyday with and for the welfare and needs of our people as directed by the Congress.
3. The Congress and party should first and foremost maintain activities with the U.S.A. and set an example for the rest of the world.
4. The Congress of the nation of Aztlan will be the governing body for the party and will handle all political questions concerning the nation de Aztlan.[18]

Though these resolutions would win no prizes for eloquence, their intent was clear. The Congreso was not limited to an electoral strategy, nor was it an electoral vehicle. The Colorado delegates were unwilling to accept a Congreso de Aztlan that would be subservient to the party. If resolutions adopted in Albuquerque impeded Gutiérrez' momentum, the Colorado representatives felt that they were saving the Congreso from becoming a deformed and reformist mutation of its original conception.

Gutiérrez was angered by his opponents' actions and was unwilling to concede to them. He realized, however, that he did not have the votes as he had in El Paso, and on Sunday, November 26 he returned to Texas. He later wrote: "In Albuquerque we became entangled in fights about ideology and structure. I ended the meeting in Albuquerque and 5 states— Illinois, Nebraska, Colorado, New Mexico, California—capriciously continued on to establish a bureaucratic, hateful and reactionary structure" for the Congreso.[19] He attributed this to his opponents' "complexes of inferiority," and criticized them on other grounds as well:

> In past months we have seen declarations from California and Colorado where they defend the struggle for a free Puerto Rico, for Lucio Cabanas [leader of a guerrilla struggle in southern Mexico], for Angela Davis, for Cuba, for Africa and others. This is fine. It would be better to defend [the struggle] of their own [people] first. Our people want help here and now. . . . My words would be futile for those from these states. But, in

the end, if they want a revolutionary party they should form one. If they want a socialist party they should join those that exist. If they want an international movement they should continue to involve themselves in affairs all over the world. For my part, I have no necessity to continue fighting with them. I will find whom I can work with in these [same] states to see who will have more success.[20]

Having founded the party, Gutiérrez was determined to continue his course. Colorado delegates were equally adamant and refused to recognize "any authority of José A. Gutiérrez to act in the name of 'national' La Raza Unida Party since no consensus of opinion or action exists within La Raza Unida due to the arbitrary action of Gutiérrez during and subsequent to the first Congreso de Aztlan meeting."[21]

The Colorado activists' anger left no room for communication with Gutiérrez, much less for compromise. They were angered by the personal nature of his reproach when he accused Colorado activists of "stupidity and hypocrisy" for having received government monies in their employment while insisting that the party remain free of the taint of government monies. "It is hypocrisy to make declarations and then not abide by them," he wrote.[22] The Coloradans were still angrier about Gutiérrez interpretation of events and positions.

Gutiérrez had not terminated the meeting in Albuquerque; he had walked out on it. He could not adjourn the meeting, since his opponents had the numbers necessary to constitute a quorum and were determined to outvote him whether he stayed or left. Perhaps Gutiérrez did not want to legitimize the proceedings with his presence. He told the Congreso delegates that he had to return to Texas on business and merely asked them to inform him of what transpired after he left. The anti-Texas voting bloc could pass whatever measures they desired based on the "authority" of their voting strength, but they had no way to enforce the vote and no resources to open the "national office" for which they voted. If Gutiérrez picked up his marbles and went home, no real option remained for his opponents except to do the same, but Gutiérrez had more marble with which to play.

Two months later, on January 24, 1973, Gutiérrez sent a letter to Tito Lucero, an Oakland Congreso delegate who was elected as a "national officer" by the anti-Texas LRUP voting bloc:

> Your letter . . . to all Congreso representatives is without any authority. I am advising all Congreso representatives that neither you nor any other "national officer" named in Albuquerque can represent the National Party in any capacity. . . . Your letter writing [as a national officer] makes me waste time and distracts us from the task at hand. I ask you to refrain from further correspondence as a "national officer."[23]

Gutiérrez then wrote another letter to all Congreso representatives, seeking to establish a steady course among those elements under his sway.

> I write you, not to cause alarm, but to caution you against letters coming your way from persons claiming to have positions and authority within our National Party. The last letter I received was from Tito Lucero in Oakland calling himself "vice-chairperson." It seems that after the Congreso meeting in Albuquerque someone held private elections. Disregard these "officers" and their letters.[24]

These communications prompted a response from Bill Gallegos of the Northern California LRUP that was devoid of the rhetoric employed by the Texas and Colorado factions: "The partido is failing to deal effectively and openly with certain basic, legitimate, and very important political differences within the Partido." Gallegos decried the fact that the two principal factions had not clarified what their ideological differences were and noted that "the election for National Chairperson of the Partido . . . was incorrectly viewed by many as a contest based on personalities and not on principle. Vague phrases making reference to 'unity' and 'no compromise' . . . were not adequately explained."[25]

A Colorado Congreso member, the author, also wrote to Gutiérrez referring to him as "highhanded . . . snide and arrogant." In retrospect, it is doubtful that such language permits resolving differences.[26] Though Colorado activists strenuously disagreed with Gutiérrez and the Texas LRUP, Gutiérrez and his allies were as deeply committed to their ideals as Colorado activists were to theirs.

To add fuel to the fire, the Crusade published an article in *El Gallo* that accused Gutiérrez of collaborating with Richard Nixon. The article, reprinted from the *San Antonio Express and News,* read in part:

> Although Raza Unida . . . claims it received no help nor wanted it from the Committee to Re-Elect the President [Richard Nixon], the party's founder did ask for "quiet" Republican help, Senate Watergate Committee files show. The thick files also set out in detail how the committee and White House operatives went about gaining support for President Nixon through grants, promises, and neutralization of La Raza Unida.[27]

The Texas paper pointed out that no proof existed that Gutiérrez received Republican money, but the Crusade was ready to believe the worst about a man for whom it now had an intense and personal dislike. The Crusade and the Colorado LRUP suspected that Gutiérrez had been communicating with Republicans, but had no proof. In 1989 historian Ignacio M. Garcia's *United We Win: The Rise and Fall of La Riza Unida Party* would detail the meetings between the Texas LRUP and the Republicans,[28] but

by that time the Crusade's leadership had itself returned to the ranks of
the Democratic Party.

Colorado and Texas were the main rivals in the struggle over the direction of the party, while other states suffered internal splits. The San Diego
County LRUP portrayed the differences in the most favorable light. In a
newsletter, issued soon after the El Paso convention, a San Diego member wrote:

> Gutiérrez said, "In politics, as in a family, we all argue. It has often been
> told to me that the Raza Unida Convention would result in a fight before
> it got started." He continued, "It hasn't happened, the enemy is not here
> but outside." National unity was emphasized during deliberation and
> discussion of issues. Unity also was stressed during Gutiérrez' election
> when he and Gonzales pledged to maintain a common front regardless
> of the outcome of the vote.[29]

Though greatly impeded by the split, various state parties continued
to meet. A meeting under a LRUP/Congreso banner took place in East
Chicago, Indiana, in September 1973 and was attended by both factions.
Another was held in Crystal City, Texas, and was attended by represen-
tatives from Arizona, California, Illinois, New Mexico, Texas, and
Wisconsin.[30]

The Colorado LRUP called for a National La Raza Unida Congreso
Conference on August 17–19, 1973, in an effort to rally its allies. The
Colorado activists planned to take positions to the left of the Texas party
in hopes that the latter would be seen as reformist by comparison. Colorado LRUP announced, "We will be inviting observers from Movement
organizations in Latin America—particularly PSP (Puerto Rican Socialist
Party), 'El Comite de Lucha' from Mexico, students from Mexico, organizations from Argentina, Bolivia, Colombia, Guatemala, other Latin
American countries, and people from the occupied nation of Aztlan."[31]

This ambitious plan fell far short of its stated goal. The Crusade and
the Colorado LRUP had neither the resources nor the contacts to hold a
gathering of such scope; the plan was impractical and unrealistic. Participants at this gathering included members of the New Mexico LRUP, activists from California and the Midwest, members of the American Indian
Movement, and PSP representatives.

Anxious to form a strong anti-Texas LRUP bloc—and to draw clear
lines on ideology and issues—the Colorado activists, the author notable
among them, were intolerant of any positions that were not supportive
of their own. The conference's seven workshops took positions on issues
ranging from political prisoners to drug trafficking. As happened in many
movement conferences, resolutions were adopted with no mechanism to

implement them. New Mexico activists and others found themselves being shouted down in the workshops. The gathering may well have alienated more people than it attracted. Gonzales later, in internal Crusade meetings, reproached Crusade activists for their behavior.

Juan José Peña, a New Mexico LRUP activist, later wrote of the effect of the division within the party. "[The] Crusade for Justice, the Chicano Rights Organization of San Diego [actually the Committee on Chicano Rights], to name a few of the largest independents, operated without any major communication or work at a national level. . . . The over-all result was that only the hard core remained, and these were badly divided." [32]

Ten

Wounded Knee as a Prelude
The Crusade for Justice and the American Indian Movement

The trend of permissiveness in this country, a trend which Edgar Hoover fought against all his life, a trend which has dangerously eroded our national heritage as a law-abiding people, is being reversed. The American people today are tired of disorder, disruption and disrespect for law. America wants to come back to the law as a way of life.
President Richard Milhous Nixon, May 4, 1972,
eulogy for FBI Director J. Edgar Hoover

At Wounded Knee . . . I saw the Chicano brothers from the state of Washington, from Nebraska, from California, and from other states but, more especially, from Colorado. We received the major supply, the major support from the Chicano. . . . It was at Wounded Knee at this time last year, when Junior Martinez suffered the assassination, we also had assassinations inside Wounded Knee of our warriors Buddy Lamont and Frank Clearwater.
Russell Means, March 17, 1974, First annual commemoration
of the death of Luis "Junior" Martinez

Upon returning from the El Paso LRUP convention, Crusade members turned to the fourth annual Mexican Independence Day walkout and settled into the school-year schedule that became its routine when Escuela Tlatelolco opened. After 1970, the Crusade was obligated to allocate the bulk of its resources to the school, which had an enrollment of over 200 students in September 1972, with many others waiting to enroll.

Though activists considered the El Paso convention a setback for the national party and movement, the Crusade itself was arguably at the peak of its influence. The same was true of the American Indian Movement (AIM), with whose Denver chapter the Crusade maintained communica-

201

tion. The initial leader of Denver AIM was Vernon Bellecourt; other members of the Denver AIM chapter were Rod Skenandore, Chick Ramirez, Jess Large, Vince Harvier, the Lakota elder Alice Blackhorse, and her relatives in the Holy Elk Face, Fobb, and Bordeaux families.

Younger members of the Crusade and the local AIM chapter were friends, and the Crusade endorsed the straggle of native people and hosted their activists at political gatherings and cultural events. Many organizations identified with AIM's struggle, and the mystique of "Aztlan" and the glorification of the mestizaje, or mixed bloodlines, of Mexico predisposed the Chicano movement to look favorably on straggles of native people seeking self-determination.

Though Colorado's only reservations are those of the Nuche (Ute), Denver's urban native population is also composed of Dine (Navajo), Lakota (Sioux), and others from the Great Plains and the Southwest. Many native activists visited Denver and met with the Crusade members in the late 1960s and early 1970s. Among them were Suzette Bridges, Roxanne Allen, Dennis Banks, Leonard Crow Dog, Anna May Aquash, Leonard Peltier, Clyde and Vernon Bellecourt, Thomas Banyacya, Larry Anderson, John Trudell, and Russell Means.

In late 1972 AIM organized the Trail of Broken Treaties, a nationwide caravan to Washington, D.C., to protest against the oppression of native people and dramatize the conditions in which they lived. The protest ended in early November with an "occupation" of the Bureau of Indian Affairs (BIA) headquarters in the nation's capital. When protestors negotiated a settlement with the federal government that involved limited amnesty and $66,500 in travel money, they evacuated the premises and returned home.

This settlement is not what one would expect of a rigid law-and-order administration. November 1972, however, was the month of the presidential elections, and the Nixon-Agnew team would have attracted messy publicity had it loosed its minions upon the impoverished descendants of the people who had been killed and whose lands were taken to build the United States. Instead, Nixon's Department of Justice ordered the FBI to investigate AIM's activities throughout the country, resulting in at least 29 file captions under eight investigative classifications. Though neither AIM nor the Crusade was aware of it, the Crusade's name, those of its associates, and allegations of gun-running were entering FBI files on AIM by January 1973.

THE CRUSADE, WOUNDED KNEE, AND THE FBI

Many of the protestors involved in the BIA takeover converged on South Dakota's Pine Ridge Reservation in late February 1973 at the invitation

of the Oglala Sioux Civil Rights Organization (OSCRO) to assist the Lakota in their protests against the reservation government of Richard
"Dick" Wilson. Protestors, many of them armed, occupied the small
hamlet of Wounded Knee on February 28, and the national media became
riveted to developments on the reservation.

The FBI Special Agent in Charge (SAC) during the confrontation at
Wounded Knee was Joseph H. Trimbach, who relocated to the Pine Ridge
Reservation from the Minneapolis FBI field office in February 1973.
Trimbach, incidentally, had some experience with Chicano activists. It
was Trimbach who while working in FBI headquarters in 1968, ordered
the internal security investigation on the National Brown Beret Organiza-
tion in Los Angeles. With time Trimbach would be joined by SACs from
other field offices: Robert W. Evans (Butte, Montana), Herbert E. Hoxie
(Milwaukee), Richard G. Held (Chicago), and Wilburn K. DeBruler
(Oklahoma City).[1]

Trimbach, moreover, was not the only SAC at Wounded Knee who had
worked in FBI headquarters. SAC DeBruler, in 1969, wrote to the Denver
SAC on Hoover's behalf to chastise him for not promptly submitting reports to Bureau headquarters in a federal antiriot law (ARL) investigation
the FBI was conducting on the Crusade's role in the West High School
protests. It was DeBruler, as well, who wrote on Hoover's behalf to order
the Denver field office to interview Rodolfo Gonzales in an investigation
about the riots at the Democratic National Convention in Chicago, an
investigation that the FBI hoped would snare Gonzales into a conspiracy
indictment.[2] No charges resulted from either investigation, and the Crusade was unaware that the investigations had been conducted.

On March 3, 1973, Lieutenant Colonel Volney Warner, Chief of Staff
for the 82nd Airborne at Ellsworth Air Force Base, arrived in South Dakota and met with SAC Trimbach. The SAC recommended that 2,000
soldiers be used to end the siege, after which the FBI would arrest the
troublemakers. Trimbach's plan was vetoed. Lt. Col. Warner's activities
on the reservation, the use of military airplanes to fly over the area, and
the provision of military supplies to law enforcement bodies were later
found to be in violation of the federal Posse Comitatus Act.

Activists throughout the country made common cause with those at
Wounded Knee. The sight of determined natives bearing arms in defense
of their sovereignty in the face of overwhelming odds stirred Chicano activists. The April 1973 *El Gallo* dedicated one and a half pages to the
protest in South Dakota under the headlines "Hands Off Wounded
Knee" and "Support Indian Rights."

The Crusade monitored media coverage of the occupation and the ma-
neuvers of the federal government. Colorado activists of all colors went to
the Pine Ridge Reservation to participate in the occupation or to smuggle

medicine, blankets, and supplies into Wounded Knee. The Crusade provided cash and supplies to activists heading north to the reservation. Chicanos from Nebraska, Colorado, Washington, and California participated in the occupation. Shortly after the occupation began, the FBI began listening to calls made on the one phone in operation in the occupied site. People in Wounded Knee called the Crusade to ask for assistance and to maintain contact with developments outside the besieged hamlet.

On March 4, attorney William Kunstler arrived in South Dakota to assist AIM and OSCRO. The same day Ralph Erickson, representing the Department of Justice, forwarded a proposal to AIM to end the occupation. AIM spent most of March 5 discussing the proposal before burning it that evening. The government extended its offer to March 6, but no one left the hamlet.

"CHICANOS AND INDIANS AGAINST THE COMMON OPPRESSOR"

When the federal government brought armored personnel carriers (APCs) to the Lakota nation, the Crusade feared that the government would use force to end the occupation. Some Crusade members felt that an attack could be forestalled if activists in urban areas demonstrated to the government that support for the native struggle was not confined to the surrounded hamlet.

AIM was in the forefront of the protest at Wounded Knee, and no group was entitled to displace indigenous leadership on their issue. Accordingly, the Crusade sent a small delegation to the local AIM office on nearby Colfax Avenue to meet with Harold Fobb and other young AIM members and offer to put Crusade resources at AIM's disposal if the Denver chapter called for a solidarity protest. AIM members were left to discuss the idea, and the proposal was accepted.

Hearing this, the Crusade called Puerto Rican contacts in New York City and Chicanos in Los Angeles and New Mexico. Jaime Rodriguez, a California activist in Denver, coordinated communication with Los Angeles activists. Calls were made to Mexico City to see if a protest could be held at the American Embassy. All activities were to take place on March 6 to maximize their impact.

Hundreds of Chicano activists gathered at the Crusade for Justice headquarters on the day of the protest. Several blocks away, at the Indian Center, the Denver AIM chapter began a march of about 200 protestors. When they arrived at the Crusade, they were joined by waiting supporters. The delegation from the Indian Center marched in the middle of the street, passing through two columns of Black Beret and Brown Beret youths who stood in formation on either sides.

Supporters from many backgrounds joined the march as it proceeded down Colfax Avenue. Native people led the way, making a clear statement: there must be justice in America for native people. The marchers arrived at the federal courthouse in downtown Denver; as the local FBI office reported:

> At approximately 1:00 p.m., this date, Mexican Americans and Indians gathered at the Crusade for Justice (CFJ) building, 16th and Downing. They were predominantly a young group including children consisting of numerous members of the CFJ (Denver based Mexican American militant organization). The group marched down Colfax Avenue, approximately one mile to the Denver Federal Building, 19th and Stout, where a rally was held. At this time the group numbered 400 to 500. There were four speakers including Rudolph (Corky) Gonzales, leader of the CFJ, and Ramon Perez, a Mexican American leader in Scottsbluff, Nebraska. All speakers announced their support for the Indians at Wounded Knee and stated that the incident highlights awareness and unity of Chicanos and Indians against the common oppressor. . . . Rally at the Federal Building lasted from 1:45 to 2:45 when at which time [*sic*] the crowd dispersed without incident.[3]

This report was teletyped to the acting director of the FBI, L. Patrick Gray, on March 6. The Denver FBI teletype's opening line shows that the teletype was sent in response to the "Pine Ridge Command Post Telephone Call to Denver, 3/6/73." SAC Trimbach was in charge of the "Pine Ridge Command Post," and no document has yet revealed the nature of the March 6 phone call to the Denver FBI field office.

AIM and the Crusade, by their estimates, had organized a march of over twelve hundred people in four or five days. Phone calls from the Crusade's contacts in other states indicated that protests took place in Los Angeles, New York, and New Mexico, but local media accounts did not reflect this. The Crusade was later told that Mexican students had attempted to hold a protest in front of the American Embassy in Mexico City, but Mexican authorities quickly responded to the embassy and dispersed the protestors. The Crusade received only a few calls from Wounded Knee and, like most of the public, had to follow developments there by reading the newspapers or watching television.

THE FBI AGAINST COMMON PROTESTORS

The FBI, on the other hand, routinely gathered information from over fifty field offices, hundreds of resident agency offices, and legal attaches in various American embassies. These offices generated blizzards of paper reports for Bureau headquarters. Had Crusade members been able to obtain FBI reports on Wounded Knee, which were often highly inaccurate, they would have read the following:

March 5: SAC Trimbach called his superior in Washington, Supervisor R. E. Gebhardt. Trimbach listed three main concerns, the third being that of "other AIM Indians arriving in the area. He has not seen any such arrivals, but this still remains a possibility."[4]

March 6: "Inquiry of an unidentified Indian male . . . revealed there would be approximately 50 AIM members from the Denver chapter who would be traveling to Wounded Knee, South Dakota, and approximately 150 from the San Francisco area on 3/7/73."[5]

March 7: "A source who has furnished reliable information in the past [one line deleted] stated that [AIM leaders] asked the AIM members and supporters at Wounded Knee not to give up hope as help was on the way regarding food, ammunition, and additional people. . . . they talk of having .30 caliber and 20 mm, armor-piercing ammunition."[6]

March 7: "Today SAC Hoxie called. [Government authorities] are preparing an affidavit to obtain a wire tap on the phone in Wounded Knee. . . . apparently the militants are telephoning out for assistance. . . . a Cesna airplane landed . . . on the road [inside Wounded Knee]. Three departed the plane armed with rifles and other material. . . . there is sufficient equipment available for [a wiretap] installation and radio men are available for such installation."[7]

March 8: "Source advised supplies being brought to WK [Wounded Knee] by AIM members and sympathizers under cover of darkness. Source indicated Indians plan to capture an Armored Personnel Carrier. . . . [Several words deleted] advised AIM members are forming units outside the WK perimeter. AIM possibly intercepting law enforcement communications."[8]

March 8: "The . . . marshals on the scene . . . belong to . . . a 'special operations group' . . . and have received extensive special training. . . . the Indians intend to ignore the 6:00 p.m., 3/8/73 deadline and will not come out of Wounded Knee."[9]

March 8: "Mr. Erickson . . . stated the situation was at this time quite grave. . . . It was pointed out to the Department of the Interior that the underlying problem . . . was a national one . . . the Department of the Interior should give consideration to building up the police force of the Bureau of Indian Affairs and in the event trouble broke out in other parts of the country it could be immediately handled."[10]

March 8: "Indians seem resigned and willing to die. . . . [A person in Wounded Knee spoke to others there] in the Sioux language and told them 60 cars from Canada . . . are preparing to move into Wounded Knee. . . . Wounded Knee inhabitants are equipped with AK-47 Chinese Communist rifles. . . . It was believed that there are at least six AK-47's ready [for] use by AIM. . . . The battle was reportedly scheduled for 6:00 p.m. this date on federal positions. . . . the Denver AIM chapter has Aero Commander Executive twin prop plane which . . . will make drop in the next 48 hours. . . . also reported that approximately 1,000 people sympathetic to AIM en route to Pine Ridge and Wounded Knee . . . Denver FBI . . . indicates no such migration. . . . Denver advised they will maintain contacts and advise. . . . Security precautions immediately in force in command post with Bureau agents on electrical power units, Bureau cars, telephone company building and roof of BIA building in which command post is located."[11]

The Crusade had no access to these documents and would have smothered in the blizzard of paper if it had. Though the Crusade heard by phone that its associates in Los Angeles had organized a solidarity protest, the FBI had more details here as well. This is not to say that the FBI knew how to interpret the data, a separate issue. The FBI reported:

On March 6, 1973, at approximately 1:00 p.m., at the Federal Building, 300 North Los Angeles Street, Los Angeles, Special Agents of the FBI observed the following: Approximately 100 people had gathered consisting primarily of Chicanos and American Indians. . . . the demonstration was a result of a coalition of Chicanos and Indians . . . to render support for their brothers at Wounded Knee. . . . On March 7 . . . the crowd peeked [*sic*] at about 75 to 100 people, again consisting primarily of Chicanos and Indians.[12]

The Crusade and Denver AIM, however, would have felt satisfaction had they read part of a March 20, 1973, FBI publication titled *FBI Summary of Extremist Activities,* covering the "Week of March 12–18, 1973." The *Summary* reported, "Some 45 demonstrations in support of AIM were reported around the country in the seven-day period beginning March 5. Most of these were small (the largest was in Denver on March 6 with an estimated 400–500 participants) and were peaceful. . . . Indians, Mexican Americans, and college-aged persons made up the bulk of the demonstrators."

Full coverage of Wounded Knee developments is missing from *El Gallo.* The death of Luis "Junior" Martinez at the hands of Denver police shortly before 1 a.m. on March 17, 1973—ten days and twelve hours after the solidarity protest—diverted the Crusade's attention from the siege at Wounded Knee. The nature of the connection between Wounded Knee and the death of Martinez, however, was something Crusade members would ponder for years to come.

Eleven

Death and Destruction on Downing Street
The March 17 Confrontation

In 1972 the Crusade purchased the Downing Terrace apartment complex adjacent to its 1567 Downing Street headquarters. The ten-unit structure, 1539 to 1547 Downing Street, was directly south of the headquarters and provided low-rent housing to Crusade members and associates. On the evening of March 16, 1973, a party was underway at 1541½ Downing Street to celebrate the birthday of a young tenant. Those attending were from different areas of the city, and many noticed a Denver police car drive slowly and repeatedly down the street while the officers observed the apartment units. Police surveillance of the Crusade headquarters was not uncommon. In this case the driver was a white male and the officer on the passenger side a black female. This was noteworthy because Denver had few minority officers at the time, and black policewomen were a rarity.

As the evening went on, arriving guests said they saw concentrations of police vehicles parked in a few locations in the area. Crusade youths discussed the reports and realized that the Crusade building and the adjacent apartments lay in the middle of a perimeter defined by those locations. Over a hundred people filled the small apartment, and refreshments soon ran out. As midnight approached, some people began to leave the crowded party, but some lingered on the common porch of the 1539–41 Downing St. apartments, in the yard in front of them, or in a parking lot directly across the street, where others loitered or sat in cars. Those on the porch included the author, Luis "Junior" Martinez, and Mario Manuel Vasquez.

The patrol car that had previously passed in front of the apartments was again passing north on Downing Street. A young man whose last

209

name was Mascareñas walked from the front yard into the street where the patrol car was passing. He appeared to argue with the driver and to have been ordered into the vehicle. The young man was from the Westside and was not one of the youth activists at the party. He had drawn attention to himself at the Fishermen's Meeting the previous Wednesday, when he entered the room with some friends who seemed more interested in the young women there than in the politics being discussed. The person addressing the crowd spoke of the need to oppose the use of hard drugs in the community, and Mascareñas made disruptive but inaudible remarks. His friends quieted him before anyone became belligerent, and the group left.

Luis Martinez did not realize that the young man in the patrol car was this person. He stepped off the porch and walked to the street to see why the man had been detained. I tried to call Martinez back, but he did not hear me. I, Mario Vasquez, and another youth walked over to the car, which was stationary in the east lane of the two-lane street.

Arriving at the patrol car, we heard Martinez and the driver, Patrolman Steve Snyder, exchange angry words. In the passenger side sat Patrolwoman Carole Hogue. We interceded in the conversation, hoping to draw Snyder's attention away from Martinez, who stood aside. When asked why he ordered Mascareñas into the patrol car, Snyder claimed the young man had jaywalked, violating a petty ordinance rarely enforced by Denver police, and that we all, by crossing the street, could be subject to the same treatment.[1] Mascareñas sat meekly in the back seat and said nothing.[2]

Angered by Snyder's attitude, we argued that there had been no problems at the party, as he could easily observe, and accused him of being there to start trouble. Hogue sat quietly in the passenger seat. As the conversation became heated, Mascareñas, who had not been frisked or handcuffed,[3] opened the rear door and ran south toward Colfax Avenue.[3] His escape surprised us and seemed to surprise the officers. When Snyder pushed open his door to give chase, he struck Martinez in the groin with the edge of the door, apparently intentionally. Angered, Martinez turned, grabbed the door, and pushed it shut before Snyder could exit. We briefly held the door shut.

I slapped Martinez' shoulder and yelled that we should run back to the apartments. Our group ran to the sidewalk, looked back toward the street, and saw that Martinez still held the car door shut. Snyder pushed his way out of the car and positioned himself between Martinez and us, leaving Martinez no way to pass without physically confronting Snyder, whose hand was on the butt of his revolver. With his way blocked, Martinez backed up into the parking lot of the apartment house across the street, telling Snyder that he did not want problems but would not let himself be arrested.[4] Officer Hogue began to follow on foot. When Snyder turned and told her to return to the car, Martinez whirled, ran east through the parking lot to the alley, turned left, and ran north out of view. Snyder pursued him into the alley.

People on the sidewalk, porch, and lawn in front of the adjoining 1539–41 Downing Street apartments stood transfixed until they saw Patrolwoman Hogue using her police radio to call reinforcements. Police records show that Hogue's radio call was made at 12:44 a.m., March 17. I had run to the porch and shoved people inside, telling them to go upstairs and tell people to leave because there was trouble and police would be coming. While on the porch I heard five shots ring out: three in one burst, a pause, then two louder shots. The shots were fired on the east side of the street, somewhere to the north, but buildings obscured the view.

Officer Hogue set the patrol car in gear and drove into the parking lot toward the alley where Martinez and Snyder had run. As she neared the alley, a young man standing by a pickup truck parked inside the lot near the sidewalk, about 20 to 30 yards behind Hogue, fired two shots at her. Immediately after the second shot, two Special Services Unit (SSU) officers, David Holt and Bruce Tow, turned onto Downing Street and pulled their car to a halt, nearly running into the gunman. Tow and Holt later testified that they saw the shooting when they turned onto Downing Street, and that I was the gunman who had shot at Hogue. I allegedly fled west across Downing Street, at which point Officer Tow shot me. The officers claimed the gunman fell near the sidewalk, got to his feet, ran to the porch at 1539–41 Downing, and was helped into the 1539 Downing apartment.

Sometime after Holt and Tow's arrival, Snyder emerged wounded between the third and fourth buildings north of the lot. Between the time Mascareñas confronted Snyder and Hogue and the time when the gunshots rang out, no more than a few minutes had elapsed, and little more than a minute passed between Hogue's radio call and the arrival of SSU Officers Holt and Tow. They, now joined by Officer Hogue, were fired on by someone shortly after the gunman allegedly entered the apartment. They crouched behind Tow and Holt's car until reinforcements arrived.

In the next few hours, Denver witnessed the bloody, controversial confrontation known to the Chicano community as the "March 17th Confrontation" or the "Saint Patrick's Day Incident."

Luis Martinez, 20 years old, had been killed. His body was found shortly after 1 a.m. at the front of a passageway between 1550 and 1560 Downing. Bricks on the northern wall of the passageway showed the impact of bullets. About 1:15 a.m, nearly 30 minutes after the incident began, I was taken from the apartment at 1543 Downing Street to Denver

General Hospital and treated for a gunshot wound. For some reason Denver newspapers reported that the wound was in the chest, though it was in the back, near the spine, with the bullet partially exiting on the top of the right shoulder. I was charged with first-degree aggravated assault on a police officer, a felony.

Other people were shot and shot at, and one dozen officers were wounded, four by gunshots. One young man with a gunshot wound was found at East Colfax and Clarkson, four blocks west of Downing, but said he had not been at the party.[5] The most seriously wounded officer, Snyder, had been shot in the face, leg, and side.

David Gonzales drove to the scene around 1 a.m. and somehow was able to drive his car into the alley behind, and to the west of, the Crusade apartments. He drove into the yard of the apartments through a gate in the long chainlink fence on the western boundary of the property. He got out of his car but then saw the police in the darkened yard of the apartments as they were entering and searching the 1539 and 1541 units. He got back into his car and tried to back into the alley, but was pulled from the car, handcuffed, and arrested by Officers Monahan, DeBruno, Brady, and others. He reported that he was choked and beaten with nunchaku sticks. The officers said they found two rifles in the car, one on the front floorboard of the vehicle and another on the rear floorboard.

Mario Vasquez was in front of the apartments when Officers Tow and Holt arrived. He said he ran away from the apartments, jumped a fence separating the Crusade apartments from a house directly to the south, and fled west toward the alley. When he found the alley filled with police, he again jumped the fence, this time into the apartments' yard, and made his way to the northernmost second-floor apartment at 1547½ Downing Street. He climbed the back stairs, entered the apartment, and hid in the darkness. Vasquez said he watched from the second-floor kitchen windows as police severely beat young men in the back yard, including his friend David Gonzales.

About one hour later, near 2 a.m., police climbed the outside stairway to a second-story balcony leading to the rear door of the apartment where Vasquez hid. They had searched the other nine units and arrested everyone they encountered. Vasquez' apartment, which he shared with Luis Martinez, was the last unit. Police entered the darkened apartment from the rear outside stairway while others sought entry from the first-floor entrance at the front. Gunshots fired from the darkened apartment wounded Officers Daniel O'Hayre, Eugene Gold, and David Dawkins. As the officers retreated, police fired volleys that shattered all the apartment's windows and riddled the ceiling. After minutes of repeated police gunfire, a tremendous explosion shook the apartment, destroying nearly two-thirds of the northern, wall of the upstairs apartment. Rubble fell on several officers who were crouched between cars parked at the base of the building.

Vasquez was found unconscious in the debris. Police theorized that he, or police gunfire, set off a cache of explosives in the apartment. The Crusade maintained that police fired an explosive device into the apartment's second-floor window. City officials declared that the damaged structure was dangerous, so a wrecking company was called on the afternoon of March 17 to demolish part of the apartment's roof and interior and exterior walls. The demolition made it impossible to determine the cause of the explosion.

Charles Garcia was called to the scene by one of the young party-goers. Around 3 a.m. he was told to leave the area by Detective Pete Diaz, who then kicked him. Luis Ramirez, a middle-aged Crusade member active in the group since the 1966 boycott of the *Rocky Mountain News,* had just arrived and started to accompany Garcia from the area. He said he berated Diaz for kicking Garcia, and Diaz then kicked him. Diaz said Ramirez turned and struck him without provocation. Several officers beat and arrested both men and charged them with assaulting Diaz and Officer Randy K. Sayles. A picture taken of Ramirez the next day shows his shirt stained with dried blood. His profile shows a shaved area on his right scalp where a deep gash is sewn together with stitches.[6] Charges against Garcia were later dropped.

Over 60 people were arrested, and many were beaten. Others arriving later were beaten or arrested as well. Five people were charged, four on felony assault charges, but only four were prosecuted because charges were later dropped against one defendant. The four March 17 defendants were Mario Manuel Vasquez, Luis Ramirez, David Gonzales, and myself. Vasquez and I were released on bonds of $25,000 each, and the others on smaller bonds.

THE MEDIA AND THE MARCH 17 CONFRONTATION

The media devoted great attention to the confrontation, focusing on weapons the police found when they searched the Downing Terrace apartments.

"A Regular Arsenal"

Detective James Jones, along with other police officials, was the source of inaccurate information about these weapons which he described as "a regular arsenal."[7] "One of the weapons was a military M-16 carbine, the latest model used by the military," Jones said.[8] An article from the *Santa Fe New Mexican* also mentioned the M-16, and added; "'More than 30 high powered rifles, many with scopes, were recovered from the apartment,' said Police Captain Robert Shaughnessy. 'There also were sawed-off shotguns, many hand guns, including .44 caliber magnums, and hundreds of rounds of ammunition.'"[9] District 2 Police Captain Doral Smith said the weapons "aren't the type generally used for target practice, but some are high-powered weapons for sniper operations. It's the tactic of revolutionaries to accuse us, to distract attention from the real thing we should be concerned about. Are we going to allow a very small number of revolutionaries to put this city in fear?"[10]

Numerous weapons were found in the 10 apartments, and four were found at 1541½ Downing, where the party had taken place. Nearly two-thirds of the total were found in the two southernmost apartments, and several were found in one apartment whose tenants were not home that evening. The tenant at this apartment was an avid hunter and amateur gunsmith who repaired guns for his friends. Contrary to the statements of Jones, Shaughnessy, and Smith, there were not "more than 30 high-powered rifles," nor were there M-16 assault rifles or .44 caliber magnum handguns in the "arsenal." There was an M-16 assault rifle, but it was apparently a police weapon, though officials denied such weapons were present that night. In fact, Deputy District Attorney William Buckley said, "The only equipment the officers had was shotguns, pistols and a couple of 30–30 rifles."[11] The police never again claimed to have found an M-16 at the scene, and the press stopped mentioning it after the first few days.

A total of 32 firearms were recovered after the confrontation, and eight were reported to be stolen, including Martinez' revolver.[12] Weapons with clear titles were released to their owners. The Crusade said many of the 17 shoulder weapons were harmless props used by the Ballet Chicano de Aztlan, the Crusade's folkloric dance troupe. Though police reported finding many expended bullet shells, implying that the spent shells were fired at police, no evidence showed that any weapons, other than Martinez' and Vasquez', were fired at police. No one was arrested in possession of firearms, although the gun with which the three officers were shot was found in the rubble near Vasquez.

Confusion and Contradictions

The confusion resulting from such incidents, as well as the large number of people involved in this particular one, makes an accurate recounting difficult. The authorities' and civilians' versions contradicted each other and, sometimes, themselves.[13] The public understood the event through the media, which relied heavily on city officials for information. The Crusade was highly critical of the way the local media covered the story. It particularly objected to the media's characterization of the incident (based on a statement by Capt. Doral Smith) as a "spontaneous confrontation" where "one thing led to another."[14]

City officials quickly accepted the police version and found no fault with their actions. Manager of Safety Dan Cronin, who was present at the confrontation, said, "The officers and commanders did an outstanding job. They used a terrific amount of control, and there was none of that deadly cross fire. People ought to be proud of them." Mayor Bill McNichols said the incident "was handled very well [though it] was unfortunate so many policemen were injured."[15] Many high-ranking officials were present at the confrontation. Captain Smith said he was called at home shortly before 1 a.m. and arrived around 1:20. Police Lt. Byrd was already on the scene and briefed Smith, who then ordered the search of the apartments after conferring with Deputy District Attorney Buckley. Buckley reportedly arrived after hearing police broadcasts on his car's police radio. Smith attested to the presence of at least 40 officers and additional command staff.[16] Police Chief Art Dill was present, and District Attorney Dale Tooley arrived shortly after the blast at Vasquez' apartment.

The Crusade criticized the police department and elected officials' remarks at a March 18 press conference at its headquarters. One newspaper wrote that Gonzales said, "'Martinez was murdered and . . . witnesses would be produced to prove it.' No witnesses were produced at the afternoon press conference, however. Rodolfo 'Corky' Gonzales, Crusade chairman, said this was because they first had to consult with their attorneys."[17] *El Gallo* later reported, "The Crusade for Justice now has undisclosed witnesses and evidence that Luis Martinez (Junior) was killed in cold blood."[18]

Though the Crusade never elaborated on this charge, it was based on statements made by a person who was released from jail Saturday night, March 17. This person claimed to have witnessed the death of Luis Martinez from an apartment window, giving an account that contradicted the police version of Martinez' death. The witness was scheduled to make a brief statement at the press conference, but, just before the conference, inexplicably claimed to have seen nothing. Now the person claimed to have made the original statement about witnessing Martinez' death because this was what people wanted to hear. This person's identity and the circumstances of the allegation will be detailed later.

The Crusade charged in its press conference that the police lied about the event. It was not the first or last time that the Crusade made such charges. Many inaccuracies were reported in the media, and it is clear in retrospect that some may have resulted from the confusion surrounding the incident or the newspapers' inclination to scoop their rivals. City officials, moreover, may have wanted to minimize some aspects of an ugly, violent encounter.

Whatever the motivation was, certain figures reported by the media and officialdom proved inaccurate. Thirty-six people were initially reported arrested, but the number was much higher. By April 1, it was finally reported that 58 people were arrested, much closer to the total, which was slightly over 60.[19] The number of police in the area was initially reported to be 60 to 72 officers, but subsequent court documents revealed a total of over 200 officers present on the 1500 block of Downing on March 17.[20] Many police, of course, arrived with the new shift that came on duty about 3 p.m. Numerous accounts, however, remarked on the speed of the police response.

These inaccuracies were not the sole basis for the Crusade's anger and suspicion. The Crusade was angry because the police claimed, and the media dutifully reported, that Luis Martinez, not the man named Mascareñas, was the person who crossed the street to confront Snyder and Hogue, who then ordered Martinez into the car. According to one front-page article, a group crossed the street to the officers' car, but Snyder told them to disperse and they complied. Martinez "then bolted from the police car. Snyder ran after him while [Hogue] called for help on the police radio. . . . [Hogue] then started to run after them, but Snyder told her to go back."[21] This version was repeated for the next 15 days. The Crusade reacted heatedly after the articles were published, stating that Martinez had never been in the police car. These assertions were not published, and it is possible that the media did not believe them.

The newspapers also provided confusing accounts about why Snyder and Hogue were in the area in the first place. The *Rocky Mountain News,* then Denver's morning newspaper, published its first account on the morning of March 17. It reported that Snyder was shot "when answering a disturbance call," and that the "disturbance erupted again when another officer was hit by automatic weapon fire from the roof of 1547 Downing St., according to a radioed call for assistance. Minutes later, officers were hurt in the blast of a bomb hurled near the Crusade for Justice, 1567 Downing St."[22] There was no disturbance call. The reference to a hurled bomb was dropped from subsequent accounts.

Another article reported that Police Chief Art Dill "said Snyder and Policewoman Hogue had parked [on Downing Street] because they could hear loud noises in the area when they issued a speeding ticket nearby a few minutes earlier."[23] This article did not cite sources for all its information, but appears to follow Officer Hogue's two statements given at police headquarters on March 17 and March 18.[24] Her March 17 statement declared:

> Okay, Officer Snyder and myself left headquarters and we drove up to the 1500 block of Downing and parked on the east side of the street, just in front of the parking lot area there, and we were parked there for, maybe, just a minute or two, and a Spanish-American male came across the street and asked us why we were sitting there, and my partner informed him that he was tired of driving.[25]

She claimed Martinez was this person, whom Snyder then ordered into the police car. The statement differed from Snyder's subsequent declaration, nor does it explain why she and Snyder were in the area.

Hogue's five-page typed statement describes how she drove into the parking lot through which Snyder and Martinez ran, heard shots fired and glass break, saw Officers Tow and Holt arrive behind her, and then ran from her car to theirs. She started to look for Snyder and found him wounded: "and he said, 'Carole, the second house, I shot him twice, and I have the gun.' I don't remember, I believe that's all he said to me, 'Call an ambulance,' and an ambulance was already called for."[26] Hogue's written accounts seem to provide the basis for media accounts and statements made by police officials, though there was some confusion about how Snyder was shot. A March 18 article, for example, reported, "Snyder said he had shot Martinez twice and had been shot himself, [Detective Sgt. Jimmy] Jones reported. It hadn't been determined by Saturday whether Snyder was shot by Martinez or someone else, Jones said."[27]

Jones played a prominent role as a police representative over the next days, but some of his statements were confusing. Jones, for example, was the person who reported that police had found "an M-16 rifle," a weapon that would later disappear, though it was shown in two photos as an officer carried it down the back stairs of 1547½ Downing.[28] Another weapon would later appear in two places at the same time, while the police claimed it to be in a third, as will be recounted in the description of the trial in which author was the defendant.

Confusion over the Shootings

The circumstances surrounding the shooting of Snyder and Martinez remained clouded. One newspaper reported, "Because of his face wound, Snyder was unable to speak with investigators Saturday [March 17], and no statement about who shot Martinez was made."[29] Hogue provided no new information about the shooting when the *Denver Post* interviewed her on March 21. "She said she has been instructed not to discuss the weekend incident," the paper reported:

> [Hogue's] career began on June 16, 1972, after she won a compromise law suit against the Denver Police Department through the American Civil Liberties Union. Hogue had charged sexual and racial discrimination against the department when her application for the June [Police] Academy class was first refused. . . . Her supervisor, Capt. Doral Smith, said he was pleased with her performance thus far.[30]

Officer Snyder's Account

On March 29, Denver newspapers reported a new account of the incident after Snyder was interviewed at Denver General Hospital on March 27. The newspapers finally reported that Martinez was not the person in the police car. The reporters did not quote Snyder directly and apparently did not see the transcript of his statement. The transcript gave Snyder's explanation of why he and Hogue were in the area and how the initial confrontation evolved.

> Uh, I'd have to go back about oh, an hour before [the confrontation] happened. We had stopped a traffic violator in the 1500 block on Downing that had made a left turn off of Colfax onto Downing, at which time we got a bunch of mouth from a bunch of kids, a bunch of punks, across the street. We went ahead and wrote the ticket, caught all this flap from them, issued the ticket and left and went to eat. Got done eatin' and I asked Carol what she wanted to do. She said, "Well, let's go and see if our friends are still out there on Downing," so I said, "Okay."[31]

When they returned to the area, Snyder said he parked at the curb across from the party, Mascareñas approached them and said, "You guys don't have to be parked here. We can handle this ourselves. We don't need you guys up here." Snyder asked for the man's identification, but he had none. Snyder told him, "You know you were just jaywalking. Why don't you get in the back seat of the car for a minute?"[32]

According to Snyder, a group of young men approached the car and told him, "'What are you doing with him? How come you're giving him a hard time? It's all right for him to go. He doesn't have to stay here,' and things like that." Then:

> about that time one of them reached back and he opened the back seat, uh, the back door. And this kid, whoever he was in the back seat, I haven't the slightest idea who he was, he started to push the door open, and the kids on the outside started to pull the door open. I reached over the seat to try to hold the door shut, but couldn't. So he got the back

door open, and all of 'em took off west, west across Downing, except for [Martinez who] was standing up a little more towards the front of the front door—the driver's side door, and I started to get out, and [Martinez] kicked the door shut on my leg. Then he took off running east through the parking lot.[33]

Parts of this statement are inaccurate, and the way it was reported compounded the problem. For example, the March 29 *Rocky Mountain News* stated,

The new version of what happened*was provided by Detective Sgt. James C. Jones after he questioned Snyder* [emphasis added] for the first time Tuesday night [March 27]. Snyder, who shot Martinez, has been hospitalized since the incident with three bullet wounds allegedly inflicted by Martinez. A facial wound prevented his talking with detectives until Tuesday. There are no other witnesses to the exchange of gunfire between the two, Jones said . . . according to Jones . . . Snyder opened his door to [chase the fleeing suspect], but Martinez kicked it shut. When Snyder did get out he began chasing Martinez, not the youth who had been in the patrol car. Snyder chased Martinez east through a parking lot to an alley where Martinez then turned and faced Snyder, pointing a gun at the officer, and began to walk backwards north through the alley. Snyder didn't draw his gun, but continued to pursue Martinez about 100 feet down the alley and then down a six-foot-wide passageway which ran west between an apartment building at 1560 Downing St.[34]

Snyder, in reality, never said Martinez drew a gun on him in the alley. He said he chased Martinez through the parking lot to the alley,

and we were about six feet away from each other. We stopped running. He turned around and was facing me. And he was walking backwards down the alley, he says, he kept saying, 'Hey man, I don't want any trouble. Just leave me alone, man. I don't want any trouble.' And every time he would comment something like this I told him, 'Friend, you and I are gonna have a little talk. I'm gonna talk to you.' So we walked down the alley like this for two or three houses, I guess.[35]

Another article inaccurately reported, "One of the persons arrested in the incident, Ernesto Vigil . . . has alleged that Martinez was backing away from Snyder, telling the patrolman he didn't want any hassle, when he was shot."[36] This added to the confusion: no one, the author included, told reporters that they saw Martinez shot. Additionally, the conversation between Snyder and Martinez ("he kept saying, 'Hey man, I don't want any trouble. Just leave me alone, man'") did not take place in the alley, but occurred when Martinez first backed away from Snyder while in the street.

Another article reported that Jones claimed that "police have a witness who saw Martinez backing down the alley, holding something in his hand, with Snyder walking after him. But the witness didn't see the shooting, since it took place between [1550 and 1560 Downing Street]. Jones refused to name the witness."[37] The police never produced the alleged witness.

Reporters were not present when Snyder gave his statement and thought Jones had interviewed Snyder. What the reporters knew, or thought they knew, was based on what Jones told them. There was something they did not know. The interview transcript clearly states: "The following is a list of persons who were present [at the interview]: Steven Snyder, Bonnie Snyder, Detective [R. C.] Callahan, Detective [Thomas] Lohr, Leonard M. Chesler, Bob Sprague."[38] Jones was not present at the interview at all.

The Crusade's attorneys did not receive a copy of Snyder's statement until several months later. No one, therefore, could ask Jones why he credited to Snyder things Snyder never said. In its March 18 press conference, the Crusade criticized public officials for their comments on the confrontation. The media published the criticisms, but wrote nothing about how the confrontation started.

"Snyder's Version Was Confirmed"

The press refused to report the Crusade's assertion that Martinez was never in police custody. Furious, the Crusade turned down subsequent requests for interviews until called by *Rocky Mountain News* reporters who said they wanted to give full coverage to the Crusade version. The Crusade agreed to an interview on the condition that a Chicano report the story.

Reporters Richard O'Reilly and Frank Moya interviewed Gonzales and myself on March 27, several hours before detectives interviewed Snyder. Moya was to write the article; O'Reilly said he was present to assist Moya by taking notes and photographs. We were told that the story would be published on March 28, but it wasn't. Further, when the story appeared on March 29 it was under O'Reilly's byline, not Moya's. Moya was embarrassed and later said he had been shunted aside.

O'Reilly's article devoted 17 paragraphs to Snyder's account and then reported:

> Snyder's version of the incident was confirmed in some respect . . . by a Chicano who witnessed part of it. The man was Ernest Vigil . . . who consented to a partial interview with the *Rocky Mountain News* Tuesday [March 27]. . . . Vigil refused to discuss what he was doing about

the time Policewoman Hogue was fired upon. . . . But he did say he was among the group that walked over to the police car with Martinez near the outset of the incident. . . . Vigil said that when he last saw them, Snyder's gun was still holstered.[39]

The reporters were not told that Snyder's gun was "still holstered," but that Snyder's hand was on its handle as he walked after Martinez, a very different description from the one O'Reilly crafted.

The article said that the Crusade's account confirmed Snyder's version. The opposite was true: Snyder's declaration on the evening of March 27 confirmed what Moya and O'Reilly were told earlier that afternoon and what the Crusade said much earlier—namely, that Martinez had not been in custody. The newspapers, having refused to publish the Crusade's account until March 29, now characterized it as a confirmation of Snyder's.

THE OFFICIAL VERSION

Transcript of Snyder's Declaration

Snyder's declaration was never directly quoted in the media or in court testimony. Snyder said he chased Martinez through the alley, and Martinez then ran through a passageway between 1550 and 1560 Downing Street with Snyder in pursuit.[40] When Snyder emerged through the passageway, he rounded the corner of 1550 Downing and saw Martinez to his left with a drawn gun and "he shot me right at that, at that instant . . . that's the [shot] I got in the side, I think, I'm almost sure it is . . . so I jumped him at this point and was wrestling with him and . . . I don't know if we both went to the ground or not."[41] Snyder's statement makes no further mention of the two men falling to the ground as they struggled, but describes both men struggling while standing. After being shot the first time, Snyder said he struggled with Martinez and was shot again, possibly in the leg.

> Now I could be mistaken about that too. I'm not sure. 'Cause that's a little bit foggy. We wrestled just a little bit more, and I grabbed hold of his hand with my left hand, and grabbed the gun 'cause I had two thoughts in my mind, if I could grab ahold of the cylinder. . . .
> **Detective:** Wait a minute now. You grabbed his left hand?
> **Snyder:** His right hand, the hand he had the gun in . . . we struggled for about . . . three or five seconds more. I tried to get the gun away from him, and I tried to get my own gun out. I, I got my gun out and I was bringing it up towards him just, and it was almost simultaneous timing that I got shot in the head, and then I shot him, within less than a second, I'm sure. . . . And when I fired he, he fell back away from me, and

> as he fell, I, tripped [*sic*] on the gun and I pulled his gun out of his hand. . . .
> Detective: Wu, let's see, did he fire when he fell back? Did he grab the gun? (I??) [*sic*] fell back and you grabbed the gun?
> Snyder: I had ahold of it all the time.
> Detective: Okay.
> Snyder: And, uh, that's [*sic*] all there was to it. I, uh, he fell and I went back out to the street . . . to get some help. I was bleedin' pretty bad.[42]

When Snyder sought help he found Hogue and four SSU Officers (Tow, Holt, Gulliksen, and Iacovetta) by Tow and Holt's car. At least nine other officers soon arrived, including two more SSU Officers, Carpenter and Gray, though it is not clear in which order they arrived. One officer, John Wycoff, reported that Snyder made statements about the shooting and handed him Martinez' gun.

In Snyder's declaration a detective remarked, "You remember a hell of a lot for all that happening." Snyder responded:

> I, I was, oh, no. It's strange, 'cause the whole, even after I'd been hit twice, I was still, though, [*sic*] of what I was doing. Like that gun. I wanted that gun 'cause you see too many times where . . . somethin' like that'll happen, and ten minutes later that gun's never to be seen again. You know, good heavens, it's gone right down the tube. . . .
> Detective: Do you remember who you gave it to?
> Snyder: No, I really don't. I got back to uh, where the cars were and there was some other shooting going on at that time, and, uh, I heard somebody say, "Call an ambulance," and somebody helped lay me down on the sidewalk, and, uh, boy from there on I get real foggy.
> Detective: You told the, they weren't quite sure what you told 'em, you said, "This is the gun that I took from the guy that shot me twice," or "this is the gun that I took from the guy that I shot twice." We weren't quite sure, but you told them this is the gun that you took from the guy.
> Snyder: I don't remember sayin' that.
> Detective: It was, it was, uh, John Wycoff.
> Snyder: I have no idea who it was. I, I was hurtin' quite a bit by then, and, uh, uh . . . I was bleedin' pretty bad, and somebody laid me down there on the sidewalk, and, uh, from then on everything's real, real foggy until the ambulance got there.[43]

After the interviewer confirmed that Martinez was not the person in Snyder's car, Snyder was asked, "Do you know which shot hit him where?"

> Snyder: No I have no idea. I couldn't see a thing, really, by this time.
> Detective: The, the last one when he shot you in the head . . . and you shot him back . . . at the same you were wrestling him, you were almost, he shot you, you was . . .

> Snyder: I had . . . hold of his gun at the time and we were . . . hand to hand together . . . and I got shot the third time, and within less than a second I shot back.
> Detective: Steve, do you know . . . when you were shooting at him, what the angle would be? Was he standing up or down?
> Snyder: I really don't. I think that he was slightly above me. . . . We were face to face, but then I think he was a little above me.
> Detective: I think that's enough . . . you were pretty hazy . . . [44]

Denver detectives prepared for Snyder's interview four days in advance, if only through written communication to each other. On March 23, Detective Lee Williams wrote a note to Detectives Lohr and Diaz:

> Officer Phil Holloway called and stated that Steve Snyder is being represented by Attorney Lyn [*sic*] Chesler and he wants Chesler present when he gives a statement. Chesler states he will make himself available to you day or night. They are not trying to throw any wrench into the machinery but are only concerned about civil liability. [45]

Three days later another note to the homicide night crew stated, "Tomorrow night 3-27-73 at 7:00 p.m. will you call [Leonard] Chesler at 222-2885. He will take you out for coffee and then you can get a statement from Snyder." [46]

"Dr. Ogura Would Like to Know . . . "

On March 27, Detective Jones wrote a note to the homicide unit night crew: "When you talk to Snyder on the Louis Martinez shooting Dr. Ogura [the coroner] would like to know—How close to Martinez he was—Angle—which wound was first?" [47] Detectives Callahan and Lohr made notes during the interview. The notes include the sentence, "We were led to believe that Snyder was unable to speak so a tape was not made. . . . Attorney Chesler had a recorder. He will make available a copy when it is typed." [48]

It is not clear why the detectives believed Snyder could not talk. If they assumed, or were told, that, it would seem pointless to interview him, unless his statement was to be written. The notes between Denver detectives were not released under rules governing disclosure of evidence, but were located in 1990 in the police department's Office of Civil Liability. Detective Jones's note does not specify when Dr. Ogura requested the information. It can be inferred from the note's date, March 27, that at that time, Ogura did not know the angles of the shots and needed answers to the questions in the note.

"Don't Know the Angle . . ."

The detectives who interviewed Snyder returned Jones's note to him with added remarks by one of the detectives. The handwritten remarks state:

> don't know the angle. He had ahold of Martinez's gun when he was shot in the head. He fired back almost simultaneously. Martinez fell backwards, and Snyder fired again. He can't recall which shot hit Martinez where. He seems to think maybe Martinez may have been above him on a step [of the 1550 Downing Street porch] or something.[49]

If the two struggled hand-to-hand as Snyder described, it is conceivable that Snyder's gunshot caused a horizontal wound as the bullet passed through Martinez' body. Martinez had such a wound, a nonfatal wound from a bullet that entered his chest near the right armpit, traveled horizontally from right to left, and exited his back. A horizontal path is also conceivable had Martinez been standing somewhat higher than Snyder. The fatal wound, however, traveled downward from the left of the throat, exited between the shoulders, and traveled from left to right, opposite the nonfatal wound.

DR. OGURA'S PREVIOUS FINDINGS

Dr. Ogura's office released a preliminary report, in the form of a letter, to District Attorney Dale Tooley, who sent a copy to attorney Ken Padilla on March 21, six days before Jones's note questioning the proximity, angle, and sequence of Martinez' wounds. Tooley made the letter public, and Denver newspapers published related articles on March 22 that stated that Ogura had performed the autopsy on Martinez on the day of his death. The *Rocky Mountain News* reported:

> A bullet through the front of the neck killed Luis Martinez . . . early last Saturday, according to George I. Ogura, chief pathologist of the Denver Coroner's Office. . . . Ogura wrote that the neck wound "lacerated the innominate artery and then exited the back. This bullet produced the primary [and fatal] injury. The course of the bullet . . . was downward at a 30-degree angle from the horizontal and from the left to right at a five-degree angle . . . from the anterior-posterior plane of the body." A second bullet wound in the right side of the chest passed through the right upper lobe of the lung and then passed out of the chest through the back. This one produced only minimal injuries to the right lung. This bullet showed a course horizontally through the body and from right to left at a 15-degree angle from the anterior-posterior plane of the body. Ogura listed the cause of death as "Massive internal hemorrhage due to laceration of the innominate artery due to gunshot wound, base of the neck."[50]

Since Ogura already knew the angle of the wounds, it is puzzling to read Jones's note seeking answers to questions already answered. Snyder's interview described the proximity of the men during the struggle and the sequence of the gunshots.

> **Detective:** How far away was he?
> **Snyder:** Uh, six feet, eight feet, that's the one I got in the side, I think, I'm almost sure it is. . . . And as soon as I looked at him he shot. So, I jumped him at this point and was wrestling with him, and. . . . I don't know if we both went to the ground or not. I really don't. But some-where during this brief struggle, which could of only been . . . maybe two or three seconds . . . that's when I got shot the second time, which I think was the one in the leg. Now I could be mistaken about that, too. I'm not sure. 'Cause that's a little bit foggy. We wrestled just a little bit more, and I grabbed hold of his hand with my left hand . . .
> **Detective:** Wait a minute now. You grabbed his left hand?
> **Snyder:** His right hand. I grabbed his right hand, the hand he had the gun in . . . and I tried to get my own gun out. I, I got my gun out and I was bringing it up towards him just, and it was almost simultaneous timing that I got shot in the head, and then I shot him, within less than a second, I'm sure . . . when I fired . . . he fell back away from me, and as he fell, I, tripped on the gun and I pulled his gun out of his hand, and as he was falling back I fired at him again. . . . I fired a second time, yeah, as he was falling away from me.[51]

Dr. Ogura's March 17 autopsy states that "unburned powder granules about the [fatal] wound in the base of the neck would indicate near con-tact with the skin at the time of discharge . . . and impregnation of the underlying soft tissues and musculature about the [nonfatal] right chest wound with dusky gray pigment would [also] indicate a contact type of wound." The report describes "pale gray disc like flakes of powder gran-ules" and "blackened dusky gray amorphous material typical of [gun] powder" in both wounds.[52]

Gunshots at close range can leave gunpowder burns on skin and cloth-ing if the gun is two feet or less from the body, especially when the gun touches, or nearly touches, the victim ("a contact type of wound"). If Martinez was grappling with Snyder at the moment he was shot, as Sny-der described, it is likely that both wounds would have powder burns.

The Contradictory Crime Lab Report

Police crime lab tests conducted on March 21 indicated that only the non-fatal wound showed powder burns. It is not known if Dr. Ogura knew of these test results. They were, however known to police detectives who figured prominently in the March 17 confrontation and its aftermath: Detectives Diaz, Lohr, Callahan, and R. H. Kasperson. Lohr and Callahan, in fact, were the detectives who interviewed Snyder in the hospital.

The test results were reported in a Supplementary Report by the four detectives, which states:

> No bullets were recovered from the body of Martinez. Nitrate tests were run on Martinez's clothing. *The wound to the neck did not show any trace of powder, indicating that the shot was fired at a distance of greater than two feet* [emphasis added]. The wound under the arm [on the right side of Martinez' chest] shows this shot had been fired at a distance of two feet or less.[53]

The fatal wound showed no powder burns, indicative that the fatal shot was fired at a distance greater than that of a hand-to-hand struggle.[54] The authorities were never questioned about this apparent discrepancy.

If Martinez fell back after the first shot, off-balance because of the step and porch behind him, it would seem that his body should have fallen on the porch and would be found with his head to the south. His body reportedly was found on the ground with his head to the north and his feet pointed south. This position was described in Coroner's Office Investigator David A. Livingston's March 17 Investigator's Report Sheet at 1:15 a.m. and is also demonstrated in a crude sketch drawn by Detective Callahan during the hospital interview, dated March 27 at 8:30 p.m., with Callahan's and Lohr's initials and badge numbers written on it. All written police accounts state that Martinez' body was found face up, with one exception. The one exception states that he was found face down and was turned over by an officer who apparently wrote no account of finding the body.

"Several Bruises on Martinez' Arm and Face"

When Snyder's version of events was published on March 29, other articles followed. A March 30 article again reported on Dr. Ogura's autopsy but revealed new data showing that Martinez' blood contained a high level of alcohol. The article reported that

> Martinez suffered two gunshot wounds which had "near contact with the skin at the time of discharge." Both wounds were from the front and exited in the back. The fatal wound was at the base of the neck and lacerated the trachea and innominate artery and fractured the spinal cord [spinal column?]. The other wound was in the right chest. . . . Ogura also reported several bruises on Martinez' arm and face "suggestive of impact with some blunt surface."[55]

Snyder's interview does not indicate that he exchanged blows with Martinez during the struggle. How Martinez sustained several bruises on his arm and face is unknown.

The *Denver Post* reported District Attorney Tooley's reaction to Ogura's autopsy and Snyder's interview: "Dist. Atty. Dale Tooley said the general direction of Martinez' wounds don't [sic] contradict Snyder's statements of the incident. Tooley said . . . he preferred not to comment on it further, pending conclusion of his office's investigation."[56]

The Firearms Work Sheet

Snyder said he thought he was first shot in the side from a distance of 6 to 8 feet. A police lab Firearms Work Sheet that documents the results of tests done on Snyder's clothing, however, reveals a different situation: "[Snyder's] shirt lower left stomach shows that the weapon was fired at a distance of 1 foot or less."[57] The test results seem to contradict Snyder's account of how he was shot.

Gonzales and other Crusade members did not believe the shooting happened as Snyder stated. A few even believed that Snyder did not kill Martinez. Many Crusade members believed that the confrontation was provoked by police as part of a government conspiracy. Admittedly, the Crusade believed in conspiracy theories and made many statements that were considered outrageous. Aside from claiming that police killed members of minority groups without justification, it asserted that the CIA overthrew governments and conducted illegal domestic operations, that J. Edgar Hoover was a vicious racist whose Bureau spied on people illegally and that Richard Nixon was a corrupt politician who abused the power of his office. The conspiracy theory held by some Crusade members about the March 17 confrontation, like the identity of the person who claimed to have witnessed Martinez' death, will be explored later.

When the Crusade defendants came to trial, the belief that police had been deployed in advance did not become an issue. A review of four radio channels that police used showed only routine broadcasts, and the defense attorneys' strategies could only address the elements of the crimes with which the defendants had been charged. Snyder and Hogue did not provide any direct testimony against the defendants. Snyder had been shot by Martinez, but Martinez was now dead, not a defendant. Someone shot at Hogue, but she never claimed to have seen the gunman. The two officers who were most central to the incident played no major role in the subsequent trials.

A FUNERAL IN SAN CRISTOBAL, NUEVO MEXICO

On March 21, Mass was held for Luis Martinez at Our Lady of Guadalupe Church in North Denver. It was estimated that over two thousand people attended the service, and the crowd overflowed into the street. The

Trio Los Alvarados played Mexican music at the church, and Gonzales spoke to the crowd and read a poem he dedicated to Martinez. Martinez' body was taken to the Crusade for Justice headquarters, where a traditional Mexican wake, or velorio, was held. The Ballet Chicano de Aztlan performed a dance that Martinez had choreographed for them. Arturo Ornelas read a poem ("Brother Louie. . . . Remember?") dedicated to Martinez. They had known each other since childhood.

On March 22, a funeral procession involving hundreds of cars proceeded from Our Lady of Guadalupe to Mount Olivet Cemetery, where Gonzales, Santiago Valdez, and Marcos Martinez, Junior's younger brother, addressed the mourners. The procession was held for the benefit of those who could not attend the final interment in the camposanto (literally "holy ground," or cemetery) of the small mountain village of San Cristobal, New Mexico.

On March 23, cars, vans, and the Crusade's school bus drove south over snow-covered mountain passes and arrived at San Cristobal. Martinez had spent summers there and had said that he wanted to be buried in New Mexico. Some of his friends arrived early and dug his grave in the frozen earth. Cleofes Vigil of San Cristobal played traditional penitente music at the funeral, and Jesse Bordeaux, originally from South Dakota's Rosebud Reservation, prayed for Martinez in the Lakota language. Martinez' friends and family then lowered his casket and buried their loved one.

LUIS "JUNIOR" MARTINEZ

Luis Martinez was born on August 21, 1952, to Luis and Anne Martinez. He was one of the most popular of the younger people in the Crusade, and he had decided to make the movement his life. It was young people like Martinez who gave hope to the older activists that the future would be brighter.

He joined the Black Berets in the summer of 1969, joined the Crusade in the fall, and was a member less than four years when he was killed at the age of 20. He said on more than one occasion that he did not expect to live to be an old man and thought he might die a violent death. When he predicted an early death for himself, he did so with a defiant laugh— but it was clearly a laugh.

Though he was usually in high spirits, he, like many others his age, resented the police. As a scrawny youngster he was manhandled by police who did not like his attitude. He found ways to avenge the mistreatment. In his early adolescence, Martinez studied the patrol habits of a particularly unpopular officer, pelted his patrol car with rocks one night, and jeered the officer when he got out to chase him. Martinez was quick-footed and knew the neighborhood's shortcuts, but he let the policeman gain on him until he reached back yard where he knew the darkness hid a clothesline. The officer ran into it at full speed, while Martinez dodged under it and got away.

In the fall of 1969, Martinez spoke at a demonstration at police head-quarters after a fellow Black Beret had been beaten and arrested. Luis Martinez never scrambled for publicity and disliked public speaking. He spoke when he felt moved to speak, and that could not be predicted. At the demonstration he was angered by the smirking officer who com-manded a riot-gear-clad crew at the building entrance. March organizers offered the microphone to anyone who wanted to speak before the dem-onstration ended. Martinez took it and slowly launched into a free-verse poem directed at the command officer while turning to face him. The poem mocked and challenged, but was so hilariously derisive that the crowd laughed, the officer averted his gaze, and his red-faced men squirmed. All who heard Martinez' poem were stunned by the words. Martinez returned the mike and walked into the crowd.

A few months after the demonstration, Martinez and Black Beret Dan Pedraza left the Crusade building shortly before midnight to buy ciga-rettes. When midnight passed, their absence was noted with concern by friends who were partying in the Crusade's lounge. But Martinez was known to go off on adventures when he was having a good time—and he had them frequently. When the two did not appear in the following days, his family and friends called the hospitals and police stations. The police said they had no information.

Martinez and Pedraza, however, had been arrested before they walked a full block that night. Police stopped them and ordered the two to pro-duce identification. As they pulled out their IDs, one officer prodded Mar-tinez in the chest with his club and Martinez protested. The cop then prodded him a second time, and all parties began to fight. When backup patrols arrived, Martinez' hands were cuffed behind his back, and he was put in the back of the car. Martinez, who was very agile, pulled himself into a ball, slid his cuffed wrists down past his feet, and pulled his hands out in front of him. He leaned over the officer seated in front, grabbed the police radio that was attached to the dashboard, and nearly pulled the radio loose. After another struggle and beating, he was again hand-cuffed with his hands behind him, and this time was fastened in the rear seat with the seat belt. The officer in the front seat then began to club Martinez in the stomach, but he tightened his stomach muscles and laughed as the club bounced off. The officer then began punching Marti-nez. He still laughed.

Martinez and Pedraza were taken to the North Denver substation, though they had not been arrested in that district, put in separate cells, and beaten. Martinez was 17 years old and should have been taken to Juvenile Hall, not to jail. At the substation, Martinez locked police out of an office when they left him alone in the room. He said they cursed and threatened him through the door's window when they returned and found themselves locked out.

As they watched, Martinez removed his shoe and pretended to use it to call for help in imitation of Special Agent Maxwell Smart, a character in a popular television comedy whose spy equipment included a "shoe-phone." Martinez put the shoe on when the officers re-entered the office and then wedged himself beneath a desk. He was pulled out by his foot after the officers' initial efforts succeeded only in pulling off his shoe. They then beat him with the shoe. He left jail days later with only one shoe; everyone believed the frustrated cops had taken the shoe to the lab to find the hidden phone.

Luis Martinez was 14 when he was taken to Juvenile Court for minor offenses, facing confinement in a youth facility. Instead, he was sent to a Vermont camp operated by Roderick P. Durkin, who operated a similar facility in Colorado. There Martinez met Puerto Rican, Dominican, and African American youths from New York City. Martinez was dark with high cheekbones, he wore a headband and a short ponytail, and he frequently went bare-chested. The New York youngsters had never met Mexicans and insisted that Martinez must be an Indian, something he took as a high compliment. He liked to walk in the forest to observe wildlife and was especially fascinated by the lively, intelligent, and mischievous raccoons who plundered the camp's supplies and were persistent, inventive, and amusing.

When Martinez was killed, Roderick and Anne Durkin wrote of their love for, and enduring friendship with, this remarkable young man. Roderick Durkin recalled:

> I first met Louis in the summer of 1967 when he attended a summer camp which I started. . . . The camp policy of not using any case history material, probation reports, or school reports in selecting campers was very important for Martinez. I had adopted this policy because professionally I question the accuracy of such material and am acutely aware how often self-fulfilling prophecies are set in motion by it. . . . Perhaps it was this coming with a clean slate that allowed Louis to be himself: a very complex, intelligent, sensitive, thoughtful, and committed person. His refusal to recognize authority unquestioningly was the trait that now seems most prominent and was perhaps his fatal flaw. This persistent trait . . . not mere insolence but combined insight and a disrespect for

pat answers, became obvious early at one of the evening [camp] meet-ings. . . . I and many others had said . . . that physical fighting would not be tolerated because most disagreements are based on misunder-standings that can be resolved by talking them out. . . . Louis raised his hand and asked "Why," if being open and candid with one another is so helpful, "do you have your staff meetings after we have gone to bed?" . . . Louis, in his impertinent way, had taught me, a professional, a valu-able lesson. . . . [In] terms of intelligence and curiosity he was noticeably exceptional. . . . One can only ask how a thoughtful, intelligent, and curious person . . . could go through a school system unnoticed. . . . [He] distrusted arrogant displays of authority and insisted that, as far as he was concerned at least, respect had to be earned and was not auto-matically deserved by those in authority. . . . [The] militant poor are questioning our assumptions about the desirability of the status quo. It is incumbent upon those in power to respond not in terms of personal antagonism, but in terms of the justice of these . . . demands to control . . . their own destinies. . . . Only if there remains the hope that social changes in this direction are possible, can I understand Louis' death, and the many others before his, and the many others to come, as any-thing but tragic and wasteful and bitter.[58]

THE AFTERMATH

In the weeks after March 17, Crusade sympathizers from coast to coast sent messages of condolence and support. A letter and a poem came from the Segregation Unit of the Federal Prison at Marion, Illinois, the prison that replaced Alcatraz. The letter ended with the exhortation, "Adelante Raza, No Hay Diablo Que Nos Rompa!" (Forward people, there is no devil who can break us!). All signers were members of the Movimiento Organizado Socialista Chicano de Aztlan (MOSCA), a prisoners' organi-zation.[59] Though the letters were appreciated, it remained a bleak winter. A bitter cold set in after March, and it snowed into June.

Escuela Tlatelolco continued; it could not stop because of death or trials. Some parents removed their children, and others withdrew from the school's waiting list. Few Crusade members left the organization, and its allies remained supportive, but the Crusade expelled over a dozen members and students in the following year for disciplinary and security reasons.

Property of the Crusade and its members was used to post bond for the Crusade defendants. A grant from the Catholic Church's Campaign for Human Development (CHD) was frozen as the CHD required the Crusade to audit its books and pay the accountants from the grant. Rubble from the bombed apartment unit filled part of the Crusade's parking lot. The tenants moved, and damage to the structure required extensive and costly repairs. The wall of the apartment had been painted with a slogan, in big sprawling letters, from the 1971 Attica prison uprising: "We are not beasts and we do not intend to be beaten or driven as such . . . what has happened here is but the sound before the fury of those who are oppressed." Only six of 10 units remained as apartments, they were never fully rented afterward, and the 1547½ unit was demolished. VISTA dismissed any volunteers who had been arrested during the confrontation. Meanwhile, in Martinez' old Eastside neighborhood, slogans of outrage over his death appeared on walls and in alleys.

LEGAL SUPPORT

Attorneys from the National Lawyers Guild and MALDEF provided the legal defense for the Crusade defendants at no cost. Investigators, photographers, and others reduced their fees. Though arrests and confrontations were frequent in the early 1970s, no defense committee was formalized until after the March 17 confrontation, when the Crusade formed the Denver Chicano Liberation Defense Committee (DCLDC). The Committee continued throughout the 1970s.[60] It found witnesses, printed stationery and mailed defense bulletins, coordinated speaking engagements and meetings for defendants, attorneys, and witnesses, and sought endorsements for its work.

Though lawyers' fees were waived, substantial costs remained. Photographers needed payment for supplies, stenographers had to transcribe court proceedings, subpoenas required fees, bills for long-distance telephone calls and postage mounted, speakers needed travel money, and the Crusade's working-class members lost time from work. Harder to calculate was the cost to the Crusade's image.

On March 6 the Crusade had orchestrated a national and international show of support for its comrades-in-arms in Wounded Knee. Now the Crusade needed a campaign for itself. On April 28, the DCLDC organized a solidarity event at Loreto Heights College, where Angela Davis and Clyde Bellecourt of AIM spoke on behalf of the Crusade defendants. The auditorium was filled with by hundreds of people, who adjourned to the Crusade headquarters for cultural activities after the presentations.

Denver Police Were Fired On

The March 17 defendants appeared in District Court for preliminary hearings in May 1973. In the same month, Eastside residents of the neighborhood where Martinez had been raised petitioned the city to rename St.

Charles Park after him. The petitions were ignored. On May 12, several hundred activists gathered to erect their own sign to rename the park. The police stayed away from the area but watched with binoculars from a distance. They drove into the park later that night and removed the sign.

Activists erected another sign the next day and cemented it into the ground. When police drove into the park that night to remove the sign, their car was hit with sustained gunfire. The officers were not hit, and the snipers escaped. The *Denver Post* reported:

> Denver police were fired on about 11:15 p.m. Sunday as they were removing a sign in St. Charles Park in the 3700 block of Lafayette St., Patrolman Larry Peters reported. . . . Peters estimated 35 to 40 shots were fired at him and Patrolmen Robert Bronough, John Brown, and Patrick Fitzgibbons as Brown and Fitzgibbons were taking down a sign renaming the park for Luis Martinez, 20, a Chicano activist slain in a gun battle between police and Chicanos in the 1500 block of Downing St. Peters said they were fired on by five persons lying behind wooden posts at the rear of 3791 Humboldt St. and two others behind a car there.[61]

It was obvious that March 17, 1973, was a date that would not soon fade from memory, neither in Denver's Chicano community nor among the police.

"Movement People Arrested in 1973"

A June 26 DCLDC letter to supporters listed the names of 15 activists who had been stopped, arrested, harassed, questioned, or followed by police. All were members of the Crusade, Denver AIM, LRUP, the Black Berets, or allied groups. An October *El Gallo* article, headlined "Movement People Arrested in 1973 As Part of Police Harassment," listed 61 activists who had encounters with the police. Of these, 58 were Mexican, three were American Indian, and 15 were women. Another article, headlined "1973 Court Calendar," listed 16 court appearances, scheduled from October 1973 to January 1974, for 24 individuals. Crusade members and Tlatelolco students were heavily represented among those listed.

THE MARCH 17 DEFENDANTS IN COURT

Acquittal of Luis Ramirez

DCLDC's efforts were rewarded on August 20 when a District Court jury found Luis Ramirez not guilty of assaulting Detectives Pete Diaz and Randy Sayles, who worked for the Intelligence Bureau.[62] Ramirez, represented by Leonard Davies, a prominent attorney, had been arrested with

Charles Garcia. The two were charged with assaulting an officer, a charge punishable by a maximum sentence of 10 years imprisonment. The DCLDC felt that the grounds for the charges were flimsy, or fabricated, and stated so well in advance of the trial. *El Gallo* reported:

> Both men arrived at the 1500 block of Downing Street . . . about 2½ hours after the incident began. Ramirez saw Garcia being pushed and kicked by plainclothes detectives Pete Diaz and Randy Sayles. When Ramirez intervened verbally and offered to escort Garcia out of the area, both men were set upon by more than a dozen officers who savagely beat and arrested them. Both required hospital attention. During the [June] preliminary hearing, both officers testified that the defendants had been ordered from the area and appeared to be complying when Ramirez, and then Garcia, abruptly turned and assaulted Detective Diaz for no apparent reason. Both cops denied pushing or kicking Garcia and say there was no excessive force. Neither officer could explain how both men's head [*sic*] were split open. Judge John Quinn, presiding judge in all defendants' trials, ruled that on the basis of the evidence presented there was no reason to have Garcia bound over for trial, since there was serious doubt as to whether Garcia knew that Diaz and Sayles were law officers, there was doubt that Garcia had caused bodily injury to Diaz, and both officers' testimony about Garcia was contradictory. Ramirez, however, was bound over for trial on August 13, 1973. Detective Diaz has been on a 2 year vendetta against Ramirez stemming from a wedding dance incident in which Diaz charged an associate of Ramirez with assault. The young man [an associate of Ramirez] was later acquitted in a trial that made Diaz look very foolish.[63]

The August *El Gallo* that announced Ramirez' acquittal showed him and other defendants standing in front of the apartments where the confrontation occurred. Behind them stands a partially obscured sign painted with the colors of the Mexican flag, an eagle, and "Luis Jr. Martinez." This was the first sign erected at St. Charles Park. The police had hauled it away and stored it in a municipal truckyard. That summer someone saw the sign through an open gate. Activists returned with a truck, drove into the truckyard, loaded the sign, drove off, and erected it.[64]

When Luis Ramirez was acquitted, he stated, "The Denver Chicano Liberation Defense Committee supplied the attorneys and proof needed in my trial, and the [remaining] defendants will also be free when the jury hears and weighs the facts."[65] Ramirez' prediction proved only partially accurate.

Because the details of Mario Manuel Vasquez' trial, conviction, imprisonment, and strange emancipation merit special treatment and attention, discussion of his September 1973 trial will be deferred, and the author's November trial recounted in its place.

Padilla and Gerash for the Defense

Attorneys Ken Padilla and Walter Gerash, long-time associates of the Crusade, with valuable assistance from law student Carlos Vigil, were co-counsel in the author's trial on charges of shooting at Officer Carole Hogue. SSU Officers Bruce Tow and David Holt, purportedly the first officers to respond to Hogue's call for assistance, claimed to have witnessed the shooting when they arrived on the scene. The trial would last two weeks.

An *El Gallo* article by Theresa Romero dedicated half a page to Padilla's courtroom activism. Padilla directed the MALDEF Regional Office from its Denver opening until he went into private practice in 1973. The article listed 18 political cases in which he had been involved, including trials in Colorado, New Mexico, and Nebraska. "Kenny's commitment and dedication in helping our people . . . is a perfect example to our young Chicanos and Chicanas of this great need for abogados del Movimiento Chicano if we, as a people are truly to get justice in a racist courtroom," Romero wrote.[66]

Walter Gerash was born in New York to immigrant Russian Jewish parents. His father was a garment worker, his mother a milliner. His parents and working-class origin were important influences on Gerash, who holds strong socialist views. After military service during World War II, Gerash joined the Labor Youth for Demócracy, a leftist youth group, while attending UCLA. His Denver law career began during the McCarthy era in 1956, when he moved to Colorado in part because California required attorneys to submit to FBI background checks before they could practice law. Gerash, a socialist, civil libertarian, and military veteran, found the procedure repugnant on all counts. Nevertheless, the FBI found Gerash in Denver and questioned him about his politics.

In Denver, he joined the American Civil Liberties Union (ACLU) and the National Lawyers Guild and practiced criminal law. He met Rodolfo Gonzales, who owned a bail bond business at the time, and noted that Gonzales was the only Mexican in that profession. When a Chicano client was convicted in Sterling, Colorado, Gerash discovered that no Spanish-surnamed person had performed jury service there in over eight years. He challenged this exclusion, and Gonzales introduced Gerash to a Chicano professor who could identify Spanish surnames on juror lists. In a case known as in *Montoya v. the People,* the Supreme Court overturned the conviction, the case was retried, the defendant acquitted, and Sterling courts obligated to include the Spanish-surnamed on juries.

Criminal Action No. 69291

Deputy District Attorney John McMullen provided a vigorous but not provocative prosecution in the November 1973 trial in which the author was the defendant. The defense team believed SSU Officer Bruce Tow would be unable to make a positive identification at the preliminary hearing in May, but Tow arrived with an attorney from the District Attorney's office before the hearing and passed the defendant and defense attorneys in the hallway. As Tow and the attorney paused before entering the court, the latter gestured at the defense team, and Tow's eyes turned to examine us. It would have been legally impermissible, of course, for a prosecutor to identify a suspect for the convenience of the prosecution's witness. After examining our group, the two entered the courtroom.

A group of supporters gathered and entered the court with the author and the defense team. The author did not take his seat at the defense table. Instead, Gerash and Padilla requested that the judge allow me to sit with young men of similar age and appearance before Tow was called to testify from the stand. Several young men had already switched articles of clothing, since Tow had seen my clothes moments before; we hoped that the switch would confuse Tow if the attorney from the DA's office had identified me to him. Tow, however, identified me as the gunman and testified that he was positive because the gunman had turned and faced the officers while illuminated in their vehicle's headlights.

I came from the spectators' gallery to the defense table after the identification, and the hearing proceeded. Tow testified that he and Officer Holt were between Pearl and Washington Streets, five and a half blocks west of Downing Street, when they heard Hogue's radio call. They arrived in less than a minute and saw the gunman twice fire a nickel- or chrome-plated revolver at Hogue as the officers stopped their car behind him. The gunman then ran west across Downing. Tow said he fired once at the suspect. The gunman fell to the sidewalk, got to his feet, ran to 1539 Downing, and was helped into the apartment.[67] Tow testified that the officers then ducked behind their car because shots "sounded like and they appeared to be coming from that first apartment [1539 Downing]."[68] Their car was hit once on the left front fender. The judge ruled that the testimony was sufficient to establish probable cause to have the case bound for trial.

The November 12, 1973, trial was in fact preceded by assorted hearings. Gerash and Padilla reviewed the transcripts of these hearings before the trial. On November 8 the following exchange occurred between Deputy District Attorney McMullen and Officer Tow.

Q: Could you describe the defendant as to his appearance when he turned and faced you?

A: Yeah, he was—The best way I could say was that he was startled to see me is the way it appeared. It looked as though I had surprised him.

Q: How about his clothing?

A: As near as I can recall he had on like a brown, leatherish-type jacket, a T-shirt—a white T-shirt—and blue jeans, and brown harness boots.

A: When you say "brown harness boots," can you describe harness boots more fully?

Q: Well, they are similar to a cowboy type boot except the toe of the boot is squared off, and there is a strap that comes around the back and a metal ring that is on each side and down to the heel of the boot.[69]

In this hearing, Tow demonstrated unique powers of recall. His memory improved. He remembered new details at every hearing. The new details, however, sometimes contradicted his earlier testimony, as demonstrated after McMullen concluded his examination and Gerash took up the questioning:

Q: Officer Tow, I believe during your direct and cross-examination as part of the identity prior to the mug shot identity, you stated that the remembrance of the shoes, white T-shirt, and tan leather jacket aided you in fixating [Vigil's] identity?

A: Yes, sir.

Q: Or you recognized that. Now, isn't it true that when you gave testimony in your preliminary examination on May 4, 1973, you were not positive about these things at all?

A: I don't remember.

Q: [Gerash hands Tow the May 4 transcript] Do you remember I asked you this question on page 41, "Question: Did he have on a white T-shirt on? Answer: I don't recall." Do you remember that?

A: Yes, sir.

Q: But now you distinctly recall he had a white T-shirt on; is that correct?

A: I believe so, yes.[70]

Tow was visibly uncomfortable when Gerash handed him the transcript. Page 41 reads:

Q: How was he dressed?

A: As I recall, I believe he had on a brown jacket and blue jeans. . . .

Q: Did he have a white T-shirt?

A: I don't recall.

Q: Did he have a shirt?

A: I don't recall. . . . All I can say positive is that he had blue jeans on, and I looked at his face.[71]

During the May 4 preliminary hearing, Tow testified that I was wearing a brown leather jacket when he saw me shoot at Hogue.[72] I had never owned such a jacket, though I wore one at the May 4 hearing when it was handed to me during the apparel switch.

After Tow identified me in that hearing, I sat with Gerash and Padilla wearing a brown buckskin jacket, which belonged to a young law school graduate, Federico Peña. When that hearing continued, Tow was asked to describe the clothing worn by the gunman on March 17. He looked at me at the defense table, looked under the table where my legs and feet were clearly visible, and then proceeded to describe the clothing I wore that day: a brown leather jacket, blue jeans, boots, etc. Though he remembered new details in subsequent hearings, his testimony about the brown leather jacket never varied. It continued at the trial, which lasted from November 12 to November 23.

Patrolwoman Hogue never testified that she saw a gunman shoot at her, but only that she heard gunfire and shattering glass as she drove through the parking lot toward the alley. A bullet hole was found through the car's rearview mirror on the driver's side. In addition to SSU Officers Tow and Holt, another prosecution witness saw the gunman.

This witness, Richard Coltrane, was a security guard and cab driver. Coltrane's cab was parked at the curb across from the Crusade's apartments, behind Snyder on the east side of the street. His testimony was intended to support the officers' testimony. Coltrane, however, described a gunman younger than myself, and, he continued: "The man I saw was 5 foot, 2 inches." The author is 5 feet, 10 inches tall.

Gerash stood behind my chair, placed his hands on my shoulders, and loudly asked, "Is my client the man you saw?"

"No, sir," Coltrane replied.

SSU Officer Donald Bruce Tow was seated at the prosecution table. He grimaced. Spectators murmured and shifted in their seats. Reporters scribbled in notepads. The jurors exchanged glances. Gerash and Padilla arched their eyebrows. The prosecution's case flew out the window.

Ray Seiber's Testimony

Ray Seiber was another witness for the prosecution. He was flown back to Colorado at the prosecution's expense. He was one of the few whites at the party. He was indoors and did not see the confrontation in the street. When the police came, he ran outside and hid in the street-level apartment at 1543 Downing. I entered this apartment and was later found there by the police. Seiber was arrested and released. He testified that he heard me tell others that I was shot when police fired at the gunman and hit me as the gunman ran toward the porch of 1539–1541 Downing.

Seiber's testimony should not have surprised the prosecution. It is possible, however, that his vague language confused the detective who took his statement (or the District Attorney's staff when they read it). Detective Joe Russell interviewed Seiber on March 17 at 9:30 p.m. The detective's notes show what Seiber told Russell; the author provides the appropriate names after the vague nouns and pronouns: "This party [Vigil] said he was [on] a porch and some guy [the gunman] ran by and a policeman shot at the guy [the gunman] and hit him [Vigil]."

Seiber's testimony contradicted the prosecution, corroborated the defense, and confirmed civilian assertions of indiscriminate police gunfire—assertions the media had refused to report. The cops fired at a gunman as he ran into a crowd, something Tow and Holt repeatedly denied. There was one thing, however, about which the cops were certain. Tow and Holt never wavered about the gunman's identity and his brown leather jacket.

The prosecution's testimony lasted one week. Defense witnesses gave another week of testimony. Ken Padilla called them to the stand. They testified about the author's clothing and gave slightly inconsistent descriptions. One described a dark windbreaker. Another said the jacket was a dark denim "jean jacket." Though descriptions varied, all described a short, dark, cloth jacket.

Other witnesses gave full descriptions, including a yellow, or gold, shirt worn with a brown sweater under the dark jacket. Some witnesses testified that they were on the porch, or near it, and saw the officers drive up and shoot at a young gunman who ran from the other side of the street toward the porch. They testified I was shot when the crowd turned to rush inside as the police shot twice, not once, at the gunman.

One young woman, Karen Gonzales, was present when police entered 1543 Downing and found the author wounded. She described an officer with rosy cheeks. She overheard a command officer ask the officer with rosy cheeks if the wounded man on the bed was the gunman at whom the officer shot. The officer with rosy cheeks said he was not sure. Officer Tow, who had rosy cheeks, blushed when she testified. She recalled something else. Though Officer Rosy Cheeks said he could not identify the author as the gunman, the command officer looked at the author and said, "It's about time we got that son of a bitch."

The Gun That Was in Two Places at Once

Officers Tow and Holt had claimed the gunman fired a nickel- or chrome-plated revolver, but no gun was found when I was arrested. At one point in the trial, detectives went to the prosecutor and claimed to have found a crime lab photograph of such a gun. The photo was shown in the judge's chambers and depicted a chrome-plated revolver lying on clothing in a dresser drawer. The detectives wanted to testify that the photo was taken in the apartment where I was found.

Defense attorneys protested against this attempt to introduce new "evidence." The law required both sides to disclose their witnesses and evidence before trial. Since the photo—and potential police testimony about it—was not made known to the defense, Judge Joseph Quinn agreed with defense objections and rejected the police attempt to enter new "evidence." As Gerash and Padilla strode from the judge's chambers, Gerash growled, "Just look at that gun! Why, it's a 'Saturday Night Special,' a piece of junk! My client wouldn't use such a gun!"

If the photo had been allowed, apartment tenants would have testified that the dresser shown in the photo was their dresser, but they had never seen this gun. The author, moreover, was not arrested in their apartment at 1545 Downing. Further, as the April 1 *Denver Post* reported, 20 weapons were reportedly seized in 1539–39½ Downing Street: the chrome-plated .32 was from this haul. A March 21 inventory by Detective John Pinder listed the chrome-plated Young American .32 caliber revolver among 20 weapons placed in the police custodian's office by Officers V. Norton and Richard Pringle. Pinder's inventory, too, suggests that the 20 weapons were found at 1539–39½ Downing, south of the apartment where I was arrested.[73] The .32 chrome revolver was either in a dresser drawer in an apartment north of where I was arrested or among weapons taken from apartments to the south, as shown in Pinder's inventory. If the photo and inventory were both accurate, the gun was obviously in two places at once.

The defense could not ask who found it, or where, when, and how it was found. The law is a double-edge sword. Because Judge Quinn ruled that the prosecution could not use the photo of the gun, the defense could not refer to it either. Listed on an inventory and photographed in a drawer, the gun was in two places at once—but not three. Denver police could not credibly establish that any guns were found at 1543 Downing (except for those in the hands or holsters of the police who entered the apartment that night).

Bloody Clothing and Leather Jackets

It seemed apparent in the last days of the trial that police had either charged the wrong person or could not prove their case. Further, though no one realized it, Gerash and Padilla had more nails for the coffin where the prosecution's case rested. The key evidence in the case was the clothing worn by the author on March 17. After I was shot and fled to the apartment at 1543 Downing, people there assisted me in removing some clothing in order to apply a cold compress to stop the bleeding. There was no ice in the refrigerator, so a frozen chicken was pressed on the wound.

The clothing was thrown onto the floor in a pile, where it lay unnoticed when officers later entered, ransacked the apartment, and tossed things around, some of which fell on the clothing. During the trial, the prosecution introduced photos of the apartment. One shows a defrosted chicken on the floor. After my release from jail, the apartment's tenants found the clothing and returned it. It was stored in plastic in a garage for eight months and turned moldy and foul-smelling. A dark blue windbreaker was the only piece of clothing not stored in the garage. It had been washed and the bullet hole covered with a small Mexican flag. I continued to wear the jacket.

When Tow claimed in the May 4 hearing that I wore a leather jacket, I told Padilla and Gerash what I wore on the night of the confrontation. I may have failed to emphasize that I still had the clothing, and no one asked me where it was. I mentioned it again in the second week of the trial, and Gerash and Padilla, a team few would describe as placid, became highly agitated. The attorneys knew, as I did not, that the defense is also bound by the rules of discovery. The judge ruled against the gun-in-a-drawer photo because the prosecution had not disclosed it to defense attorneys in a timely manner. The law required that the prosecution be told that I had the bloody undershirt, sport shirt, sweater, and jacket with a hole. The clothing was crucial to the defense, but now it could have been excluded. Contrary to our expectation, however McMullen did not object to the new evidence.

Almost weirdly, brown leather jackets were mentioned by many witnesses. Luis Martinez wore a leather jacket that night. Clyde Martinez wore a light-colored suede jacket. Ironically, Clyde Martinez' testimony was needed to confirm what the author wore that evening. We had never met until that night, and Clyde was driving to the party with a friend who knew me. They gave me a ride when they saw me walking. Clyde remembered what I wore: jeans, windbreaker, etc. Reporter Richard O'Reilly wrote:

> Another youth, Clyde Martinez told of being found by the police hiding from the shooting in a closet at 1539 Downing St. and being accused of being the gunman. He was jailed, and policemen tried to beat a confession out of him before he was released, Martinez said. Police officers testified they went into 1539 Downing Street and found Vigil only after an ambulance was called for him at 1543 Downing St.[74]

Nearly nine months to the day after O'Reilly wrote the first article revealing that Luis Martinez was never in Snyder's custody—a tardy revelation, since the Crusade had repeatedly told the media this—O'Reilly now reported the disintegration of police testimony and the prosecution's case.

> Several jurors said afterward they felt the state was unable at any point in the two-week trial to make a case against Vigil. . . . Jury foreman Mike Williams . . . said the deliberation took only 30 seconds. The rest of the 14 minutes the jury was out was spent in rest-room visits and choosing a [jury] foreman, he said. . . . Dist. Judge Joseph R. Quinn denied a defense motion for a judgement of acquittal at the end of prosecution testimony. But when the defense renewed its motion after its own case had been presented, Quinn postponed his ruling until after the jury's verdict, thus revealing doubts in his own mind about whether the prosecution had made a case. Indeed, Deputy Dist. Atty. John McMullen appeared to have his own doubts that Vigil was the right man when he addressed the jury briefly in closing arguments. . . . McMullen merely told the jurors, "I'm sure you will reach a fair and just verdict, and that's all we seek." . . . . Tow and Holt both identified Vigil as the gunman. They said he was wearing an unbuttoned brown leather jacket with a white T-shirt beneath. . . . The strongest defense testimony centered on the clothing he wore that night, which was introduced as evidence. The blood-stained tank-style undershirt, bright yellow sport shirt, and green-gold pullover sweater were convincing arguments that Vigil wasn't the gunman in the white T-shirt. Also introduced as evidence was a navy blue jacket with a bullet hole in the back, which Vigil said he was wearing that night. . . . The clothing caught McMullen by surprise. He said later that had he known of it, the charge against Vigil might well have been dropped.[75]

The trials were not reported with sensational headlines, and the newspapers paid less attention to the trials than they did to the initial incident, described by Captain Smith as a "spontaneous confrontation" in which "one thing led to another."[76] The Crusade and its supporters, on the contrary, assumed that Wounded Knee was a factor in the equation. Before that assumption can be examined, the deferred narrative of Mario Manuel Vasquez will be recounted.

MARIO MANUEL VASQUEZ: TRIAL, CONVICTION, AND LIBERATION

Mario Manuel Vasquez, a former college student, came to Denver from Michigan in 1971. He lived on low-paying job, as did many young people who took to the road, drawn by the adventure and mystique of the Chicano movement. He attended political meetings and events but was not noted for his work or leadership. He was more a footloose camp-follower who spent time at parties and socializing with activists. To help him out, Martinez invited Vasquez to share accommodations and rent at Martinez' 1547½ Downing Street apartment.

Vasquez, 20 years old, was the youngest defendant. He was arrested when three policemen, Officers O'Hayre, Dawkins, and Gold, were shot after they entered the back door of his upstairs apartment shortly after 2 a.m. The apartment was the last to be searched. The three officers entered the darkened apartment while others tried to enter the first-floor, front stairway ascending to it. The three were hit by gunfire from the interior and retreated outside and down the stairs. Police fired massive volleys of gunfire into the apartment. An explosion blew out its northern wall, and Vasquez was found in the rubble. The gun with which the police were shot was found nearby. It showed no fingerprints, and a paraffin test later administered to Vasquez proved negative.

The Trial

Vasquez was defended by Leonard Davies. The prosecution had to prove beyond a reasonable doubt that Vasquez, and no one else, shot the officers. One prosecution witness testified that he thought he saw someone peer from a small attic window above Vasquez' apartment, so the possibility existed that the officers were shot by someone who fled through a crawl space to adjoining attics before the explosion and escaped in the subsequent confusion. The police and prosecutors did not know that a crawl space ran the length of the apartment building. Not all second-floor apartments had a trap door allowing access to the crawl space, but Vasquez' apartment did.

After the witness testified about the face in the attic window, the prosecutor called three additional police witnesses who testified that they had searched the attic two hours after Vasquez was arrested. One officer said he searched the attic by entering it from 1545½ Downing but found no one. This must have been difficult, since the 1545½ Downing apartment had no trap door to the attic. Another officer testified that he examined the crawl space and found that a brick partition made it impossible for someone to escape from one unit to another. Attorney Davies later went to the scene with the officer. The cop returned to court the next day, resumed his testimony, and now admitted that there was no brick partition in the crawl space.

Vasquez did not testify in his own defense in the week-long trial. The jury evidently felt that the prosecution met the burden of proof. Vasquez was found guilty on three charges of first-degree assault and given an indeterminate-to-15-year sentence on each, to run concurrently. At the time of his conviction, *El Gallo* reported:

> The DA systematically excused from jury duty anyone with long hair, anyone with a college level education, all young Blacks and Chicanos, and young people in general. The final 12 jurors were generally middle-aged or elderly, conservative, lower middle-class and 11 of them were White with one older Black man. The only Mexican was a young Chicana who was the 13th member of the jury, an alternate who would have no say . . . in deciding the verdict. . . . As the case went to the jury, the Chicana alternate came to the apartments to see the scene for herself. She would not be deliberating the verdict. But when asked what her opinion was, having heard all the evidence, she said she immediately would have voted for acquittal.[77]

The Crusade was seldom defeated in court. It appealed Vasquez' conviction.

Like all Crusade cases, the Vasquez case bore certain trademarks. Crusade defendants had top-notch attorneys and were freed on bond shortly after their arrests. The courts were always packed with supporters, and those who could not get in lined the hallways until seats were available. Defendants' supporters were serious and well-behaved, but not humble. They did not attend court to intimidate, but did not attend court to make new friends, either. They did not believe courts were neutral arenas where justice was decided in an even-handed manner, or that the law was synonymous with justice. They felt that sides had been chosen, that sides had to be chosen, and they knew which side they were on.

Vasquez' supporters came from the Crusade, UMAS and MEChA, Black Berets and Brown Berets, independent community groups like Escuela Aztlan and Casa del Barrio, and other groups. His case was unique in other respects. It was the most tense of the trials, and hostility was pervasive. Uniformed cops and plainclothes detectives would stand on one side of the court hallway and Vasquez' supporters on the other. Both sides exchanged menacing glares, sometimes muttering loud insults.

Loud, angry remarks were muttered in the prosecutor's direction at different times in the case. Deputy D. A. Peter Bornstein's manner seemed calculated more to antagonize the spectators than to rattle witnesses on the stand. His closing remarks emphasized that Vasquez was the only person found at the scene, comparing this to finding dog's tracks in wet cement and following them to the dog. His repeated use of the word "dog," and the relish with which he used it, was insulting and provocative.[78]

Another unique and troubling aspect of the trial was that Vasquez' attitude indicated that he expected to lose. Crusade members were boxing fans, and knew that a fighter who expects to lose rarely wins. This perception was not widely discussed, since defense efforts were uphill struggles anyway, and it was easier to motivate people by emphasizing the positive. Equally disturbing was Vasquez constant partying.

Exactly four weekends passed between Vasquez' March 17 arrest and his late night arrest on April 15. Police stopped the car in which he was a passenger and arrested Vasquez, who was very drunk, but released his companions. Since he was drunk, alone, and on bond for shooting three cops the previous month, Crusade members assumed he would be a good candidate for a serious beating. They were making arrangements for his bond when Vasquez walked into the Crusade building without a scratch. He reported no abuse but said police let him sleep off the alcohol and released him without charge. A 1973 rap sheet does not reflect the names of the arresting officers.

Second Felony Indictment

Seven days later, on April 22, Vasquez was again arrested on felony aggravated assault charges for shooting an acquaintance in an early morning dispute after a night spent partying. Vasquez allegedly shot the unarmed man after being knocked down in a fight that began when Vasquez escorted a woman home. She was involved in divorce proceedings, and the husband was at the residence when Vasquez arrived. The unarmed man was shot five times, once in the heart. The victim, a popular, well-respected young man from Denver's Eastside, survived his wounds. He was active in the Crusade's social and political circles, and the incident could have been very divisive had he been bitter or vindictive. Or had he died.

Vasquez' 1973 rap sheet shows that the arresting officers in this shooting were Officers O'Dell and Campbell. O'Dell was present at the March 17 confrontation, as were two officers named Campbell: Charles and R. K. The County Court Warrant issued against Vasquez for the April 22 shooting lists 13 police witnesses, 12 of whom were present on March 17, including Detectives Diaz and Callahan.

The Crusade and DCLDC did not support Vasquez in his second felony case. Whether he was guilty or not, the charges were not politically motivated, and the DCLDC was not a public defender's office. Vasquez had been scheduled for trial on both cases in September, but the case involving the unarmed man resulted in a mistrial and was rescheduled. The case stemming from the Downing Street confrontation started on September 19, Vasquez was found guilty on September 26, and he was scheduled for sentencing on December 6.

Imprisonment

In December 1973, Judge Quinn, after refusing to let Vasquez remain free on an appeal bond, sent him to the State Reformatory at Buena Vista to serve three concurrent indeterminate-to-15-year sentences, a considerably more lenient sentence than the judge could have imposed. The DCLDC found attorneys to appeal the conviction, but Vasquez notified the committee shortly before Christmas that he wanted to drop the appeal, a decision made after less than one month's confinement. People familiar with prisons know that a prisoner's first priority is to regain freedom and that few abandon any option to do so. Vasquez, however, told the DCLDC that the appeal would consume undue time and resources, that prisoners with indeterminate Reformatory sentences were usually paroled after a few years, and that he might be released before an appeal would be heard. The young man who seemed apathetic in defending himself in court now appeared selfless in his concern for conserving the movement's resources. His three points were valid. The last one soon proved true.

"Vasquez Was Released"

Vasquez was imprisoned in December 1973, but was returned to Denver to stand trial on June 17, 1974, for the second shooting. The initial 1973 proceedings resulted in a mistrial when the victim could not identify his assailant and recanted a statement he made under medication while hospitalized. The Crusade assumed that the district attorney proceeded with the case for punitive reasons only, since convictions are unlikely when assailants cannot be identified. The victim, himself an activist, was well known to be reluctant to prosecute any Chicano in the establishment's court. The Crusade was not surprised when the victim remained unable to identify his assailant, a second mistrial was declared, and the district attorney was forced to drop the charges. Something else, however, was surprising.

After the second mistrial, Vasquez was taken to the Denver County Jail in preparation for his return to the Reformatory. Instead, he was released from the County Jail and never returned to custody. In fact, he was rumored to have escaped. The escape is not confirmed by any records, which, few as they are, tend to confuse more than they confirm. Consider the following.

Reformatory Records Officer Mary J. Sharpe wrote to Captain E. A. Torrey of the Denver Sheriff's Department in March 1977 to address a discrepancy in Reformatory records. An inmate had been registered at the Reformatory, but the inmate, Mario Manuel Vasquez, was not there. He had not been there for nearly three years, and nothing accounted for his absence. Years later these records on Vasquez would also disappear. But why, in March 1977, was Vasquez' name was still on the Reformatory confinement list? Why did Denver newspapers, not to mention the police, fail to notice his escape, inadvertent release, or disappearance? Records Officer Sharpe wrote to Captain Torrey:

> On June 7, 1974, the Denver County Sheriff's Department removed Mr. Vasquez from the Colorado State Reformatory on a Writ of Habeas Corpus Ad Prosecuendem in reference to Case #69738, CR 12 [the April 22 shooting]. To date, the only correspondence received on subject is attached which indicates Mr. Vasquez was released from custody by the court while he still had a commitment to this institution. The Reformatory is still carrying subject on their count and as being under your jurisdiction. In talking to Mr. Nelson, the previous records supervisor, he indicates he talked to Captain Hayes of the Denver County Sheriff's Department, and it was agreed Denver County would take the responsibility to find subject and return him to the custody of the Reformatory. I would like to know what progress has been made by your department to apprehend subject and return him to our custody. Your assistance is appreciated.[79]

Documents covering the period from Vasquez' June 1974 release to Sharpe's March 1977 inquiry do not seem to exist. The reference in Sharpe's letter to "correspondence received on subject" is puzzling. Other than Captain Torrey's response, only Sharpe's letter, with no attached correspondence, remains in the Reformatory's file. Whatever the attached correspondence would have revealed is therefore unknown. Sharpe's inquiry was indirectly answered by Captain Torrey, who, instead of responding to Sharpe, wrote to Reformatory Warden C. Winston Tanksley.

> Our records indicate that [Vasquez] was received at Denver County Jail on 7 June 1974. He was taken before court on 17 June 1974 and it appears that he was released from custody without proper clearance. Please be advised that on 20 August 1974 this department placed a pick up on the subject (see attached sheet). We will advise you of any further developments. Thank you for your cooperation in this matter.[80]

Though Torrey's letter refers to "a pick up on the subject (see attached sheet)", the "attached sheet" no longer exists. If the sheriff's "pick up" is synonymous with an escape or arrest warrant, no such warrant exists either. A thorough, and discreet, inquiry at Denver City and County offices shows no warrant for Vasquez' "pick up." Attempts to verify whether arrest warrants were ever issued are inconclusive. Neither the police nor the FBI ever inquired about Mario Manuel Vasquez.

"We Should Have the File, but We Don't"

Handwritten and typed notes were added to Vasquez' Writ of Habeas Corpus on June 17, 1974, when the second case was dismissed. The notes state, "Case Dismissed, Return to B. V. [Buena Vista]," and, "This order of court executed as hearin [sic] directed and this case was dismissed this date 6/17/74 and same ordered returned to State Reformatory at Buena Vista Colo on next trip." These data, however, are found in Denver District Court records, not in Reformatory records. In fact, records about Vasquez from the Denver Sheriff's Department, the State Reformatory, and the Colorado Department of Corrections are hard to find.

In November 1990 a letter was sent to the Denver Sheriff's Department and the State Reformatory to request copies of Vasquez' records. Both responded that they maintained no records that old. The Reformatory forwarded the inquiry to the Department of Correction's History and Records Section at the Territorial Corrections Facility in Canon City, Colorado, where old records are archived, but the section took no action. Finally, after my repeated calls to the History and Records office on March 15, 18, 22, and 25, 1991, Supervisor Anna Vellar, in a phone conversation, announced some results. Sort of.

> All we have is that his file was, uh, there was a place for it, but it never, there was nothing there for it. It's either, uh, somebody's, uh, taken it, or they didn't microfilm it, or something's, something's happened. We don't know where it's at; we've looked through all our filing and cannot locate it. . . . We should have the file, but we don't . . . somebody may have destroyed it by accident, or it's just somewhere; it could be anywhere. It's not in this office, because we've looked.[81]

Supervisor Vellar was cordial and informative. She said Vasquez' file should contain his presentence report, a "judgement and conviction," a case summary, and a "ticket of leave" or discharge papers if he completed his sentence. When asked if the "pick up" referred to in Torrey's 1977 letter to the State Reformatory was the same thing as an arrest or escape warrant, she responded affirmatively. When asked if Vasquez' name would be kept on the FBI's National Crime Information Center (NCIC) computer (and its clone, the Colorado Crime Information Center [CCIC] computer) if he had escaped, she said it would or should. When asked what would happen if Vasquez had escaped, she responded:

> [They] have to put a hold on him, so that they can have him picked up again because he's out on the streets improperly. See, he still has another sentence to serve, so they have to arrest him again. . . . Even if he's on escape, I think the [original] sentence stops. . . . I think what they do is

that if they're on escape they stop their time, and then when they're brought back, I think they start [the original sentence] again.[82]

If Vasquez did not "escape," perhaps he was released. Supervisor Vellar said Ms. Paula Watson of the Territorial Correction Facility's "Time and Release Office" was the person to contact for records of his release. Watson found no information about Vasquez, but said Ms. Judy Sutton, the Colorado Department of Corrections' "Fugitive Coordinator" in Colorado Springs, might shed light on the matter. Sutton worked in the office where information on fugitive prisoners would be found. Usually.

The Liberation of Mario Manuel Vasquez

Sutton was initially cordial, but soon seemed to become irritated. She was inquisitive herself: "First of all, who are you? . . . Are you recording this phone conversation? . . . What did Anna [Vellar] tell you? Did she find any records on this guy?" After I explained who was calling and why, she put the call on hold for nearly three minutes. When she returned, it was apparent that she was viewing data on a computer terminal. Though her tone was curt, her words may actually have masked an undue modesty. Sutton professed a lack of knowledge and underestimated her ability to be helpful and informative. In response to an initial question, she said, "I could not help you at all. According to our [computer] terminal, he discharged [his prison sentence] January the 3rd, 1981, so all of his records would be in History Records [Anna Vellar's office], whatever we maintained."

When I asked what should be in his file, if he had one, which he did not, Sutton responded:

> I can't answer that because you're talking 10 and 12 years ago, and I didn't deal with it then, so I don't know. You know, I'm sure his commitment documents, his institutional adjustment, any disciplinary hearings, all of that information would be in the file, and if there was an escape, that would be in the file. . . . You don't send [any further written inquiry] to me 'cause I don't have it [information]. It all has to go to Anna Vellar in History Records. What did Anna tell you? Did she find any records on this guy? . . . [Reading from her computer terminal] It looks to me like he had three counts of first-degree assault, zero to fifteen years from Denver County.[83]

When I asked, "So for all intents and purposes, this is a free man?" she answered:

> Absolutely, absolutely. He has no obligation to any, to this department, according to the [computer] terminal. Now, see, I have no paperwork to

substantiate that, all I can tell you is that is what it says [on the computer terminal] so I have to believe it.[84]

How a prisoner can discharge his sentence while "on escape" was something no one could explain.

A FAULTY RECOLLECTION

On March 17, after being shot, I ran from the porch shared by 1539 and 1541 Downing and climbed the stairs to the second-floor 1541½ Downing apartment. I pushed through the crowded apartment to the backdoor and stood on the iron balcony outside. In the alley were police vehicles with flashing lights. Somewhere dogs were barking, and bulky figures scurrying in the alley seemed to wear police flak jackets. Gunshots were echoing. Downing Street was filled with police on the east, and prospects for escape to the west seemed dim. Escape would require climbing a six-foot fence, then getting through the officers on the other side. Instead, I ran down the stairway and knocked on the back door of a dark apartment: 1543 Downing. I was let in.

I lay on a small bed in the apartment, frozen chicken compress and all, and waited for an ambulance. People who huddled in the darkness or scurried on the floor were asked if anyone had seen Junior. No one had. Soon thereafter someone crawled across the floor from the front of the apartment. A woman put her hand on my chest, as though to comfort me, and said that maybe everything was going to be all right. She had moved the drawn shades of the apartment window and thought she saw Martinez standing handcuffed across the street, surrounded by police. She glanced out briefly because she feared being shot. She whispered that she was not sure if it was Martinez, but the person stood in profile, and she thought she recognized his leather jacket and short ponytail. Gunfire continued until nearly 3 a.m., long after I was taken from the apartment to Denver General Hospital.

Penetrating the back between the shoulder blades, the .38 Special slug had missed the spine by án inch, traveled upward to the right, and broke the skin on the right shoulder, near the top, after breaking the collarbone where the arm and shoulder join the torso. Only the top half of the slug emerged. Doctors cut it free and saved it as evidence.

The slug hit no vital organs and severed no arteries. In spite of the trauma to the body that results from being shot through the back, the injury was not life-threatening. A jail cell was as appropriate as a hospital bed for suspected felons. I was put in a cell at the hospital with Luis Ramirez and did not recognize him at first. We were later put in a patrol wagon to be taken from the hospital to the jail. Vasquez was also in the patrol wagon on the drive to the old City Jail. I did not recognize him until he spoke. His face was swollen, his hair scorched, and his clothes encrusted with dust and debris.

I was held in an isolated cell on the fourth floor of the old City Jail, in an area with which I was not familiar and in which I was never held again in subsequent arrests. Sheriffs periodically came to peer at me where I lay. The early morning brought a cold breakfast and colder coffee served in a big aluminum bowl. After breakfast, a Chicano jail trustee pulled a mop and bucket to the passageway outside the cell and began to mop the floor. He carried a small transistor radio and, when asked if he heard anything on the radio about the disturbance, he responded that Chicanos and police had "shot it out," and one person was killed. When asked if he knew the name of the person who was killed, he said, "Yeah, some guy named Martinez." The trustee knew no other details.

The words of the woman who thought she saw Luis Martinez alive were enough to keep hope flickering. Much later that day, in the City Jail's small arraignment court, I turned to someone sitting behind me and asked about Martinez. "He's dead," I was told. In 1990, I spoke with the woman I thought told me she saw Martinez. She said I was mistaken, she had no memory of this conversation. She spoke sincerely. Whoever the woman was that night, she said Martinez stood near the sidewalk in front of a brick building that served at the time as an art school. It was one of the two building between which Martinez ran.

It was the same location described by Mario Manuel Vasquez when he said he saw Martinez and police officers before Martinez was shot, the story he told upon his release from jail in the late evening of March 17. He told two people within an hour of his release on bond that he saw Martinez shot between the buildings, and later said he thought this was what people wanted to hear. He recanted on March 18, before the Crusade press conference. Still, the story had possibilities that could have been exploited had he stuck to it.

The police were quickly in control of the eastern side of the street, where the body was found, except for members of the Coroner's Office, who were on the scene but were evacuated when the apartment blew up after 2 a.m. Though Vasquez later graphically described the beating of David Gonzales in the apartment's backyard as Vasquez peered from the second-floor, rear kitchen window, he never again said he saw anything while peering out the front window. The front window of the apartment where Vasquez hid for over an hour provided a birds-eye view of the porch area where the fatal encounter between Snyder and Martinez took place and where Martinez' body was later found.

I went to the Crusade's March 18 afternoon press conference after Gonzales called me at home and, with few details, said that Martinez was not killed in the manner police claimed. Though my recollection is unclear, in a subsequent, personal visit I was told that Vasquez saw Martinez shot between the buildings where his body was found and that more than one cop was involved. I wondered how such information would be presented and felt that the minimum should be told, concerned about putting the witness in jeopardy. Gonzales was in the downstairs cafeteria when I arrived and asked him for details of what Vasquez saw and how it would be recounted. Gonzales responded that Vasquez would say nothing because he now said he did not witness Martinez' death.

Gonzales said Vasquez had asked him earlier what to say at the approaching press conference. Gonzales, puzzled and surprised by the question, told Vasquez to tell what he saw. Vasquez then said that he had not witnessed Martinez' death and had said that he did only because he thought it was what people wanted to hear. "But that doesn't make any sense," I told Gonzales. "Why would he think this is what anyone wanted him to say?" Gonzales, angered or exasperated, glared and said, "That's it exactly. It doesn't make any sense." He pushed back his chair and walked away. At the press conference speakers chose not to recount specific details about the incident.

When the press conference ended, Vasquez stood alone by the cafeteria wall. He was asked if he had said that he saw Martinez killed while he watched from the apartment window. He said he had, but he volunteered nothing more. When asked if he really saw Martinez killed, he hung his head and said, "No," and again volunteered nothing more. He was asked if he said this "because that's what you thought we wanted to hear." He smiled weakly, looked at the floor, and said, only "Yes." He stood looking at the floor with head hung and a worried, sheepish look that stayed with him over the coming months.

The Crusade was angry when the *Rocky Mountain News* reporters requested an exclusive March 27 interview, delayed publishing what they were told, and then, on March 29, reported selective details merely as a confirmation of Snyder's belated admission. The Crusade held an afternoon press conference on March 30 to criticize the media coverage. That evening Gonzales had one more interview with the *Denver Post,* after which the Crusade dropped its efforts to ascertain or clarify the circumstances of the death of Luis Martinez. The *Denver Post* reported:

> At an interview Friday, Gonzales produced two color photographs, a front and back view of what he said was Martinez' body. The front view

showed a large ragged hole in the right side of the chest near the armpit and a large hole in the middle of the front of the chest in the area of the breastbone. The view of the back of the body showed two smaller wounds, about three inches apart near the middle of the back, at about the level of the shoulder blades. Earlier, Gonzales said he had "knowledgeable witnesses" [Vasquez] who have alleged that Martinez was "shot in the back on the ground between the two buildings and left to die." Asked by the *Denver Post* Saturday [March 31] if Martinez could have been shot in the back, a Denver coroner's spokesman said, "This is wrong." The "skellied" neat holes were in the front of Martinez' body, and there is no doubt that he was shot from the front, the spokesman said.[85]

The nameless spokesman's words, or the reporters' rendition of them, clouded the issue. At least one of the three reporters evidently spelled things as he heard them, because the autopsy never mentioned "skellied" holes, but described "stellate," or star-shaped, wounds. By definition stellate wounds are ragged, not neat, making "skellied [stellate] neat holes" a nonsensical term that hides the facts, whatever they were, by obscuring the nature and location of the wounds. The reporter, however, saw the photographs and described large and ragged wounds in front and smaller ones in back.

The photos the reporters saw were taken by an independent pathologist whose findings, like the photos themselves, contradicted the official autopsy. Martinez' mother was traumatized by his death, and the family asked the Crusade to drop the matter. The organization never again explored Martinez' death, but Gonzales and other Crusade members believed his death resulted from a conspiracy.

CONSPIRACY THEORY

The Crusade never accepted the police version of Martinez' death, or the confrontation. If the March 17 confrontation occurred the way police claimed, Martinez' death would have been ruled a justifiable homicide, and so it happened. There were some things, however, that the Crusade never tried to contradict. For example, it never denied that Martinez shot Snyder.

Several years after Martinez' death, Gonzales and I spoke briefly about initial copies of FBI files that he obtained through the Freedom of Information Act (FOIA).[86] Our discussion turned to March 17, 1973. It was necessarily speculative because, unlike the police and FBI, the Crusade had limited staff and resources to investigate matters, no authority to subpoena evidence or compel testimony, and no capacity to use the media to sway public opinion. We discussed Snyder's declaration, the sequence and direction of the gunfire, the positions of the men as they struggled, and two impact marks left by bullets on the northern wall of the passageway through which they ran. The following account is based on that discussion.

Snyder said Martinez stood to his left, to the south, as he emerged from the passageway through which he had chased Martinez. Snyder said he was first shot "in the side, I think," from a distance of "six feet, eight feet." He "jumped [Martinez] at this point and was wrestling with him," though he did not know if they "went to the ground or not." He said he was shot in the leg as they struggled, but, "I could be mistaken about that too. I'm not sure." Snyder, using his left hand, grabbed Martinez' "right hand, the hand he had the gun in." Snyder drew his own gun, "was bringing it up towards him . . . and it was almost simultaneous timing that I got shot in the head, and then I shot him, within less than a second . . . and as he was falling back I fired at him again."

The author heard five shots in two bursts: three rapid shots, a pause, then two louder ones.[87] Though it is likely that the two struggled, my recollection of the gunfire does not support the idea that they wrestled between each of Martinez' three shots, or that Snyder's first shot was "simultaneous" with Martinez' third. Recollections, whether mine or Snyder's, are not foolproof. The crime lab test on Snyder's shirt indicates that he was not six to eight feet away when Martinez shot him, but much closer. Physical evidence does not lie, although it may not tell the entire story.

Martinez was standing south of Snyder and, as Snyder said, was backed against a porch when Snyder fired. Someone's bullets caused two impact marks on bricks of the passageway's north wall, but Snyder's bullets traveled south, so neither should be attributed to his gunfire. One mark, probably the result of Martinez' gunfire, was at face level and the other near waist level. If Martinez' gunfire accounted for one mark on the wall and his other two slugs were recovered from Snyder at the hospital, what accounted for the second mark? Additional shots could account for that mark, but Snyder only told of five shots and I only heard five shots at that time. The second mark makes no sense unless there was additional, subsequent gunfire in the passage.

If the crime lab report on Martinez' clothing was accurate and the autopsy inaccurate, then the shot that produced Martinez' nonfatal wound was fired within two feet of his body, and the fatal shot was fired at a greater distance. If Snyder fired his second shot immediately after the first, why did the slug travel in the opposite direction from the gunshot immediately preceding it? Snyder did not say Martinez fell down, which would account for a downward path for the fatal bullet. Snyder said Martinez was "falling back." If powder burns on the fatal wound were lacking because he fell away from Snyder, why did the bullet enter at a downward angle as though the gun were above him? What scenario made sense?

We believed that Martinez realized the predicament he was in as Snyder, probably with gun in hand, chased him through the passageway. When Snyder emerged from the passage, did Martinez draw his gun and try to kill Snyder with a first shot to the head? Snyder was shot in the side of his face, and the bullet exited the other side of his jaw. If Martinez' first shot was to Snyder's face, did Snyder's momentum carry him into Martinez as Martinez fired twice more? This would account for all Snyder's wounds, the powder burns on his shirt, and one impact mark on the wall.

The bullets that killed Martinez passed through his body and were not recovered, so tests could not show if both came from one gun. Did Snyder struggle for Martinez' gun, fire twice, but miss? Did one shot hit Martinez, but only incapacitate him? Dead bodies do not bruise. Was Martinez captured by officers who became angry when they saw Snyder gravely wounded, and then beat and killed Martinez? This would explain the bruises on Martinez' face and arms that were described in the autopsy. Shots fired by another officer would account for the angles of Martinez' wounds and for the second mark on the wall.

Did the two men fall to the ground? Did Martinez, who was strong and exceptionally agile, pin Snyder down, and was he then was shot by another policeman who came upon them? A standing officer could inflict the fatal downward shot, though this explanation might not account for the second mark on the wall. Other officers were at the scene very quickly. SSU Officers Tow and Holt testified that they arrived within a minute of hearing Hogue's call.

Other cops, if they were deployed in advance, might arrive as quickly, or quicker, and come upon Martinez as he struggled with Snyder in the passageway. If another officer fired the fatal shot, why would he remain silent about his heroism? The only answer we could surmise was related to Snyder and Hogue's earlier presence on Downing Street and to the sightings of police concentrations earlier in the evening. If police were deployed in advance with Snyder and Hogue serving as bait, the incident was a provocation, not a "spontaneous confrontation." A provocation would be a felonious conspiracy by those involved, and a felony leading to someone's death can be prosecuted as homicide.

We theorized that the confrontation was sparked by the Crusade's support for Wounded Knee. It was not the first time the Crusade had supported such radical causes. It had done so repeatedly, effectively, and would continue to do so. If the Crusade could not be coopted, it had to be stopped, and any thorough narrative of its history shows a campaign to dismantle the Crusade and the movement it represented. Although law enforcement and intelligence gathering at Wounded Knee were orchestrated at the federal level, not by Denver cops, the long history of antagonism between police and the Crusade would incline elements of the police to do the dirty work. According to this conjecture, the FBI at the field office, regional, and national levels was the guiding hand in a conspiracy involving elements of the Denver police: district command officers, the Special Services Unit, and the Intelligence Bureau. An emergency call from Snyder or Hogue would summon extra unwitting but willing troops. The media, in turn, would rely on police for the official story.

All this, of course, was mere speculation. Only Vasquez claimed to have seen Martinez killed, and he quickly recanted.[88] Vasquez, however, was seen in Denver in the late 1970s, risky behavior for a prison escapee. Through the 1980s and 1990s, some activists have hosted events to honor "martyrs" of the Chicano movement. They count Vasquez among these "martyrs."

In the late 1970s, Gonzales and I could not fit Wounded Knee and the FBI into the puzzle. There was no evidence, not even circumstantial evidence, in the copies we had of FBI documents. At least, not at that time.

Rodolfo "Corky" Gonzales holds a reprint of famed Mexican photographer Agustin Casasola depicting Zapatista soldiers during 1910 Mexican Revolution. The photo was a gift given to Gonzales by Mario (Mauro) Cantu, a San Antonio activist. Photograph by Antonio Sanchez.

Rodolfo "Corky" Gonzales being arrested during a protest at Denver West High School, March 1969. Photograph by Duane E. Howell.

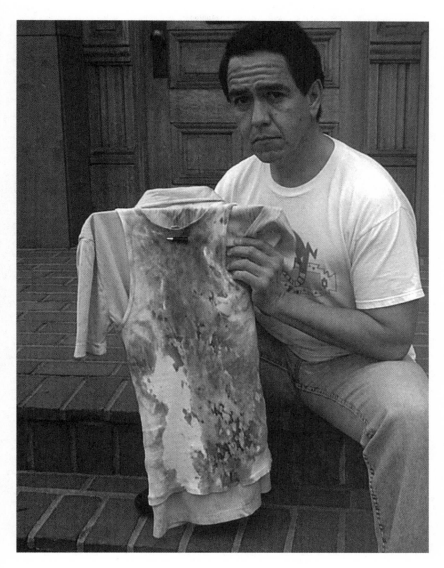

Author with March 17 evidence.

Activists gather in front of Crusade headquarters for a march to the state capitol to protest the incarceration of Rodolfo Gonzales in Los Angeles for charges stemming from the August 29, 1970, National Chicano Anti-war Moratorium. Photograph by Pablo Castro.

Luis "Junior" Martinez, August 21, 1952–March 17, 1973. Photograph by Dino Castro.

View of the Crusade's apartment building as seen from the parking lot through which Officer Snyder pursued Luis "Junior" Martinez on March 17, 1973. Snyder's car was parked in the street in the area of the van seen at the left; a young man fired at Officer Hogue from the area of the sidewalk near the tree at right of photo. Photograph by Pablo Castro.

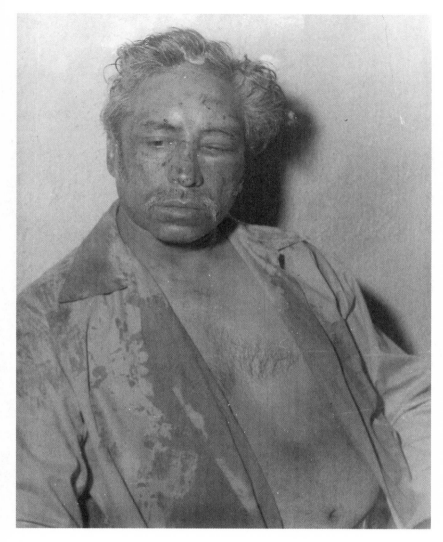

Luis Ramirez after beating by Denver police on March 17, 1973. Photograph by Pablo Castro.

Emilia, Manuel, and Ray Alvarado lead the procession bearing coffin of Luis "Junior" Martinez for burial in San Cristobal, New Mexico. Photograph by Pablo Castro.

The apartment at 1547 1/2 Downing Street. The greater part of the unit's damage
stemmed from demolition ordered by city officials on March 17, 1973. Slogan on wall
originated from uprising at New York's Attica prison. Photograph by Pablo Castro.

Slogan painted on wall of La Raza Park in Denver's Northside around 1972–73.
Photograph by Pablo Castro.

Activist attorneys Ken Padilla and Walter Gerash with newspaper recounting the record-setting acquittal in the author's trial over allegations of attempting to shoot police on March 17, 1973. Photograph by Jay Alire.

Angela Davis, shown here with Rodolfo Gonzales and Ernesto Vigil, spoke in Denver at Loretto Heights College on April 28, 1973, to raise funds for the March 17 defendants. Photograph by Pablo Castro.

Radical priest James Groppi of Milwaukee, Wisconsin, poses with Ernesto Vigil, Rodolfo Gonzales, and Mario Manuel Vasquez after a June 10, 1973, fund-raiser in support of the Crusade's legal defense committee. Photograph by Pablo Castro.

Ricardo Falcon: UMAS leader, community organizer, and Colorado's first Chicano activist to meet a violent death, August 30, 1972. Photograph by Pablo Castro.

Several of the Crusade's most prominent women activists are captured in this photo. From left to right: Deborah Montoya, Audrey Luera, Cecilia "Tuni" Garrison, Josie Salinas, Teresa Romero, Maria Subia, Shirley Castro, and Geraldine Gonzales. Photograph by Pablo Castro.

Ed Montour, Brown Beret leader, addresses education conference in the wake of racial conflict and police violence during student unrest at Centennial High School in Pueblo, Colorado, in October 1974. Photograph by Pablo Castro.

William Kunztler of the Center for Constitutional Rights holding bullhorn. Rodolfo Gonzales, partially obscured by microphone stand, at right, and California's Bert Corona in upper right, applauding, during the 1974 commemorative protest marking the death of Luis "Junior" Martinez. Photograph by Pablo Castro.

AIM leader John Trudell, Rodolfo Gonzales, and Kwame Ture (formerly Stokeley Carmichael) of the All-African Peoples Revolutionary Party at the Denver Indian Center auditorium in March 1976 at the third annual commemoration of Luis Martinez's death. Photograph by Pablo Castro.

June 1976 press conference protests release of intelligence bulletins alleging conspiracy of Crusade, AIM, SDS, and Brown Berets to kill police during American Bicentennial. From left to right: Anita Gonzales; Rodolfo Gonzales; Harold Fobb, of Colorado Warrior Society; Maria Subia, of the Crusade's legal defense committee; Gary Garcia, seated on window ledge. Photograph by Pablo Castro.

The Crusade, AIM, and Leonard Peltier

Crusade officials, noting the speed with which scores of Denver police were able to get to the area well-armed and prepared for attack, . . . speculate that the reason for the attack was much larger than a jay-walking incident. They point to a recent demonstration organized by the Crusade for Justice and the American Indian Movement in which over 1,200 Chicanos and Indians marched in support of Wounded Knee.

Ernesto Vigil, *El Gallo*, April 1973

The government of this state is bent on destroying the Chicano liberation struggle and the form of progress made by the Crusade for Justice. It is no secret that the Crusade is locked in a struggle for survival. We are witnessing the work of a conspiracy, a conspiracy to destroy the Crusade and render it ineffective. . . . When they see the revolutionary face of the Crusade for Justice, they, the rulers and the criminals, feel that their system is being threatened. Now I think that everyone who is here today and has experienced the tremendous presence and inspiration of the Crusade, everyone who has experienced this, can say that, brothers and sisters, they are quite right, their system is being threatened.

Angela Davis, April 1973

Capt. Doral Smith described the events of March 17 as a "spontaneous confrontation" in which "one thing led to another." Crusade members and other activists viewed the confrontation as an attempt to crush the Crusade, and believed that the Crusade's support for Wounded Knee prompted federal officials to manipulate a willing police department to do its bidding that day.[1] These beliefs were never raised in the March 17 trials. No concrete evidence existed, and the Crusade's suppositions were irrelevant. Or were they?

THE SCOTTSBLUFF INCIDENT

After AIM activists occupied the BIA headquarters in Washington, in November 1972, FBI headquarters ordered its field offices to monitor AIM activity for violations of federal laws. On January 12, 1973, the Denver FBI field office reported on Denver AIM's leadership. Other than noting that "Alice Blackhorse was killed in an automobile accident," the Denver FBI had little to report.[2]

This changed on January 14, when AIM Coordinator Russell Means was arrested in Scottsbluff, Nebraska, at "a disturbance which occurred at the Park Motel . . . where a meeting between AIM and Chicanos was being held. . . . AIM at Scottsbluff has been in contact with the Governor's office at Lincoln re arrest of above individuals and charges of brutality on the part of Scottsbluff PD officers."[3] On January 18 an FBI Domestic Intelligence Division "Informative Note" reported that a junior high school in Scottsbluff was firebombed and five AIM members were arrested, and that "on 1/17/73, Mexican Americans and AIM followers scuffled with police when asked to leave an office in Scottsbluff, resulting in the arrest of leader Ramon J. Perez and four others. One Deputy Sheriff receiving knife wound in back is hospitalized in good condition."[4]

The names of Russell Means and Ramon Perez are frequently mentioned in FBI documents from Scottsbluff, where AIM members and local Chicanos met for a unity conference. This rural area is bordered on the south by the North Platte River and on the north by the southern lands of South Dakota's Pine Ridge Reservation, lands over which the Lakota, Cheyenne, Arapaho, and other horse-culture nations of the northern Great Plains had long ranged and where much blood was shed in the latter half of the nineteenth century in U.S. wars against them.

Perez, a Chicano from Scottsbluff, left Nebraska for employment in Denver, where he was associated with the Crusade but was also active with a North Denver group. He maintained ties with his home state, and his Nebraska associates often visited Denver. A delegation of Nebraska activists attended the national LRUP convention, at which they voted with the Colorado LRUP. By late January 1973 these Nebraska activists and AIM members were headquartered in a "building formerly-utilized as a recreation center for Mexican Americans belonging to Our Lady of Guadalupe Church in Scottsbluff. . . . The use of this building, rent free, was given some months ago to Ramon Perez . . . for use by a group he headed known as New Congress for Community Action."[5] Though it was noteworthy that Mexicans and Indians were uniting in small towns like Gering, Alliance, and Scottsbluff, Nebraska, the FBI received even more ominous reports from South Dakota after Wesley Bad Heart Bull was stabbed to death on January 21 in Buffalo Gap by a white service station operator from Custer. AIM called for an "Indian Rights Day" gathering in Custer, to be held on February 6.

The affair ended in a riot in which the local courthouse was set afire and the Chamber of Commerce building burned to the ground. Dennis Banks and Russell Means were among 27 people arrested. AIM then called for supporters from Colorado, Kansas, Nebraska, and Wyoming to send 7,000 reinforcements; Minneapolis AIM said it was sending caravans for the protest. Subsequent AIM meetings and protests followed in Custer, Rapid City, Sturgis, and Hot Springs, South Dakota, until mid-February, when AIM focused its attention and energies on the Pine Ridge conflict that led to the Wounded Knee takeover.

Federal, state, and local police collaborated to gather intelligence and maintain control. They were also concerned about the collaboration between Indian and Chicano activists. The Minneapolis FBI office reported to Bureau headquarters that "AIM members, while in Scottsbluff . . . reportedly made a deal [with their Chicano allies] for approximately sixty automatic weapons which resemble the Thompson submachine gun of Mexican manufacture." This, at least, was the information gathered by the FBI from Custer Sheriff Ernie Pepin, who got his information from the Scottsbluff chief of police.[6] The Scottsbluff chief of police also reported that of 38 cars with out-of-state license plates belonging to AIM sympathizers, 12 were from Colorado; South Dakota placed second with 11. Bad omens?

Though the Crusade was in touch with activists at Wounded Knee in the early days of the siege that started on February 28, 1973, Crusade members, at least, realized the danger of talking on tapped phones. Few calls were received from Wounded Knee after the Denver solidarity protest on March 6, though the Crusade continued to receive information from the media and from people who journeyed to South Dakota and returned to Denver. Few of these individuals, however, had been able to get past law enforcement roadblocks, so the Crusade's knowledge was limited.

Lacking access to FBI communications, the Crusade did not know, for example, that a key speaker at Denver's March 6 protest, Ramon Perez, was among the Scottsbluff Chicanos mentioned by the FBI in connection with the deal "for approximately sixty automatic weapons." Perez and some Denver associates, further, were among those who had entered Wounded Knee. No one, however, could have easily smuggled in the "Thompson submachine gun of Mexican manufacture." The Thompson .45 caliber submachinegun was never produced in Mexico.[7]

WOUNDED KNEE AND THE WATERGATE ERA

The mounting crisis at Wounded Knee was in the national headlines and seemed sure to be a public relations disaster no matter how authorities handled it. Conservatives demanded that the law be enforced, Indians demanded that treaties be enforced, and if one treaty was honored, then, logically, so must the next—and where would it all end? President Richard Nixon's administration sent high officials to negotiate with Indians during the 1969 Indian occupation of Alcatraz Island in the San Francisco Bay, but he could not afford the headache in 1973. Nixon, who campaigned for re-election on law-and-order themes, was in his bunker at the White House. The Watergate burglary of June 17, 1972, was unraveling even before his January 1973 inauguration. Other problems existed as well.

FBI Director J. Edgar Hoover died on May 2, 1972, and his Bureau remained in the hands of his loyalists until Nixon appointed L. Patrick Gray to head it. Gray, who helped Nixon's advisors subvert the Watergate probe, was resented by FBI administrators for being an outsider. Nixon was worried about Hoover's secret files and needed a Nixon loyalist in charge at the FBI. The FBI shredded, or hid, these files rather than provide them to Gray. Senate hearings on Gray's appointment coincided with the Wounded Knee takeover. Meanwhile, in South Dakota, SAC Trimbach took charge at Wounded Knee and promptly banned the media from the area. The media in turn complained to the White House, generating publicity that Nixon was anxious to dodge.

Professor Rolland Dewing's *Wounded Knee II,* from which this chapter draws much of the Wounded Knee chronology, notes that the federal government had gone into the initial phases of a civil disturbance repression plan called Operation Garden Plot.[8] Under Garden Plot the 82nd Airborne would be used to put down the rebellion, a real attention-getter for a besieged president whose use of military force against domestic dissidents would heighten his public profile. Officials at Wounded Knee were informed that White House advisors wanted to avoid bloodshed. The team of FBI SACs there bumped heads over strategy and tactics with Director Wayne Colburn of the U.S. Marshals, a Nixon appointee with his own clout at the White House. Leadership in the field bogged down in squabbles over the law enforcement pecking-order.

On March 9, 1973, the day the FBI believed AIM would attack agents' positions, negotiations appeared to be successful, and tensions eased. The agreement stipulated that nonresidents at Wounded Knee would leave and identify themselves, but would not be subject to immediate arrest. Federal forces were to withdraw. FBI roadblocks, which had drawn gunfire and publicity and were not entirely effective in preventing the entry of people and supplies, briefly came down.

Local ranchers, upon hearing that the roadblocks were down, crossed through the area, but were detained on March 10 by AIM members, who found them in possession of three guns. They were reportedly struck and menaced. The ranchers' detention was another alleged violation of the law. On March 11 a gun battle erupted seven miles north of Wounded Knee between FBI agents and men in a van that the agents attempted to stop. An FBI agent was shot in the hand during the chase, and the van crossed the perimeter into Wounded Knee, where the chase ended.

The roadblocks went back up, the truce ended, and all FBI SACs at Wounded Knee recommended to Bureau headquarters that the U.S. Army be used to put down the Indians by overrunning their positions with armored personnel carriers (APCs). Ralph Erickson, a Justice Department official, said that AIM had taken advantage of the removal of the roadblocks "to fortify their positions with more weapons and ammunition."[9] Wayne Colburn, former chief of the San Diego Police Department and architect of the U.S. Marshals Service Special Operations Group (SOG), said, "We have observed changes in the type and number of weapons there and changes in the type of people, meaning they are importing people." Colburn said the government would consider "starving them out, freezing them out, everything to prevent them from normal comfort. I'm sure as hell planning on changing their life-style."[10]

ROY MOORE AND THE WEEKEND OF MARCH 17–18

At this point FBI Acting Director Gray ordered that SAC Trimbach be relieved by veteran FBI SAC Roy Moore and rotated SAC Hoxie out of the area. SAC DeBruler was instructed by superiors to concentrate on intelligence gathering and told, "The safety of one Agent is not worth a thousand dirty militant bedraggled Indians."[11] Trimbach's replacement by Moore meant that the FBI's Wounded Knee operations would be guided by a man with very special skills and a unique reputation.

Moore was one of the best-known FBI SACs. In March 1973 he was stationed as SAC in the Chicago field office, was one year from retirement, and was known for his participation in FBI "specials." This term was used to describe special investigations conducted by elite squads of FBI agents and led by an experienced agent. The squads had the authority to make instant decisions on the scene and could ignore field office boundaries. Moore had a reputation for taking whatever measures he believed were effective to get results. Two books, in fact, report that FBI agents under Moore were responsible for the kidnapping and armed interrogation of a suspect in order to extract a confession.[12] Moore organized the "special" investigation of the March 1971 burglary of FBI offices in Media, Pennsylvania—a burglary that uncovered the extent of the FBI's domestic spying and first revealed the FBI's illegal counterintelligence programs, COINTELPROs.[13]

Assistant Attorney General Harlington Wood took charge of negotiations on March 13. SAC Moore took charge in South Dakota on March 14, the day the Sioux Falls grand jury returned 31 sealed indictments against Wounded Knee leaders. Moore left press relations and siege negotiations to Justice Department officials while the FBI concentrated on intelligence gathering and arrests. One FBI report cited in *Wounded Knee II* indicates that AIM members from Wounded Knee arrived in California on March 13 to purchase guns, ammunition, and explosives.[14] According to Dewing, "Moore reported that a consensus of federal law enforcement . . . agreed that the confrontation should be ended the weekend of March 17–18 by direct attack if necessary. Moore suggested that a force of twelve armed APC's with ten men in each could take the compound if the attack were preceded by a gas attack from the helicopters."[15]

On March 16 Moore organized 60 law enforcement officers, with three APCs, and stepped up pressure on AIM by expelling 70 supporters from the Pine Ridge Community Hall after a three-hour standoff. The supporters were forced to leave behind one ton of food gathered for Wounded Knee occupants. Meanwhile, 10 BIA officers ordered a dozen clergymen, representatives of the National Council of Churches, to leave Pine Ridge because they were not clearing their activities with Dick Wilson's Pine Ridge tribal government, AIM's bitter enemy. Elsewhere, federal officers arrested 16 persons in Nevada for crossing state lines with intent to assist in the takeover.

The FBI monitored AIM sympathizers in Denver, where two people were reported to have taken weapons to Wounded Knee on March 15. The Denver FBI was also concerned about the activity of a woman and a Mexican male suspect named "Rocky" whose surname was unknown. "Rocky . . . left Denver Friday 3–16–73 to take emergency medical supplies to Wounded Knee, S. D. Rocky allegedly had made arrangements for [his companions] and supplies to be flown by Lear jet to South Dakota."[16]

The Los Angeles FBI field office notified Acting Director Gray in an urgent teletype sent on March 16 at 4:53 p.m. that a source had informed the Los Angeles field office that "several Chicanos [plan] to participate in American Indian Movement caravan reportedly departing Los Angeles today for Wounded Knee, South Dakota." The FBI was monitoring the activity of someone named "Rodriguez" who "indicated Chicano group would first meet with 'Corky' Gonzales, Crusade for Justice leader, in Denver, Colorado, before proceeding to Wounded Knee."[17]

Another document demonstrates federal law enforcement attitudes and priorities 24 hours before the confrontation on the 1500 block of Downing Street. The document reads:

> To: All SAC's and SAC's, Wounded Knee Command Post (Personal Attention)
> From: Acting Director, FBI
> Re [Bureau teletype] to all SAC's, 3/15/73
> As stated in [3/15/73 teletype], Government interested in preventing outside elements from infiltrating troubled area of Wounded Knee. It is desirous to arrest members of such groups before they reach South Dakota. . . . Where probable cause cannot be established or purpose of trip ascertained without disclosing highly placed informant, *other action must be considered to try to prevent these groups from traveling interstate to Wounded Knee. . . . [When] probable cause cannot be established to stop group, these groups are to be put under physical surveillance 24 hours a day* [emphasis added]. . . . It is responsibility of each SAC in whose territory they are to pass at any given time (day or night) to keep FBI [headquarters], the Wounded Knee Command Post . . . and each SAC in the adjoining division which the group is approaching fully advised. . . . US Attorney is to be consulted when sufficient facts developed by investigation establishing there is probable cause a federal violation has been committed . . . arrest warrants should be obtained and individuals responsible arrested in territory which they are in at that time. *The object is to make lawful arrests as far from Wounded Knee, South Dakota, as possible* [emphasis added]. . . . All SAC's are to personally coordinate implementation of these instructions. FBI HQ and Command Post at Wounded Knee are to be kept informed by telephone or other expedite communication. . . . Assistant General Harlington Wood is desirous to prevent subversive elements from supporting the militant Indians. . . . Coordinated with [Special Agent] Arthur B. Fulton, [Internal Security-1], Intelligence Division.[18]

Though it is clear that the FBI took measures to deal with the siege at Wounded Knee, no documentation proves FBI involvement in the March 17 confrontation in Denver. The available documents, however, show the FBI's concern about Chicano–AIM connections, what the Bureau heard, and some of the options it entertained.

THE FBI IN DENVER

Though it is known that the FBI maintained communications with police department intelligence squads (and FBI reports on Wounded Knee show that the FBI communicated with Denver Intelligence officers), no documents show that the FBI and Denver police planned any action against the Crusade. The FBI files, however, pose more questions than they answer, if only because reading hundreds, or thousands, of pages of documents on the Crusade and AIM is only a start if one wants to see the whole picture. For example, Rolland Dewing's collection of FBI documents on Wounded Knee, archived at Chadron State College, contains over 25,000 pages. Many other case files exist, and few of them have been adequately researched.

As previously mentioned, Crusade members had no way to know—when Ramon Perez spoke at the March 6 Denver solidarity protest—that the FBI suspected their associates in Denver and Nebraska of having made a deal with AIM for machine guns in January 1973. If they had known, they might well have laughed at the FBI's notions, or shrugged, feeling no obligation to educate the FBI or correct its misconceptions. The FBI knew who Perez was. It had been monitoring LRUP activity in the Midwest since 1970, but found none in Nebraska until June 14, 1972, when Denver FBI agents sent the Omaha field office a letter that included a copy of a letter by Perez in the May 1972 *El Gallo*. The letter identified Perez as being from Scottsbluff and voiced his intent to begin LRUP in Nebraska. A subsequent Omaha field office document concludes that La Raza Unida did not exist, but identified Perez as being part of a group working "with a few other minority groups, principally local American Indians, to form a group named New Congress for Community Development." [19]

The Denver FBI field office, moreover, saw the Colorado LRUP as synonymous with the Crusade for Justice as early as July 9, 1971, or so it implies: "[LRUP] was organized and was and is directed by the CFJ [Crusade]. . . . Plans for improving coverage of CFJ will affect future coverage of the LRU." [20] This Denver field office Letter-head Memorandum (LHM) was written under the Mexican American Militancy caption and seems to be in response to an order to survey Colorado Chicano organizations the FBI deemed potentially violent. It reveals that the Denver FBI was then focusing on UMAS, the GI Forum, LRUP, and the Crusade for Justice.

The LHM's assessment of the Crusade, however, is revealing: "Time devoted to developing other organizations would seem to detract from Denver's primary goal of obtaining additional live coverage at the CFJ. It is felt also that if any other Mexican American groups in the Denver Division developed a potential for violence, this fact would be uncovered through increased coverage at the CFJ." [21]

"CHICANO GROUPS AND MEXICAN SUBVERSIVE ORGANIZATIONS"

The Mexican American Militancy (MAM) caption surfaced again in relation to the Crusade on August 29, 1972, when the FBI Legal Attache

(Legat) in the American Embassy in Mexico City sent a "Nitel" to the acting director notifying him that a radical Mexican human-rights attorney who had previously supported Chicano causes was invited to attend the national LRUP convention in El Paso.[22]

The same caption is found on other FBI documents concerning conferences in Mexico in the last months of 1972 at which Chicano activists met Mexican activists and high government officials. One FBI document stated that the purpose of the November 21 conference was "to internationalize [the] Chicano movement."[23] LRUP leaders had been invited to attend, and many accepted. Gonzales and the Crusade, however, did not attend. Another MAM-captioned document pertaining to the same conference was routed to Denver on January 31, 1973. This LHM noted that its purpose was "to demonstrate the inter-relation between U.S. Chicano groups and Mexican subversive organizations" at the Mexico City conference.[24] By this date, incidentally, the FBI had been told by Scottsbluff police that Chicano activists in Scottsbluff were to supply Mexican-manufactured machine guns to AIM. The Scottsbluff activists, however, had not attended the Mexico City conference either.

On the other hand, one FBI report showed that Crusade associates who held a March 7 Wounded Knee solidarity protest in Los Angeles did attend the Mexico City conference. This document went to 15 field offices in the Southwest, Midwest, and Florida. Another FBI document shows that Rodolfo Gonzales spoke at a rally organized by some of these same Los Angeles activists on February 5, 1973.[25]

These activists belonged to the Committee to Free Los Tres, the Centro de Accion Social Autonomo (CASA), and the Casa de Carnalismo. FBI files indicate that the Bureau believed some of these activists were involved with the Chicano Liberation Front, a clandestine group that was reportedly responsible for bombings in Los Angeles in the early 1970s. These activists had previously invited Gonzales to attend a December 15, 1972, fundraising dance sponsored by LRUP on behalf of Ricardo Chavez-Ortiz, an immigrant Mexicano who hijacked an airliner to publicize his complaints of discrimination. Activists briefly rallied around Chavez-Ortiz; the gun he used in the hijacking was not loaded, and he surrendered peacefully.[26] At this fundraising dance, Gonzales and the author encountered an old acquaintance, Antonio El Guerrillero Medina (see Chapter 6).

The FBI was also concerned with the Crusade's perceived links to two groups, the "Committee of Solidarity with Latin America (COLAS)" and the "Latin American Pro-independence Movement, Known in California as Instituto de Investigacion Mexico-Aztlan (PIM-IIMA)," as revealed in two FBI documents dated March 14 and March 15, 1972. Copies of one document, cross-filed in other files captioned "109–653 (Cuban Subversion)" and "157–8887 (La Raza Unida)," were filed with (La Raza Unida)," were filed with FBI field offices in San Antonio, Denver, Sacramento, San Diego, and Albuquerque. One document is a highly censored letter from headquarters to the Los Angeles SAC, and one of two remaining paragraphs in the two-page letter reads, "San Francisco, Los Angeles, and San Antonio [should] be alert to the formation of an above-ground apparatus for PIM-IIMA known as Partido Nacional de Aztlan. Be particularly alert for activities by Chicano groups such as those mentioned above and others on behalf of the Cubans in the United States."

A San Francisco LHM dated September 20, 1972, reported, "The Instituto de Investigacion Mexico-Aztlan (IIMA), formerly known as Latin American Pro-Independence Movement, is a semi-covert Latin American organization in the United States whose purpose is to create such turmoil in the United States that the United States would be unable to intervene in the affairs of any Latin American country, including Cuba, for fear of urban guerrilla warfare in the United States resulting from such intervention."

The next sentence merely reads, "The Crusade for Justice is a militant Mexican American organization founded in Denver in 1968 [actually 1966] with headquarters in Denver, Colorado. Its political arm is known as 'La Raza Unida.'" The rest of the document, serialized as 105-176910-56, is blacked out. Documents available to the author show that the FBI sought to explore the Crusade's perceived ties to the preceding individuals and groups, but give no indication how, when, or if, the investigations ended.

SAC TRIMBACH'S TESTIMONY: THE CRUSADE–AIM CONNECTION

The FBI's interest in links between the Crusade and AIM continued for years. On March 5, 1974, the Denver FBI field office wrote FBI Director Clarence Kelley about Crusade plans to commemorate the death of Luis Martinez. The Denver FBI teletype reported, "Information in reference teletype indicates possibility of violence including attacks on police officers in connection with captioned rally."[27]

Among the speakers the Crusade invited to the event were names that must have kept the FBI's copy machines in constant use: Hortensia de Allende, widow of the martyred Chilean president Salvador Allende, Ramon Arbona of the Puerto Rican Socialist Party (PSP), attorney William Kunstler of New York, Bert Corona of CASA, Mario Cantu of San Antonio, Jaime Rodriguez of the Los Angeles–based National Committee to

Free Los Tres. This particular FBI teletype, however, was particularly concerned with the invitation extended to Dennis Banks and Russell Means of AIM.

> [Five lines deleted.] In view of the past violent activities by Banks and Means and the information contained in referenced teletype, UACB [Unless Advised to the Contrary by Bureau headquarters], it is requested that [the] Minneapolis [field office] contact US District Judge, St. Paul, Minnesota, who is currently handling the trial of Banks and Means and advise of the potential for violence in Denver involving the militant Crusade for Justice. Determine whether travel restrictions have been placed or can be placed on Means and Banks to prevent their travel to Denver to participate in the March 17, 1974, events.[28]

In response to the Denver FBI's suggestion, SAC Joseph Trimbach's Minneapolis FBI office reported to the FBI director in a March 8 teletype. Though half of its 48 sentences were blacked out when released by the FBI, the remaining text states:

> There are no travel restrictions on Banks and Means. They have been traveling considerably during days their trial is not in session. . . . District Court Judge Fred J. Nichol, who is handling their trial in St. Paul, Minnesota, was not contacted relative to the possibility of imposing travel restrictions. . . . The current attitude of . . . Judge Nichol of St. Paul and recent comments by him in open court which were not complimentary to the FBI, is another reason why no contact was made with him relative to possible travel restrictions for Banks and Means.[29]

What the Minneapolis teletype did not detail was the serious criticism of SAC Trimbach that resulted from discoveries of FBI misconduct at the federal trial of Banks and Means that started in January 1974. Judge Nichol found discrepancies in the prosecution's testimony and was irritated at the prosecutors' delay in releasing information to the defense attorneys as he had ordered. Nichol was amazed when Trimbach testified that he had never applied for authorization to tap the sole telephone at Wounded Knee. When Trimbach was presented with a copy of the wiretap request that bore his signature, he responded, "I don't know if that's my signature."[30]

Nichol's anger at Trimbach increased as the trial progressed and Douglas Durham, a government informant who had infiltrated AIM and its defense committee, was exposed. Trimbach had already given sworn testimony that the FBI had no such informers. The Justice Department later asked Judge Nichol to bar himself from further AIM trials because they feared he was biased against the FBI.

LEONARD PELTIER AND THE CRUSADE FOR JUSTICE

The Crusade's 1975 commemoration of Luis Martinez' death at the Denver Indian Center included many speakers. Among them were Jesse Bordeaux, a Lakota who worked with the Crusade and Denver AIM, and AIM leaders John Trudell and Larry Anderson.[31] Trudell spoke again at the 1976 commemoration at the Denver Indian Center. Among the 1977 commemoration speakers was Dino Butler, whose FBI file was probably very thick.

Dino Butler, Bob Robideau, and Leonard Peltier, all AIM members, had been charged in the death of two FBI agents on the Pine Ridge Reservation on June 26, 1975, when the FBI became embroiled in a shootout with AIM members. Butler and Robideau were tried in federal court in 1976, and among the defense witnesses was Rodolfo Gonzales, who testified about FBI misconduct affecting the Crusade and AIM. The trial was unique because FBI Director Clarence Kelley was called to give testimony, the first time an FBI director had ever given testimony in court. Butler and Robideau were acquitted.

Leonard Peltier, however, was arrested separately and subsequently convicted in a controversial trial. He is presently serving life sentences in federal prison.

The Crusade had suffered a terrible blow on March 17, 1973, but the tragedy strengthened the resolve of its core members. They continued to support the sovereignty of native peoples. Crusade members met with Leonard Peltier when he was a fugitive in the late summer of 1975 and once more in late September or October. Peltier recounted what happened in the FBI shootout on the Pine Ridge Reservation. He spoke of the intense FBI harassment of AIM, of his fears for his life, and of his conviction that he would not get a fair trial in South Dakota. He spoke freely, and he claimed no responsibility for the FBI agents' deaths. He was given financial support, and he said he would try to communicate in the near future.

On November 14, 1975, Oregon state troopers halted a motor home and a station wagon on Interstate 80. One state trooper described a man who got out of the mobile home as a "large Mexican-appearing person," whom the trooper ordered to lie spread-eagled in the road.[32] The man complied. The trooper claimed that another person in the motor home then drove off while firing a weapon. In the confusion the "Mexican-appearing person" jumped up and ran into the night, but not before the trooper fired at him twice with a shotgun and wounded him. Leonard Peltier had escaped again.

Between the time of Peltier's escape and his later capture in Canada, a rumor reached the Crusade for Justice over the "Moccasin Trail," the term one AIM member used to describe what others would call the "grapevine." The rumor was that the large Mexican-appearing person, needing a name, not being able to use his own, and perhaps—in keeping with Lakota tradition—wanting to honor a brave warrior, chose a new name. He later purchased a car, actually a station wagon, the white 1970 Plymouth station wagon that was stopped in Oregon (Colorado license plates PW 949). The registration papers were rumored to be under the name Luis Martinez. This, however, may just be a rumor. Maybe FBI files would reveal the name of the person to whom the car was registered. Maybe not. FBI files on AIM and the Crusade for Justice—if revealed in their entirety—would surely shed light on the death of Luis "Junior" Martinez, Wounded Knee, and the trial and conviction of Leonard Peltier, although many reports would be alarmist and inaccurate. But if respecting one treaty means honoring them all, then completely opening one FBI file could mean opening them all—and where would it all end?

If Leonard Peltier honored Luis Martinez by using his name, Peltier may have been doing in 1975 what Kwame Ture suggested at a commemorative event in Denver in 1977.

> When a man or woman dies in the service of the people, the people can never forget that man or woman. This is a memorial, but we cannot cry. How can you be sad when a man has given his life for you? We can't be sad. All we can do is perfect that act for which he died. We must work to become a perfect struggler for the people. History shapes us whether we like to admit it or not. You have but one alternative; either fight against oppression or to help oppression. There is no middle ground. When you're not fighting oppression to liberate the people, even if you're standing still, you're fighting against the people. We must wake the people up, make them conscious. It's the only way we can give a proper memorial to Junior.[33]

Thirteen

Conflicts, Deaths, and Indictments, 1973–1974

Activists and organizations throughout Colorado experienced conflicts, confrontations, arrests and court cases paralleling those that affected the Crusade for Justice in the mid-1970s. Though the Crusade was the most prominent movement organization in the state, with the largest membership, experience, and resources, other groups confronted similar problems, without the human and financial resources to deal with them.

ESCUELA AZTLAN

Activists from Escuela Aztlan, an independent alternative school in West Denver, were in the news on December 11, 1973, because of their support for student protests at Baker Junior High School. Baker students, with Escuela Aztlan supporters, complained about heavy police patrols at the school and in the neighborhood. The student council invited Escuela Aztlan members to participate in an assembly to address student grievances. Students subsequently walked out of the assembly, charging that it was being manipulated by the principal. As they left school to march to nearby Hector Florez Park, they encountered firemen, the police canine corps, and the Special Services Unit (SSU), who had been called to the scene.[1]

Protestors said that while marching to Florez Park, they overheard orders broadcast on police radios calling for the identification and arrest of protest leaders. Chuck Koehler and Juan Avila, a student leader from Escuela Aztlan, were specifically mentioned. Scuffles between police and protestors occurred when the march arrived at Florez Park. Each side blamed the other for the violence. Patrolman David Holt allegedly struck a young woman, Wendy Aragon, with his fist while attempting to arrest her. Holt, however, alleged that he was dragged from his car by students, was beaten without provocation, and lost a fingertip when he was disarmed and shot in the hand with his own gun by 15-year-old Juan Avila.

Protestors said Holt, who arrived in a Volkswagen and wore civilian clothes, was wounded when his gun discharged as he drew the weapon while scuffling with students who went to the young woman's defense. Holt, a member of the SSU, was one of two officers who were the first to arrive on Downing Street in response to Officer Hogue's call during the March 17 confrontation. Escuela Aztlan activists said their office was surveilled after the incident by plainclothes officers using cabs and trucks belonging to the telephone and Public Service companies.

Denver District Attorney Dale Tooley's office requested that Avila be held without bond and tried in District Court for conspiracy, theft of Holt's revolver, and first-degree assault, which carried a potential 4 to 50 year prison sentence. The judge concurred with the prosecutor only on the assault charge, which was tried in Juvenile Court. Tooley's office then requested a $20,000 bond. The judge, after hearing evidence at a detention hearing, set a $4,500 bond over the prosecutor's protest. Westside activists organized a defense committee for Avila, who was defended by Ken Padilla in a trial that bore similarities to the author's March 17 trial. Holt was as certain that Avila was the person who fired the weapon as he and Tow were that the author was the gunman who fired at Officer Carole Hogue. As in the March 17 case, a prosecution witness hurt the prosecution's case by testifying that Avila was not the person the witness saw shoot Holt. Juan Avila was acquitted on September 5, 1974.[2]

COLORADO SCHOOL PROTESTS: 1974

School protests and disturbances erupted elsewhere in Colorado. On October 9, 1974, young Chicanas fought with young black women at Centennial High School in Pueblo. The fighting grew to involve 300 students, and then pitted Chicanos against teachers, police, administrators, and black and white students. Chicano students charged that knives were pulled on them, but teachers who intervened merely told the students with weapons to put their knives in their pockets and continue their fighting elsewhere. The Chicano students then turned on the teachers at the school.[3] Tensions had been building there: it was alleged that an athletics coach once drew a bean on a blackboard and asked students to tell him what it was. The answer to the question, according to the coach, was "a Mexican brain." Over 30 patrol units responded to the October

9 disturbance, and 16 students were arrested, all of them Mexican. A photograph of the disturbance in a Pueblo newspaper showed a Chicana teenager being dragged on the ground by a plainclothes officer. The next day a press conference was held. Community activists from the Pueblo chapter of LRUP, the Pueblo Brown Berets, the Eastside Planning Council, and the Mothers of Casa Verde condemned the school administration and blamed teachers and police for the escalation of violence. The next day over 300 Chicano students walked out of Centennial in support of the arrested students. Students and parents, in company with community activists, attended an educational conference hosted by Southern Colorado State College on Saturday, October 12.

The community delegation, led by Brown Beret Eddie Montour, included students, parents, LRUP members, the Mothers of Casa Verde, and the Eastside Planning Council. They took the podium to address the situation at Centennial and other Pueblo public schools. The audience responded with a standing ovation when Montour concluded. Conference participants wrote a formal statement that read, "We, the participants in the Pueblo Conference toward Quality Education for the Mexican American in Colorado completely support the Chicano community in Pueblo in condemning the actions of the administration of Centennial High School in the manner they handled the recent incident there." Participants also endorsed demands for the release of arrested students, for rescinding their suspensions, for suspension of policemen involved, and for the removal of the school principal.[4]

Meanwhile vandals entered Centennial High School and painted the walls with graffiti that read, "Fuck Chicanos," and "Spics and Dirty Greasers Get Out of Our School." The Pueblo activists said the media and local government blamed conflicts on ethnic rivalry to divert attention from the dereliction of school authorities. The activists wrote, "The fact that incidents of this type have continued to reoccur since 1969 makes it clearly evident that the fault does not lie with the student body, but with the teachers, administrators, hiring practices, and the continuation of an irrelevant and inadequate educational system. The only thing our young people are guilty of is practicing self-defense and having pride in being Chicano."[5]

In the spring of 1974, school disturbances between Chicano and white students closed schools for one week in the southern Colorado town of Monte Vista. In an attempt to prevent recurrences, Community Relations Service mediators from the U.S. Justice Department drew up a ten-point agreement, which was signed by school officials and Raymond Gallegos, a senior at Monte Vista High School. The agreement was to clarify policies on suspensions, expulsions, corporal punishment, locker searches, and school security. The schools endorsed an expansion of a bilingual, multicultural education program that would include Southwestern cultural studies. The agreement's last point read, "Every effort will be made to emphasize the role played by various cultures in the development of the Southwest and will emphasize the worth and dignity of individuals of these cultures."[6]

CONFLICT IN BRIGHTON

That summer, on July 13, 29 people from Brighton and Fort Lupton were arrested by 50 officers from eight jurisdictions at Veterans Roadside Park, a secluded gathering spot for local Chicanos in Brighton. Charges included inciting to riot, obstructing a police officer, third-degree assault, and disobeying a public safety order under riot conditions. The incident occurred shortly before midnight when officers drove to the area with police dogs and began asking for people's identification. Police said many underage youths were drinking and carousing at the park.

Civilians reported that they were Maced, clubbed, and attacked by the police dogs as reinforcements quickly arrived from the widely dispersed municipalities of Broomfield, Fort Lupton, Commerce City, Thornton, Northglenn, and Westminster, and from the Adams County Sheriff's Department. People were arrested at other parks hours after the initial incident. Civilians charged police with initiating the violence and on July 18 held a press conference at the park to announce a July 26 march and rally. The city formed a board of inquiry with local and federal officials and community representatives, including Brighton Brown Berets. Diane Romero and Charlotte Bonsell of Brighton led a defense committee, and Gerald Lucero submitted an article to *El Gallo:* "Brighton Chicanos needed to show the Brighton Police Department that when they call in other police agencies from this state to support an attack against Chicanos, Chicanos in Brighton can also call on Chicanos from throughout this state for support."[7]

"KNOCKING AT THE DOORS OF THE ESTABLISHMENT"

Though most protests involved working-class Chicanos, others were led by those entering professional fields. Law students and medical students challenged the Colorado State Board of Bar Examiners, the Colorado Supreme Court, and the University of Colorado Medical Center.

The law students protested because the Board of Bar Examiners failed eight of 10 Chicanos and Chicanos who took the bar exam in February

1974. The students that alleged the real reason for the failure rate was that Mexicans were now "knocking at the doors of the establishment for jobs traditionally held by white professionals," and "that to allow [Mexicans] to enter into the Establishment, especially if they have roots in the barrio, is a direct threat to the economic, social, political, and legal status quo of the established professions."[8] Some of these students supported organizations like the Crusade and gave their time and talent to activist causes. Carlos Vigil, for example, who provided invaluable assistance to the Crusade in the March 17 trials, played a key role in the bar exam protests.

Students at the University of Colorado Medical Center (UCMC) voiced similar sentiments. Guided by the National Chicano Health Organization, these students protested against UCMC practices and shortcomings in serving the community and Chicano medical students. Like the law students, they called upon the Crusade to endorse their demands.

A student and community delegation met with UCMC administrators, including the deans of the dentistry, nursing, and medical departments, on May 15, 1974. The students said that UCMC had, since 1893, graduated only 14 Spanish-surnamed doctors and had "no known" statistics for Spanish-surnamed nursing graduates. Hospital employees were reprimanded for speaking Spanish on the job, but were often called upon to translate for doctors and nurses, after which they were sometimes criticized for neglecting their regular duties. In 1974, 16 Chicanos and Chicanas applied to UCMC, but none attended because they were more readily accepted in California, New Mexico, Utah, and California.[9] An article submitted to *El Gallo* by the students ended:

> The Crusade for Justice has come to the support of our students at the UCMC, as it has—and does—for Chicano students everywhere. However, we remind our Chicano brothers and sisters that they must never forget their origin, where they came from. You must never forget who needs you most, if not your own Raza. The community rallies behind you, hermanas y hermanos, but you must rally behind your community when you finally leave that university. That is where the need is, that is where you belong. Companeros, companeras, unidos—Venceremos![10]

ARRESTS AT THE DENVER PUBLIC LIBRARY

By 1973, the Crusade had organized five Mexican Independence Day walkouts, which popularized the September 16 holiday and legitimized community pride in Mexican history and culture. The Crusade felt that such accomplishment needed to be defended from encroachments by the establishment and by opportunists as other groups began to sponsor their

own events. The involvement of business owners, politicians, social service agencies, and promoters in those activities served to dilute the political focus that initially sparked the event. An *El Gallo* editorial explained:

> The Establishment itself has not been able to dilute the intent of Sep-
> tember 16th to create political awareness . . . or co-opt the leading
> forces. . . . On the negative side, we have the Boomerang Chicanos who
> resisted the identity, the culture, the association [with their people], but
> who come back home to reap in the program profits; we have the poverty
> pimps who take care of themselves instead of the poor; we have busi-
> nessmen and money jugglers who identify based on profits and gain and
> not on any dedication to our people's cause. . . . We have the opportun-
> ists who make an industry out of the movement and line their pockets
> with green while they shout Brown Power! . . . September 16th, Chicano
> Liberation Day, will remain in the hands of the people at any cost![11]

The Crusade's concerns stemmed from the Denver Public Library's
"Viva Mejicano!" program of September 1973. The Crusade was angered
to learn that the program would open with a proclamation by Mayor Bill
McNichols on Friday, September 7, at the Greek Amphitheater in Civic
Center Park. Dozens of people attended the event, which commenced
with Mexican folkloric dancers and musicians. The *Denver Post* reported
that "10 Chicana women shouted insults in an outdoor ceremony at Civic
Center that opened the library's month-long salute to Mexican Americans. They left when they failed to halt the celebration."[12]

The article, written six days after the Civic Center protest, was inaccurate and misleading. The protestors did not leave when they failed to halt
the ceremony; the mayor left when the protestors succeeded in doing so.
Most of the crowd, about 70 people, were protestors from the Crusade,
from Westside or Northside groups, or elsewhere, and they waited until
the performances were over. When McNichols was called to the microphone, he was booed so loudly that he could not finish his speech. The
article did not mention that the mayor was present, that he was the target
of the protest, or that he had been booed from the stage. The protest was
lead by Maria Serna and Nita Gonzales.

Protests continued the next week, when a panel of middle-class women
discussed "The Past and Present of the Mexican Woman." The September
12 discussion was attended by 40 to 50 people, of whom 80 percent were
protestors. It ended when protestors shouted down the panelists. Police
Captain Glenn Reichart, who headed the Intelligence Bureau in 1968,
told reporters that Patrolman Eugene McGuire "saw a suspect in a
kidnap-rape case" in the crowd and attempted to arrest him, but was
"jumped" by 35 to 40 people, disarmed, and had his walkie-talkie stolen.

He was treated for bruises at the hospital, and nine people were arrested.[13] Protestors said they intervened in the arrest when McGuire used undue force and disarmed him when he drew his weapon on the crowd.

Among those arrested were Northside activists Frank "Kiko" De Claw and Frank Luevano and Crusade members Ray Alvarado, José Gonzales, Eloy Espinoza, and Nita Gonzales, who was charged with second-degree assault and conspiracy one week after the incident.[14] Charges were later dropped for all, except for Luevano, who pled no contest to disturbance charges. The *Rocky Mountain News* reported, "McGuire apparently knew many of the ones who allegedly hit him and gave their names to fellow officers."[15] McGuire was indeed familiar with Chicano activists. He worked for the Intelligence Bureau, as was revealed when a briefcase was stolen from a patrol car. Its contents included a police intelligence report on people the police believed were linked to the Crusade.

CLANDESTINE ORGANIZATIONS AND A "POSSIBLE WEAPONS CONNECTION"

On February 12, 1975, Officer McGuire issued an "Intelligence Information Sheet" concerning 14 persons the Intelligence Bureau believed were linked to the Crusade. This document was found in a briefcase stolen in West Denver and brought to the Crusade building by those who took it. Crusade members who reviewed the sheet did not know five of the individuals, knew four others only vaguely, and heartily disliked two others. By the Crusade's definition, only one person of the 14 was an activist. By this person's name police noted, "Strong Crusade ties—Possible weapons connection." That the others were considered associates or co-conspirators of the Crusade was laughable.

The document reported that Detective J. C. Tyus told the Intelligence Bureau that the key suspect in the group, a 19-year-old, was believed to have "rifles and guns" and was waiting for "armor piercing ammunition before he starts sniping at police. . . . He has shot at officers in the past, as have the following associates. All below parties have had connections with the Crusade for Justice and seem to congregate at La Casa De Barrios, 935 W. 11th Ave. They hang around in Lincoln Park and Las Casitas Projects."[16] The Intelligence Information Sheet was circulated to all police districts, the Street Crime Attack Team (SCAT), the SSU, the burglary detail, the vice bureau, and Crimes Against Persons detectives.

During the 1960s and 1970s, some clandestine groups employed violence to oppose the government. Among the better-known groups were the Weather Underground, the Black Liberation Army, and the Fuerzas Armadas de Liberacion Nacional Puertoriqueña (FALN), who claimed responsibility for their actions in communiques to the media. In the

1970s, *El Gallo* often received such announcements and reprinted them without editorial comment.

Communiques were received from the Northern California Frente de Liberacion Chicano; the Chicano Liberation Front in El Paso; the Continental Revolutionary Army in Colorado; the Emiliano Zapata Unit of the People's Forces in California; and the People's United Liberation Army of America, a guerrilla army in the southern Mexican state of Guerrero led by the Mexican revolutionary Florencio Medrano Mederos. This last group, based among the exploited campesinos and Mexican Indians of traditionally rebellious southern Mexico, was the only group to develop the political and organizational sophistication to pose a serious threat to its government. This group continued the guerrilla war launched by Genaro Vasquez Rojas and Lucio Cabañas, whose names were legendary among Mexico's poor in the 1960s and 1970s. The Mexican communique read in part:

> The imperialists use their military force to control our countries at all levels: politically they support fascism in countries like Chile; economically they impose prices and tariffs on our agricultural products as in Central America; they strip our countries of their natural resources as in Venezuela and Peru and they force us into humiliating and cruel economic submission as in the case of Puerto Rico; culturally they have deformed our history, robbing us of our culture and separating us from our origins, using the "divide and conquer" tactic they have caused false divisions among the poor people as in the case with the Chicanos of the United States. The divisions which the great powers have imposed on the whole continent are nothing more than an organized way to better exploit us, and it is clear that we are all suffering the same political, economic, and cultural exploitation everywhere, which makes us see that we are one people without borders. . . . Liberty and Unity for all America![17]

The Continental Revolutionary Army operated in Colorado. In the spring of 1975 the group claimed responsibility for placing a pipe bomb outside the home of James M. Somerville, who was in Texas on business. Local newspapers reported that Somerville was chief of the Central Intelligence Agency's Denver field office. What Somerville was doing in Texas is unknown—he referred all questions to CIA headquarters in Washington. As far as anyone knew, this bombing marked the first time the CIA was physically attacked in the United States.[18]

DEATHS IN BOULDER

Mystery enshrouds other events of the mid-1970s. The death of six activists in Boulder is a case in point. There were two powerful explosions on

May 27 and May 29, 1974. The first three to die were Reyes Martinez, 25, a young attorney who previously worked with the Colorado Rural Legal Services; Neva Romero, 21, a UMAS leader; and Una Jaakola, 23, a University of Colorado student and Martinez' girlfriend. Both women lived in Boulder. Martinez was the younger brother of activist attorney Francisco "Kiko" Martinez, sons of a southern Colorado family with roots among the Nuevo Mexicano settlers of Colorado's Valle de San Luis in the mid-1800s.

Neva Romero, with her small-town background and middle-class roots, was as unlikely a bomb victim, or alleged bomber, as most people could imagine. She had been elected to the University of Colorado Student Senate and was prominent in UMAS after the 1972 expulsion from the Boulder campus of Florencio Granados, Ricardo Falcon, and others. Her father was the mayor of Ignacio, a southwestern Colorado town. Though many activists left the university after the 1972 expulsions, others, like Romero, remained.

Una Jaakola's political orientation was largely unknown. She was the product of a small-town midwestern upbringing, and the sole Anglo victim. Reyes Martinez lived and worked in southern Colorado. Romero was involved in a student occupation of a university building, a protest that was still in progress at the time of their deaths. Why Martinez, Romero, and Jaakola were together on that night is not known.

Just over 48 hours after the first group died, three more people were killed and one person critically injured in another explosion. The dead were Florencio "Freddie" Granado, 32, former UMAS leader and LRUP candidate; Heriberto Teran, 24, poet, former UMAS activist, and employee of the Colorado Pinto Project, which worked with Colorado parolees; and Francisco Dougherty, 22, a Vietnam veteran from Laredo, Texas. The sole survivor was Antonio Alcantar, of Texas, who suffered severe burns and the amputation of his left leg. Traumatized and wary, Alcantar was able to recall only the blinding flash of the explosion that took his friends' lives.

These four were natives of Texas. Teran and Granado enrolled at Boulder through community-oriented recruitment programs directed by Chicano students and staff. Several prominent members of UMAS, and instructors and staff of the programs that served them, arrived in Boulder from Texas in this manner. Among those from the El Paso–Juárez and Rio Grande Valley areas, in addition to Teran and Granado, were Salvador Ramirez, Carlos Rosas, and Abelardo "Lalo" Delgado.

Granado and Teran had been prominent members of the Boulder UMAS chapter and, like Neva Romero, were dedicated activists and effective organizers who were known and respected on campuses and in rural and urban communities throughout Colorado. Leaving Boulder after the 1972 student protests, Granado moved to Denver to work at the Platte Valley Action Center, a social service agency. He was editor and chief writer for the newspaper *El Escritor del Pueblo*. Teran was involved in the 1972 Boulder UMAS protests and was known for his Spanish and bilingual poetry, including poems about the death of his friend Ricardo Falcon, and another poem in tribute to those who died in the first bomb blast. This poem, "Aztlan Esta De Luto," was written on May 28, one day before his own death.[19] Dougherty and Alcantar, friends of Teran whom they knew from Texas, were recent arrivals in Colorado.

These bloody events fueled media headlines in the weeks after the blasts. Local, state, and federal authorities investigated and speculated that the dead were killed when bombs they themselves had constructed exploded accidentally. Each of the blasts completely destroyed the vehicle that carried the bomb, and identification of the remains was difficult. It is not known if the two groups had been in communication; it is not deemed likely by those who knew them well. Yet local media accounts attempted to detail links between the young activists. One account was published with the headline, "Woman Tied to Blast Seized with Timing Device." It reported:

> [Francisco] Luevano, who had been using the name Francisco Dougherty, was being sought by police on a Boulder County Court bench warrant issued when he failed to appear for a probation hearing. He was sentenced to three months in jail in connection with a campus disturbance in August 1973. Franke Martinez was Luevano's attorney. . . . Then Reyes Martinez started representing Luevano. . . . Luevano was one of 10 persons taken into custody after a Columbus Park disturbance last summer. He was arrested in September 1973 in connection with the assault of a Denver patrolman outside the Denver Public Library. Rodolfo "Corky" Gonzales, head of Denver's Crusade for Justice, said Friday he suspected the bombings were the actions of "right-wing" groups. Gonzales criticized press coverage of the bombings and the Boulder Police Department investigation. . . . Searches at the homes of Alcantar, Mrs. Freida Bugarin [whose car Granado, Dougherty, Teran, and Alcantar had borrowed] and Teran turned up evidence relating to the explosion, according to police sources. Batteries, a pocket watch, and heavy gauge wire were among the items taken from Alcantar's home, a source said. . . . Reyes Martinez, an attorney for Colorado Legal Services, has appeared frequently in Boulder County Court as Luevano's attorney. . . . A graduate of the University of Colorado Law School, Martinez often spent weekend [*sic*] in Boulder visiting Miss Jaakola at her apartment at the Lazy-J Motel. . . . Miss Jaakola, an August graduate of the University of Colorado, had been working as a waitress at a

Holiday Inn. She and Martinez were seen leaving the motel apartment with a woman who fit the description of Miss Romero.[20]

The items taken from Alcantar's home could be found in many households. The article confused one victim, Francisco Dougherty, with Francisco Luevano, a Denver native and a former Black Beret. Though Luevano knew some of the people who died in Boulder, he was obviously alive and had not been present in Boulder at the time of the bombings.

Activists criticized the authorities and media for assuming that the blast victims were responsible for their own deaths, for the many inaccuracies reported, and for what they viewed as a deliberate campaign of negative innuendo. Some believed that the dead were victims of a conspiracy that targeted them for their activism. But if this was true, who was responsible and how was it done? No one had a comprehensive theory, and no one had proof. If, as some thought, mysterious forces were somehow involved in domestic political assassinations, why focus on student activists, young lawyers, and college dropouts? If a young attorney, a UMAS leader, University of Colorado students, a former LRUP candidate, a member of the Colorado Pinto Project, and a Vietnam vet could be killed for unknown reasons, who could be next?

Although the Crusade was but one of many groups that spoke up in the outcry that followed the deaths, its criticisms were typical of activists' concerns.

> The press, by insinuation and imaginary journalism, has maligned not only the dead but the living. Although it is stated over and over again that no one saw the immediate explosion in the first case, we quote from the mouths of Radio Hams and newspaper clippings, "It was assumed that they were assembling a bomb." Who is assuming? We say the press is the speculator, with an eye toward indicting the dead. . . . On Friday, May 31 [1974], Rita Montero, 23, of Denver was arrested by the Colorado State Patrol in Boulder after they attempted to stop her after seeing a "La Raza Unida" bumper sticker on her car. She was charged with traffic violations and released but not until after Boulder Police called out the bomb squad to search her car. . . . Police told the press the bomb squad was called because police had found "a timing device in her car which police said could be used in a bomb." It was further described as "a clock with wires attached to it." The headlines read, "Woman Linked to Victim of Car Blast Is Arrested," "Woman Tied to Bomb Blast Seized with Timing Device," and "Suspected Bomb Leads to Arrest." These headlines were used on Friday, Saturday, and Sunday with pictures of Rita. . . . After the police and press had created enough hysteria, an article in Monday's paper gave about 2 inches of print to the incident, calling it a "false alarm" and saying that the timing device was admitted by Boulder police to be an ordinary egg timer. Boulder police refused to

say why this wasn't reported earlier and the press gave no big headlines on this story. Is this just a case of bungling?[21]

As news of the Boulder tragedy spread, telegrams and letters of protest and solidarity poured in to Colorado from the National Alliance Against Racist and Political Repression in New York City; the national field director of AIM in St. Paul; the Centro de La Raza in Seattle; the Houston 12 Defense Committee; the Houston Youth Against War and Fascism; Luis "Tingo" Archuleta, vice-president of LADS at the Colorado State Penitentiary; Hortensia de Allende; Eileen Klemr, vice-chairperson of the October League of Detroit; and others. The Eugene Coalition of Eugene, Oregon, reported:

> We extend to all our sisters and brothers of the Crusade for Justice and the Chicano Movement in Colorado our total solidarity to you in the present attack on your organizations. . . . Here in Eugene, Oregon, we have demonstrated in protest of the bombing deaths in Boulder. On June 1, the day of the memorial services in Colorado, we picketed the Post Office in Eugene demanding an end to the attack on the Chicano people of Colorado and to protest the west coast [*sic*] suppression of all news from the Denver-Boulder area. In Salem on June 5, seventy people from all over the state met and demonstrated in front of the State Capitol building in solidarity with the Crusade for Justice and the Chicano Movement. In an effort to tell the people of Oregon about the vicious attacks in Boulder, we took to the streets of Portland, Salem, Corvaillis, Woodboro, Mt. Angel, and Eugene and distributed over 7,000 leaflets to inform the people when the corporate news media ignored this attack. . . . We believe as we know you do that the only solution to the oppression and racism in this country and throughout the world is in unity of all freedom loving people.[22]

If the authorities had evidence that the dead were victims of their own actions, it was not presented. It appeared, at least to the activists, that authorities were interested in using the six deaths for a much larger investigation of Colorado's activist network. Several women were subpoenaed by federal authorities investigating the bombing deaths.

On July 11, Freida Bugarin, Lee Teran, Patricia Alcantar, Rita Montero, and Guadalupe Granado were ordered to appear before the federal grand jury. The women—three of them widows of the Boulder blast victims—and their supporters protested against the subpoenas, the focus of the investigation, and the conduct of law enforcement bodies. On the day of their scheduled appearance, the women, friends of the blast victims, and hundreds of supporters demonstrated at the U.S. Courthouse in Denver. "Also waiting," according to *El Gallo*, "were over 50 U.S. Marshals, FBI Agents, security guards from the Post Office, from the Customs house, from the U.S. Courthouse complex, and dozens of Denver Police, including undercover men [and] members of the specially trained Street Crime Attack Team (SCAT) and the Special Services Unit."

The investigating authorities had already taken a public posture based on the assumed guilt of the dead, but subpoenaing grief-stricken family members angered those who could not accept the official story. On the day the women appeared at the Federal Courthouse, local attorneys filed a complaint in Federal Court on behalf of four individuals and three groups: Boulder students John Espinoza and Judy Sandoval; Freida Bugarin, who lent Granado the car in which he died; Rita Carmen Montero, a former UMAS member living in Denver; and the Crusade for Justice, Boulder UMAS, and the DCLDC. Attorneys from the National Lawyers Guild, MALDEF, and others represented the subpoenaed women. Among these attorneys were Ruth Buechler, Jeanne Busacca, Carlos Vigil, Scott Keating, Barry Roseman, Manuel Ramos, David Vela, Jacobo Pacheco, Jerry Gerash, Bill Hazleton, Sander Karp, Federico Peña, and Rudy Schware, a life-long activist and veteran attorney for progressive causes.

The defendants were agents of the Bureau of Alcohol, Tobacco, and Firearms (ATF), local federal attorneys, Attorney General William B. Saxbe and Treasury Secretary William E. Simon. The complaint charged the defendants with "the continuous and malicious harassment, intimidation and illegal surveillance of Plaintiffs . . . for the illegal purpose of chilling and punishing the constitutionally protected political activities of the Plaintiffs." Specifically, the complainants stated that they were subjected to

> (a) threats; (b) excessive, continuous, open and unjustifiable "surveillance"; (c) illegal searches and limitations of freedom of movement; (d) illegal electronic surveillance and/or wiretapping; (e) illegal harassment through intimidation of friends, neighbors, and associates; (f) denial of the right to counsel; and (g) illegal and bad faith utilization of the grand jury.[24]

Student journalist John Espinoza declared that he was harassed and threatened by federal agents. He submitted an affidavit that detailed his visit with federal agents and wrote:

> I was told that if I wanted an attorney present "you must have something to hide." Additionally, I was informed that I was not a suspect at the time and therefore the agents did not have to read me my rights. . . . I was told that if I did not answer the agents' questions, I would be subpoenaed before the Federal Grand Jury. . . . [The Federal agents] began calling me a "commander" of Chicanos in Boulder with the clear intent

of classifying myself and other Chicanos, with whom I associate, as members of a military or paramilitary political organization.[25]

Espinoza further reported that the agents told him that "I could become an informer and be granted immunity from prosecution and would 'be set up for the rest of my life.'"[26] Judy Sandoval submitted a similar affidavit: "I believe that if I am called before the Grand Jury, it will be to harass me solely because I am a Chicana and politically active. I have avoided meetings with other Chicanos, whom I have been politically active with because I believe I am under surveillance."[27] Before the issues in the complaint could be decided, around 4:30 p.m. on the date of the scheduled appearance, the federal attorneys dropped the grand jury subpoenas and merely announced that the subpoenas were satisfied. The plaintiffs' complaint against the government was subsequently dismissed. No cause for the deaths was ever established, but the tragedy continued to furnish cause for conjecture. Denver District Attorney Dale Tooley wrote: "The classic example of the gang that couldn't shoot straight was the activist bombers' group who made Denver the bombing capital of the nation in the 1970's. Several of its members apparently could not tell red wires from green ones, and blew themselves up in the process of planting bombs."[28]

The Crusade intervened in the controversy to defend the names of the dead activists and those subpoenaed by the grand jury. None were Crusade members, though Bugarin's children attended Escuela Tlatelolco. Still, the Crusade bore a burden of innuendo through its association with the activists involved. In the aftermath of the bombing that killed Granado, Teran, and Dougherty, the media reported that police found materials from the Crusade for Justice in the car in which they were riding. The police and media never clarified that the material found was merely a homework folder left in the car by one of Bugarin's children.

As the oldest and most visible of Colorado's "militant" organizations, the Crusade already bore the weight of negative publicity and police surveillance. The last March 17 felony case ended in November 1973, but the Crusade had no rest. Indeed, at the time of the Boulder bombing deaths, the Crusade was already embroiled in a bombing controversy that began in January 1974. Crusade member Gary Garrison was the defendant in this new case.

THE TRIAL AND ACQUITTAL OF GARY GARRISON

On January 15, 1974, the *Rocky Mountain News* published a story headlined "Bomb Recipient, Crusade for Justice Connection Traced." The article reported that a homemade bomb, which failed to detonate, had been tossed through the window of a paint store owned by James A. Boone on Sunday, January 13. The article reported that Boone had sold the Crusade for Justice an apartment building, the site of the March 17 confrontation, but foreclosed on the property in August 1973 because the Escuela Tlatelolco Education Fund, which held title to the property, failed to make two monthly payments of $453.94 each. The property had been purchased for $67,000, but damage to the property from the confrontation alone was estimated at $60,000. Though Gonzales signed the checks to pay Boone, his daughter forgot to mail them, and they lay unnoticed on a desk at the Crusade's office.

The owner stopped the foreclosure one month later when the Crusade paid the $50,000 balance, draining the organization's resources. Gonzales met with Boone and Boone's attorney, who insisted on the full balance rather than monthly payments. Boone commented in the article, "I felt, what with the condition of the building [following the explosion] that the only agreement I could accept was payment in full."[29]

Boone said that his meeting with Gonzales had been "totally business-like." His attorney told the reporter that Gonzales "always conducted himself like a gentleman" in the course of the negotiations. Boone concluded, "It was just like any other real estate transaction. It's all forgotten and there are no hard feelings. They had a problem, I had a problem, and we worked it out to our satisfaction."[30]

Police Captain Robert Shaughnessy said the dynamite used in the unexploded bomb thrown through the paint store window was the same as that used in most of 15 alleged bombings and bombing attempts in the Denver area since September 17, 1973, including alleged attacks targeting a Northside motorcycle shop across from La Raza Park and a letter-bomb allegedly sent to Officer Carole Hogue by Francisco "Kiko" Martinez, a fugitive attorney charged with these bombing attempts. The *Rocky Mountain News* described him as

> a known associate of officials of the Colorado La Raza Unida party, which was established by Gonzales and whose headquarters are in the Crusade building. Martinez served as an informal spokesperson for Mrs. Priscilla Falcon during the trial of a man accused of manslaughter in connection with the shooting death of her husband, Richard.[31]

The article named no suspect in the paint store incident, but the Crusade angrily complained that it was the target of a defamatory publication. On January 16, the day after the article appeared, the Crusade held a press conference to announce a $10 million suit against the owners of the *Rocky Mountain News.*[32] The Crusade's criticism of press coverage was joined by representatives of the National Lawyers Guild, MALDEF,

Servicios de La Raza, a North Denver social service agency, the director and staff of the Platte Valley Action Center, and others. The MALDEF statement said, "Yesterday's story virtually accused the Crusade of bombing the Boone Paint Store." MALDEF described the *News* article as "another slanted report in a pattern of systematic, intentional, and willful 'misreportings.'"[33] The National Lawyers Guild press release stated, "The sole journalistic purpose of placing such disparate items of information in juxtaposition is to create a false and misleading impression. . . . This intent to create false impressions constitutes actual malice which is the distinguishing feature of this article."[34] The Crusade suit charged:

> The article published in said Newspaper . . . was intended to convey and did convey that the Plaintiffs, as organizations, by and through their members and/or teachers and students, and/or associates were engaged in an active pattern of intentional violence and bombing of police and other persons whose interests were or had been antagonistic to the interests of either the plaintiff, Crusade for Justice, or the plaintiff, Escuela Tlatelolco and in particular, that plaintiff organizations were responsible for a bomb thrown into the business establishment known as Boone's Paint Store.[35]

The Crusade alleged that the article was one of many that had been wholly or partly false, defamatory, published with malice, and intended to hurt the organization's reputation in the community. The suit included a three-page summary of articles dating back to April 1, 1966. This civil case was overshadowed by more serious legal concerns.

Gary Garrison was arrested for the bombing of Boone's Paint Store several hours after the Crusade press conference. He was charged with attempted murder, first- and second-degree arson, and criminal mischief. Garrison had been active in the Crusade since its earliest days. In the 1960s he performed in Gonzales' play "The Revolutionist." At the time of his arrest Garrison was a part-time caretaker at the Crusade and an instructor at Escuela Tlatelolco. After his arrest, the district attorney proposed a bond of $100,000, but Garrison was released from custody on his own recognizance two days later.

Garrison's case added to the legal burdens on the Chicano movement. A schedule of court dates for activists from November 1 to December 17, 1973, showed 12 persons with a total of 15 separate court appearances. These resulted in 11 dismissals, two acquittals, and two continuances. Five people were Crusade members; one was a state officer of LRUP from northern Colorado; one was a Boulder UMAS activist; two were Westside associates of the Crusade; one was a former Northside Black Beret; and two were members of LADS from the State Penitentiary at Canon City. These months were not exceptional; 20 people had six court appearances in Brighton, Boulder, Fort Collins, and Denver from August 20 to September 16, 1974.[36]

Garrison was scheduled to appear before the Denver grand jury conducted by District Attorney Dale Tooley on January 24, but he was dismissed without giving testimony. That night the grand jury charged Garrison with criminal attempt of first-degree arson, criminal mischief, and conspiracy. When the indictment was issued, Garrison was arrested and bond set at $50,000. Garrison reported that, while in custody, the District Attorney's office invited him to enter a guilty plea to criminal mischief in return for dropping the remaining charges. Garrison's attorneys, Walter Gerash and Ken Padilla, requested a bond reduction. Denver Judge Joseph Lilly reduced the bond to $7,500 over the district attorney's objection. The authorities alleged that Garrison's fingerprints were found on a paper sack that contained a brick and the dynamite bomb reportedly tossed through the store window.

On January 24, grand jury investigator James Visser went looking for Garrison at his North Denver residence. Visser said he noticed loose bricks in a barbecue pit at the home, thought they were "similar" to the brick found in the paint store, and took a brick with him. A search warrant was issued, other bricks were taken from the residence by authorities, and the original brick was returned. On May 3, defense attorneys filed motions before Judge Lilly asking that the bricks be suppressed as evidence because the first brick was taken without a warrant. The bricks were banned from the case, saving Gerash and Padilla the trouble of summoning witnesses to testify about how brickyards produce untold millions of "similar" bricks that could be found in countless places throughout the city. *El Gallo* reported that Deputy District Attorney William Buckley, who subsequently withdrew from the case, said the bricks were merely "the frosting on the cake," adding that "their loss isn't going to ruin the case."[37] The defendant, defense attorneys, and the defense committee thought the use of the bricks was laughable, but worried that newspaper headlines implied that evidence of guilt had been suppressed, publicity that would make a fair trial extremely difficult.

The Garrison trial began in Denver on September 16. Judge Lilly barred Garrison's supporters from the courtroom during the jury selection process, and they had to vacate the corridors near the courtroom. The next day, Gerash and Padilla, protesting against *Rocky Mountain News* coverage that detailed the evidence to be used in the trial, asked for a mistrial and the dismissal of charges on the grounds that the District Attorney's office had improperly discussed the case with reporters and made it impossible for Garrison to have an impartial jury. Deputy District Attorney Charles Murray countered by introducing a defense committee flyer that itself publicized details of the case. Judge Lilly declared a mistrial when a prospective juror reported seeing the flyer and then ordered the case moved to another town. Gerash and Padilla protested against the change of venue to no avail.

After many procedural delays, the Garrison case was set for trial in Fort Morgan before Judge Waino Johnson. The trial lasted from August 13 to August 29, 1975. The Crusade and DCLDC organized transportation for supporters and did intensive work in the defense effort. No eyewitness tied Garrison to the crime scene. One Anglo woman called by the prosecution testified that police had shown her photos of Garrison, but that he did not fit the description of men she saw in the area of the paint store after she heard glass break and looked out her window. None of the men she saw were Mexican.[38] An expert witness called by the defense contradicted the police claim that Garrison's fingerprint was found on the paper sack that held the dynamite and brick tossed through the paint store window. Garrison's family testified that he was home on the night of the incident. The Fort Morgan jury found Garrison not guilty.

The Crusade had little time to savor the victory, nor did the activists have time to assess the substantial cost of the setbacks of the previous three years. The national La Raza Unida Party once linked an expanding Chicano movement in the Southwest and Midwest, but was now being dismembered. In 1972, Ricardo Falcon, Florencio Granado, and other UMAS activists left the Boulder campus after confrontations with the university over control of student programs. Falcon and Granado's subsequent deaths deprived Colorado of energetic, talented, and charismatic young leaders. On March 17, 1973, Luis Martinez was killed in a confrontation that caused huge losses to the Crusade's finances and its already controversial public image. In January 1974, Gary Garrison was arrested and charged with an attempted bombing. In April, six young people died in two explosions that left the sole survivor burned and maimed. No account of their deaths satisfactory to the authorities or to their friends, families, and associates was ever given. The Crusade's most sympathetic supporters were now confronted with upholding an organization whose members and teachers were portrayed as bomb-throwers and terrorists.

Though the Crusade saw the victory in Fort Morgan as a vindication, the troubles and controversy that plagued it did not end. Within three weeks, Crusade members were again indicted on felony charges involving the use of explosives and charges of conspiracy to kill police officers. The September 1975 arrest of John Haro and Anthony Quintana, within a month of the Garrison acquittal, linked the Crusade to another sensational controversy.

Fourteen

The Conspiracy Case
Against John Haro

Longtime Denverites will remember that in the mid-70's, Denver was the
bombing capital of the U.S. It was my belief at the time that the Crusade
for Justice, a militant group, was responsible for the bombings. With the
assistance of a brave informer, Detective J. C. Tyus, Officer Mike Klawonn,
and agents from the Bureau of Alcohol, Tobacco and Firearms, we were
able to infiltrate the group and obtain bombs from [John] Haro. . . . Haro
was arrested in a stolen vehicle transporting a dynamite bomb to the District 4 police substation. . . . This was the first time in U.S. history that a
bomber was apprehended en route with a live bomb. As a result of this
investigation, the Crusade was exposed for what it was—a terrorist
organization.

Ex-Patrolman Daril F. Cinquanta, letter to the editor,
Rocky Mountain News, June 21, 1989

In a government of laws, existence of the government will be imperiled if it
fails to observe the law scrupulously. Our Government is the potent, the
omnipresent teacher. For good or for ill, it teaches the whole people by its
example. Crime is contagious. If the Government becomes a lawbreaker, it
breeds contempt for law. . . . To declare that . . . the Government may commit crimes in order to secure the conviction of a private criminal—would
bring terrible retribution.

Justice Louis Brandeis, dissent in *Olmstead v. U.S.* (1928)

On December 12, 1978, the Denver Chicano Liberation Defense Committee (DCLDC) informed its supporters that John Haro, a former vice
chairperson of the Crusade, had exhausted his last court appeal and
started a federal prison sentence after being sentenced to four concurrent
six-year terms on 1975 charges of possessing explosive devices. This conviction, in 1976 in federal court, was related to a more serious state case

in which Haro and Anthony Quintana, a Crusade member and employee of Haro, were charged with several felonies, including unlawful use of explosives, theft, and conspiracy to commit murder.

A BRAVE INFORMER

According to press accounts, the arrests resulted from the state's biggest investigation and surveillance operation of its kind and involved both local and federal law enforcement bodies.[1] Police and prosecution sources alleged that members of the Crusade for Justice conspired to place time-bombs at police facilities to protest against a September 1975 gathering in Denver of the International Association of Chiefs of Police. Police claimed that they uncovered the conspiracy when an informer, Joseph Cordova, Jr., gained a position of trust within the Crusade.

Haro met Joseph Cordova, Jr., after being introduced to Cordova's father by Rodolfo Gonzales. While his vehicle was being serviced at Haro's filling station in the summer of 1975, Gonzales encountered Varolin Joseph Cordova, Sr., the informer's father. The elder Cordova recalled, "I went to [Lake Junior High School] with Corky. I always admired Corky because he was one hell of an athlete."[2] Cordova, Sr., with his stocky son following behind, approached Gonzales. The father introduced his son, saying that Cordova, Jr., wanted to meet Gonzales.

The younger Cordova told Gonzales he had belonged to a Brown Beret chapter in California after being discharged from the military and wanted to get involved in the movement in Denver. Haro approached at that moment, and Gonzales introduced the Cordovas to him. Gonzales walked away from this chance encounter with an old acquaintance and his son. Months later he would recall the incident.

Joseph Cordova, Jr., later claimed he received hand grenades from Haro, gaining his confidence by faking a bombing attempt at the Cut Rate Meat Market on 13th Avenue and Kalamath Street, five blocks from Haro's station. Cordova claimed to have a grudge against the store owner, and said Haro assisted him by giving him a hand grenade to use. Police Captain Robert Shaughnessy testified that Cordova was supposed to have been provided with a hand grenade by Haro that was supposed to have been used against an Arab store in West Denver on August 13, 1975, in order for Cordova to gain credibility with Haro.[3] The allegation that Haro provided Cordova with grenades, on August 13 and, later, on September 13, led to criminal charges against Haro in federal court in early 1976. A subsequent, more serious case followed in state courts in a trial that ended in April 1977.

District Attorney Dale Tooley's autobiography, *I'd Rather Be in*

Denver, recounts that police went to his house in August 1975 to ask him to approve a plan for Cordova to toss a grenade (presumably a dud) through the store window (presumably with the owner and customers inside).[4] Tooley said he vetoed the plan. Instead, a simulated grenade was laid on the store's floor, police responded to the scene, and the incident was treated as a real bombing attempt and reported as such in the newspaper. Exact details, however, are difficult to follow. Detective Tyus, for example, said he met Cordova around May or June of 1975. He remembered that it was during Denver's mayoral campaign, but he did not know the exact date.

Tyus had reason to remember the 1975 mayoral election. In the spring of 1975, Tyus campaigned against a Democratic mayoral contender who had angered police earlier that year by opposing the police use of hollow-point bullets. Public debate was heated and became hotter when a Denver officer subsequently was killed during a robbery. Police mobilized a show of mourning for their comrade, then followed it with a show of force.

After church ceremonies for the officer, hundreds of police, most in uniform and some in patrol cars with flashing lights, proceeded in the middle of the street to the campaign headquarters of the politician who opposed hollow-point ammunition. A photo in a Denver newspaper showed Tyus marching at the head of a column of police protestors. One person who was present when the protesting police arrived at District Attorney Dale Tooley's campaign headquarters told reporters, "I was in Chicago in 1968 [when police beat demonstrators at the Democratic National Convention], and I didn't see that kind of hatred there. [Denver police] were shouting things like 'castrate the bastard' and things like that. It was really ugly."[5]

The police demanded that the politician meet with them. He did. They vowed to defeat him on Election Day. They did. In May 1975 D. A. Dale Tooley lost his second attempt to be elected mayor, so Tyus was probably correct when he recalled meeting Cordova sometime during the mayoral election, although his murkiness about dates sometimes carried over to his memory for identities.

Haro had allegedly given Cordova a hand grenade, which was turned over to police, who substituted a harmless dud in its place. Police simulated the destruction of the grenade, which the media then reported. Detective Tyus participated in the sham destruction of that grenade. When Tyus was questioned during a hearing on December 4, 1975, he testified that the whole charade was done without Cordova's assistance. When he was asked to name the participants at an August 1975 meeting involving the substitution and simulated destruction of the dummy grenade, he responded: "Captain Shaughnessy, a couple guys in the bomb squad,

Detective Weyand, I can't remember exactly everybody's name, and somebody from the District Attorney's office, but I don't know his name or, excuse me, I don't know if he worked for the District Attorney's office or what he was."[6]

This person did not work for the District Attorney's Office; he worked for the police. Tyus was shown a document dated from August 1975, that listed the names of those present at the meeting, including one referred to as "C. I.," as in "Confidential Informer."

After having his memory refreshed by the document, Tyus recalled that Cordova was indeed present. After 20 more questions about Cordova's involvement, Tyus continued to argue that Cordova, by Tyus' standards, was not involved: Cordova did not simulate a grenade, the police did; Cordova did not place the simulated grenade at the store, the police did; Cordova did not obtain the simulated grenade, the police did. Therefore, by Tyus' definition, Cordova was not involved in the sham bombing of the store.[7] The main case against Haro, however, did not involve grenades he allegedly gave Cordova, but more serious charges, including attempted murder.

Cordova notified Tyus on September 17, 1975, that Haro intended to bomb a police substation in Southwest Denver. Cordova said he went to Haro's station that day, and Haro told him that the bombing would occur that night. Cordova volunteered to help. Haro allegedly told Cordova to be prepared. Cordova left to inform the police and ATF, and he later returned with a "body mike" and instructions.

Accomplices were allegedly planning to bomb other facilities. Haro reportedly ordered the theft of two cars to use as car bombs, so Cordova and Anthony Quintana, Haro's employee, allegedly stole two cars that day. One car was a Ford; the other a brown, 1967 Plymouth. Haro and other, unnamed suspects were closely watched throughout the day, including aerial surveillance from a police helicopter.

Cordova said he called Haro's home that evening and left a message with Haro's wife, Irene, saying that he—Cordova—was having problems with his car. His message asked Haro to meet him at a shopping center where the Plymouth was parked. Haro received the message and drove to the shopping center. After starting the vehicle, Haro and Cordova went in their separate cars to Haro's home. Cordova parked the Plymouth nearby. They met Anthony Quintana at Haro's home. Quintana allegedly provided an electrical blasting cap and a timing device that the three allegedly used to make a 26-stick dynamite bomb.

Though Cordova said the three men were supposed to coordinate their drive to the substation in three cars, Quintana drove off alone. Haro and Cordova allegedly took the bomb in Haro's car and then transferred it to the Plymouth. Police and ATF agents surrounded Haro and Cordova as they drove their cars away and arrested Haro. Quintana's car was stopped later at a different location, and he too was arrested.

Early accounts of the arrests were based on information provided by police and prosecution sources, who claimed Haro had been arrested in the stolen car with the bomb. They also claimed that Cordova had gained a position of trust in the Crusade for Justice:

> "[Cordova] came forward realizing the lives that were going to be taken if he didn't," according to one source on the prosecution side. According to that source, Cordova wasn't pressed into service as an informant under the threat of prosecution of some offense, as is sometimes the case with police informers. "We didn't bust him with anything," the source said.[8]

Capt. Robert Shaughnessy, the bomb squad commander, testified at Haro and Quintana's preliminary hearing on September 22, 1975. Attorney Walter Gerash asked Shaughnessy if Cordova had a record of criminal convictions. He answered, "I know of none, no sir. I have only seen the Denver record, but apparently he has lived here all his life and there is no conviction on it."[9]

Others challenged this version of events, and Cordova's role in them. Attorney Ken Padilla asserted that Cordova "is paid by the Denver Police Department, including Cinquanta and Tyus, or other law enforcement agencies, to commit illegal acts and then to get others charged who are not involved in the planning and commission of the crimes."[10]

"Cinquanta" was Daril Frank Cinquanta, one of Denver's most controversial police officers. Cinquanta, who recruited Cordova as an informer, claimed to have told Haro during the arrest that he would face first-degree murder charges if the bomb killed officers. A frightened Haro allegedly blurted, "Let me take it apart, I can take it apart because I put it together, and then no one will be hurt."[11] Haro denied making the statement. Denver newspapers reported that the authorities anticipated more arrests, but none occurred.

Cordova's history seemed to indicate that he was less than a model citizen. He had left the military with a bad conduct discharge. He was imprisoned at the Colorado State Reformatory in 1969 for armed robbery, having unsuccessfully pled not guilty by reason of insanity.[12] This was not his last entanglement with the law.

Haro and Quintana were jailed with bonds set at $250,000 each. Though the bonds were subsequently lowered, the cases tied up over $170,000 in personal and organizational property until the trials and appeals ended. By that time Haro and Quintana had been assisted by attorneys Walter Gerash, Harold Haddon, Sander Karp, Jeff Goldstein, David Manter, Kenneth Padilla, Normando Pacheco, Alfredo Peña, and Stan Marks.

The DCLDC sent a letter dated September 25, 1975, to its supporters: "Hardly have we gotten on our feet long enough to share our movement's victory [in the Gary Garrison trial] and we've got another trumped-up case on our hands."[13] The constant arrests, costly trials, and bad publicity were taking a toll on the Crusade. It was hard to put a pleasant face on allegations that Haro and Quintana were involved in a plot to car-bomb a police substation, other police facilities, and a national police chiefs' convention.

With time, cracks appeared in the bomb plot story. After Haro and Quintana's arrest, police also announced they were seeking John Maestas. Media accounts reported that "Maestas is known to have strong ties with militant Chicanos in Colorado's San Luis Valley," and police believed Maestas was "driving a car with 17 grenade-type bombs in the trunk."[14] A week later, the *Denver Post,* on information from Captain Shaughnessy, announced: "Police have canceled a search for a car believed to belong to John C. Maestas . . . in connection with [Haro's] bomb investigation." The three-paragraph article gave no explanation.[15] Maestas' only link to the alleged conspiracy was that his car was repaired at Haro's filling station during the time of the alleged conspiracy.

At the December 4 hearing, defense attorney Ken Padilla questioned Detective Tyus about the initial focus of the police investigation of the Crusade and Cordova's role in it. Tyus responded, "I asked [Cordova] if he could get next to anybody who would be handling explosives, hiding out escapees, mainly the AIM people, where they were keeping stolen weapons, how the weapons were transported down to Mexico, you know, things like that." Detective J. C. Tyus said police did not want to expose Cordova as an informer, preferring instead to have him infiltrate police agents into the Crusade and then move him to California or "back East, that area, or even down into Mexico."[16]

Tyus acknowledged that Cordova received $100 from the Denver police, $300 from the District Attorney's office, a $700 car, the promise of "a new life," and the possibility of "thousands and thousands of dollars."[17] Defense attorney Stan Marks said, "The question is whether Cordova had a story he had to come up with. And if the story wasn't right, he wouldn't get the pot of gold at the end of the line."[18] Denver police, however, said that only minimal payments were made. They denied that they suppressed criminal cases against Cordova.[19] Yet after Haro and Quintana's arrests it was revealed that Cordova had worked to entrap a man named Newton J. McVickers the previous spring.

On April 21, Cordova, McVickers, and Allen "Tex" Jacobs were followed from Denver's jurisdiction by the cops. Two parties, one being Cordova, burglarized the Wishbone Restaurant in suburban Thornton. After the burglary, the suspects led police on a high-speed chase exceeding 100 miles per hour and fired three shots while fleeing. The chase ended in a wreck in which three civilians and two cops, one being Cinquanta, were injured. Police reports again contained conflicts about who committed the burglary and drove the car. Cordova committed the burglary and apparently fired the shots. No charges were filed against him.[20]

In a subsequent incident, Tyus, Cinquanta, Sgt. Ed Hansen, and other Denver officers followed a car containing McVickers and Cordova to Greeley, in Weld County. Cordova wore a body mike in an attempt to record McVickers. Tyus testified at the December 4 hearing that Cordova told police he "had uncovered a [kidnapping] plot that might be committed against [Mayor Bill McNichols] during [the mayoral] campaign and (inaudible) [sic] McVickers was the prime suspect."[21] The officers were again operating outside their jurisdiction. Tyus and other officers claimed that McVickers burglarized two residences while Cordova remained uninvolved. When McVickers was arrested, he told Weld County authorities, "I've been set up. Cinquanta set me up. He's been after me. Cordova has been knocking on my door 3 or 4 times a week. I didn't hit the house. . . . I want to take a polygraph."[22] The polygraph was unnecessary. Weld County officers who assisted Denver police reported that Cordova committed the burglaries while McVickers sat in a parked car or drove around the area.

Weld County D. A. Robert Miller considered filing charges against Denver officers for misrepresenting the facts, but changed his mind after Investigative Division Chief Tom Rowe wrote an apology on Denver Police Chief Dill's behalf to Weld County Sheriff Ernest Bower. The letter stated: "What I regret even more than [the bungling of charges on McVickers] was the feeling that our officers more or less put you all on the spot. . . . Apparently, some of the [Denver] officers thought that they saw more than they actually did."[23] Miller concluded "The actual burglary was committed by CORDOVA who was working for the Denver PD."[24] McVickers' charges were dropped, and none were ever filed on Cordova.

When Chief Dill was asked whether his officers were disciplined over the matter, he first said he "couldn't recall." He added, "I'm not going to bother checking it out. If you're trying to infer that some sort of disciplinary action should have been taken, then you should be doing my job."[25] When District Attorney Tooley was questioned about Cordova's activities, he said he was unaware of them until reading the newspapers.

Cordova was apparently not working for the police when he and Russell Billings burglarized the suburban Lakewood home of auto dealer Vern Hagestad on February 3, 1975. Cordova carried a loaded 12-gauge shotgun, with which they planned to force residents to open a safe. When they were surprised by a guest, both men fled, leaving behind the shotgun. It was traced to Cordova, who had bought it in California in 1973.[26]

Though Officer Cinquanta was not supervising Cordova in this burglary, he was still linked to the case. Billings and Cordova were to have been helped in the Hagestad burglary by Lloyd Steven Dalrymple, an informer for Sgt. Ed Hansen and Cinquanta. When Billings and Cordova concluded that Dalrymple was an informer, Cordova took action. On April 15, he visited Dalrymple's home and shot him in the head.[27] On April 21, Cordova confessed to the attempted murder of Dalrymple to Officer Cinquanta. This was the same date Cordova, under police direction, participated in the burglary at the Wishbone Restaurant in Thornton.

Cordova's unique relationship to the police was not fully revealed prior to Haro's trial before Federal Judge Sherman Finesilver on four counts of possessing unregistered explosive devices. The federal grand jury returned the indictment against Haro on Cordova's testimony that he obtained additional grenades from Haro on September 13, four days before his arrest in the alleged car-bombing attempt.

THE FEDERAL TRIAL

When the federal trial began on January 19, 1976, Finesilver ordered special measures. Spectators passed through metal detectors, were accompanied to the courtroom by U.S. marshals, and could not use the building's cafeteria or stairwells. Court was held from 9 a.m. to 10 p.m., and all spectators were barred from the jury selection process. Denver's Special Services Unit was deployed throughout the building and used the roof to watch Haro's supporters, looking down at them through the scopes of sniper rifles. For entertainment, SSU officers threw snowballs from the roof at spectators.

Cordova testified that Haro gave him grenades on September 13, the transaction that resulted in the federal charges. The grenades had been kept in a box on the shelf of a desk at Haro's filling station. Cordova was accompanied to the filling station by Robert "Beto" Valadez, an undercover ATF agent. Cordova said Valadez was present when the conversation about—and transfer of—the grenades took place. Valadez, however, testified that he was not present because Cordova asked him to leave the station to open Cordova's car trunk. Haro denied the allegations. The filling station desk was later brought into court. No box the size described by Cordova (3 feet by 2 feet by 8 inches) would fit on its shelves.

Though Detective Tyus had testified on December 4 that he spoke to Cordova "about the possibility of receiving thousands of dollars and a new identity, a new life,"[28] Cordova testified that he did not speak with authorities about receiving money for his cooperation.

When ATF Agent Valadez was asked what was the objective of the police and ATF operation, he responded that it was "to get the Crusade for Justice, to get John Haro and Corky Gonzales."[29] When defense attorneys questioned Cordova about criminal involvements, he repeatedly refused to answer based on Fifth Amendment rights against self-incrimination.

The only eyewitness to the alleged grenade transaction was Cordova. The jury consisted of eleven whites and one African American. On January 22, 1976, John Haro was found guilty of illegal possession of explosive devices after the jury deliberated one hour and 17 minutes. Judge Finesilver ordered Haro to report to court for sentencing on February 18.

Haro's attorneys were again in court on February 13. Attorneys Marks and Manter requested a new trial or acquittal for Haro because of a "deliberate attempt to suppress the truth" by ATF Agent Al Gleason, an expert witness in Haro's January trial. Gleason "testified in the Judge's chambers that he had constructed a device identical to the devices allegedly possessed by [Haro] and he showed slides of a car in which grenades had been exploded to show the force and impact of the devices."[30] The testimony was an element of the federal case and was needed to demonstrate that the grenades were destructive devices fitting the definition prescribed by law. Gleason testified during the trial that he had duplicated grenades similar to those allegedly obtained from Haro and exploded them in a car selected at random. The testimony was shown to be untrue after the trial had concluded. The slides shown in court were evidence presented in a previous federal case in Wichita, Kansas, involving members of AIM.

The Wichita case involved Bob Robideau and other AIM members who were fleeing FBI raids in South Dakota in the aftermath of a June 26, 1975, confrontation on the Pine Ridge reservation in which FBI Agents Ronald Williams and Jack R. Coler were killed. Coler was an FBI SWAT team member recently transferred to South Dakota from the FBI office in Colorado Springs. A damaged tailpipe caused the AIM members' car to catch fire, and ammunition and explosives being transported in the car detonated. Police recovered the .308 rifle that belonged to Agent Coler and an AR-15 rifle that the government claimed was used to kill the FBI agents. Robideau was tried and convicted in December 1975 on nine counts of illegally transporting firearms and explosives. The photos used in Haro's trial were from Robideau's December 1975 trial in Wichita.[31]

The ATF witness's expert testimony in the judge's chambers led defense attorney Marks to stipulate for the jury that the grenades fit the legal definition of explosive devices. Had the ATF witness testified before the jury and then been confronted with the facts of his misrepresentation, it would have supported the defense contention that the case involved governmental impropriety and deceit. Federal Prosecutor John Kobayashi refused to speak with the press about the matter, and reporters were unable to contact Gleason, who was based in Washington, D.C. Judge Finesilver, however, ruled that the misrepresentation did not constitute misconduct by the witness or affect the defense's ability to conduct its case. Haro's conviction was upheld, and the judge sentenced him to four concurrent six-year sentences. The DCLDC immediately appealed the conviction.

During the 1976 federal case, Cordova denied he was paid for informing and said that, aside from "subsistence" money, his only compensation was protection. He explicitly denied receiving immunity from criminal charges.[32] However, when he was tried in Jefferson County for the Hagestad burglary, over two months after Haro's conviction, he admitted that he had received immunity in exchange for his testimony, not only against his partner, Russell Billings, but against Haro and Quintana as well. Cordova also testified that he received only $125 from ATF prior to January 1976. The Crusade suspected that the true amount was much larger. It was subsequently revealed that Cordova received $961.84 prior to January 1976, and got over $12,000 from city and federal agencies between October 1975 and July 1976.[33]

THE STATE TRIAL

While the DCLDC appealed Haro's federal conviction, it was also busy with the more serious state case involving charges of conspiracy to commit murder. Denver District Court Judge George McNamara twice moved the trial against the wishes of defense attorneys. Haro's attorneys protested against sensational publicity in pretrial hearings, saying that it made an unbiased jury impossible, and urged the judge to limit police and prosecution involvement in actions that would fuel publicity before the trial. McNamara agreed that the publicity could hurt Haro's chances for an unbiased jury but turned down defense requests to dismiss the charges or postpone the trial.

Instead, McNamara transferred the case to the Western slope town of Durango, which would oblige Haro's supporters to travel more than 350 miles over the Continental Divide in mid-winter. The DCLDC did not like the idea of trying the case before a conservative, small-town jury.

An article in the August 1976 *El Gallo* complained that though Mc-Namara transferred the trial to Durango in a conspiracy with the prosecution, he remained as the presiding judge in order to bring "his ex-policeman, prosecutor bias" to the case.[34] McNamara, a former FBI agent and Denver deputy district attorney, called the article false, inflammatory, and irresponsible. He criticized defense attorneys for not disavowing it, saying that their failure to do so "compounds the situation."[35]

On December 9, Judge McNamara changed his mind about moving the trial to Durango, because of the expense and difficulty winter travel would impose. He rescheduled the trial for January 1977 and transferred it to Akron.[36] This transfer also displeased the defense team. Akron, a Washington County farming community 115 miles east of Denver, was smaller than Durango, and had few people of color. Research done by the defense showed that the county's population was only 0.36 percent Chicano.[37] There were no Spanish-surnamed people among 150 selected for the panel from which Haro's jury would be chosen. Moreover, a motion filed by Marks showed that no Chicanos had been called to jury service in Washington County in the previous 10 years. McNamara denied another defense request to return the trial to Denver and insisted that it would begin on January 12. McNamara's decision, however, would not hold.

Denver and Akron news accounts reported that Akron merchants feared an upsurge in shoplifting during the trial, and Akron Judge Royal Donnen acknowledged concerns that the courthouse might be bombed. The DCLDC's concern about the area's conservatism was confirmed when a Denver paper, citing Akron news accounts, reported that the Washington County Committee to Restore the Constitution had "urged the county's residents to meet [January 8] to discuss 'the Chicano Bomber Trial.'"[38] Fifty-one people reportedly attended the meeting during a blizzard, and their spokesperson, Loren R. Lodwig, predicted a good turnout should Haro's allies cause trouble. He said it was "up to the individuals" in his group to decide whether to bring firearms.[39]

The publicity about the Committee to Restore the Constitution, a John Birch Society affiliate, caused Judge McNamara, on January 11, to cancel the trial he had set to start the following day. He returned the case to Denver, where it was tentatively set for March 14. McNamara described the Akron newspaper advertisements of the Committee to Restore the Constitution as "inflammatory." At the same time he also condemned the August 1976 *El Gallo* article criticizing the original transfer to Durango.

On January 13 McNamara disqualified himself as the trial judge, saying that the *El Gallo* article made him fear that trying the case would give students from Escuela Tlatelolco, who were in frequent attendance at Haro's court appearances, a warped view of the courts.

Trials also started for Joseph Cordova, Jr. On October 2, 1975, nearly eight months after the crime and about six months after he attempted to murder Lloyd Steven Dalrymple, the *Rocky Mountain News* revealed that Cordova would be charged for the Hagestad burglary. The Crusade believed that embarrassing publicity had forced the authorities to act. The charges and arrest warrant were based on information Dalrymple gave to Denver Patrolman Greg Meyer, "the [former] partner of Patrolman Daril Cinquanta." Dalrymple revealed that "Russell Billings and Joseph Cordova were the two subjects who entered the [Hagestad] residence."[40]

At their burglary trial, Billings and Cordova took the stand against one another. Some of Billings' allegations had nothing to do with the burglary. He testified that he was present in early 1975 when Cordova argued over a drug deal with Orlando "Orlie" Quintana, a Denver tavern owner. Billings said Cordova threatened Quintana's life and threw a hand grenade into Quintana's car as they left (it did not detonate). Cordova denied the allegation. Sometime after these incidents were alleged to have happened, the owner was murdered. Though his death was attributed to a group called the "Texas Mafia," Billings' testimony raised the possibility that Cordova had access to explosives many months before meeting Haro.

In court proceedings on the attempted Hagestad burglary, Cordova admitted that he carried the shotgun during the incident. The admission did not hurt Cordova, who by this time had been granted immunity by the district attorney for testifying against Billings. Cordova testified that Billings wanted him as a crime partner because of Cordova's potential for violence. When Cordova was facetiously questioned by Billings' attorney about Billings' "erroneous impression" that Cordova was "cold-blooded enough to kill somebody," Cordova responded, "I didn't say it was erroneous." When asked if he would kill Billings, if necessary, Cordova responded, "I believe I would." When questioned about his motive for testifying, Cordova admitted that he "was at least partly motivated by his fear that prosecutors might send him to prison."[41]

Cordova's attempt to murder Dalrymple was an interesting episode. Police records show that Cordova entered Dalrymple's home about 11:30 p.m. to ask him to hide stereos taken in a burglary. Police were called by Dalrymple's wife around 11:45 p.m. and found Dalrymple unconscious on the living room floor. He was taken to Denver General Hospital, where doctors found a gunshot wound in his left forearm that broke two bones.

A second bullet entered his head near the left ear and was lodged at the base of the skull. . . . [Sgt. Ed] Hansen then interviewed Dalrymple: "He gave Sgt. Hansen the same story he [previously] gave Detective Lohr although he [now] identified the shooter as Joseph Cordova. . . ." [Dalrymple had first told Lohr he did not know his assailant.] Cordova subsequently was interviewed by Denver Patrolman Daril Cinquanta.[42]

The police reports on the attempted murder specifically stated, "Information from Detective Cinquanta, vice bureau: Cordova admitted to [Cinquanta] that he was the one that shot Dalrymple."[43]

Newspaper articles revealed that Lloyd Dalrymple informed on Newton McVickers and Solomon Vigil in a February 15, 1975, robbery case. Dalrymple was present, but stayed outside the victim's home. He informed Hansen about the robbery, and about Cordova and Billings' February 3 burglary and robbery attempt. Apparently, Dalrymple was supposed to participate in the latter crime but informed instead. Dalrymple's testimony against Cordova did Cordova no harm. The district attorney in Golden decided that Dalrymple's testimony against Cordova was unsatisfactory, so Dalrymple found himself facing conspiracy charges for planning the Lakewood crime. The deal between Cordova and the district attorney in the Hagestad case allowed him to turn state's evidence against both Billings and Dalrymple.

During Cordova and Billings' trial in Golden, newspaper articles reported that precautions were being taken because, police claimed, "a $20,000 price has been put on [Cordova's] head" as a result of the Haro case.[44] Police snipers were posted on rooftops for his protection. The publicity cast this burglar, informer, felon, armed robber, and attempted murderer in the role of endangered witness.

Police dealings with Cordova, however, were subject to criticism in legal circles. Truman Coles, in a letter to Denver D. A. Dale Tooley, petitioned for the appointment of a special prosecutor to investigate the relationship of Denver police to Cordova. Coles, former director of the Denver Public Defender's office, wrote: "I have never ceased to wonder why persons holding positions of trust continue to cover up police illegality and corruption when it is in the interest of law enforcement that bad policemen be gotten rid of."[45] Pete Reyes and Patrick Stanford, attorneys from MALDEF and the National Lawyers Guild, supported Coles and criticized Tooley. Reyes said Tooley's office "is becoming merely a tool of the police department and isn't fulfilling its obligation to fairly prosecute those who break the law."[46] Tooley brushed off these criticisms as "overzealous attempts to defend (persons accused) in upcoming criminal cases by way of attack on law enforcement agencies"; it was, he said, an "extremist tactic. I don't intend to get down to responding to these unfounded charges."[47] Denver police and Tooley claimed that Cordova had not been prosecuted for the attempted murder of Dalrymple because Dalrymple did not want to pursue the matter.

Attorneys Padilla, Coles, and Rudy Schware went before Denver District Judge Robert Kingsley on December 11, seeking the appointment of a special prosecutor to prosecute Cordova. Robert Schmalzer, Dalrymple's attorney, said police who interviewed Dalrymple after he was shot persuaded him that prosecution of Cordova would be difficult because of Dalrymple's criminal record. There was also an evidence problem: police claimed that the gun Cordova used was not recovered. Though Cordova confessed to Officer Cinquanta, police had decided—without the customary consultation with the District Attorney's office—not to prosecute the case. Tooley's office asked Schmalzer if Dalrymple would repeat his charges, but Schmalzer refused to allow his client to do so because the "Denver D. A.'s office at this point in time is a party of interest," since Cordova was their key witness in the Haro trial.[48]

The search warrant used to seize material from Haro's residence after his arrest was based on an affidavit prepared by Officer Cinquanta, who said Cordova provided him with information on the night of Haro's arrest. However, in a February 28, 1977, proceeding, Cordova testified that he had not spoken with Cinquanta at all that day. When Cordova was questioned by Padilla about his career as a police informer, Cordova testified that it started at the point of Cinquanta's gun. "He stuck a gun in my face and threatened to blow me away. I'd heard about him and that gun. It looked like a pretty good reason to become an informer."[49]

Both Cinquanta and Cordova say Cordova was pressed into service after his attempt to murder Lloyd Dalrymple on April 15, 1975. However, the search warrant for Haro's home, drawn up before Judge Edward A. Simons by Cinquanta on September 18, 1975, declared, "During the past twelve months, I have received information from the informant which has led to the arrest of suspects involved in burglaries, armed robberies, and the use of narcotic drugs, and escapees from state institutions. . . . Information from this informant has always proved to be correct and has never proved to be untrue." (If Cinquanta's affidavit is correct, his relationship with Cordova went back to September 1974, not April 1975.) The search of Haro's home revealed no evidence of explosives, nor were traces of explosives found on his clothes or person.

During Haro's state trial Cordova claimed to have constructed a dynamite bomb with Anthony Quintana and John Haro at the latter's residence. Quintana left the residence with Cordova and Haro but drove off alone, and Cordova did not see him again that night. Cordova claimed that he and Haro carried the bomb to Haro's car, drove the short distance to the parked 1967 Plymouth, and placed the bomb in the back seat. Cordova started the Plymouth and drove off. Haro followed in his own Oldsmobile. The authorities then made the arrests.

Cordova's testimony at trial confirmed an ongoing defense contention: Haro never drove—nor was he a passenger in—the car where the bomb was found. Numerous pretrial articles reported that Haro was the driver (or, by other accounts, the passenger). Articles written after Cordova's testimony continued to repeat this nonfact, as does Cinquanta's letter to the *Rocky Mountain News* cited at the opening chapter.

Tooley's account of the arrest also blurs the record. His autobiography, *I'd Rather Be in Denver,* completed in the months before his death from cancer in 1985, recalls, "Several others placed a bomb in the back seat of a car in which they planned to drive to a district police station in North-west Denver [Haro was charged with conspiring to blow up the South-west, not the Northwest, substation]. . . . Ever mindful of details, the bombers started the timing device on the bomb as they began to drive to the police station target. Coincidentally, they were stopped by police officers en route. The police officers casually questioned the suspects while the bomb continued to tick in the back seat. Only this twist of fate caused the bomb to be detected and the timing device turned off before it exploded." [50]

Cordova's testimony in state court did not have the same weight it was given in federal court, and it may have given jurors reason to doubt. The *Denver Post* reported that "at one point during the lengthy examination by Padilla, Cordova said he first suggested to Haro and Rodolfo (Corky) Gonzales, leader of the militant Chicano organization, that Denver police substations be bombed. . . . But when asked again about who suggested destroying the substations, Cordova said he didn't. And he contended that he misunderstood the earlier question." [51] Though Cordova said during his testimony on March 22 that he had minimal knowledge of explosives, on March 23 he boasted about his familiarity with explosive devices from Marine basic training and wartime Vietnam.

Haro's defense strategy was simply to deny Cordova's assertions. Haro said his only dealings with Cordova on September 17 consisted of helping him with a car with which he claimed to be having trouble—the 1967 Plymouth driven by Cordova, the car where the bomb was found.

The ATF and Denver officers gave lengthy testimony about meeting with Cordova, surveilling Haro and Quintana, observing the filling sta-tion, trailing Haro with a helicopter, etcetera. They witnessed no vehicle thefts. The recording device Cordova wore revealed only garbled conver-sation and off-hand remarks about "pigs," but no discussion of stealing cars or blowing things up, police or otherwise. On September 17, the day of Haro's arrest, Cordova left the device in the stolen car, thinking, he said, to use it to help police locate the car. He said he then accompanied Quintana in preparations for the attack. Police thus lost track of Cordova and any opportunity to record what was said or done by the defendants. Or by Cordova.

Cordova, who had reportedly infiltrated the Crusade and risen to a position of trust, attended, at most, one or two Fishermen's Meetings and a few Wednesday fundraising luncheons that were open to the public. He was seen once at La Raza Park, where he strolled into the park in July 1975 wearing a black karate uniform. On September 16, he attended the Mexican Independence Day protest at the State Capitol in Denver, where he wore a brown beret and mingled with the crowd as though providing security. These activities, in addition to the time he spent loitering at Haro's gas station, account for Cordova's participation in the Crusade and the Chicano movement in Denver.

On April 1, 1977, John Haro was found not guilty by the Denver jury after five hours of deliberation. Eleven days later all charges were dismissed against Anthony Quintana, who declared, "It was a big frame up from the beginning. I was a scapegoat for Cordova."[52]

Jury foreman Daniel Worthington said the jury had not "ruled out" the possibility that the case resulted from a government conspiracy, saying, "We also vaguely knew of the possibility of a frame. We knew that the FBI has kept files on people." He felt that the government's case was not credible and said the jury never "seriously considered Cordova's testimony."[53] The massive visual and electronic surveillance proved nothing. "No one ever saw Mr. Haro with the bomb. They couldn't show us evidence (of dynamite) on his clothes. They couldn't show us anything."[54]

In his closing remarks, Haro's attorney Stan Marks had declared, "We haven't proved and we haven't said the police planted this bomb. We cannot present to you how that dynamite got there, but given the character of Joseph Cordova, we'll leave it to your imagination."[55] Haro later said, "The charges were created by the Denver District Attorney and the Denver Police Department, but not just to get me. I see every count as the police and the District Attorney going out to hurt the Crusade."[56]

Haro's federal conviction remained, and his appeal ended unsuccessfully in August 1978. He began his first day of confinement on November 1, was released in late 1979, and successfully completed his parole.

DARIL "SUPERCOP" CINQUANTA

Haro's case was not the only alleged bombing conspiracy involving Cinquanta. On March 23, 1976, police surrounded Our Lady of Guadalupe

Church in North Denver, where local and federal agents, including Cinquanta, conducted a search for explosives that an informer said were hidden there. The priest was handcuffed in the sacristy during the 90-minute search. Nothing was found.

Cinquanta continued as a Denver policeman until 1989. His career, almost from its beginning in 1970, was marked by charges of brutality, perjury, procedural violations, frame-ups, and quests for recognition. His biggest critics are found in the Chicano community, but he steadfastly denies their charges: "That was a myth. It developed because I specialized in Spanish neighborhoods. If I had specialized in black neighborhoods, I would have been accused of being prejudiced against blacks. The only people complaining were the criminals and their relatives and friends and who gives a (expletive deleted) about them?"[57]

Cinquanta first made headlines on October 3, 1971, after he approached a parked vehicle in Denver's Northside around 9:30 a.m. He ordered a man out of the car for an ID check. The man exited the car, drew a gun, shot Cinquanta, and escaped on foot after dropping a cap on which was pinned a Crusade for Justice button. The other passengers, one a Crusade member, were arrested, questioned, and released after saying they did not know the man's identity and had met him when barhopping the previous evening.

Some Crusade members attribute Cinquanta's anti-Chicano bias to this incident. Ironically, Cinquanta's assailant was not Mexican but, like Cinquanta himself, Italian American. His name was Lawrence Carbone Pusateri, his barrio nickname was "Tingo," and his alias in Denver was Luis Archuleta. He was born in the Bronx in New York City, moved to Los Angeles as a child, and was raised in the barrios of East Los Angeles. He considered himself Chicano. He was sentenced to prison in California, escaped in May 1971, and made his way to Denver and a confrontation with Daril F. Cinquanta. A May 1973 Denver "Presentence Investigation" report states, "Although of Italian extraction, this defendant was reared in a Mexican American environment and has taken on the characteristics of that sub-culture. . . . he tended to identify with a delinquent Mexican American peer group and commenced getting into difficulties with the law in his early teens."

Tingo fled Colorado after shooting Cinquanta in October and was captured in Monterey, Mexico, in December 1971. He said he was tortured as a suspected soldier in the guerrilla army of Lucio Cabanas. He was returned to Denver in March 1972, convicted for shooting Cinquanta in March 1973, and sent to the State Penitentiary, where he was elected chairman of LADS. Sent for medical treatment to the State Hospital in Pueblo, he made a daring escape in 1974. He was not recaptured.

On June 3, 1981, Cinquanta was charged with brutality by Barbara Maes, whom he had arrested. He discounted her charges saying, "I have just gone out there and done my job. This is another ploy trying to render me ineffective."[58] The charges of excessive force were backed by witnesses in the area where the arrest took place. One article reported:

> [Cinquanta] was demoted in May [1981] to a patrolman after a seven-month [internal] investigation into a drug bust Cinquanta made last October. [Chief] Dill found that Cinquanta violated "departmental regulations" because he failed to get clearance prior to talking with his attorneys and a grand jury on the case, in which another officer alleged [Cinquanta] lied on a search warrant affidavit. Charges of lying were not substantiated, but Dill said Cinquanta also delayed turning over evidence in another unrelated case. Dill recommended closer supervision for the 11-year police veteran.[59]

Though police–community conflicts continued, the time came when Cinquanta was no longer at center stage. In 1988 his career ended in a scandal in which he faced 19 criminal counts, including several felonies. In a plea-bargain arrangement, Cinquanta pled guilty to two misdemeanors. The other charges were dropped.

A local television station, wanting to film a news special, featured Cinquanta and Larry Subia, his partner, who were called "The Supercops." The reporters accompanying the officers were treated to a special photo opportunity when the officers responded to a burglary and arrested some "bad guys." One suspect escaped. The "bad guys" were not the only ones nabbed. It was later revealed by a police informer, the "escaped suspect," that the burglary was planned by the informer to allow Cinquanta to make a live "bust" for television cameras. The informer said the burglary was set up at Cinquanta's initiative, and charges were dropped against those who were arrested.

Cinquanta resigned from the force in August 1989 but collects a yearly disability payment of $19,000. He is providing a ghost-writer with information for a book on his life:

> I promised the public the truth and they're going to get it. I don't give a (expletive deleted) if they sue me. My book will tell the truth. It has romance, violence, corruption, politics. It shows policemen's private lives. It's really heavy about informants . . . and in nearly 20 years I had only one or two complaints of police brutality. I wasn't a bad cop. I was an honest cop. I'd make a great police chief. I loved police work. I miss it. You bet.[60]

Though Cinquanta said in 1990 that he was the subject of brutality complaints only once or twice, a May 1978 article on Cinquanta for *Den-*

ver Magazine contradicts his recollection. Journalist John White reported that "police officers join street people and the Chicano community in their dislike for the twenty-nine-year-old Italian American detective. His citizens' complaint file is a foot thick."[61]

THE AFFIDAVIT OF VAROLIN JOSEPH JOHN CORDOVA, SR.

The DCLDC was told that the gun used in Lloyd Dalrymple's shooting was seized in a raid on Cordova's residence after Dalrymple identified him as the gunman. The officer who took the weapon figured prominently in Haro's arrest. No hard evidence existed, however, to show that the gun had been seized. Those who gave the information to the DCLDC were unable, or unwilling, to substantiate their account—one of many unverifiable accounts brought to the committee's attention.

The most unique account was a signed statement of 29 typewritten pages given to the DCLDC at 1:50 p.m. on August 2, 1977. It was never used. Varolin Joseph John Cordova, Sr., the informer's father, gave the statement after calling the Crusade and asking to speak with Rodolfo Gonzales. He wanted Gonzales to know about a police conspiracy against the Crusade. Gonzales referred him to the DCLDC. Cordova then asked to speak with the author. Instead, he was interviewed in person by Maria Subia and Alberto Mares. The father was distraught, appeared to have been drinking, and said he had recently been charged with two felonies. He gave a long, rambling account of his son's activities.

> **Alberto Mares:** Mr. Cordova, your son Joseph Cordova, Jr., you said he made the statement to you that the government wanted to pay him $1,000 for each stick of dynamite that he procured for the law enforcement agencies?
> **Answer:** Yes. . . . He approached me, sir, when he said, he says, "If I could only . . . ," he said he was working for the police department because he got in trouble. . . . He told me he could get a thousand [dollars]. "Look," he said, "they're paying me so much but they said they'd give me a thousand dollars for each stick of dynamite that I find."[62]

When his son said no one would get hurt, his father proposed obtaining dynamite from a mining camp, but his son was not interested in the scam. The father referred to his son as "retarded" as a result of a childhood injury: "He's got a plate in his head. The best neurosurgeon saved his life, but I had a retarded boy. The government used that retarded boy for their purposes and they lost." The elder Cordova also lamented his son's military career, saying, "He came with the recruiter. I told him,

'You can't take him, he's got a plate in his head.' You know the answer he gave me? 'It's all right, they wear helmets.'"[63] Cordova, Sr., said he did not take his son seriously until after the Haro arrest, which he described as a "set-up," The father talked about the money his son earned as an informer, money apparently paid *before* Haro's arrest in September 1975:

> All of a sudden he comes out with a roll of bills, all hundreds, I lived with them [his son and daughter-in-law], I mean they went on a spree. He said something about the federals had given him his first payment or something, I mean, with a roll of bills, yeah, we lived good that day, ate good, too.[64]

He continued:

> Ah, there was this Daril, Daril, Daril Cinquanta, Cinquanta's behind it all, I didn't even know his name until I read it in the paper. . . . I met with one, two, three, four, five, six Federal agents . . . they took me to the Federal building, they asked me all kinds of questions, if I want to cooperate, and they'd give me protection, and they was giving me a bunch of bullshit.
> **Mares:** Cooperate in what way, Mr. Cordova?
> **Cordova, Sr.:** Testimony. That, against the Crusade. . . . that, ah, let's see, wait a minute, to go along with Joey's testimony. They'd fill me in on Joey's testimony. . . . they'd fill me in on what they wanted me to say.[65]

It was never clear to the Crusade where the affidavit of Cordova, Sr., would lead. It seemed, however, to confirm its assumptions and assertions about governmental criminality.

Initial news reports on the Haro and Quintana arrests, based on information provided by Denver police, hinted at a bombing conspiracy involving people besides Haro and Quintana, though these unnamed parties were never arrested. These alleged co-conspirators, however, were mentioned in the younger Cordova's statement to ATF Agent Charles Baylor.

> Corky Gonzales was there [at Haro's filling station] at the the time the [stolen] car was being wiped clean and he asked me, 'What was happening, Joe?' . . . He asked what I was doing with that Ford [the second stolen vehicle], it was a pretty nice-looking Ford. And I answered him that the car was fresh off the street, fresh on the license plate [i.e, the license plates had been switched], and fresh back on the street, at which we smiled at each other in a knowing kind of way that meant my way of hinting to him that the car was stolen.[66]

Another of Cordova's statements to ATF Agent Baylor is of special interest to the author.

John Haro briefed me on the way over that Ernesto [Vigil] was getting ready to do his bomb devicing at 9:15, and at that time, he also mentioned that there were going to be five targets that night. . . . John Haro caught himself mentioning Ernesto's name and said that he meant to say "this other guy." And I told him, "That's cool, I didn't hear that."[67]

Cordova, however, never stated that he saw, spoke to, or smiled at me that day. Not even in a "knowing kind of way."

AN OLD QUESTION ANSWERED:
"RECORDED OR NOT?"

Further revelations surfaced in the course of Haro's state trial, which, all told, lasted from September 1975 until April 1977. These revelations suggested answers to some older questions.

The Crusade believed that the March 17 confrontation stemmed from a deliberate provocation by elements of the police department in collaboration with federal authorities. Special police units must have been deployed in advance, but how did all those dispersed police units coordinate their movements? The only answer the Crusade could surmise was communication by police radio. A motion was made in court to examine police radio broadcasts, but the tapes of the four police district frequencies showed only routine Friday night broadcasts, so the matter was never pursued. Unknown to the Crusade and its attorneys until 21 months after Martinez' death, however, was that there was a fifth frequency.

In the case against John Haro, police alleged that on September 17, 1975, Joseph Cordova, Jr., and Anthony Quintana took the second stolen car—the Ford with the "fresh" license plate—and parked it by Children's Hospital on 18th and Downing Street, two blocks from Crusade headquarters. They were allegedly followed by police, who radioed their movements to other officers involved in the surveillance. Walter Gerash questioned Detective J. C. Tyus about this surveillance:

Q: Where was this being broadcast over?
A: Our Intelligence Frequency.
Q: Was this being recorded?
A: No sir.
Q: So this doesn't go through normal police frequency, I guess you mean by Intelligence Frequency, is that what you mean?
A: I don't know, we just call it Intelligence Frequency, it's got a different frequency than our normal four channels.
Q: The normal four channels are recorded while they are being broadcast?

A: I believe so, I have been told that.

Q: You don't know whether this Intelligence Frequency is recorded or not?

A: No, I know it isn't.

Q: You know that it is not?

A: Yes.[68]

Fifteen

The System Weathers the Storm

FBI Director J. Edgar Hoover died in 1972, Richard Nixon resigned before he could be impeached or indicted in 1974, and Gerald Ford replaced Nixon in the White House until the November 1976 election of moderate Democrat Jimmy Carter. Although administrations changed, some things remained the same. An incident in mid-1976, for example, indicated that the government's intelligence agencies had not changed their practices. The incident coincided with America's Bicentennial and began with the leaked release of intelligence bulletins to the media. The first was a Connecticut State Patrol Criminal Intelligence Division bulletin that became known to the Crusade as the "Kill a Cop Day memo." [1]

NATIONAL ALERT: "PLANS TO KILL A COP EACH DAY"

Although the bulletin circulated among law enforcement officials throughout the nation, its exact origins later proved untraceable. According to the bulletin:

> A spokesman for the Bureau of Indian Affairs stated that they had received information the American Indian Movement had made contact with the Brown Beret [*sic*], a militant Chicano group in the Denver area with the idea of joining forces at least in instances benefiting both groups. The SDS [Students for a Democratic Society] is also re-emerging as a militant force and has been in contact with AIM and the Brown Beret. Rodolfo "Corky" Gonzales, a leader of the Brown Beret, reportedly has a rocket launcher and rockets either in his possession or available to him along with explosives, hand grenades, and ten to fifteen M-16 rifles with banana clips. The objectives of the group are disturbance and terrorism. They are reported to have plans to kill a cop each day in each state. Two vehicles have been identified as being used to lure law enforcement officers into an ambush. False reports of family

disturbances, drunken drivers, and other traffic violations are to be used. When an officer arrives on the scene of a family disturbance or stops a reported vehicle, armed members will cut down the officer when he approaches.[2]

The bulletin was issued on June 18, 1976, and coincided with Rodolfo Gonzales' birthday. It was remarkably similar to another bulletin sent to Washington State's Colville Indian Agency soon thereafter. The subject of the second bulletin was AIM, whose members referred to it as the "Dog Soldier memo." This bulletin was distributed by the FBI internally and sent to other agencies, including the Secret Service, the U.S. Marshals Service, and the Department of the Interior. It read, in part:

> "Dog Soldiers," who are pro–American Indian Movement (AIM) members who will kill for the advancement of AIM objectives, have been training since the Wounded Knee, South Dakota, incident in 1973. These Dog Soldiers, approximately 2,000 in number, have been training in the Northwest Territory (not further described) [sic] and also an unknown number have been training in the desert of Arizona. These Dog Soldiers are undergoing guerrilla warfare training experiences (not further described) [sic]. The Dog Soldiers are to arrive at the Yankton Sioux Reservation, South Dakota (Wagner, South Dakota), in order to attend the traditional Sioux Sun Dance and International Treaty Conference. The Sun Dance and Conference are to occur on the Yankton Reservation in early June of 1976, and this Sun Dance and Conference are to serve as a cover for the influx of Dog Soldiers. . . . At the conclusion of the activities at the Sioux reservation the Dog Soldiers are to meet on June 25, 1976, or immediately thereafter. . . . At this meeting final assignments will be given the Dog Soldiers for targets throughout the state on the Fourth of July weekend.[3]

Among the alleged assignments were the assassination of the governor of South Dakota, an assault on the state penitentiary in Sioux Falls, and "sniping at tourists on the interstate highways in South Dakota . . . to be carried out between July 1 and July 5, 1976."[4]

The release of these memos did not occur in a vacuum. The Crusade for Justice, the Pueblo Brown Berets, and other Colorado activists, as well as AIM, had announced their intention to protest against America's Bicentennial on July 4, 1976. The Pueblo Brown Berets had been approached by people offering them money to participate in the Bicentennial celebration. A Pueblo activist formerly associated with the Pueblo Brown Berets, Al Gurule, denounced the Bicentennial as hypocritical. His remarks were attacked on a Pueblo radio talk show:

> Gurule says his people have suffered 200 years. If Gurule wants to experience suffering, perhaps he should live under the dictatorial govern-

ments of Mexico or Spain, or in the communist regimes of the African
nations, or the so-called republics of poverty-stricken Latin America. . . . Anyone willing to work hard can make it in America and that
includes Italians, Slovenians, Polacks, Blacks, Chicanos, and Indians . . .
it is the Chicano, Black, and Indian community that has most benefitted
by such programs as food stamps, welfare, grants to go to college, and
a variety of other standards that give minorities an advantage over everyone else. What they are saying is this, "This country has treated us
badly. . . . By the way, my welfare check was late this week."[5]

The Crusade planned to participate in a Fourth of July protest in conservative Colorado Springs. A Colorado Springs newspaper reported on
the protest and noted that the Crusade held a July 2 press conference
denouncing the release of the bulletins. Gonzales stated that the intent
behind the release was to instigate:

"mentally unbalanced, overzealous, fanatical right-wing 'patriots' to do
the actual job for [law enforcement agencies], that is, to murder us in
the name of freedom, democracy, and patriotism. We don't want any
violence. You don't march with women and children and old people and
say we want to take on the whole armed forces," Gonzales stated. The
Crusade was joined at the press conference by Harold Fobb who spoke
for the Colorado Warrior Society and who declared that the release of
the memos was motivated by a desire to direct an attack at all Chicano
and Native American organizations protesting the Bicentennial.[6]

One newspaper insinuated that the Fourth of July might be commemorated by more than the usual fireworks. *The Sun* reported, "While state
officials from the governor on down are making rosy predictions for a
peaceful Fourth of July in Colorado, Jefferson County officials [west of
Denver] are trying to find who stole a large cache of explosives from a
construction site six days ago. Some law enforcement officials suspect
radical groups in the theft."[7] This theft reportedly took place in Deer
Creek Canyon in Jefferson County on June 25. The newspaper reported
that Capt. Robert Shaughnessy of the Denver bomb squad said he had no
leads about the thieves' identity or motive:

[Shaughnessy] noted intelligence reports indicating a Denver militant is
slated to be out of town on the nation's 200th birthday. "It seems whenever that guy is out of town, we have a bombing here—so we can't ever
pin it on him or his friends," Shaughnessy said. Colorado Springs police
sources indicate they have heard the stolen explosives have fallen into
the hands of radical groups. However, Lt. Noel Fryburger of the Jefferson County Sheriff's Office said although his men haven't arrested any

suspects in the case, he doesn't believe radicals stole the dynamite. For months, radical groups around the nation have been threatening to "blow out the candles" on the nation's birthday cake and to "bring the fireworks" to the celebration. However, Colorado Springs intelligence officers have said they expect no trouble locally.[8]

According to a United Press International article headlined "Police Warned of 'Kill a Cop a Day' Conspiracy," Denver FBI SAC Ted Rosack said, "We've heard all kinds of rumors, but we're not making any special arrangements"—an interesting attitude given the FBI's role in circulating one of the memos.[9] SAC Rosack, incidentally, had a very distinguished FBI career. He joined the FBI in Washington, D.C., in 1950, worked in Bureau headquarters from 1960 to 1970, and was assigned to the Denver field office in July 1975. FBI documents cited by David J. Garrow in *The FBI and Martin Luther King Jr.* reveal that Rosack served under J. Edgar Hoover and other FBI bureaucrats from May 1964 to October 1964, and was involved in surveillance campaigns against King at the time the FBI was wiretapping his phones and planting electronic devices in hotels and motels he used.[10]

The release of the two bulletins generated nationwide media attention. Police in Utah and Idaho were alerted, and members of the Brown Beret organization in Lubbock, Texas, were reportedly questioned by the FBI.[11] The Texas National Guard was reported to be "standing by" because "police are taking the entire thing very seriously."[12] A UPI article reported police preparations in New York, Vermont, and Maine, where "the Brown Berets were reportedly traveling in two vans with Colorado and Wyoming license plates. The vans were reportedly spotted at a restaurant in the Portsmouth, New Hampshire, area, not far from Pease Air Force Base."[13] The *Detroit Free Press* reported that the Connecticut State Police had received "unverified information" from the BIA about the alleged plot and that Detroit police had "instituted a secret elaborate procedure—called Operation Hailstone"—in response to the memo. Police would reveal no details about "Operation Hailstone."[14]

After the Crusade and AIM denounced the sensational allegations, police departments and the FBI downgraded the memos. Connecticut's *Hartford Courant* reported, "State police here erroneously sent a confidential message seven weeks ago to law enforcement agencies around the country. . . . The message turned out to be 'very erroneous' and 'probably shouldn't have been sent,' said a policeman who asked not to be identified and is a member of the criminal intelligence division which sent the message."[15] Though the exact number of recipients is unknown, it is interesting to note that the Idaho Department of Law Enforcement, the Denver, Salt Lake City, Detroit, and Albuquerque police departments, and the

State Police of Vermont, Maine, and Connecticut all have intelligence
units or bureaus that belong to the Law Enforcement Intelligence Unit.[16]
George O'Toole quotes FBI informer Douglass Durham on the LEIU:

> "The LEIU is so secret that, until recently, even its existence was usually
> denied," says Douglass Durham, a former Des Moines police officer who
> claims to have worked as an undercover investigator for the group. . . .
> Douglass Durham, an accomplished pilot, safe cracker, photographer,
> scuba diver, and electronic eavesdropping specialist, said he was part of
> an LEIU-sponsored exchange program in which undercover officers
> were traded between police departments in the Midwest. Durham says
> he was lent by the Des Moines police to work undercover for the police
> departments of Lincoln, Nebraska, and Cedar Rapids, Iowa.[17]

Rodolfo Gonzales and Harold Fobb of the Colorado Warrior Society
(formerly Denver's AIM chapter), denounced the release of the bulletins.[18]
Gonzales and the National American Indian Movement—represented by
Ken Padilla of Denver, Ken Tilsen of St. Paul, and William Kunstler of
New York—filed a $3 million suit against the Connecticut State Police
Department and the U.S. Immigration and Naturalization Service (INS) in
the U.S. District Court in Connecticut, as will be subsequently recounted.

Though the Crusade and AIM had bonds of solidarity, neither was
plotting to kill policemen. Though some activists surmised that the bulletins were designed to prejudice the jury in an important federal case
against AIM activists (and to slander the Crusade and make it vulnerable
to attack by law enforcement bodies), the bulletins had some unintended
consequences.

The uproar over the two bulletins did not prevent one further show of
Crusade solidarity in the 1976 trial of two members of AIM, Darelle
"Dino" Butler and Robert "Bob" Robideau. Both were charged with killing two FBI men in a 1975 gun battle on the Pine Ridge reservation. Gonzales, called by the defense attorneys, testified about the government's history of deceit, disruption, and harassment of political dissidents. He cited
the two bulletins as evidence of his allegations.

In an unprecedented move, the defense attorneys called FBI Director
Clarence Kelley to the witness stand. In spite of the vigorous efforts of
the FBI to target AIM, arrest AIM leaders, and disrupt AIM's efforts,
Director Kelley gave testimony that displeased his own agency: "It is my
definite knowledge that the American Indian Movement is a movement
which has many fine goals, has many fine people, and has as its general
consideration of what needs to be done, something that is worthwhile;
and it is not tabbed by us an un-American, subversive, or otherwise

objectionable organization."[19] On August 1, 1976, the *New York Times* reported:

> Last month the Justice Department was unable to quash a subpoena for Mr. Kelley's appearance—the first of its kind—at a criminal trial in Iowa where two Indians stood accused of killing two FBI agents in South Dakota. In the view of the defense attorneys, it was Mr. Kelley's admission on the witness stand that the FBI had issued a nationwide alert of possible violence over the Bicentennial Weekend without any evidence that such violence would occur that tipped the scales in the defendants' favor.[20]

Butler and Robideau were subsequently acquitted.

THE IMMIGRATION "PROBLEM"

The focus on immigration and "illegal aliens" in the 1970s almost uniformly portrayed Mexicans as the "problem." States bordering Mexico had a much larger influx of immigrants than did Colorado, where "manitos" and other U.S.-born Mexicans were a big part of the Latino community. Though southwestern states are affected by the influx of undocumented immigrants, the perspective of Chicano activist groups was quite different from that of the INS. Mexican immigration to the United States was not always seen as a "problem."

Older members of the Chicano community who were familiar with the border could remember when it was, in effect, open. Mexicans on both sides crossed freely with little government control or concern. Activists were aware that Mexican immigration was encouraged in times of economic expansion, when labor was needed in the fields and cities of the Southwest and the nation. The Crusade viewed U.S. immigration policy as racist, knew that mass deportations of Mexicans and their U.S.-citizen children had happened before, believed that the U.S. economy was losing steam after the Vietnam war, and feared that Mexicans would be convenient scapegoats. Critics of the INS pointed to poverty in Mexico as a factor pushing immigrants out of their country. Until this was solved, INS efforts amounted to spitting in a windstorm.

The Crusade's position on immigration was based on its understanding of U.S.–Mexican history. Members viewed the relationship between the two countries as one of neocolonialism and held the United States responsible for the "immigration problem," since its intervention in the Mexican economy resulted in unfavorable trade balances, depleted Mexico's natural resources and capital, and kept Mexico from developing its economy and keeping its work force gainfully employed. How could the INS stem this immigration flow when the United States itself was at fault for plundering the Mexican economy?[21]

"Mexican Racists" and the KKK

In the late 1970s, the Crusade developed close ties with the Committee on Chicano Rights (CCR), headed by Herman Baca of National City, California, near San Diego. Baca's National City La Raza Unida chapter had collaborated earlier with the Colorado LRUP, helping to cement ties between the two groups.

In the 1970s growing pressure to "control" the border led to proposals to "solve" the "immigration problem" by granting "amnesty" to certain undocumented immigrants while drying up the employment base for others by making it illegal to hire them. While Congress debated the new proposal and its various versions (Simpson-Rodino, Simpson-Mazzoli, Rodino-Kennedy, etc.), opposition increased among immigration activist groups like the Centro de Accion Social Autonomo–Hermandad General de Trabajadores (CASA–HGT), the CCR, and Arizona's Manzo Council. In an *El Gallo* article, Baca was questioned about the CCR's position on the proposed immigration amnesty law:

> We are not against amnesty. In fact we were one of the first organizations to propose it in the early 70's. What we are against is the false promise of amnesty. . . . The Carter proposal does not talk about "amnesty." It outlines an "adjustment of status" for undocumented persons who entered the country before 1970. Such adjustment is not anything new— it already exists in the form of INS State 8 USC 1254. This statute provides that an alien with seven years continuous residency and equity . . . can petition for permanent resident status. Very few will benefit for two reasons. First, a 1976 Department of Labor Study found that few of the undocumented apprehended by the Border Patrol or INS have been in the country for longer than two years. Therefore, the vast majority of the undocumented will not be affected. Second, [referring to existing INS backlogs] right now the INS' incompetence and racism has resulted in a seven year waiting period. It will take years before anyone will benefit [from the provisions of the newly proposed laws].[22]

Baca was equally skeptical of proposals to outlaw the employment of undocumented immigrants by providing sanctions for their employers:

> The proposal is as phony as a three dollar bill. We don't oppose punishing employers, we oppose punishing our people. The result of the proposal would be . . . punishment by discrimination at the hands of employers who will simply refuse to hire any person of Mexican or Latin

ancestry. If Carter and (INS director Leonel) Castillo were sincere about penalizing employers they would enforce all existing laws designed to protect workers, laws dealing with wages, health and safety, social security, etcetera. . . . Everyone agrees that the immigration problem is caused by social, economic, and political factors. The solution is not to be found in law enforcement.[23]

The Crusade participated in an October 29, 1977, march in San Ysidro, California, at which the CCR protested against the Ku Klux Klan's plan to help the INS and Border Patrol apprehend "illegal aliens" via a "Klanwatch program."[24] The Klanwatch program was announced by KKK Grand Dragon David Duke after a meeting with Allen Clayton of the San Diego Port Authority during which Duke toured INS facilities and was shuttled to a border checkpoint via helicopter. Over 300 protestors turned out to hear Baca, Gonzales, Mario Cantu of San Antonio, and Bert Corona denounce the Klanwatch.

Gonzales' participation in this demonstration figured in an attempt by KKK members from Fallbrook, California, to sue the Chicano activists in early 1978. The Fallbrook KKK, under the leadership of Tom Metzger in northern San Diego County, was prominent in racist activities. The Klan alleged:

> The plaintiffs are Mexican racists who are laying the political, criminal, and manpower foundation for a guerilla war against the United States government for a political separation of California and southwestern states from the United States of America. . . . Another essential phase of the plaintiffs' conspiracy is to cower the United States Border Patrol and to neutralize any really meaningful enforcement of the immigration laws of the United States.[25]

When the Chicano plaintiffs moved to dismiss the KKK suit, the Klan filed additional court papers detailing their version of the illegal Chicano conspiracy. "Sources in Denver, Colorado, report that Corky Gonzales, identified above, has a long history of arrest for the possession of hand grenades and narcotics, and is a Mexican racist," the Klan alleged.[26] The Klan's suit was thrown out of court, but immigration-related controversies were not over. An especially ugly incident in Arizona had already occurred.

The Hannigan Case

On August 18, 1976, three undocumented workers from Mexico were kidnapped at gunpoint in southern Arizona by a prominent cattleman, George Hannigan, and his two sons, Pat and Tom. The Mexicanos were tied, had their hair cut off with hunting knives, were beaten, threatened with castration, and left naked after being menaced with knives and guns. One was branded and hanged, saving himself by supporting his weight against a ravine wall where he was strung up. The others were told to run and then sprayed by shotguns blasts. One was hit by 47 shotgun pellets and the other by 127. The Hannigans were indicted, but the judge and county prosecutors refused to bring them to trial. Catholic bishops interceded, and the Hannigans were eventually charged with 22 felony counts, including kidnapping assault, robbery, and conspiracy. Ultimately the Hannigans were found not guilty by an all-white jury.[27]

In late 1978, the U.S. government announced plans to build a specially designed steel fence along the U.S.–Mexican border in the areas of San Ysidro and El Paso. In early 1979 Gonzales spoke in San Diego at another CCR-sponsored protest to denounce the militarization of the border and the steel fence, which activists called the "Carter Curtain." Gonzales said:

> Anti-Castro Cubans receive relocation funds the minute they come from Cuba. . . . Indo-Chinese right-wing elements are immediately welcomed to these shores, but those who have roots, who have history, those related to this part of occupied Mexico and Mexico are set aside as criminals, are placed in jails, are deported, are harassed and harangued, and even those of us who think we have documents are treated the same. . . .
>
> Mexico indeed was rich in resources and minerals but has always been subject to foreign exploitation . . . we must teach not only ourselves but also our hermanos de Mexico of this exploitation, of the economic political controls by a capitalistic society, and that Mexico is in danger of being raped once more [for its oil].[28]

The vigorous activism of the 1960s and 1970s was a factor in preventing the implementation of restrictive immigration measures. Such measures were later implemented under Ronald Reagan in the 1980s: some federal laws, in fact, evolved from prototypes developed in California when Reagan was governor. The 1986 Immigration Reform and Control Act that Reagan signed into law, for example, was patterned after California's Dixon-Arnett Law, passed when Reagan was governor.

PRISON AND POLICE BRUTALITY

Freedom for Andres Figueroa

Though mass protests and organization in communities of color declined in the late 1970s, the Crusade's involvement with various causes continued. The focus on criminal justice issues increased as conservative forces successfully implemented their law-and-order agenda.

In October 1977, the Puerto Rican Nationalist Andres Figueroa, political mentor of Crusade member Alberto Mares, was released from federal prison. Figueroa had reported medical problems to prison authorities while he was being held in solitary confinement for participating in prison protests. His requests for medical attention went unheeded, and upon his release from solitary confinement, he was found to have inoperable cancer. Prior to his release from prison, during the summer of 1977, Andres sent a statement to supporters:

> At present I have a very bad cough and I cough blood every time I cough, but my spirit is at the height of all those men who struggle with vigor for the national liberation of all the peoples of the world. . . . I am very grateful for the White, Chicano, Afro-American, and Indian movements who are struggling for our freedom and the struggle of all the political prisoners in the Yankee prisons.[29]

A rally was held at the federal prison in Marion, Illinois, in October 1977 to demand the release of the remaining Puerto Rican Nationalists. Among the 300 protestors were participants from Denver, including the Metropolitan State College MEChA, Buena Mata, a West Denver group, and the Crusade for Justice.[30] In the summer of 1979, the remaining Nationalists were released.

Police Killings Continue

Police–community controversies continued. Gilberto Jasso, of the American GI Forum's National Office of Civil Rights, cited the cases of 49 Chicanos killed by police from 1972 to 1976, during the Nixon and Ford administrations. The killings continued during the Carter presidency: Jasso documented 43 killings from 1976 to 1978.[31] On February 9, 1978, MALDEF submitted a letter to Attorney General Griffin Bell that listed 30 incidents of police misconduct and killings of Chicanos. The Jasso and MALDEF lists covered incidents in all southwestern states, but Texas was especially prominent. In 1978, protests against police brutality occurred in Dallas, Odessa, Big Spring, Austin, Waco, Laredo, Kingsville, El Paso, Weslaco, Corpus Christi, and elsewhere in the state. Chicanos and police clashed violently in Mathis, Houston, Austin, and Weslaco. Among these cases were those of Ricardo Morales, Santos Rodriguez, and José Campos Torres.

The 1973 killing of 11-year-old Santos Rodriguez drew national attention. Rodriguez was killed by a Dallas policeman who believed the boy had information about a service station burglary. While Santos sat handcuffed in the patrol car, Officer Darrell Cain drew his .357 magnum revolver, put it to the boy's head, and pulled the trigger. Cain said he thought he had removed the bullets and was merely trying to scare the child into divulging information. The officer, who was previously involved in the shooting death of an 18-year-old youth, was convicted and sentenced to five years for criminally negligent homicide.

On September 9, 1975, Ricardo Morales was killed in Castroville, Texas, by Marshal Frank Hayes who was investigating a series of burglaries. After arresting Morales, Hayes drove the unarmed man into the Texas countryside, where he shot and killed him. Hayes's wife and a friend later took the body away from the scene of the killing and buried it. Hayes was later convicted of aggravated assault and sentenced to 10 years.

The killing of José Campos Torres also drew national attention and inspired a song by the African American singer Gil Scott Herron. On May 5, 1977, Torres was arrested by six Houston police officers on disturbance charges. He was kicked and beaten with flashlights while handcuffed after he reportedly became unruly in the police car. Upon arrival at jail, the duty sergeant ordered that Torres be taken to a hospital. Instead, he was taken to a bayou and thrown into the water. His body was recovered several days later. The officers were found guilty of criminally negligent homicide and sentenced to one year's probation.

The Colorado Prison Case

Controversies were not lacking in Colorado, and many centered on the state's law enforcement and penal systems. Since the early 1970s, notably with the demise of prisoner-based self-help groups, the Colorado State Penitentiary at Canon City was the scene of several controversies over the treatment of its prisoners. Chicanos, the largest ethnic group, were approximately 40 percent of the prison population.

Fidel "Fifi" Ramos filed suit in Denver Federal Court over conditions at the state's maximum security prison. On November 15, 1979, his suit received a favorable ruling in the court of Federal Judge John Kane. Ramos and other convicts were represented in a month-long case by the Denver Chapter of the ACLU, whose attorneys argued that the prison was structurally unmanageable and unfit for housing human beings. In his ruling, Kane criticized the state legislature for allowing such conditions to develop.

The court was overwhelmed by an abundance of witnesses and experts who decried conditions prevalent in the "joint"—inadequate living space, sanitation, ventilation, and light, "massive, pervasive idleness" caused by lack of programs and jobs, as well as "gross over-classification into restricted and oppressive living conditions."

"The basic human needs must be met or the state must surrender its exercise of power to deprive confined individuals of their liberty," Judge Kane ruled. "The US Constitution does not stop at the prison gate. Our whole system is based on the idea that individuals do count, that personal integrity has to be required, insured and protected." [32]

The victory in the Ramos case was not complete. The conservative Colorado state legislature delayed payment of lawyers' fees to the ACLU well into the 1980s. The legislature increased the length of prison sentences, lowered the age at which juveniles can be punished as adults, imposed mandatory minimum sentences to limit judges' sentencing discretion, and dropped all pretense that prisons were intended to rehabilitate. Prisons now serve one purpose: they punish.

Frustration with efforts to reform prisons is shown in two *El Gallo* articles on the Ramos case by the author:

> [While] Ramos initiated the court action, it wasn't until some other brother inmates and the American Civil Liberties Union got involved that the actual case started progressing. . . . There was a time when the Chicano Movement was very active in prisoners rights. Where then are all those movement Chicano lawyers and organizations born out of the movement? Why must our Chicano brothers depend on the ACLU? This is not to say that all Chicano lawyers have turned their backs on unpopular Chicano issues, but that despite the increase of Chicano [attorneys], Chicanos need help more than ever. MALDEF at one time not only led, but initiated many Chicano legal and prisoner rights cases. To all organizations and individuals I say do not fear to back unpopular issues or make waves. You are where you are today because your brothers made waves and worked for and supported unpopular issues. [33]

A similar sentiment was expressed two years earlier in "Cellhouse 3: A Hell," which reported on "cruel physical and mental treatment and conditions" at the state penitentiary.

> Many prisoners feel they have grounds for legal complaints and action but need legal advice and information on filing lawsuits and petitioning the courts to do something . . . seldom is there an attorney who will take the case for prisoners at the penitentiary without payment and sometimes even with payment because of the travel it would involve. Law students don't seem to be able to get away from the university and so-called progressive law groups are too limited to help so prisoners are left by themselves to do what they can. [34]

The article quoted one prisoner who complained of "senseless rules and regulations" in force in Cellhouse 3, the maximum security "prison within a prison":

> The senseless rules and regulations titled "security" are both silly and dangerous because they cause tension and bitterness. For example, [we are allowed] one roll of toilet paper a week, no mirrors are allowed, no canned food, no access to the prison library. Never in all my prison experience has anyone ever been killed or assaulted with an extra roll of toilet paper or law books. It seems that everything that is for convicts is denied.[35]

The efforts to remedy these problems were frustrating and made little progress. Prison riots, work stoppages, racial violence, and lockdowns occurred frequently. The people who were caught in these "oppressive living conditions" were convicted felons, mostly poor and nonwhite, factors the Crusade saw as intimately linked to their incarceration in the first place. Prisons were located in remote areas, and the fundamentals of organizing—finances and communication, for example—were always lacking. The Crusade formed the Colorado Prisoners Rights Organization (CPRO) to work on prison issues. A key organizer was Alberto Conrad Mares, who joined the Crusade in 1975, soon after his parole from the state penitentiary. He later paid a high price for his activism.

The Death of Dennis Lucero

On May 5, 1976, Dennis Lucero, 23, was killed by James Emmett Connely, 37, after an argument in front of Connely's home. Connely had allegedly called Lucero a "dirty Mexican." Connely grabbed a rifle from his home, and Lucero was fatally shot. Contending that the rifle discharged accidentally, because of a hair-trigger, Connely was charged with manslaughter and released after posting 10 percent of a $1,000 bond—$100.

When the Lucero family and the Crusade criticized the charges as too lenient at a June 10 press conference, District Attorney Tooley charged Connely with second-degree homicide but continued the same bond. On June 30 the charges were again reduced to manslaughter. Connely's trial, after postponements, was scheduled for June 21, 1977. Before the jury was chosen, his attorney called for the dismissal of charges because the custodian of evidence at the police building had sent an invoice to Patrolman Lance Halverson earlier that month asking for permission to destroy the weapon. Halverson, one of the officers who investigated the killing, okayed the rifle's destruction in what the police called a "goof-up." The destruction of the weapon led Judge John Plank to dismiss the charges.[36] On June 23, 200 protestors, including members of the Lucero family, picketed Tooley's office and charged him with negligence. Tooley took no further action.

The Deaths of Artie Espinoza and James Hinojos

Another controversy involved the fatal shooting of Artie Espinoza and James Hinojos by plainclothes officers in Mestizo Park in the late afternoon of July 30, 1977. Police responded to the scene looking for Espinoza as a suspect in an earlier shooting in which Kerry Ulibarri was wounded.

Witnesses reported that a patrol car drove onto the grass at the park, which was full of children and bystanders. Espinoza and Hinojos were passed out on the lawn. Plainclothes officers and a uniformed patrolman approached them, shouting orders. As the men began to sit up, police fired a volley of shots, killing both. The police said they fired after seeing Espinoza pass a gun to Hinojos, who pointed it at them.

Numerous civilian witnesses heatedly disputed this story. Additional officers responded to the scene, where a disturbance nearly erupted between officers and Chicano and African American bystanders. Police, including SSU members, used teargas and dogs to disperse the crowd around 8:30 p.m. Around 11 p.m. police lobbed teargas canisters at the entrance to the Curtis Park Community Center, where a dance was underway; they were pouring teargas into the nearby housing projects as late as 3 a.m. the following morning.[37]

Espinoza suffered one gunshot wound, Hinojos was shot more than six times, and the autopsy seemed to support witnesses' contentions that the men were too drunk to have responded as police described. Colorado law presumes that a person with a .10 blood alcohol level is intoxicated. Espinoza's blood alcohol content was .140 after 13 blood transfusions; Hinojos' registered .290.[38]

The day after the killings, the staff of Mestizo Park organized a rally there under the direction of Van Lucero, a former Black Beret and Gonzales' son-in-law. He was assisted by Dino Castro, an 18-year-old Tlatelolco graduate and witness to the killings, who distributed news releases and later testified before the grand jury. The two young men were members of Crusade families, unassuming working-class families that were the backbone of the Crusade.

Gonzales spoke to a crowd of nearly 500 at the rally. The next day several hundred protestors marched through downtown Denver to police headquarters to demand the indictment of officers involved in the killings. After months of investigation, the grand jury, in an unprecedented action, indicted Officer David Neil, although the other officers were cleared.

On May 24, 1978, Neil was acquitted of charges of manslaughter and criminally negligent homicide for killing Artie Espinoza, whose family later won a civil suit over his death. *El Gallo* sarcastically reported, "Killing Mexicans has never been a crime [for the police]; [Mexicans] provide good target practice, and there are always plenty of them around." [39]

The Shooting of Felix Jaramillo

The Denver District Attorney's office and the Sheriff's Department were harshly criticized by the Chicano community in the shooting of Felix Jaramillo on February 12, 1979. Jaramillo, 17 years old, had a juvenile record for theft, truancy, and walking away from a youth farm. He was critically wounded by Sheriff Russell McGilvery, who was transporting him to Juvenile Hall, when he attempted to escape upon arrival. Escape would have been difficult; Jaramillo was handcuffed to another youth at the time. Jaramillo suffered two wounds, one in the chest and one in the back. The director of surgery at Denver General Hospital reported that it was impossible to determine where the bullet entered. Officials contended that the bullet ricocheted and caused two wounds.

District Attorney Tooley was criticized when he announced that the shooting would be investigated by the grand jury. Grand juries seldom charged officers involved in controversial shootings. The indictments in the Hinojos and Espinoza killings were exceptions. No charges resulted from the Jaramillo shooting.

Shootings by law enforcement officers leave city governments open to being sued, and for this reason, if no other, controversial shootings become highly political matters. Grand juries are conducted behind closed doors, and the prosecutor is the only attorney present. The grand jury has the power to subpoena witnesses and compel testimony, but the prosecutor conducts the proceedings and decides which questions to ask. And which ones not to ask.

An article by attorney Ken Padilla implied that the grand jury condoned criminal acts by police officers by concealing the facts from public scrutiny:

> Mr. Tooley has the power, authority, and responsibility to file cases directly against persons alleged to have committed crimes and does so routinely, on a daily basis . . . [including] shootings that result in charges of first degree murder or first degree assault if the victim is not killed. Of the shooting cases that occur in Denver, it appears that the only ones that are referred to the Grand Jury are those in which a peace officer is the person who is doing the shooting or killing, and most frequently, the victim is a member of a minority group, Chicano, Black, or American Indian. Mr. Tooley's usual excuse for referring these cases to the Grand Jury is that he needs subpoena power to obtain witnesses. Clearly this is not the case in the present Jaramillo shooting for the witnesses even appeared on television and given their statement as to what occurred.

This is not a complicated factual situation . . . since the Colorado Legislature, on July 1, 1977, passed a law stating that assault in the first degree is committed by a person under circumstances manifesting extreme
indifference to the value of human life if he knowingly engages in conduct which creates a grave risk of death to another person and thereby
causes serious bodily injury to any person. Further, the law is clear that
a peace officer may only use deadly physical force to effect an arrest or
prevent an escape upon a person who had committed a felony involving
the use, or threatened use, of a deadly weapon. . . . Nonetheless, District
Attorney Tooley wants to take this matter behind closed doors before a
Grand Jury and deny all public access to this inquiry. In addition, if this
is not enough, Mr. Tooley has directed that no disciplinary action be
taken against the Deputy Sheriff because it will "complicate the Grand
Jury probe."[40]

The article charged Tooley's office with various motives for sending the
matter to the grand jury. Among them were to "delay the matter for several months so that the public sentiment and interest will end," and "to
deny Felix Jaramillo and his attorneys any opportunity to investigate or
otherwise obtain statements and police accounts of the incident."

For example, with the use of the Grand Jury in the Curtis Park killing
of two Mexican Americans in the summer of 1977, Mr. Tooley has effectively kept all police reports, physical evidence and transcripts of the
Grand Jury proceedings from those attorneys representing the families
in their lawsuits against police officers. . . . When is Mr. Tooley ever going to quit running for the mayor's office and start doing his job as District Attorney and protect all the people in the community, regardless of
race or national origin, and quit using the D.A.'s office to appease or
otherwise solicit support from special interest groups for his own political ambitions?

The Chicano community's anger stemmed from the belief that the
grand jury was used to deflect truth and justice, rather than to seek it.
This was not the first time the charge was made.

State Grand Juries, whether regular or special, have been notoriously
ineffective in Denver. . . . Their success is so minuscule it must be mea-
sured through a microscope. . . . In recent years, the panel's main responsibility has been to hear testimony and weigh evidence in cases involving confrontations between policemen and civilians, particularly
when the latter are injured or killed in such disputes. In a sense, the
Grand Jury has become a civilian review board in police matters. The
system, as it operates in Denver, has also been used as an escape
hatch. . . . A Grand Jury moreover, can, and has been used, politically.
City administrations have found that it can be a bottomless well into

which irritating issues can be dropped without fear of splash or retribution. Rather than use the open-to-the-public investigative authority available by City Charter, municipal leaders are inclined to refer ticklish but serious problems to the Grand Jury. The secret nature of the proceedings offers administrators an attractive way to avoid airing dirty linen, without seeming to do so.[41]

The Death of Joey Rodriguez

Joey Rodriguez, 16, was killed on May 27, 1979, by Patrolman Robert Silvas in the Sun Valley Housing Projects in Denver's Westside. Accounts of the killing given by community residents contradicted those of the police, though the versions concurred on some details.

Rodriguez, accompanied by Richard Sandoval, was seen by Officer Silvas and Officer Marcos Vasquez as Rodriguez was inhaling paint vapors near the sidewalk on the southern boundary of the projects. The officers left their patrol car with guns drawn and attempted to apprehend the young men, who fled. Officer Vasquez apprehended Sandoval at the entrance to an apartment. Officer Silvas chased Rodriguez into a housing unit, where he drew his gun and fatally shot the youngster.

The police and civilian versions then diverged. Silvas claimed Rodriguez drew a .25 caliber automatic and pointed it at Silvas, who then killed Rodriguez. Mary Rojas saw Officer Silvas and Rodriguez run into her apartment and looked into the room where Rodriguez fled after hearing the fatal shot fired. The police, the District Attorney's office, and the media reported that Rojas said Rodriguez was armed, a statement she vehemently denied. She saw no weapon in the Rodriguez' hand or on the floor where he had fallen. She saw no gun on Rodriguez at any time.

Richard Sandoval, in a taped statement to Tooley's office, said the .25 caliber pistol was in his possession and that it fell to the sidewalk when he struggled with Officer Vasquez. Manuel Vasquez, the son of public housing resident Mary Vasquez, also stated that he saw Sandoval drop the gun on the sidewalk. This was further confirmed by Judy Arellano, another project resident. Another resident stated that she had lent the gun to Sandoval. Two other witnesses stated that they had seen a metal object drop as Sandoval struggled with Officer Vasquez, but they could not confirm that it was a pistol.

Ken Portuese, a Crusade member, and I visited the Rodriguez family and spoke with witnesses and project residents. A march was organized the week after the killing, and protestors went from the projects to Tooley's office. The Rodriguez family demanded that the officers involved be suspended without pay, but they remained on duty and continued to patrol the area. The family asked for an independent investigation of the killings, but Tooley proceeded with a grand jury investigation.

On July 6 Tooley announced that no charges would be brought against the officers. He released details of Rodriguez' juvenile record and the autopsy showing that Rodriguez was under the influence of alcohol and paint vapors when he died. The angry Rodriguez family demanded that the record of brutality complaints against the two officers also be made public. Less than two weeks before the killing, a local tavern operator complained to the Police Department about harassment of customers by Officers Silvas and Vasquez, saying that if they were not removed from duty, someone would eventually be killed. *El Gallo* pointed to controversies surrounding the killings of Carl Newland, an African American, and Sidney Whitecrane, a Native American—other police killings that had gone unpunished.

In mid-June of 1979, Officer Silvas was issuing traffic tickets in the early evening near La Raza Park when someone shot at him. *El Gallo* quoted an anonymous barrio resident who stated, "If the police freely break the law and justice isn't to be found in the courts, then people are justified by seeking justice in the streets through their own hands."[42] Silvas, incidentally, was subsequently involved in three other fatal shootings.

Ken Padilla sent Tooley an open letter criticizing the conduct of his office in Rodriguez' death:

> The press has reported that you have personally released some selected statements and evidence in the case to the press. I am seriously questioning your motives in releasing these selected statements and evidence and hereby request that all statements and evidence be released immediately to the public including the evidence that I am aware you have in your possession that does not corroborate with the police officer's statements and specifically shows that the gun or weapon was outside the residence . . . at the time Robert Silvas shot and killed Joseph Rodriguez inside the home. . . . As you are most aware, since you obtained changes in the legislation regarding the appointment of special prosecutors as a result of pressure brought upon your office by the Mexican American community in the past, because of your inaction to protect the rights of Mexican Americans, such an appointment must be made by the Court. We ask that you set aside your ego and request that the Court make such an appointment since anyone with even a minimum amount of intelligence could recognize that you and your office have zero credibility with the Chicano community in regard to this investigation. In addition, you and your office have intentionally prevented the victims of such killings and assaults by police officers to obtain redress in the court system by denying access to any of the records, reports or investigations of these killings and beatings by authorized representatives. . . . All that has ever been requested of your office is that when a peace officer commits a killing or assault that justice will require that he will have to face the criminal justice system just like any other citizen and will not receive this

special treatment as they have in the past by your office. If there are issues of fact in dispute, why don't you let the jury trial process determine these facts as is the normal procedure? Why is it always that your office becomes the judge and jury just as the police officer becomes the judge, jury and executioner on the street?[43]

Padilla's letter concluded with six requests, including an independent investigation, divulging of all reports and evidence on Rodriguez' death, and polygraph examinations of the officers involved. The requests were never granted.

This was not Padilla's first experience with grand juries in controversial killings. He was involved in a 1972 protest over the death of Albert Lucero, who was allegedly beaten to death by sheriffs at the Denver County Jail. Protestors demanded that charges be filed against two sheriffs who they believed were responsible. The district attorney at that time, Jarvis Seccombe, refused to meet with the protestors. The case went to the grand jury. No charges resulted.[44]

By the late 1970s, local grand juries were not the only ones that confronted Padilla and Crusade activists. Crusade members Van and Steve Lucero would face subpoenas to appear before a federal grand jury in New York, and Alberto Mares would be indicted in a savings and loan robbery.

Though the pattern of police killings and official response remained the same, other things had changed. The Crusade continued to defend its membership successfully, but there were fewer decisive victories in mass-based struggles involving the larger interests of youth and barrio communities. Nothing in the late 1970s, for example, rivaled the successful 1969 school protests.

The Crusade still played a role in local conflicts, but its base was shrinking. An evolving moderate middle class vied for recognition and constituencies, and the Crusade's energy and resources were now centered on its own organizational needs. Some Crusade members sought out the Rodriguez family and attempted to help them, but key Crusade leaders, who at one time would have been outraged, now demonstrated attitudes of futility and resignation. In earlier times the Crusade's leaders and rank-and-file threw their full weight into such efforts and rallied larger constituencies to the struggle. Rodriguez' name was merely added to a long list of fatalities, and city government twiddled its thumbs and waited for the protests to blow over. And they did.

Sixteen

Witch Hunts and Grand Juries

THE LUCERO BROTHERS

On December 23, 1977, two young Crusade members, brothers Van and Steve Lucero, were subpoenaed to appear before a New York federal grand jury investigating a clandestine Puerto Rican independence group, the Fuerzas Armadas de Liberacion Nacional (FALN). In late 1974, the FALN exploded several bombs in New York City and became a high priority for FBI investigation and apprehension.

The FALN claimed responsibility for bombings carried out throughout the United States, but mostly in New York City and Chicago. Law enforcement bodies had been unable to identify FALN members, much less apprehend them, since the group's emergence in late 1974. In late 1976, the FBI identified Carlos Alberto Torres of Chicago as a suspected FALN member. In time, federal authorities subpoenaed various individuals who they believed were associated with Torres and who, the FBI reasoned, knew about the FALN.

By 1977 a growing number of Latino activists—Chicano, Puerto Rican, and others—had become the center of grand jury attention in Chicago and New York. Unable to apprehend the FALN members via investigative techniques, the federal government appeared to be ready to use grand juries in a fashion critics characterized as a witch hunt.

FBI agents visited the parents of the Lucero brothers in December 1977 to inquire about their sons. Their inquiries were referred to attorney Kenneth Padilla. Crusade members assumed that the organization's activities were routinely monitored, knew that the authorities had been asking questions about the Crusade since its inception, and assumed that such activity was related to government counterintelligence efforts targeting the Crusade.

Alfredo Peña, Padilla's law partner, phoned the FBI on December 9 to discuss the visit to the Lucero family. Peña initially spoke with Agent

Donald Halter, who said that the FBI wanted to speak to the brothers "concerning a 'Top Ten' fugitive investigation, and that the names of the Lucero brothers had come up repeatedly in their investigation."[1] Halter said he was new to the area and would speak to his partner on the case. The two agents would get back to Peña.

On December 12, Agent Halter and Agent Robert E. Bishop visited Peña at his office. They showed Peña a "Wanted" poster and informed him that

> their [FBI] investigation revealed that one of the individuals on the "Wanted" poster sheet was known to them to have been visited by Rodolfo "Corky" Gonzales in the past few years, and also in recent months. They told me that either through their personal knowledge, or through information they gathered from fellow agents, that Rodolfo "Corky" Gonzales had, in the past years, repeatedly visited one of the fugitives on their "Wanted" poster sheet while this particular fugitive was in Chicago, Illinois, and that this same fugitive had visited Rodolfo "Corky" Gonzales in Denver, Colorado, in recent months.

The "Wanted" poster showed pictures of suspected members of the FALN: Carlos Alberto Torres, Haydee Beltran Torres, Oscar Lopez Rivera, and Ida Luz Rodriguez. In addition to mentioning "that Mobil Oil Company had a $10,000 reward" for the capture of any of the fugitives, the agents told Peña "that they had no desires to serve any grand jury subpoena on either of the Luceros, but were only interested in meeting with the Luceros in hopes of securing more information [regarding the suspects]. The fact that the Lucero brothers were members of the Crusade for Justice, and that Rodolfo 'Corky' Gonzales was its Chairman, concerned the Agents in their fugitive investigation."

Padilla contacted Bishop on December 15, but Bishop "refused to inform [him] as to the purpose or reasons the FBI wanted to interrogate [his] clients."[2] Padilla met with Bishop and Halter on January 17, 1978, who repeated that they were interested in speaking with the Luceros about the Puerto Rican fugitives.

> These Agents further stated that there were several major companies in New York who desired to apprehend these persons, including the Mobil Oil Company, the American Bankers Association, the Manufacturers Association of New York, and other groups, and that there would be at least $100,000 available to anyone providing information regarding the whereabouts of the four persons.

The agents threatened the brothers with subpoenas to appear before a grand jury in New York if they did not provide information. Then they left Padilla's office:

FBI Agents [Halter and Bishop] in the meeting of January 17, 1978, stated that they did not have sufficient information to arrest or charge Van or Stephen with any crimes, and if they did, they would be "here with warrants instead of subpoenas." The FBI Agents further stated that they felt that Van and Stephen Lucero might have some information regarding the whereabouts of these fugitives because they belong to the Crusade for Justice, and the chairman of the Crusade for Justice, Rodolfo "Corky" Gonzales is known to have known and been associated with Oscar Lopez Rivera, one of the persons contained in the FBI "Wanted" poster sheet.

The subpoenas delivered to Van and Steve Lucero on December 23, ordered them to appear in New York City on January 9, 1978. Maybe it was not a coincidence that their attorney, Kenneth Padilla, was scheduled to appear that day in Denver Federal Court to represent Crusade member Alberto Mares on charges of robbing a savings and loan office.

Van Lucero was 22 years old and had been active in the Crusade since he was about 15. He had been a Black Beret, and all nine members of his family—parents, brothers, and sisters—belonged to the Crusade. An older brother, Tony, had been involved with the Crusade since 1968. At the time of the subpoenas, Van was married to Rodolfo Gonzales' daughter, Gail, and they had two children. He was a Tlatelolco graduate and a Crusade board member, and worked summers at Mestizo Park. His older brother Steve had been an instructor at Escuela Tlatelolco in the 1972–73 school year and remained active in the Crusade.

Steve was known for his courteous intelligence and his soft-spoken, unassuming demeanor. He married Gonzales' oldest daughter, Nita, in the early 1980s. An affidavit written on his behalf by the author stated, "A multi-talented person, Steve is known to all as a person who will put his varied skills at the service of anyone while seeking no personal gain even to the point of doing menial or arduous tasks, whether it's shoveling snow at the organization's headquarters, helping people do their tax returns or repairing someone's car."[3]

THE MEXICAN CONNECTION?
THE PUERTO RICAN CONNECTION?

The FBI attempted to establish links between the Crusade and the clandestine FALN as early as the spring of 1975 and even sought to link Crusade activist Alberto Mares with bombings and thefts of explosives allegedly used by the FALN. In one instance the FBI contacted a young man, Hilbert Martinez, whose only tie to the Crusade was that a friend with whom he shared an interest in photography was a Crusade member.

In the fall of 1976, Hilbert Martinez was visited by an FBI agent whose name he thought was Simmons or Simons, a tall, thin older man. Martinez had been an explosives handler and rock driller for Winslow Construction before 1976. The agent told him that an informer had told the FBI that Martinez, in company with a former employee of Winslow Construction, was selling dynamite to the Crusade. The FBI wanted to know if "I knew about bombings in Chicago and New York."[4] Martinez denied the allegations and later learned that his former wife and her family had been questioned about him.

In the fall of 1977, the FBI again visited Martinez and told him that an informer had said that Martinez had attempted to sell explosives in Lincoln (Alma) Park. When he challenged the FBI to name the informant, Martinez was told "they couldn't tell me who the informant is because it was a police informant and they had this agreement or something with the Police Department here in Denver." The FBI hinted that a lack of cooperation by Martinez could result in incarceration. "I guess they were trying to intimidate me by telling me that there was one man in Northern New Mexico that didn't want to give any type of help and they put him in jail."

Though Martinez did not know who the FBI was talking about, Pedro Archuleta, a former Alianza member from Tierra Amarilla, was jailed in June 1977 for refusing to cooperate with a federal grand jury investigating the FALN. Under FBI pressure, and without an attorney's guidance Martinez, agreed to take a polygraph test and passed the examination. In a subsequent affidavit he recounted:

> I am not a member of the Crusade, but I had stated to [the FBI] that I had one friend who works there and I used to come down [to the Crusade] to take pictures with him. Sometimes me and my friend would go out to have a few beers, and I go to the Crusade to pick him up. At the time the FBI first talked to me I'd visited the Crusade maybe six times. Even now I'm not a member of the Crusade. [The FBI] didn't offer me money, they just told me that it was more or less an offer for my freedom. If I talked, then I wouldn't go to jail.

Another Crusade member, Richard Tapia, was approached by two FBI agents in the spring of 1977 after he left work. Tapia, to his recollection, had never met a Puerto Rican. He was questioned about an alleged explosives theft in the mountains west of Denver. The FBI said some of the explosives were used in bombings in Chicago and New York. Tapia said that the FBI "knew who I was," and that they told him:

> "We know your ties with the Crusade and your friends in that organization and everything," and that someone had informed them that I could

lead them to dynamite, or weapons, or ammunition, or a storage place. They did say that I was a member of the Crusade and that their sources had told them that I was a person that could lead them to all that stuff. . . . They told me that a group that had been using [dynamite] in Chicago and New York was, I believe, the FLAN [sic]. I'm not too sure, but they did name a name and letters, but I can't remember exactly.[5]

With the Lucero brothers scheduled to appear in New York City, the Crusade organized for another legal battle in an atmosphere of negative publicity.[6]

Since its inception in late 1974, the FALN had carried out numerous bombings. Investigating the group was an FBI priority. The FBI purportedly found its initial lead in 1976, when explosives were discovered in a safe house linked to Carlos Alberto Torres of Chicago. The explosives were reportedly stolen in Colorado. Torres had been a member of the Episcopalian Church's National Commission on Hispanic Affairs, a grant-making committee of church- and community-based Latino activists from all over the country. The commission reviewed hundreds of proposals from church and community activists throughout the United States and Puerto Rico in the several years of its existence.

The commission's records were confiscated, and some staff and commission members were subpoenaed by the federal grand jury. Several were jailed for refusing to cooperate with the investigation. Ricardo Romero, the younger brother of Geraldine Gonzales, belonged to both the commission and the Crusade in 1974. (The author replaced Romero on the commission in 1975.) Romero, a founder of the Crusade, remained active with the organization until 1974, when he was dismissed by the board of directors. In September 1977 Romero was subpoenaed to appear before a federal grand jury in Chicago. He was jailed for contempt of the grand jury when he refused to testify on November 9.

In early 1977 Crusade members were invited to a conference in Chicago regarding grand jury proceedings there and in New York. The National Committee Against Grand Jury Oppression was formed at the conference, although the Crusade maintained its autonomy and did not join it. The legal entanglements the Crusade had endured since 1973 had drained its resources and made it increasingly wary.

The Crusade was aware that the government suspected it of illegal acts and conspiracies and would go to any lengths to prove its suspicions—or to invent proof if necessary. The "Kill a Cop a Day" and "Dog Soldier" bulletins of 1976 were fresh memories. Still, the two Lucero brothers had almost no connection to Puerto Rico or Puerto Ricans other than via their membership in the Crusade.

"ATTACKED BY THE FBI"

Demonstrations were held at the Denver Federal Courthouse to protest against the subpoenas. The Crusade collected numerous affidavits demonstrating the FBI's long and persistent interest in the organization. On December 29, 1977, the Crusade issued a press statement in response to Van Lucero's subpoena (Steve Lucero had not yet been subpoenaed):

> We feel that once more the Crusade for Justice has been singled out to be attacked by the FBI. In this case they are attempting to punish an innocent man for the position and philosophy of an organization that they have been unable to destroy. . . . We see that the Grand Jury is a tool of the FBI which is attempting to prove that there is a link or alliance between the Puerto Rican Independence Movement and the Chicano Movement. We . . . have always supported worthwhile human rights causes, and especially that of the struggle of progressive groups, organizations, and countries. We support the philosophy and concepts not only for Puerto Rican Independence, but the right for all people who struggle for liberation to determine their own sociopolitical destiny.[7]

Attached to the press release were telegrams of support for the Crusade from Ken Portuese of the Denver Metropolitan State College MEChA group; from Luis Talamantez, a former political prisoner and defendant in the San Quentin Six case in California; the Committee to Free the Puerto Rican Nationalist Prisoners; William Kunstler and Margaret Ratner of the Center for Constitutional Rights; Professor Rudy Acuna of Cal State Northridge; the People's Law Office of Chicago; the National Alliance Against Racist Political Repression; and Bert Corona of the National Immigration Coalition.

On January 23 the DCLDC called for a protest to be held at the Denver Federal Courthouse on January 27 to coincide with the scheduled appearance of the Lucero brothers in New York. "The Crusade further supports the position taken by the seven remaining [non-Crusade] people who have already taken a principled position against cooperation with this witch hunt and are now jailed in Chicago and New York," the letter announced, "and we call for an end to these Grand Juries and their abuses."[8]

The effects of the publicity cannot be fully estimated. Though the Crusade had a considerable following in the barrios, the majority of Denver's population may well have been confounded by the trail of controversies to which the Crusade's name had been linked. Investigations by federal grand juries in these years, however, were also linked to controversy. Frank Donner writes that the Justice Department's Internal Security Division

converted the federal grand jury proceeding from its traditional and recognized function, deciding whether the prosecutor has presented sufficient evidence to justify an accusation of law violation, into a cover for
a variety of intelligence-related pursuits divorced from legal ends. The
effectiveness of the grand jury proceeding as an intelligence instrument
is directly traceable to its subpoena power, the power to compel testimony and the production of documents on pain of contempt. A dominant aim of such compelled testimony was to force a witness to name
associates and friends in an ever-widening inquisition.[9]

According to Donner, the ISD "exploited the grand jury format to develop information for the ISD's intelligence unit, the IDIU (Interdivisional
Intelligence Unit)."[10] The IDIU in turn shared its "intelligence" with other
governmental spy agencies, including the CIA. Donner details ISD misconduct involving informers who spied on the legal defense efforts of subpoenaed individuals, thus violating the privilege of confidentiality between attorneys and clients. Other abuses involved warrantless wiretaps.
When individuals who appeared before the grand jury alleged government misconduct via wiretaps, federal prosecutors often dropped subpoenas, nervous about placing themselves in jeopardy if caught in illegal
activity.

Defense attorneys prepared motions calling for the Luceros' subpoenas
to be quashed. Other motions called on the government to disclose informers and electronic surveillance. The attorneys intended to enter motions in federal court to subpoena any relevant records of the FBI, CIA,
and National Security Council on the Crusade for Justice. If the motions
were granted, the directors of these agencies would be summoned to
testify.

Van Lucero's affidavit cited indications of electronic surveillance of his
personal phone, that of the Crusade, and those of his family members.
His five-page affidavit cited eight time periods in six years when he believed he was wiretapped.[11]

A similar affidavit was drawn up by Steve Lucero detailing apparent
tampering with his home phone and that of his parents, as well as times
his parents got busy signals when they called the Crusade, though the
Crusade phones were not in use. Steve's affidavit cited phone interference
whenever he called his friend Jesse Bordeaux. Steve's phone calls were
marred by clicking sounds, static, and faint background conversations by
other parties; often he got busy signals when calling other parties, only
to find out later that they were at home but had not heard the phone ring.
At other times operators came on line to ask where he was calling from
and who he was. Steve's phone problems started in June 1977 and persisted to January 1978.[12]

A five-page motion to quash the subpoena was prepared by attorneys Kenneth Padilla and Robert Bloom.

> In light of Van Lucero's and Stephen Lucero's extensive exercise of their legitimate First Amendment rights, the government's long history of COINTELPRO activity, and illegal harassment of persons exercising First Amendment rights, and the unnecessary harassment of the Lucero family, the Court should examine closely the government's motivation in subpoenaing Van and Stephen Lucero, and quash the subpoenas in that they chill legitimate First Amendment rights of the subpoenaed witnesses. The Federal Bureau of Investigation has a documented history of attempting to sabotage, discredit, falsely charge, falsely label members of groups as informers, to misuse judicial process, to create antagonisms among ethnic groups and organizations seeking civil rights, and to generally dissipate and discredit efforts of minority groups and civil rights organizations as part of their COINTELPRO program and the Federal Bureau of Investigation has practiced this program against the Crusade for Justice, its Chairman, Rodolfo "Corky" Gonzales, its members and its members' families, and those who associate with said organization.[13]

On January 27, the Crusade marched in the bitter Denver cold at the local Federal Courthouse in solidarity with the Luceros. Upon returning to the Crusade's headquarters, they received word that the government prosecutors had dismissed the subpoenas. The Luceros were not subpoenaed again. Whether the federal judge in New York would have granted the defense motions to open the government's records on the Crusade was a question that was never answered because it was never asked. When the prosecution dropped the subpoenas, there was no need for the judge to rule on the defense motions.

The legal scuffle over the Lucero brothers' subpoenas coincided with another case affecting the Crusade, that of Alberto Mares. The clock on this case started ticking on April 7, 1977. Or did it? This case, too, left more questions in its wake than answers.

"WHY WOULD THE GOVERNMENT DO THIS?"

On October 1, 1977, Alberto Conrad Mares was arrested by the FBI in Denver and charged with robbery of the Colorado Federal Savings and Loan at 6460 E. Yale Avenue in Denver. The robbery, however, had occurred on April 7.

Alberto was born in Antonito, Colorado, and moved to Denver in the summer of 1951. His adjustment to city life was difficult. In April 1966 Mares was convicted of bank robbery and sentenced to 18 years imprisonment in the federal penitentiary. Though he did not serve the full sentence, his imprisonment included nearly four and a half years in the prison at Marion, Illinois. He was paroled and joined the Crusade in 1975 and found himself again under indictment in 1977.

The 1977 case never received the same scrutiny as other Crusade cases. Mares never went to trial. He fled Denver sometime in December 1977 or January 1978, and did not return until the spring of 1982, when he would revile those responsible for his exile:

> I declare that I didn't commit this crime and knew nothing about it, but over 5 years of [my] life have been severely disrupted, and my liberty and life have been in danger. I firmly believe—and am willing to document for the media—that my being charged with this crime was a deliberate act by government authorities who knew I was innocent yet were willing to fabricate a case against me. Why would the government do this?[14]

Prison Experiences

When Mares was first sent to prison in the mid-1960s, he drew the attention of prison authorities. Hearing a guard yelling obscenities at a Mexicano prisoner who did not understand English, Mares tried to translate for the prisoner. Angered, the guard called for reinforcements.

The two prisoners were beaten and taken to the isolation section. Alberto was charged with "disrupting the orderly running of the prison." In isolation he heard other prisoners being beaten, gassed, and thrown into the "hole" for complaining about prison conditions. He was transferred to the U.S. Medical Center in Springfield, Missouri, for minor surgery on May 1, 1969.

In Springfield, Alberto helped organize a work stoppage and was placed in the "hole" two cells away from the Mafia informer Joe Valachi. Mares was beaten for refusing Thorazine, which was administered to prisoners who were then forced to work while under its influence. He urged prisoners to refuse the medication.

On August 27, 1969, Mares was transferred from Springfield to Leavenworth, Kansas. The ranks of political activists in prisons were growing. With Raul "Tapon" Salinas, Ramon Chacon, Rafael Cancel Miranda, and others, Mares helped form Chicanos Organizados Rebeldes de Aztlan (Organized Rebel Chicanos of Aztlan), (CORA) and *Aztlan,* a newspaper they exchanged with Chicano Press Association newspapers across the country. The Puerto Rican socialist newspaper, *Claridad* was circulated in prison. CORA once tried to arrange for Rodolfo Gonzales to address the prisoners, but the Federal Bureau of Prisons canceled the visit. Over time, CORA organized five major work stoppages in prison.

Among the reforms Mares credits to CORA were the increase in Chicano enrollment in the prison educational department, higher pay for Chicanos employed in the prison factory, access to vocational training programs, the hiring of Spanish-speaking staff, twice weekly servings of Mexican food, and recognition of the Cinco de Mayo and September 16 as holidays for the prisoners.

In March 1972 Chicano prisoners organized a major work strike to protest against prison conditions. The prisoners were locked down for seven days with no change of clothing or showers. On April 8, many prisoners were taken by prison buses to federal prisons throughout the country. Mares was returned to Marion, along with Raul "Tapon" Salinas, "Beto" Gudino, and others. Rafael Cancel Miranda had been transferred to Marion about three months earlier because, he was told by prison officials, he had too many friends at Leavenworth.

Mares continued organizing after his release into the general population at Marion in April. In July 1972 he helped organize a strike to protest against the beating of Jesse Lopez by prison guards. The entire prison was locked down. Mares, Salinas, Gudino, Miranda, and several others were segregated from the general population and placed in the Control and Rehabilitation Effort (CARE) unit, a behavior modification program. They filed a successful suit in federal court to stop the program but spent more than 18 months locked down. They were beaten, gassed, and forced to take drugs like Thorazine.[15]

The suit filed by Mares and the other prisoners was his hardest-won victory, a milestone in his political development and education. As he later wrote:

> It was in prison that I asked why there were so many Chicanos, so many blacks, so many minorities and poor people in prison. In prison I was fortunate to learn that the prison only reflected society in general and I understand that my being in prison was the end result of a process that discriminates against the poor, working-class minorities because the economy, the government and society in general is structured to benefit the rich at the expense of the poor. In prison I came to understand that society's conditions can be changed by people. I dedicated my life to being active in seeking that change.[16]

In federal prison Mares met four men he credited with having educated him: Rafael Cancel Miranda, mentioned previously, Andres Cordero, Oscar Collazo, and Irving Flores Rodriguez, four of five famed Puerto Rican Nationalist prisoners. Lolita Lebron, the fifth, was confined at a federal women's prison.

In separate incidents, the Puerto Rican Nationalists attacked Blair

House, a temporary residence of the president, and entered Congress, where they drew pistols and fired them to protest against the suppression of the Puerto Rican independence movement. The Nationalists were sentenced to long prison terms, and their freedom became a demand of Puerto Rican independence activists. The Nationalists did not concede that their acts were criminal, but considered them patriotic.

"Albert Conrad Mares—Subversive Matter"

The Crusade was familiar with Mares through attorneys who handled his cases and through prisoners' correspondence with the Crusade. After his release from federal prison in December 1974, Mares was paroled to the state penitentiary at Canon City to finish a robbery sentence dating to 1966. While confined in the medium security prison in Canon City, he started a Chicano Studies class where guests, including Crusade members, spoke at the classes.

Mares joined the Crusade when he was released in April 1975 and became one of its most dedicated and tireless workers. He taught history at Escuela Tlatelolco, was chairperson of the Raza Association of Media Advocates, program director for the Colorado Recreation and Boxing Coaches Association, committee member of the Denver Chicano Liberation Defense Committee, and founder of the Colorado Prisoners Rights Organization, a prisoner advocacy group.

The authorities' treatment of Alberto was unique. His parole officer never allowed him to leave Colorado without putting his request for out-of-state travel through special processing. Rather than simply grant permission, as was in his power, the parole officer forwarded the request to the regional parole director in California, thereby imposing a three-week delay on every trip.

The FBI also had a special interest in Mares. In an October 1975 FBI file captioned "Albert Conrad Mares—Subversive Matter," an agent wrote:

> This investigation was initiated upon receipt of information that [Mares'] activities could involve a violation of Title 18 U.S. Code 2383 (Rebellion and Insurrection), Section 2385 (Advocating Overthrow of the Government), Section 837 (Unlawful Possession and Receipt of Firearms), and Section 844(d) (Explosive and Incendiary Devices).[17]

The FBI inquired about Mares shortly after his release from state prison in 1975. His sister, Anna, was contacted by FBI Agent Bishop, who asked if Alberto made trips to Chicago, if he participated in demonstrations against the government, if he was on the Crusade's board of directors, and what work he did for the Crusade. Bishop also questioned his

stepmother, asking additional questions about the involvement of Mares'
younger sisters with the Crusade. Anna Mares wrote:

> When I was living at 1914 E. 16th Avenue, Denver, an agent from the
> FBI named Bishop called my home wanting information about my
> brother, Alberto Mares. . . . This happened around May 1975, or early
> that summer. At this time I'd only lived at the above address for a short
> time and I can't understand how the agent would know it. The landlord
> at the apartments is Corky Gonzales, Chairman of the Crusade for
> Justice.[18]

In early 1976, the FBI visited Hector Subia, a prisoner at the state
penitentiary in Canon City. The agent asked if "it was true that Alberto
had come to visit me in prison . . . [and] what I knew about some revolutionary group in Chicago, and the bombing they were claiming, and if
Alberto was tied in with them." Subia refused to talk to the agent and
recounted:

> I tried to leave [the meeting room], but the door was locked. He kept
> trying to ask questions, and I told him "Fuck you, I have nothing to say
> to you," and he started getting indignant. He told me I could go to prison
> for not cooperating, and he could make me talk. I thought that was
> funny because I was already in prison. . . . I continued to have corre-
> spondence with the Crusade for Justice Prisoners Rights Committee,
> and there are a couple of other instances when it was called to my atten-
> tion that because of my correspondence with the Crusade for Justice,
> my actions and visits were closely scrutinized.[19]

Indictment for Armed Robbery

On the day of Mares' arrest for a robbery that took place six months
earlier, the phone at his residence showed signs of being monitored.
Shortly before the arrest, someone made calls from his phone to various
Crusade members. The calls did not go through. Sometimes the phone
appeared to ring, but no one answered. Other calls were answered by
phone recordings or operators who came on line saying the numbers were
out of order. Calls made to the Mares residence met similar treatment.[20]

On the day of the robbery, Mares was teaching his daily schedule of
classes and meeting with parents over lunch in the school cafeteria. He
was mindful of his work that day because it had been announced that
classes might be filmed by a local television station. The filming was later
canceled. April 7 was a routine day, except that a robbery was committed
on the other side of town by someone whose identity the authorities still
refuse to reveal.

When preliminary hearings were held, Mares was identified by a bank teller as the man who committed the robbery. The eyewitness identification astounded him. Although students, parents, and others were ready to testify that his whole day was accounted for, he faced the reality that his witnesses were Mexican activists involved with the "radical" Crusade for Justice.[21] The government's case would proceed before a white jury with a white judge and prosecutor. FBI agents in business suits and police would attend and testify. A white woman, the bank teller, would swear under oath that Mares was the culprit. Unfortunately for Mares, the security camera at the savings and loan company was not working on the day of the robbery.

Should he testify, he would face grueling questions about his bank robbery conviction, his long years in prison, and his status as a parolee and felon. His credibility and integrity would be impugned before a jury that held his life in the balance. What could Mares say in his own defense, other than that he had spent the day with a large number of Mexicans and fellow radicals? Would he tell his life story with his characteristic bluntness? Would he say:

> During the days of my imprisonment I not only had an opportunity to read various books either written by or about great guerrilleros . . . but also had the honor and privilege of having met and been taught by those great Puerto Rican revolutionaries, Rafael Cancel Miranda, Oscar Collazo, Irving Flores Rodriguez, and Andres Cordero, who taught me the true meaning of Yankee Imperialism. Little did I know then that the influence of the above great men attributed to my total involvement that seeks the total destruction of that monster, capitalism-imperialism, that causes the death in so many ways of so many people in this world. In the Southwest this movement is the Chicano Movement.[22]

Alberto Mares disappeared shortly before his slated court date on January 9, 1978. The FBI conducted an extensive investigation in Colorado, Wyoming, California, Illinois, New York, and San Juan, Puerto Rico. FBI headquarters issued a "Fugitive Robber Flyer" on him on February 7, 1978.[23]

An envelope was delivered to the Crusade with the message quoted above after Mares failed to appear in court. It concluded:

> I'll try to wrap this up by telling each of you that the repressive forces of the multinational corporation dealers have forced my departure from you by accusing me of a crime I had nothing to do with or know anything about. I have no confidence whatsoever in the judicial system of this country. . . . History will someday prove my innocence. Until then I will make my departure from you and serve my people somewhere else. . . . I will not disappoint any of you, this "Lousy Thing" [a nickname] will never allow the real criminals to be comfortable.[24]

With this message, Alberto Mares dropped from sight until the spring of 1982. Shortly after his disappearance, his photo appeared on local television stations along with a notice that classified Mares as one of Colorado's 10 "most wanted" criminals.

Charges are Dropped

On November 12, 1981, Kenneth Padilla notified Nita (Gonzales) Marquez, who posted bond for Mares before his disappearance, that the attorney had received notice from Assistant U.S. Attorney Jimmye Warren advising that the charges against Alberto Mares had been dropped. On October 14, the federal attorney filed a Motion and Order to Dismiss in Denver's federal court, stating, "The undersigned counsel [for the federal government] has determined that the interests of justice would best be served by the dismissal of said Indictment."[25]

On December 17, federal probation officials in Denver notified officials in the California regional office that charges had been dropped. The Denver officials noted that the Mares family sought legal counsel from Carlos Vigil, a New Mexico attorney who studied law in Colorado and had previously worked on several cases for the DCLDC.[26] No one, including Gonzales and the Crusade, gave the family detailed information. Federal officials never contacted the family.

Attorney Carlos Vigil confirmed that charges against Alberto had been dropped. He received a copy of the letter Denver probation officials sent to the California officials:

> Mr. Vigil was advised that the parole violation warrants [resulting from Mares' flight] remains [*sic*] outstanding and parolee will be taken into custody when located. [Vigil] was further advised that the Parole Commission may still consider the Failure to Appear as new criminal behavior and that there are other technical violations of parole, such as Failure to Report Change in Residence, Failure to Report Change in Employment, and Failure to Submit Written Monthly Reports, since January 9, 1978.[27]

New doubts and questions arose. Would Mares now face charges for parole violation?

On February 16, 1982, an attorney with the U.S. Attorney's office mailed an affidavit of FBI Agent Walter F. Scott to Kathy Bonham, an attorney for Nita Marquez. The affidavit read:

> In July, 1981, an individual whose identity must remain confidential confessed to a total of nine federal savings and loan robberies . . . dating from August 30, 1976, to August 16, 1979. Included in these nine robberies is the April 7, 1977, robbery of the Colorado Savings and

Loan. . . . Agents WFS and BWJ of the Denver office of the FBI conducted sufficient additional investigation to corroborate this confession
and are satisfied beyond doubt that Mares is not responsible for this
robbery.[28]

Questions persisted. Who had confessed? Why did the government re-
fuse to reveal the robber's identity? Why did the bank teller identify
Mares? Why did the authorities wait six months from the time of the
robbery to arrest Mares? This last question was answered in 1992 after
Mares received copies of FBI files through the Freedom of Information
Act.

The authorities had waited six months to indict Mares because there
was insufficient evidence to arrest him. A Denver FBI memorandum to
the headquarters, dated September 22, 1977, stated:

> This case has received continuous investigative attention. All logical in-
> vestigation has been conducted resulting in the fact that successful pros-
> ecution of MARES is not imminent unless further evidence is developed.
> This case has received continuous attention since Mares was considered
> a suspect. Numerous discussions have been held between the case Agent
> and the U.S. Attorney's office. Discussions have also taken place between
> the ASAC [Assistant Special Agent in Charge], Denver Division, and the
> Bank Robbery Squad and also among the Bank Robbery Squad in Den-
> ver. All logical investigation has been conducted, and there is not enough
> evidence to present this matter to the Denver Federal Grand Jury to seek
> indictment against MARES.[29]

Shortly after this memorandum was sent, the bank teller identified
Mares. Another Denver FBI memorandum to the FBI director stressed the
need to develop evidence against Mares and other Crusade members:

> MARES . . . is a ranking member in the militant organization known as
> the Crusade for Justice (CFJ). . . . [He] is an avowed Communist known
> to have associates in other militant-revolutionary type organiza-
> tions. . . . A number of CFJ activists have been involved in violent crimi-
> nal activity in the Denver area. . . . MARES has been developed as a
> suspect in transporting stolen dynamite from the Denver area to Chi-
> cago. . . . A number of other bank robbery violations have been commit-
> ted in Denver by an individual meeting the same general description and
> using the same general MO [modus operandi] as MARES and/or his
> associates. . . . [One sentence deleted] the possibility exists that MARES
> and/or his associates are involved directly or indirectly in these robber-
> ies. Consequently, captioned bank robbery is being designated a priority
> target case inasmuch as the identification, apprehension, and prosecu-
> tion of MARES for bank robbery would have a positive impact on bank
> robberies in the Denver metropolitan area. An investigation regarding

MARES and associates could develop evidence regarding additional
Federal and state prosecutable violations being perpetrated by other
CFJ activists.[30]

Some questions were never answered. Why did the FBI hound Mares
after his release from prison in Colorado and try to link him to bombings
involving Puerto Rican independence? Why did the government wait four
months to drop the charges after the culprit's confession in July 1981?
Moreover, Denver police and the FBI continued to harass the Mares family as late as July 27 in the very month the robber confessed.

Remigio Mares, Alberto's father, died in July 1981 and was buried on
July 27. According to the Reverend Patrick Valdez, an "unholy atmosphere" prevailed at the funeral due to "the presence of local and federal
police [FBI], both during the Mass and at the internment service at Mount
Olivet Cemetery," Valdez wrote:

> These officers behaved as if they had never been to a church before nor
> to a funeral. Their lack of respect for the dead man and his mourning
> family and friends included both the inordinate number of officers as
> well as their unrestrained movement and the crackling noise of walkie-
> talkies throughout the ceremonies.[31]

Over 20 Denver police and FBI agents attended the services, still seeking
to arrest Mares even though the robber had already confessed.

In April 1982, after Denver attorney Harold Haddon confirmed that
the remaining parole violation warrants had been dropped, a press conference publicized the new developments in Mares' case. The hope was
that some would know how to contact Mares.

Alberto Mares appeared at a June 21 news conference at Servicios de
La Raza, a North Denver social service agency. He refused to discuss his
whereabouts after his 1978 disappearance. Reading from a prepared
statement, he said:

> The indictment against me in October 1977 is an experience that shows
> that the government stands ready to persecute people who fight for so-
> cial change because this endangers the privilege of those who oppress
> us. . . . When the right-wing comes to power it brings with it a program
> of so-called law and order that defines as criminal those people and ac-
> tivities that challenge it. The right-wing has come to power with Ronald
> Reagan. Nixon used COINTELPRO to smash people's movements
> when he was president. In a similar way I have been persecuted since my
> release from prison in 1975. And now Reagan is in power with a pro-
> gram far more reactionary than Nixon ever was. He threatens war in El
> Salvador and is foolish enough to believe that our youth will be cannon
> fodder without us resisting.[32]

Angered at the false accusations that forced him to live as a fugitive for over four years—during which time his father died and his marriage broke up—Mares returned to Denver hoping to continue in the Crusade. In less than five months, however, he took a job in property management and dedicated himself to his family and finances, which had greatly suffered since his flight from Denver.

Alberto Mares had returned to a city and political circumstances very different than when he left. He joined the Crusade in 1975, when the Crusade had reached, and was passing, the peak of its fortunes. By the time of his flight, the signs of the Crusade's decline were evident, and its effectiveness and once impressive grassroots support had faltered.

By 1982, Mares and others saw the Crusade's structure, programs, influence, and morale plummet. Once willing to sacrifice his freedom and his life for the movement the Crusade embodied—a movement to which he wholeheartedly gave himself—Mares now decided to go his own way.

Seventeen

Sliding Backwards

Alberto Mares returned to Denver in the spring of 1982, but *El Gallo* did not report on his case, Escuela Tlatelolco students did not assemble in the Crusade auditorium to welcome him, and his return was not discussed at a Wednesday Fishermen's Meeting. The Denver Chicano Liberation Defense Committee did not rally around his case, and he did not resume teaching at Escuela Tlatelolco or working with the Colorado Prisoners' Rights Organization.

El Gallo was last published on a regular basis in 1980, Escuela Tlatelolco now enrolled only elementary level students (the spring of 1982 was Tlatelolco's last semester at the Crusade's headquarters), the DCLDC and the CPRO were defunct, and there had been no Fishermen's Meeting since 1979.

Escuela Tlatelolco relocated to Servicios de La Raza, a North Denver social service agency where Gonzales' oldest daughter was employed in 1982. There it remained until the mid-1990s. As far as is known, the last issue of *El Gallo* was published in 1985 to attack then Mayor Federico Peña (ironically, a Democrat whom the Gonzales family and Crusade members worked to elect).

The Crusade functioned, but its activities, constituency, and effectiveness had greatly declined since Mares fled Colorado in early 1978. By the late 1970s few new members joined the organization, though the experience of its veteran members was a substantial asset. In the four and a half years that followed Mares' departure, the Crusade, unable to grapple effectively with the changing political environment and its loss of human and material resources—ceased to be a powerful organization.

Various sources can be used to reconstruct the rise of the Crusade for Justice, but records reflecting the causes of its decline are less accessible. The preceding chapters recount the issues in which the Crusade was involved, but no one incident, date, or information source fully accounts for the Crusade's decline.[1]

364

The election of Ronald Reagan in 1980 continued the consolidation of power by conservatives first attained in 1968 by Richard Nixon's election. To say that the political climate changed, however, is not to say that it improved. Issues that stirred controversies and community activism in the early 1960s persisted into the late 1970s.

PATROLMAN JAMES "BUSTER" SNIDER

In 1979 homeowners living near Sloan Lake Park complained about youths congregating in the area. To discourage young people from gathering in the park, Denver police stopped youngsters on their way there and issued scores of traffic tickets and other citations. Patrolman James "Buster" Snider, for example, would step into the street and stop oncoming cars, then cite the drivers for impeding traffic by stopping. He ticketed people for jaywalking on streets within the park that were closed to vehicular traffic anyway.

The Sloan Lake Committee Against Police Harassment, an ad hoc group led by Dolores "Dolly" Lucero and Judy Cisneros, organized protests over the park situation. "The police attitude toward the younger Chicanos can only mean trouble," Cisneros said "These are beautiful kids [and] I hate to see them start getting police records just for using the parks that their parents are paying for." Snider, one of city's most notorious policemen, was "Denver's most prolific ticket writer" according to a *Denver Post* article on Snider's activities at Sloan Lake Park in early May 1979.

The article reported that Snider "stopped dozens of persons, almost all of whom were Chicanos." Snider denied singling out Chicanos and said, 'I'd say it was about half and half. I think about half were white.' He started to show a book of tickets as proof of his statement, but said it was in his car." Snider then admitted that the people ticketed were Mexicans, but explained, "This is a Chicano area. You know yourself that if I'm at a disturbance at [the University of Denver] that most of the people I stop are going to be those seditious ones. If I'm over in Five Points, then most of those I stop are going to be the coloreds."[2] No city official objected to Snider's practices, and some voiced hearty approval. Snider continued on the force until he was fired in 1984, charged with second-degree sexual assault on a 36-year-old Chicana.

Community meetings to organize the youths who were harassed by police at Sloan Lake were held in North Denver. Police informers in attendance showed quiet hostility. One was a woman who operated a bar on West Colfax Avenue near Sloan Lake; others were relatives of Spanish-surnamed police officers.[3]

Though the Sloan Lake Committee Against Police Harassment included Crusade members, the Crusade's involvement was mostly passive. Similarly, the controversy over the killing of 16-year-old Joey Rodriguez by Patrolman Robert Silvas on May 27, 1979, and protests over inadequate recreation facilities in the unincorporated "Goathill" neighborhood on Denver's northern boundary drew little Crusade support. As with the Sloan Lake protests, the Goathill organizing was begun by women, Teresa Tenorio and Virginia Salazar, who sought the Crusade's support for their efforts.

Activists continued to meet violent deaths. Carlos Zapata, 29, was killed in an explosion at 9th Avenue and Bannock Street in the early morning of March 22, 1978. The body was so mutilated that it had to be identified through dental charts. Police theorized that the dead man was placing a bomb at the time of his death.

> When asked by the media about a possible identification of the body, Capt. Robert Shaughnessy told reporters that he would wait to see which one of "Corky's guys" would show up missing and then he would know who the person was. Before the identification of the body, which the media said was that of a "Hispano" based on police reports that, at that time, had no basis . . . the news media used the names of Chicano activists and organizations, especially the Crusade for Justice, and hinted at a pattern of the bombing of "non-militant" Chicanos by "militant" Chicanos.[4]

Carlos Zapata had been employed at the Platte Valley Action Center as an administrative assistant for three years. Though associated with the Crusade since the early 1970s, when he'd been a North Denver Brown Beret, Zapata was not a Crusade member.

"THE UMBILICAL CORD OF THE ESTABLISHMENT"

Though the Crusade loaned its building to the Sloan Lake and Goathill organizers for meetings and fund raisers, the organization was now preoccupied with internal affairs, in contrast to earlier times when it sought out community issues in which to become involved. It is likely that the Crusade's harsh and strident criticism of mainstream organizations was motivated by an uncomfortable recognition that its resources were diminishing while the fortunes of those it viewed as political opportunists were on the upswing.

The Crusade criticized the moderate politics of the Chicano community's emerging middle class, many of whom were tied to political parties, government programs, and affirmative action.[5] The Crusade realized that ethnic solidarity and nationalism had mobilized a disorganized community to push for reforms, but the Crusade felt that the popularization of ethnic pride could be—and was—used by interest groups who did not share the goals of Chicanos activists, groups the Crusade described as "still tied to the umbilical cord of the Establishment; two party politics, capitalism, economic dependency, and right-wing social classism [sic] . . . who have made economic gains [but] done so at the expense of the movement, but [who] have never nourished or supported those who have maintained the spirit of resistance and progress."[6]

Aside from the merits of the Crusade's criticism of its rivals, the fact remained that other avenues to power, prestige, and employment were opened up to the budding leadership elements in Denver's Mexican-origin community. Grievances could be expressed—and resolutions sought—through party politics and other channels. Those in need of employment and social services were better served at funded agencies, since the Crusade never had the resources for such a task, but in providing such services others could develop political constituencies. This uncomfortable fact would not go away.

Efforts at social reform by mainstream minority politicians, however, often fared no better through the system than those of activists who operated outside it. Councilman Sal Carpio, described by the *Rocky Mountain News* in 1979 as "more likely to be haggling over sewer bond issues and zoning changes than fighting for Chicano rights," provides one such example.[7]

Amendment A

In November 1978, Charter Amendment A was put before Denver voters. Drawn up by Councilman Carpio, it proposed to create a civilian board to review police misconduct complaints. Supporters raised $3,000, to promote its passage. The police Staff Inspection Bureau (SIB), had, in the five preceding years, evaluated 522 citizen complaints against the police, responsibility that the Colorado Bar Association thought should be transferred outside the SIB. A mayor's advisory panel itself said that the SIB spent more energy trying to disprove complaints than investigating them.[8]

A pro-police group, the Committee for Professional Law Enforcement, worked against Amendment A, raising $55,000. The Police Protective Association, the Police Union, and the (Police) Brotherhood, as well as police families, also campaigned against it. The Police Protective Association had a budget of $500,000 and spent $30,000 on this campaign.[9]

Joe Sandoval, a college instructor and former Arvada policeman, said, "This proposal will not eliminate the very things we are complaining about—police misconduct, police rudeness, police killings." Sandoval said that the Los Angeles police commission—on which the Denver proposal was patterned—was viewed by the city's Chicanos and blacks as part of the police department and not the community.[10] Voters turned down Amendment A by a two-to-one margin, and police announced that they intended to be involved in future elections.

The Crusade did not participate in efforts to pass the charter amendment because it considered the proposed remedy ineffective and it did not support efforts whose leadership it distrusted. Nonparticipation meant that the Crusade had little influence on public opinion because it offered no independent course of action. As mainstream politicians were elected from the barrio, the Crusade's nonparticipation fed its growing isolation.

THE STRUGGLE FOR ECONOMIC SELF-SUFFICIENCY

Aside from this isolation and drumbeat of negative publicity and innuendo, other factors led to the Crusade's decline. Inability to fund its activities and staff was, obviously, a crucial problem. Less obvious was the Crusade's failure to confront, much less resolve, the question of how it would generate its own resources.

The Crusade had walked a tightrope between political independence and economic vulnerability since its inception. When membership swelled in the late 1960s, its clout increased, a fact that was especially significant because the Crusade operated outside mainstream channels. Gonzales, with his long familiarity with politics, bureaucracy, and the funding processes of social programs, proved adept at devising ways to take advantage of that clout.

The Crusade, for example, was approached in the early 1970s by lower-level administrators of the Volunteers in Service to America, who offered to place VISTA volunteers at the Crusade. Volunteers were paid $200 a month for their work in low-income communities. Rather than accept the placement of outsiders, usually well-meaning Anglos, Gonzales made a counterproposal. The Crusade would recruit people (its members), refer them to VISTA for training, and then allow them to be placed at the Crusade. Such stop-gap measures sustained many people with subsistence incomes, but they were no real substitute for economic self-sufficiency. At the time of the March 17 confrontation, 17 Crusade members were employed at Escuela Tlatelolco as VISTA volunteers. Those whose names were publicized in connection with the confrontation were dismissed by the VISTA administration.

As membership declined in the late 1970s, the Crusade developed separately incorporated entities under its direction: Tlatelolco Credit Union, which received its state charter on November 1, 1977; the Circulo Infantil Doña Teresina Romero, Escuela Tlatelolco's day-care center; the Colorado Prisoners Rights Organization (CPRO);[11] the Colorado Recreation and Boxing Coaches Association (CRBCA);[12] the Raza Association of Media Advocates (RAMA) in the summer of 1976;[13] the Denver Chicano Liberation Defense Committee (DCLDC); and the Ballet Chicano de Aztlan dance troupe. Though the Crusade's core membership had developed diverse talents by the late 1970s—as shown by the diversity of the Crusade's involvements—the advanced skills did not translate into greater economic resources as much as they allowed for more specialized organizational development.

The Case of the Missing Documentary

A minor controversy involving RAMA illustrates some aspects of the Crusade's growing concern with economic resources. RAMA became involved in a dispute with one of Denver's major television channels, KMGH, in the spring of 1977. Ironically, the dispute was the result of a RAMA initiative in which the group, under the direction of its coordinator, Nita (Gonzales) Marquez, approached KMGH in an attempt to gain publicity for work involving the Crusade's separately incorporated groups under city-funded job training programs. Marquez, ever watchful for opportunities to get favorable publicity, proposed that KMGH produce a news documentary on the job-training programs. This documentary, produced by independent producer Sue Kinney, subsequently disappeared from the television station.

The money for the programs was allocated by the Denver Manpower Administration and was part of a national program initiated under President Jimmy Carter to reduce unemployment by using federal money to subsidize local job training and placement. Local project sponsors were to identify unmet needs and recruit unemployed workers to staff projects once they were funded. The CRBCA used the monies "to provide unmet public service to the community by creating jobs for people who have existing skills in the area of recreation and who have been unable to secure employment." Under this program the CRBCA had 15 employees who received their checks from the Denver Manpower Administration and not from the Crusade for Justice.[14] The sponsors, however, had to provide funds and resources for the start-up phase of the projects. The Crusade's nonprofit branches submitted several proposals that were funded in 1976, and they looked forward to continued funding in 1977. The programs paid a modest hourly wage, but Crusade members, who were accustomed to living on less, actually enjoyed a modest increase in income. The increase in income would have been greater, but all Crusade members employed on the programs donated a portion of their wages to the Crusade.

RAMA sought media coverage for the jobs programs described in proposals submitted, but not yet approved, for funding in the autumn of 1977. At the time RAMA approached KMGH, the contracts for the job programs were still being negotiated.

Marquez and RAMA were not happy with the subsequent documentary, referred to it as "terrible," and demanded changes to make it "more positive." The changes Marquez and RAMA wanted concerned an interview done with Marquez' father, Rodolfo Gonzales, and references to federal money received by the Crusade to pay employees of the CPRO and CRBCA programs.

The Crusade did not in fact receive federal money, and this characterization angered the RAMA activists. The separately incorporated CPRO and CRBCA had been, and were to be, the recipients of the money, through contracts drawn up with a city government office that was set up to negotiate and monitor such projects. When the CPRO and CRBCA were incorporated and submitted proposals for funding, both groups had numerous officers and employees who were not Crusade members.

When RAMA approached Channel 7 with the idea for the news documentary, it did not bargain for the attention that Sue Kinney gave to the project. Kinney was an independent producer noted for her exposés. Members of RAMA, the Crusade, the CRBCA, and the CPRO showed Kinney and the film crew around the Crusade headquarters, where filming and interviews were done. All parties were cordial to Kinney, but many noted that she was distant and cool toward her hosts.

Kinney was inquisitive about the identities of job program employees and officers and their relationship to the Crusade. Some Crusade members wondered if this was her main concern; she showed little interest in the work of the job programs on which she purportedly was to focus. Among those employed on the job programs, and on the boards of the nonprofit groups, were members of Gonzalez' family. The job programs had rules forbidding nepotism, but those employed by the job projects were not working under the direction of relatives or spouses, though some relatives were employed as co-workers.

When Kinney interviewed Gonzales, she sharply and persistently questioned him about the number of the program participants who were members of his family. He terminated the interview. After this, the Crusade assumed that Kinney's reporting had nothing to do with the merits of the programs, but sought to imply nepotism in their operation.

The question arose among some Crusade members about how (and why) Kinney—a middle-aged, middle-class, professional white woman was questioning the relationships of a large number of people she was meeting for the first time. The time she spent at the Crusade was marked by a perfunctory attitude apart from the intense interest she had shown in family relationships. It seemed unlikely that Kinney had stumbled upon appearances of nepotism, or the finagling of monies through Crusade front groups, in the four-month span from RAMA's approaching the station to the disappearance of the film. It also seemed unlikely that Channel 7 was unaware of Kinney's intentions, assumptions, or focus.

When RAMA met with Channel 7 to review the film, the filming was complete. If in fact Sue Kinney sought to mislead the Crusade, the organization and RAMA had been caught napping. Hard feelings arose when RAMA and Crusade representatives reviewed the film on March 28, 1978, did not like what they saw, and asked for changes.

Marquez returned to Channel 7 on the night of March 28, at 7 p.m. and asked to see Mr. Ted Barros, a station employee, about those changes.[15] Barros was not there, but a secretary allowed Marquez, Roberto "Che" Luera, and Reba Garcia, members of RAMA and of the Channel 7 Minority Advisory Committee, into the station.

A newspaper later reported, "Once in the room where the film was kept, they asked an employee if the changes had been made. The employee said he didn't know, [Marquez] said. The three [RAMA] members then went back down to the guard and asked to see another station official. They briefly returned to the film room and then left."[16]

Channel 7 subsequently looked for the film and couldn't find it. The station believed the film had been stolen. No one at the station, however, could say they had seen anyone in possession of the film. The television station believed the disappearance—or theft—was linked to RAMA's displeasure with its content. Marquez and RAMA members angrily denied involvement.

> Three Chicano activists said Wednesday they had no part in the disappearance Tuesday evening of a video tape about the Crusade for Justice from a local television station. They accused the station of deliberately losing the film to discredit them. Nita Marquez, daughter of Crusade leader Rodolfo "Corky" Gonzales, Robert [sic] Luera, and Reva [sic] Garcia acknowledged entering the studios of KMGH-TV shortly before 7 p.m. Tuesday to view the half-hour feature film [KMGH official Bob] Hart did not discount the possibility that a station employee may have accidentally misplaced the tape. And the Denver police, who privately said they were less than enthusiastic about getting involved in the argument between the Chicanos and the station, said they had no leads.[17]

The film was never found, but the station aired lower-quality copy of the film on March 28. The Crusade and job program participants and supporters held a demonstration in front of KMGH in protest against the broadcast.

It was reported that "[RAMA] suggested the station do a feature on the Crusade as a way of meeting its requirement for public service broadcasting and the station agreed. This is the last point upon which the station and [RAMA] agreed." The activists stated that they had considered seeking an injunction to stop the broadcast because the film had "discrepancies," "misrepresentation of fact," "false information," "false statements", and other flaws.[18]

Whether or not the broadcast was flawed, other factors fueled the heat of the Crusade's displeasure, things that may not have been clearly understood by the Crusade at the time. One additional aspect of the controversy left the Crusade with lingering suspicions.

In the spring of 1978, shortly after the KMGH feud, the Denver Manpower Administration announced that it would not fund any of the Crusade-affiliated programs. The CPRO and CRBCA had been negotiating with the Denver Manpower Administration since the fall of 1977 for the release of anticipated funds. As they waited, the Crusade dipped into its own dwindling reserves to fund the projects.

The program sponsors had been told that the funds would be forthcoming, but delays stretched into the spring of 1978. Then funding was denied. All this caused economic hardship to the employees of the programs and to the sponsoring groups.

The Crusade had not anticipated problems when it geared up its programs in the fall. The various groups used their savings to employ people on the assumption that the groups would eventually be reimbursed for the outlay. When funding was denied in 1978, the groups, having nearly exhausted their resources, were now told that no money would be forthcoming, not even reimbursements.

Some Crusade members became suspicious when the initial delays became prolonged. The Denver Manpower Administration asked job program participants to provide copies of birth certificates and reveal how people on the programs were related to each other. Crusade members denied that they were related to each other, but it seemed evident that the administration knew otherwise. One family scurried around making copies of birth and marriage certificates, whiting out or changing data, and then submitting the altered copies to avoid entanglements that would hinder the approval for funding—an example of financial vulnerability undermining political independence.

One Crusade member, Rob Cisneros, sought a night job as a janitor. A co-worker employed at the Manpower Administration office during the day told him that the Manpower Administration was keeping an eye on the Crusade-associated projects and even had a woman employee gathering information about the identities and relationships of Crusade members. This person in fact routinely attended the Crusade's weekly fundraising luncheons. Cisneros' co-worker believed Manpower had no intention of funding the programs. When this information was brought to the Crusade's attention, some older Crusade members—friends of the woman who attended the Wednesday luncheons—shrugged it off. After all, she was a former member, spent money at the Wednesday luncheon, and was a friend of one of the organization's prominent women. Other Crusade members remained suspicious.

Some Manpower Administration employees were former Crusade members who had left the organization about four years before when a group of their friends and relatives were expelled. One person was a recipient of job-training funds on a project where his numerous relatives were employed. The Crusade noted that his project had no problems with its funding.

When the Crusade for Justice began in the 1960s, it sought to be economically independent. The Crusade, however, never charged membership or service fees. Many, if not most, of the organization's members subsisted for years on poverty-level stipends. The Manpower jobs boosted their income, but the young, single activists of the late 1960s and early 1970s were now married with children and financial obligations.

The underlying tension in the Crusade's heated response to the Channel 7 film was caused by its own financial crisis. From its original insistence on economic—and therefore political—independence, the Crusade had become an organization with many bills to pay and a core membership dependent on it for their income. The Crusade's work at this time was made possible as much by government and foundation money as by its own efforts.

"I BELIEVE WE ARE SLIDING BACKWARDS"

The Crusade's greatest expense was Escuela Tlatelolco, where no tuition was charged, books were free, and a free lunch was provided four days a week. Its bills for lights, gas, phones, wages, and building upkeep were now being paid for the eighth year as the school continued to consume more resources than it provided. An additional problem was one of unforeseen consequences.

Many of the students enrolled in Escuela Tlatelolco in the early 1970s were young activists or children of Crusade members who related to the teachers and administrators as fellow activists, as "family," not as authority figures. It was hoped that Tlatelolco graduates would attend college and return to their communities—and to the Crusade—as a new generation of leaders and workers. The 17 years it takes to go from kindergarten to a bachelor of arts degree, however, meant a long wait before a return on this investment would arrive.

In spite of its activist orientation, Tlatelolco accepted students who were not activists or whose families remained uninvolved in the organization. Some students came to the Escuela after being kicked out of public school or after having problems with the juvenile courts as an alternative to confinement. Tlatelolco found itself trying to be three different things: a training ground and leadership academy for young activists, an alternative school for barrio youth, and a private school for Crusade members' children and Tlatelolco's staff.[19]

Individuals who had been the Crusade's best organizers were now employed for nine months out of 12 as teachers or support staff. If the teachers were waiting to be replaced by the next generation of activists, the replacements were slow to arrive. Further, Tlatelolco was founded in response, or in reaction, to the treatment of Mexican youth in public schools, but these problems did not end because the Crusade had its own school. The number of pushouts from one barrio high school in one semester exceeded the Crusade's total enrollment. In its peak school year, 1972–73, Tlatelolco enrolled 178 students from kindergarten to twelfth grade.

If Tlatelolco drained the Crusade's resources, it also served as a barometer of its well-being. From the fall of 1971 to the spring of 1975, Tlatelolco graduated 51 students, including eight who obtained bachelor's degrees through a special program in collaboration with Goddard College. From the fall of 1975 to the spring of 1979, however, Tlatelolco had only 21 students graduate, less than half of the previous four-year total.

The sinister stresses confronting the Crusade continued, as shown in a 1979 deposition in a federal court suit in Bridgeport, Connecticut, over the release of the "Kill a Cop a Day" memo in 1976. The plaintiffs (initially Rodolfo Gonzales, the Crusade, and AIM) alleged that damages to their reputations included financial loss.[20] Gonzales, in person and as the Crusade's chief representative, had to prove the nature and extent of damages. Since he had been self-employed nearly his entire life, and the Crusade was a nonprofit organization, it was difficult to specify damages.

At the beginning of Gonzales' deposition, attorney William Kunstler stated:

> [We] want to indicate that we will resist any inquiry into the make-up, membership, of the Crusade. I'm not going to have [Gonzales] do here

what he would resist doing in front of a Federal Grand Jury. . . . I just want to put you [the attorney for the Connecticut State Police] on notice of that in case you want names of membership, where sources of income come from, etcetera.[21]

Yet the 81-page deposition is full of inquiries about these topics. Surprisingly, Gonzales proceeded to answer the questions Kunstler said would be resisted. Many of his answers seem vague, while others seem resentful, befuddled, and inaccurate.

When asked why there were fewer Crusade board members in the late 1970s than in the early 1970s, Gonzales responded, "Because I think we have more or less developed an administrative ability in the core leadership and they represent different areas we work in," implying that the Crusade board had enhanced leadership qualities and functioned well with fewer persons, not that its numbers had declined.[22] When asked about the Crusade's activity in 1979, Gonzales answered that it was active in educational, cultural, and social service programs, and said, "[We] have been active in family instruction. We are also active in labor organizations."[23] What Gonzales meant by "family instruction" is unclear. The Crusade never had a "family instruction" program, much less any such effort in 1979. Nor was it involved with labor unions in 1979; it had been only minimally involved with them since the late 1960s.[24]

Gonzales' confusing or contradictory claims are illustrated in the following exchange on pages 70 and 71:

Q: But you still continue to draw enormous crowds?
A: Well, at one time we have drawn 15,000, but we have declined quite a bit on that.
Q: You no longer draw that many?
A: I don't know that we can. If the press would help us, I'm sure we could.
Q: Are you saying the movement has not lost forces since the early 1970's?
A: No, in the Chicano movement it hasn't. There are more involved today than there were in the 60's.[25]

Gonzales' remarks also reflect the financial crisis affecting the organization.

There is not that much money to distribute . . . if we have funds we can do many things. If we don't have funds, we have to slow down. . . . The financial picture is that we're broke. . . . We have less money on hand than we did in 1976. We owe more money than we did in 1976. We tried to run the organization the way I run my personal life which is not to owe debts. The Crusade is supported—is the main support of our school, not only by the providing [of] the building but also by helping to pay stipends for the school and teachers. At this time we have to borrow on our property and I think that's very serious. I believe we are sliding backwards.[26]

Gonzales also commented on menacing pressures that he attributed to the government intelligence agencies and the personal burden of fear and stress he bore. At several points in his remarks he addressed this burden:

I think that where I go, whether it be Mexico City or New York, I have surveillance or people watching me. . . . Anything I do out of hand, how I speak, what I say may constitute belligerence and also constitute my death warrant. . . . I don't think [the memo] was used so much to stop, to stop, my credibility, but I think it was used to have me assassinated, in a sense, murdered by proxy.[27]

Gonzales was also a husband, the father of eight children, and now grandfather to numerous grandchildren. His concerns and fear as a family man were evident.

I think we've suffered a lot of undue pressure and a lot of undue harassment. Our invasion of our privacy, the different threats on our lives. My children have grown up understanding how to handle these situations. I have a large family. . . . These are not day-dreams. We live with these every day. We have been followed and we have a series of license numbers and descriptions and photos of people that have followed us and harassed us. People that surveil us at demonstrations and at our private work. They take pictures of our houses, of our yards and children. It's not that I'm just saying this. It's a serious matter and this is not something you play around with and make up. This is the type of life we lead.[28]

The full impact of this pressure is difficult to gauge or state. Though Gonzales would seek the advice of his most trusted organizational confidants, he seldom revealed his innermost thoughts. Numerous comments in his deposition refer to the bad publicity the Crusade received and its effect on the organization. A composite of these remarks follows:

I think that because of the slander and some of the things which have been printed . . . has tried to destroy our credibility, and within the community has placed fear in people of the Crusade for Justice in itself. It has heightened our dedication of the core group, but the influence [of the Crusade] on the totality [of the community] has probably waned and I feel that this has been purposely done . . . we have been attacked in many areas through the press, through these types of bulletins that have come out in the press and come out on TV and come out in radio to destroy our credibility. . . . If this credibility is destroyed fewer people are going to give to that organization.[29]

The constant battles with adversaries, including those within the Chicano movement, caused the Crusade gradually, if unconsciously, to withdraw from involvements where the outcome was uncertain. The Crusade, for example, declined to attend a national conference in Salt Lake City and a subsequent gathering on immigration policy in San Antonio in October 1977. Participating in the immigration conference were members of the Texas LRUP, the Socialist Workers Party, and the Centro de Accion Social Autonomo, groups with whom the Crusade had previous disputes.

The Crusade, however, continued to support its local allies. In 1979 MEChA students from Denver's Metropolitan State College sought its support for their plans to host a national student conference.[30]

The April 1979 conference drew students from throughout the country. Crusade members participated as panelists, and the Crusade hosted a cultural event for the students in its auditorium. The opening was marked by a confrontation in which MEChistas and Crusade members physically ejected members of two Anglo leftist groups from the literature tables they had set up at the entrances to the conference site. The Metro MEChistas and Crusade members resented what they viewed as the opportunism of the groups and twice asked them to leave.

When the groups were approached the third time, their literature tables were overturned, causing a brief brawl. Leftist-oriented students criticized the brawl and the ejection of the two groups. Heated debate ensued. Leftist-oriented students felt that the free exchange of political thought was being repressed and that ideological competition was best dealt with through debate. The other side felt that the time for debate was over and that the opportunism and intervention they perceived from the ejected groups—groups with no vested interest in the community—caused division and futile debates within Chicano ranks. A resolution was adopted at the conference in reference to the dispute.

> Unity With Other Oppressed People: While recognizing that the struggle of our people is the first priority, we recognize that as oppressed people we have common goals of liberation with other oppressed peoples, and that alliance with these people are [*sic*] a necessity in order to facilitate our liberation. We also recognize that there are elements in this society who disguise themselves as friends and liberators of all people and who seek to use the Chicano Movement to further their own aims. We reject the opportunistic and unprincipled tactics of these groups.[31]

The conference, which became an annual event hosted each year in a different state, adopted resolutions on immigration, the arts, communica-

tions, and student protests and called for a boycott of *Boulevard Nights*
and *Walk Proud,* Hollywood movies about Chicano gangs that students
criticized for stereotyping barrio youth and glamorizing gang violence.
Though the Crusade was increasingly isolated, it did not retreat from being outspoken.

The Crusade became concerned when anti-Iranian graffiti appeared on
barrio walls during the hostage crisis at the American Embassy in Iran in
1980. If there was to be a war, members reasoned, this one was not worth
fighting. The Crusade called a press conference and recounted how the
shah of Iran was brought to power by the CIA and had run a corrupt
dictatorship notorious for human rights violations—the basis for the Ira-
nians' fury. Part of the Crusade's statement read:

> Taking the past history of oppression into consideration, it is not hard
> to understand the determination and emotional fervor that is part of
> Iran's present revolution. . . . We ask the people of America . . . to reason
> for yourselves to decide if you support [the U.S.] corruption of foreign
> governments, exploitation of under-developed countries' natural re-
> sources, the torture, imprisonment, and murder of oppressed peoples
> for the benefit of Capitalism and Imperialism. If the majority of America
> is willing to swallow lies and gird for war to defend the economic inter-
> ests of the transnational corporations and the political goals of hypocrit-
> ical politicos, it is not in our interest to give ourselves to war as we have
> in the past.[32]

The political climate since the late 1960s—increased military spend-
ing, deregulation of business, tax breaks for the corporate world, and
cutbacks in social services to the middle and working classes—confirmed
the Crusade's belief that society put militarism and profit before human
needs. The consolidation of political power by conservative forces from
Nixon's 1974 downfall to Reagan's 1980 election was a phenomenon that
the Crusade had not analyzed or even watched closely. Skeptical that the
poor would receive social justice under either major party, the Crusade
was indifferent to Reagan's election.

The increasing power of conservatism was symbolized in Colorado by
Joseph Coors, who became a member of Reagan's informal "Kitchen
Cabinet" in the 1980s. In the mid-1960s, Paul Gonzales, leader of a local
G. I. Forum chapter, and Rodolfo Gonzales called for a boycott of Coors
beer because of the brewery's discriminatory employment practices. The
Crusade, however, was even more opposed to Coors' funding of right-
wing politics. The boycott spread throughout the Southwest until Coors
began to donate money to groups that supported the boycott. Some organizations, primarily middle-class groups, began to announce the end of

a boycott that very few of them had any role in starting. Coors wielded its economic power to reward its friends and to instruct its adversaries.

> A $50,000 grant by the Coors Foundation for the G. I. Forum was canceled after the Forum rescinded its plans to drop the boycott and support the strike [of Coors' brewery workers]. Gordon Jones, Coors Foundation executive manager, said the Forum's strike support, "was like biting the hand that feeds you . . . I didn't like that attitude." Furthermore, Jones said the foundation also seeks to be sure that any potential recipient of its funds is stable and non-political. He said the G. I. Forum's decision to back the strike made it a political group and indicated its policies might not be as stable as the foundation would want them to be.[33]

On April 25, 1980, the Crusade picketed in front of the Denver Hilton Hotel to protest against a fundraising scholarship dance conducted by various Hispanic groups in conjunction with the Coors Brewing Company.

THE RETURN OF GANGS AND GANG HYSTERIA

Another sign of the declining influence of the Chicano movement was the return of gang violence to Denver barrios. Lou Lopez, a police "gang specialist," writes:

> The [gang] problem developed in several ways. In Denver, the Los Angeles gang influence can be traced back to the late 1970s when Denver Police officers started to notice young Hispanic youth dressed in "chollo" attire (endearing name for Hispanic gang members) [*sic*]. It was determined that many of these youths were from East Los Angeles. . . . These "chollos" who were born in the Los Angeles gang scene were introducing the gang phenomenon in the form of dress, talk, hand signals, and graffiti to the Hispanic youth of Denver.[34]

The insight by which Denver police "determined that many of these youth were from East Los Angeles" was due mostly to the California parole authorities' practice of relaying information to Denver police about parolees coming to Colorado. Or so stated Lopez and other police in the winter, spring, and summer of 1980, after Crusade members and others found out that "community meetings" about gangs had been scheduled. Few participants at the "community meetings" were community residents; most were on the city payroll: police officers, City Council members, and member of the Commission on Community Relations. The Crusade was intrigued about "community meetings" scheduled with no advance publicity.

Lopez then worked with Denver's first police gang squad, officially known as the Juvenile Delinquency Prevention Unit, which was created by a $3000,000 grant to the Police Department from the Justice Department's Law Enforcement Assistance Administration. Oddly, at the time of the grant (around June 1979), Denver's barrios had no identifiable gangs. By the time politicians and police had held their "community meetings," the police were telling receptive politicians that Denver's alleged gangs were 99 percent "Hispanic."[35]

The first indications of renewed gang activity appeared in Denver in the fall of 1980, after the release of Hollywood "gang" movies in the city's discount theaters. Within days of the first movie's release, copycat graffiti began to appear in the barrio. Denver's first gang-related death of a Spanish-surnamed youth occurred in November 1982. Though Lopez gives his version of how gangs "developed" in Denver in the late 1970s, his booklet, *Gangs in Denver*, conveys no hint about how gangs had once been done away with.[36]

The disappearance of gangs in Denver's barrios in the late 1960s is not traceable to legislation, to the juvenile justice system, to the creation of police gang squads, or to efforts of the schools or the business world. Gangs existed in the 1950s and 1960s, and their decline coincided with work to establish unity by the Crusade for Justice and groups like the Black Berets and Brown Berets. An equal role in the decline was played by the student walkout leaders and their associates at West High School on a warm day in March 1969. They were supported by those who walked out from at least five barrio high schools and seven junior high schools in solidarity with their peers and their people.

In two short days a whole generation set aside "gang" and neighborhood rivalries. They set aside self-doubt and self-hatred and unified in a spirit of struggle against forces that previously seemed too formidable to surmount. They were beaten, gassed, shot, and jailed. They were not intimidated, and they did not run away. They stood on the stairs at West High School and demanded that those who lived on the salaries their taxes paid cease to call them racist names—and more. They demanded that they be allowed to know themselves, to learn about themselves, to be themselves, and to have their culture, history, and rights respected, if not by others, then by themselves.

They wanted to see their history recounted in the schools of the state, a state which was named in their language, in a nation that had been built by the sweat, blood, and misery of humble, hard-working people like themselves—contributions for which they had never been thanked, or acknowledged, as though they did not exist or did not count. These young people demanded no longer to be treated as foreigners in the only land they had ever known, in the land where untold generations of their ancestors had been buried. They demanded an end to humiliation at the hands of strangers who had arrived here but yesterday.

On that day they put aside their petty differences and the appearances of apathy, indifference, and fatalism in which they had so long been cloaked. They would fight the schools, and they would fight the police who maintained law and order—laws in which they found no justice and an established order in which they found no dignity and no hope. They fought with anger, at first, but then fought with exhilaration because they saw and felt that the world could finally be different for them, and that they themselves could make the difference. They sought to obtain the power to determine their own destiny. They wanted more than brief mention in some book, more than for "one of their own" to sit in a suit behind a desk and to kick them out of school as others had done before— as though this humiliation would not hurt because it was done by a "Hispanic." They wanted more. They wanted the truth, and they wanted justice.

They had been brought to this point through the Chicano movement and, more than any other group or person, by an organization called the Crusade for Justice and by the Crusade's founder—Rodolfo "Corky" Gonzales. But Gonzales and the Crusade for Justice, in reality, were no more than reflections of this community and its potential. Gonzales was not a god, and the Crusade was not infallible. Like the people, Gonzales and the Crusade had their vanities, errors, and shortcomings as well as inspired hopes and remarkable strengths. On the site where the Crusade for Justice building stood there now stands a U.S. Post Office. The vacant building and adjacent property were sold by Gonzales around 1987. The local police and power structure apparently no longer fear or abhor the Crusade, and an optimist could presume the FBI no longer spies on it.

In the fall of 1987 Gonzales became ill while driving and lost control of his car. The resulting wreck left him with serious head injuries and impaired memory, from which he will not recover. As of this writing Gonzales has entered his seventy-first year. The Crusade still exists as a nonprofit corporation with limited membership and a board composed mostly, if not entirely, of members of Gonzales' family. Their efforts continue to center on the operation of their school.

The Crusade for Justice, for a span of 15 years, was the most powerful and effective organization to fight for the rights of people of Mexican descent in the state of Colorado in this century. It is hoped that this work can adequately convey the conditions of the Chicano people in Denver and Colorado, the nature of their struggle, and the role played by the Crusade for Justice. In the end, this work is written in the belief that no organization will rise to match the Crusade, much less surpass it, until it first learns the lessons from the legacy of the Crusade's rich and largely unrecognized history.

Notes

Index

Notes

CHAPTER I. RODOLFO GONZALES' CRUSADE
FOR JUSTICE

1. Quoted in *Denver Post*, August 8, 1924, as cited in Robert Alan Goldberg, *Hooded Empire: The Ku Klux Klan in Colorado* (Urbana: University of Illinois Press, 1981), p. 34.

2. Frank Moya, "Corky Gonzales Has Changed Little," *Rocky Mountain News*, September 11, 1977.

3. Ibid.

4. "Gonzales Is Accused of Assault, Battery," *Rocky Mountain News*, July 29, 1958.

5. "Gonzales Seeks $1 Million from Police Officer," *Rocky Mountain News*, April 17, 1959.

6. George Kelly, *The Old Gray Mayors of Denver* (Boulder: Pruitt, 1974), pp. 53, 43.

7. Tom Gavin, "Liberty and the Law: Police Assailed For 'Checkout' System," *Rocky Mountain News*, August 30, 1955.

8. Kelly, *Old Gray Mayors*, pp. 72–76.

9. Richard Gardner, *Grito! Reies Tijerina and the New Mexico Land Grant War of 1967* (Indianapolis and New York: Bobbs-Merrill, 1970), p. 197. Time and space do not permit a summary of the Indian-Spanish-Mexican history of the "American Southwest." Nor is this the place to explain the confusion of, or preference for, terms such as "Mexican American," "Hispanic," etc., by people of Mexican descent. The term "Chicano" is a variant of "Mexicano," which in turn derives from the Nahuatl word "mexica." (The Mexica are often mistakenly called "Aztecs.") The word "Chicano" emerged in the 1920s and 1930s along the border, probably in Ciudad Juárez–El Paso. In the 1940s a generation of urban youths also called "pachucos" used "Chicano" to describe themselves. The term was in wide usage in the Southwest by the 1950s and 1960s. As used in this work, "Chicano" or "Chicana" describes a person of Mexican descent who is born in the United States or a person of such descent who prefers the term. I use "Mexicans" interchangeably with "Chicano." "Mexicano," however, is used for people born in Mexico. It is, after all, what they call themselves. They, unlike some of their

relatives in the American Southwest, know who they are and know their own name.

CHAPTER 2. POLITICS, POLICE CONTROVERSIES, SURVEILLANCE: THE ADVENT OF THE CRUSADE FOR JUSTICE

1. "Unarmed Boy Shot in Chest," *Denver Post,* July 7, 1962. In the 1960s Denver's liquor establishments included some that sold 3.2 percent beer, a low-alcohol beer that was a consequence of the Prohibition era, when it was called "near-beer." These establishments were popular with youths, who only needed to be 18 years old to enter. Denver police seeking to augment their incomes were often employed to check identification and to serve as bouncers, a controversial practice.

2. Ibid.

3. "Policeman Who Killed Youth Suspended Pending Probe," *Denver Post,* July 8, 1962.

4. Ibid.

5. Charles C. Vigil, "Los Voluntarios," *Viva!* May 20, 1964, p. 6. The pre-amble of Los Voluntario's charter stated, "We, the members of Los Voluntarios, realizing that the Spanish-speaking people of Colorado are in need of an active political organization dedicated to its complete social, economic, and political advancement, do hereby join together to establish a state organization to be known as Los Voluntarios." Vigil wrote that "the group was formed from among leaders of various cultural, educational, and fraternal groups as well as those who had political party affiliation," and recounted that Los Voluntarios had supported an unidentified candidate (or candidates) only to find that "A promise made is a debt unpaid." Los Voluntarios and *Viva!,* its newspaper, were precursors of the Crusade for Justice and *El Gallo.* Another article (ibid., p. 2) reported that *Viva!* was founded because "of frustration and determination for the truth. . . . This newspaper will not only inform, but advise the public on political issues, educational advantages, social acceptance. Where there is a cause to be fought and there is no leadership, this newspaper will champion that cause. Where there is ignorance, this newspaper will educate. Where there is misunderstanding, this newspaper will guide. Where there is hypocrisy, this paper will tell the truth."

6. "The Hispanic Community Speaks," *Viva!* May 20, 1964, pp. 1, 2.

7. "Grand Jury Says, 'No Brutality,' Suggests 15-Man Citizen Board," *Viva!* June 16, 1964, p. 8.

8. The letterhead shows the first use of the name "Crusade for Justice" and gives Gonzales' bail bond business at 1961 Larimer Street as its address. The Crusade, however, was not formally incorporated until 1966, and it appears that Gonzales used the name to circumvent the need for approval from more moderate (or timid) middle-class members who would have found it hard to approve the highly critical remarks found in the letter. Letter, Rudolph "Corky" Gonzales to Mayor Thomas G. Currigan, July 5, 1964.

9. "Hats Off to Tom Gavin: The First Objective News Article on the Police Brutality Issue," *Viva!* May 20, 1964, p. 6.

10. Jack Gaskie, "Gonzales Views His Poverty Role," *Rocky Mountain News,* September 29, 1965. Gonzales had been prosperously self-employed since the age of 18 except for appointments to the directorship of Denver's War on Poverty (thereafter renamed the Office of Economic Opportunity) and the Neighborhood Youth Corps, a low-income youth employment program. His history of self-employment was undoubtedly responsible for much of his sense of self-reliance and political independence.

11. Ibid.

12. Clark Secrest, "Capra Deletes 'Spanish' on Booking Slips," *Denver Post,* February 17, 1966. The official racial designation used for Asians was originally "Yellow," then changed to "Mongolian." A representative of the mayor's office said the term used would be "Yellow."

13. "Mayor Hails Capra, Dill on Decision," *Denver Post,* February 17, 1966. The Mexican community's sensitivity to racial terminology (or its confusion over its own identity) was raised with Mayor Currigan in a meeting on police–community relations. The mayor had previously (in 1964) ordered police to stop using the words "Mex.," "Mexican," and "U. S. Mexican." See "Currigan, Gonzales Confer," *Viva!* May 20, 1964, p. 1.

14. Del W. Harding, "Police to Halt Nationality Identification in Arrests," *Rocky Mountain News,* February 17, 1966.

15. Barbara Browne, "Angry Callers Berate Capra for Remarks," *Rocky Mountain News,* February 25, 1966.

16. Ibid. Apart from the crudeness of Capra's remarks, it appears that the issue generated emotion because it questioned who and what Chicanos were at a time of prevailing racial conservatism, before the Chicano movement had raised the words "Mexican" and "Chicano" as banners of ethnic pride. The May and June 1964 issues of *Viva!* give insight into the Chicano community's self-perception in the early 1960s: "Hispanic," "Chicano," "Mexican American," "Spanish American," "Spanish-speaking people," "Mexican," "Spanish," "Latinos," and "Latin American" are all used to refer to the community.

17. "Chief Dill Asserts Charge Is Hearsay," *Denver Post,* February 25, 1966.

18. John Morehead, "Plan to Recruit and Train Minority Policemen Studied," *Denver Post,* August 24, 1967.

19. "Attacks on Police Department Harm Race Relations," *Denver Post,* March 2, 1966.

20. Rudolph "Corky" Gonzales, "Address to Coalition" (mimeographed paper, Denver, April 23, 1966), pp. 1, 3. After breaking with the Democratic Party, Gonzales campaigned in the spring of 1967 as an independent mayoral candidate against Mayor Currigan, who was re-elected (as Gonzales had anticipated). After the election, Gonzales' attorneys—Walter Gerash, Harry Nier, and Eugene Deikman—sued Currigan, unsuccessfully, for violating the City Charter campaign expenditure limit, which was set at $1,000. This limit, set by City Charter in 1913, was routinely ignored by candidates as campaign costs mounted over the years; it

is a fact, nevertheless, that the City Charter established the limit and Currigan violated it.

21. John Toohey, "Gonzales Issues Reply to Ex-aide's Charges," *Denver Post,* February 14, 1966.

22. Dan Thomasson, "Poverty Chief's Acts Under Scrutiny," *Rocky Mountain News,* April 21, 1966. The next day another Thomasson article, headlined "Denver's Poverty War Under Watch," reported that a Washington official had called Gonzales "quite a wild man," although the official strongly protested against that wording, and "the content and interpretation" of both *News* articles, in an interview he gave the *Denver Post,* on April 23; see John Toohey, "Sen. Allott Requests Shriver Probe Denver War on Poverty," *Denver Post,* April 23, 1966. The dispute in Denver erupted at a time of national contention between Democrats who favored "war on poverty" efforts and Republicans who had been charging since the previous year that the poverty programs were marred by waste, fraud, and political abuses; see "Antipoverty Probe Resisted by Dems," *Denver Post,* March 6, 1966.

23. "Gonzales Brands Currigan 'Gutless,'" *Cervi's Journal,* April 27, 1966, p. 3. Eugene Cervi had been a *Rocky Mountain News* journalist, a former state chairperson of the Democratic Party, and a partner in a public relations firm. He published *Cervi's Journal,* which served his role as a political gadfly.

24. Ibid.

25. Robert Kistler, "1,200 Cheer Gonzales at 'Vote Revolt' Rally," *Denver Post,* April 30, 1966.

26. R. "Corky" Gonzales, "A Message to the Democrat [*sic*] Party," *El Gallo,* June 23, 1967, p. 2. The letter was actually written to Tooley on May 15, 1967.

27. Denver FBI Special Agent in Charge (SAC), Nonprosecutive Summary Report, to J. Edgar Hoover, January 22, 1968, Rudolph Gonzales Field Office File 100-9290, p. 9; filed in headquarters as Bufile 105-176910 [hereafter referred to as "NSR"]. The digits "105" denote internal security matters. The FBI obtained two pages of Gonzales' three-page antiwar speech. Gonzales' opposition to the war grew as the war escalated. In the spring of 1965, there were 25,000 U.S. troops in Vietnam. By the end of 1965 the number had grown to 184,000; it totaled 385,000 at the end of 1966.

28. Ibid. Exactly when, or how, Gonzales evolved his antiwar position is unknown. Though he was not a military veteran, Gonzales did belong to the American GI Forum—probably for social and political reasons, since the forum was founded as an advocacy group for Chicanos, not as an endorsement of militarism. The June 15, 1964, issue of *Viva!* pictures Gonzales with Denver GI Forum officers and Colorado Governor John Love, who proclaimed June 15–21, 1964, as "GI Forum Week." The proclamation noted that "more than half a million Spanish-Americans served in the United States armed forces during World War II and the Korean conflict; . . . these brave men received more Congressional Medals of Honor than any other group of our great nation, and more than two hundred and fifty thousand either lost their lives or were wounded on the field of battle." At the same time, however, *Viva!* announced a conference on "Youth and

Morality in a Nuclear Age," sponsored by the pacifist American Friends Service Committee.

29. Esequiel "Kelly" Lovato, Jr., "Police and Peace," *El Gallo*, August 31, 1967, p. 1.

30. Denver SAC to Hoover, NSR, p. 7.

31. Ibid., p. 8.

32. Ibid., p. 15.

33. Translated by the author. The potential for legal entanglements posed by Tijerina's letter was clear to Gonzales. There were times when publicity defused danger and times when it was imprudent. Gonzales was carefully building the Crusade's core; the invitation to send people to the takeover was interesting, but not prudent. Seasoned Crusade activists were guided by a saying: "The fish that gets caught is the one that opens its mouth." Tijerina's letter was published in *El Gallo* on June 23, 1967, when it would not give advance notice to law enforcement authorities.

34. Peter Nabokov, *Tijerina and the Courthouse Raid* (Albuquerque: University of New Mexico Press, 1969), pp. 150–51.

35. Ibid. The theft of land grants was a violation of the Constitution because the Treaty of Guadalupe Hidalgo, whose provisions safeguarding the property of Mexicans who stayed in the conquered territory were promptly violated, is also the "supreme law of the land." This argument, fundamental to the Alianza's position, is based on the Constitution's Article VI, paragraph two: "This Constitution, and the Laws of the United States which shall be made in Pursuance thereof; *and all Treaties made, or which shall be made, under the Authority of the United States, shall be the supreme Law of the Land.*" Starting in the early 1600s, land grants were made by Spain, and then by Mexico, to entice settlers into Mexico's northernmost provinces—the present U.S. Southwest. There are 1,715 land grants in the United States, including some in Louisiana and Florida. The New Mexico grants, for which the Alianza fought, and southern Colorado's Mexican-era land grants, have been the most hotly contested. The legal argument based on Article VI applies to all treaties (but would require the government to respect its own laws).

36. Ibid.

37. Denver FBI SAC to Hoover, NSR, p. 17.

38. "Viva Tijerina," *El Gallo*, June 23, 1967, pp. 1, 3.

39. Ibid. Crusade women organized a dinner in Denver on July 17, 1967. Donations for the Alianza were solicited, and $286.75 was raised. Present were "former members of the Alianza. The San Luis Valley Friendship Club was represented by their president, Lionel Ruybal and many of their members. Also present were many notable guests which included Los Valientes, the Crusaders who traveled to New Mexico and marched in Santa Fe." *El Gallo*, named the Denver "valientes": Betty and Waldo Benavidez, Desiderio "D. C." de Herrera, Eugene Deikman, Emilio and Robbie Dominguez, Gary Garrison, Corky, Anita, Charlotte, and Rudy Gonzales, John Haro, Anthony and David Hermosillo, Amy Lizt, Bill Longley, Eloisa, Larry, Kelly, and Sue Lovato, Don Martinez, Henry Montoya,

Lorraine Quintana, Joe Perea, Jr., Louis Ramirez, Richard Romero, Robert Trujillo, Al Sanchez, Bob Sandison, and Eloy Espinoza.

40. "Gonzales To Take Over Group," *Denver Post,* June 29, 1967, cited in the Denver FBI SAC, NSR.

41. "Gonzales Speaking Schedule," *El Gallo,* July 28, 1967, p. 4.

42. Jose Madril, "Dear Juanita Dominguez," *El Gallo,* July 28, 1967, p. 6.

43. Garcedan Madrid, "Letters to the Editor," *El Gallo,* July 28, 1967, p. 2.

44. Waldo Benavidez, "Letters to the Editor," *El Gallo,* July 28, 1967, p. 2. The resurrection of the New Mexico land struggle affected Colorado, where, in November 1967, land grant heirs filed an unsuccessful suit in Denver's U.S. District Court over grants in southern Colorado and northern New Mexico. Colorado's San Luis Valley is home to a land grant dispute dating from 1960, when J. T. Taylor, Jr., sought to purchase and clear title to 77,524 acres of the 1844 Sangre de Cristo Land Grant in Costilla County. Taylor closed access roads to local people who had formerly hunted, fished, and gathered firewood on communal lands. This led to violence, and the legal struggle continues as of this writing. See "Spanish Lands Lawsuit Filed" and "Land Claims Based on 1848 Peace Pact," *Denver Post,* November 28, 1967, p. 36.

45. "Protest Staged at Police Building," *Denver Post,* July 23, 1967, p. 4. The *Denver Post,* article was cited by the Denver FBI Field Office when preparing its NSR for FBI headquarters and starting the internal security investigation on Gonzales and the Crusade for Justice. The Denver FBI submitted the report to headquarters on January 22, 1968 when Gonzales was already listed on the local Rabble Rouser Index (RRI). Headquarters notified the Denver office on February 28, 1968 that Gonzales was approved for inclusion on the national RRI and stated, "His activities also warrant inclusion on the Security Index." Gonzales was now deemed a threat to the nation's internal security.

46. "Pinedo Shot in Back," *El Gallo,* July 28, 1967,p.1.

47. *El Gallo* published a photograph of Pinedo's death certificate, which showed the cause of death to have been a gunshot in the back: July 28, 1967, p. 3.

48. "Time for Action,"*El Gallo,* July 28, 1967, p. 2.

49. "Andrew Garcia Shot by Police Bouncer at Tavern," *El Gallo,* August 31, 1967, p. 1.

50. Rodolfo Gonzales, "What Now?" *El Gallo,* August 31, 1967, p. 2.

51. "Tijerina Arrested in Denver," *El Gallo,* October 1, 1967, p. 1.

52. "Tijerina Extradition Dismissed!" *El Gallo,* November 1967, p. 1.

53. Denver FBI SAC Field Office, NSR, p. 20.

54. "The Letter That Has Never Been Printed or Answered," *El Gallo,* December, 1967, p. 2.

55. Rodolfo Gonzales, "Concern or Control?" *El Gallo,* October 1, 1967, p. 2. One target of Gonzales' derision, "an old left-winger," was said to have belonged to a communist-front organization in the early 1950s until McCarthyism made this perilous. This person remained apart from social protest movements thereafter but is now, ironically, hailed for pioneering advocacy for Denver's Spanish-surnamed community. Derision of those "still dancing to the tune of the power structure," of weak "leaders" who fail to confront issues squarely, is not

new. Similar criticism was voiced nearly a generation earlier: "The working class Mexican who bears the brunt of police brutality cannot look for assistance to the self-styled Mexican leaders. Few of these middle-class Mexicans are able to face squarely the fact of police dereliction. . . . The middle-class Mexican, aspiring to leadership of the Mexican people, still feels so basically insecure in status that his primary concern is to demonstrate his own superiority to the Mexican masses." Lloyd H. Fisher, "Observation on Race Conflict in Los Angeles, The Problem of Violence," published by the American Council on Race Relations, p. 14, cited in Beatrice Griffith, *American Me* (Boston: Houghton-Mifflin, 1948).

56. Eugene Deikman, "Killer Cop Cleared in 'Mock' Trial," *El Gallo*, November 1967, pp. 1, 6.

57. Ibid., p. 6. The same issue of *El Gallo* (see "Police Shoot Youth in His Own House," p. 6) records the Crusade's anger over another police shooting that occurred within two weeks of Officer Vandervelde's acquittal. On October 27, 1967, Richard Medina, 20, was shot three times by Denver Officer Edwin James during a domestic dispute between Medina and his girlfriend in which Medina grabbed an unloaded rifle. When police arrived, his girlfriend reported, "I ran back into the bedroom and grabbed the gun away from Richard and threw it on the bed and, while I was holding him, the policeman came in without any kind of warning and started shooting. After he stopped, Richard dropped from my arms onto the floor. The police should have been able to see that Richard no longer had the gun." Medina was lucky; he lived and was held for investigation of assault.

58. Denver FBI SAC, NSR, p. 11.

59. Frank J. Donner, *The Age of Surveillance* (New York: Knopf, 1980), pp. 404, 430. The informers included an operative from the Senate Internal Security Subcommittee, police and their informers, and people like David Gumaer, a John Birch Society member and Chicago police informer who became a member of the staff of Birchite Congressman John Schmitz.

60. Todd Gitlin, *The Sixties: Years of Hope, Days of Rage* (New York: Bantam Books, 1987), p. 245.

61. In December 1967 the Crusade convened a national Chicano youth gathering in Denver, but a blizzard struck and few attended. Two who did were Ignacio "Nacho" Perez of the Mexican American Youth Organization (MAYO) in Texas and Francisco Martinez of Los Angeles. This effort was the forerunner of four national youth conferences the Crusade organized. The small December 1967 gathering focused on developing an information center and planning a national gathering of Chicano activists in the spring of 1968—the project that drew so much FBI scrutiny when first proposed in Chicago in August 1967. Very little information is available on the December 1967 Denver gathering. *El Gallo* refers to this meeting in "Crusade Conference," January 1968, p. 4, and "Martinez Arrested," *El Gallo*, April 1968, p. 3.

62. Gonzales did not attend the subsequent meeting, and Eloy Espinoza was sent to represent the Crusade in Gonzales' place. A review of these highly censored FBI documents indicates that the FBI confused Espinoza with Gonzales based on a few physical similarities.

63. Chicago FBI Airtel to Director FBI, dated April 24, 1968, but stamped

"Not Recorded April 26, 1968," under the caption "Mexican American Militancy," accompanied by an Chicago FBI Letter-head Memorandum [LHM] of the same date and caption, noted that the "[proposed] national convention in Denver is to be hosted by an organization headed by a militant Latin named 'Corky' Gonzales. At this point it was unknown what name the convention will utilize." Thirteen pages of the LHM were withheld "to protect third party and also that information which would identify source." Copies of the Chicago Airtel, however, were sent to FBI field offices in Albuquerque, Denver, El Paso, Los Angeles, Milwaukee, Phoenix, Sacramento, San Antonio, San Diego, San Francisco, and Chicago. The Chicago Airtel, moreover, was cross-filed in a headquarters file, or "Bufile," captioned "DEMCON" [Democratic Convention] with file serial number 157-8589, the digits "157" denoting a "Racial Matter." Chicago's April 24 Airtel and LHM referred to previous communication between Chicago and headquarters on April 10 and 17, 1968, under the "DEMCON" caption. The FBI believed that the conference had been postponed until June. A Denver FBI LHM to "Director, FBI," dated May 23, 1968, and captioned "Rudolph 'Corky' Gonzales," file serial 105-176910, included a one-page cover sheet, but five and a half paragraphs of seven were blacked out. The remainder reads, "Reference is made to Chicago FBI letter dated April 24, 1968, entitled 'Mexican American Militancy' which stated subject and his organization, Crusade for Justice, was to host a National conference in Denver [five-and-a-half-paragraph deletion]. It should be noted that the recent editions of *El Gallo,* the official publication of the Crusade for Justice, have not mentioned the national conference to be held in Denver or the Crusade for Justice owning a ranch in the Southwest."

64. Denver LHM to Hoover, May 23, 1968. Headquarters Supervisor S. S. Mignosa, writing on Hoover's behalf in a May 1, 1968, FBI headquarters Airtel to the Denver SAC, noted the presence of a "Rudolph Gonzales" at a Poor People's Campaign protest on April 29 and wrote, "It is quite possible 'Rudolph Gonzales' mentioned . . . is subject [of the Denver field office file of the same name]. . . . You should determine whereabouts of subject . . . so that current whereabouts and activities of subject can be regularly followed and reported. You should specifically determine if subject was in Washington D.C. on 4/29/68 and if he participated in the Poor People's Campaign." Additionally, the Santa Fe, New Mexico, District Attorney claimed on June 5, 1968, that the Alianza had a guerrilla training camp in the Taos area. Gonzales frequently visited San Cristobal, New Mexico, just north of Taos. It appears FBI suspicions were related to reports of Gonzales' visits to San Cristobal by Alan Stang, published in *American Opinion,* a John Birch Society publication.

65. Hoover to Denver FBI SAC, February 7, 1968, Rudolph Gonzales file, 105–176910.

66. Hoover to Denver FBI SAC, Rodolfo Gonzales file, 105-176910, February 28, 1968. Though the FBI's Internal Security investigation on Gonzales began in late 1967, the January 22, 1968, NSR shows that the FBI was gathering data on Gonzales as early as April 30, 1964, when he attended two meetings apparently related to the death of Alfred Salazar. One meeting was sponsored by the Socialist Workers Party at the Unitarian Church on 14th and Lafayette Streets in Denver.

The investigation on Gonzales was number 176, 910, the one-hundred and seventy-sixth thousand, nine-hundred and tenth such investigation. Internal Security investigations were then codified with the digits "100" or "105," so Gonzales' headquarters file ("Bufile") is serialized as "105-176910."

67. Hoover to Denver FBI SAC, February 29, 1968.

68. Denver FBI SAC, NSR, p. 23.

69. "Crusade's Anniversary Dinner!" *El Gallo*, December 1967, p. 4.

70. Denver FBI SAC, NSR, pp. 20, 21.

71. Ibid., p. 12.

72. Ibid., p. 21.

73. "Spanish American Dissension Hinted," *Rocky Mountain News*, October 26, 1967.

74. "Plan de La Raza Unida Preamble" (mimeographed paper, El Paso, 1967), p. 1.

75. Inter-agency Committee on Mexican American Affairs, *Cabinet Committee Hearings on Mexican American Affairs: Labor Standards* (El Paso, Tex.: Inter-agency Committee on Mexican American Affairs, 1967), pp. 1, 2.

76. "Crusade News Flashes," *El Gallo*, November 1967, p. 2.

77. Rodolfo Gonzales, "Chicano on the Move!" *El Gallo*, December 1967, p. 5.

78. Ibid.

79. Ibid.

80. [Manuel Martinez], "Chicano Power: La Raza Youth Resolution," *El Gallo*, December 1967.

81. Denver FBI SAC, NSR, pp. 13, 14.

82. Ibid., p. 20.

83. "Chavez Spent Full Day in Denver," *El Gallo*, January 1968, p. 3.

84. Al Nakkula, "Harold Dill: A Cop's Cop—First of a Series," *Rocky Mountain News*, January 1, 1968.

85. Ibid.

86. Ibid.

87. Al Nakkula, "Harold Dill: A Cop's Cop—Second of a Series," *Rocky Mountain News*, January 2, 1968. Another cause of the rift was Dill's persistent support for a police pay raise Currigan opposed. Recent Denver history suggests that the Police Department rarely has trouble increasing its budget.

88. *El Gallo*, December 1967, p. 1.

89. Ibid., p. 2.

90. "Chicanos Power Takes Over Police Meeting," *El Gallo*, November 1967, p. 5.

91. "Chief Seaton off to a Good Start," *Denver Post*, January 4, 1968; "Seaton Impresses Minority Leaders;" *Denver Post*, January 15, 1968.

92. Francis R. Salazar, "All Citizens Urged to Support New Denver Police Chief," *Denver Post*, January 4, 1968.

93. Michael Rounds, "Police Shakeup Is Announced by Seaton," *Rocky Mountain News*, January 4, 1968.

94. Ibid.

95. Bob Saile, "Gonzales Predicts 'Guerilla Warfare,'" *Denver Post,* January 29, 1968.

96. "Will Mexican Minority Riot?" *Rocky Mountain News,* January 29, 1968.

97. Denver FBI field office, Rudolph Gonzales file 100-9290, April 22, 1968, p. 3.

98. Ibid., p. 4.

99. Kenneth Stiles, "$150,000 Ford Grant Increasing Native Spanish-American Lawyers," *Denver Clarion,* November 10, 1967.

100. Rees Lloyd and Peter Montague, "Ford's Pacification Program for La Raza," *El Grito del Norte,* August 29, 1970, pp. 8–11. This article was published simultaneously by *El Grito* and *Ramparts* magazine.

CHAPTER 3. THE POOR PEOPLE'S CAMPAIGN

1. Denver FBI field office enciphered wire dated March 13, 1968, to Director J. Edgar Hoover with copies to Atlanta and Washington, D.C., FBI field offices; Albuquerque FBI field office advised by mail.

2. Paul Valentine, "Tijerina Assails Key March Aides," *Denver Post,* July 12, 1968.

3. Bruce Johansen and Roberto Maestas, *Wasi'chu: The Continuing Indian Wars* (New York: Monthly Review Press, 1979,) pp. 183–93. The tribal nations of North America are usually known by incorrect names given them by colonizing forces. The Lakota-Dakota-Nakota, for example, are frequently referred to as the "Sioux." Even "Native American," presently used to designate these nations instead of "Indian," is still a name imposed by others. Although I attempt to use correct names, at times I reluctantly use the general terms "Native American" and "Indian." These tribal nations, like people of Mexican descent, are rightfully resentful of the distortion of their histories and identities. I owe a debt of gratitude to the late "Granny" Alice Blackhorse, her son Jesse Bordeaux, and her granddaughters Jessica and Linda for sharing their knowledge.

4. [Ernesto Vigil], "Washington D.C. Report: Supreme Court Demonstrators and Arrests," *El Gallo,* July 1968, p. 4.

5. Ibid.

6. FBI headquarters Airtel to Denver FBI SAC, May 1, 1968. Rudolph Gonzales file no. 105-176910. Recipients of the Airtel included the 113th Military Intelligence Group, the CIA, the State Department, the Secret Service, and the Justice Department's Interdivisional Information Unit (IDIU).

7. Washington, D.C., FBI field office SAC "Plaintext teletype" to Hoover, June 4, 1968, Washington field office POCAM [Poor People's Campaign] file no. 157-1395. Other information came from author's interviews with Carlos Montes, Summer 1990.

8. POCAM file no. 157-1395.

9. FBI SAC, Washington, D.C., field office [WFO] teletype to Hoover, June 10, 1968, filed as [Rodolfo Gonzales] 105-176910, Not Recorded, June 18, 1968. Two copies were cross-filed in WFO POCAM file 157-1395.

10. Ibid.

11. Ibid.

12. Gene Cooper, "Poor People Campaigners Plan Specific Demands," *Denver Post*, June 10, 1968.

13. Ibid.

14. Ibid.

15. With his income plummeting, Gonzales sold his home in the middle-class Park Hill area and moved his large family to a modest apartment in a building he owned at 16th Avenue and High Street in Denver's Capitol Hill neighborhood. The Deed of Trust for the old Calvary Baptist Church stipulated that after the initial downpayment, the Crusade was to spend $5,000 to recondition the building in the first year, and would thus be free of any payments in that period. The price of the building and property was $86,000, and it sold in 1986 for nearly $1,000,000. The purchase of the church building was a collective effort of the Crusade, which owned the building. Members donated money or made loans, and most were repaid. Known initially as "El Centro de La Cruzada," with time the facility became simply, and widely, known as "The Building."

16. WFO Letterhead Memorandum (LHM) to J. Edgar Hoover, July 15, 1968, WFO file no. 100-47866, pp. 5–6.

17. [Vigil], "Washington D.C. Report," p. 4, Montes interview.

18. "Poor People's Coalition Wins Gonzales' Praise," *Denver Post*, September 11, 1968.

19. Paul W. Valentine, "Civil Rights Leaders Set Up 'Poor People's Embassy,'" *Washington Post and Times Herald*, September 7, 1968, cited in a September 24, 1968, WFO LHM on Rudolph Gonzales.

20. "Poor People's Coalition Wins Gonzales' Praise."

CHAPTER 4. YOUTH ACTIVISM AND THE CRUSADE'S
NEW HEADQUARTERS

1. Juan Gomez-Quinones, *Mexican Students por La Raza: The Chicano Student Movement in Southern California 1967–1977* (Santa Barbara, Calif.: Editorial La Causa, 1978), pp. 16, 23.

2. Ernie [Ernesto] Vigil, "UMAS at Boulder," *El Gallo*, September 1968, p. 7.

3. [Ernesto Vigil], "Minority Farce," *El Gallo*, September 1968, p. 7.

4. Denver SAC, Airtel to J. Edgar Hoover, October 4, 1968, Rudolph Gonzales field office file no. 100-9290.

5. J. Edgar Hoover, Airtel to Denver and Chicago SACs October 10, 1068, with Rudolph Gonzales and ARL as subject(s), and references to Denver and Chicago file nos. 176-2 and 176-885.

6. Denver FBI field office report on Rudolph Gonzales to J. Edgar Hoover, field office file no. 100-9290, dated January 15, 1969. Copies sent to the Denver Secret Service office, the Naval Intelligence Service Regional Agency in Denver, the Office of Naval Intelligence, the Denver office of the 113th Military Intelligence Group, the State Department, the CIA, and others.

7. Andres Valdez, "Attention Chicanos," *El Gallo*, January 1969, p. 1.

8. "Chicano Press Association," *El Gallo*, September 1968, p. 8. The 13 listed included California's *Carta Editorial, El Malcriado, Inside Eastside, Chicano Student Movement,* and *La Hormiga.* Texas was represented by *Compass* and *Inferno;* Colorado by *El Gallo;* Arizona by *El Paisano;* and New Mexico by *El Papel.*

9. Ernesto Vigil, "Student Action: Chicano on the Move," *El Gallo*, December 1968, p. 5.

10. Ibid.

11. "Al Sanchez Leads Grape Boycott at Lincoln High," *El Gallo*, October 1968, p. 2.

12. "Crusade Supports Florist Strikers," and "Things Get 'Hot' for Kitayama Bros.," *El Gallo*, September 1968, p. 2.

13. "Washington Indians in Denver," *El Gallo*, October 1968, p. 6.

14. "Melville in Denver," *El Gallo*, October 1968, p. 3.

15. Ibid. The articles on Mexico and the 1968 massacre in Mexico D. F., "An Analogy" and "Venceremos," show that CPA newspapers monitored events in Mexico and supported Mexican movements for social change. The December 1968 *El Gallo* printed a small article ("Chicanos Picket at Mexican Consulate") on a demonstration by UMAS members in Los Angeles to protest against the Tlatelolco massacre. The students declared their "utmost solidarity" with their compañeros in Mexico.

16. I made no copy of the letter sent with the draft card to the office of the Selective Service System. After learning from lawyers and draft counselors that it was important to keep copies for later reference, I wrote to the draft board to request a copy of the original and used parts of it to write an article captioned "First Chicano in Southwest Refuses to Kill in Vietnam," *El Gallo*, May 1968, pp. 1, 2.

17. These little-noted facts are found in Richard Tucker, "Hispanos Set Sights High for Election," *Rocky Mountain News,* November 3, 1966.

CHAPTER 5. SCHOOL PROTESTS AND YOUTH LIBERATION

1. [Ernesto Vigil,] "Racist West High Teacher Must Go," *El Gallo*, March 1969, p. 4.

2. Groppi gained national attention for his outspoken support of the Milwaukee African American community during civil disorders. The Crusade met Father Groppi at the Poor People's Campaign. He had accompanied activists from the Milwaukee Youth Council of the National Association for the Advancement of Colored People, whom he served as an advisor.

3. Annette Chandler, "Father Groppi: A Modern Priest Looks at a Racist Society," reprinted in *El Gallo*, March 1969, p 8.

4. [Vigil,] "Racist West High Teacher Must Go."

5. [Ernesto Vigil,] "West High Blowout," *El Gallo*, April 1969, p. 1.

6. Vernon Rowlette worked for KLZ-TV and was filming a particularly violent arrest when police yelled for him to stop. When he continued filming, he was thrown to the ground, arrested, and later charged with assault.

7. State Senator Roger Cisneros said events indicated "a deep underlying deficiency" in the school system. Two liberal attorneys were running for school board positions. One, A. Edgar Benton said that the majority community believed "that the Mexican isn't worth a damn, so they don't give [Mexicans] the . . . opportunity [they] deserve"; the other, Monte Pascoe, said, "Anglos are now prepared to take the first important step toward understanding." The mayor and manager of safety, however, said that police, "if anything, have been restrained" in their response to the situation. Mayor Bill McNichols subsequently said that police did "a wonderful job . . . they acted magnificently." A *Denver Post* editorial said police operated with "commendable efficiency" and that "adult militants" manipulated the situation and "must bear a significant share of the responsibility." As police and school officials laid the blame on "outside agitators" and "anarchists," the City Council passed a resolution commending police performance. See "West Disturbance 'Symbol of Errors'" *Denver Post,* March 21, 1969; John Morehead, "McNichols, [Governor John] Love Meet on Problems at West," *Denver Post,* March 22, 1969; Al Nakkula, "Mayor Praises Conduct of Police," *Rocky Mountain News,* March 23, 1969; "Denver's Violence Tragic, Avoidable," *Denver Post,* March 24, 1969; "Law Officers Lauded in West Boycott," March 25, 1969; Michael Rounds, "West High Troubles Cost City $25,000," *Rocky Mountain News,* March 26, 1969.

8. See "From East to Manual to West," *Denver Post,* March 21, 1969.

9. [Vigil,] "West High Blowout," p. 7.

10. Ibid.

11. John Dunning, "Chief Seaton Looks at Today's Police," *Denver Post,* July 22, 1969.

12. Ibid.

13. Ibid.

14. Clemens Work, "Seaton: Will Enforce Law," *Rocky Mountain News,* September 27, 1968.

15. Ibid.

16. Richard O'Reilly, "Seaton Vows Better Police Protection," *Denver Post,* September 27, 1968.

17. Work, "Seaton: Will Enforce Law."

18. Ibid.

19. John Morehead, "Mayor OKs Firm Police Reaction," *Denver Post,* September 30, 1968.

20. "No Full-scale Rioting Expected for Denver," Denver Post February 8, 1968.

21. Harry Gessing, "Seaton Won't Tolerate Reported Police Assault," *Denver Post,* January 28, 1968.

22. "Riot Control Squads Slated," *Denver Post,* January 14, 1968. The SWAT prototype originated in Los Angeles in late 1967 under Police Chief Tom Reddin, Deputy Chief Ed Davis, and future chief Daryl F. Gates, who was then LAPD's resident riot-control expert. Gates previously served as captain of the LAPD Intelligence Division under Chief William Parker. LAPD's SWAT-team was trained in counterinsurgency and guerrilla warfare at the Naval Armory in Chavez Ravine

and at the Marines' Camp Pendleton. The LAPD SWAT-team and Denver's SSU made headlines in Denver on May 30, 1975, when a simulated hostage scenario went wrong and led to a "panic scene" at the Denver City and County building. The LAPD SWAT team was in town training Denver police.

23. Michael Rounds, "Denver to Get Specialized Police Unit," *Rocky Mountain News,* March 7, 1968.

24. Ibid.

25. Harry Gessing, "Seaton Reorganizes Police Department," *Denver Post,* January 3, 1968; and "Police Chief Shifts Bureaus, Officers," *Denver Post,* January 4, 1968. Jerry Kennedy and his partner, Duane "Fatback" Borden, gained reputations as street-smart narcotics officers in the early 1960s. Kennedy was involved in the death of a suspect who attempted to swallow drugs when stopped. Kennedy grabbed him by the throat, and the suspect choked to death. Juvenile Court Judge Ted Rubin once chastised Kennedy for "reprehensible police conduct," and for "harassment and intimidation . . . and interferrence with . . . constitutional right to counsel" in the questioning of a 16-year-old boy. Elvis Presley gave Kennedy a new car because he was pleased by security services Kennedy had provided. The officer received further publicity in 1982 when Dr. Gerald Starkey reportedly told him that the socially prominent *Rocky Mountain News* editor Michael B. Howard was snorting cocaine at a party attended by Kennedy, Police Chief Art Dill, and officials of the Colorado Bureau of Investigation. Kennedy denied seeing any wrong doing. When another officer later approached Chief Dill and said, "Chief, there's something I want to tell you" (about Howard), Dill said he responded, "If I don't know it now, I don't want to know it." Dill and other high-ranking Denver police officials resigned, or retired, from the force in the early-1980s over a scandal involving proceeds from bingo games where police provided security. See "Juvenile Case Handling 'Reprehensible': Judge," *Denver Post,* February 25, 1970; and Louis Kilser, "Kennedy Implicated in Probe," *Rocky Mountain News,* May 25, 1982.

26. Harry Gessing, "Seaton Shifts Police District," *Rocky Mountain News,* September 24, 1968.

27. Jay Whearley, "Army 'Infiltrated' Colo. Groups in '60s," *Denver Post,* September 14, 1975. The article further reported, "It has been charged that the Pentagon had files, such as those maintained in Denver, placed in a computer network instead of destroying them, as instructed by a federal court order . . . a breakthrough that will enable the government to compile swiftly an individual's military, medical, tax, and FBI records. . . . Previous published accounts of Army intelligence . . . indicated the [military] units operated strictly on their own or in cooperation with the FBI."

28. The FBI headquarters file on the Crusade for Justice is Bureau file (Bufile) 105-178283. The Rodolfo Gonzales Bufile is 105-176910. The last digits of the Bufile filing code indicate the chronological and/or numerical order in which reports were added. The 113th MIG's activities in conjunction with the Chicago police intelligence unit (a member of the Law Enforcement Intelligence Unit, LEIU), the FBI, and a neo-Fascist group called the Legion of Justice are docu-

mented in Frank J. Donner, *The Age of Surveillance* (New York: Knopf, 1980), pp. 287–320, 427–30.

29. Donner, *Age of Surveillance*, p. 288. Proponents of the 1878 Posse Comitatus Act defend it by saying that military intervention into domestic affairs threatens democratic processes. The erosion of the act through allowing the use of militay personnel to "interdict" drugs was an early legislative victory of the Reagan–Bush administration, which painted drug use as an internal security threat. Or, as one general argued, "The Latin American drug war is the only war we've got." He was apparently unaware of Reagan's Contra war.

30. Chicago FBI field office Letterhead Memorandum (LHM) to Director J. Edgar Hoover, April 24, 1968, Bufile 105-176910, Not Recorded 4/24/68; 13 of 16 pages were deleted by the FBI before release under a Freedom of Information Act request.

31. The mysterious reference to "Mexican American Militancy" is first found in an April 24, 1968, Airtel from the Chicago SAC to Director, FBI, in Gonzales' Bufile. The caption "Mexican American Militancy, [MAM] IS [Internal Security]–Spanish American" is referred to in the first paragraph. The Chicago FBI field office was responding to an April 17, 1968, Airtel from headquarters that apparently initiated the Mexican American Militancy caption. The contents of headquarters Airtel were referred to but not revealed. The MAM caption was not assigned a file number at that time, merely being designted as "105-new," but the caption was subsequently designated as Bufile 105-180564 (Denver file 105–3958).

The FBI maintained files on individuals, organizations, and specific events, but broad programs like the Black Nationalist Hate Group COINTELPRO targeted entire social movements for unconstitutional, illegal FBI activity, and files on individuals, groups, and events were cross-filed under these broader captions. The Black Nationalist Hate Group COINTELPRO was initiated on August 25, 1967, five days before Rodolfo Gonzales first met Dr. Martin Luther King in Chicago, and, after a trial run, Hoover ordered this COINTELPRO to be conducted on a national scale on March 4, 1968. One month and 13 days after the launching of the antiblack COINTELPRO, the FBI created the broad "Mexican American Militancy" caption, but no document reveals its scope or intent. Numerous references in files on Chicano activism show cross-filings of various reports under this caption. The proposed (but postponed) 1968 conference and the 1969, 1970, and 1971 Denver conferences are cross-filed under the MAM caption, though the caption is sometimes written as "Mexican American Militants" or "Mexican American Matters." Other FBI files cross-filed under MAM include those on the Crusade for Justice (CFJ), the Mexican American Youth Organization (MAYO), the United Mexican American Students (UMAS), La Raza Unida (including its 1972 national convention), the Movimiento Estudiantil Chicano de Aztlan (MEChA), the Instituto de Investigacion Mexico-Aztlan (IIMA), the Committee to Free Los Tres, the Young Chicanos for Community Action (YCCA, a.k.a. Brown Berets); files on Rodolfo Gonzales, José Angel Gutiérrez, Reies Tijerina, Carlos Munoz, Jaime and Antonio Rodriguez, Juan Gomez [Gomez-Quinones], Humberto (Bert) Corona; and, significantly, files on Wounded Knee and Chicano activist gatherings in Mexico. It appears that the FBI had changed the MAM caption to "Mexican American Extremism" by February 1975, possibly due to pressures resulting from Watergate-era revelations of FBI scandals and illegalities. A Freedom of Information Act/Privacy Act (FOI/PA) request filed with the FBI by the author on July 29, 1994, included a request for MAM data. After acknowledging receipt of my request (and offering in the spring of 1997 to drop the request because they had not acted on it), my 400-page Bufile was released in September 1998.

32. Reference to the August 25, 1967, trial run of the Black Nationalist Hate Group COINTELPRO is found in Director, FBI Airtel to SAC, Albany [Georgia], dated March 4, 1968, and captioned "Counterintelligence Program, Black Nationalist Hate Groups–Racial Intelligence." This document ordered the expansion of COINTELPRO from 23 FBI field offices to 40 FBI field offices (41 if FBI headquarters is added).

33. FBI documents on the Black Nationalist Hate Group COINTELPRO worry about "the rise of a leader who might unify and electrify . . . violence-prone groups." Goal 2 of Director, FBI, Airtel to SAC, Albany [Georgia], March 4, 1968, Counterintelligence Program, Black Nationalist Hate Groups–Racial Intelligence, specifically sought to "prevent the rise of a 'messiah'" who would have "the necessary charisma to be a real threat in this way." Interestingly, a LHM of the Denver FBI to FBI headquarters in Crusade Bufile 105-178283-32, p. 6, dated "7/30/69," possibly quoting an informer or an unwitting interviewee, describes Gonzales as "a charismatic person, that is, one who by his personality and style attracts a substantial following."

34. Director, FBI, Airtel to Denver FBI SAC, March 13, 1969, Bufile 105-178283-4.

35. Denver FBI to Director, Bufile 105-178283-5, March 26, 1969. This document deleted data about what the Denver FBI office did. Interestingly, the first and second volumes of four volumes of FBI documents on the Crusade deal overwhelmingly with Denver youth conferences of 1969–71. Three documents (105-178283-5 through 8) change from the Crusade file number to an uncaptioned file, 176-1397-1, where reports on the 1969 conference appear to be cross-filed. The digits "176" denote concern with riots. Documents 105-178283-9 through 31 deal with the 1969 Denver walkouts and youth conference. Sprinkled throughout the volume are numerous "Not Recorded" documents with various dates. Documents 105-178283-34 through 69 focus largely on the 1970 youth conference, and a few deal with the 1971 conference. Documents frequently indicate that field offices had difficulty finding informers. In essence, half of the FBI documents in the purported Crusade file deal with the Denver youth conferences and various youth-based protests.

36. On March 16, 1970, the Bufile on the youth conferences was recaptioned "Second Annual Youth Conference, Denver, Colorado, March 25–30, 1970, aka National Chicano Youth Liberation Conference of Aztlan, IS [Internal Security]–Spanish American." The report was filed in Chicago FBI file 105-30180, Denver file 100-10061, Los Angeles file 100-71172, etc. A 1990 FOIPA request resulted in the release, in 1992, of nearly one thousand pages that the FBI claims are the

Crusade Bufile, but one document indicates that the Denver FBI file is 10 times larger than the Bufile. Approximately two-thirds of FBI data is blacked out, and hundreds of FBI pages were not released at all. Other related Crusade files and subfiles were not released, nor were files on other organizations wherein Crusade data was cross-filed. Reports on the Crusade from military sources, with the exception of a handful, were also withheld, as were files from the CIA, the Denver Police Intelligence Bureau (and other LEIU members), nor were "private sector" spy group files released. Scores of pages on the Crusade that are not found in the purported FBI Crusade Bufile have been found in other FOIPA-released documents. Former Crusade member Alberto Mares received about 160 pages of FBI documents on himself, nearly 50 pages were withheld entirely, and files where he reasonably believed himself to be mentioned were denied him. The FBI maintained files on dozens (possibly scores) of Crusade members.

37. In 1978 Crusade activists, including myself, filed FOI/PA requests for FBI files. Gonzales had filed a request early the previous year. I did not pursue my request because of the paperwork and bureaucratic delays involved in the process. Initial government responses indicated that not much data existed and I had little confidence in their truthfulness or in the prospects for a meaningful response. Documents came into Gonzales' possession from other sources by 1979, and—around 1980—one trusted confidant of the Crusade recalled seeing a box of documents that had been released to Gonzales. I recall seeing a stack about six inches high on his desk, which he was reviewing when I entered his office to discuss an unrelated matter. He asked what had happened with my FOI/PA request, and I told him why I had dropped it. He said that the FBI documents in his hand requested the Denver FBI office to list 10 Crusade members whom that office considered the most violence prone. He laughed and said my name was among the 10. We then discussed the matter about which I wanted to speak with him—after he laid the document down, never offering to show it to me.

38. George Lane and Clem Work, "Economics Is Pertinent Root of Hispano Problem," *Rocky Mountain News,* 1969.

39. Ibid.

40. "Chicano Youth Conference," *El Gallo,* March 1969, p. 12.

41. M. E. [Maria] Varela, "And So We Are, Again, Aztlan," *El Gallo,* April 1969, pp. 4–5 of eight-page conference insert.

42. Manuel J. Martinez, "Los Artistas de Aztlan," *El Gallo,* April 1969, page 7 of eight-page insert. Martinez in 1968 adapted a three-faced symbol (Spanish-Indian-mestizo) representing the Mexican people. The "mestizo head," inspired by a mural Martinez saw in Mexico, became popular with Chicanos as a cultural, social, and historical symbol.

43. "El Proposito Para Implementar y Ensenar El Plan de Aztlan," *El Gallo,* April 1969, p. 11.

44. "A Marriage in Aztlan," *El Gallo,* April 1969, p. 10.

45. Patricia Borjon was the young woman who raised the issue of sexism during the 1969 Denver youth conference. She was interviewed about her role in the conference in the first hour of a four-hour-long documentary entitled *Chicano! History of the Mexican American Civil Rights Movement* (1996), produced by

Galan Productions and the National Latino Communications center. Her role was further elaborated to me by Professor Raul Ruiz in a February 1990 interview.

46. *El Gallo,* April 1969, pp. 2, 8, of insert. The proclamation reflected the nationalist consciousness of activists who had studied the history of the 1910 Mexican Revolution with its myriad plans: Zapata's *Plan de Ayala,* Francisco Madero's *Plan de San Luis Potosi,* Venustiano Carranza's *Plan de Guadalupe,* among others.

47. "The Program of El Plan Espiritual de Aztlan," *El Gallo,* April 1969, p. 12.

48. "Crusade News Flashes" and "Regional News," *El Gallo,* April 1969, pp. 2, 8.

49. This FBI document is not found in the four-volume FBI Bufile 105–178283 released in 1992, but is probably from files released in the late 1970s. It is dated July 30, 1969, and the informant's data are on page 6. The document has the Crusade for Justice caption without a file number. It may be missing from the 1992-released Bufile because Ronald Reagan's administration successfully restricted access to FBI data in the 1980s, even data that had previously been released. Also see *El Gallo,* June–July 1969, p. 1; Marjorie Heins, *Strictly Ghetto Property: The Story of Los Siete de La Raza* (Berkeley: Ramparts Press, 1972) p. 161.

50. The FBI began an internal security file on the Committee to Free Los Siete de La Raza soon after its inception. One reference to the group, for example, is found in a November 19, 1970, LHM to Director, FBI, in response to headquarters' instructions to conduct "a survey of Mexican American organizations in the San Francisco territory" and to submit a response under "Subject: Mexican American Militancy," headquarters file number 105-197022, San Francisco field office file number 100-60797. On p. 15 of the report, the San Francisco field office stated that members of the defense committee were "reportedly planning to bomb targets . . . and to be preparing for guerilla warfare . . . studying firearms and . . . reported to possess firearms [two and a half lines deleted]. This group has a newspaper, *Basta Ya!* . . . The Bureau file number is 105-198431, and San Francisco is the Office of Origin, file 100-63425."

51. Copy of unnumbered Denver FBI document, July 30, 1969, p. 6.

52. Copy of unnumbered Denver FBI document, November 28, 1969, p. 6.

53. "District 14 Boycott Threatened by Minority Group," *El Gallo,* June–July 1969, p. 8. El Guerrillero made similar threats on November 18, 1969, during a dispute at Denver's Kepner Junior High School. A Denver FBI unnumbered report, dated November 28, 1969, p. 6, citing the November 19, 1969, *Rocky Mountain News,* reported that "MEDINA was reported as stating that his group would close down the school."

54. According to Heins, *Strictly Ghetto Property,* p. 146, citing a "reliable source," Gio Lopez was arrested three times in various parts of the country but used aliases and was always released before fingerprints showed his true identity. He reportedly hijacked a plane to Cuba in July 1970; over the years, mutual acquaintances have said they saw him in Cuba or knew people who did.

55. Unnumbered Denver FBI report, June 30, 1969, p. 8.

56. "Young Hispanos Feel Sense of Pride," *Rocky Mountain News,* October 28, 1969.

57. Reference to the FBI Internal Security file on "Chicano Liberation Day" is found in FBI Bufile document "105-178283-NOT RECORDED, SEP 10 1969." The Bufile number for "Chicano Liberation Day" is 105-197022, and the Denver file number is 105-4231. The initial entry in this Bufile is 105-197022-1, copies of which were sent to FBI field offices in Albuquerque, Chicago, Los Angeles, Houston, New York, Phoenix, Sacramento, San Antonio, and San Francisco. High-ranking FBI officials whose signatures are found on this document include those of [W. Raymond] Wannall and C. D. [Charles] Brennan.

58. The "Synopsis" in the July 30, 1969, Denver FBI report is found in Bufile 105-178283-32.

59. *El Gallo,* April 1969, special insert of *Plan Espiritual de Aztlan, punto tercero,* Action item 2, p. 8.

60. Unnumbered Denver FBI report, November 28, 1969, p. 3.

61. "Women Assume Key Roles in Community Leadership," *Viva!.* June 15, 1964, p. 7.

62. "Hispanos Set Denver Parade," *Rocky Mountain News,* September 13, 1969.

63. Ibid.

64. Ken Love, "Parade Peaceful Protest Attract 3,000 in Denver," *Rocky Mountain News,* September 17, 1969.

65. Richard O'Reilly, "Chicano Unity Marchers' Theme," *Denver Post,* September 17, 1969. The Crusade's crowd estimate was between 6,500 and 8,000.

66. Ibid.

67. Ibid.

68. Orrin Brown, "Big March Celebrates Chicano Day in Denver," *The Militant,* October 3, 1969, p. 9.

69. Articles on the September 16 walkout are found in *El Gallo,* September–October 1969, pp. 1, 2, 8, 9, and 11. Though walkouts were reported in other states, written confirmation was sketchy. For September 16 walkouts in Hayward, California, see Steve Chainey, "Hayward Chicanos in School Walkout," *The Militant,* October 10, 1969, p. 11.

70. [Ernesto Vigil,] "What Has Been Accompolished [*sic*]," *El Gallo,* September–October 1969, p. 1.

71. Beatrice Griffith, *American Me* (Boston: Houghton Mifflin, 1948), p. 153.

CHAPTER 6. MILITANCY AND COUNTERREACTION

1. The Denver Black Berets and Brown Berets took their lead from groups that started in California. The Black Berets started in San Jose and had chapters around San Jose and the San Francisco Bay Area. The Brown Berets started in East Los Angeles, were known as the National Brown Beret Organization, and initially emulated the Black Panthers, as seen in their leaders' titles: "Prime Minister," "Minister of Information," etc. Other Brown Beret chapters formed in the Southwest, Midwest, and elsewhere. Some were affiliated with the East Los

Angeles Brown Berets but operated autonomously. Only one group of Denver Brown Berets, a small, ineffectual group from the Westside, was affiliated with the National Brown Beret Organization.

2. Details of the September 26 riot are found in "Community Defense Stops Police Riots," *El Gallo*, September–October 1969, p. 10, and Rocky Hernandez, "Los Black Berets por la Justicia," *El Gallo*, undated [January 1970], p. 8. The latter article announces the Black Berets' intention to collaborate with the Crusade for Justice and with the Eastside Berets, states criteria for membership, and lists the 10 points of the Black Berets' Chicano Code of Aztlan. Many names of members of this Black Beret chapter, as well as details of the role they played in the September 16 walkout, were provided in an interview with former Black Beret Dan Pedraza, March 16, 1990.

3. Ray Saragosa, "The Brown Berets," *El Gallo*, undated [March 1970], p. 4. The Eastside Brown Berets organized youths living on East 23rd Avenue, the St. Charles Park/Annunciation area, and other neighborhoods east of Downing Street, as well as the Swansea-Elyria-Globeville neighborhoods.

4. James R. Sena, "Hispano Role in U.S. History Corrected," *The Register,* Denver Archdiocesan edition, September 25, 1969, pp. 1, 8.

5. Hernandez, "Brown Berets por la Justicia"; "25 Hispano Students Walk Out of Classes," *Rocky Mountain News,* October 8, 1969; "35 Stage Walkout at Junior High," *Rocky Mountain News,* October 9, 1969.

6. "25 Hispano Students Walk Out."

7. "Young Hispanos Feel Sense of Pride," *Rocky Mountain News,* October 28, 1969.

8. The information on the Crusade's participation in the San Francisco Moratorium is included in an 18-page report from the Denver FBI field office to FBI headquarters covering August 1 to November 21, 1969, Crusade Bufile no. 105–178283–33. Further, the FBI opened internal security files captioned "La Raza" and "La Raza Unida" in early 1968, and as these files expanded, additional data about Chicano antiwar activism was archived in them and in similar files. Censored San Francisco FBI field office reports of November and December 1969 include captions and file numbers for "La Raza" (100-62747) and "La Raza Unida" (100-62368). One unnamed FBI Special Agent's report (document 100-62747-32) to the San Francisco SAC, dated March 31, 1970, stated, "La Raza Oneida [*sic*] does have leanings toward the left. Many of its members are uneducated, and the leaders take advantage of them by setting themselves up as the saviors of the Mexican Americans." The documents in the author's possession are brief, highly censored, and include clippings from the *Daily Review* (Hayward, Calif.) and the campus paper of California State College (now University) at Hayward. The articles report on the effort to establish "La Raza Unida Independent Political Party," and one article (San Francisco FBI document 100-62747-24) shows that the San Francisco antiwar protest was criticized because it "does not . . . relate directly to the Chicanos." Associated Student Body Representative-at-Large Ron de la Cruz reportedly said, "We are finally taking a stand on the war in Vietnam: we recognize that we should call our people back from the war; we realize the fact that in reality we are not Americans."

9. Ralph Guzman, "Mexican American Casualties in Vietnam," *La Raza* 1, no. 1 (1971): 12, 15.

10. Research Triangle Institute, "Contractual Report of Findings," in *The National Vietnam Veterans Readjustment Study* (Research Triangle Park, N.C.: Research Triangle Institute, November 7, 1988), p. 16.

11. Roberto Elias, "Draft Conference," *El Gallo*, undated, [January 1970], p. 3.

12. Juan Gomez [Ernesto Vigil], "Crime on the Street: A Report on the Denver Police Department," *El Gallo*, undated [January 1970], pp. 3–4. In this incident I hid behind a tree until the pursuing officers passed. I started to double back and was seen by one officer when I slipped and fell on some snow. I stood up and put out my hands to be handcuffed, but the cop first hit me on the forehead with a blackjack. The gash required nine stitches. The penname used for this article, "Juan Gomez," was that of a fictional character adopted by Crusade members when the need arose. Crusade members met Juan Gomez-Quinones, then a student and now a well-known historian, in 1968; Gonzales had met him in 1967. In February 1969 Crusade members were picketing in support of greenhouse workers in Brighton, Colorado, when Gonzales' daughter Gina was hit and knocked to the ground by a car crossing the picket line. Later, a foreman at the location was punched and fell to the ground. When law enforcement officials at the scene asked the crowd who had thrown the punch, someone quickly responded, "Juan Gomez." (The only connection between the fictional Gomez and the real Juan Gomez-Quinones is that the latter's name came to mind when picketers were asked who had punched the foreman; Gomez-Quinones, of course, was not present at the confrontation.) The officers were given a fictional description of Gomez and told that he had left the scene. A picture of the unconscious foreman is shown on page 7 of the March 1969 *El Gallo*. The caption reads, "Flattened by the notorious Juan Gomez (the Brown Avenger)." When Gio Lopez of Los Siete de La Raza arrived in Denver after the first national youth conference, he was automatically given the name "Juan Gomez."

13. The description of the fundraiser is on p. 3 of uncaptioned Denver FBI LHM numbered 105-176910-61, dated "3/21/73," and covering "Investigative period 11/21/72–3/6/73": "[They] were in Los Angeles on December 15, 1972, through December 17, 1972, attending a fund raising dance on December 15, 1972, for RICARDO CHAVEZ-ORTIZ who was convicted of air piracy in July, 1972. The dance was sponsored by the La Raza Unida Party and was held at St. Peters Hall in Los Angeles, California."

14. Gonzales' December 1972 visit to California, accompanied by the author, is mentioned on page 3 of the document cited just above. In this period Gonzales and the Crusade were apparently subject to more rigorous scrutiny than usual. El Guerrillero is not mentioned in the heavily censored document, as far as can be ascertained, but he was present at the event reported upon. A casual reader would have difficulty determining which individuals or groups were being monitored, since nearly all names have been blacked out. Additionally referenced on the cover page of the Denver FBI LHM were a January 24, 1973, "letter to Acting Director . . . entitled CHICANO CONFERENCE, UNIVERSIDAD NACIONAL AUTO-

NOMO DE MEXICO, 11/21–25/72, Mexico City, Mexico, D.F.," a Denver to Bureau "1/20/73" teletype regarding "PROTESTS DURING PRESIDENTIAL INAUGURAL CEREMONIES, 1973," and a Los Angeles "2/6/73" teletype to the Bureau . . . entitled 'RALLY SPONSORED BY COMMITTEE TO FREE LOS TRES.'" The Denver report, a copy of which went to the CIA, referred to six previous communications involving FBI offices in Washington, Mexico City, Los Angeles, and Denver. The FBI communication from Mexico City to headquarters is referenced as the "letter to the Bureau 1/31/73, [LHM] entitled 'MEXICAN AMERICAN MILITANCY.'"

15. The student demands were tallied as follows: 38 from the 1968 East L. A. walkouts; 9 from the 1969 West High School student walkout; 13 from the Adams City Junior and Senior High Schools and Kearney Junior High School 1969 walkout in solidarity with West; 17 from the Horace Mann Junior High School walkout on September 16, 1969; and 17 from the Black Beret– and Brown Beret–led student walkouts in February 1970. Republican antibusing activists James Perrill and Frank Southworth ran against Democrat integrationists A. Edgar Benton and Monte Pascoe for the Denver school board on May 20, 1969, and won 15 of 18 election districts. Southworth and Perrill narrowly won in the Westside's District 7, but had comfortable victory margins in West and Northwest Denver Districts 2, 3, and 6. Their strongest support, however, came from Southeast and Southwest Denver, areas that then had few people of color. Benton and Pascoe were unable to win even in the districts where they resided.

16. Ernesto Vigil, "Baltazar Martinez Frame-up: Yellow Journalism at Work," *El Gallo*, undated [March 1970], pp. 1, 2.

17. Ibid. The quotations cited in the *El Gallo* account were taken from the *Denver Post* and *Rocky Mountain News* of February 8, 1970. It would be an understatement to describe Baltazar Martinez as a colorful character. Though he was a Vietnam veteran, Martinez was mainly the product of his rural upbringing in northern New Mexico. He reportedly escaped into the mountains on foot after the courthouse raid and successfully evaded capture by a combination of skills learned in Vietnamese jungles and New Mexican mountains. He is said to have disguised his scent when being tracked by dogs and to have slept in trees while his puzzled pursuers passed by underneath. Knowing that he could not be a fugitive permanently, Martinez decided to surrender, and since a cash reward was offered for his arrest, reportedly arranged for his mother to turn him in. Martinez came to Denver seeking employment as generations of Nuevo Mexicanos had done. Like those before him, Martinez used connections with family and friends, not political connections, to help him find work and lodging in Denver. The Crusade, therefore, did not know Martinez was in Colorado and was surprised to see his name in the bombing headlines.

18. Ibid. The Alianza building, which doubled as the Tijerina family's residence, was subjected to vandalism and bombings on several occasions. On April 17, 1968, William Fellion, described as "an ex-Sheriff's deputy," was seen driving from the scene after the Alianza office was bombed. The building sustained little damage because the culprit apparently stumbled before placing the dynamite, prematurely detonating it. Fellion seemed a likely suspect. When police

stopped him, he had a bloody stump where his right hand and wrist had previously been. Outside the Alianza's shattered window, scattered to a distance of 30 feet, were pieces of a right hand and wrist. In spite of this evidence, charges were reduced to "careless driving" after Fellion was held in a hospital and spent 15 days in the Bernalillo County Jail.

On February 2, 1969, Reies Tijerina announced that a ranch in San Cristobal, New Mexico, owned by Craig and Jennie Vincent would be used as a cultural center. Craig Vincent had retreated from Denver to the isolated mountain valley village in the 1950s to escape the pressures of the McCarthy era. Hours after Tijerina's announcement, a fire destroyed buildings at the mountain ranch. In March 1969 the Alianza's office was bombed while its members met there. The doorway of a member's home was bombed two hours later. See "Campaign of Terror Against Alianza," *El Grito del Norte*, July–August 1973, p. 10; Peter Nabokov, *Tijerina and the Courthouse Raid* (Albuquerque: University of New Mexico Press, 1969), p. 243.

19. Vigil, "Martinez Frame-up," pp. 1–2.

20. Ibid.

21. Ibid.

22. Baltazar Martinez, "Baltazar Martinez' Letter," *El Gallo*, undated [March 1970], p. 2.

23. Doug Vaughn, Ron Wolf, and Rosemary Cowles, "The Redfearn File," *Straight Creek Journal*, March 24, 1977, pp. 1–6. The revelations about Redfearn and his federal and Denver spymasters appear in a five-part series by Vaughn, Wolf, and Cowles that ran in the *Straight Creek Journal* between March 24 and April 21, 1977.

24. Ibid.

25. Ibid.

26. Gilbert Quintana, "Students Stage Walkout February 11, 1970," *El Gallo*, undated [March 1970], pp. 3, 4.

27. Ibid.

28. A photograph with the students' names is found ibid., p. 4.

29. An article on the February 1970 moratorium was written by Della Rossa and John Gray for the *People's World* and reprinted as "ELA Chicano Moratorium: Dec. 20, '69, Feb. 28 '70," *El Gallo*, undated [March 1970], p. 9.

30. Ibid.

31. "Chicano Conference Politics Workshop Resolutions," *El Gallo*, June 1970, p. 9.

32. See *El Gallo*, June 1970, pp. 8, 9, 10, and 12, for conference resolutions.

33. "Resolution from Chicana Workshop," *ibid.*, p. 10.

34. "Political Prisoners," *ibid.*, pp. 8, 9.

35. This wording is found as No. 4 under the caption "Introduction: Raza, Raza, Raza," *ibid.*, p. 10.

36. Ibid.

37. "Anti-war Resolutions," *ibid.*, p. 12.

38. Gonzales' emphasis on electoral politics independent of mainstream parties is further illustrated by his 1967 independent mayoral campaign and the

workshop on independent politics in urban areas he conducted at the National Conference on New Politics in Chicago on August 31, 1967.

39. Rodolfo Gonzales, "Why Do We Need La Raza Unida Party?" *El Gallo,* June 1970, p. 1.

40. Joseph Sanchez, "La Raza Candidate Concerned with 'Needs of People,'" *ibid.,* p. 3. This article was originally published in the *Denver Post,* May 17, 1970.

41. Officer Harold E. McMillan had been involved in a brutality controversy on August 20, 1967, when, while moonlighting at a Westside bar, he shot and critically wounded Andrew Garcia, 23. (See Chapter 2.)

42. John Morehead, "Brutality Probe Continues," *Denver Post,* April 22, 1970.

43. James Crawford, "Group to Present Demands in Brutality Probe," *Rocky Mountain News,* April 23, 1970.

44. John Morehead, "Mayor Favors Body as 'Impartial,'" *Denver Post,* April 27, 1970.

45. "Changos Attack," *El Gallo,* June 1970, p. 4. This *El Gallo* account is inaccurate in describing the initial stage of the conflict. Some of the young Brown Berets had been drinking and horsing around in the park, and one allegedly drove his car onto the lawn. The article stated that "officers reported to the scene of a reported accident . . . the victim of the pedestrian-auto accident told the pigs that he was okay and did not need assistance, etc."

46. John Morehead, "Hispanos Jam Council Meeting," *Denver Post,* April 28, 1970. Miller's letter to the *Post* relating police brutality allegations to Asian Communists and race war in the United States ("Attacks on Police Department Harm Race Relations," March 2, 1966) is quoted in Chapter 2.

47. Morehead, "Hispanos Jam Council Meeting."

48. "Lawyer Says Castro Passed Lie Test," *Denver Post,* April 29, 1970.

49. "Jury Delays Brutality Probe Action," *Rocky Mountain News,* April 29, 1970.

50. "Clarification Asked in Police Probe," *Rocky Mountain News,* May 8, 1970.

51. Rykken Johnson, "Hispano Group Plans Further Police Probe," *Rocky Mountain News,* May 11, 1970.

52. Sanchez, "La Raza Candidate Concerned With 'Needs of People,'" *Denver Post,* May 17, 1970.

53. George Lane, "Garcia Tells of His Ouster," *Denver Post,* May 24, 1970.

54. "Cisneros, Atencio Resign Positions," *Rocky Mountain News,* May 28, 1970.

55. "Jury Finds No Brutality Evidence," *Rocky Mountain News,* June 6, 1970.

56. "Changos Attack," p. 4.

57. "Jury Finds No Brutality Evidence."

58. Significantly, Richard Castro was elected to the state legislature in the 1970s and directed the Commission on Community Relations for Mayor Federico Peña's administration from the 1980s to 1991. He was a widely respected political figure in Denver until his death in the 1990s. He spoke out against immigrant-

bashing in the 1970s, criticized U.S. intervention in Central America and "English Only" laws in the 1980s, and advocated for a police civilian review board.

59. "Police Request Jury Probe of Shooting Incident," *Rocky Mountain News*, May 13, 1970.

60. "Fort Collins Brutality Case," *El Gallo*, June 1970, p. 5.

61. Ibid.

62. Christopher Smith, "Chicanos Stage Protest Against Fort Lupton Police," *Rocky Mountain News*, August 11, 1970.

63. Ibid.

CHAPTER 7. EAST LOS ANGELES, AUGUST 29, 1970

1. "Rosalio Muñoz Refuses Induction," *El Gallo*, September–October 1969, pp. 4–5.

2. In August 1990, while in Los Angeles, I was given access to a copy of the FBI file on Ruben Salazar by an acquaintance who came into possession of it while researching the Chicano Moratorium. This acquaintance gave me ample time to read the file, which consisted of hundreds of pages. This was the first time I thoroughly reviewed FBI files obtained through the Freedom of Information Act (FOIA). We agreed that I could make copies of any documents that mentioned the Crusade for Justice and that I could copy by hand any information I desired from other documents but could not copy the documents themselves. Lastly, I was allowed to photocopy one lengthy, but highly-censored, CIA document that was included in Salazar's FBI file. These 40 pages of handwritten notes and copies are cited below as "Author's notes on Salazar FBI file."

3. Davis is quoted in Edward J. Escobar, "The Dialectics of Repression: The Los Angeles Police Department and the Chicano Movement, 1968–1971," *Journal of American History* 79 (1993): 1499; Salazar's article is reprinted in Mario T. Garcia, ed., *Ruben Salazar: Border Correspondent, Selected Writings, 1955–1970* Berkeley and Los Angeles: (University of California Press, 1995), pp. 246–248.

4. "Schools Demands Met by Clubs, Cops," *El Gallo*, undated [March 1970], p. 8. The article is reprinted from People's World, March 14, 1970.

5. The line cited in the narrative is taken from an undated 1970 *Los Angeles Times* clipping Ruben Salazar, "A Beautiful Sight: The System Working the Way It Should." Most of the *Los Angeles Times* clippings in this chapter were copied from the clippings collection of Ralph Arriola, a trade unionist and community activist who first met Salazar in the early 1960s. This clipping unfortunately, lacked the date. The article was not reprinted in the collection of Salazar's articles published by the *Times* after his death, nor in Garcia, ed., *Border Correspondent*. The article referred to the killing of Guillermo and Beltran Sanchez, Mexican nationals and cousins, by five LAPD officers and two others officers on July 16, 1970. The Chicano Moratorium Committee called a rally at the Federal Building on July 20, and the July 22 *Los Angeles Times* ("Seven Policemen Charged in Killing of Mexican Pair in Raid") reported that the seven officers had been charged in the killings. Acting Chief of the Police Daryl Gates warned that the

indictments would have a "devastating effect on [police] morale." It can be assumed that Salazar's article was published after the July 22 article reporting the indictments and before his own death on August 29, 1970.

6. Escobar, "Dialectics of Repression," p. 1501.

7. Garcia, *Ruben Salazar: Border Correspondent,* p. 32.

8. Curt Gentry, J. *Edgar Hoover: The Man and the Secrets* (New York: 1992), p. 263n.

9. Notes taken from FBI files on the Young Chicanos for Community Action (YCCA), a.k.a. Brown Berets, obtained by Professor José Angel Gutiérrez under the FOIA and archived at the University of Texas at Arlington.

10. Declaration of Robert Acosta, sworn and signed December 1978, in author's possession.

11. Declaration of Fernando Sumaya, December 1, 1978, three pages, unsigned copy in author's possession.

12 Declaration of Abel Armas, December 1, 1978, three pages, unsigned copy in author's possession.

13. Declaration of Carlos Montes, *People of the State of California v. Carlos Montes,* Case No. A 244 906, State of California, County of Los Angeles, 10-page draft, signed, March 1, 1979.

14. Acosta's seven-point campaign program is found in Oscar Acosta, "Protection Department," *La Vida Nueva,* April 29, 1970, p. 4. This article was reprinted in Garcia, *Ruben Salazar: Border Correspondent,* pp. 258–60.

15. Interview with former Crusade members Antonio and Josefina "Josie" Salinas, August 19, 1990.

16. "Free 'Corky' Rally Held Feb. 8th," *El Gallo,* February 1972, p. 2; Antonio and Josefina Salinas interview.

17. Thompson recounts the adventures of Oscar Zeta Acosta, Rodolfo Gonzalez, and others during Moratorium. See Hunter S. Thompson, "Strange Rumblings in Aztlan," originally published in *Rolling Stone* magazine and reprinted in *The Great Shark Hunt: Strange Tales from a Strange Time* (New York: Fawcett Popular Library, 1980), pp. 136–74.

18. Doug Shuit and John Scheibe, "Vandals Set Fires, Smash Windows; East L. A. Quiet," *Los Angeles Times,* August 31, 1970.

19. "River Peaceful After 4 Officers Are Wounded by Shots," *Los Angeles Times,* September 1, 1970.

20. Jerry Mandel and Jay Alire, *The Police Use of Force in Hispanic Communities,* draft of publication for the National Conference of La Raza, 1982.

21. The total arrested was given as 29 in the August 30 *Los Angeles Times,* but the August 31 issue indicates that Gonzales and 25 others were arrested. Two of the arrested were Californians who were identified as former UCLA MEChA leader Anthony R. Salazar, 28, and Ernesto Moreno, 23, of West Los Angeles and Cardiff-by-the-Sea, respectively.

22. Charles T. Powers and Jeff Perlman, "40 Hurt, One Dead in East L. A. Riot," *Los Angles Times,* final edition, August 30, 1970.

23. Robert Kistler, "Police Reports Over Militant's Arrest Conflict," *Los Angeles Times,* August 31, 1970. Though the discrepancies in the *Los Angeles*

Times coverage were pointed out by *Times* reporters on August 31, the *Denver Post*, citing Lt. Robert Keel, reported new ones on August 31 in a page 2 article headlined "Legal Aid Rally Helps Colo. Hispanos in L. A. Arrests." In this article Keel said the truck was stopped because it carried too many passengers to operate safely, that three people (not two) had firearms, and that two people (not Gonzales alone) had "several hundred dollars in their possession." Keel told the *Denver Post* reporter "that during the rioting, robberies had been committed, and some of the individuals in the truck appeared to fit the description of the persons involved."

24. Ibid.

25. "Grab Guns, 3, 'Brown Berets,'" *Los Angeles Herald-Examiner*, August 31, 1970.

26. "Relative Calm of Riot Areas Marked by Sporadic Incidents," *Los Angeles Times*, September 2, 1970.

27. Paul Houston, "Newsman's Family Will File Claim for $1 Million in Slaying," *Los Angeles Times*, September 2, 1970.

28. Paul Houston, "U.S. Says It Is Probing Reports That Outsiders Fomented Riot," *Los Angeles Times*, September 2, 1970.

29. Houston, "Newsman's Family Will File Claim."

30. Denver SAC to Director, Crusade Bufile document 105-178283-42, dated May 22, 1970, and Chicago FBI field office Airtel to FBI Director, June 2, 1970, Crusade Bufile document 105-178283-44. Copies of the Chicago Airtel were filed in LA FBI office file 100-71172 under a "Racial Matters" caption and filed in Chicago field office file "105-30180 (P)" [i.e., "pending"]."

31. Sam Kushner, "LA Police and Officials Add 2 Notches to Guns," *People's World*, September 5, 1970, p. 1.

32. Charles T. Powers and Jeff Perlman, "40 Hurt, One Dead in East L. A. Riot," *Los Angeles Times*, August 30, 1970, final edition.

33. For information on the weaponry that killed Salazar, see Jerry Cohen, "Fatal Gas Missile Not Intended for Riot Control Use," *Los Angeles Times*, September 1, 1970. For details of Salazar's death, see *La Raza Magazine*, special issue, September 1970; "Ruben Salazar Murdered," *La Raza: Chicano Press Association Special*, undated [early September 1970]; Houston, "Newsman's Family Will File Claim"; "L.A. Police Attack Chicano Moratorium: Two Die," *El Gallo*, June 1970 *sic:* actually September 1970, p. 3.

34. Salazar, "A Beautiful Sight."

35. Ibid.

36. United Press International, "Davis Blames Subversives for East L. A. Riot," *Los Angeles Herald-Examiner*, August 31, 1970.

37. Kistler, "Police Reports Over Militant's Arrest Conflict."

38. "Judge Jails Attorney in East L. A. Riot Case," *Los Angeles Times*, November 14, 1970.

39. Thompson, "Strange Rumblings in Aztlan," in *The Great Shark Hunt*, p. 148.

40. Della Rossa, "Colorado Chicano Leaders on Trial in Frame-up," *The Militant*, December 18, 1970, p. 7.

41. Ibid.

42. Antonio Salinas interview.

43. Rossa, "Colorado Chicano Leaders on Trial," p. 7; Rudy Villaseñor, "Chavez Gives Testimony for Gun Suspect," *Los Angeles Times*, November 26, 1970.

44. "Jury Deadlocks, Gonzales Retrial on Gun Charge Set," *Los Angeles Times*, December 5, 1970; "Jurors' Belief Assures Gonzales a New Trial," *La Verdad*, December 1970, p. 5. Judge Grillo said he was originally inclined to dismiss the charges, a statement neither Gonzales nor Acosta believed. Gonzales felt that Grillo was unsympathetic to the defendants because of their militant nationalist politics, but the judge himself displayed an Italian flag in his chambers. Gonzales noted this irony in a phone call to the Crusade headquarters. The next day, back in the judge's chambers, Gonzales noticed that the flag was gone. He concluded that the phone had been tapped.

45. "National Chicano Moratorium Goes Sour in Last Effort," *La Causa*, August 29, 1970, p. 5.

46. Declaration of Carlos Montes, interview with Carlos Montes, summer 1970. Carlos Montes allowed the author to copy many documents from his personal archives and granted me lengthy interviews during which he recounted the early days of the country's first Brown Beret organization. Montes attributed some of the turmoil in which the Berets sometimes found themselves to the volatility of the population they organized: the tough youth of the inner city. At the same time, he was openly critical of the leadership style of "Prime Minister" David Sanchez, a leadership style to which Montes attributed much of the group's factionalism, male chauvinism, lack of discipline, etc. He noted that the undercover police agents who infiltrated the Brown Berets sought to isolate Sanchez from other Beret leadership by becoming his bodyguards, a tactic to which he seems to have been vulnerable.

47. Uncaptioned nine-sentence paragraph, *La Causa*, August 29, 1970, p. 5.

48. Declaration of Carlos Montes: Carlos Montes interview.

49. Declaration of Fernando Sumaya.

50. Declaration of Abel Arms.

51. Ibid.

52. Officer A. I. Priest, Los Angeles Police Department Employee's Report, Special Operations Conspiracy Squad, April 30, 1969.

53. Declaration of Robert Acosta.

54. Citizens Research and Investigation Committee (CRIC) and Louis E. Tackwood, *The Glass House Tapes: The Story of an Agent-Provocateur and the New Police-Intelligence Complex* (New York: Avon 1973), pp. 137–39. Also see Rodolfo Acuña, *Occupied America: A History of Chicanos*, 3d ed. (New York: Harper Collins, 1988), pp. 350–52. Acuña also details Sumaya's efforts to infiltrate MEChA, Chicano student organization at San Fernando Valley State College, now California State University at Northridge.

55. CRIC and Tackwood, *Glass House Tapes*, pp. 138–39.

56. Ibid., pp. 136–37.

57. Frank Donner, *The Age of Surveillance* (New York: Knopf, 1980), p. 348.

58. CRIC Tackwood, *Glass House Tapes*, p. 25.

59. Ibid., p. 93.

60. Ibid., pp. 207–8.

61. Elizabeth Thompson, "'Police Spying' on L. A. Activist Groups Scored," *Los Angeles Times*, July 19, 1978, quotes Gates as saying he didn't know what police spying was, but his comments seem misleading in light of subsequent revelations. The *Los Angeles Times* published articles on LAPD political spying on July 7, 1983; July 22, 1983; July 31, 1983; August 12, 1983; September 2, 1983; September 23, 1983; September 29, 1983; October 1, 1983; October 18, 1983; October 19, 1983; October 20, 1983; October 27, 1983; November 28, 1983; December 12, 1983; February 29, 1984; July 11, 1992; and more. The revelations in *L.A. Secret Police: Inside the LAPD Elite Spy Network* by Mike Rothmiller and Ivan G. Goldman (New York: Pocket Books, 1992) are comprehensive, current, and chilling. The *Los Angeles Times* articles seem to offer mere inklings of a very ominous reality.

62. Author's notes on Salazar FBI file.

63. Ibid.

64. Garcia, *Ruben Salazar: Border Correspondent*, p. 34.

65. Dial Torgerson, "Reds Seek to Use Latin Youths as 'Prison Fodder,' Davis Says," *Los Angeles Times*, January 15, 1971.

66. Donner, *Age of Surveillance*, pp. 397–98.

67. Garcia, *Ruben Salazar: Border Correspondent*, pp. 246–48.

68. Kushner, "LA Police and Officials Add 2 Notches," p. 7.

69. Garcia, *Ruben Salazar: Border Correspondent*, p. 34.

70. Mario Garcia, *Memories of Chicano History: The Life and Narrative of Bert Corona* (Berkeley and Los Angeles: University of California Press, 1994), pp. 276–85. For details of the LAPD's relationship with, and antagonism to, militant Chicanos from 1968 to 1971, see Escobar, "Dialectics of Repression," For a history of the LAPD's authoritarian leadership and its "red" squads' attendant violence, corruption, persistent racism, and ties to groups like the John Birch Society, see Frank Donner, *Protectors of Privilege: Red Squads and Police Repression in Urban America* (Berkeley and Los Angeles: University of California Press, 1990).

CHAPTER 8. COLORADO IN THE EARLY 1970S:
EDUCATION, ELECTIONS, PARKS, AND PRISON ACTIVISM

1. The brochure can be approximately dated because it gives the Crusade's address as "P.O. Box 50503 1265 Cherokee Street," a location not used after the Crusade departed for the Poor People's Campaign. Certain people listed as board members in the brochure were no longer active in the first months of 1968. As far as is known, this was the only brochure the Crusade ever printed about itself.

2. The plaza is also referred to as the Plaza de Las Tres Culturas because it is surrounded by colonial, modern, and pre-Columbian structures representing three cultures.

3. Kelly Lovato, a founding member of the Crusade for Justice, was known for his witty (and sometimes caustic) remarks. His free-thinking unorthodoxy

antagonized older Crusade members. Lovato moved to New Mexico in 1969, but Gonzales continued to harbor a stubborn resentment against his perceived lack of "respect" or "loyalty."

4. This project, serving Chicanos, Native Americans, and Taos-area progressives, was also an organizing vehicle. In one instance, Lovato and the writer John Nichols leveraged money from the actor Dennis Hopper to finance the appearance in Taos of Luis Valdez' activist theater troupe, Teatro Campesino. Nichols later wrote an account of bizarre plot to pressure Lovato to move from the Taos area through a rumor campaign linking him to a conspiracy to launch an armed takeover of Taos. The rumors seemed to stem from law enforcement circles, including one officer later involved in the shooting deaths of two Albuquerque Black Berets. See [John Nichols], "Ted Drennan in Taos" and "Albuquerque Beret Killings: An In-Depth Report and an Alternate Theory," *New Mexico Review,* March 1972.

5. The 1973 brochure provides other data about Escuela Tlatelolco:

"*Physical Plant:* Tlatelolco is presently located where it was founded, the Crusade for Justice Building, at 1567 Downing Street in Denver, Colorado, Aztlan. The facilities house an auditorium, a gymnasium, a cafeteria, classrooms, a photography laboratory, a silk-screening shop, a newspaper library, the *El Gallo* office, an art gallery, two machine reproduction rooms, a combination curio shop and book-store, a lounge, Tlatelolco administration offices, and the Crusade for Justice organization offices.

"*Administration:* Escuela Y Colegio Tlatelolco is governed by a twenty-one member Board of Directors—Chicano students, parents, faculty, and other community residents. The functional responsibility of this Board is to establish operational policies and procedures for the program, identify program needs and problems, determine program priorities, coordinate program planning with staff and students, monitor program activities, recruit, select, and evaluate personnel, generate community resources, and secure other contributive services.

"*Operational Support:* Volunteer Personnel, Parental and Community Contributions, Fund-raising Campaigns, Private Foundation Grants (minimal), Campaign for Human Development, Goddard College (limited), Local MDTA Programs, Proceeds from the sale of *I Am Joaquin,* Commission on Film, *I Am Joaquin,* Consultantships and Speaker Honorariums, Ballet Chicano de Aztlan Benefit Performances." The list of staff, administration, and consultants totaled 21 names, without including kitchen, janitorial, and other support staff.

6. Gary Gebhardt, "Seven Students Arrested in West High Disturbance," *Rocky Mountain News,* October 23, 1970; "West Closes After Violence," *Denver Post,* October 23, 1970.

7. Martin Moran, "School Board Partially Yields to Protestors," *Rocky Mountain News,* October 23, 1970.

8. Ibid.

9. Ibid.

10. Cindy Parmenter, "Board Will Try to Remove Police at GW," *Denver Post,* October 23, 1970.

11. "South Pupils Ask Removal of Principal," *Rocky Mountain News,* October 30, 1970.

12. For Carpio's remarks see "La Raza Candidate Hits Foes' Verbiage," *Rocky Mountain News,* October 26, 1970. Other information on Colorado LRUP's early history and candidates is found in "La Raza Candidates Concerned About the 'Needs of People,'" *El Gallo,* June 1970 [September 1970], pp. 10, 11.

13. Ibid.

14. Martin Moran, "Minority Help Regent Candidate's Aim," *Rocky Mountain News,* October 27, 1970.

15. See "Rosales Scores 'Dangerous Precedent,'" *Rocky Mountain News,* October 2, 1970; Richard Tucker, "La Raza Man Withdraws, Blasts Dems," *Rocky Mountain News,* October 10, 1970.

16. Tucker, "La Raza Man Withdraws."

17. "Avila Quits Race for Post," *Denver Post,* October 9, 1970.

18. Tom Gavin "La Raza Candidate Keeps the Faith in System," *Denver Post,* October 11, 1970.

19. Bob Whearley, Fred Gillies, and Chuck Green, "'Juvenile Policy Lenient,'" *Denver Post,* September 21, 1970.

20. Ibid.

21. "Judge Rubin Retention Poll Conducted by DCTA," *Denver Post,* October 23, 1970.

22. "DCTA to Poll Teachers on Judge Rubin," *Rocky Mountain News,* October 30, 1970.

23. "Letters from the People: Change Needed," *Rocky Mountain News,* October 30, 1970. For the results of the DCTA poll, "DCTA Action Seeks Judge Rubin Ouster," *Denver Post,* October 27, 1970. For Ballinger's allegations about classroom assaults, see "Teachers Vote Judge Rubin's Ouster," *Rocky Mountain News,* October 28, 1970.

24. "Teachers Blast Anti-Rubin Poll," *Rocky Mountain News,* October 31, 1970.

25. Dick Thomas "Rubin Harbors No Rancor, Bitterness—Only Sadness," *Rocky Mountain News,* November 5, 1970.

26. The art work and life of Manuel (Emanuel) Martinez is beautifully captured in 141 pages in *Emanuel Martinez: A Retrospective,* edited by Teddy Dewalt (Denver: Museo de Las Americas, 1995).

27. The 1971 staff at La Raza Park included Antonio Archuleta, Ed Prado, Julian Mazzoti, Donny Marquez, Frank "Kiko" De Claw, and Arturo Rodriguez. Many women's talents and energies contributed to the successful community organizing at La Raza Park. Those employed at the park over the years included Georgeanne Archuleta, Diane Garcia, Sally Morehouse, sisters Patricia "Pati" Salas and Joan "Tinko" Salas, Cecilia "Tuni" Garrison, Josie Salinas, Jeanette Marquez, and many others.

28. [Ernesto Vigil,] "Police Terrorism in Denver," *El Gallo,* August 1972, pp. 1, 2.

29. This account of the police tactical maneuvering is based on personal ob-

servation. A similar account of police tactics is given by Arturo "Bones" Rodriguez, a Crusade member and La Raza Park's first Chicano manager. Rodriguez is quoted extensively in a master's thesis by Anthony Sisneros, probably the most extensive account of the DiManna recall effort: "The DiManna Recall" (M.A. thesis, University of Colorado at Boulder, 1974).

30. [Ernesto Vigil,] "Police Terrorism in Denver," *El Gallo,* September 1971, pp. 3, 4, The original *El Gallo* article was written from an eyewitness perspective. The shooting of Tomas Rios, the apparent pilfering of the personal property of those arrested, the subsequent gunfire at the Lincoln Housing Projects, and other events were related to me by those who experienced them, Rios' account of his shooting was confirmed by those who tried to come to his assistance—people whose names I have long since forgotten. Rios lived next door to me as a child and later graduated from Escuela Tlatelolco.

31. Ibid., p. 3.

32. George Lane, "Chicano Protest on Pool, Parks," *Denver Post,* March 24, 1972.

33. [Ernesto Vigil,] "Attention Chicanos," *El Gallo,* August 1972, p. 2.

34. [Vigil,] "Police Terrorism in Denver" (August 1972).

35. [Vigil,] "Attention Chicanos," pp. 3, 4. DiManna's letters on behalf of Woolverton and Pauldino were cited in Cecil Jones, "DiManna Note Fails to Avert Sentence," *Rocky Mountain News,* July 11, 1972.

36. [Vigil,] "Attention Chicanos," p. 2.

37. *El Gallo* dedicated four pages to the controversy over La Raza Park. The June 28 battle and the events described in the following pages are reported in [Vigil,] "Attention Chicanos," pp. 2–4.

38. "Petitions Again Short for DiManna Recall," *Denver Post,* December 13, 1972.

39. Arturo Rodriguez is quoted in Sisneros, "The DiManna Recall," p. 26.

40. *Denver Post,* June 13, 1973.

41. *Santiago H. Valdez, Arthur Rodriguez, and David Madrid* v. *Election Commission of the City and County of Denver.*

42. Two-page copy entitled "Community Development Act Programs in the Sunnyside, Highlands, Globeville, and Jefferson Park Neighborhoods," hand-dated "June 28th–1981."

43. The prisoners wanted to use the words "Mexican" or "Chicano" in its name, but prison authorities forbade this.

44. [Ernesto Vigil,] "Prison Strike," *El Gallo,* January 1972, p. 7.

45. Ibid.

46. The scandal provoked an investigation into affairs at the State Penitentiary that lasted into 1974. Seek Jack Olsen, "Prison Ranch Boss Admits Discrepancies," *Rocky Mountain News,* October 10, 1973; "Prison Probe May Bring New Charges," *Rocky Mountain News,* August 8, 1974.

CHAPTER 9. LA RAZA UNIDA PARTY: FIGHTS ABOUT
IDEOLOGY AND STRUCTURE

1. Frank Del Olmo, "Independent Party for Latins Backed by Chicano Caucus,"*Los Angeles times,* April 23, 1972.

2. Ibid.

2. Carlos Penichet, "Reflections on the Chicano Political Caucus Held in San Jose, April 21–23, 1972," undated three-page manuscript, pp. 1, 2.

3. Ibid., p. 2.

4. José Angel Gutiérrez' letter to the San Jose gathering was published in the UCLA *LA Gente,* May 26, 1972, and reprinted in "Colorado's La Raza Unida Party Position Statement," *El Gallo,* November–December 1973/January 1974, p. 6.

5. Letter of José Angel Gutiérrez to Vicente Gonsalez, La Raza Unida Party Coordinator from Newark, California, dated June 12, 1972.

6. [Ernesto Vigil,] "La Raza Unida," *El Gallo,* undated [October 1972], p 2.

7. Ibid.

8. The October 1972 *El Gallo* printed a two-page article on Falcon's death, criticizing the grand jury that indicted Brunson for manslaughter, not murder, and further criticizing District Attorney, Norman Bloom, who knew Brunson and frequented his filling station. *El Gallo* stated that a special prosecutor should have been brought in, citing a press release that revealed that the Officer Cunningham who arrested Brunson was his neighbor and a fellow member of the American Independent Party. The O'Brien who performed the autopsy was also Brunson's doctor. District Attorney Bloom insisted that there were no racial overtones in the killing, even though Brunson admitted calling Falcon derogatory names. Ironically, the *El Gallo* issue that covered Falcon's death has pictures of three young men who would die before the 1970s were over: Mike Licon, Martin Serna, and Florencio "Freddy" Granado, the friend who witnessed Falcon's death in Orogrande.

9. Rodolfo Gonzales, "Speech Delivered to La Raza Unida National Convention: Liberty Hall, El Paso, Texas, September 2, 1972," *El Gallo,* undated [October 1972], pp. 3, 4, 11.

10. Activists throughout the Southwest were aware of Texas activists' efforts to build a third party based in their own state. Gonzales was also aware of the reluctance of Texas leaders to be enmeshed in a political strategy decided by others. Gonzales had favored third-party politics since his run for mayor against Tom Currigan in the mid-1960s. Other activists, principally from California, also favored a third party, and Gonzales formed a lobby with them to sway Texas in favor of the national party strategy.

11. Elias Castillo, "S. J. Caucus Called Chicano 'Awakening,'" *Mercury News [San Jose],* April 22, 1972.

12. Letter of Reies Lopez Tijerina to "Dear Brothers," dated October 15, 1972.

13. Reies Tijerina, *Mi Lucha por la Tierra* (Mexico: Fondo de Cultura Economica, 1978), p. 403 (translated by the author).

14. "Rodolfo Gonzales' Letter to Reis (sic) Lopez Tijerina," *El Gallo*, undated [October 1972], p. 12.

15. Rodolfo Gonzales "Message to El Congreso on Land and Cultural Reform: I. Land and Its Relationship to Our People and Movement," *El Gallo*, undated [October 1972], p. 12.

16. The November–December 1973/January 1974 *El Gallo* devoted over five pages to its position on the conflict within LRUP. The article, "Colorado La Raza Unida Party Position Statement," provides a lengthy chronological narrative detailing the Colorado party's perspective. The interpretation that Gutiérrez had been elected Congreso Chairman and National [La Raza Unida] Convention Chairman, not "National La Raza Unida Party Chairman," is found on p. 8.

17. The June 1970 *El Gallo* that reported the resolutions pertaining to the Congreso de Aztlan and LRUP offered a one-paragraph summary of the political workshop discussion, along with four brief paragraph's calling for the establishment of Aztlan, the Congreso, and the party. The November–December 1973/January 1974 issue reprinted the entire workshop discussion summary, which was much longer than reported in 1970. This summary, on p. 6, reveals doubt that the electoral process and media access would work in the party's favor once it gained strength: "What direction do we want the Party to take? . . . Do we hold our own elections in our own nation and ignore them [American elections] completely? . . . Probably for now we will have to run in their elections. This, in itself, is not the answer, but will give us equal time . . . on their mass communications media to politicize and radicalize our people. Equal time to tell the truth to our people, and for a lot of them it will be the first time in their lives they've heard the truth. . . . Of course, they will not allow to use their media for long and will begin passing laws, but we will, while we could, have used their media as a forum for the truth. . . . A lot of our people already no longer respect this government or judicial system. Hell, they don't even vote because they already know it's meaningless."

18. "Report on Political Workshop: Resolutions," *El Gallo*, June 1970, p. 9.

19. From a letter of José Angel Gutiérrez to the *La Gente*, November-December, 1973, reprinted as "José Angel Speaks out," in *El Gallo*, November–December 1973/January 1974, p. 7.

20. José Angel Gutiérrez to "Hermano de Raza," 1973 (no day or month specified).

21. Colorado La Raza Unida Party to "Congreso Representatives," July 13, 1973.

22. Gutiérrez to "Hermano de Raza," 1973.

23. José Angel Gutiérrez to Tito Lucero of Oakland, California, January 24, 1973.

24. José A. Gutiérrez to "Congreso Representatives," January 24, 1973.

25. Northern California LRUP Correspondence Secretary Bill Gallegos to Congreso members, February 11, 1973.

26. Author to José A. Gutiérrez, February 21, 1973, published without caption in *El Gallo*, April 1973, pp. 6, 7.

27. Jim Wood, "La Raza Sought Nixon Cash," *San Antonio Express and*

News, November 18, 1973, reprinted in *El Gallo,* November–December 1973/ January 1974, p. 8.

28. This history of La Raza Unida Party, including details of the Texas party's dealings with the Republicans in 1972, is recounted in Ignacio M. Garcia, *United We Win: The Rise and Fall of La Raza Unida Party* (Tucson: Mexican American Studies and Research Center, 1989), and Armando Navarro, *The Cristal Experiment: A Chicano Struggle for Community Control* (Madison: University of Wisconsin Press, 1998).

29. San Diego County, *La Raza Unida Party Newsletter,* no. 5 (October 1972).

30. Juan José Peña in "Discussion Bulletin Number One: The Chicano Movement, the Southwest, and the Role of the National and State Partido De La Raza Unida in the Southwest" (undated, but around 1980 or 1981), wrote: "The split was decisively made at the East Chicago, Indiana meeting, with the Partido's aligned Texas Raza Unida continuing under the party banner, while the Crusade-affiliated Partidos either left the Partido for new tendencies or let the Partido fall into disuse as a means of struggle for Chicano liberation" (p. 7). Peña was chair of the New Mexico LRUP.

31. "La Raza Unida Party Convention," *El Gallo,* July 1973, p. 6.

32. Peña, "Discussion Bulletin Number One," p. 8. Juan José Peña attended the El Paso LRUP Convention, the November 1972 "Congreso" gathering in Albuquerque, and the abortive August 1973 "La Raza Unida Congreso Conference" in Denver. He sought to work with both rival LRUP groups, who would not work with each other, and was a mainstay within the New Mexico LRUP.

CHAPTER 10. WOUNDED KNEE AS A PRELUDE:
THE CRUSADE FOR JUSTICE AND THE AMERICAN
INDIAN MOVEMENT

1. An FBI document shows the names of SACs transferred to South Dakota in addition to Trimbach. The copy is headed "Minneapolis SAC Airtel to Acting Director (Attention: Movement Unit), FBI, March 7, 1973." The name of the subject being investigated is deleted from the caption of this FBI document, but the letters "CIR" (Crime on Indian Reservation) were not deleted. The document is serialized as 176-2404-66. Rolland Dewing's 1995 book *Wounded Knee II* (Chadron, Neb.: Great Plains Network), states that SAC Trimbach was newly appointed to his Minneapolis SAC post when he was sent to South Dakota on February 13, 1973. Dewing says (p. 70) that Acting Associate Director Mark Felt ordered SACs DeBruler and Hoxie to South Dakota to assist Trimbach. Professor Dewing's collection of FBI documents on Wounded Knee is archived at Chadron State College in Chadron, Nebraska. The guide to the microfilm edition of the document collection cites an FBI memorandum dated April 24, 1975, in which DeBruler is listed as the SAC of the Atlanta FBI field office, possibly because of a subsequent transfer from Oklahoma City. Mark Felt, who ordered the additional SACs to South Dakota, served as the FBI Deputy Associate Director—the FBI's third most powerful position—under J. Edgar Hoover at the time of Hoover's death in the spring of 1972. Felt and Edward S. Miller, another high-ranking FBI

executive, were convicted of felonies in 1980 for authorizing illegal FBI burglaries in the 1970s, but both were promptly pardoned by the recently elected Ronald Reagan.

2. The FBI brought promising field agents to Bureau headquarters for training. Some remained in Washington and, learning bureaucratic politics, began the long climb through the hierarchy. Others were rewarded with SAC positions and plum posting in the field. Various FBI documents show that DeBruler wrote directives under Hoover's name in 1968 and 1969. DeBruler's name is found in "Director, FBI [by W. K. DeBruler], to SAC, Denver, 3/24/69." The caption is given as "Unsubs [Unknown Subjects]; Interference With Denver, Colorado, Police Officers During Mexican-American Demonstrations at West High School, 3/21/69," with the document serialized as 176-1356-1. DeBruler's name is likewise found in a related April 11, 1969, FBI document serialized as 176-1356-2. Gonzales was a subject of the 1968 FBI investigation that resulted in the Chicago Seven conspiracy trial (see Chapter 4). The Airtel sent to the Denver field office ordering Gonzales to be interviewed is headed. "To: S. A.'s [possibly SAC's] Denver (176-2) Chicago (176-885 [886?]), From: Director, FBI [by W. K. DeBruler], RUDOLPH GONZALES, ARL [Anti-Riot Law], OO [Office of Origin], Chicago, October 7, 1968," The Airtel was channeled to Gonzales' Bufile (105-176910) and the original filed as 176-1209-1.

3. Denver FBI field office Nitel to FBI Acting Director and the Minneapolis FBI field office, March 6, 1973, 7:45 p.m. The FBI headquarters file number for the Crusade is 105-187283. FBI headquarters logged individual entries to the file with sequential numbers, e.g., 105-187283-44, 105-187283-45, 105-187283-46, etc. This March 6, 1973, Nitel, rather than being assigned a sequential number, was instead stamped as "Not Recorded" on March 21, 1973. The 'Not Recorded' on FBI Documents is reportedly used to designate and count documents during release under the FOI/PA process.

4. FBI document 176-2404-51, R. E. Gebhardt to Mr. [Mark] Felt, March 5, 1973, captioned "Disorder by American Indians in South Dakota, Crime on Indian Reservation; Extremist Matters—American Indian Activities."

5. San Francisco FBI field office to Acting Director, Denver (157-529), Minneapolis (176-87), March 6, 1973, serialized as 100-462483—Not Recorded March 19, 1973.

6. SAC, Minneapolis Summary Teletype to Acting Director, FBI, March 7, 1973, serialized as 176–2404–63.

7. R. E. Gebhardt to Mr. Felt, March 7, 1973, captioned "Disorder by American Indians in South Dakota, Crime on Indian Reservation; Extremist Matters—American Indian Activities," serialized as 176-2404-62. Since the phone line at Wounded Knee went through Pine Ridge, where the FBI and BIA had their command post, the FBI had already been listening in on Wounded Knee phone calls, though, technically speaking, this was a "party-line" arrangement in which the agents actively overheard conversations, not a "wiretap" in which calls were recorded. The judge to whom the FBI applied for the wiretap denied the affidavit and believed the information cited in it had been obtained by wiretapping, which, of course, would have been illegal.

8. Two one-page notes to "General Investigative Division," both dated March 8, 1973, initialed by "JBL" as the sender.

9. R. E. Gebhardt to Mr. Felt, March 8, 1973, serialized as 176-2404-76.

10. R. J. Gallagher to Mr. Gebhardt, March 8, 1973, serial illegible.

11. SAC, Minneapolis [Joseph Trimbach], "Urgent Teletype" to Acting Director, FBI, March 8, 1973, serialized as 176-2402-86.

12. SAC, Los Angeles Letterhead Memorandum to Acting Director, FBI, dated March 13, 1973, pp. 5, 6, 9, serialized as 100-462483-383.

CHAPTER 11. DEATH AND DESTRUCTION ON DOWNING
STREET: THE MARCH 17 CONFRONTATION

1. Officer Carole Hogue gave a statement to Denver Detective Lohr on March 17, 1973, at 2:50 a.m. This typed statement reflects Snyder's threat to arrest us all for jaywalking. The statement reads, "Just at that time, when the other guys came across the street, [Snyder] told [Mascareñas] to get in the car, and then he got into the back seat of the car, and the other guys were asking why we were taking him and my partner said, 'For the same reason, you jaywalked across the street, what you are doing right now,' and the next thing I heard him say was, 'You three guys,' and some words went back and forth."

2. My recollection is that Mascareñas said nothing during the time we argued with Snyder. Officer Hogue's typed statement reports that Mascareñas told the officers he wanted to leave the car "and [Snyder] said, 'No, you stay there,' and [Mascareñas] said, 'I'm going, man,' and he bolted out of the car and Steve jumped out after him." I did not hear Mascareñas give police advance notice that he intended to escape their custody. I later saw Mascareñas swagger from a West-side bar in the summer of 1973 and spoke to him. He stared at me insolently when I stopped him till he recognized me. I asked him to testify. His expression changed, and he nearly wailed that he could not testify because he was on parole, he claimed, "and the police will get me."

3. Various witnesses saw Mascareñas run from the car but did not accurately recollect the direction he fled in. These witnesses were not close by, and some mistakenly said he ran east. Mascareñas ran south to East Colfax Avenue.

4. Under advice of attorneys, no one who was charged gave details about what they were doing when arrested because we believed that the police would use the information to tailor their version of events. When the media reported that Martinez was the person who was in Snyder and Hogue's car, Crusade representatives phoned reporters to state that Martinez was not this person. This correction was never reported.

5. Documents released from police files to defense attorneys include two handwritten pages by Officers Catalina (badge #64-33) and Isenhart (#63-44) regarding this shooting victim, a man named Montoya. The two pages are addressed to Captain Shaughnessy and dated March 17, 1973. The officers reported that the shooting victim said he was shot for no reason in the 3100 block of West 16th Avenue and drove nearly four miles to seek police assistance. He walked up to a policeman on East Colfax Avenue, a few blocks west of Downing Street, and

422   Notes to Pages 213–215

was taken to the hospital. He could have driven less than six blocks west from where he was shot and been attended at St. Anthony's Hospital. His truck was searched at 4:00 a.m., but no blood was found in it. A 17-year-old woman was also shot and hospitalized around the same time, and the press and police surmised that she may have been present during the Downing Street confrontation. This woman's husband was intoxicated when she was shot and could not give details of the shooting for police. The two told police that she was shot at a bar, the Red Turkey. The bar was two blocks from where Montoya was shot on West 16th Avenue. These shootings may have been linked, but, as with many other matters, subsequent police and media reports never clarified what happened.

6. A picture of Luiz Ramirez' injuries is found in the April 1973 *El Gallo*, p. 4.

7. Frank Moya, "Chicano-Police Gunfight, Bombing Kill 1, Injure 18," *Rocky Mountain News,* March 18, 1973.

8. "'Martinez' Revolver 'Stolen,'" *Denver Post,* March 19, 1973.

9. "Snipers Fight Cops in Denver," *Santa Fe New Mexican,* March 18, 1973.

10. Fred Gillies, George Lane, and John Ashton, "Disputed Denver Shootout Questions Persists," *Denver Post,* April 1, 1973.

11. Ibid.

12. Weapons seized in the 10 apartments were inventoried by Detective John Pinder on March 21, and a copy of the inventory was turned over to defense attorneys months after the incident. The inventory, written on stationery captioned "Denver Police Department Inter-department Correspondence," is dated March 21, 1973, and is addressed to "Sgt. J. Jones" from Detective Pinder. The inventory lists 17 shoulder weapons (three shotguns, six 22-caliber rifles, eight higher-caliber rifles), and 15 handguns. Among the handguns were five .22 calibers, but no .44 magnums. The highest caliber handguns were four .38 Specials.

13. The sheer number of statements from police and civilians easily results in confusion. Most people arrested that night, more than 60 people, did not see the confrontation in the street because they were inside the apartment. Some young people, for example, said an attractive African American woman briefly attended the party, and rumors spread that Carole Hogue had been present at the party in civilian clothes. No one could say they saw this unknown woman, they had only heard about her from someone else. Early defense committee meetings stressed the need to maintain composure, to keep quiet until things were better organized, and to keep to the facts no matter how heated the emotions. Rumors and silly statements made without substantiation could make the Crusade seem less credible.

14. Jay Whearley and Jack R. Olsen, "Gun Battle 'Spontaneous,'" *Denver Post,* March 18, 1973.

15. George Lane, "Police Actions Condemned, Lauded," *Denver Post,* March 18, 1973.

16. Captain Smith's estimate of the number of police on the scene when he arrived is found in "Memorandum Brief in Opposition to Defendant's Motions to Suppress and Dismiss," *People of the State of Colorado v. Mario Vasquez,* Criminal Action no. 69292, Courtroom 17 in the District Court in and for the City and County of Denver, September 11, 1973.

17. Frank Moya, "Police Blamed by Chicanos for Shootout on Saturday,"

Rocky Mountain News, March 19, 1973. Among those who spoke were Rodolfo Gonzales, Louie Ramirez, attorneys Ken Padilla and Bill Hazleton, Marcos Martinez (Luis' brother), and myself.

18. [Ernesto Vigil], unheadlined article, *El Gallo,* April 1973, p. 4. This article begins on page 3 at the bottom of column 1.

19. The names of over 60 people, adults and juveniles, are found in offense reports and lists of people arrested that were turned over to defense attorneys.

20. The March 17, 1973, *Denver Post* reported: "About 30 police cars and 60 police officers were sent to the scene"; the March 27 *Denver Post* referred to "statements of 117 witnesses, including 72 policemen"; and the April 1 *Denver Post* reported that "about 50 police officers would be in the area." Two typewritten lists later given to defense attorneys, totaling more than 10 pages, reveal about 236 names of officers involved in the March 17 confrontation. If we deduct the names of police who worked in the crime lab and detectives at headquarters who interviewed witnesses but were not present at the scene, the number of officers on the 1500 block of Downing on March 17 still totals over 200.

21. Harry Gessing and John Ashton, "1 Killed, 19 Hurt, 36 Held in Denver Gunfight, Blast: 12 Policemen, 7 Others on Injury List," *Denver Post,* March 17, 1973.

22. "Main Slain, Officers Wounded in Denver Shooting, Bombing," *Rocky Mountain News,* March 17, 1973.

23. Gessing and Ashton, "1 Killed, 19 Hurt, 36 Held."

24. Officer Carole Hogue's account of the confrontation is found in documents released to defense attorneys about five months after the incident. These statements claim that Luis Martinez was the belligerent young man who was put in custody for jaywalking after confronting Snyder and Hogue. The main document is a five-page typed account described as "Statement taken in the Criminal Investigation Division, Room 305, Police Building . . . on March 17, 1973, at approximately 2:50 a.m., in the presence of [Detective] Thomas Lohr [and] Terry H. Jaeckel, Hearings Reporter." It is signed by Hogue and Lohr and concluded at 2:55 a.m. The account was apparently preceded by two other documents. One is a 13-sentence paragraph denoted as "Start of statement from Carol [*sic*] Hogue." It is unsigned, undated, and no time is indicated. Following this document, but preceding the typed statement, are two handwritten pages on stationery captioned "Denver Police Department Inter-office Correspondence," addressed to Captain Smith from "C. C. Hogue." The document refers to "Incident 1500 block Downing St., at approximately 12:45, 3-17-73." These two pages are unsigned and untimed. Lastly, Officer Hogue made statements included in Offense Reports written by Officer Rennert on March 18, 1973. The Offense Reports are signed by Hogue and listed as Case Nos. 083041 and 083043 (at 0400 and 0345 hours).

25. Officer Hogue's typed statement, March, 1973, p. 2. Hogue could have confused Mascareñas and Martinez when Mascareñas jumped from the rear door and ran, since Martinez was on the same side of the car and in the small cluster of people by the car's rear left door. Hogue claims, however, that the group at the car dispersed on Snyder's order before Mascareñas jumped from the car.

26. Ibid., p. 3.

27. Moya, "Chicano-Police Gunfight, Bombing Kill 1, Injure 18."

28. Though the *Rocky Mountain News* referred to the M-16 assault rifle, no picture of it was shown. The *Denver Post*, however, published two photos in the March 17 issue, on p. 10.

29. Whearley and Olsen, "Gun Battle 'Spontaneous.'"

30. "City Policewoman Has Praise for Job," *Denver Post*, March 21, 1973.

31. Officer Steve Snyder's interview at Denver General Hospital, March 27, 1973, pp. 1, 2. Civilians saw Hogue and Snyder slowly cruise by the apartments at least twice that night. No one saw them issue a ticket to anyone, and no one harassed them. The interviewing detectives did not tape Snyder's interview. The detectives were later given a typed transcript of Snyder's statement by Chesler, who had taped the interview, but the tape was never made available. Detectives made several pages of handwritten notes during the interview, including a sketch of the shooting scene that shows the location and the position where police say they found Martinez' body. This material was released to defense attorneys several months after the incident. Some documents were uncovered in police files only 17 years later, through the assistance of a skilled researcher. The transcript of Snyder's tape is six pages long; it is cited verbatim, with no changes other than adding commas where the transcriber used dashes—, correcting some misspellings, and deleting minor repetitions. At one point, example, the transcript reads: "we got a bunch of mouth from a bunch of kids—a bunch of punks—across the street." I quote the passage as: "We got a bunch of mouth from a bunch of kids, a bunch of punks, across the street."

32. Ibid., p. 2.

33. Ibid. No one attempted to open the door to enable Mascareñas to escape, and no one said it was "all right" for Mascareñas "to go."

34. Richard O'Reilly, "Police Reveal New Version of Slaying in Shootout," *Rocky Mountain News*, March 29, 1973.

35. Snyder hospital interview, p. 2. The conversation Snyder reported with Martinez ("he kept saying, 'Hey man, I don't want any trouble. Just leave me alone, man. I don't want any trouble'") occurred not in the alley, but as Martinez first backed away from Snyder on Downing Street.

36. "Officer Details Shooting Events," *Denver Post*, March 29, 1973.

37. O'Reilly, "Police Reveal New Version of Slaying in Shootout." Jones's statements about a witness are not substantiated by a review of 75 police offense reports or civilians' statements released to defense attorneys. Only one witness, Richard Coltrane, gives an account somewhat similar to that of Jones's purported witness. At 2:40 p.m. on March 20. Coltrane gave Denver police a statement that said, in part, that Snyder and Hogue had "a suspect in the back of the car . . . the suspect jumped out of the car, the right rear door, and ran northeast down Downing Street. I thought I saw the suspect shoot at the policeman. It looked like the suspect had a gun in his right hand. He turned around towards [Snyder]. He pointed the gun at the policeman at about 30 feet away. Then they both went out of my sight." This, however, is not what Snyder (or anyone else except Detective Jones) described.

38. Snyder hospital interview, p. 1.

39. O'Reilly, "Police Reveal New Version of Slaying in Shootout."
40. Snyder hospital interview. p. 2.
41. Ibid., p. 3.
42. Ibid., pp. 3, 4.
43. Ibid., p. 6.
44. Ibid., p. 4. At two places in the transcript the parties appear to stop, then resume, taping. This quotation ends where the second apparent occurs.
45. Photocopy of signed note of Detective Williams to "night crew" Detectives Lohr and Diaz, March 23, 1973.
46. Photocopy of handwritten note to the "night crew" signed by "Joe [Russell] & Lee [Williams]"; from the note's wording, it was apparently written on March 26.
47. Photo copy of Detective Jones's note to the night crew, March 27, 1973.
48. Photo copy of handwritten notes of Detectives Lohr and Callahan during Snyder hospital interview, March 27, 1973.
49. Ibid.
50. "Bullet in Neck Killed Martinez, Ogura Says," *Rocky Mountain News*, March 22, 1973. Additionally, Coroner's Office Investigator David A. Livingston made an initial investigation around 1:15 a.m. on March 17 at the scene where Martinez' body was found. Martinez was pronounced dead by Dr. Ogura, who arrived shortly after Livingston began the investigation, which was then delayed for over an hour by gunfire and the explosion at the apartment of Mario Manuel Vasquez.
51. Snyder hospital interview, pp. 3, 4. Snyder did not explain what he meant, nor did the detectives ask, when he said, "As he fell, I *tripped on the gun* and I pulled his gun out of his hand."
52. Dr. George I. Ogura Denver Department of Health and Hospitals Autopsy Report No. C-117-73: Louis Martinez, March 17, 1973, pp. 1, 2. I paid a search fee on Friday, June 25, 1993, and then found that the original autopsy may no longer exist. I was told that the staff should be able to locate it by the following Monday or Tuesday, June 28 or June 29. I waited until after the Fourth of July holiday to give the staff extra time and called the Coroner's Office on July 5 or July 6. I was told that they could not find the report. The person I yelled at, Michelle, said that the files had been moved; the space for archiving had been reduced; the storage area was flooded twice; the files were in disarray; files sometimes were lost; entire years of autopsies were missing; old files crumbled in their hands; etc. Hours later, I received a call from Michelle. She told me she had spoken with Dr. Ogura, who had a copy of the autopsy in his personal files. She sent me a copy.
53. Detectives T. L. Lohr, P. Diaz, R. C. Callahan, and R. H. Kasperson, Supplementary Report, with entries on March 17 and March 21, 1973. The tests of the crime lab are entered with the date March 21, 1973. This Supplementary Report has no handwritten signature.
54. Gunshots can leave evidence that indicate the proximity of a firearm at the time of its firing. Shots fired at close or intermediate ranges can leave a residue of gunpowder in or near the wounds the gunfire inflicts. The appearance of a

wound also gives clues to forensic pathologists. In general, an entry wound looks smaller and neater than an exit wound, but direct-contact entry wounds can also be large and ragged. An entry wound resulting from a gunbarrel's direct contact with the skull, for example, could be ragged. A non-contact wound on softer flesh is often small and round. In general, pistol shots fired at a distance of more than two feet are unlikely to leave powder traces, and shots fired from closer than two feet usually leave powder traces or powder residue. This commentary, however, does not pretend to be comprehensive.

55. "Autopsy Report Shows Slain Man Drunk," *Rocky Mountain News,* March 20, 1972.

56. "Officer Details Shooting Events." It should be clarified that I did not see Martinez "when he was shot," nor had I said so.

57. Another document, dated two days after Martinez' autopsy and two days before the above-cited Supplementary Report, seems to be linked to the Supplementary Report. In this document Detective G. Schaffer and Sergeant R. Nicoletti wrote, "Holes in [Martinez] knit shirt marked 1 through 6 shows [*sic*] that the weapon was fired at a distance of 2 feet or more. Holes 1 and 2 in [Martinez'] leather jacket shows that the weapon was fired at a distance of 2 feet or more. Hole no. 3 in the leather jacket shows that the weapon was fired at a distance of 2 feet or less." This document is designated as Denver Police Department Firearms Work Sheet, Lab. No. 73-1525, Custodian No. 161620, March 19, 1973. It is hard to decipher the significance of the information because Martinez' clothes were never released by the police. The confusion is increased by another Firearms Work Sheet with the same lab and custodian's number and signed by Schaffer and Nicoletti on the same day. This document showing the results of tests done on Snyder's clothing, seems to contradict Snyder's account of his own shooting. Snyder claimed he thought he was first shot in the side from a distance of 6 to 8 feet and shot the second time, in the leg, while he struggled hand-to-hand with Martinez. In examining Snyder's clothing, Schaffer and Nicoletti found the following: "[Snyder's] shirt lower left stomach shows that the weapon was fired at a distance of 1 foot or less. The right pants leg shows that the weapon was fired at a distance of two feet or more."

58. Roderick P. Durkin, with Anne B. Durkin, "The Real Louis Martinez— Reflections on His Death" (Perspective Section), *Denver Post,* July 10, 1973.

59. Letters of support and condolence came from Washington, D.C., El Paso, Mission, Texas, from Idaho, and from organizations and individuals elsewhere. The letter cited in the narrative was signed by Victor Gerardo Bono, Chairman, Movimiento Organizado Socialista Chicanos de Aztland (MOSCA) at the U.S. Penitentiary at Marion, Illinois, March 25, 1973; reprinted in *El Gallo,* April 1973, p. 14. The letter and poem were signed by Rafael Cancel Miranda, Alberto C. Mares, José Antonio Perez, Victor Bono, Alberto Gudino, Gil Leano, Javier Ramer, Salvador Vasquez, Manuel Estrada, Gumersindo Tony Gomez, Raul Estrada, an Afredo Molina.

60. The Crusade had an ad hoc legal defense committee after the 1970 Los Angeles Moratorium, but its work remained informal until 1973. Among the attorneys who came forward after March 17 were Leonard Davies, Walter Gerash,

Ken Padilla, Stanley Marks, and Rudy Schware, a leading figure in the Denver chapter of the National Lawyers Guild. Others members of the defense team were law students like Carlos Vigil and future Denver mayor Federico Peña. The Crusade's legal defense efforts were remarkably successful, and Gonzales' contributions to this success must not be underestimated. He was the movement's chief figure in Colorado and one of the three most visible national leaders. Many in the organization had referred to him as "El Jefe," the Chief, since the 1968 Poor People's Campaign, a practice he did not discourage. On his shoulders fell the responsibility of being the tactician and strategist, the economic planner, and the lightning rod for hostile forces. His years of experience were invaluable to the Crusade's community organizing success.

The DCLDC's first logo came from a Mexican protest poster produced in the aftermath of the 1968 Tlatelolco massacre in Mexico City, it shows the boots of rifle- and club-wielding men kicking a civilian laying prone in the street. The slogan read, "No Mas Aggresion." Among the DCLDC endorsers were Colegio Jacinto Treviño of Texas, MEChA groups in California and Colorado, Angela Davis, Allen Ginsberg, Dennis Banks, Russell Means, and Clyde Bellecourt of AIM, Mario Obledo of MALDEF, the Puerto Rican Solidarity Committee, the Olga Talamante Defense Committee, Catholic priests Daniel and Philip Berrigan and James Groppi, Cesar Chavez, the Puerto Rican independentista Carlos Feliciano, and many others.

61. "Police Report Sniper Fire," *Denver Post,* May 14, 1973. This shooting was not the first time police were the target of community anger in the aftermath of the March 17 confrontation. Within 24 hours of Martinez' death, the front entrance of the North Denver Police Substation at 22nd Avenue and Decatur Street was bombed, and the North Denver Police Storefront office at 4379 Tejon was fire bombed. Three other locations were fire bombed, including the Coors Distributing Co. at 1280 West 47th Avenue in the Northside. Gonzales was asked if these incidents were linked to Martinez' death. He denied any connection with the Crusade and surmised that the incidents were "acts of God." These incidents are recounted in Moya, "Police Blamed by Chicanos for Shootout on Saturday."

62. Diaz and Sayles were minority officers, and Sayles had been my friend in junior and senior high school. He joined the police force after a brief period of military service from which he was released because his mother was involved in an accident in which another person was killed. He went from being a patrolman to working for the Intelligence Bureau, during which time he was assigned to monitor the Crusade. He then went on to fulfill a goal he had held since his adolescence, becoming an agent for the FBI. The growing number of minority officers in the Denver Police Department is traceable to recruitment drives in response to a court ruling to remedy employment discrimination, following Carole Hogue's 1972 suit against the department. Most minority officers in 1973 were new to the force and had not risen to positions with political and bureaucratic clout. The Crusade felt that many minority cops were drawn to police work (as they had been to the military) because of an inferiority complex and a wish to achieve acceptance by proving their "Americanism."

63. [Ernesto Vigil], "DCLDC News Release," *El Gallo,* May 1973, p. 2.

64. Photos of the sign are found in *El Gallo,* [August] 1973, on pp. 1, 7, and 8.

65. Roman Dueñez, "Luis Ramirez Found Not Guilty," *El Gallo,* August 1973, p. 7.

66. Theresa Romero, "Un Abogado Del Movimiento Chicano," *El Gallo,* November–December 1973–January 1974, p. 11.

67. Contrary to police testimony, the gunman did not fall by the sidewalk, nor did anyone help him into the 1539 Downing apartment.

68. The officer's testimony is found in Reporter's Transcript of Preliminary Hearing, *People of the State of Colorado v. Ernesto Vigil,* Criminal Action no. 69291, May 4, 1973. For reasons best known to Tow and Holt, both testified that only one shot was fired at the gunman. Two shots, not one, were fired, the first as the gunman ran west across Downing Street, and the second as he neared the front of 1539–41 Downing Street.

69. Ibid., p. 22.

70. "Motion to Suppress (Excerpt of Proceedings: Recross-examination of Officer Tow)," *People of the State of Colorado Ernesto Vigil,* Criminal Action no. 69291, November 8, 1973, p. 6.

71. Ibid., pp. 11, 12.

72. Tow's testimony about the leather jacket, or leather coat, was confirmed by SSU Officer David Holt in his testimony.

73. Pinder was one of the targets of the 1967 protest at police headquarters by the Crusade and the Denver Black Panther chapter after he killed an African American man in an Eastside after-hours nightclub. Officer Pringle had infiltrated the Socialist Workers Party and the Young Socialist Alliance for the Denver police after being recruited for the job when he was still in the police academy.

74. Richard O'Reilly, "Jury Acquits Vigil in 30 Seconds," *Rocky Mountain News,* November 24, 1973. The defense team thought Tow gave testimony describing a leather coat to make his identification more credible, and that he was not very imaginative when Gerash pressed him for details at the May 4 preliminary hearing. We felt that he testified about the jacket only because I wore a brown leather jacket at the preliminary hearing. Various witnesses identified various parties as wearing brown jackets or brown leather jackets on the night of the confrontation. Officer Carole Hogue's five-page typed statement of March 17, 1973, says the first person to approach her car Mascareñas, "had on a brown coat, jacket." Another civilian witness, Richard Coltrane, gave a three-page statement to police on March 20, 1973, which states that the gunman shooting at Hogue wore a "brown coat." Further, Mitchell Walker, a 17-year-old party-goer sitting in his truck in the parking lot on the east side of Downing Street, saw the confrontation develop. It was at the rear of his parked truck that the gunman fired at Officer Hogue. Walker's five-page typed statement given to police on March 17, includes a physical description of the gunman that could describe the author ("about 5 feet 10 inches, long, either dark brown or black hair, and he wore glasses"). Walker stated that "the guy in the tan leather jacket reached inside of his jacket and pulled out a gun and started shooting at the police car in which the police woman was driving, and after that I just ducked down." (Walker's description contradicted Coltrane, who told defense investigator Charles Denman on

May 7, 1973, that the gunman was "about 5'2", short curly black hair.") Lastly, Luis Martinez wore a brown leather jacket on the night of his death. Confusion about the roles, identities, and clothing of Martinez, Mascareñas, and the gunman may have been a factor in Officer Tow's swearing I wore a brown leather jacket on March 17.

75. O'Reilly, "Jury Acquits Vigil in 30 Seconds."

76. Whearley and Olsen, "Gun Battle 'Spontaneous'."

77. [Ernesto Vigil], "Racism Prevails in a Courtroom," *El Gallo*, October 1973, p. 2.

78. Among those who noted Bornstein's glee in using the term "dog" was Florencio "Freddy" Granado, who mentioned it in his article, "Vasquez Railroaded," *El Escritor del Pueblo*, October 1973, p. 1.

79. Photocopy of letter of Mary J. Sharpe, Reformatory Records Officer, to Captain Torrey of the Denver County Sheriff's Department, March 25, 1977.

80. Photocopy of letter of Denver Sheriff Captain E. A. Torrey to State Reformatory Warden C. Winston Tanksley; Attention: Ms. Sharpe, April 7, 1977.

81. Taperecording of Ms. Anna Vellar, Colorado Department of Corrections History and Records Supervisor at the Territorial Corrections Facility in Canon City, Colorado, March 29, 1991, approx. 10:00 a.m. This tape also records subsequent calls on the same day to two other Colorado Department of Corrections employees suggested by Ms. Vellar. Ms. Paula Watson and Ms. Judy Sutton.

82. Ibid.

83. Ibid.

84. Ibid.

85. Fred Gillies, George Lane, and John Ashton, "Disputed Denver Shootout Questions Persist," *Denver Post*, April 1, 1973.

86. Other than a handful of documents, Gonzales never shared the entire collection of FBI files with the Crusade membership, including its leadership. The initial FOIA release, some of which he did share at this time, showed, that the FBI used the Internal Revenue Service to audit the Crusade's taxes. Though this was illegal, it was minor harassment compared with what the FBI is known to have done to other groups and individuals.

87. The standard police revolver at that time was the .38 Special, the same caliber Martinez carried. Police testimony revealed that their ammunition carried an extra charge of powder, and this accounts for the louder sound of the second burst of fire. It also confirms part of Snyder's declaration—Martinez fired first.

88. I heard two second-hand accounts of Vasquez' claims, one from Gonzales, but neither fully recounted his tale. My grasp of Vasquez' story was incomplete, and my questions to him after he recanted were paraphrasings to which he responded with one-word answers.

CHAPTER 12. THE CRUSADE, AIM, AND LEONARD PELTIER

1. Jay Whearley and Jack Olsen, "Gun Battle 'Spontaneous,'" *Denver Post*, March 18, 1973.

2. Denver SAC to Acting Director, Letter-head memorandum (LHM) on

American Indian Movement, Extremist Matters—American Indian Activities, January 12, 1973, Bufile 100-462483-253, Denver field office serial 157-529.

3. Omaha FBI field office to Acting Director, January 15, 1973, Bufile document 100-462483-174[?].

4. The January 18, 1973, FBI Domestic Intelligence Division Informative Note bore the initials "EM" and "GCM": Edward Miller, head of the FBI Domestic Intelligence Division, and George C. Moore, who worked in the Racial Intelligence Section.

5. Omaha FBI Nitel to FBI Acting Director L. Patrick Gray, dated February 2, 1973, American Indian Movement—Extremist Matter, OO (Office of Origin): Denver, Bufile 100-462483-233 (copy to Edward Miller).

6. January 30, 1973, Minneapolis field office teletype to Acting Director, FBI, in Bufile 100-462483-208, American Indian Movement (AIM); Extremist Matter—American Indian Activities, Office of Origin: Denver.

7. The Scottsbluff chief of police was the source of the rumor about the "deal" between Chicanos and AIM for 60 tommy guns. By January 30, 1973, the date of the FBI report, the Scottsbluff chief may not have been the most objective source of information. Relations between local police and AIM and its Chicano allies in previous encounters had been less than friendly. Russell Means was charged with carrying a concealed weapon after his arrest. Means claimed that police tossed the weapon in his cell and taunted him to make a run for it. The local newspaper defended police actions and, in response to AIM's allegations of Scottsbluff racism, responded, "The shoe fits and we'll wear it." However, three days later a federal judge ruled in favor of AIM and Chicano defendants and granted a temporary order restraining Scottsbluff authorities from denying minority rights. All charges were later dropped because of illegal police procedures.

8. Rolland Dewing, *Wounded Knee II* (Chadron, Neb.: Great Plains Network, 1995). Dewing's work is based on 25,000 pages of FBI documents released to him under the FOIA. Prof. Dewing's collection is archived at Chadron State College in Chadron, Nebraska. His book, unfortunately, has not been widely read, but it is a fair and very detailed account of the siege at Wounded Knee. His assistance in facilitating access to these FBI records is greatly appreciated.

9. "Wounded Knee Roadblocks Rise Anew," *Rocky Mountain News,* March 13, 1973.

10. Ibid. Federal officials said the declaration of sovereignty might lead them to consider charges of seditious conspiracy against takeover leaders. About 85 supporters had already been arrested. Colburn ordered U.S. marshals, including the SOG, to the Pine Ridge Reservation on February 12, 1973, over two weeks in advance of the Wounded Knee siege.

11. Gebhardt to Felt, March 12, 1973, cited in Dewing, *Wounded Knee II,* p. 82.

12. Sanford J. Ungar, *FBI* (Boston: Little, Brown, 1975), p. 415; Curt Gentry, *J. Edgar Hoover: The Man and the Secrets* (New York: Plume, 1992), pp. 556, 567.

13. Though FBI improprieties and crimes were disclosed because of the scandal that commenced with the Watergate burglary in June 1972, dramatic evidence had surfaced on March 8, 1971, when unknown persons burglarized an FBI office

in Media, Pennsylvania, carted off FBI files, and began to systematically mail copies to the media, politicians, and the activists who were spied upon. An observant reporter became interested in an acronym on one document: COINTELPRO. Subsequent revelations showed that it stood for "counter-intelligence program." All COINTELPROs were coordinated by the FBI Domestic Intelligence Division ("Division Five"), as were most FBI investigations of the Chicano movement. "Counterintelligence" is premised on the assumption that domestic dissidents are knowingly or unknowingly in the service of a hostile foreign power. To counter the enemy, the FBI and similar groups conduct "counterintelligence" efforts. Implicit in this terminology is the logic that those who serve an enemy are themselves the enemy. The FBI's first formal COINTELPRO targeted the Communist Party USA and was the model for subsequent COINTELPROs. The Watergate-related investigations showed that COINTELPROs employed illegal, politically motivated attacks against targets. This, however, does not mean that COINTELPROs were rare aberrations confined to a particular era. The illegal activities associated with COINTELPROs—burglaries, blackmail, illegal wiretaps—are tactics that were employed throughout the history of the FBI. Martin Luther King, Jr., for example, was the victim of such tactics years before the beginning of the Black Nationalist Hate Group COINTELPRO in 1967. Technically speaking, the FBI conducted few "counter intelligence programs" because the Bureau defines such FBI programs as those in which the words "counterintelligence program" are part of the official file caption—for example, the "New Left Counterintelligence Program," the "Black Nationalist Hate Group Counterintelligence Program." By this definition, the Crusade for Justice was not targeted in an FBI "counterintelligence program" because the words are not found on its file caption.

14. Dewing, *Wounded Knee II*, p. 87.

15. Ibid., p. 88.

16. Denver FBI field office "urgent" teletype to Acting Director, copies to Minneapolis, Charlotte [North Carolina], and Pine Ridge, March 18, 1973, Bufile document 176-2404-226, p. 3.

17. Los Angeles FBI field office "urgent" teletype to Acting Director, copies to Denver field office and E. S. Miller of the FBI Domestic Intelligence Division, March 16, 1973, at 4:53 p.m., Bufile document 176-2404-190.

18. FBI Acting Director [by J. C. Gauzen] plaintext teletype to All SAC's and SAC Wounded Knee Command Post (Personal Attention), copies to E. S. Miller, March 19, 1973, in reference to a previous teletype "to all SAC's, [sent] 3/15/73," Bufile document 176-2404-257.

19. Omaha SAC to Acting Director, November 8, 1972, "La Raza Unida" caption, Bufile document 157-8887-39. The FBI document that shows the Denver field office sent the Omaha field office information on Perez is LHM of Omaha SAC to Acting Director, July 21, 1972, under the La Raza Unida caption and serialized as 157-8887-29.

20. Denver LHM to Acting Director, July 9, 1971, "Mexican American Militancy" caption, released with corresponding file serial deleted, and the document subfiled as 157-8887-15 Not Recorded July 12, 1971.

21. Ibid.

22. Legat Mexico City Nitel to Acting Director, August 29, 1972, under "Mexican American Militancy" caption, Bufile document 105-180564-157.

23. Los Angeles FBI field office to Acting Director, November 13, 1972, copies to Denver, San Antonio and Albuquerque, under "Mexican American Militancy" caption, Bufile document 105-180564-165.

24. Legat Mexico City LHM to Acting Director, January 31, 1973, under "Mexican American Militancy" caption and serialized as 105-180564-167.

25. Los Angeles FBI field office Nitel to Acting Director, February 5, 1973, captioned "Rally Sponsored by Committee to Free Los Tres . . . Los Angeles, California . . . 2/5/73, Internal Security—SA, [Office of Origin]: Los Angeles." The Los Angeles serial number was 105-34112, and the Bufile document number seems to be 100–0-44268.

26. The document showing Gonzales' attendance at the Chavez-Ortiz dance is a report of the Denver field office on Rodolfo Gonzales covering November 21, 1972, to March 6, 1973. It is serialized as 105-176910-61, but Gonzales' name is blanked out. Copies were sent to four military intelligence bodies, to San Antonio and Los Angeles field offices, to Bureau headquarters, and to the CIA. As its references for these reports, the Denver field office cites six FBI documents with information on Gonzales' activity or related investigations. Two documents originate in Denver, one in Mexico City, and three in Los Angeles. All references to Gonzales' name are deleted and only the serial number reveals that it is the FBI Bufile on him. Most periodic reports sent by the FBI to Bureau headquarters show that the reports are sent to headquarters within a week or less of the last day cited under the box on the report forms that designates "Investigative Period." This report, however, was mailed two weeks and one day after March 6, 1973—on March 21, 1973. No mention of the March 17 confrontation is found in the highly censored copy.

27. Denver field office to Director with Denver serial 157-529 (P), dated March 5, 1974, captioned "Dennis James Banks; Russell Charles Means; American Indian Movement. EM [Extremist Matter]—AIM," Bufile document 105-178283 Not Recorded March 11, 1974.

28. Ibid. This Denver teletype refers to a previous February 26, 1974, teletype, captioned "Proposed Rally in Solidarity with the Crusade for Justice, Denver, Colorado, March 17, 1974; EX [Extremist Matter]—Potential Civil Unrest." The copy of the latter document—Bufile document 105-178283-85—released by the FBI shows it was sent by the Denver FBI to 12 other field offices, FBI headquarters, the CIA, State Department, and others. The teletype is composed of 102 sentences, 83 of which were blacked out.

29. Minneapolis field office "urgent" teletype to Director, under Minneapolis serial 157-3656, dated March 8, 1974, with handwritten "G. C. Moore" as one of the Bureau Supervisors who read the document, and serialized as Bufile document 105-178283-87 Not Recorded March 14, 1974.

30. Peter Matthiessen, *In the Spirit of Crazy Horse,* (New York: Penguin Books, 1991), p. 123.

31. Among the other speakers at the event were Fernanda Navarro, a Mexican representative who brought a taped solidarity message from Hortensia de Al-

lende, Ramon Arbona, Mrs. Ann Chavez, the mother of Junior Martinez, attorney William Kunstler, Russell Means of AIM, Bert Corona, Mario Cantu, Jaime Rodriguez, and Ricardo Longoria, Denver director of the United Farm Workers. At the rally at the State Capitol, written statements of solidarity were read from Juan José Peña of the New Mexico LRUP; the Eugene Coalition of Eugene, Oregon; the Committee to Defend Carlos Feliciano, from New York; Cesar Chavez; James Larson, president of the National Lawyers Guild; the Teatro Campesino, from California; Angela Davis; the San Quentin Six Defense Committee; Escuela Antonio José Martinez in Montezuma, New Mexico; the Houston 12 Defense Committee; and the Survival of American Indians Association, from Tacoma, Washington. Three hundred people attended a solidarity rally in Albuquerque, New Mexico, heard speakers Petra Jimenez and Margaret Garcia, and saw a performance by El Teatro del Norte.

32. Matthiessen, *In the Spirit of Crazy Horse*, p. 249.

33. "Luis Martinez Remembered: Unity Keys March 17ᵗʰ Rally," *La Cucaracha*, April 1977, p. 13.

CHAPTER 13. CONFLICTS, DEATHS, AND INDICTMENTS, 1973–1974

1. "Chicano Community Activists in the State of Colorado Continue to Be Special Targets of Police Repression," *El Gallo*, May–June 1974, p. 5.

2. A brief article on Avila's trial and acquittal is found in "Avila Acquitted," *El Gallo*, September 16, 1974, p. 3.

3. "Justicia Para los Estudiantes," *El Gallo*, October–November 1974, p. 8.

4. Ibid. For the Pueblo activists' negotiations with school officials for parity of employment for Chicano teachers, see "Pueblo Walkouts," *El Gallo*, December 1974, p. 4.

5. Ibid.

6. "Monte Vista," *El Gallo*, May–June, 1974, p. 2.

7. "Si Chingan Con Mi Hermano, Chingan Conmigo," *El Gallo*, July–August 1974, p. 13.

8. "Law Students Push(ed) Out?" *El Gallo*, May–June 1974, p. 3. Law students who signed the statement were Margaret Martinez, David Cordova, Juan Vigil, Ernie Lopez, Daniel Anchondo, Doug Vasquez, Bob Romero, Carlos Vigil, and Jacob Pacheco.

9. "Chicano Students Confront UCMC," *El Gallo*, May–June 1974, p. 2.

10. Ibid.

11. "Editorial," *El Gallo*, September 16, 1974, p. 2.

12. Pat Bray, "7 Chicano Activists Arrested in Library Ceremony Fracas," *Denver Post*, September 13, 1973. Two additional people were cited after the initial seven arrests. All charges were subsequently dropped.

13. Ibid.

14. Ibid. See also "Gonzales' Daughter Arrested," *Denver Post*, September 19, 1973.

15. *Rocky Mountain News*, September 13, 1973.

16. Denver Police Department Intelligence Bureau Officers McGuire, Kennedy, Wattles, and Mollohan, two-page typed Intelligence Information Sheet re "Sniping Activity Involving Militants," February 12, 1975.

17. Miguel Enriquez Brigade of the People's United Liberation Army of America, "To the Workers, the Farmers, and the Exploited and Oppressed Peoples of the Americas," *El Gallo*, January–February 1975, p. 11. Vásquez Rojas and Cabañas were Mexican teachers from southern Mexico, an area rich with revolutionary tradition, the land of Zapata, Ruben Jaramillo, and other agrarian martyrs. Vasquez Rojas and Cabañas were radicalized in Mexican social reform movements. These guerrilla groups saw themselves as part of a greater revolutionary movement aiming to free Latin America from foreign economic and political domination. They found inspiration in the ideals and examples of José Maria Morelos, Simon Bolivar, José Artigas, Tupac Amaru, Augusto César Sandino, Bernardo O'Higgins, José Marti, and Ernesto "Che" Guevara.

18. "CIA Regional Member's House Bombed: The First Direct Attack on a CIA Person," *El Gallo*, May–June 1975, p. 11.

19. Teran's poem "Aztlan Esta De Luto" is found in *El Gallo*, July–August 1974, p. 5.

20. "Woman Tied to Blast Seized with Timing Device," *Rocky Mountain News*, June 1, 1974; "We Will Endure" and "Aztlan Esta de Luto," *El Gallo*, July–August 1974, pp. 3.

21. Ernesto Vigil, "Aztlan Esta De Luto: H. Teran," *El Gallo*, July–August 1974, p. 3.

22. Letter of solidarity, undated, Eugene Coalition Liberation Support Movement to the Crusade for Justice, accompanied by a June 9, 1974, letter addressed to "The Colorado Ruling Class," reprinted in *El Gallo*, July–August 1974, p. 6.

23. "U. S. Gov't vs Chicano People: Chicanos Win!" *El Gallo*, July–August 1974, p. 16.

24. Complaint, United Mexican American Students; Crusade for Justice, Inc., a non-profit Corporation; Denver Chicano Liberation Committee; John Espinoza; Judy Sandoval; Freida Bugarin, Rita Carmen Montero, Plaintiffs, v. R. G. Breese, Lopez, Rodriguez, individually and as agents for the Bureau of Alcohol, Tobacco, and Firearms of the United States Department of Treasury, John Doe - 1 and other John Does . . . as agents for the [ATF]; Richard Roe - 1 and Richard Roes . . . as detectives of the University of Colorado, Boulder, Colorado; William Simon . . . Secretary of the Treasury of the United States; Rex Davis . . . Director [ATF]; William Gaunt [as ATF Regional Director]; William Saxby . . . Attorney General of the United States; James Treece . . . United States Attorney for the District of Colorado, Defendants, Civil Action No. 74-W-604 in the United States District Court for the District of Colorado, filed July 11, 1974. Although five women were issued subpoenas, the subpoena for Patricia Alcantar was dropped for medical reasons before the court date.

25. Ibid. John Espinoza's July 10, 1974, affidavit served as Exhibit A of the above-cited complaint.

26. Ibid.

27. Ibid. Judy Sandoval's July 10, 1974 affidavit served as Exhibit B of the above-cited complaint.

28. Dale Tooley, *I'd Rather Be in Denver: Dale Tooley's Own Story* (Denver: Colorado Legal Publishing Co., 1985), p. 149.

29. Frank Moya, "Bomb Recipient, Crusade for Justice Connection Traced," *Rocky Mountain News,* January 15, 1974.

30. Ibid.

31. Ibid.

32. "Crusade Threatens News with $10 Million Libel Suit," *El Gallo,* November–December 1973/January 1974, p. 2.

33. MALDEF Press Release, *El Gallo,* November-December 1973/January 1974, p. 2.

34. "National Lawyers Guild [Denver Chapter] Press Release," *El Gallo,* November–December 1973/January 1974, p. 2.

35. Draft of Complaint of Crusade for Justice, a Colorado non-profit corporation, Escuela Tlatelolco, a Colorado non-profit corporation, and Rodolfo Gonzales, Plaintiffs, v. The Denver Publishing Company, a Colorado corporation doing business as *The Rocky Mountain News,* Defendant. The draft available to the author is not signed or dated.

36. "Court Calendar," *El Gallo,* February–March 1974, p. 11; "Court Calendar for August and September," *El Gallo,* July–August 1974, p. 14.

37. "Garrison Case on Sept. 16," *El Gallo,* July–August 1974, p. 14.

38. Numerous editions of *El Gallo* chronicled the Garrison case as it went through its various delays and changes of venue. See "Garrison: Change of Venue," *El Gallo,* October–November 1974, p. 7; "Colorado Cases," *El Gallo,* December 1974, p. 8; "Support Gary Garrison," *El Gallo,* January–February 1975, p. 3; "Garrison Court Case," *El Gallo,* July 1975, p. 2.

CHAPTER 14. THE CONSPIRACY CASE AGAINST JOHN
HARO

1. "Big Dynamite Bomb Seized, Two Men Held," *Rocky Mountain News,* September 19, 1975. In this article, Capt. Robert Shaughnessy stated that "twenty police officers, four police intelligence detectives, and eight federal Alcohol, Tobacco, and Firearms (ATF) agents were working on various aspects of the operation."

2. Notarized affidavit of Varolin Joseph John Cordova, Sr., August 2, 1977, p. 10.

3. Cindy Parmenter, "Grenade Plans Disclosed," *Denver Post,* December 5, 1975.

4. Dale Tooley, *I'd Rather Be in Denver: Dale Tooley's Own Story* (Denver: Colorado Legal Publishing Co., 1985), p. 126.

5. "Police Ask Special Prosecutor in Slaying," *Rocky Mountain News,* January 28, 1975. Tooley called the demonstration "an understandable emotional response."

6. Tyus' testimony is found in Transcriber's Transcript, *People of the State of Colorado v. Juan Haro and Anthony Quintana,* December 4, 1975, Criminal Action No. 92797, pp. 257, 258. (Hereafter cited as "Tyus testimony.")

7. Ibid.

8. Frank Moya, "Informant in Alleged Bomb Plot Taped Talks," *Rocky Mountain News, September 28, 1975.*

9. Captain Shaughnessy's testimony before Judge L. P. Weadick on September 12, 1975, is found in the Transcriber's Transcript, *People of the State of Colorado v. Juan Haro and Anthony Quintana,* Criminal Action No. 92797, p. 23. (Hereafter cited as Shaughnessy testimony.)

10. Frank Moya, "Informer, Denver Police Implicated in Burglary," *Rocky Mountain News,* September 30, 1975.

11. Shaughnessy testimony, September 22, 1975, p. 14.

12. Frank Moya, "Police Informant's 1969 Insanity Plea an Issue Again," *Rocky Mountain News,* December 7, 1975.

13. Maria Subia, DCLDC Letter to Supporters, September 25, 1975.

14. Jay Whearley and Sandra Dillard, "Dynamite Bomb Found in Car: Three Arrested," *Denver Post,* September 18, 1975.

15. "Police Cancel Search for Car," *Denver Post,* September 25, 1975.

16. Tyus testimony, pp. 164, 243.

17. Ibid., p. 172.

18. Cindy Parmenter, "Grenade Plans Discussed," *Denver Post,* December 6, 1975.

19. Moya, "Informant in Alleged Bomb Plot Taped Talks."

20. Frank Moya, "Denver Police Also Watched Informant in Restaurant Burglary," *Rocky Mountain News,* October 1, 1975, p. 16; Moya, "Informer, Denver Police Implicated in Burglary."

21. Tyus testimony, p. 134.

22. Copy of May 13, 1975, offense report of Weld County Sheriff Lt. Clyde Bennetts, found in Weld County D. A. Robert Miller's May 14, 1975, Motion to Dismiss, *State of Colorado v. Newton J. McVickers,* Criminal Case No. 9358.

23. Letter, Chief Art Dill (actually written by Thomas E. Rowe) to Weld County Sheriff Ernest D. Bower, May 19, 1975. One month after writing the letter on Chief Dill's behalf, Rowe retired from the Denver Police Department after 27 years. Like many others involved in cases against Crusade members, his career involved work with the Intelligence Bureau. Rowe's career began in 1948, and he was a sergeant with the Intelligence Bureau in 1959. By 1972 he was chief of the Investigations Division, and a 1975 article on his retirement credited him with reorganizing the Crimes Against Person's section of the Investigations Division. Detectives from the aforementioned bureau, section, and division figured prominently in the controversies and trials involving police and Crusade members. See Spence Conley, "Denver Consolidates Three Police Bureaus," *Rocky Mountain News,* August 30, 1959; Al Knight, "Evidence Indicates Price of Police Informers Heavy," *Rocky Mountain News,* December 19, 1972; and "Police Captain Rowe Ends Long Service," *Denver Post,* June 20, 1975.

24. Weld County D. A. Robert Miller, unsigned Synopsis Report from the Motion to Dismiss, *People of the State of Colorado v. Newton McVickers.*

25. Moya, "Informer, Denver Police Implicated in Burglary."

26. Frank Moya, "Bomb Case Informant Faces Burglary Charge," *Rocky Mountain News,* October 2, 1975.

27. Though the Crusade for Justice was extremely skeptical about and critical of the news media, *Rocky Mountain News* reporter Frank Moya reported extensively on the Haro trial and wrote numerous articles on the Denver Police Department's dubious relationship with Joseph Cordova, Jr. These articles exposed the details of Cordova's criminal involvements and served somewhat to counterbalance the repeated publication of inaccurate information about the Haro case. Moya was the Chicano reporter who gained access to Crusade representatives for an exclusive interview on the March 17 confrontation in which Luis Martinez was killed (see Chapter 11). At the time, the Crusade wrongly suspected Moya of deliberate deception. Moya left journalism and now practices law in Denver. Among his many excellent articles on Cordova and the Denver police for the *Rocky Mountain News* are: "Informer, Denver Police Implicated in Burglary," September 30, 1975; "Denver Police Also Watched Informant in Restaurant Burglary," October 1, 1975; "Bomb Case Informant Faces Burglary Charge," October 2, 1975; "Police Informant Admits Shooting, but Is Not Charged," November 16, 1975; "Witness Testifies About Threat Against Tavern Owner," November 21, 1975; "Special Prosecutor Demanded on Cordova," *Rocky Mountain News,* November 26, 1975; "Police Informant's 1969 Insanity Plea an Issue Again," December 7, 1975; "'Victim' in Cordova Case Ready to Testify," December 12, 1975.

28. Tyus testimony, p. 172.

29. [Ernesto Vigil], "Juan in Kangaroo Court," *El Gallo,* undated pp. 2, 3. This *El Gallo* was a special edition and bears no date, but was published in late February or early March 1976.

30. [Ernesto Vigil], "DCLDC Appeals 6 Year Sentence," *El Gallo* January–February 1976, p. 1; Frank Moya, "Haro Attorneys Claim Trial Witness Lied," *Rocky Mountain News,* February 14, 1976.

31. The Crusade had long assumed that its relationship with AIM was the subject of intelligence gathering by the federal government, but no documentary evidence was then available to the Crusade to prove this point. The AR-15 rifle that was recovered in Kansas and purportedly used in the death of the two FBI agents in the summer of 1975 in South Dakota served as evidence to convict AIM member Leonard Peltier. FBI documents obtained by defense attorneys subsequent to Peltier's conviction showed that the AR-15 could not in fact be linked to the AR-15 shell casing found at the scene of the agents' deaths, though that link was crucial to the government's case. The Peltier case is the subject of Peter Matthiessen's *In the Spirit of Crazy Horse* (New York: Penguin, 1992).

32. Appellant's Opening Brief—Consolidated Appeal, *United States of America (Plaintiff-Appellee) v. John Haro (Defendant-Appellant),* Case No. 77-1263, May 12, 1977, p. 3.

33. Ibid., pp. 4, 5. Cordova's admission occurred on April 9, 1976.

34. "Forced Change of Venue," *El Gallo,* August 1976, p. 11.

35. Jack Olsen, Jr., "Judge Disqualifies Himself in Haro Trial," *Rocky Mountain News,* January 14, 1977.

36. "Judge Moves Bomb-plot Trial to Akron," *Rocky Mountain News,* December 10, 1976.

37. Cindy Parmenter, "Judge Won't Shift Haro Trial," *Denver Post,* January 5, 1977.

38. Cindy Parmenter, "Judge to Review Haro Trial Site," *Denver Post,* January 11, 1977.

39. Jack Olsen, Jr., "'Vigilante' Report Threatens Haro Trial," *Rocky Mountain News,* January 11, 1977.

40. Moya, "Bomb Case Informant Faces Burglary Charge."

41. Moya, "Witness Testifies About Threat Against Tavern Owner."

42. Moya, "Police Informant Admits Shooting, but Is Not Charged."

43. Ibid.

44. Jonathan Dedmon, "Expected Witness Brings Tight Security," *Rocky Mountain News,* November 19, 1975.

45. Frank Moya, "Special Prosecutor Wanted to Study Police–Cordova Ties," *Rocky Mountain News,* November 19, 1975.

46. Moya, "Special Prosecutor Demanded on Cordova."

47. Ibid.

48. "Moya, 'Victim' in Cordova Case Ready to Testify."

49. Cindy Parmenter, "Informant Admits Suggesting Bomb," *Denver Post,* March 2, 1977.

50. Tooley, *I'd Rather Be in Denver,* p. 149.

51. Parmenter, "Informant Admits Suggesting Bomb."

52. Anthony Polk, "Charges Against Activist Quintana Are Dismissed," *Rocky Mountain News,* April 12, 1977.

53. Cindy Parmenter, "Haro Acquitted of Bomb-Plot Charges," *Denver Post,* April 2, 1977.

54. Anthony Polk, "Haro Is Acquitted of All Plot Charges," *Rocky Mountain News,* April 2, 1977.

55. Ibid.

56. Parmenter, "Haro Acquitted of Bomb-Plot Charges."

57. Richard Johnson, "Ex-'Supercop' Puts It in Writing," *Denver Post,* July 2, 1990.

58. Sharon Stewart, "Cinquanta Under Probe Again in Alleged Assault," *Rocky Mountain News,* July 9, 1981.

59. Ibid.

60. Johnson, "Ex-'Supercop' Puts It in Writing."

61. John G. White, "Zealot on a Tightrope," *Denver Magazine,* May 1978, p. 38.

62. Notarized affidavit of Varolin Joseph John Cordova, Sr., August 2, 1977. (Hereafter referred to as Varolin Cordova, Sr., affidavit.) The quotations from Mr. Cordova, Sr., are found on various pages of his affidavit, but the ellipses in this passage often represent pauses in his statement as well as deleted material. The DCLDC showed the affidavit to Rodolfo Gonzales and discussed the advisability of calling upon the father to give evidence. An obvious concern was his reliability as a witness. Would he repeat his statement or would he change his mind and denounce the Crusade, saying, for example, that the Crusade had bribed or threatened him to make the statement? Was he emotionally fit? And what about

the felony charges for which he claimed to have been recently arrested? Though his statement seemed to give detailed information about his son's involvement with police, details the Crusade surmised to be true, was this another set-up? The Crusade doubted the wisdom of calling upon an emotionally distraught person like Cordova, Sr., but met with John Haro before making the decision. Haro's filling station business was mired in deep financial problems, and he was experiencing domestic problems as well. At the meeting he was glum and said little. He asked almost no questions about the elder Cordova's statement before rejecting the idea of pursuing the matter.

63. Varolin, Cordova, Sr., affidavit, p. 9.

64. Ibid., p. 11.

65. Ibid., p. 17.

66. Statement of Joseph Cordova, Jr., to ATF Agent Charles Baylor, September 18, 1975, p. 8.

67. Ibid.

68. Tyus testimony, p. 207.

CHAPTER 15. THE SYSTEM WEATHERS THE STORM

1. Though the Crusade referred to the law enforcement communique as a "memo," it was technically a "bulletin."

2. [Rodolfo Gonzales], "Attempted Murder by Proxy," *El Gallo*, July 1976, pp. 1, 2, 9. A copy of the memo accompanied p. 2.

3. Quoted in Bruce Johansen and Roberto Maestas, *Wasi'chu: The Continuing Indian Wars* (New York: Monthly Review Press, 1979), pp. 46–48.

4. Ibid.

5. Steve Henson, transcript of "Steve Henson Report," Pueblo KCSJ, February 12, 1976.

6. "Gonzales Denies Plotting Murder of Police," *El Gallo*, July 1976, p. 2.

7. Bill McBean, "Dynamite theft Triggers Riot Concerns," *Sun* (Colorado Springs), July 2, 1976.

8. Ibid.

9. "Police Warned of 'Kill a Cop a Day' Conspiracy," *Sun*, (Colorado Springs), July 2, 1976. Though the exact source of the "Kill a Cop a Day" bulletin was never ascertained, it may have been related to comments made by Douglass Durham, who appeared before the Internal Security Subcommittee of the U.S. Senate on April 6, 1976. Durham, a former Des Moines policeman and FBI infiltrator, claimed that for AIM, "any patriotic symbol in the United States would be an immediate target for attack" during the Bicentennial. After being uncovered as a police spy, Durham testified before the Internal Security Committee and then went on a speaking tour sponsored by the John Birch Society. For more on Durham see Johansen and Maestas, *Wasi'chu;* "Profile of an Informer," *Covert Action Intelligence Bulletin*, no. 24 (Summer 1985): 18–21.

10. David J. Garrow, *The FBI and Martin Luther King, Jr.* (New York: Penguin Books, 1981), pp. 264n–268n. FBI agents do more than investigate violations of federal law and arrest felons. They are involved in political intelligence

gathering (i.e., spying), and their desire for anonymity makes information about their careers and backgrounds hard to find. Rosack seems to have served in Bureau headquarters or the Washington field office early in his career and worked in the Chicago and New York field offices, important postings for someone climbing the FBI career ladder, until 1960. Rosack's transfer to Denver is reported in "FBI Chief in Denver Office Is Being Transferred," *Rocky Mountain News,* July 17, 1975.

11. [Gonzales], "Attempted Murder by Proxy," p. 1.

12. "Teletype Radical (6/29/76)," *El Gallo,* July 1976, pp. 2, 9. This radio or television news script from Lubbock, Texas, was obtained by the Crusade and printed verbatim in *El Gallo.* The reporter is identified in *El Gallo* only as "Richard Griffing, News 28."

13. "Police Call Off Warning About Plot," *El Gallo,* July 1976, p. 2. This article was a United Press International release and was clipped and reprinted in *El Gallo* without its original date of publication.

14. Robert Ostmann, Jr., "'Kill a Copy a Day' Plot Reported; Police Wary," *Detroit Free Press,* June 21, 1976.

15. J. Herbert Smith, "State Police Error Alerts Others to 'Plot,'" *Hartford Courant,* August 12, 1976.

16. See George O'Toole, "America's Secret Police," *Penthouse,* December 1976, for a listing of police departments whose intelligence units belong to LEIU.

17. For more on the LEIU, see George O'Toole, *The Private Sector: Rent-a-Cops, Private Spies, and the Police-Industrial Complex* (New York: W. W. Norton, 1978), pp. 127–48, quotations from pp. 127, 132.

18. Vernon Bellecourt was the leader of the Denver AIM chapter until shortly before the siege at Wounded Knee. His growing responsibilities took him away from the Denver area, and his place was taken by Vince Harvier and Jess Large. In the aftermath of Wounded Knee, many AIM leaders were tied up in court and some internal disputes affected the Denver AIM chapter. Two younger men, Harold Fobb, a Choctaw-Seminole, and Frank Dillon, a Lakota, assumed leadership and opted to use the name "Colorado Warrior Society" in order to sidestep some of the internal AIM problems.

19. Peter Matthiessen, *In the Spirit of Crazy Horse* (New York: Penguin Books, 1991), p. 307.

20. *New York Times,* August 1, 1976, as cited in Johansen and Maestas, *Wasi'chu,* p. 51.

21. The Crusade also distrusted the Mexican government, dominated by the Partido Revolucionario Institucional (PRI), and viewed its corruption as symptomatic of dependency. Government jobs in Mexico were a source of "stable" employment, and jobholders often used their authority to enrich themselves while neglecting their duties. Crusade leaders noted that the CIA knew that Luis Echeverria would be Mexico's president before the Mexican public voted for him in a PRI-controlled election. Echeverria had served as a "liaison contact" for Mexico City's CIA station and was referred to by the CIA cryptonym LITEMPO-14. For Echeverria and the CIA, see Philip Agee, *Inside the Company: CIA Diary* (New York: Bantam Books, 1976), p. 522. By October 1966 the CIA knew that Luis Echeverria would be Mexico's president in 1970.

22. "CCR Interview," *El Gallo,* August–October 1977, p. 6.

23. Ibid.

24. "3,000 Protest KKK" and "KKK Racists to Begin Border Patrol," *El Gallo,* November 1977, pp. 3, 6.

25. An Additional More Definitive Statement Based on Defendants' Investigation, Tom Metzger in Propia Persona for the Defense, *Margaret Navarro et al., Plaintiffs. v. David Duke et al., Defendants,* Civil No. 77–0676-S, filed in the U.S. District Court in the Southern District of California, February 6, 1978.

26. Answer and Affidavits of Tom Metzger and Kathleen Metzger and a Supplementary More Definitive Statement and Exhibits and Points in Opposition of Plaintiffs' Motion to Dismiss, *Navarro et al. v. Duke et al.,* undated.

27. "The Hannigan Torture Case," *El Gallo,* January 1979, p. 4.

28. "National Protest March Against the Militarization of the Border," *El Gallo,* February–March 1979, p. 4. The El Paso–Juárez area, like San Diego–Tijuana, has long been a major entry point for Mexican immigrants and figured prominently in INS plans to restrict such entry. Chicano activists participated in a protest on the El Paso–Juárez border in March 1979 after 150 Mexican workers were deported on March 9 on charges of having illegal or fraudulent border-crossing cards. It was later admitted that only 11 of the border-crossing cards were invalid. These workers, mostly women employed as maids in El Paso, initiated the protest by stopping traffic on the bridge crossing from Juárez to El Paso. Protests at the border blocked traffic over the weekend. An estimated 500 Juárez residents participated on the Mexican side, and about 75 Chicano sympathizers protested on the El Paso side, including Chicanos Unidos and other community organizations. American flags were taken down from the international bridge and thrown into the river. See "El Paso–Juarez Bridge Unblocked," *Rocky Mountain News,* March 12, 1979.

29. "Message from Andres Figueroa: 'I Ask of the Movements . . . ,'" *El Gallo,* August–October 1977, p. 3.

30. "Rally at Marion, Illinois Prison," *El Gallo,* November 1977, p. 15.

31. Gilberto Jasso, "The World Is Watchful of U.S. Govt. Permissiveness of Massive Constitutional Violations and Terrorism Against Hispanics in America," *Chicano National Immigration Tribunal Documentation Submitted to Be Presented to U.S. President Reagan and Mexico's Presidente Portillo,* San Diego, Calif., April 11, 1981.

32. [Ernesto Vigil], "Prisoners Sue Canon City," *El Gallo,* October––November 1979, p. 3.

33. Ibid.

34. [Ernesto Vigil], "Cellhouse 3: A Hell," *El Gallo,* July 1977, p. 6.

35. Ibid.

36. [Ernesto Vigil], "Lucero Murderer Still Free," *El Gallo,* July 1977, pp. 2, 15.

37. [Ernesto Vigil], "Two Killed in Park Didn't Fire at Police," *El Gallo,* July 1977, four-page unnumbered insert.

38. Ibid.

39. [Ernesto Vigil], "Police Terrorism," *El Gallo,* July 1978, pp. 2, 10.

40. [Ken Padilla], "Police Shoot Hand-cuffed Youth", *El Gallo,* February–March 1979, p. 2, 11.

41. George Kelly, *The Old Gray Mayors of Denver* (Boulder: Pruett, 1974), pp. 130–31.

42. [Ernesto Vigil], "Justice for Joey Rodriguez," *El Gallo,* June–July 1979, p. 2.

43. Ken Padilla, "Open Letter to Tooley," *El Gallo,* June–July 1979, pp. 2, 4.

44. "Chicano Beaten to Death in Jail" and "Chicanos Demonstrate at Jail," *El Gallo,* June 1972, p. 4.

CHAPTER 16. WITCH HUNTS AND GRAND JURIES

1. Peña's account is from Affidavit of Alfredo E. Peña, subscribed and sworn January 9, 1978.

2. Affidavit of Kenneth Padilla Regarding Meeting with FBI Agents, subscribed and sworn January 20, 1978.

3. Affidavit of Ernesto Vigil re Grand Jury Subpoena of Stephen John Lucero, subscribed and sworn January 25, 1978.

4. Affidavit of Hilbert Martinez, January 19, 1978.

5. Affidavit of Richard E. Tapia, undated copy. It was my responsibility, as DCLDC co-chairperson, to coordinate the legal defense effort for the Luceros. The DCLDC taped interviews with Hilbert Martinez, Richard Tapia, and others, which were then transcribed as affidavits and signed. The Martinez and Tapia interviews were particularly interesting because both were also questioned by the FBI about a cache of explosives supposedly found by Denver police in a burial crypt at Riverside Cemetery around the spring of 1977. The local newspapers gave prominent coverage to this discovery. My parents, siblings, maternal grandparents, and second-born child are buried at Riverside Cemetery; most of them about a hundred yards away from where the explosives were supposedly "found." The crypt can be seen from where most of my relatives are buried. The cemetery is about a quarter mile from where I lived at the time. It was a quiet, tree-shaded place with winding dirt roads. I used to jog there before the police "discovery" of the explosives. After the sensational publicity, the police became quickly and curiously quiet about it. They never mentioned it again, and I quit jogging at Riverside Cemetery.

6. The FALN exploded bombs in mid-October 1977 in New York City, and *Time* magazine published a strange article by James Willwerth shortly thereafter. "Dynamite used by the FALN has been traced to thefts from construction sites in Colorado and New Mexico," the article noted. And: "Puerto Rican terrorism tends to be a family enterprise." Willwerth purported to have interviewed a "former terrorist from a similar [to the FALN] terrorist group." This "Puerto Rican familiar with FALN tactics" was "'Jose,' a muscular, mustachioed sometime terrorist who now lives in Colorado." Jose was allegedly "sent to Cuba to learn guerrilla tactics." Further, "among other jobs, he was involved in the murder of an informer." He was now "retired." This "retired" terrorist/murderer somehow chose Colorado as his new home. The number of Puerto Ricans in Colorado is

very small; they are probably outnumbered by Guatemalans and Salvadoreños. The 1980 census indicates that 0.5 percent of Colorado Latinos reported Puerto Rico as their place of birth, yet Willwerth somehow found one who was a "retired" terrorist/murderer and was willing to talk. A number of questions come to mind. How did Willwerth find this terrorist in Colorado? Who made the introductions? Didn't "Jose" fear arrest for murder, a capital crime with no statute of limitations? Maybe Jose came to Colorado to enjoy the ski slopes at Aspen or Vail on a terrorist "retirement" pension. The story seemed completely implausible, as if taken from a bad Hollywood movie on the terrorist underground. See James Willwerth, "Forecast: More Bombs Ahead. A Former Puerto Rican Terrorist Talks," *Time*, October 24, 1977, pp. 39–40.

7. Crusade for Justice Press Statement, December 29, 1977.

8. [Ernesto Vigil], Denver Chicano Liberation Defense Committee letter to supporters, January 23, 1978.

9. Frank Donner, *The Age of Surveillance* (New York: Knopf, 1980), p. 356.

10. Ibid., p. 364.

11. Affidavit of Van Sy Lucero, subscribed and sworn January 20, 1978. Van Lucero's affidavit listed the following dates as those during which he detected phone monitoring: March 12, 15, and 17, 1973; March 13–20, 1974; October 30, 1974; September 14, 15, 16, and 17, 1975; June 28–July 3, 1976; "on or about the second of December [of 1977]"; December 4, 6, and 31, 1977; and January 12, 1978.

12. Affidavit of Steve J. Lucero, subscribed and sworn January 20, 1978.

13. Attorneys Kenneth A. Padilla and Robert Bloom for Van and Steve Lucero, Verified Motion to Quash Subpoena for Abuse of Grand Jury Process, subscribed and sworn January 20, 1978.

14. Statement of Alberto C. Mares at press conference, Servicios de La Raza, June 21, 1982, 10 a.m. (Hereafter cited as Mares press conference statement.)

15. The account of Alberto Mares' prison activism is constructed from a 23-page handwritten chronology of events that is, in turn, based on the extensive files Mares maintains. This prudent practice goes back to habits he developed as a jailhouse lawyer.

16. Mares press conference statement.

17. Denver FBI SAC to FBI Director Clarence M. Kelley, October 24, 1975, Albert[o] Conrad Mares—Subversive Matter, Denver FBI File no. 100-12441 and FBI Headquarters File no. 100-484144, p. 1.

18. Undated copy of Affidavit of Anna Mares on behalf of Van and Steve Lucero, approximately January 1978.

19. Affidavit of Hector L. Subia on behalf of Van and Steve Lucero, January 20, 1978.

20. Attorney Kenneth Padilla's file on Alberto Mares, now in Mares' possession. One typewritten page captioned "Documentation of Telephone Disorders Which Led to Suspicion That Telephone Conversations at the Residence of Alberto Mares Are Being and Have Been Monitored Through Wire Taps, Bugs, or Other Means for Over Three Months to the Present," dated December 13, 1977.

21. Padilla file on Alberto Mares. Memorandum, December 7, 1977. Among

the numerous Crusade witnesses who expected to testify on his behalf were Antonio and Josefina Salinas, Arturo "Bones" Rodriguez, Nita Marquez (Gonzales), Shirley Castro, and Roberto Luera.

22. Alberto Mares' letter delivered to the Crusade for Justice after his flight from Denver, published as "Message to the People," El Chicano Boxing, the magazine of the Colorado Recreation and Boxing Coaches Association (CRBCA), approximately February 1978.

23. Affidavit of FBI Agent Walter F. Scott, February 16, 1982.

24. Mares, "Message to The People."

25. Letter of Kenneth Padilla to Nita Marquez (Gonzales), Re: United States v. Albert Conrad Mares Criminal Action No. 77-CR-298 on November 12, 1971; and Criminal Case No. 77-CR-298 Motion and Order to Dismiss of Assistant U.S. Attorney Jerome C. Ramsey on October 14, 1981.

26. William D. Graves, Chief U.S. Probation Officer, to Mrs. Audrey A. Kaslow, Regional Commissioner, U.S. Parole Commission, 330 Primrose Road—5th Floor, Burlingame, California 94010, December 17, 1981. Re: Albert Mares, Reg. No. 85831-132; Status of Warrant.

27. Ibid.

28. Assistant U.S. Attorney Jimmye Warren's Criminal Case No. 78-CR-07 Certificate of Filing and Mailing, sent to Kathy P. Bonham, attorney for Nita Marquez (Gonzales) February 16, 1982.

29. Denver FBI SAC Airtel to FBI Director [and FBI Criminal Intelligence Division], September 22, 1977, FBI Headquarters File No. 91-66030-9, pp. 2, 7.

30. Denver FBI SAC Airtel to FBI Director [and Criminal Investigation Division], May 25, 1977, FBI Headquarters File No. 91-66030-7, p. 2. Many events that occurred during the time period covered by this book are not subject to verification by ink on paper and have, therefore, been omitted from the main narrative. Certain memories, however, remain very vivid. I was contacted by phone in the spring or summer of 1975 by a person who identified himself as an FBI agent. He asked if Alberto Mares had been in Chicago at the time of a bank bombing, and if Mares had worked at a dam construction site in northern New Mexico where explosives had been stolen. When I asked why he wanted the information, he responded that Mares' picture was shown to a witness who had seen a man in the area of the bombing, and this witness said Mares resembled the potential suspect. Why the FBI would include Mares' picture among those shown to the witnesses is an intriguing question. I told the FBI agent that I had nothing to say. Alberto was informed of the FBI's inquiry, and he reported it to his parole officer. Alberto was confined in the state prison at the time of the reported dynamite theft, and was in a Denver halfway house on the weekend of the Chicago bombing. His parole required that he enter the facility on Friday and not leave until the following Monday.

Denver Police Department intelligence officers were also interested in Mares, as shown when I was approached by an old acquaintance in January 1976. This person said that two detectives and one officer (all of whom, coincidentally, figured prominently in the John Haro case) tried to pressure him to provide information on the Crusade and on myself. They promised this acquaintance favorable consideration on charges they said were pending against him. The officers told him that I was responsible for the murder of a Chicano teenager. They wanted to know if I maintained another residence. The acquaintance said that he denied knowing me to convince the police he would be of little help. They then showed him a picture of himself talking to me at an entrance to the Crusade building. The photo appeared to have been taken in 1969 or 1970, the last time he had been at the Crusade. He said the police had federal money to "buy or bust" explosives and arms caches. Informers who assisted police were to receive rewards whose amount depended on whether the information led to weapons, explosives, or arrests. The police said they would pay for information leading to weapons or explosives even if no arrests could be made. He said he entertained the idea of obtaining weapons or explosives by himself and then revealing their whereabouts (but without identifying a culprit, for obvious reasons). It would have been an easy way to earn quick money, he reasoned. He was a heroin addict. He said he revealed this information because he wanted me to know that the police were keenly interested in me and nine others whom they believed were involved with weapons and explosives. Rodolfo Gonzales' name was not on the list. When I asked why Gonzales was overlooked, the acquaintance said that police told him "Corky was too smart to get busted red-handed." The way to undermine the Crusade, they said, was "by busting the guys that the cops think are his 'lieutenants.'"

Among the names of these "lieutenants" were Tony "Big T" Marquez, Van Lucero, Eddie Montour, and Alfredo "Freddie" Archer (from Pueblo), Alberto Mares, myself, and four others. Five were not Crusade members. If the old acquaintance's account was accurate, the police were trying to link Mares with weapons and explosives less than a year after his release from prison. The story was very interesting. I ended communications with my old acquaintance after I was subtly (actually not so subtly) asked to participate in the murder of the officers involved.

These conversations took place after I returned from a brief trip to Arizona in January 1976. I was accompanied by one of the Crusade's "lieutenants," and we had been photographed by a plainclothes officer immediately upon arriving in Arizona. Four or five plainclothes officers were waiting in the boarding area when we returned to the Arizona airport. They walked onto the tarmac, where they appeared ready to board the plane to Denver. Instead, they remained in Arizona. One man who boarded may have been part of the group. Unknown to the Crusade at the time, the FBI believed the organization was involved in a conspiracy to bomb a federal facility in Denver. Upon arriving in Denver, ahead of schedule because of a strong tail wind, we saw several officers whom we recognized as part of the Denver Police Department Intelligence Bureau. They had missed our arrival at the gate and milled around until they saw me and others observing them. They gestured to us with upraised middle fingers. We returned the greeting.

We never knew the identities of the men in Arizona or whether they were Arizona law enforcement officers or federal authorities. However, some educated guesses might be made after reading the FBI Bufile document, 105-178283-118, dated June 3, 1976, and covering the Investigative Period of 12/6/75–5/28/76. Captioned "Crusade for Justice, Extremist Matter—Spanish American," it refers to a "Denver report of "SA [Special Agent] [name deleted] dated 12/16/75. Bureau teletype to Denver, dated 1/26/76, captioned 'Crusade for Justice; ALLEGED PLOT TO BOMB FEDERAL FACILITY, DENVER, COLORADO, ABOUT JANUARY 28–31, 1976." This document, and Bufile document 105-178283-118X, refer to my name twice and Alberto Mares' name once. The documents reveal interest in the March 1976 commemoration of the death of Luis Martinez and the involvement of AIM activists. Deciphering this document is difficult because it is heavily blacked out and 26 pages were not released at all. The author, therefore, will not indulge in idle speculation.

31. Rev. Patrick Valdez, Pastor of Our Lady of Guadalupe Church, Denver, "To Whom It May Concern," May 24, 1982.

32. Mares press conference statement.

CHAPTER 17. SLIDING BACKWARDS

1. The Crusade's extensive financial records would be the best indicator of the Crusade's rising or declining fortunes, because they should show sources of income, expenditures for staff wages, etc. These records were not made available to the author.

2. The quotations are taken from a May 7, 1979, *Denver Post* article, reprinted—without page number, byline, or original headline—under the headline "Chicano Harassment at Sloan's Lake," in *El Gallo,* April–May 1979, p. 11. The *Denver Post* reporter counted at least 13 officers (with three police dogs) who were active in issuing tickets and citations at the park. City Councilman Larry Perry initially boasted of using his influence to have Snider assigned to the park, then amended his remarks to say he wasn't responsible for Snider's presence, but was happy about it. The article did not mention that a "Hispanic" city councilman also looked on approvingly until his son handed him a ticket he himself had gotten. Judy Cisneros, holder of a master's degree in social work, was employed as a community worker at the Youth Component of Servicios de La Raza and was noted for her sensitivity to the community and her commitment to youth. Her work and that of her predecessor, Paul Roybal, laid the base for the service agency's development of its Youth Component.

Snider was dismissed from the Denver police force in 1984 after being charged with sexual assault on a woman he arrested. After his dismissal, he was again arrested in 1988 for forcing a young woman into his vehicle at gunpoint and attempting to assault her before she escaped from the car. Both women were Mexican. He was accused of a similar crime in 1980, but no charges were brought. Though he was subsequently acquitted of the 1984 charges, his victim was awarded a $75,000 settlement in 1996. He was found guilty of felony menacing and misdemeanor assault in the 1988 incident and given four years probation.

3. Mayor McNichol promised to ease the four-week crackdown and indicated that Snider would be removed from the area. McNichol's timing was interesting: the mayoral primary was one week away. The police reaction was also typical: "Dill said he might remove Snider because the patrolman has been threatened and because his presence—rightly or wrongly—might provoke adverse reactions from

some park patrons. 'Buster's not being driven out,' Dill said." *Rocky Mountain News,* May 9, 1979.

4. "Chicano Activist Dies in Mysterious Bomb Blast," *El Gallo,* March–April 1978, p. 15.

5. If the word "Chicano" was the banner of the Chicano movement, the generic word "Hispanic" was the banner of this rising middle class.

6. Rodolfo Gonzales, "The Past, Present, the Future of the Chicano Movement," speech (undated, but mid-1970s).

7. Pamela Avery, "Carpio Unopposed in District 9 City Race," *Rocky Mountain News,* May 9, 1979. The article reported that Carpio "argues that he hasn't sold out, that he simply learned how to work within the system."

8. The 1978 struggle to pass Charter Amendment A generated much attention from the print media. See "Mayor's Panel Opposes Civilian Control of Police," *Rocky Mountain News,* July 15, 1978; "Mayor Opposes Police Commission," *Rocky Mountain News,* July 23, 1978; John Ashton, "Tooley Rips Police Commission Plan," *Rocky Mountain News,* August 8, 1978; Louis Kilzer, "Policemen Oppose Commission," *Rocky Mountain News,* September 2, 1978; Bill Pardue, "Police Panel Foes Raise $24,000 Fund," *Denver Post,* October 27, 1978; Andrew Schlesinger, "Police Commission, Parks Plan Defeated," *Rocky Mountain News,* November 8, 1978; and "Mayor in No Rush to Create Proposed Safety Commission," *Rocky Mountain News,* August 31, 1979. After nearly three decades of seeking to establish a civilian police review board, community activists were at last partially successful in 1992 when the Public Safety Review Commission was finally installed. The commission, however, confronts resistance from individual officers and from a highly political (and politically powerful) police department with deep pockets, as seen in Howard Pankratz, "Court Curbs Police-review Panel," *Denver Post,* September 4, 1998. Significantly, the administrations of Hispanic Mayor Federico Peña and African American Mayor Wellington Webb in the 1980s and 1990s were unreceptive to the establishment of a police oversight panel.

9. Gary Delsohn, "Police Plan Assailed at Rally," *Rocky Mountain News,* July 31, 1978.

10. Ibid. This same article showed that relatives of a man killed at Mestizo Park in 1976 were themselves divided on Amendment A. One said, "What are the alternatives? Do we stand in the street and holler? We're damn lucky to get this thing. And if it doesn't pass, Denver police are going to take it as a mandate from the people that they can beat more people on the heads. Everybody should consider that." The quoted man's uncle said, "Any appointee of Mayor McNichols, who's kept his mouth shut throughout all these killings, would be ineffective. The way [Amendment A] is now, it isn't worth a thing. It won't end police abuse." Another participant said, "This bill is a bunch of crap. It's just an effort by city council to get people off their backs about all these killings [by police]. The council has been in turmoil with people coming in and screaming at them and now they can say they did something." *Rocky Mountain News,* July 31, 1978.

11. The CPRO, was started by Crusade for Justice activists—principally Alberto Mares and Maria Subia—in August 1976 in response to a 1976 lockdown

at the State Penitentiary. The CPRO was composed of Crusade members and associates who sought to organize prisoners' families to pressure for prison reform and to advocate on behalf of individual prisoners.

12. The CRBCA, formed by the Crusade for Justice on May 26, 1976, was founded after a brawl at the Pre-Olympic Amateur Boxing Trials in Denver on May 8, when Ricky Romero, a young Crusade amateur boxer and nephew of Rodolfo Gonzales, lost a controversial decision. Gary Kenny, a Native American boxer, fought next and also lost by a questionable decision. In the intermission that followed Kenny's fight, *El Gallo* reported: "One official, Ray Ulmer, an ex-heavyweight, became abusive and belligerent, provoking an incident that resulted with Ulmer being left with bruises and black eyes. . . . Misdemeanor charges were later filed against Corky [who was charged with assaulting Ulmer]. Denver police responded to the area with their canine patrol and riot squad, but after estimating the mood of the crowd, they quietly withdrew and left only their command officers who negotiated with friends of Gonzales. After watching the remainder of the tournament, Gonzales turned himself over to the police." See "The Rise and Fall of the Colorado Boxing Empire," *El Gallo,* June 1976, p. 2.

13. RAMA started when Crusade members and other activists attended a conference organized by the Colorado Committee on the Mass Media and the Spanish Surnamed (CCMMSS). The activists criticized the CCMMSS, charging that it was dominated by television employees seeking to promote their careers, not advocate for the community. The activists called for an election and voted in new leadership. Gonzales' oldest daughter, Nita Marquez, coordinated RAMA's efforts. It monitored the electronic media to ensure compliance with Federal Communications Commission regulations.

14. RAMA and CRBCA statement of March 29, 1978. See also *Rocky Mountain News,* March 30, 1978.

15. In the uproar over the Sue Kinney film, RAMA criticized Chicano employees of the station, declaring that they were "advocating their own professional status [within the stations] and [promoting] management policies rather than the community [interests] they purport to represent." The targets of this criticism were Ted Barros and Jeannie Olguin; the latter was a supporter of Nita Gonzales in her 1992 and 1994 campaigns for a position on the Denver school board.

16. Louis Kilzer, "Chicanos Deny Involvement in Channel 7 Film Case," *Rocky Mountain News,* March 30, 1978.

17. Ibid.

18. Ibid.

19. Some students who went from primary to secondary school at Tlatelolco lacked the political passion that motivated many earlier students, because the later cohort had been sheltered from what their peers experienced in public schools. Meanwhile, the student activism sparked by the Crusade had declined in the public schools. It was once proposed in a staff meeting that Tlatelolco's secondary school be open only to youth activists, whose course of studies would require periodic re-enrollment in public schools to keep them from losing touch with the everyday reality of their peers and give them an opportunity to politicize and to organize. The look of shocked disbelief on the faces of several women from a prominent family whose children were enrolled at Tlatelolco ("What? Send *my*

kids back to public school? No way!") quickly revealed that the idea would not be considered, much less seriously discussed.

20. In 1979 AIM's case was separated from the Crusade's in the civil suit filed in Bridgeport, and Gonzales proceeded to court by himself.

21. Deposition of Rodolfo Gonzales, June 21, 1979, Bridgeport, Connecticut, Civil Case No. H-76-530, pp. 3, 4, (hereafter cited as "Gonzales deposition). The questioning of Gonzales by opposing attorneys reads like an intelligence interrogation. They asked about sources of income (his and that of the Crusade), the number of Crusade members, the board members' names and addresses, income received from the organization by board members, the Crusade's relationship to the larger Chicano movement and the Chicano community, the nature and extent of the Crusade's relationship to the Brown Berets, SDS, AIM, Gonzales' views on capitalism, and any international travel by Gonzales related to antiwar activism. Further, he was questioned about Crusade applications for federally funded grants; his own activities as a lecturer (monies received, the places he had spoken, accessibility of records of his lectures, etc.); Crusade payroll records; and the financial status of Escuela Tlatelolco.

22. Ibid., p. 22.

23. Ibid., p. 42.

24. The Crusade's views on organized labor are complex. Though the Crusade believed unions served the interests of working people, it was critical of conservative labor leadership. Perhaps a 1967 brochure stated the Crusade's relationship to organized labor as clearly as the Crusade ever bothered to state it: "Labor Movement: Complete liaison and cooperation will be maintained with existing labor unions which are dedicated to the same objectives as the Crusade for Justice."

25. Gonzales, deposition pp. 70, 71.

26. Ibid., pp. 18, 45.

27. Ibid., pp. 28, 31, 74.

28. Ibid., pp. 29, 47.

29. Ibid., pp. 15, 28, 44.

30. The sponsoring MEChA group came from a campus that combined three separate institutions (Metropolitan State College, the University of Colorado Denver Center, and Community College of Denver) with three MEChA chapters. The Metro MEChA students wanted the Crusade to help them gain the support of the other MEChA chapters. At least one of the latter had fallen under the control of "born-again Christians" eager for workshops and speakers to address their spiritual concerns.

31. The resolutions from the 1979 National Chicano Student Conference were compiled on April 8 but were not widely disseminated in Colorado. A copy was provided to the author by Seferino Garcia of the Orange County (California) chapter of the National Brown Berets de Aztlan.

32. Rodolfo Gonzales, "Chicanos and the Iranian Question," *El Gallo,* January–February 1980, pp. 2, 14.

33. *Rocky Mountain News,* July 2, 1978; ad by Colorado supporters of the Coors boycott, signed by Herbert M. Gallegos.

34. Denver Police Department, *Gangs in Denver* (City and County of Denver,

1989), cited in James Patrick Walsh, "Young and Latino in a Cold War Barrio: Survival, the Search for Identity, and the Formation of Street Gangs in Denver, 1945–1955" (thesis, University of Colorado at Denver, 1996), p. 13. Academic or nonpolice training that qualifies Lopez as a "specialist" are unknown, but more than one error escapes his detection. Lopez refers to a gang composed of "Mexican Nationalists." "Nationalist" is a political term, and no gang of "Mexican Nationalists" existed in Denver. Lopez may be referring to Mexican "nationals" (i.e., citizens of Mexico). Other minor errors involve the spelling and meaning of the word "cholo," which has only one "l" and is not a term of endearment. How the word came to be used to describe Chicano youth-gang members is unknown (as is true of "pachuco," similarly used in the 1940s). As used in various Latin American countries, "cholo" refers to the lower classes, usually with negative racial connotations in reference to Indians and mestizos. It has never been used—or thought of—as a term of endearment other than in Lopez' booklet.

35. Reports of the Commission on Community Relations of March 31, June 11, and June 28, 1980.

36. Similarly, the Commission on Community Relations acknowledged on June 11, 1980, that "our [Denver] youth activity in terms of gang formation was done away with in the late 60's," but does not state how this happened.